A HISTORY OF

THE

MW01603081

OF

THE MIDDLE AGES

BY
HENRY CHARLES LEA*IN THREE*
VOLUMES
VOL. I

PREFACE.

THE history of the Inquisition naturally divides itself into two portions, each of which may be considered as a whole. The Reformation is the boundary-line between them, except in Spain, where the New Inquisition was founded by Ferdinand and Isabella. In the present work I have sought to present an impartial account of the institution as it existed during the earlier period. For the second portion I have made large collections of material, through which I hope in due time to continue the history to its end.

The Inquisition was not an organization arbitrarily devised and imposed upon the judicial system of Christendom by the ambition or fanaticism of the Church. It was rather a natural—one may almost say an inevitable—evolution of the forces at work in the thirteenth century, and no one can rightly appreciate the process of its development and the results of its activity without a somewhat minute consideration of the factors controlling the minds and souls of men during the ages which laid the foundation of modern civilization. To accomplish this it has been necessary to pass in review nearly all the spiritual and intellectual movements of the Middle Ages, and to glance at the condition of society in certain of its phases.

At the commencement of my historical studies I speedily became convinced that the surest basis of investigation for a given period lay in an examination of its jurisprudence, which presents without disguise its aspirations and the means regarded as best adapted for their realization. I have accordingly devoted much space to the origin and development of the inquisitorial process, feeling convinced that in this manner only can we understand the operations of the Holy Office and the influence which it exercised on successive generations. By the application of the results thus obtained it has seemed to me that many points which have been misunderstood or imperfectly appreciated can be elucidated. If in this I have occasionally been led to conclusions differing from those currently accepted, I beg the reader to believe that the views presented have not been hastily formed, but that they are the outcome of a conscientious survey of all the original sources accessible to me.

No serious historical work is worth the writing or the reading unless it conveys a moral, but to be useful the moral must develop itself in the mind of the reader without being obtruded upon him. Especially is this the case in a history treating of a subject which has called forth the fiercest passions of man, arousing alternately his highest and his basest impulses. I have not paused to moralize, but I have missed my aim if the events narrated are not so presented as to teach their appropriate lesson.

It only remains for me to express my thanks to the numerous friends and correspondents who have rendered me assistance in the arduous labor of collecting the very varied material, much of it inedited, on which the present work is based. Especially do I desire to record my gratitude to the memory of that cultured gentleman and earnest scholar, the late Hon. George P. Marsh, who for so many years worthily represented the United States at the Italian court. I never had the fortune to look upon his face, but the courteous readiness with which he aided my researches in Italy merit my warmest acknowledgments. To Professor Charles Molinier, of the University of Toulouse, moreover, my special thanks are due as to one who has always been ready to share with a fellow-student his own unrivalled knowledge of the Inquisition of Languedoc. In the Florentine archives I owe much to Francis Philip Nast, Esq., to Professor Felice Tocco, and to Doctor Giuseppe Papaleoni; in those of Naples, to the Superintendent Cav. Minieri Riccio and to the Cav. Leopoldo Ovary; in those of Venice to the Cav. Teodoro Toderini and Sig. Bartolomeo Cecchetti: in those of Brussels to M. Charles Rahlenbeck. In Paris I have to congratulate myself on the careful assiduity with which M.L. Sandret has exhausted for my benefit the rich collections of MSS., especially those of the Bibliothèque Nationale. To a student, separated by a thousand leagues of ocean from the repositories of the Old World, assistance of this nature is a necessity, and I esteem myself fortunate in having enlisted the co-operation of those who have removed for me some of the disabilities of time and space.

Should the remaining portion of my task be hereafter accomplished, I hope to have the opportunity of acknowledging my obligations to many other gentlemen of both hemispheres who have furnished me with unpublished material illustrating the later development of the Holy Office.

PHILADELPHIA, *August*, 1887.

THE INQUISITION

BOOK I.
ORIGIN AND ORGANIZATION.
CHAPTER I.
THE CHURCH.

AS the twelfth century drew to a close, the Church was approaching a crisis in its career. The vicissitudes of a hundred and fifty years, skilfully improved, had rendered it the mistress of Christendom. History records no such triumph of intellect over brute strength as that which, in an age of turmoil and battle, was wrested from the fierce warriors of the time by priests who had no material force at their command, and whose power was based alone on the souls and consciences of men. Over soul and conscience their empire was complete. No Christian could hope for salvation who was not in all things an obedient son of the Church, and who was not ready to take up arms in its defence; and, in a time when faith was a determining factor of conduct, this belief created a spiritual despotism which placed all things within reach of him who could wield it.

This could be accomplished only by a centralized organization such as that which had gradually developed itself within the ranks of the hierarchy. The ancient independence of the episcopate was no more.

Step by step the supremacy of the Roman see had been asserted and enforced, until it enjoyed the universal jurisdiction which enabled it to bend to its wishes every prelate, under the naked alternative of submission or expulsion. The papal mandate,{2} just or unjust, reasonable or unreasonable, was to be received and implicitly obeyed, for there was no appeal from the representative of St. Peter. In a narrower sphere, and subject to the pope, the bishop held an authority which, at least in theory, was equally absolute; while the humbler minister of the altar was the instrument by which the decrees of pope and bishop were enforced among the people; for the destiny of all men lay in the hands which could administer or withhold the sacraments essential to salvation.

Thus intrusted with responsibility for the fate of mankind, it was necessary that the Church should possess the powers and the machinery requisite for the due discharge of a trust so unspeakably important. For the internal regulation of the conscience it had erected the institution of auricular confession, which by this time had become almost the exclusive appanage of the priesthood. When this might fail to keep the believer in the path of righteousness, it could resort to the spiritual courts which had grown up around every episcopal seat, with an undefined jurisdiction capable of almost unlimited extension. Besides supervision over matters of faith and discipline, of marriage, of inheritance, and of usury, which belonged to them by general consent, there were comparatively few questions between man and man which could not be made to include some case of conscience involving the interpellation of spiritual interference, especially when agreements were customarily confirmed with the sanction of the oath; and the cure of souls implied a perpetual inquest over the aberrations, positive or possible, of every member of the flock. It would be difficult to set bounds to the intrusion upon the concerns of every man which was thus rendered possible, or to the influence thence derivable.

Not only did the humblest priest wield a supernatural power which marked him as one elevated above the common level of humanity, but his person and possessions were alike inviolable. No matter what crimes he might commit, secular justice could not take cognizance of them, and secular officials could not arrest him. He was amenable only to the tribunals of his own order, which were debarred from inflicting punishments involving the effusion of blood, and from whose decisions an appeal to the supreme jurisdiction of distant Rome conferred too often virtual immunity.{3} The same privilege protected ecclesiastical property, conferred on the Church by the piety of successive generations, and covering no small portion of the most fertile lands of Europe. Moreover, the seignorial rights attaching to those lands often carried extensive temporal jurisdiction, which gave to their ghostly possessors the power over life and limb enjoyed by feudal lords.

The line of separation between the laity and the clergy was widened and deepened by the enforcement of the canon requiring celibacy on the part of all concerned in the ministry of the altar. Revived about the middle of the eleventh century, and enforced after an obstinate struggle of a hundred years, the compulsory celibacy of the priesthood divided them from the people, preserved intact the vast acquisitions of the Church, and furnished it with an innumerable army whose aspirations and ambition were necessarily restricted within its circle. The man who entered the service of the Church was no longer a citizen. He owed no allegiance superior to that assumed in his ordination. He was released from the distraction of family cares and the seduction of family ties. The Church was his country and his home, and its interests were his own. The moral, intellectual, and physical forces which, throughout the laity, were divided between the claims of patriotism, the selfish struggle for advancement, the provision for wife and children, were in the Church consecrated to a common end, in the success of which all might hope to share, while all were assured of the necessities of existence, and were relieved of anxiety as to the future.

The Church, moreover, offered the only career open to men of all ranks and stations. In the sharply-defined class distinctions of the feudal system advancement was almost impossible to one not born within the charmed circle of gentle blood. In the Church, however much rank and family connections might assist in securing promotion to high place, yet talent and energy could always make themselves felt despite lowliness of birth. Urban II. and Adrian IV. sprang from the humblest origin; Alexander V. had been a beggar-boy; Gregory VII. was the son of a carpenter; Benedict XII., of a baker; Nicholas V., of a poor physician; Sixtus IV., of a peasant; Urban IV. and John XXII. were sons of cobblers, and Benedict XI. and Sixtus V. of shepherds; in fact, the annals of the hierarchy are full of those who rose from{4} the lowest ranks of society to the most commanding positions. The Church thus constantly recruited its ranks with fresh blood. Free from the curse of hereditary descent, through which crowns and coronets frequently lapsed into weak and incapable hands, it called into its service an indefinite amount of restless vigor for which there was no other sphere of action, and which, when once enlisted, found itself perforce identified irrevocably with the body which it had joined. The character of the priest was indelible; the vows taken at ordination could not be thrown aside; the monk, when once admitted to the cloister, could not abandon his order unless it were to enter another of more rigorous observance. The Church Militant was thus an army encamped on the soil of Christendom, with its outposts everywhere, subject to the most efficient discipline, animated with a common purpose, every soldier panoplied with inviolability and armed with the tremendous weapons which slew the soul. There was little that could not be dared or done by the commander of such a force, whose orders were listened to as oracles of God, from Portugal to Palestine and from Sicily to Iceland. "Princes," says John of Salisbury, "derive their power from the Church, and are servants of the priesthood." "The least of the priestly order is worthier than any king," exclaims Honorius of Autun; "prince and people are subjected to the clergy, which shines superior as the sun to the moon." Innocent III. used a more spiritual metaphor when he declared that the priestly power was as superior

2

to the secular as the soul of man was to his body; and he summed up his estimate of his own position by pronouncing himself to be the Vicar of Christ, the Christ of the Lord, the God of Pharaoh, placed midway between God and man, this side of God but beyond man, less than God but greater than man, who judges all, and is judged by none. That he was supreme over all the earth—over pagans and infidels as well as over Christians—was legally proved and universally taught by the mediæval doctors.[1] Though the power thus vaingloriously asserted was fraught with evil in many ways, yet was it none the less a service to humanity that, in those rude ages, there existed a{5} moral force superior to high descent and martial prowess, which could remind king and noble that they must obey the law of God even when uttered by a peasant's son; as when Urban II., himself a Frenchman of low birth, dared to excommunicate his monarch, Philip I., for his adultery, thus upholding the moral order and enforcing the sanctions of eternal justice at a time when everything seemed permissible to the recklessness of power.

Yet, in achieving this supremacy, much had been of necessity sacrificed. The Christian virtues of humility and charity and self-abnegation had virtually disappeared in the contest which left the spiritual power dominant over the temporal. The affection of the populations was no longer attracted by the graces and loveliness of Christianity; submission was purchased by the promise of salvation, to be acquired by faith and obedience, or was extorted by the threat of perdition or by the sharper terrors of earthly persecution. If the Church, by sundering itself completely from the laity, had acquired the services of a militia devoted wholly to itself, it had thereby created an antagonism between itself and the people. Practically, the whole body of Christians no longer constituted the Church; that body was divided into two essentially distinct classes, the shepherds and the sheep; and the lambs were often apt to think, not unreasonably, that they were tended only to be shorn. The worldly prizes offered to ambition by an ecclesiastical career drew into the ranks of the Church able men, it is true, but men whose object was worldly ambition rather than spiritual development. The immunities and privileges of the Church and the enlargement of its temporal acquisitions were objects held more at heart than the salvation of souls, and its high places were filled, for the most part, with men in whom worldliness was more conspicuous than the humbler virtues.

This was inevitable in the state of society which existed in the early Middle Ages. While angels would have been required to exercise becomingly the tremendous powers claimed and acquired by the Church, the methods by which clerical preferment and promotion were secured were such as to favor the unscrupulous rather than the deserving. To understand fully the causes which drove so many thousands into schism and heresy, leading to wars and persecutions, and the establishment of the Inquisition, it is necessary{6} to cast a glance at the character of the men who represented the Church before the people, and at the use which they made, for good or for evil, of the absolute spiritual despotism which had become established. In wise and devout hands it might elevate incalculably the moral and material standards of European civilization; in the hands of the selfish and depraved it could become the instrument of minute and all-pervading oppression, driving whole nations to despair.

As regards the methods of election to the episcopate there cannot be said at this period to have been any settled and invariable rule. The ancient form of election by the clergy, with the acquiescence of the people of the diocese, was still preserved in theory, but in practice the electoral body consisted of the cathedral canons; while the confirmation required of the king, or semi-independent feudal noble, and of the pope, in a time of unsettled institutions, frequently rendered the election an empty form, in which the royal or papal power might prevail, according to the tendencies of time and place. The constantly increasing appeals to Rome, as to the tribunal of last resort, by disappointed aspirants, under every imaginable pretext, gave to the Holy See a rapidly-growing influence, which, in many cases, amounted almost to the power of appointment; and Innocent II., at the Lateran Council of 1139, applied the feudal system to the Church by declaring that all ecclesiastical dignities were received and held of the popes like fiefs. Whatever rules, however, might be laid down, they could not operate in rendering the elect better than the electors. The stream will not rise above its source, and a corrupt electing or appointing power is not apt to be restrained from the selection of fitting representatives of itself by methods, however ingeniously devised, which have not the inherent ability of self-enforcement. The oath which cardinals were obliged to take on entering a conclave—"I call God to witness that I choose him whom I judge according to God ought to be chosen"—was notoriously inefficacious in securing the election of pontiffs fitted to serve as the vicegerents of God; and so, from the humblest parish priest to the loftiest prelate, all grades of the hierarchy were likely to be filled by worldly, ambitious, self-seeking, and licentious men. The material to be selected from, moreover, was of such a character that even the most exacting friends of the Church had to content themselves{7} when the least worthless was successful. St. Peter Damiani, in asking of Gregory VI. the confirmation of a bishop-elect of Fossombrone, admits that he is unfit, and that he ought to undergo penance before undertaking the episcopate, but yet there is nothing better to be done, for in the whole diocese there was not a single ecclesiastic worthy of the office; all were selfishly ambitious, too eager for preferment to think of rendering themselves worthy of it, inflamed with desire for power, but utterly careless as to its duties.[2]

Under these circumstances simony, with all its attendant evils, was almost universal, and those evils made themselves everywhere felt on the character both of electors and elected. In the fruitless war waged by Gregory VII. and his successors against this all-pervading vice, the number of bishops assailed is the surest index of the means which had been found successful, and of the men who thus were enabled to represent the apostles. As Innocent III. declared, it was a disease of the Church immedicable by either soothing remedies or fire; and Peter Cantor, who died in the odor of sanctity, relates with approval the story of a Cardinal Martin, who, on officiating in the Christmas solemnities at the Roman court, rejected a gift of twenty pounds sent him by the papal chancellor, for the reason that it was notoriously the product of rapine and simony. It was related as a supreme instance of the virtue of Peter, Cardinal of St. Chrysogono, formerly Bishop of Meaux, that he had, in a single election, refused the dazzling bribe of five hundred marks of silver. Temporal princes were more ready to turn the power of confirmation to profitable account, and few imitated the example of Philip Augustus, who, when the abbacy of St. Denis became vacant, and the provost, the treasurer, and the cellarer of the abbey each sought him secretly, and gave him five hundred livres for the succession, quietly went to the abbey, picked out a simple monk standing in a corner, conferred the dignity on him, and handed him the fifteen hundred livres. The Council of Rouen, in 1050, complains bitterly of the pernicious custom by which ambitious men accumulated, by every possible means, presents wherewith to gain the favor of the prince and his courtiers in order to obtain bishoprics, but it could suggest no remedy.[8] The council was directly concerned only with the Norman dukes, but the contemporary King of France, Henry I., was notorious as a vendor of bishoprics. He had commenced his reign with an edict prohibiting the purchase and sale of preferment under penalty of forfeiture of both purchase-money and benefice, and had boasted that, as God had given him the crown gratis, so he would take nothing for his right of confirmation, reproaching his prelates bitterly for the prevalence of the vice which was eating out the heart of the Church. Yet in time he yielded to the custom, and a single instance will illustrate the working of the system. A certain Helinand, a clerk of low extraction and deficient training, had found favor at the court of Edward the Confessor, where he had ample opportunities of amassing wealth. Happening to be sent on a mission to Henry, he made a bargain by which he purchased the reversion of the first vacant bishopric, which chanced in course of time to be Laon, where he was duly installed. Henry's successor, Philip I., was known as the most venal of men, and from him, by a similar transaction, Helinand purchased, with the money acquired from the revenues of Laon, the primatial see of Reims. Such jobbers in patronage were accustomed to enter into compacts with each other for mutual assistance, and to consult astrologers as to expected vacancies. The manipulation of ecclesiastical preferment was reduced to a system, calling forth the indignant remonstrance of all the better class of churchmen. Instances of these abuses might be multiplied indefinitely, and their influence on the character of the Church cannot easily be overestimated.[3]

Even where the consideration paid for preferment was not actually money, the effect was equally deplorable. Peter Cantor assures us that, if those who were promoted for relationship were[9] required to resign, it would cause general destruction throughout the Church; and worse motives were constantly at work. Though Philip I., for his adultery with Bertrade of Anjou, was nominally deprived of the confirmation, or, rather, nomination, of bishops, there were none to prevent his exercise of the power. About the year 1100 the Archbishop of Tours, having gratified the king by disregarding the excommunication under which he lay, claimed his reward by demanding that the vacant see of Orleans should be given to a youth whom he loved not wisely but too well, and who was so notorious for the facility with which he granted his favors (the preceding Archbishop of Tours had likewise been one of his lovers) that he was popularly known as Flora, in allusion to a noted courtesan of the day, and ribald love-songs addressed to him were openly sung in the streets. Such of the Orleans clergy as threatened trouble were put out of the way by false accusations and exiled, and the remainder not only submitted, but even made a jest of the fact that the election took place on the Feast of the Innocents—

"Elegimus puerum, puerorum festa colentes,
Non nostrum morem sed regis jussa sequentes."[4]

Under such influences it was in vain that the better class of men who occasionally appeared in the ranks of the hierarchy, such as Fulbert of Chartres, Hildebert of Le Mans, Ivo of Chartres, Lanfranc, Anselm, St. Bruno, St. Bernard, St. Norbert, and others, struggled to enforce respect for religion and morality. The current against them was too strong, and they could do little but protest and offer an example which few were found to follow. In those days of violence the meek and humble had little chance, and the prizes were for those who could intrigue and chaffer, or whose martial tendencies offered promise that they would make the rights of their churches and vassals respected. In fact, the military character of the mediæval prelates is a subject which it would be interesting to consider in more detail than space will here admit. The wealthy abbeys and powerful bishoprics came to be largely regarded as appropriate means to provide for younger sons of noble houses, or to increase the influence of[10] leading families. By such methods as we have seen they passed into the hands of those whose training had been military rather than religious. The mitre and cross had no more scruple than the knightly pennon to be seen in the forefront of battle. When excommunication failed to bring to reason restless vassals or encroaching neighbors, there was prompt recourse to the fleshly arm, and the plundered peasant could not distinguish between the ravages of the robber baron and of the representative of Christ. One of the early adventures of Rodolph of Hapsburg, by which he won the reputation which elevated him to the imperial throne, was the war declared by Walter, Bishop of Strassburg, against his burghers, because they had refused to aid him in gratuitously interfering in a quarrel between the Bishop of Metz and a troublesome noble. As they disregarded his excommunication, Bishop Walter attacked them vigorously, when they placed themselves under the command of Rodolph, and utterly defeated their pastor, after a war which desolated every portion of Alsace.

The chronicles of the period are full of details of this nature. Worldly and turbulent, there was little to differentiate the prelate from the baron, and the latter had no more scruple in making reprisals on Church property than on secular possessions. In the dissensions which reduced the wealthy Abbey of St. Tron to beggary, the pious Godfrey of Bouillon, shortly before the crusade which won for him the throne of Jerusalem, ravaged the abbey lands with fire and sword. The people, on whom fell the crushing weight of these conflicts, could only look upon the baron and priest as enemies both; and whatever might be lacking in the military ability of the spiritual warriors, was compensated for by their seeking to kill the souls as well as the bodies of their foes. This was especially the case in Germany, where the prelates were princes as well as priests, and where a great religious house like the Abbey of St. Gall was the temporal ruler of the Cantons of St. Gall and Appenzel, until the latter threw off the yoke after a long and devastating war. The historian of the abbey chronicles with pride the martial virtues of successive abbots, and in speaking of Ulric III., who died in 1117, he remarks that, worn out with many battles, he at last passed away in peace. All this was in some sort a necessity of the incongruous union of feudal noble and Christian prelate, and though more marked in Germany than elsewhere, it{11} was to be seen everywhere. In 1224 the Bishops of Coutances, Avranches, and Lisieux withdrew from the army of Louis VIII. at Tours, under an agreement that the king should make legal investigation to determine whether the bishops of Normandy were bound to serve personally in the royal armies; if this was found to be the case, they were to return and pay the amercement for deserting him. The decision apparently went against them, for in 1272 we find them serving personally under Philippe le Hardi. This indisposition to fight the battles of others was not often shown when the cause was their own. Geroch of Reichersperg inveighs bitterly against the warlike prelates who provoke unjust wars, attacking the peaceful and delighting in the slaughter which they cause and witness, giving no quarter, taking no prisoners, sparing neither clergy nor laity, and spending the revenues of the Church on soldiers, to the deprivation of the poor. Such a prelate was Lupold, Bishop of Worms, whose recklessness provoked his brother to say, "My lord bishop, you scandalize us laymen greatly by your example. Before you were a bishop you feared God a little, but now you care nothing for him," to which Bishop Lupold flippantly retorted that when they both should be in hell he would exchange seats if his brother desired. During the wars between the emperors Philip and Otho IV. he personally led his troops in support of Philip, and when his soldiers hesitated about sacking churches, he would tell them that it was enough if they left the bones of the dead. The story is well known of Richard of England, and Philippe of Dreux, the warlike Bishop of Beauvais, who had shown himself equally skilful and ruthless in the predatory warfare of the age, and who, when at last captured by Earl John, complained to Celestin III. of his imprisonment as a violation of ecclesiastical privileges. When Celestin, reproving him for his martial propensities, interceded for his release, King Richard sent to the pope the coat of mail in which the prelate had been captured, with the inquiry made to Jacob by his sons, "Know, whether it be thy son's coat?" to which the good pontiff responded by abandoning the appeal. A different result, not long afterwards, attended a similar experience of Theodore, Marquis of Montferrat, when he defeated and captured Aymon, Bishop of Vercelli. It happened that Cardinal Tagliaferro, papal legate to Aragon, was tarrying at Geneva, and, hearing of the sacrilege,{12} wrote in threatening wise to the marquis, who responded with the same inquiry as King Richard, sending him the martial gear of the prelate, including his sword still stained with blood. Yet the proud noble felt his inability to cope with his spiritual foes, and not only liberated the bishop, but surrendered to him the fortress which had been the occasion of the war. Even more instructive is the case of the Bishop-elect of Verona, who, in 1265, when marching at the head of an army, was taken prisoner by the troops of Manfred of Sicily. Although Urban IV. was busily urging forward the crusade which was to deprive Manfred of life and kingdom, he had the assurance to demand the liberation of his bishop, telling Manfred that if he had a spark left of the fear of God he would dismiss his prisoner. When Manfred replied, evading the demand with exuberant humility, Clement IV., who had meanwhile succeeded to the papacy, called upon Jayme I. of Aragon to intervene. Neither pope seemed to imagine that there could be any hesitation in acceding to the preposterous claim, and King Jayme interposed so effectually that Manfred offered to release the bishop on his swearing not to bear arms against him in future. Even this condition was not accepted without difficulty. When the spiritual character thus only served to confer immunity for acts of violence, it is easy to understand the irresistible temptation to their commission.[5]{13}

The impression which these worldly and turbulent men made upon their quieter contemporaries was, that pious souls believed that no bishop could reach the kingdom of heaven. There was a story widely circulated of Geoffroi de Péronne, Prior of Clairvaux, who was elected Bishop of Tournay, and who was urged by St. Bernard and Eugenius III. to accept, but who cast himself on the ground, saying, "If you turn me out, I may become a vagrant monk, but a bishop never!" On his death-bed he promised a friend to return and report as to his condition in the other world, and did so as the latter was praying at the altar. He announced that he was among the blessed, but it had been revealed to him by the Trinity that if he had accepted the bishopric he would have been numbered with the damned. Peter of Blois, who relates this story, and Peter Cantor, who repeats it, both manifested their belief in it by persistently refusing bishoprics; and not long after an ecclesiastic in Paris declared that he could believe all things except that any German bishop could be saved, because they bore the two swords, of the spirit and of the flesh. All this Cæsarius of Heisterbach explains by the rarity of worthy prelates, and the superabounding multitude of wicked ones; and he further points out that the tribulations to which they were exposed arose from the fact that the hand of God was not visible in their promotion. Language can scarce

5

be stronger than that employed by Louis VII. in describing the worldliness and pomp of the bishops, when he vainly appealed to Alexander III. to utilize his triumph over Frederic Barbarossa by reforming the Church.[6]

In fact, the records of the time bear ample testimony to the rapine and violence, the flagrant crimes and defiant immorality of these princes of the Church. The only tribunal to which they were amenable was that of Rome. It required the courage of desperation to cause complaints to be made there against them, and when such complaints were made, the difficulty of proving charges, the length to which proceedings were drawn out, and the notorious venality of the Roman curia, afforded virtual immunity. When a resolute and incorruptible pontiff like Innocent III. occupied the {14} papal chair, there was some chance for sufferers to make themselves heard, and the number of such trials alluded to in his epistles show how wide-spread and deep-rooted was the evil. Yet, even under him, the protraction of the proceedings, and the evident shrinking from final condemnation, show how little encouragement there was for prosecutions likely to react so dangerously on the prosecutor. Thus, in 1198, Gérard de Rougemont, Archbishop of Besançon, was accused by his chapter of perjury, simony, and incest. When summoned to Rome the accusers did not dare to prosecute the charges, though they did not withdraw them, and Innocent, charitably quoting the woman taken in adultery, sent him back to purge himself and be absolved. Then followed a long course of undisturbed scandals, through which religion in his diocese became a mockery. He continued to live in incest with his relative, the Abbess of Remiremont, and other concubines, one of whom was a nun, and another the daughter of a priest; no church could be consecrated or preferment conferred without payment; by his exactions and oppressions his clergy were reduced to live like peasants, and were exposed to the contempt of their parishioners; and monks and nuns who could bribe him were allowed to abandon their convents and marry. At last another attempt was made, in 1211, to remove him, which, after more than a year, resulted in a sentence that he should undergo canonical purgation; *i.e.*, find two bishops and three abbots to join him in an oath of disculpation, when negotiations as to the character of the oath ensued, lasting until 1214. Finally the citizens rose and drove him out; he retired to the Abbey of Bellevaux, where he died in 1225. Maheu de Lorraine, Bishop of Toul, was a prelate of the same stamp. Consecrated in 1200, within two years his chapter applied to Innocent for his deposition, alleging that he had already reduced the revenues of the see from a thousand livres to thirty. It was not until 1210 that his removal could be effected, after a most intricate series of commissions and appeals, interspersed with acts of violence. He was wholly abandoned to debauchery and the chase, and his favorite concubine was his daughter by a nun of Épinal, but he retained a valuable preferment, as Grand-prévôt of Saint-Dié. In 1217 he caused his successor Renaud de Senlis to be murdered, soon after which his uncle, Thiebault, Duke of Lorraine, happening to meet him, slew him on the spot. Ordinary {15} justice, apparently, could do nothing with him. Very similar was the case of the Bishop of Vence, whom Celestin III. had ordered suspended and sent to Rome to answer for his enormities, and who had defiantly continued in the exercise of his functions. On Innocent's accession, in 1198, his excommunication was ordered, which was equally ineffectual; and at length, in 1204, Innocent sent peremptory orders to the Archbishop of Embrun to investigate the charges, and, if they were found correct, to depose him. Meanwhile the diocese had been brought to the verge of ruin, the churches were demolished, and divine service was performed in only a few parishes. So in Narbonne, the headquarters of heresy, the Archbishop, Berenger II., natural son of Raymond Berenger, Count of Barcelona, preferred to live in Aragon, where he held a rich abbey and the bishopric of Lerida, and never even visited his province. Consecrated in 1190, he had never seen it in 1204, though he drew large revenues from it, both in the regular way and by the sale of bishoprics and benefices, which were indiscriminately bestowed on children or on men of the most abandoned lives. The condition of the province, the highest ecclesiastical dignity of France, was consequently shocking in the extreme, through the misconduct of the clergy, the boldness of the heretics, and the violence of the laity. As early as the year 1200, Innocent III. summoned Berenger to account. In 1204 he made another attempt, continued during the following years, as no amendment was visible, and as the farce of appeals from legate to pope was persistently kept up. At length, in 1210, we find Innocent still writing to his legate to investigate the archbishops of Narbonne and Ausch and execute without appeal whatever the canons require, but it was not until 1212 that Berenger was removed. It is probable that even then he might have escaped had not the legate, Arnaud of Citeaux, been desirous of the succession, which he obtained. We can readily believe the assertion of a writer of the thirteenth century, that the process of deposing a prelate was so cumbrous that even the most wicked had no dread of punishment.[7] {16}

Even where the enormity of offences did not call for papal intervention, the episcopal office was prostituted in a thousand ways of oppression and exaction which were sufficiently within the law to afford the sufferers no opportunity of redress. How thoroughly its profitable nature was recognized, is shown by the case of a bishop who, when fallen in years, summoned together his nephews and relatives that they might agree among themselves as to his succession. They united upon one of their number, and conjointly borrowed the large sums requisite to purchase the election. Unluckily the bishop-elect died before obtaining possession, and on his death-bed was heartily objurgated by his ruined kinsmen, who saw no means of repaying the borrowed capital which they had invested in the abortive episcopal partnership. As St. Bernard says, boys were inducted into the episcopate at an age when they rejoiced rather at escaping from the ferule of their teachers than at acquiring rule; but, soon growing insolent, they learn to sell the altar and empty the pouches of their subjects. In thus exploiting their office the bishops only followed the example set them by the papacy, which, directly or through its agents, by its exactions, made itself the terror of the Christian churches. Arnold, who was Archbishop of Trèves from 1169 to 1183, won great credit for his astuteness in saving his people from spoliation by papal nuncios, for whenever he heard of their expected arrival he used to go to meet them, and by heavy bribes induce them to bend their steps elsewhere, to the infinite relief of his own flock. In 1160 the Templars complained to Alexander III. that their labors for the Holy Land were seriously impaired by the extortions of papal legates and nuncios, who were not content with the free quarters and supply of necessaries to which they were entitled, and Alexander graciously granted the Order special exemption from the abuse, except when the legate was a cardinal. It was{17} worse when the pope came himself. Clement V., after his consecration at Lyons, made a progress to Bordeaux, in which he and his retinue so effectually plundered the churches on the road that, after his departure from Bourges, Archbishop Gilles, in order to support life, was obliged to present himself daily among his canons for a share in the distribution of provisions; and the papal residence at the wealthy Priory of Grammont so impoverished the house that the prior resigned in despair of being able to reestablish its affairs, and his successor was obliged to levy a heavy tax on all the houses of the order. England, after the ignominious surrender of King John, was peculiarly subjected to papal extortion. Rich benefices were bestowed on foreigners, who made no pretext of residence, until the annual revenue thus withdrawn from the island was computed to amount to seventy thousand marks, or three times the income of the crown, and all resistance was suppressed by excommunications which disturbed the whole kingdom. At the general council of Lyons, held in 1245, an address was presented in the name of the Anglican Church, complaining of these oppressions in terms more energetic than respectful, but it accomplished nothing. Ten years later the papal legate, Rustand, made a demand in the name of Alexander IV. for an immense subsidy—the share of the Abbey of St. Albans was no less than six hundred marks—when Fulk, Bishop of London, declared that he would be decapitated, and Walter of Worcester that he would be hanged, sooner than submit; but this resistance was broken down by the device of trumping up fictitious claims of debts due Italian bankers for moneys alleged to have been advanced to defray expenses before the Roman curia, and these claims were enforced by excommunication. When Robert Grosseteste of Lincoln found that his efforts to reform his clergy were rendered nugatory by appeals to Rome, where the offenders could always purchase immunity, he visited Innocent IV. in hopes of obtaining some change for the better, and on utterly failing, he bluntly exclaimed to the pope, "Oh, money, money, how much thou canst effect, especially in the Roman court!" This special abuse was one of old standing, and complaints of its demoralizing effect upon the priesthood date back from the time of the establishment of the appellate jurisdiction of Rome under Charles le Chauve. Prelates like Hildebert of Le Mans, who honestly sought to better the depraved lives{18} of their clergy, constantly found their efforts frustrated, and had scant reticence in remonstrating. Remonstrances, however, were of little avail, though occasionally an upright pope like Innocent III., whose biographer finds special cause of praise in his refusal of "propinas"—gifts or bribes for issuing letters—would sometimes recall a letter of remission avowedly issued in ignorance of the facts, or would even grant to a prelate the right to punish without appeal, while other popes were found who sought to neutralize the effects of their letters without diminishing the business and fees of the chancery. Even when papal letters were not of this demoralizing character, they were never issued without payment. When Luke, the holy Archbishop of Gran, was thrown in prison by the usurper Ladislas, in 1172, he refused to avail himself of letters of liberation procured from Alexander III., saying that he would not owe his freedom to simony.[8]

This was by no means the only mode in which the supreme jurisdiction of Rome worked inestimable evil throughout Christendom. While the feudal courts were strictly territorial and local, and the judicial functions of the bishops were limited to their own dioceses so that every man knew to whom he was responsible in a tolerably well-settled system of justice, the universal jurisdiction of Rome gave ample opportunity for abuses of the worst kind. The pope, as supreme judge, could delegate to any one any portion of his authority, which was supreme everywhere; and the papal chancery was not too nice in its discrimination as to the character of the persons to whom it issued letters empowering them to exercise judicial functions and enforce them with the last dread sentence of excommunication—letters, indeed, which, if the papal{19} chancery is not wronged, were freely sold to all able to pay for them. Europe thus was traversed by multitudes of men armed with these weapons, which they used without remorse for extortion and oppression. Bishops, too, were not backward in thus farming out their more limited jurisdictions, and, in the confusion thus arising, it was not difficult for reckless adventurers to pretend to the possession of these delegated powers and use them likewise for the basest purposes, no one daring to risk the possible consequences of resistance. These letters thus afforded a *carte blanche* through which injustice could be perpetrated and malignity gratified to the fullest extent. An additional complication which not unnaturally followed was the fabrication and falsification of these letters. It was not easy to refer to distant Rome to ascertain the genuineness of a papal brief confidently produced by its bearer, and the impunity with which powers so tremendous could be assumed was irresistibly attractive. When Innocent III. ascended the throne he found a factory of forged letters in full operation in Rome, and although this was suppressed, the business was too profitable to be broken up by even his vigilance. To the end of his pontificate the detection of fraudulent briefs was a constant preoccupation. Nor was this industry confined to Rome. About the same period Stephen, Bishop of Tournay, discovered in his episcopal city a similar nest of counterfeiters, who had invented an ingenious instrument for the fabrication of the papal seals. To the people, however, it

7

mattered little whether they were genuine or fictitious; the suffering was the same whether the papal chancery had received its fee or not.[9] {20}

Thus the Roman curia was a terror to all who were brought in contact with it. Hildebert of le Mans pictures its officials as selling justice, delaying decisions on every pretext, and, finally, oblivious when bribes were exhausted. They were stone as to understanding, wood as to rendering judgment, fire as to wrath, iron as to forgiveness, foxes in deceit, bulls in pride, and minotaurs in consuming everything. In the next century Robert Grosseteste boldly told Innocent IV. and his cardinals that the curia was the source of all the vileness which rendered the priesthood a hissing and a reproach to Christianity, and, after another century and a half, those who knew it best described it as unaltered.[10]

When such was the example set by the head of the Church, it would have been a marvel had not too many bishops used all their abundant opportunities for the fleecing of their flocks. Peter Cantor, an unexceptionable witness, describes them as fishers for money and not for souls, with a thousand frauds to empty the pockets of the poor. They have, he says, three hooks with which to catch their prey in the depths— the confessor, to whom is committed the hearing of confessions and the cure of souls; the dean, archdeacon, and other officials, who advance the interest of the prelate by fair means or foul; and the rural provost, who is chosen solely with regard to his skill in squeezing the pockets of the poor and carrying the spoil to his master. These places were frequently farmed out, and the right to torture and despoil the people was sold to the highest bidder. The general detestation in which these gentry were held is illustrated by the story of an ecclesiastic who, having by an unlucky run of the dice lost all his money but five sols, exclaimed in blasphemous madness that he would give them to any one who would teach him how most greatly to offend God, and a bystander was adjudged to have won the money when he said, "If you wish to offend God beyond all other sinners, become an episcopal official or collector." Formerly, continues Peter Cantor, there was some decent concealment in absorbing the property of rich and poor, but now it is publicly and boldly seized through infinite devices and frauds and novelties of extortion. The officials of the prelates are not only their leeches, who suck and are squeezed, but {21} are strainers of the milk of their rapine, retaining for themselves the dregs of sin.[11]

From this honest burst of indignation we see that the main instrument of exaction and oppression was the judicial functions of the episcopate. Considerable revenues, it is true, were derived from the sale of benefices and the exaction of fees for all official acts, and many prelates did not blush to derive a filthy gain from the licentiousness universal among a celibate clergy by exacting a tribute known as "cullagium," on payment of which the priest was allowed to keep his concubine in peace, but the spiritual jurisdiction was the source of the greatest profit to the prelate and of the greatest misery to the people. Even in the temporal courts, the fines arising from litigation formed no mean portion of the income of the seigneurs; and in the Courts Christian, embracing the whole of spiritual jurisprudence and much of temporal, there was an ample harvest to be gathered. Thus, as Peter Cantor says, the most holy sacrament of matrimony, owing to the remote consanguinity coming within the prohibited degrees, was made a subject of derision to the laity by the venality with which marriages were made and unmade to fill the pouches of the episcopal officials. Excommunication was another fruitful source of extortion. If an unjust demand was resisted, the recalcitrant was excommunicated, and then had to pay for reconciliation in addition to the original sum. Any delay in obeying a summons to the court of the Officiality entailed excommunication with the same result of extortion. When litigation was so profitable, it was encouraged to the utmost, to the infinite wretchedness of the people. When a priest was inducted into a benefice, it was customary to exact of him an oath that he would not overlook any offences committed by his parishioners, but would report them to the Ordinary that the offenders might be prosecuted and fined, and that he would not allow any quarrels to be settled amicably; and though Alexander III. issued a decretal pronouncing all such oaths void, yet they continued to be required. As an illustration of the system a case is recorded where a boy in play accidentally killed a comrade with an arrow. The father of the slayer chanced to be wealthy, and {22} the two parents were not permitted to be reconciled gratuitously. Peter of Blois, Archdeacon of Bath, was probably not far wrong when he described the episcopal Ordinaries as vipers of iniquity transcending in malice all serpents and basilisks, as shepherds, not of lambs, but of wolves, and as devoting themselves wholly to malice and rapine.[12]

Even more efficient as a cause of misery to the people and hostility towards the Church was the venality of many of the episcopal courts. The character of the transactions and of the clerical lawyers who pleaded before them is visible in an attempted reformation by the Council of Rouen, in 1231, requiring the counsel who practised in these courts to swear that they would not steal the papers of the other side or produce forgeries or perjured testimony in support of their cases. The judges were well fitted to preside over such a bar. They are described as extortioners who sought by every device to filch the money of suitors to the last farthing, and when any fraud was too glaring for their own performance they had subordinate officials ever ready to play into their hands, rendering their occupation more base than that of a pimp with his bawds. That money was supreme in all judicial matters was clearly assumed when the Abbey of Andres quarrelled with the mother-house of Charroux, and the latter assured the former that it could spend in any court one hundred marks of silver against every ten livres that the other could afford; and in effect, when the ten years' litigation was over, including three appeals to Rome, Andres found itself oppressed with the enormous debt of fourteen hundred livres *parisis*, while the details of the transaction show the most unblushing bribery. The Roman court set the example to the rest, and its current reputation is visible in the praise bestowed on Eugenius III. for rebuking a prior who commenced a suit before him by offering a mark of gold to win his favor.[13]{23}

There was another source of oppression which had a loftier motive and better results, but which was none the less grinding upon the mass of the people. It was about this time that the fashion set in of building magnificent churches and abbeys, and the invention of stained glass and its rapid introduction show the luxury of ornamentation which was sought. While these structures were in some degree the expression of ardent faith, yet more were they the manifestation of the pride of the prelates who erected them, and in our admiration of these sublime relics of the past, in whatever reverential spirit we may view the towering spire, the long-arched nave, and the glorious window, we must not lose sight of the supreme effort which they cost—an effort which inevitably fell upon suffering serf and peasant. Peter Cantor assures us that they were built out of exactions on the poor, out of the unhallowed gains of usury, and out of the lies and deceits of the *quæstuarii* or pardoners; and the vast sums lavished upon them, he assures us, would be much better spent in redeeming captives and relieving the necessities of the helpless.[14]

It was hardly to be expected that prelates such as filled most of the sees of Christendom should devote themselves to the real duties of their position. Foremost among these duties was that of preaching the word of God and instructing their flocks in faith and morals. The office of preacher, indeed, was especially an episcopal function; he was the only man in the diocese authorized to exercise it; it formed no part of the duty or training of the parish priest, who could not presume to deliver a sermon without a special license from his superior. It need not surprise us, therefore, to see this portion of Christian teaching and devotion utterly neglected, for the turbulent and martial prelates of the day were too wholly engrossed in worldly cares to bestow a thought upon a matter for which their unfitness was complete. In 1031 the Council of Limoges expressed a wish that preaching should be done, not only at the episcopal seat, but in other churches, when the will of God inspires a competent doctor to the task; but the Church slumbered on until the spread of heresy aroused it to a sense of its unwisdom in neglecting so powerful a source of influence. In 1209 the Council of Avignon ordered the bishops to preach more{24} frequently and diligently than heretofore, and, when opportunity offered, to cause preaching to be done by honest and discreet persons. In 1215 the great Council of Lateran admitted the impracticability of bishops attending to this among so many more pressing avocations, and directed them to provide and pay proper persons to visit their parishes and edify the people by word and example. Yet little improvement could be expected from exhortations such as these, and the heretics had the field virtually to themselves until the Preaching Friars arose and were steadily rebuffed by those whose negligence they replaced. The Troubadour Inquisitor Izarn does not hesitate to declare that heresy never could have spread had there been good preachers to oppose it, and that it never could have been subdued but for the Dominicans.[15]

The character of the lower orders of ecclesiastics could not be reasonably expected to be better than that of their prelates. Benefices were mostly in the gift of the bishops, though, of course, advowsons were frequently held by the laity; special rights of patronage were held by religious bodies, and many of these latter filled vacancies in their own ranks by co-optation. Whatever was the nominating power, however, the result was apt to be the same. It is the universal complaint of the age that benefices were openly sold, or were bestowed through favor, without examination into the qualifications of the appointee, or the slightest regard as to his fitness. Even the rigid virtue of St. Bernard did not prevent him, in 1151, from soliciting a provostship for a graceless youth, the nephew of his friend the Bishop of Auxerre, though repentance induced by cooler reflection led him to withdraw his application, which he could the more easily do on learning that his friend, in dying, had left no less than seven churches to his beloved nephew. In the same year he was more cautious in refusing Count Thibaut of Champagne some preferment which he had asked for his son, a child of tender years; but the mere request for it shows how benefices, when not sold, were wont to be distributed; and it is safe to say that there were few like St. Bernard, with courage and conviction to reject the solicitations of the powerful. It is true that the{25} canon law was full of admirable precepts respecting the virtues and qualifications requisite for incumbents, but in practice they were a dead letter. Alexander III. was moved to indignation when he learned that the Bishop of Coventry was in the habit of giving churches to boys under ten years of age, but he could only order that the cures should be intrusted to competent vicars until the nominees reached a proper age, and this age he himself fixed at fourteen; while other popes charitably reduced to seven the minimum age for holding simple benefices or prebends. No effectual check for abuses of patronage, of course, could be expected of Rome, when the curia itself was the most eager recipient of benefit from the wrong. Its army of pimps and parasites was ever on the watch to obtain fat preferments in all the lands of Europe, and the popes were constantly writing to bishops and chapters demanding places for their friends.[16]

That pluralities, with all their attendant evils and abuses, should be habitual under such a system follows as a matter of course. In vain reforming popes and councils issued constitutions prohibiting them; in vain indignant moralists inveighed against the scandals and injuries which they occasioned, the ruin of the temporalities, the sacrifice of souls, and the general contempt excited for the Church. Forbidden by the canon law, like all other abuses they were a source of profit to the Roman curia, which was always ready to issue dispensations when the holders of pluralities found themselves likely to be disturbed in their sin; or they could

9

be used for purposes of statecraft, as when Innocent IV., in 1246, by skilful use of such dispensations broke up the menacing combination of the nobles of France. In fact, learned doctors of theology were found to defend the lawfulness of the abuse, as was done in a public disputation about the year 1238 by Master Philip, Chancellor of the University of Paris, who was a notorious pluralist himself. His fate, however, was a solemn warning to others. On his death-bed his friend, William of Auvergne, Bishop of Paris,{26} urged him to resign all his benefices but one, promising to make good the sacrifice if he should recover, but Philip refused, on the ground that he wished to experience whether he should be subjected to damnation on that account. The disputatious ardor of the schoolman was gratified. Soon after his death a dusky shade appeared to the good bishop at his prayers, announced itself to be the chancellor's soul, and declared that it was damned to eternity; though it must be admitted that habitual licentiousness was super-added to pluralism as a cause of hopeless perdition.[17]

A clergy recruited in such a manner and subjected to such influences could only, for the most part, be a curse to the people under their spiritual direction. A purchased benefice was naturally regarded as a business investment, to be exploited to the utmost profit, and there was little scruple in turning to account every device for extorting money from parishioners, while the duties of the Christian pastorate received little attention.

One of the most fruitful sources of quarrel and discontent was the tithe. This most harassing and oppressive form of taxation had long been the cause of incurable trouble, aggravated by the rapacity with which it was enforced, even to the pitiful collections of the gleaner. It had proved the greatest of the obstacles to Charlemagne's proselyting efforts among the Saxons, and, as we shall see, in the thirteenth century it led to a most devastating crusade against the Frisians. The resistance of the people to its exaction in some places was such that its non-payment was stigmatized as heresy, and everywhere we see it the cause of scandalous{27} altercation between pastor and flock, and between rival claimants, giving rise to a very intricate branch of canon law. Carlyle states that at the outbreak of the French Revolution there were no less than sixty thousand cases arising from tithes then pending before the courts, and though the statement may be exaggerated, it is by no means improbable. Anciently the tithe had been divided into four parts, of which one went to the bishop, one to the parish priest, one to the fabric of the Church, and one to the poor, but in the prevailing acquisitiveness of the period, bishop and priest each seized and held all they could get, the Church received little, and the poor none at all.[18]

The portion of the tithe which the priest could retain in this scramble was rarely sufficient for his wants, addicted as he frequently was to dissolute living, and exposed to the rapacity of his superiors. The form of simony which consists in selling his sacred ministrations therefore became general. Thus confession, which was now becoming obligatory on the faithful and the exclusive function of the priest, afforded a wide field for perverse ingenuity. Some confessors rated the sacrament of penitence so low that for a chicken or a pint of wine they would grant absolution for any sin, but others understood its productiveness far better. It is related of Einhardt, the priest of Soest, by a contemporary, that he sharply reproved a parishioner who, in preparation for Easter, confessed incontinence during Lent, and demanded of him eighteen deniers that he might say eighteen masses for his soul. Another came who said that during Lent he had abstained from his wife, and he was fined the same amount for masses because he had lost the chance of begetting a child, as was his duty. Both men had to sell their harvests prematurely to raise money to pay the fine, and, happening to meet upon the market-place, compared notes, when{28} they complained to the Dean and Chapter of St. Patroclus, and the story came out, to the scandal of the faithful, but Einhardt was permitted to continue his speculative career. Every function of the priest was thus turned to account, and the complaints of the practice are too frequent and sweeping for us to doubt that it was a general custom. Marriage and funeral ceremonies were refused until the fees demanded were paid in advance, and the Eucharist was withheld from the communicant unless he offered an oblation. To the believer in Transubstantiation nothing could be more inexpressibly shocking, and Peter Cantor well describes the priests of his day as worse than Judas Iscariot, who sold the body of the Lord for thirty pieces of silver, while they do it daily for a denier. Not content with this, many of them transgressed the rules which forbade, except on special occasions, the celebration by a priest of more than one mass a day, and it was almost impossible to enforce its observance; while those who obeyed the rule invented an ingenious evasion through which, by repeating the Introit, they would split a single mass up into half a dozen, and collect an oblation for each.[19]

If the faithful Christian thus was mulcted throughout life at every turn, the pursuit of gain was continued to his death-bed, and even his body had a speculative value which was turned to account by the ghouls who quarrelled over it. The necessity of the final sacraments for salvation gave rise to an occasional abuse by which they were refused unless an illegal fee or perquisite was paid, such as the sheet on which the dying sinner lay, but this we may well believe was not usual. More profitable was the custom by which the fears of approaching judgment were exploited and legacies for pious uses were suggested as an appropriate atonement for a life of wickedness or cruelty. It is well known how large a portion of the temporal possessions of the Church was procured in this manner, and already in the ninth century it had become a subject of{29} complaint. In 811 Charlemagne, in summoning provincial councils throughout his empire, asks them whether that man can be truly said to have renounced the world who unceasingly seeks to augment his possessions, and by promises of heaven and threats of hell persuades the simple and unlearned to disinherit their heirs, who are thus compelled by poverty to robbery and crime. To this pregnant question the Council of Chalons, in 813, responded by a canon forbidding such practices, and reminding the clergy that the Church should succor the needy rather than despoil them; that of Tours replied that it had made inquiry and could find no one complaining of exheredation; that of Reims prudently passed the matter over in silence; and that of Mainz promised restoration in such cases. This check was but temporary; the Church continued to urge its claims on the fears of the dying, and finally Alexander III., about 1170, decreed that no one could make a valid will except in the presence of his parish priest. In some places the notary drawing a will in the absence of the priest was excommunicated and the body of the testator was refused Christian burial. The reason sometimes alleged for this was the preventing of a heretic from leaving his property to heretics, but the flimsiness of this is shown by the repeated promulgation of the rule in regions where heresy was unknown, and the loud remonstrances against local customs which sought to defeat this development of ecclesiastical greed. Complaints were also sometimes made that the parish priest converted to his personal use legacies which were left for the benefit of pious foundations.[20]

Even after death the control which the Church exercised over the living and the profit to be derived from him were not abandoned. So general was the custom of leaving considerable sums for the pious ministrations by which the Church lightened the{30}torments of purgatory, and so usual was the bestowal of oblations at the funeral, that the custody of the corpse became a source of gain not to be despised, and the parish in which the sinner had lived and died claimed to have a reversionary right in the ashes which were thus so profitable. Occasionally intruders would trespass upon their preserves, and some monastery would prevail upon the dying to bequeath his fertilizing remains to its care, giving rise to unseemly squabbles over the corpse and the privilege of burying it and saying mortuary masses for its soul. As early as the fifth century Leo the Great did not hesitate to condemn in the severest terms the rapacity which led the monasteries to invite the living to their retreats for the sake of the possessions which they would bring with them, to the manifest detriment of the parish priest, thus deprived of his legitimate expectations. Leo therefore ordered a compromise, by which one half of the goods and chattels thus acquired should be transferred to the church of the deceased, whether he had entered the monastery dead or alive. The parish churches at last came to claim the bodies of their parishioners as a matter of right, and to deny to the dying the privilege of electing a place of sepulture. It required repeated papal decisions to set aside claims so persistently urged, but these decisions invariably conceded to the churches a portion of one fourth, one third, or one half the sum the deceased had set apart for the care of his soul. In some places the parish church asserted a right by custom to certain payments on the death of a parishioner, and the Council of Worcester, in 1240, decided that when this claim would reduce the widow and orphans to beggary, the Church should mercifully content itself with one third of the estate and relinquish the other two thirds to the family of the defunct; while in Lisbon the last consolations of religion were denied to any one who refused to leave a portion, usually one third, of his property to the Church. Under other local customs, the priest claimed as a perquisite the bier on which a corpse was brought to his church, leading, in case of resistance, to quarrels more lively than edifying. In Navarre the law stepped in to define the amount which the poorer classes should give as an offering in the mortuary mass, being two measures of corn for a peasant. Among the caballeros the usual offering was the incongruous one of a war-horse, a suit of armor, and jewels; and the cost of this was frequently defrayed{31} by the king to honor the memory of some distinguished knight. That the amounts were not small is evident when we see that, in 1372, Charles II. of Navarre paid to the Franciscan Guardian of Pampeluna thirty livres to redeem the charger, armor, etc., offered at the funeral of Masen Seguin de Badostal. With the rise of the mendicant orders and their enormous popularity, the rivalry between them and the secular clergy for the possession of corpses and the accompanying fees became more intense than ever, creating scandals of which we shall have more to say hereafter.[21]

On no point were the relations between the clergy and the people more delicate than on that of sexual purity. I have treated this subject fully in another work, and can be spared further reference to it, except to say that at the period under consideration the enforced celibacy of the priesthood had become generally recognized in most of the countries owing obedience to the Latin Church. It had not been accompanied, however, by the gift of chastity so confidently promised by its promoters. Deprived as was the priesthood of the gratification afforded by marriage to the natural instincts of man, the wife at best was succeeded by the concubine; at worst by a succession of paramours, for which the functions of priest and confessor gave peculiar opportunity. So thoroughly was this recognized that a man confessing an illicit amour was forbidden to name the partner of his guilt for fear it might lead the confessor into the temptation of abusing his knowledge of her frailty. No sooner had the Church, indeed, succeeded in suppressing the wedlock of its ministers, than we find it everywhere and incessantly busied in the apparently impossible task of compelling their chastity—an effort the futility of which is sufficiently demonstrated by its continuance to modern times. The age was not particularly sensitive on the subject of female virtue, but yet the spectacle of a priesthood professing ascetic purity as{32} an essential prerequisite to its functions, and practising a dissoluteness more cynical than that of the average layman, was not adapted to raise it in popular esteem; while the individual cases in which the peace and honor of families were sacrificed to the lusts of the pastor necessarily tended to rouse the deepest antagonism. As for darker and more deplorable crimes, they were sufficiently frequent, not alone in monasteries from which women were rigorously excluded; and, moreover, they were committed with virtual immunity. Not the least of the evils involved in the artificial asceticism ostensibly imposed on the priesthood was the erection of a false standard of morality which did infinite harm to the laity as well as to the Church. So long as the priest did not defy the canons by marrying, everything could be forgiven. Alexander II., who labored so strenuously to restore the rule of celibacy, in 1064

11

decided that a priest of Orange who had committed adultery with the wife of his father was not to be deprived of communion for fear of driving him to desperation; and, in view of the fragility of the flesh, he was to be allowed to remain in holy orders, though in the lower grades. Two years later the same pope charitably diminished the penance imposed on a priest of Padua who had committed incest with his mother, and left it to his bishop whether he should be retained in the priesthood. It would be difficult to exaggerate the disastrous influence on the people of such examples.[22]

Yet perhaps the most efficient cause of demoralization in the clergy, and of hostility between them and the laity, was the personal inviolability and the immunity from secular jurisdiction which they succeeded in establishing as a recognized principle of public law. While this was doubtless necessary for the independence, and even for the safety of a presumably peaceful class in an age of violence, it worked unhappily in a double sense. The readiness with which acquittal was obtainable in ecclesiastical procedure by canonical purgation, or the "wager of law," and the comparative mildness of the penalties in case of conviction, relieved the ecclesiastic in great measure from the terrors of the law, and removed from him the necessity of restraining his evil{33} propensities. At the same time it attracted to the Church vast numbers of worthless men, who, without abandoning their worldly pursuits, entered the lower grades and enjoyed the irresponsibility of their position, to the injury of its character and the detriment of all who came in contact with them. How, in maintaining its privileges, the Church habitually threw its ægis over those least deserving of sympathy, is well illustrated by the intervention of Innocent III. in favor of Waldemar, Bishop of Sleswick. He was the natural son of Cnut V. of Denmark, and had headed an armed insurrection against Waldemar II., the reigning king, on the suppression of which he was cast into prison. Innocent demanded his liberation, as his incarceration was a violation of the immunities of the Church. Waldemar naturally hesitated thus to expose his kingdom to the repetition of revolt, and Innocent at first modified his command in so far as to order the offender conveyed to Hungary and liberated there, promising that he should not be permitted again to disturb the realm; but he subsequently evoked the case to Rome, where, in spite of the bishop being the offspring of a double adultery and thus ineligible to holy orders, and in spite of the representations of the Danish envoys that he had been guilty of perjury, adultery, apostasy, and dilapidation, Innocent, in behalf of the liberties of the Church, restored him to his bishopric and patrimony, with the special privilege of administering it by deputy if he feared that residence would endanger his personal safety. When requested to decide whether laymen could arrest and bring before the episcopal court a clerk caught red-handed in the commission of gross wickedness, Innocent replied that they could only do so under the special command of a prelate—which was tantamount to granting virtual impunity in such cases. A sacerdotal body, whose class-privileges of wrong-doing were so tenderly guarded, was not likely to prove itself a desirable element of society; and when the orderly enforcement of law gradually established itself throughout Christendom, the courts of justice found in the immunity of the ecclesiastic a more formidable enemy to order than in the pretensions of the feudal seigniory. Indeed, when malefactors were arrested, their first effort habitually was to prove their clergy, that they wore the tonsure, and that they were not subject to the jurisdiction of the secular courts, while zeal for ecclesiastical rights, and possibly{34} for fees, always prompted the episcopal officials to support their claims and demand their release. The Church thus became responsible for crowds of unprincipled men, clerks only in name, who used the immunity of their position as a stalking-horse in preying upon the community.[23]

The similar immunity attaching to ecclesiastical property gave rise to abuses equally flagrant. The cleric, whether plaintiff or defendant, was entitled in civil cases to be heard before the spiritual courts, which were naturally partial in his favor, even when not venal, so that justice was scarce to be obtained by the laity. That such, in fact, was the experience is shown by the practice which grew up of clerks purchasing doubtful claims from laymen and then enforcing them before the Courts Christian—a speculative proceeding, forbidden, indeed, by the councils, but too profitable to be suppressed. Another abuse which excited loud complaint consisted in harassing unfortunate laymen by citing them to answer in the same case in several spiritual courts simultaneously, each of which enforced its process remorselessly by the expedient of excommunication, with consequent fines for reconciliation, on all who by neglect placed themselves in an apparent attitude of contumacy, frequently without even pausing to ascertain whether the parties thus amerced had actually been cited. To estimate properly the amount of wrong and suffering thus inflicted on the community, we must bear in mind that culture and training were almost exclusively confined to the ecclesiastical class, whose sharpened intelligence thus enabled them to take the utmost advantage of the ignorant and defenceless.[24]

The monastic orders formed too large and important a class not to share fully in the responsibility of the Church for good or for evil. Great as were their unquestioned services to religion and culture, they were peculiarly exposed to the degrading tendencies{35} of the age, and their virtues suffered proportionally. At this period they were rapidly obtaining exemption from episcopal jurisdiction and subjecting themselves immediately to Rome. This inevitably stimulated conventual degeneracy. Richard, Archbishop of Canterbury, complained bitterly to Alexander III. of the fatal relaxation thus induced in monastic discipline, but to no purpose. It abased the episcopate; it increased the authority of the Holy See, both directly and indirectly, through the important allies thus acquired in its struggles with the bishops; and it was, moreover, a source of revenue, if we may believe the Abbot of Malmesbury, who boasted that for an ounce of gold per year paid to Rome he could obtain exemption from the jurisdiction of the Bishop of Salisbury. In too many cases the abbeys thus became centres of corruption and disturbance, the nunneries scarce better than houses of prostitution, and the monasteries feudal castles where the monks lived riotously and waged war upon their neighbors as ferociously as the turbulent barons, with the added disadvantage that, as there was no hereditary succession, the death of an abbot was apt to be followed by a disputed election producing internal broils and outside interference. Thus in a quarrel of this kind occurring in 1182, the rich abbey of St. Tron was attacked by the Bishops of Metz and Liège, the town and abbey were burned, and the inhabitants put to the sword. The trouble lasted until the end of the century, and when it was temporarily patched up by a pecuniary transaction, the wretched vassals and serfs were reduced to starvation to raise the funds which bought the elevation of an ambitious monk. It is true that all establishments were not lost to the duties for which they had received so abundantly of the benefactions of the faithful. In the famine of 1197, though the monastery of Heisterbach was still young and poor, the Abbot Gebhardt distributed alms so lavishly that sometimes he fed fifteen hundred people a day, while the mother-house of Hemmenrode was even more liberal, and supported all the poor of its district till harvest-time. At the same time a Cistercian abbey in Westphalia slaughtered all its flocks and herds and pledged its books and sacred vessels to feed the starving. It is satisfactory to be assured that in each case the expenditures were more than made up by the donations which the establishments received in consequence of their charity. Such instances go far to redeem the institution of monachism, but{36} for the most part the abbeys were sources of evil rather than of good.[25]

This is scarce to be wondered at if we consider the material from which their inmates were drawn. It is the severest reproach upon their discipline to find so enthusiastic an admirer of the strict Cistercian rule as Cæsarius of Heisterbach asserting as an admitted fact that boys bred in monasteries made bad monks and frequently became apostates. As for those who took the vows in advanced life, he enumerates their motives as sickness, poverty, captivity, infamy, mortal danger, dread of hell or desire of heaven, among which the predominance of selfish impulses was not likely to secure a desirable class of devotees. In fact, he assures us that criminals frequently escaped punishment by agreeing to enter monasteries, which thus in some sort became penal settlements, or prisons, and he illustrates this with the case of a robber baron in 1209, condemned to death for his crimes by the Count Palatine Henry, who was rescued by Daniel, Abbot of Schonau, on condition of his entering the Cistercian order. Scarcely less desirable inmates were those who, moved by a sudden revulsion of conscience, would turn from a life stained with crime and violence to bury themselves in the cloister while yet in the full vigor of strength and with passions unexhausted, finding, perhaps, at last their fierce and untamed natures unfitted to bear the unaccustomed restraint. The chronicles are full of illustrations of this passionate religious energy in natures wholly untrained in self-control, and they explain much that otherwise would seem incredible to the calmer and more self-contained world of to-day. For instance when, in 1071, Arnoul III. of Flanders, fell at Montcassel in defending his dominions against his uncle, Robert the Frisian, Gerbald, the knight who slew his suzerain, was seized with remorse for his act and wandered to Rome, where he presented himself before Gregory VII. with the request that his hands be stricken off as a fitting{37} penance. Gregory assented, and ordered his chief cook to do the service, secretly instructing him that if, when the axe was raised, Gerbald shrank or wavered, he was to strike without mercy, but if the penitent was firm, then he was to announce that he was spared. Gerbald did not blench, and the pope declared to him that the hands thus preserved were no longer his but the Lord's, and sent him to Cluny to be placed under the charge of the holy Abbot Hugh, where the fierce warrior peacefully ended his days. If, as sometimes happened, these untamable souls chafed under the irrevocable vow, after the fit of repentance had passed, they offered ample material for internal sedition and external violence.[26]

Among these ill-assorted crowds it was impossible to maintain the community of property which was the essence of the rule of Benedict. Gregory the Great, when Abbot of St. Andreas, denied the last consolations of religion to a dying brother, and kept his soul for sixty days in the torments of purgatory, because three pieces of gold had been found among his garments. Yet the good monks of St. Andreas, of Vienne, found it necessary to adopt a formal constitution segregating as a sacrilegious thief any of the brethren detected in stealing clothing from the dormitory, or cups or plates from the refectory, and threatening to call in the intervention of the bishop if the offence could not be otherwise suppressed. So it is mentioned that in the Abbey of St. Tron, about the year 1200, each monk had a locked cupboard behind his seat in the refectory, wherein he carefully secured his napkin, spoon, cup, and dish, to preserve them from his brethren. In the dormitory matters were even worse. Those who could procure chests threw into them their bed-clothes on rising, and those who could not were constantly complaining of the thievish propensities of their fellows.[27]

The name of monk was rendered still more despicable by the crowds of "gyrovagi" and "sarabaitæ" and "stertzer"—wanderers and vagrants, bearded and tonsured and wearing the religious habit, who traversed every corner of Christendom, living by begging{38} and imposture, peddling false relics and false miracles. This was a pest which had afflicted the Church ever since the rise of monachism in the fourth century, and it continued unabated. Though there were holy and saintly men among these ghostly tramps, yet were they all subjected to common abhorrence. They were often detected in crime and slain without mercy; and in a vain effort to suppress the evil, the Synod of Cologne, early in the thirteenth century, absolutely forbade that any of them should be received to hospitality throughout that extensive province.[28]

13

It was not that earnest efforts were lacking to restore the neglected monastic discipline. Individual monasteries were constantly being reformed, to sink back after a time into relaxation and indulgence. Ingenuity was taxed to frame new and severer rules, such as the Premonstratensian, the Carthusian, the Cistercian, which should repel all but the most ardent souls in search of ascetic self-mortification, but as each order grew in repute for holiness, the liberality of the faithful showered wealth upon it, and with wealth came corruption. Or the humble hermitage founded by a few self-denying anchorites, whose only thought was to secure salvation by macerating the flesh and eluding temptation, would become possessed of the relics of some saint, whose wonder-working powers drew flocks of pious pilgrims and sufferers in search of relief. Offerings in abundance would flow in, and the fame and riches thus showered on the modest retreat of the hermits speedily changed it to a splendid structure where the severe virtues of the founders disappeared amid a crowd of self-indulgent monks, indolent in all good works and active only in evil. Few communities had the cautious wisdom of the early denizens in the celebrated Priory of Grammont, before it became the head of a powerful order. When its founder and first prior, St. Stephen of Thiern, after his death in 1124, commenced to show his sanctity by curing a paralytic knight and restoring sight to a blind man, his single-minded followers took alarm at the prospect of wealth and notoriety{39} thus about to be forced upon them. His successor, Prior Peter of Limoges, accordingly repaired to his tomb and reproachfully addressed him: "O servant of God, thou hast shown us the path of poverty and hast earnestly striven to teach us to walk therein. Now thou wishest to lead us from the straight and narrow way of salvation to the broad road of eternal death. Thou hast preached the solitude, and now thou seekest to convert the solitude into a market-place and a fair. We already believe sufficiently in thy saintliness. Then work no more miracles to prove it and at the same time to destroy our humility. Be not so solicitous for thy own fame as to neglect our salvation; this we enjoin on thee, this we ask of thy charity. If thou dost otherwise, we declare, by the obedience which we have vowed to thee, that we will dig up thy bones and cast them into the river." This mingled supplication and threat proved sufficient, and until St. Stephen was formally canonized he ceased to perform the miracles so dangerous to the souls of his followers. The canonization, which occurred in 1189, was the result of the first official act of Prior Girard, in applying for it to Clement III., and as Girard had been elected in place of two contestants set aside by papal authority, after dissensions which had almost ruined the monastery, it shows that worldly passions and ambition had invaded the holy seclusion of Grammont, to work out their inevitable result.[29]

In the failure of all these partial efforts at reform to rescue the monastic orders from their degradation, we hardly need the emphatic testimony of the venerable Gilbert, Abbot of Gemblours, about 1190, when he confesses with shame that monachism had become an oppression and a scandal, a hissing and reproach to all men.[30]

The religion which was thus exploited by priest and monk{40} had necessarily become a very different creed from that taught by Christ and Paul. Doctrines are beyond my province, but a brief reference is requisite to certain phases of belief and observance to render clear the relation between clergy and people, and to explain the religious revolt of the twelfth and thirteenth centuries.

The theory of justification by works, to which the Church owed so much of its power and wealth, had, in its development, to a great extent deprived religion of all spiritual vitality, replacing its essentials with a dry and meaningless formalism. It was not that men were becoming indifferent to the destiny of their souls, for never, perhaps, have the terrors of perdition, the bliss of salvation, and the never-ending efforts of the arch-fiend possessed a more burning reality for man, but religion had become in many respects a fetichism. Teachers might still inculcate that pious and charitable works to be efficient must be accompanied with a change of heart, with repentance, with amendment, with an earnest seeking after Christ and a higher life; but in a gross and hardened generation it was far easier for the sinner to fall into the practices habitual around him, which taught that absolution could be had by the repetition of a certain number of Pater Nosters or Ave Marias accompanied by the magical sacrament of penitence; nay, even that if the penitent himself were unable to perform the penance enjoined, it could be undertaken by his friends, whose merits were transferred to him by some kind of sacred jugglery. When a congregation, in preparation for Easter, was confessed and absolved as a whole, or in squads and batches, as was customary with some careless priests, the lesson taught was that the sacrament of penitence was a magic ceremony or incantation, in which the internal condition of the soul was a matter of virtual indifference.[31]

More serviceable to the Church, and quite as disastrous in its influence on faith and morals, was the current belief that the posthumous liberality of the death-bed, which founded a monastery or enriched a cathedral out of the spoils for which the sinner had no further use, would atone for a lifelong course of cruelty and rapine; and that a few weeks' service against the enemies of a{41} pope would wipe out all the sins of him who assumed the cross to exterminate his fellow-Christians. The use, or abuse, of indulgences, indeed, is a subject which would repay extended investigation, and a brief reference to it may be pardoned here, in view of the frequent allusions to it which will occur hereafter.

That sin, confessed and repented, could be remitted through penance, was a doctrine dating back to primitive times. That penance could be redeemed by sacrifices made for the Church was a corollary of later origin, but yet well established at this period. Thus, in 1059, we see Guido, Archbishop of Milan, imposing on himself a penance of one hundred years, to atone for rebellion against Rome, and redeeming it at a certain sum for each year—a transaction which satisfied even so stern a moralist as St. Peter Damiani. Then the schoolmen invented the theory of the treasure of salvation, accumulated through the merits of the Crucifixion and of the saints, and the pope, as the vicar of God, had the unlimited dispensation of that treasure. It was for him to prescribe the methods by which the faithful could partake of it, and no theologian before Wickliffe was hardy enough to question his decisions. In the administration of this treasure the pope issued "pardons," either plenary or partial, the former releasing the soul absolutely from the purgatorial punishment of its sins after their guilt had been wiped out in the sacrament of penitence, the latter shortening the punishment by the equivalent of the penance remitted by the terms of the concession. At first this partial indulgence was granted in return for pious works, pilgrimages to shrines, contributions towards the building of churches, bridges, etc.—for a spiritual punishment could be commuted to a corporal or to a pecuniary one, and the power to grant such indulgence was a valuable franchise to the church which obtained it, for it served as a constant attraction to pilgrims. Abuses, of course, crept in, denounced by Abelard, who vents his indignation at the covetousness which habitually made a traffic of salvation. Alexander III., about 1175, expressed his disapproval of these corruptions, and the great Council of Lateran, in 1215, sought to check the destruction of discipline and the contempt felt for the Church by limiting to one year the amount of penance released by any one episcopal indulgence. At length St. Francis of Assisi was said to have procured, in 1223, from Honorius III. the celebrated "Portiuncula" indulgence,[42] whereby all who visited the Church of Santa Maria de Portiuncula, at Assisi, from the vespers of August 1st to the vespers of August 2d, obtained complete and entire remission of all sins committed since baptism; and even the fact that St. Francis had been directed by God to apply to Honorius for it, and the admission of Satan that this indulgence was depopulating hell, did not serve to reconcile the Dominicans to so great an advantage given to the Franciscans. Boniface VIII., when he conceived the fruitful idea of the jubilee, carried this out still further by promising to all who should perform certain devotions in the basilicas of St. Peter and St. Paul, during the year 1300, not only "*plena venia*," but "*plenissima*," of all their sins. By this time the idea that an indulgence might avert the entire penalty of all sins had become familiar to the Christian mind. When the Church sought to arouse Europe to supreme exertion for the redemption of the Holy Sepulchre some infinite reward was requisite to excite the enthusiastic fanaticism requisite for the crusades. If Mahomet could stimulate his followers to court death by the promise of immediate and eternal bliss to him who fell fighting for the Crescent, the vicegerent of the true God must not be behindhand in his promises to the martyrs of the Cross. It was to be a death-struggle between the two faiths, and Christianity must not be less liberal than Islam in its bounty to its recruits. Accordingly when Urban II. held the great Council of Clermont, which resolved on the first crusade, and where thirteen archbishops, two hundred and fifteen bishops, and ninety mitred abbots represented the universal Church Militant, the device of plenary indulgence was introduced, and the military pilgrims were exhorted to have full faith that those who fell repentant would gain the completest fruit of eternal mercy. The device was so successful that it became an established rule in all the holy wars in which the Church engaged; all the more attractive, perhaps, because of the demoralizing character of the service, for it was a commonplace of the *jongleurs* of the period that the crusader, if he escaped the perils of sea and land, was tolerably sure to return home a lawless bandit, even as the pilgrim who went to Rome to secure pardon came back much worse than he started. As the novelty of crusading wore off, still greater promises were necessary. Thus, in 1291, Nicholas IV. promised full remission of sins to every one who would send a crusader or go at another's[43] expense; while he who went at his own expense was vaguely told that in addition he would have an increase of salvation—a term which the Decretalists perhaps could not find it easy to explain. Finally, forgotten sins were included in the pardon, as well as those confessed and repented.[32][44]

As an additional inducement to crusaders they were, moreover, released from earthly as well as heavenly justice, by being classed with clerks and subjected only to spiritual jurisdiction. When accused, the ecclesiastical judge was directed to take them from the secular courts by the use of excommunication, if necessary, and when found guilty of enormous crime, such as murder, they were merely divested of the cross, and punished with the same leniency as ecclesiastics. This became embodied in secular jurisprudence, and its attraction to the reckless adventurers who formed so large a portion of the papal armies is readily conceivable. When, in 1246, those who had taken the cross in France were indulging themselves in robbery, murder, and rape, St. Louis was obliged to appeal to Innocent IV., and the pope responded by instructing his legate that such malefactors were not to be protected.[33]

Still further rewards were offered when personal ambition and vindictiveness were to be gratified in the crusade preached by Innocent IV. against the Emperor Conrad IV., after the death of Frederic II., when he granted a larger remission of sins than for the voyage to the Holy Land, and included the father and mother of the crusader as beneficiaries in the assurance of heaven. A profitable device had also been introduced by which crusaders, unwilling or unable to perform their vow, were absolved from it on a money payment proportioned to their ability, and very large sums were raised in this manner, which were expended, nominally at least, for the furtherance of the holy cause. The development of the system continued until it came to be employed in the pettiest private quarrels of the popes as masters of the patrimony of St. Peter. If Alexander IV. could use it successfully against Eccelin da Romano, the next century saw John XXII. have recourse to it, not only in making war against a formidable antagonist like Matteo Visconti or the Marquis of Montefeltre, but even when he wished to reduce the rebellious citizens of little places like Osimo and Recanati, in the March of Ancona, or the turbulent[45] people of Rome itself. The ingenious method of granting indulgences to those who took the cross, and then releasing them from service for a sum of money, had become too cumbrous, and the purchase of salvation simplified itself into a direct payment, so that John was able to raise funds for his private wars by thus distributing the treasures of salvation over Christendom, and ordering the prelates everywhere to establish coffers in the churches by which the pious could help the Church while they saved their souls. The prelates who saw with regret the coins of their parishioners disappear into the never-satisfied maelstrom of the Holy See, in vain endeavored to resist. They were no longer independent, and the slender barriers which they sought to erect were easily swept away.[34]

These money payments were doubtless more practically efficacious than an indulgence, remitting a certain number of days of penance, offered to all who would earnestly pray to God, especially during the solemnity of the mass, for the success of the same pope in his death-struggle with Louis of Bavaria. This is a specimen of the minor indulgences which were frequently granted as a stimulus to acts of devotion, such as visiting cathedrals on the anniversaries of their patron saints; reciting, for the peace and prosperity of the Church, on bended knees, the Pater Noster five times, in honor of the five wounds of Christ; the Ave Maria seven times, in honor of the seven joys of the Virgin, and other similar practices.[35][46]

A more demoralizing system of indulgences was that of sending out "quaestuarii," or pardoners, sometimes furnished with relics, by a church or hospital in need of money, and sometimes merely carrying papal or episcopal letters, by which they were authorized to issue pardons for sin in return for contributions. Though these letters were cautiously framed, yet they were ambiguous enough to enable the pardoners to promise, not only the salvation of the living, but the liberation of the damned from hell for a few small coins. Already, in 1215, the Council of Lateran inveighs bitterly against these practices, and prohibits the removal of relics from the churches; but the abuse was too profitable to be suppressed. Needy bishops and popes were constantly issuing such letters, and the business of the pardoner became a regular profession, in which the most impudent and shameless were the most successful, so that we can readily believe the pseudo Peter of Pilichdorf, when he sorrowfully admits that the "indiscreet" but profitable granting of indulgences to all sorts of men weakened the faith of many Catholics in the whole system. As early as 1261 the Council of Mainz can hardly find words strong enough to denounce the pestilent sellers of indulgences, whose knavish tricks excite the hatred of all men, who spend their filthy gains in vile debauchery, and who so mislead the faithful that confession is neglected on the ground that sinners have purchased forgiveness of their sins. Complaint was useless, however, and the lucrative abuse continued unchecked until it aroused the indignation which[47] found a mouthpiece in Luther. Subsequent councils are full of complaints of the lies and frauds of these peddlers of salvation, who continued to flourish until the Reformation; and Tassoni fairly represents the popular conviction that this was an unfailing resort of the Church in its secular aims—

"Le cose della guerra andavan zoppe;
I Bolognesi richiedean danari
Al Papa, ad egli rispondeva coppe,
E mandava indulgenze per gli altari."[36]

The sale of indulgences illustrates effectively the sacerdotalism which formed the distinguishing feature of mediæval religion. The believer did not deal directly with his Creator—scarce even with the Virgin or hosts of intercessory saints. The supernatural powers claimed for the priest interposed him as the mediator between God and man; his bestowal or withholding of the sacraments decided the fate of immortal souls; his performance of the mass diminished or shortened the pains of purgatory; his decision in the confessional determined the very nature of sin itself. The implements which he wielded—the Eucharist, the relics, the holy water, the chrism, the exorcism, the prayer—became in some sort fetiches which had a power of their own entirely irrespective of the moral or spiritual condition of him who employed them or of him for whom they were employed; and in the popular view the rites of religion could hardly be more than magic formulas which in some mysterious way worked to the advantage, temporal and spiritual, of those for whom they were performed.

How sedulously this fetichism was inculcated by those who profited from the control of the fetiches is shown by a thousand stories and incidents of the time. Thus a twelfth-century chronicler piously narrates that when, in 887, the relics of St. Martin of Tours were brought home from Auxerre, whither they had been[48] carried to escape the Danish incursions, two cripples of Touraine, who earned an easy livelihood by beggary, on hearing of the approach of the saintly bones, counselled together to escape from the territory as quickly as possible, lest the returning saint should cure them and thus deprive them of claims on the alms of the charitable. Their fears were well founded, but their means of locomotion were insufficient, for the relics arrived in Touraine before they could get beyond the bounds of the province, and they were cured in spite of themselves. The eagerness with which rival princes and republics disputed with each other the possession of these wonder-working fetiches, and the manner in which the holy objects were obtained by force or fraud and defended by the same methods, form a curious chapter in the history of human credulity, and show how completely the miraculous virtue was held to reside in the relic itself, wholly irrespective of the crimes through which it was acquired or the frame of mind of the possessor. Thus in the above case, Ingelger of Anjou was obliged to reclaim from the Auxerrois the bones of St. Martin at the head of an armed force, more peaceful means of recovering the venerated relics having failed; and in 1177 we see a certain Martin, canon of the Breton church of Bomigny, stealing the body of St. Petroc from his own church for the benefit of the Abbey of St. Mevennes, which would not surrender it until the intervention of King Henry II. was brought to bear. Two years after the capture of Constantinople the Venetian leaders, in 1206, forcibly broke into the Church of St. Sophia and carried off a picture of the Virgin, said to have been painted by St. Luke, in which popular superstition imagined her to reside, and kept it in spite of excommunication and interdict launched against them by the patriarch and confirmed by the papal legate. Fairly illustrative of this belief is a story told of a merchant of Groningen who in one of his voyages coveted the arm of St. John the Baptist belonging to a hospital, and obtained it by bribing heavily the mistress of the guardian, who induced him to steal it. On his return the merchant built a house and secretly encased the relic in a pillar forming part of the structure. Under its protection he prospered mightily and grew wealthy, till once in a conflagration he refused to take measures to save the house, saying that it was under good guardianship. The house was not burned, and public curiosity was so much excited{49} that he was forced to reveal his talisman, when the people carried it off and deposited it in a church, where it worked many miracles, while the merchant was reduced to poverty. It was a superstition even less rational than that which led the Romans to conjure into their camp the tutelary deity of a city which they were besieging; and the universal wearing of relics as charms or amulets had in it nothing to distinguish it from the similar practices of paganism. Even the images and portraits of saints and martyrs had equal virtue. A single glance at the representation of St. Christopher, for instance, was held to preserve one from disease or sudden death for the rest of the day—

"Christophori sancti speciem quicumque tuetur
Illo namque die nullo languore tenetur—

and a huge image of the gigantic saint was often painted on the outside of churches for the preservation of the population. The custom of selecting a patron saint by lot at the altar is another manifestation of the same blindness of superstition.[37]

The Eucharist was particularly efficacious as a fetich. During the persecution of heresy in the Rhinelands by the inquisitor Conrad of Marburg, in 1233, one obstinate culprit refused to burn in spite of all the efforts of his zealous executioners, until a thoughtful priest brought to the roaring pile a consecrated host. This at once dissolved the spell by a mightier magic, and the luckless heretic was speedily reduced to ashes. A conventicle of these same heretics possessed an image of Satan which gave forth oracular responses, until a priest entering the room produced from his bosom a pyx containing the body of Christ, when Satan at once acknowledged his inferiority by falling down. Not long afterwards St. Peter Martyr overcame, by the same means, the imposture of a Milanese heretic in whose behalf a demon was wont to appear in a heterodox church in the shape of the Virgin, resplendent and holding in her arms the holy Child. The evidence in favor of heresy seemed to be overwhelming, until St. Peter dispelled it by presenting to the demon a host, and saying, "If thou{50} art the true Mother of God, adore this thy Son," whereupon the demon disappeared in a flash of lightning, leaving an intolerable stench behind him. The consecrated wafer was popularly believed to possess a magic efficacy of incomparable power, and stories are numerous of the punishment inflicted on those who sacrilegiously sought thus to use it. A priest who retained it in his mouth for the purpose of using it to overcome the virtue of a woman of whom he was enamoured, was afflicted with the hallucination that he had swelled to the point that he could not pass through a doorway; and on burying the sacred object in his garden it was changed into a small crucifix bearing a man of flesh and freshly bleeding. So when a woman kept the wafer and placed it in her beehive to stop an epidemic among the bees, the pious insects built around it a complete chapel, with walls, windows, roof, and bell-tower, and inside an altar on which they reverently placed it. Another woman, to preserve her cabbages from the ravages of caterpillars, crumbled a holy wafer and sprinkled it over the vegetables, when she was at once afflicted with incurable paralysis. This particular form of fetichism was evidently not regarded with favor, but it was the direct evolution of orthodox teaching. It was the same in respect to the water in which a priest washed his hands after handling the Eucharist, to which supernatural virtues were ascribed, but the use of which was condemned as savoring of sorcery.[38]

The power of these magic formulas, as I have said, was wholly disconnected with any devotional feeling on the part of those who employed them. Thus the efficacy of St. Thomas of Canterbury was illustrated by a story of a matron whose veneration for him led her to invoke him on all occasions, and even to teach her pet bird to repeat the formula "Sancte Thoma adjuva me!" Once a hawk seized the bird and flew away with it, but on the bird uttering the accustomed phrase, the hawk fell dead and the bird returned unhurt to its mistress. So little, indeed, of sanctity was requisite, that wicked priests employed the mass as an incantation and execration, mentally cursing their enemies while engaged in its solemnization, and expecting that in some way the malediction{51}would work evil on the person against whom it was directed. Nay, it was even used in connection with the immemorial superstition of the wax figurine which represented the enemy to be destroyed, and mass celebrated ten times over such an image was supposed to insure his death within ten days.[39]

Even confession could be used as a magic formula to escape the detection of guilt. As demons professed a knowledge of every crime committed, and would reveal them through the mouth of those whom they possessed, demoniacs were frequently used as detectives in case of suspected persons. Yet when sins were confessed with due contrition, the absolution wiped them forever from the demon's memory, and he would

17

deny all knowledge of them—a fact which was regularly acted on by those afraid of exposure; for even after the demon had revealed the guilt, the perpetrator could go at once and confess, and then confidently return and challenge a repetition of the denunciation.[40]

Examples such as these could be multiplied almost indefinitely, but they would only serve to weary the reader. What I have given will probably suffice to illustrate the degeneracy of the Christianity superimposed upon paganism and wielded by a sacerdotal body so worldly in its aspirations as that of the Middle Ages.

The picture which I have drawn of the Church in its relations with the people is perhaps too unrelieved in its blackness. All popes were not like Innocent IV. and John XXII.; all bishops were not cruel and licentious; all priests were not intent solely on impoverishing men and dishonoring women. In many sees and abbeys, and in thousands of parishes, doubtless, there were prelates and pastors earnestly seeking to do God's work, and illuminate the darkened souls of their flocks with such gospel light as the superstition of the time would permit. Yet the evil was more apparent than the good; the humble workers passed away unobtrusively, while pride and cruelty and lust and avarice were demonstrative and far-reaching in their influence. Such as I have{52} depicted the Church it appeared to all the men of the time who had the clearest insight and the loftiest aspirations; and its repulsiveness must be understood by those who would understand the movements that agitated Christendom.

No more unexceptionable witness as to the Church of the twelfth century can be had than St. Bernard, and he is never weary of denouncing the pride, the wickedness, the ambition, and the lust that reigned everywhere. When fornication, adultery, incest, palled upon the exhausted senses, a zest was sought in deeper depths of degradation. In vain the cities of the plain were destroyed by the avenging fire of heaven; the enemy has scattered their remains everywhere, and the Church is infected with their accursed ashes. The Church is left poor and bare and miserable, neglected and bloodless. Her children seek not to bedeck, but to spoil her; not to guard her, but to destroy her; not to defend, but to expose; not to institute, but to prostitute; not to feed the flock, but to slay and devour it. They exact the price of sins and give no thought to sinners. "Whom can you show me among the prelates who does not seek rather to empty the pockets of his flock than to subdue their vices?" St. Bernard's contemporary, Potho of Pruhm, in 1152, voices the same complaints. The Church is rushing to ruin, and not a hand is raised to stay its downward progress; there is not a single priest fitted to rise up as a mediator between God and man and approach the divine throne with an appeal for mercy.[41]

The papal legate, Cardinal Henry of Albano, in his Encyclical letter of 1188 to the prelates of Germany, is equally emphatic though less eloquent. The triumph of the Prince of Darkness is to be expected in view of the depravity of the clergy—their luxury, their gluttony, their disregard of the fasts, their holding of pluralities, their hunting, hawking, and gambling, their trading and their quarrels, and, chief of all, their incontinence, whence the wrath of God is provoked to the highest degree and the worst scandals are created between the clergy and the people. Peter Cantor, about{53} the same time, describes the Church as filled to the mouth with the filth of temporalities, of avarice, and of negligence, so that in these points it far surpasses the laity; and he points out that nothing is more damaging to the Church than to see laymen superior, as a class, to the clergy. Gilbert of Gemblours tells the same tale. The prelates for the most part enter the Church not by election, but by the use of money and the favor of princes; they enter, not to feed, but to be fed; not to minister, but to be ministered to; not to sow, but to reap; not to labor, but to rest; not to guard the sheep from the wolves, but, fiercer than wolves, themselves to tear the sheep. St. Hildegarda, in her prophecies, espouses the cause of the people against the clergy. "The prelates are ravishers of the churches; their avarice consumes all that it can acquire. With their oppressions they make us paupers and contaminate us and themselves.... Is it fitting that wearers of the tonsure should have greater store of soldiers and arms than we? Is it becoming that a clerk should be a soldier and a soldier a clerk?... God did not command that one son should have both coat and cloak and that the other should go naked, but ordered the cloak to be given to one and the coat to the other. Let the laity then have the cloak on account of the cares of the world, and let the clergy have the coat that they may not lack that which is necessary."[42]

One of the main objects in convoking the great Council of Lateran, in 1215, was the correction of the prevailing vices of the clergy, and it adopted numerous canons looking to the suppression of the chief abuses, but in vain. Those abuses were too deeply rooted, and four years later Honorius III., in an Encyclical addressed to all the prelates of Christendom, says that he has waited to see the result. He finds the evils of the Church increasing rather than diminishing. The ministers of the altar, worse than beasts wallowing in their dung, glory in their sins, as in Sodom. They are a snare and a destruction to the people. Many prelates consume the property committed to their trust and scatter the stores of the sanctuary throughout the public places; they promote the unworthy, waste the revenues of the Church on the wicked, and convert the churches into conventicles of their kindred. Monks and{54} nuns throw off the yoke, break their chains, and render themselves contemptible as dung. "Thus it is that heresies flourish. Let each of you gird his sword to his thigh and spare not his brother and his nearest kindred." What was accomplished by this earnest exhortation may be estimated from the description which Robert Grosseteste, Bishop of Lincoln, gave of the Church in the presence of Innocent IV. and his cardinals in 1250. The details can well be spared, but they are summed up in his assertion that the clergy were a source of pollution to the whole earth; they were antichrists and devils masquerading as angels of light, who made the house of prayer a den of robbers. When the earnest inquisitor of Passau, about 1260, undertook to

18

explain the stubbornness of the heresy which he was vainly endeavoring to suppress, he did so by drawing up a list of the crimes prevalent among the clergy, which is awful in the completeness of its details. A church such as he describes was an unmitigated curse, politically, socially, and morally.[43]

This is all ecclesiastical testimony. How the clergy were regarded by the laity is illustrated in a remark by William of Puy-Laurens, that it was a common phrase "I had rather be a priest than do that," just as one might say "I had rather be a Jew." It is true that the priests had the same contempt for the monks, for Emeric, Abbot of Anchin, tells us that a clerk would never associate with any one whom he had once seen wearing the black Benedictine habit. But priest and monk were both comprehended in the general detestation of the people. Walther von der Vogelweide sums up the popular appreciation of the whole ecclesiastical body, from pope downward:

"St. Peter's chair is filled to-day as well
As when 'twas fouled by Gerbert's sorcery;
For he consigned himself alone to hell,
While this pope thither drags all Christentie.
Why are the chastisements of Heaven delayed?
How long wilt thou in slumber lie, O Lord?
Thy work is hindered and thy word gainsaid,
Thy treasurer steals the wealth that thou hast stored. {55}
Thy ministers rob here and murder there,
And o'er thy sheep a wolf has shepherd's care."[44]

Walther's echo is heard from the other end of Europe in the Troubadour Pierre Cardinal, who enlarges on the same theme in a manner to show how popular were these invectives and how completely they expressed the general feeling:

"I see the pope his sacred trust betray,
For, while the rich his grace can gain alway,
His favors from the poor are aye withholden.
He strives to gather wealth as best he may,
Forcing Christ's people blindly to obey,
So that he may repose in garments golden.
The vilest traffickers in souls are all
His chapmen, and for gold a prebend's stall
He'll sell them, or an abbacy or mitre.
And to us he sends clowns and tramps who crawl
Vending his pardon briefs from cot to hall—
Letters and pardons worthy of the writer,
Which leave our pokes, if not our souls, the lighter.

"No better is each honored cardinal.
From early morning's dawn to evening's fall,
Their time is passed in eagerly contriving
To drive some bargain foul with each and all.
So, if you feel a want, or great or small,
Or if for some preferment you are striving,
The more you please to give the more 'twill bring,
Be it a purple cap or bishop's ring.
And it need ne'er in any way alarm you
That you are ignorant of everything
To which a minister of Christ should cling,
You will have revenue enough to warm you—
And, bear in mind, that lesser gifts won't harm you.

"Our bishops, too, are plunged in similar sin,
For pitilessly they flay the very skin
From all their priests who chance to have fat livings.
For gold their seal official you can win
To any writ, no matter what's therein.
Sure God alone can make them stop their thievings. {56}
'Twere hard, in full, their evil works to tell,
As when, for a few pence, they greedily sell
The tonsure to some mountebank or jester,
Whereby the temporal courts are wronged as well,
For then these tonsured rogues they cannot quell,
Howe'er their scampish doings may us pester,
While round the church still growing evils fester.

19

"Then as for all the priests and minor clerks,
There are, God knows, too many of them whose works
And daily life belie their daily preaching.
Scarce better are they than so many Turks,
Though they, no doubt, may be well taught—it irks
Me not to own the fulness of their teaching—
For, learned or ignorant, they're ever bent
To make a traffic of each sacrament,
The Mass's holy sacrifice included;
And when they shrive an honest penitent,
Who will not bribe, his penance they augment,
For honesty should never be obtruded—
But this, by sinners fair, is easily eluded.
   "'Tis true the monks and friars make ample show
Of rules austere which they all undergo,
But this the vainest is of all pretences.
In sooth, they live full twice as well, we know,
As e'er they did at home, despite their vow,
And all their mock parade of abstinences.
No jollier life than theirs can be, indeed;
And specially the begging friars exceed,
Whose frock grants license as abroad they wander.
These motives 'tis which to the Orders lead
So many worthless men, in sorest need
Of pelf, which on their vices they may squander,
And then, the frock protects them in their plunder."[45]
   It was inevitable that such a religion should breed dissidence and such a priesthood provoke revolt.[57]

CHAPTER II.

HERESY.

THE Church, which we have seen so far removed from its ideal and so derelict in its duties, found itself, somewhat unexpectedly, confronted by new dangers and threatened in the very citadel of its power. Just as its triumph over king and kaiser was complete a new enemy arose in the awakened consciousness of man. The dense ignorance of the tenth century, which followed the evanescent Carlovingian civilization, had begun in the eleventh to yield to the first faint pulsations of intellectual movement. Early in the twelfth century that movement already shows in its gathering force the promise of the development which was to render Europe the home of art and science, of learning, culture, and civilization. The stagnation of the human mind could not be thus broken without leading to inquiry and to doubt. When men began to reason and to ask questions, to criticise and to speculate on forbidden topics, it was not possible for them to avoid seeing how woful was the contrast between the teaching and the practice of the Church, and how little correspondence existed between religion and ritual, between the lives of monk and priest and the profession of their vows. Even the blind reverence which for generations had been felt for the utterances of the Church began to be shaken. Such a book as Abelard's "Sic et Non," in which the contradictions of tradition and decretal were pitilessly set forth, was not only an indication of mental disquiet ripening to rebellion, but a fruitful source of future trouble in sowing the seeds of further investigation and irreverence. Vainly, at the command of the Roman curia, might Gratian seek to show, in his famous "Concordantia Discordantium Canonum," that the contradictions might be reconciled, and that the canon law was not merely a mass of clashing rules called forth by special exigencies, but an harmonious body of spiritual law. The fatal word had been spoken, and the efforts of[58] the Glossators, of Masters of Sentences, of Angelic Doctors, and of the innumerable crowd of scholastic theologians and canon lawyers, with all their skilful dialectics, could never restore to the minds of men the placid and unbroken trust in the divine inspiration of the Church Militant. Few as were the assailants as yet, and intermittent as were their attacks, the very number of the defenders and the vigor of the defence show the danger which was recognized as dwelling in the spirit of inquiry which had at last been partially aroused from its long slumber.

   That spirit had received a powerful impulse from the school of Toledo, whither adventurous scholars flocked as to the fountain where they could take long draughts of Arabic and Grecian and Jewish lore. Even in the darkness of the tenth century Sylvester II., while yet plain Gerbert of Aurillac, had acquired a sinister reputation as a magician, owing to his asserted studies of forbidden science at that centre of intellectual activity. Towards the middle of the twelfth century Robert de Rétines, at the instance of Peter the Venerable of Cluny, laid aside for a while his studies in astronomy and geometry, in order to translate the Koran, and enable his patron to controvert the errors of Islam. The works of Aristotle and Ptolemy, of Abubekr, Avicenna, and Alfarabi, and finally those of Averrhoes, were rendered into Latin, and were copied with incredible zeal in all the lands of Christendom. The Crusaders, too, brought home with them fragmentary remains of ancient thought

20

which met with an equally warm reception. It is true that judicial astrology was the chief subject of study and speculation among these new-found treasures, but the earnestness with which more fruitful topics were investigated and the danger which lurked in them are evidenced by the repeated prohibitions of the works of Aristotle and the denunciations of their use in the University of Paris. Even more menacing to the Church was the revival of the Civil Law. Whether or not this was caused by the discovery of the Pandects of Amalfi, the ardor with which it came, by the middle of the twelfth century, to be studied in all the great centres of learning is incontestable, and men found, to their surprise, that there was a system of jurisprudence of wonderful symmetry and subtle adjustment of right, immeasurably superior to the clumsy and confused canon law and the barbarous feudal customs, while drawing its authority from immutable justice as represented{59} by the sovereign, and not from canon or decretal, from pope or council, or even from Holy Writ. The clearsightedness of St. Bernard was not in fault when, as early as 1149, he recognized the danger to the Church, and complained that the courts rang with the laws of Justinian rather than with those of God.[46]

To understand fully the effect of this intellectual movement upon the popular mind and heart, we must picture to ourselves a state of society in many respects wholly unlike our own. It is not only that in civilized lands settled institutions have rendered men more submissive to law and custom, but the diffusion of intelligence and the training of generations have brought them more under the control of reason and rendered them less susceptible to impulse and emotion. Even in modern times we have seen, in outbursts like the Revolution of '89, the possibilities of popular frenzy when reason is dethroned by passion. Yet the madness of the Reign of Terror is no unapt illustration of the violent emotions to which mediæval populations were subject, for good or for evil, giving occasion to the startling contrasts which render the period so picturesque, and relieve the sordidness of its daily life with splendid exhibitions of the loftiest enthusiasm or with hideous deeds of brutality. Unaccustomed to restraint, vigorous manhood asserted itself in all its greatness and its littleness, whether in wreaking cruel vengeance upon the defenceless or in offering itself joyfully as a sacrifice to humanity. Thrills of delirious emotion spread from land to land, arousing the populations from their lethargy in blind attempts to achieve they scarcely knew what—in crusades which bleached the sands of Palestine with Christian bones, in wild excesses of flagellation, in purposeless wanderings of the Pastoureaux. In the deep and hopeless misery which oppressed the mass of the people there was an ever-present feeling of unrest which constantly saw in the near future the coming of Antichrist, the end of the world, and the Day of Judgment. In the deplorable condition of society, torn with unceasing and savage{60} neighborhood-war and ground under the iron heel of feudalism, the common man might indeed well imagine that the reign of Antichrist was ever imminent, or might welcome any change which possibly might benefit, and scarce could injure, his condition. The invisible world, moreover, with its mysterious attraction and horrible fascination, was ever present and real to every one. Demons were always around him, to smite him with sickness, to ruin his pitiful little cornfield or vineyard, or to lure his soul to perdition; while angels and saints were similarly ready to help him, to listen to his invocations, and to intercede for him at the throne of mercy, which he dared not to address directly. It was among a population thus impressionable, emotional, and superstitious, slowly awakening in the intellectual dawn, that orthodoxy and heterodoxy—the forces of conservatism and progress—were to fight the battle in which neither could win permanent victory.

It is a noteworthy fact, presaging the new form which modern civilization and enlightenment were to assume, that the heresies which were to shake the Church to its foundations were no longer, as of old, mere speculative subtleties propounded by learned theologians and prelates in the gradual evolution of Christian doctrine. We have not to deal with men like Arius or Priscillian, or Nestorius or Eutyches, scholars and prelates who filled the Church with the disputatious wrangles of their learning. Hierarchical organization was too perfect, and theological dogma too thoroughly petrified, to admit of this; and the occasional deviations, real or assumed, of the schoolmen from orthodoxy, as in the case of Berenger of Tours, of Abelard, of Gilbert de la Porée, of Peter Lombard, of Folkmar von Trieffenstein, were readily suppressed by the machinery of the establishment. Nor have we, for the most part, to deal with the governing classes, for the alliance between Church and State to keep the people in subjection had been handed down from the Roman Empire, and however much monarchs like John of England or Frederic II. had to complain of ecclesiastical pretensions, they never dared to loosen the foundations on which rested their own prerogatives. As a rule, heresy had to be thoroughly disseminated among the people before those of gentle blood would meddle with it, as we shall see in Languedoc and Lombardy. The blows which brought real danger to the hierarchy came from obscure{61}men, laboring among the poor and oppressed, who, in their misery and degradation, felt that the Church had failed in its mission, whether through the worldliness of its ministers or through defects in its doctrine. Among these lost sheep of Israel, like the Goim, whom, neglected and despised by the rabbis, it was Christ's mission to bring into the fold, they found ready and eager listeners, and the heresies which they taught divide themselves naturally into two classes. On the one hand we have sectaries holding fast to all the essentials of Christianity, with antisacerdotalism as their mainspring, and on the other hand we have Manichæans.

In briefly reviewing these and their vicissitudes, it must be borne in mind that, with scarce an exception, the authorities are exclusively their antagonists and persecutors. Saving a few Waldensian tracts and a single Catharan ritual, their literature has wholly perished. We are left, for the most part, to gather their doctrines from those who wrote to confute them or to excite popular odium against them, and we can only learn their struggles

21

and their fate from their ruthless exterminators. I shall say no word in their praise that is not based upon the admissions or accusations of their enemies; and if I reject some of the abuse lavished upon them, it is because that abuse is so manifestly conscious or unconscious exaggeration that it is deprived of all historical value. In general, the *prima facie* case may be assumed to be in favor of those who were ready to endure persecution and face death for the sake of what they believed to be truth; nor, in the existing corruption of the Church, can it be imagined, as the orthodox controversialists assumed, that any one would place himself outside of the pale for the purpose of more freely indulging disorderly appetites.

The fact is, as we have seen, that the highest authorities in the Church admitted that its scandals were the cause, if not the justification, of heresy. An inquisitor who was actively engaged in its suppression enumerates among the efficient agents in its dissemination the depraved lives of the clergy, their ignorance, leading to the preaching of false and frivolous things, their irreverence for the sacraments, and the hatred commonly entertained for them. Another informs us that the leading arguments of the heretics were drawn from the pride, the avarice, and the unclean lives of clerks and prelates. All this, according to Lucas, Bishop of Tuy, who laboriously confuted heterodoxy, was exaggerated by false{62} stories of miracles skilfully directed against the observances of the Church and the weaknesses of its ministers; but if so this was a work of surplusage, for nothing that the heretics could invent was likely to be more appalling than the reality as stated by the most resolute champions of the Church. Not many controversialists, indeed, were capable of the frank assurance of the learned author of the tract which passes under the name of Peter of Pilichdorf, in answering the arguments of the heretics, that the Catholic priests were fornicators and usurers and drunkards and dicers and forgers, by boldly saying, "What then? They are none the less priests, and the worst of men who is a priest is worthier than the most holy layman. Was not Judas Iscariot, on account of his apostleship, worthier than Nathaniel, though less holy?" The Troubadour Inquisitor Isarn only uttered a truth generally recognized when he said that no believer would be misled into Catharism or Waldensianism if he had a good pastor:

"Ja no fara crezens heretje ni baudes
Si agues bon pastor que lur contradisses."[47]

The antisacerdotal heresies were directed against the abuses in doctrine and practice which priestcraft had invented to enslave the souls of men. One feature common to them all was a revival of the Donatist tenet that the sacraments are polluted in polluted hands, so that a priest living in mortal sin is incapable of administering them. In the existing condition of ecclesiastical morals this was destructive to the functions of nearly the whole body of the priesthood, and its readiness as a means of attack had been facilitated by the policy of the Holy See in its efforts to suppress clerical marriage and concubinage. In 1059 the Synod of Rome, under the impulsion of Nicholas II., had adopted a canon forbidding any one to be present at the mass of a priest known to keep a concubine or wife. This was inviting the flock to sit in judgment on the pastor; and though it remained virtually a dead letter for fifteen years, when it was revived and effectually put in{63} force by Gregory VII., in 1074, it produced immense confusion, for continent priests were rare exceptions. So violent was the contest excited that, in 1077, at Cambrai, the married or concubinary priesthood actually burned at the stake an unfortunate who resolutely maintained the orthodoxy of the papal rescripts. The orders of Gregory were reiterated by Innocent II. as late as the Council of Reims, in 1131, and in that of Lateran, in 1139, and Gratian embodied the whole series in the canon law, where they still remain. Although Urban II. had endeavored to point out that it was merely a matter of discipline, and that the virtue of the sacraments remained unaltered in the hands of the worst of men, still it was difficult for the popular mind to recognize so subtle a distinction. A learned theologian like Geroch of Reichersperg might safely declare that he paid no more attention to the masses of concubinary priests than if they were those of so many pagans, and yet be unimpeached in his orthodoxy, but to minds less robust in faith the question presented insoluble difficulties. Albero, a priest of Mercke, near Cologne, shortly afterwards, when he taught that the consecration of the host was imperfect in sinful hands, was forced, by the unanimous testimony of the Fathers, to recant; but he adopted the theory that such sacraments were profitable to those who took them in ignorance of the wickedness of the celebrant, while they were useless to the dead and to those who were cognizant of the sin. This was likewise heretical, and Albero's offer to prove its orthodoxy by undergoing the ordeal of fire was rejected on the logical ground that sorcery might thus enable false doctrine to triumph. The question continued to plague the Church until, about 1230, Gregory IX. abandoned the position of his predecessors, and undertook to settle it by an authoritative decision that every priest in mortal sin is suspended, as far as concerns himself, until he repents and is absolved, yet his offices are not to be avoided, because he is not suspended as regards others, unless the sin is notorious by judicial confession or sentence, or by evidence so clear that no tergiversation is possible. To the Church it was, of course, impossible to admit that the virtue of the sacrament depended upon the virtue of the ministrant, but these fine-drawn distinctions show how the question troubled the minds of the faithful, and how readily the heresy could suggest itself that transubstantiation might fail in the hands of the wicked. In fact,{64} even without the suggestive commands of Gregory and Innocent, to a thoughtful and pious mind there was a grievous incompatibility between the awful powers vested by the Church in her ministers and the flagitious lives which disgraced so many of them. That the error should be stubborn was unavoidable. As late as 1396 it was taught by Jean de Varennes, a priest of the Remois, who was forced to recant, and in 1458 we find Alonso de Spina declaring it to be common to the Waldenses, the Wickliffites, and the Hussites.[48]

One or two of the earlier antisacerdotal heresies may be mentioned which were local and temporary in their character, but which yet have interest as showing how ready were the lower ranks of the people to rise in revolt against the Church, and how contagious was the enthusiasm excited by any leader bold enough to voice the general feeling of unrest and discontent. About 1108, in the Zeeland Isles, there appeared a preacher named Tanchelm, who seems to have been an apostate monk, subtle and skilled in disputation. He taught the nullity of all hierarchical dignities, from pope to simple clerk, that the Eucharist was polluted in unworthy hands, and that tithes were not to be paid. The people listened eagerly, and after filling all Flanders with his heresy, he found in Antwerp an appropriate centre of influence. Although that city was already populous and wealthy through commerce, it had but a single priest, and he, involved in an incestuous union with a near relative, had neither leisure nor inclination for his duties. A people thus destitute of orthodox instruction fell an easy prey to the tempter and eagerly followed him, reverencing him to that degree that the water in which he bathed was distributed and preserved as a relic. He readily raised a force of three thousand fighting men, with which he dominated the land,{65} nor was there duke or bishop who dared withstand him. The stories that he pretended to be God and the equal of Jesus Christ, and that he celebrated his marriage with the Virgin Mary, may safely be rejected as the embroideries of frightened clerks; nor could Tanchelm have really considered himself as a heretic, for we find him visiting Rome with a few followers for the purpose of obtaining a division of the extensive see of Utrecht and the allotment of a portion of it to the episcopate of Terouane. On his return from Rome, in 1112, while passing through Cologne, he and his retinue were thrown in prison by the archbishop, who the next year summoned a synod to sit in judgment on them. Several of them purged themselves by the water-ordeal, while others succeeded in escaping by flight. Of these, three were burned at Bonn, preferring a frightful death to abandoning their faith, while Tanchelm himself reached Bruges in safety. The anathema which had been pronounced against him, however, had impaired his credit, and the clergy of Bruges had little difficulty in procuring his ejectment. Yet Antwerp remained faithful, and he continued his missionary career until 1115, when, being in a boat with but few followers, a zealous priest piously knocked him on the head, and his soul went to rejoin its master, Satan. Even this did not suppress the effect of his teaching and his heresy continued to flourish. In vain the bishop gave twelve assistants to the lonely priest of St. Michael's in Antwerp; it was not until 1126, when St. Norbert, the ardent ascetic who founded the Premonstratensian order, was placed in charge of the city with his followers, and undertook to evangelize it with his burning eloquence, that the people could be brought back to the faith. St. Norbert built other churches and filled them with disciples zealous as himself, and the stubborn heretics were docile enough to pastors who taught by example as well as by words their sympathy for those who had so long been neglected. Consecrated hosts which had lain hidden for fifteen years in chinks and corners were brought forth by pious souls, and the heresy vanished without leaving a trace.[49]{66}

Somewhat similar was the heresy propagated not long afterwards in Brittany by Éon de l'Étoile, except that in this case the heresiarch was unquestionably insane. Sprung from a noble family, he had gained a reputation for sanctity by the life of a hermit in the wilderness, when, from the words of the collect, "per *eum* qui venturus est judicare vivos et mortuos," he conceived the idea that he was the Son of God. It was not difficult to find sharers in this belief who adored him as the Deity incarnate, and he soon had a numerous band of followers, with whose aid he pillaged the churches of their ill-used treasures, and distributed them to the poor. The heresy became sufficiently formidable to induce the legate, Cardinal Alberic of Ostia, to preach against it at Nantes in 1145, and Ilugues, Archbishop of Rouen, to combat it with dreary polemics; but the most convincing argument used was the soldiery despatched against the heretics, many of whom were captured and burned at Alet, refusing obstinately to recant. Éon retired to Aquitaine for a season, but in 1148 he ventured to appear in Champagne, where he was seized with his followers by Samson, Archbishop of Reims, and brought before Eugenius III. at the Council of Rouen. Here his insanity was so manifest that he was charitably consigned to the care of Suger, Abbot of St. Denis, where he soon after died, but many of his disciples were stubborn, and preferred the stake to recantation.[50]

More durable and more formidable were the heresies which about the same time took stubborn root in the south of France, where the condition of society was especially favorable for their propagation. There the population and civilization were wholly different from those of the north. The first wave of the Aryan invasion of Europe had driven to the Mediterranean littoral the ancient Ligurian inhabitants, who had left abundant traces of their race in the swarthy skins and black hair of their descendants. Greek and Phœnician colonies had still further crossed the blood. Gothic domination had been long continued, and the Merovingian conquest had scarce given to the Frank a foothold in the soil.{67} Even Saracenic elements were not wanting to make up the strange admixture of races which rendered the citizen of Narbonne or Marseilles so different a being from the inhabitant of Paris—quite as different as the Langue d'Oc from the Langue d'Oyl. The feudal tie which bound the Count of Toulouse, or the Marquis of Provence, or the Duke of Aquitaine to the King of Paris or the Emperor was but feeble, and when the last named fief was carried by Eleanor to Henry II., the rival pretensions of England and France preserved the virtual independence of the great feudatories of the South, leading to antagonisms of which we shall see the full fruits in the Albigensian crusades.

23

The contrast of civilization was as marked as that of race. Nowhere in Europe had culture and luxury made such progress as in the south of France. Chivalry and poetry were assiduously cultivated by the nobles; and, even in the cities, which had acquired for themselves a large measure of freedom, and which were enriched by trade and commerce, the citizens boasted a degree of education and enlightenment unknown elsewhere. Nowhere in Europe, moreover, were the clergy more negligent of their duties or more despised by the people. There was little earnestness of religious conviction among either prelates or nobles to stimulate persecution, so that there was considerable freedom of belief. In no other Christian land did the despised Jew enjoy such privileges. His right to hold land in *franc-alleu* was similar to that of the Christian; he was admitted to public office, and his administrative ability rendered him a favorite in such capacity with both prelate and noble; his synagogues were undisturbed; and the Hebrew school of Narbonne was renowned in Israel as the home of the Kimchis. Under such influences, those who really possessed religious convictions were but little deterred by prejudice or the fear of persecution from criticising the shortcomings of the Church, or from seeking what might more nearly respond to their aspirations.[51]{68}

It was in such a population as this that the first antisacerdotal heresy was preached in Vallonise about 1106, by Pierre de Bruys, a native of the diocese of Embrun. The prelates of Embrun, Gap, and Die endeavored in vain to stay his progress until they procured assistance from the king, when he was driven out and took refuge in Gascony. For twenty years he continued his mission, and the openness and success with which he taught is shown by the story that in one place, to show his contempt for the objects of sacerdotal veneration, he caused a great pile of consecrated crosses to be accumulated, and then, setting fire to them, deliberately roasted meat at the flames. Persecution at length became more active, and about the year 1126 he was seized and burned at St. Gilles.

His teaching was simply antisacerdotal—to some extent a revival of the errors of Claudius of Turin. Pædo-baptism was useless, for the faith of another cannot help him who cannot use his own—a far-reaching proposition, fraught with immeasurable consequences. For the same reason offerings, alms, masses, prayers and other good works for the dead are useless and each will be judged on his own merits. Churches are unnecessary and should be destroyed, for holy places are not wanted for Christian prayer, since God listens to those who deserve it, whether invoked in church or tavern, in temple or market-place, before the altar or before the stable; and the Church of God does not consist of a multitude of stones piled together, but in the united congregation of the faithful. As for the cross, as a senseless thing it is not to be invoked with foolish prayers, but is rather to be destroyed as the instrument on which Christ was cruelly tortured to death. His most serious error, however, was his rejection of the Eucharist. Transubstantiation had not yet had time to become immovably fixed in the perceptions of all men, and Pierre de Bruys went even further than Berenger of Tours. His only recorded utterance is his vigorous rejection of the sacrament: "O people, believe not the bishops, the priests, and the clerks, who, as in much else, seek to deceive you as to the office{69} of the altar, where they lyingly pretend to make the body of Christ and give it to you for the salvation of your souls. They plainly lie, for the body of Christ was but once made by Christ in the supper before the Passion, and but once given to the disciples. Since then it has been never made and never given."[52]

There was evidently nothing to do with such a man but to burn him, but even this did not suffice to suppress his heresy. The Petrobrusians continued to diffuse his doctrines, secretly or openly, and, some five or six years after his death, Peter the Venerable of Cluny considered them still so formidable as to require his controversial tract, to which we are indebted for almost all we know about the sect. This is dedicated to the bishops of Embrun, Arles, Die, and Gap, and urges them to renewed efforts for the suppression of the heresy by preaching and by the arms of the laity.

All their efforts might well be needed, for Peter was succeeded by a yet more formidable heresiarch. Little is known of the earlier life of Henry, the Monk of Lausanne, except that he left his convent there under circumstances for which St. Bernard afterwards reproached him, but which may well have been but the first ebullition of the reformatory spirit to which he finally fell a victim. We next hear of him at Le Mans, perhaps as early as 1116, but the dates are uncertain. Here his austerities gained him the veneration of the people, which he turned with disastrous effect upon the clergy. We know little of his doctrines at this time, except that he rejected the invocation of saints, but we are told that his eloquence was so persuasive that under its influence women abandoned their jewels and sumptuous apparel, and young men married courtesans to reclaim them. While thus teaching asceticism and charity, he so lashed the vices of the Church that the clergy throughout the diocese would have been destroyed but for the active protection of the nobles. Henry had taken advantage of the absence in Rome of the bishop, the celebrated Hildebert of Le Mans, who, on his return, overcame the heretic in disputation and forced him to abandon the field, but could not punish him. We have glimpses of his activity in Poitiers and Bordeaux, and then lose sight of him till we{70} find him a prisoner of the Archbishop of Arles, who took him to the presence of Innocent II. at the Council of Pisa, in 1134. Here he was convicted of heresy and condemned to imprisonment, but was subsequently released and sent back to his convent, whence he departed with the intention of entering the strict Cistercian order at Clairvaux. What led to his resuming his heretical mission we do not know, but we meet him again, bolder than before, adopting substantially the Petrobrusian tenets, rejecting the Eucharist, refusing all reverence for the priesthood, all tithes, oblations, and other sources of ecclesiastical revenue, and all attendance at church.

24

The scene of this activity was southern France, where the embers of Petrobrusianism were ready to be kindled into flame. His success was immense. In 1147 St. Bernard despairingly describes the condition of religion in the extensive territories of the Count of Toulouse: "The churches are without people, the people without priests, the priests without the reverence due them, and Christians without Christ. The churches are regarded as synagogues, the sanctuary of the Lord is no longer holy; the sacraments are no more held sacred; feast days are without solemnities; men die in their sins, and their souls are hurried to the dread tribunal, neither reconciled by penance nor fortified by the holy communion. The little ones of Christ are debarred from life since baptism is denied them. The voice of a single heretic silences all those apostolic and prophetic voices which have united in calling all the nations into the Church of Christ." The prelates of southern France were powerless to arrest the progress of the bold heresiarch, and imploringly appealed for assistance. The nobles would not aid them, for, like the people, they hated the clergy and were glad of the excuses which Henry's doctrines gave them for spoiling and oppressing the Church. The papal legate, Alberic, was summoned, and he prevailed upon St. Bernard to accompany him with Geoffrey, Bishop of Chartres, and other men of mark. Though St. Bernard was sick, the perilous condition of the tottering establishment aroused all his zeal, and he unflinchingly undertook the mission. What was the condition of popular feeling and how boldly it dared to express itself may be gathered from the reception of the legate at Albi, where the people went forth to meet him with asses and drums in sign of derision, and when they were convoked to be present at his celebration of mass scarcely thirty attended.{71} If we may believe the accounts of his disciples, the success of Bernard was immense. His reputation had preceded him, and it was heightened by the stories of miracles which he daily performed, no less than by his burning eloquence and skill in disputation. Crowds flocked to hear him preach, and were converted. At Albi, two days after the miserable failure of the legate, St. Bernard arrived, and the cathedral was scarcely able to hold the multitude which assembled to listen to him. On the conclusion of his discourse he adjured them: "Repent, then, all ye who have been contaminated. Return to the Church; and that we may know who repents, let each penitent raise his right hand"—and every hand was raised. Scarce less effective was his rejoinder when, after preaching to an immense assemblage, he mounted his horse to depart and a hardened heretic, thinking to confuse him, said, "My lord abbot, our heretic, of whom you think so ill, has not a horse so fat and spirited as yours." "Friend," replied the saint, "I deny it not. The horse eats and grows fat for itself, for it is but a brute and by nature given to its appetites, whereby it offends not God. But before the judgment seat of God I and your master will not be judged by horse's necks, but each by his own neck. Now, then, look at my neck and see if it is fatter than your master's, and if you can justly reprehend me." Then he threw down his cowl and displayed his neck, long and thin and wasted by maceration and austerities, to the confusion of the misbelievers. If he failed to make converts at Verfeil, where a hundred knights refused to listen to him, he at least had the satisfaction of cursing them, which we are assured caused them all to perish miserably.

St. Bernard challenged Henry to a disputation, which the prudent heretic declined, whether through fear of his antagonist's eloquence or a reasonable regard for the safety of his own person. It mattered little which, for his refusal discredited him in the eyes of many of the nobles who had hitherto protected him, and thenceforth he was obliged to lie in hiding. Orthodoxy took heart and was soon on his track: he was captured the next year and brought in chains before his bishop. His end is not known, but he is presumed to have died in prison.[53]{72}

We hear no more of the Henricians as a definite sect, though in 1151 a young girl, miraculously inspired by the Virgin Mary, is said to have converted many of them, and they probably continued to exist throughout Languedoc, furnishing material in the next generation for the spread of the Waldenses. We have scanty indications, however, in widely separated places, of the existence of sectaries probably Henrician, showing how, in spite of persecution, the antisacerdotal spirit continued to manifest itself. Contemporary with St. Bernard's mission to Languedoc is a letter addressed to him by Evervin, Provost of Steinfeld, imploring his aid against heretics recently discovered at Cologne—some Manichæans and others, evidently Henricians, who had betrayed themselves by their mutual quarrels. These Henricians boasted that their sect was numerously scattered throughout all the lands of Christendom, and their zeal is shown by an allusion to those among their number who perished at the stake. Probably Henrician, too, were heretics who infested Perigord under a teacher named Pons, whose austerities and external holiness drew to them numerous adherents, including nobles and priests, monks and nuns. Besides the antisacerdotal tenets described above, these enthusiasts anticipated St. Francis in proclaiming poverty to be essential to salvation and in refusing to receive money. The impression which they produced upon a worldly generation is shown by the marvellous legends which grew around them. They courted persecution and sought for persecutors who should slay them, yet they could not be punished, for their master, Satan, liberated them from chains and prison. Thus if one should be fettered hand and foot and placed under an inverted hogshead watched by guards, he would disappear until it pleased him to return. We know nothing as to the fate of Pons and his disciples, but their numbers and activity were a manifestation of the pervading disquiet and yearning for a change.[54]

Arnald of Brescia's heresy was much more limited in its scope. A pupil of Abelard, he was accused of sharing his master's errors,{73} and incorrect notions respecting pædo-baptism and the Eucharist were attributed to him. Whatever may have been his theological aberrations, his real offence was the energetic way in which he lashed the vices of the clergy and stimulated the laity to repossess the ample wealth and extended privileges which the Church had acquired. Profoundly convinced that the evils of Christendom arose from the worldliness of the ecclesiastical body, he taught that the Church should hold neither temporal possessions nor jurisdiction, and should confine itself rigidly to its spiritual functions. Of austere and commanding virtue, irreproachable in his self-denying life, trained in all the learning of the schools, and gifted with rare persuasive eloquence, he became the terror of the hierarchy, and found the laity ready enough to listen and to act upon doctrines which satisfied their worldly aspirations as well as their spiritual longings. The second Lateran Council, in 1139, endeavored to suppress the revolt which he excited in the Lombard cities by condemning and imposing silence on him; he refused obedience, and the next year Innocent II., in approving the proceedings of the Council of Sens, included him in the condemnation of Abelard, and ordered both to be imprisoned and their writings burned. Arnald had fled from Italy to France, and now he was driven to Switzerland, where we find his restless activity at work in Constance and then in Zurich, pursued by the sleepless watchfulness of St. Bernard. According to the latter, his conquests over souls in Switzerland were rapid, for his teeth were arms and arrows, and his tongue was a sharp sword. After the death of Innocent II. he returned to Rome, where he seems to have been reconciled to Eugenius III. in 1145 or 1146. The new pope, speedily wearied with the turbulence of the city which had exhausted his predecessors, abandoned it and finally sought refuge in France. Arnald was not idle in these movements, and was generally held responsible for them. Vain were the remonstrances of St. Bernard to the Roman commonalty, and equally vain his appeals to the Emperor Conrad to restore the papal power by force. At the same time Conrad treated with disdain envoys sent by the Roman republic, protesting that their object was to restore the imperial supremacy as it had existed under the Cæsars, and inviting him to come and assume the empire of Italy. Eugenius, on his return to Italy, in 1148, issued from Brescia a condemnation{74} of Arnald, directed especially to his supporters among the Roman clergy, who were threatened with deprivation of preferment; but the citizens stood firm, and the pope was only allowed to return to his city on condition of allowing Arnald to remain there. After the death of Conrad III., in 1152, Eugenius III. hastened to win the support of the new King of the Romans, Frederic Barbarossa, by intimating that Arnald and his partisans were conspiring to elect another emperor and make the empire Roman in fact as well as in name. The papal favor seemed necessary to Frederic to secure his coveted coronation and recognition. Blindly overlooking the irreconcilable antagonism between the temporal and spiritual swords, he cast his fortunes with the pope, swore to subdue for him the rebellious city and regain for him the territory of which he had been deprived; while Eugenius, on his side, promised to crown him when he should invade Italy, and to use freely the artillery of excommunication for the abasement of his enemies. The domination of the Roman populace has not been wholly moderate and peaceful. In more than one emeute the palaces of noble and cardinal had been sacked and destroyed and their persons maltreated, and at length, in 1154, in some popular uprising, the cardinal of Santa Pudenziana was slain. Adrian IV., the masterful Englishman who had recently ascended the papal throne, took advantage of the opportunity and set the novel example of laying an interdict on the capital of Christianity until Arnald should be expelled from the city; the fickle populace, dismayed at the deprivation of the sacrament, indispensable to all Christians at the approaching Easter solemnities, were withdrawn from his support, and he retired to the castle of a friendly baron of the Campagna. The next year Frederic reached Rome, after entering into engagements with Adrian which included the sacrifice of Arnald, and he lost no time in performing his share of the bargain. Arnald's protectors were summoned to surrender him, and were obliged to obey. For the cruel ending the Church sought to shirk the responsibility, but there would seem to be no reasonable doubt that he was regularly condemned by a spiritual tribunal as a heretic, for he was in holy orders, and could be tried only by the Church, after which he was handed over to the secular arm for punishment. He was offered pardon if he would recant his erroneous doctrines, but he persistently refused, and passed his last moments in silent{75}prayer. Whether or not he was mercifully hanged before being reduced to ashes is perhaps doubtful, but those ashes were cast into the Tiber to prevent the people of Rome from preserving them as relics and honoring him as a martyr. It was not long before Frederic had ample cause to repent the loss of an ally who might have saved him from the bitter humiliation of his surrender to Alexander III.[55]

Though the immediate influence of Arnald of Brescia was evanescent, his career has its importance as a manifestation of the temper with which the more spiritually minded received the encroachments and corruption of the Church. Yet, though he failed in his attempt to revolutionize society, and perished through miscalculating the tremendous forces arrayed against him, his sacrifice was not wholly in vain. His teachings left a deep impress in the minds of the population, and his followers in secret cherished his memory and his principles for centuries. It was not without a full knowledge of the position that the Roman curia scattered his ashes in the Tiber, dreading the effect of the veneration which the people felt for their martyr. Secret associations of Arnaldistas were formed who called themselves "Poor Men," and adopted the tenet that the sacraments could only be administered by virtuous men. In 1184 we find them condemned by Lucius III. at the so-called Council of Verona; about 1190 they are alluded to by Bonaccorsi, and even until the sixteenth century their name occurs in the lists of heresies proscribed in successive bulls and edicts. Yet the complete oblivion into which they fell is seen in the learned glossator Johannes Andreas, who died in 1348, remarking that perhaps the name of the sect may be derived from some one who founded it. When Peter Waldo of Lyons endeavored, in more pacific wise, to carry out the same views, and his followers grew into the "Poor{76} Men of Lyons," the Italian brethren were ready to welcome the new reformers and to co-operate with them. Though there were some unimportant points of difference between the two schools, yet their resemblance was so great that they virtually coalesced; they were usually confounded by the Church, and were enveloped in a common anathema. Closely connected with them were the Umiliati, described as wandering laymen who preached and heard confessions, to the great scandal of the priesthood, but who were yet not strictly heretics.[56]

Far greater in importance and more durable in results was the antisacerdotal movement unconsciously set on foot by Peter Waldo of Lyons, in the second half of the twelfth century. He was a rich merchant, unlearned, but eager to acquire the truths of Scripture, to which end he caused the translation into Romance of the New Testament and a collection of extracts from the Fathers, known as "Sentences." Diligently studying these, he learned them by heart, and arrived at the conviction that nowhere was the apostolic life observed as commanded by Christ. Striving for evangelical perfection, he gave his wife the choice between his real estate and his movables. On her selecting the former, he sold the latter; portioned his two daughters, and placed them in the Abbey of Fontevraud, and distributed the rest of the proceeds among the poor then suffering from a famine. It is related that after this he begged for bread of an acquaintance who promised to support him during his life, and this coming to the ears of his wife, she appealed to the archbishop, who ordered him in future{77} to accept food only from her. Devoting himself to preaching the gospel through the streets and by the wayside, admiring imitators of both sexes sprang up around him, whom he despatched as missionaries to the neighboring towns. They entered houses, announcing the gospel to the inmates; they preached in the churches, they discoursed in the public places, and everywhere they found eager listeners, for, as we have seen, the negligence and indolence of the clergy had rendered the function of preaching almost a forgotten duty. According to the fashion of the time, they speedily adopted a peculiar form of dress, including, in imitation of the apostles, a sandal with a kind of plate upon it, whence they acquired the name of the "Shoed," Insabbatati, or Zaptati—though the appellation which they bestowed upon themselves was that of Li Poure de Lyod, or Poor Men of Lyons.[57]{78}

It was not possible that ignorant zeal could thus undertake the office of religious instruction without committing errors which acute theologians could detect. It is not likely, moreover, that it would spare the vices and crimes of the clergy in summoning the faithful to repentance and salvation. Complaint speedily arose of the scandals which the new evangelists disseminated, and the Archbishop of Lyons, Jean aux Bellesmains, summoned them before him, and prohibited them from further preaching. They disobeyed and were excommunicated. Peter Waldo then appealed to the pope (probably Alexander III.), who approved his vow of poverty and authorized him to preach when permitted by the priests—a restriction which was observed for a time and then disregarded. The obstinate Poor Men gradually put forward one dangerous tenet after another, while their attacks upon the clergy became sharper and sharper; yet as late as the year 1179 they came before the Council of Lateran, submitted their version of the Scriptures, and asked for license to preach. Walter Mapes, who was present, ridicules their ignorant simplicity, and chuckles over his own shrewdness in confusing them when he was delegated to examine their theological acquirements, yet he bears emphatic testimony to their holy poverty and zeal in imitating the apostles and following Christ. Again they applied to Rome for authority to found an order of preachers, but Lucius III. objected to their sandals, to their monkish copes, and to the companionship of men and women in their wandering life. Finding them obstinate, he finally anathematized them at the Council of Verona in 1184, but they still refused to abandon their mission, or even to consider themselves as separated from the Church. Though again condemned in a council held at Narbonne, they agreed, about 1190, to take the chances of a disputation held in the Cathedral of Narbonne, with Raymond of Daventer, a religious and God-fearing Catholic, as judge. Of{79} course the decision went against them, and of course they were as little inclined as before to submit, but the colloquy has an interest as showing what progress at that period they had made in dissidence from Rome. The six points on which the argument was held were, 1st. That they refused obedience to the authority of pope and prelate; 2d. That all, even laymen, can preach; 3d. That, according to the apostles, God is to be obeyed rather than man; 4th. That women may preach; 5th. That masses, prayers, and alms for the dead are of no avail, with the addition that some of them denied the existence of purgatory; and 6th. That prayer in bed, or in a chamber, or in a stable, is as efficacious as in a church.[58] All this was rebellion against sacerdotalism rather than actual heresy; but we learn, about the same period, from the "Universal Doctor," Alain de l'Isle, who, at the request of Lucius III., wrote a tract for their refutation, that they were prepared to carry these principles to their legitimate but dangerous conclusions, and that they added various other doctrines at variance with the teachings of the Church.

Good prelates, they held, who led apostolic lives, were to be obeyed, and to them alone was granted the power to bind and loose—which was striking a mortal blow at the whole organization of the Church. Merit, and not ordination, conferred the power to consecrate and bless, to bind and to loose; every one, therefore, who led an apostolic life had this power, and as they assumed that they all led such a life, it followed that they, although laymen, could execute all the functions of the priesthood. It likewise followed that the ministrations of sinful priests were invalid, though at first the French Waldenses were not willing to admit this, while the Italians boldly affirmed it. A further error was, that confession to a layman was as efficacious as to a priest, which was a serious attack upon the sacrament of penitence; though, as yet, the Fourth Council of Lateran had not made priestly confession indispensable, and Alain is willing to admit that in the absence of a priest, confession to a layman is sufficient. The system{80} of indulgences was another of the sacerdotal devices which they rejected; and they added three specific rules of morality which became distinctive characteristics of the sect. Every lie is a mortal sin; every oath, even in a court of justice, is unlawful; and homicide is under no circumstances to be permitted, whether in war or in execution of judicial sentences. This necessarily involved non-resistance, rendering the Waldenses dangerous only from such moral influence as they could acquire. Even as late as 1217, a well-informed contemporary assures us that the four chief errors of the Waldenses were, their wearing sandals after the fashion of the apostles, their prohibition of oaths and of homicide, and their assertion that any member of the sect, if he wore sandals, could in case of necessity consecrate the Eucharist.[59]

All this was a simple-hearted endeavor to obey the commands of Christ and make the gospel an actual standard for the conduct of daily life; but these principles, if universally adopted, would have reduced the Church to a condition of apostolic poverty, and would have swept away much of the distinction between priest and layman. Besides, the sectaries were inspired with the true missionary spirit; their proselyting zeal knew no bounds; they wandered from land to land promulgating their doctrines, and finding everywhere a cordial response, especially among the lower classes, who were ready enough to embrace a dogma that promised to release them from the vices and oppression of the clergy. We are told that one of their chief apostles carried with him various disguises, appearing now as a cobbler, then as a barber, and again as a peasant, and though this may have been, as alleged, for the purpose of eluding capture, it shows the social stratum{81} to which their missions were addressed. The Poor Men of Lyons multiplied with incredible rapidity throughout Europe; the Church became seriously alarmed, and not without reason, for an ancient document of the sectaries shows a tradition among them that under Waldo, or immediately afterwards, their councils had an average attendance of about seven hundred members present. Not long after the Colloquy of Narbonne, in 1194, the note of persecution was sounded by Alonso II. of Aragon, in an edict which is worthy of note as the first secular legislation, with the exception of the Assizes of Clarendon, in the modern world against heresy. The Waldenses and all other heretics anathematized by the Church are ordered, as public enemies, to quit his dominions by the day after All-Saints'. Any one who receives them on his lands, listens to their preaching, or gives them food shall incur the penalties of treason, with confiscation of all his goods and possessions. The decree is to be published by all pastors on Sundays, and all public officials are ordered to enforce it. Any heretic remaining after three days' notice of the law can be despoiled by any one, and any injury inflicted on him, short of death or mutilation, so far from being an offence, shall be regarded as meriting the royal favor. The ferocious atrocity of these provisions, which rendered the heretic an outlaw, which condemned him in advance, and which exposed him without a trial to the cupidity or malice of every man, was exceeded three years later by Alonso's son, Pedro II. In a national council of Girona, in 1197, he renewed his father's legislation, adding the penalty of the stake for the heretic. If any noble failed to eject these enemies of the Church, the officials and people of the diocese were ordered to proceed to his castle and seize them without responsibility for any damages committed, and any one failing to join in the foray was subjected to the heavy fine of twenty pieces of gold to the royal fisc. Moreover, all officials were commanded, within eight days after summons, to present themselves before their bishop, or his representative, and take an oath to enforce the law.[60]

The character of this legislation reveals the spirit in which{82} Church and State were prepared to deal with the intellectual and spiritual movement of the time. Harmless as the Waldenses might seem to be, they were recognized as most dangerous enemies, to be mercilessly persecuted. In southern France they were devoted to common destruction with the Albigenses, though the distinction between the sects was clearly recognized. The documents of the Inquisition constantly refer to "heresy and Waldensianism," designating Catharism by the former term as the heresy *par excellence*. The Waldenses themselves regarded the Cathari as heretics to be combated intellectually, though the persecution which they shared forced them to associate freely together.[61]

In a sect so widely scattered, from Aragon to Bohemia, consisting mostly of poor and simple folk, hiding their belief in the lowlands, or dwelling in separate communities among the mountain fastnesses of the Cottian Alps or of Calabria, it was inevitable that differences of organization and doctrine should arise, and that there should be variations in the rapidity of independent development. The labors of Dieckhoff, Herzog, and especially of Montet in recent times, have shown that the early Waldenses were not Protestants in our modern sense, and that, in spite of persecution, many of them long continued to regard themselves as members of the Church of Rome, with a persistence proving how real were the abuses which had forced them to schism, and finally to heresy. Yet, in others, the spirit of revolt ripened much more rapidly, and it is impossible, within our limited space, to present a definite scheme of a doctrine which differed in so many points according to time and circumstance.

In the crucial test of belief in transubstantiation, for instance, as early as the thirteenth century, an experienced inquisitor, in drawing up instructions for the examination of Waldenses, assumes disbelief in the existence of the body and blood in the Eucharist as one of the points whereby to detect them, and in 1332 we hear of such a denial among the Waldenses of Savoy. Yet about this latter date Bernard Gui assures us that they believed in it, and M. Montet has shown from their successive writings how their views on the subject changed. The inquisitor who{83} burned the Waldenses of Cologne in 1392 tells us that they denied transubstantiation, but they added, that if it occurred it could not be wrought in the hands of a sinful priest. So it was with regard to

28

purgatory—which for a long while was regarded as an open question, to be definitely decided in the negative by the close of the fourteenth century—together with the suffrages of the saints, the invocation of the Virgin, and the other devices of which it was the excuse. The antisacerdotalism in which the sect took its rise, naturally, in its development, tended to do away with all that interposed mediators between God and man, although this progress was by no means uniform. The Waldenses burned in Strassburg, in 1212, rejected all distinction between the laity and the priesthood. In Lombardy, about the same time, the community elected ministers either temporary or for life. Both the French and Lombard Waldenses of this period held that the Eucharist could only be made by an ordained priest, though they differed as to the necessity of his not being in mortal sin. Bernard Gui speaks of three orders among them—deacons, priests, and bishops; M. Montet has found in a MS. of 1404 a form of Waldensian ordination; and when the Unitas Fratrum of Bohemia was organized in 1467, it had recourse, as we shall see hereafter, to the Waldensian Bishop Stephen to consecrate its first bishops. Yet the antisacerdotal tendencies were so strong that the difference between the laity and priesthood was greatly diminished, and the power of the keys was wholly rejected. About 1400, the Nobla Leyczon declares that all the popes, cardinals, bishops, and abbots since the days of Silvester could not pardon a single mortal sin, for God alone has the power of pardon. As the soul thus dealt directly with God, the whole machinery of indulgences and so-called pious works was thrown aside. It is true that faith without works was idle—"*la fe es ociosa sensa las obras*"—but good works were piety, repentance, charity, justice, not pilgrimages and formal exercises, the founding of churches and the honoring of saints.[62]{84}

The Waldensian system thus created a simple church organization with a tendency ever to grow simpler. As a general proposition it may be stated that the distinction between the clergy and laity was reduced to a minimum, especially when transubstantiation was rejected. The layman could hear confessions, baptize, and preach. In some places it was the custom for each head of a family on Holy Thursday to administer communion in a simple fashion, consecrating the elements and distributing them himself. Yet of necessity there was a recognized priesthood, known as the Perfected, or Majorales, who taught the faithful and converted the unbeliever, who renounced all property and separated themselves from their wives, or who had observed strict chastity from youth, who wandered around hearing confessions and making converts, and were supported by the voluntary contributions of those who labored for their bread. The Pomeranian Waldenses believed that every seven years two of these were transported to the gate of Paradise, that they might understand the wisdom of God. One marked distinction between them and the laity was that, when on trial before the Inquisition, the prohibition of swearing was relaxed in favor of the latter, who might take an oath under compulsion, while the Perfects would die rather than violate the precept. The inquisitors, while complaining of the ingenuity with which the heretics evaded their examination, admitted that all were much more solicitous to save their friends and kindred than themselves.[63]

With this tendency towards a restoration of evangelical simplicity, it followed that the special religious teaching of the Waldenses {85} was to a great extent ethical. The reply of an unfortunate before the Inquisition of Toulouse, when questioned as to what his instructors had taught him, was "that he should neither speak nor do evil, that he should do nothing to others that he would not have done to himself, and that he should not lie or swear"—a simple formula enough, but one which practically leaves little to be desired; and a similar statement was made to the Celestinian Peter in his inquisition of the Pomeranian Waldenses in 1394. A persecuted Church is almost inevitably a pure Church, and the men who through those dreary centuries lay in hiding, with the stake ever before their eyes, to spread what they believed to be the unadulterated truths of the gospel in obedience to the commands of Christ, were not likely to contaminate their high and holy mission with vulgar vices. In fact, the unanimous testimony of their persecutors is that their external virtues were worthy of all praise, and the contrast between the purity of their lives and the depravity which pervaded the clergy of the dominant Church is more than once deplored by their antagonists as a most effective factor in the dissemination of heresy. An inquisitor who knew them well describes them: "Heretics are recognizable by their customs and speech, for they are modest and well regulated. They take no pride in their garments, which are neither costly nor vile. They do not engage in trade, to avoid lies and oaths and frauds, but live by their labor as mechanics—their teachers are cobblers. They do not accumulate wealth, but are content with necessaries. They are chaste and temperate in meat and drink. They do not frequent taverns or dances or other vanities. They restrain themselves from anger. They are always at work; they teach and learn and consequently pray but little. They are to be known by their modesty and precision of speech, avoiding scurrility and detraction and light words and lies and oaths. They do not even say *vere* or *certe*, regarding them as oaths." Such is the general testimony, and the tales which were told as to the sexual abominations customary among them may safely be set down as devices to excite popular detestation, grounded possibly on extravagances of asceticism, such as were common among the early Christians, for the Waldenses held that connubial intercourse was only lawful for the procurement of offspring. An inquisitor admits his disbelief as to these stories, for which he had never found a basis worthy of credence, nor does anything of the kind make its appearance {86} in the examinations of the sectaries under the skilful handling of their persecutors, until in the fourteenth and fifteenth centuries the inquisitors of Piedmont and Provence found it expedient to extract such confessions from their victims.[64]

There was also objected to them the hypocrisy which led them to conceal their belief under assiduous attendance at mass and confession, and punctual observance of orthodox externalities; but this, like the ingenious evasions under examination, which so irritated their inquisitorial critics, may readily be pardoned to those with whom it was the necessity of self-preservation, and who, at least during the earlier period, had often no other means of enjoying the sacraments which they deemed essential to salvation. They were also ridiculed for their humble condition in life, being almost wholly peasants, mechanics, and the like—poor and despised folk of whom the Church took little count, except to tax when orthodox and burn when heretic. But their crowning offence was their love and reverence for Scripture, and their burning zeal in making converts. The Inquisitor of Passau informs us that they had translations of the whole Bible in the vulgar tongue, which the Church vainly sought to suppress, and which they studied with incredible assiduity. He knew a peasant who could recite the Book of Job word for word; many of them had the whole of the New Testament by heart, and, simple as they were, were dangerous disputants. As for the missionary spirit, he tells of one who, on a winter night, swam the river Ips in order to gain a chance of converting a Catholic; and all, men and women, old and young, were ceaseless in learning and teaching. After a hard day's labor they would devote the night to instruction; they sought the lazar-houses{87} to carry salvation to the leper; a disciple of ten days' standing would seek out another whom he could instruct, and when the dull and untrained brain would fain abandon the task in despair they would speak words of encouragement: "Learn a single word a day, in a year you will know three hundred, and thus you will gain in the end." Surely if ever there was a God-fearing people it was these unfortunates under the ban of Church and State, whose secret passwords were, "*Ce dit sainct Pol, Ne mentir,*" "*Ce dit sainct Jacques, Ne jurer,*" "*Ce dit sainct Pierre, Ne rendre mal pour mal, mais biens contraires.*" The "Nobla Leyczon" scarce says more than the inquisitors, when it bitterly declares that the sign of a Vaudois, deemed worthy of death, was that he followed Christ and sought to obey the commandments of God.

"Que si n'i a alcun bon que ame e tema Yeshu Xrist,
Que non volha maudire ni jurar ni mentir,
Ni avoutrar ni aucir ni penre de l'altruy,
Ni venjar se de li seo enemis,
Ilh dion qu'es Vaudes e degne de punir,
E li troban cayson en meczonja e engan."

In fact, amid the license of the Middle Ages ascetic virtue was apt to be regarded as a sign of heresy. About 1220 a clerk of Spire, whose austerity subsequently led him to join the Franciscans, was only saved by the interposition of Conrad, afterwards Bishop of Hildesheim, from being burned as a heretic, because his preaching led certain women to lay aside their vanities of apparel and behave with humility.[65]

The sincerity with which the Waldenses adhered to their beliefs is shown by the thousands who cheerfully endured the horrors of the prison, the torture-chamber, and the stake, rather than return to a faith which they believed to be corrupt. I have met with a case in 1320, in which a poor old woman at Pamiers submitted to the dreadful sentence for heresy simply because she would not take an oath. She answered all interrogations on points of faith{88} in orthodox fashion, but though offered her life if she would swear on the Gospels, she refused to burden her soul with the sin, and for this she was condemned as a heretic.[66]

That all antisacerdotalists should agree, even under persecution, in a common creed, is not to be expected. In the decrees against heretics and in the writings of controversialists we meet the names of other sects, but they are of too little importance in numbers and duration to require more than a passing notice. The Passagii ("all-holy" or "vagabond") or Circumcisi were Judaizing Christians, who sought to escape the domination of Rome by a recourse to the old law and denying the equality of Christ with God. The Joseppini were still more obscure, and their errors appear mostly to lie in the region of artificial and unclean sexual asceticism. The Siscidentes were virtually the same as the Waldenses, the only difference being as to the administration of the Eucharist. The Ordibarii and Ortlibenses, followers of Ortlieb of Strassburg, who flourished about the year 1216, were likewise externally akin to the Waldenses, but indulged in doctrinal errors to which we shall have to recur hereafter. The Runcarii appear to have been a connecting link between the Poor Men of Lyons and the Albigenses or Manichæans; an intermediate sect whose existence might be presupposed as an almost necessary result of the common interests and common sufferings of the two leading branches of heresy.[67]{89}

CHAPTER III.

THE CATHARI.

THE movements described above were the natural outcome of antisacerdotalism seeking to renew the simplicity of the Apostolic Church. It is a singular feature of the religious sentiment of the time that the most formidable development of hostility to Rome was based on a faith that can scarce be classed as Christian, and that this hybrid doctrine spread so rapidly and resisted so stubbornly the sternest efforts at suppression that at one time it may fairly be said to have threatened the permanent existence of Christianity itself. The explanation of this may perhaps be found in the fascination which the dualistic theory—the antagonism of co-equal good and evil principles—offers to those who regard the existence of evil as incompatible with the supremacy of an all-wise and beneficent God. When to Dualism is added the doctrine of transmigration as a means of reward and retribution, the sufferings of man seem to be fully accounted for; and in a period when those sufferings were so universal and so hopeless as in the eleventh and twelfth centuries, it is possible to understand that many might be predisposed to adopt so ready an explanation. Yet this will not account for the fact that the Manichæism of the Cathari, Patarins, or Albigenses, was not a mere speculative dogma of the schools, but a faith which aroused fanaticism so enthusiastic that its devotees shrank from no sacrifices in its propagation and mounted the blazing pyre with steadfast joy. A profound conviction of the emptiness of sacerdotal Christianity, of its failure and approaching extinction, and of the speedy triumph of their own faith may partially explain the unselfish fervor which it excited among the poor and illiterate.

Of all the heresies with which the early Church had to contend, none had excited such mingled fear and loathing as Manichæism. Manes had so skilfully compounded Mazdean Dualism with Christianity{90} and with Gnostic and Buddhist elements, that his doctrine found favor with high and low, with the subtle intellects of the schools and with the toiling masses. Instinctively recognizing it as the most dangerous of rivals, the Church, as soon as it could command the resources of the State, persecuted it relentlessly. Among the numerous edicts of both Pagan and Christian emperors, repressing freedom of thought, those directed against the Manichæans were the sharpest and most cruel. Persecution attained its end, after prolonged struggle, in suppressing all outward manifestations of Manichæism within the confines of the imperial power, though it long afterwards maintained a secret existence, even in the West. In the East it withdrew ostensibly to the boundaries of the empire, still keeping up hidden relations with its sectaries scattered throughout the provinces, and even in Constantinople itself. It abandoned its reverence for Manes as the paraclete and transferred its allegiance to two others of its leaders, Paul and John of Samosata, from the first of whom it acquired the name of Paulicianism. Under the Emperor Constans, in 653, a certain Constantine perfected its doctrine, and it maintained itself under repeated and cruel persecutions, which it endured with the unflinching willingness of martyrdom and persistent missionary zeal that we shall see characterize its European descendants. Sometimes driven across the border to the Saracens and then driven back, the Paulicians at times maintained an independent existence among the mountains of Armenia and carried on a predatory warfare with the empire. Leo the Isaurian, Michael Curopalates, Leo the Armenian, and the Regent Empress Theodora in vain sought their extermination in the eighth and ninth centuries, until at length, in the latter half of the tenth century, John Zimiskes tried the experiment of toleration, and transplanted a large number of them to Thrace, where they multiplied greatly, showing equal vigor in industry and in war. In 1115 we hear of Alexis Comnenus spending a summer at Philippopolis and amusing himself in disputation with them, resulting in the conversion of many of the heretics.[68]{91} It was almost immediately after their transfer to Europe by Zimiskes that we meet with traces of them in the West, showing that the activity of their propagandism was unabated.

In all essentials the doctrine of the Paulicians was identical with that of the Albigenses. The simple Dualism of Mazdeism, which regards the universe as the mingled creations of Hormazd and Ahriman, each seeking to neutralize the labors of the other, and carrying on interminable warfare in every detail of life and nature, explains the existence of evil in a manner to enlist man to contribute his assistance to Hormazd in the eternal conflict, by good thoughts, good words, and good deeds. Enticed by Gnostic speculation, Manes modified this by identifying spirit with the good and matter with the evil principle—perhaps a more refined and philosophical conception, but one which led directly to pessimistic consequences and to excesses of asceticism, since the soul of man could only fulfil its duty by trampling on the flesh. Thus in the Paulician faith we find two co-equal principles, God and Satan, of whom the former created the invisible, spiritual, and eternal universe, the latter the material and temporal, which he governs. Satan is the Jehovah of the Old Testament; the prophets and patriarchs are robbers, and, consequently, all Scripture anterior to the Gospels is to be rejected. The New Testament, however, is Holy Writ, but Christ was not a man, but a phantasm—the Son of God who appeared to be born of the Virgin Mary and came from Heaven to overthrow the worship of Satan. Transmigration provides for the future reward or punishment of deeds done in life. The sacraments are rejected, and the priests and elders of the{92} Church are only teachers without authority over the faithful. Such are the outlines of Paulicianism as they have reached us, and their identity with the belief of the Cathari is too marked for us to accept the theory of Schmidt, which assigns to the latter an origin among the dreamers of the Bulgarian convents. A further irrefragable evidence of the derivation of Catharism from Manichæism is furnished by the sacred thread and garment which were worn by all the Perfect among the Cathari. This custom is too peculiar to have had an independent origin, and is manifestly the Mazdean *kosti* and *saddarah*, the sacred thread and shirt, the wearing of which was essential to all believers, and the use of which by both Zends and Brahmans shows that its origin is to be traced to the prehistoric period anterior to the separation of those branches of the Aryan family. Among the Cathari the wearer of the thread and vestment was what was known among the inquisitors as the "hæreticus indutus" or "vestitus," initiated into all the mysteries of the heresy.[69]{93}

Catharism thus was a thoroughly antisacerdotal form of belief. It cast aside all the machinery of the Church. The Roman Church indeed was the synagogue of Satan, in which salvation was impossible. Consequently the sacraments, the sacrifices of the altar, the suffrages and interposition of the Virgin and saints, purgatory, relics, images, crosses, holy water, indulgences, and the other devices by which the priest procured salvation for the faithful were rejected, as well as the tithes and oblations which rendered the procuring of salvation so profitable. Yet the Catharan Church, as the Church of Christ, inherited the power to bind and to loose bestowed by Christ on his disciples; the Consolamentum, or Baptism of the Spirit, wiped out all sin, but no prayers were of use for the sinner who persisted in wrong-doing. Curiously enough, though Catharism translated the Scripture, it retained the Latin language in its prayers, which were thus unintelligible to most of the disciples, and it had its consecrated class who conducted its simple services. Some regular form of organization, indeed, was necessary for the government of its rapidly increasing communities and for the missionary work which was so zealously carried forward. Thus there came to be four orders selected from among the "Perfected," who were distinguished from the mass of believers, or simple "Christians"—the Bishop, the Filius Major, the Filius Minor, and the Deacon. Each of the three higher grades had a deacon as an assistant, or to replace him; for the functions of all were the same, though the Filii were mostly employed in visiting the members of the church. The Filius Major was elected by the congregation and promotions were made to the episcopate as vacancies occurred. Ordination was conferred by the imposition of hands or Consolamentum, which was the equivalent of baptism, administered to all who were admitted to the Church. The belief that sacraments were vitiated in sinful hands gave rise to considerable anxiety, and to guard against it the Consolamentum was generally repeated a second and a third time. It was generally, though not universally, held that the lower in grade could not consecrate the higher, and therefore in many cities there were habitually{94} two bishops, so that in the case of death consecration should not be sought at the hands of a filius major.[70]

The Catharan ritual was severe in its simplicity. The Catholic Eucharist was replaced by the benediction of bread, which was performed daily at table. He who was senior by profession or position took the bread and wine, while all stood up and recited the Lord's Prayer. The senior then saying, "The grace of our Lord Jesus Christ be with us," broke the bread, and distributed it to all present. This blessed bread was regarded with special reverence by the great mass of the Cathari, who were, as a rule, merely "crezentz," "credentes," or believers, and not fully received or "perfected" in the Church. These would sometimes procure a piece of this bread and keep it for years, occasionally taking a morsel. Every act of eating or drinking was preceded by prayer; when a "perfected" minister was at the table, the first drink and every new dish that was tasted was accompanied by the guests with "Benedicite," to which he responded *Diaus vos benesiga*. There was a monthly ceremony of confession, which, however, was general in its character and was performed by the assembled faithful. The great ceremony was the "Cossolament," "Consolamentum," or Baptism of the Holy Ghost, which reunited the soul to the Holy Spirit, and which, like the Christian baptism, worked absolution of all sin. It consisted in the imposition of hands, it required two ministrants, and could be performed by any one of the Perfected not in mortal sin— even by a woman. It was inefficacious, however, when one of these was involved in sin. This was the process of "heretication," as the inquisitors termed the admission into the Church, and except in the case of those who proposed to become ministers was, as a rule, postponed until the death-bed, probably for fear of persecution; but the "credens" frequently entered into an agreement, known as "la covenansa," binding himself to undergo it at the last moment, and this engagement authorized its performance even though he had lost the power of speech and was unable to make the responses. In form it was exceedingly simple, though it was generally preceded by{95} preparation, including a prolonged fast. The ministrant addressed the postulant, "Brother, dost thou wish to give thyself to our faith?" The neophyte, after several genuflexions and blessings, said, "Ask God for this sinner, that he may lead me to a good end and make me a good Christian," to which the ministrant rejoined, "Let God be asked to make thee a good Christian and to bring thee to a good end. Dost thou give thyself to God and to the gospel?" and after an affirmative response, "Dost thou promise that in future thou wilt eat no meat, nor eggs, nor cheese, nor any victual except from water and wood; that thou wilt not lie or swear or do any lust with thy body, or go alone when thou canst have a comrade or abandon the faith for fear of water or fire or any other form of death?" These promises being duly made, the bystanders knelt, while the minister placed on the head of the postulant the Gospel of St. John and recited the text: "In the beginning was the Word," etc., and invested him with the sacred thread. Then the kiss of peace went round, the women receiving it by a touch of the elbow. The ceremony was held to symbolize the abandonment of the Evil Spirit, and the return of the soul to God, with the resolve to lead henceforth a pure and sinless life. With the married, the assent of the spouse was of course a condition precedent. When this heretication occurred on the death-bed, it was commonly followed by the "Endura" or "privation." The ministrant asked the neophyte whether he desired to be a confessor or a martyr; if the latter, a pillow or a towel (known among the German Cathari as Untertuch) was placed over his mouth while certain prayers were recited; if he chose the former he remained without food or drink, except a little water, for three days; and in either case, if he survived, he became one of the Perfected. This Endura was also sometimes used as a mode of suicide, which was frequent in the sect. Torture at the end of life relieved them of torment in the next world, and suicide by voluntary starvation, by swallowing pounded glass or poisonous potions, or opening the veins in a bath, was not uncommon—and, failing this, it was a kind office for the next of kin to extinguish life when death was near. The ceremony known to the sectaries as "Melioramentum," and described by the inquisitors as "veneration," was important as affording to them a proof of heresy. When a "credens" approached or took leave of a minister of the sect, he{96} bent the knee thrice, saying "benedicite," to which the minister replied, "*Diaus vos benesiga*." It was a mark of respect to the Holy Ghost assumed to dwell in the minister, and in the records of trials we find it eagerly inquired into, as it served to convict those who performed it.[71]

32

These customs, and the precepts embodied in the formula of heretication, illustrate the strong ascetic tendency of the faith. This was the inevitable consequence of its peculiar form of Dualism. As all matter was the handiwork of Satan, it was in its nature evil; the spirit was engaged in a perpetual conflict with it, and the Catharan's earnest prayer to God was not to spare the flesh sprung from corruption, but to have mercy on the imprisoned spirit—"*no aias merce de la carn nada de corruptio, mais aias merce de l esperit pausat en carcer.*" Consequently, whatever{97} tended to the reproduction of animal life was to be shunned. To mortify the flesh the Catharan fasted on bread and water three days in each week, except when travelling, and in addition there were in the year three fasts of forty days each. Marriage was also forbidden except among a few, who permitted it between virgins provided they separated as soon as a child was born, and the mitigated Dualists who confined the prohibition to the Perfect and permitted marriage to the believers. Among the rigid, carnal matrimony was replaced by the spiritual union between the soul and God effected by the rite of Consolamentum. Sexual passion, in fact, was the original sin of Adam and Eve, the forbidden fruit whereby Satan has continued his empire over man. In a confession before the Inquisition of Toulouse in 1310, it is said of one heretic teacher that he would not touch a woman for the whole world; in another case a woman relates of her father that after he was hereticated he told her she must never touch him again, and she obeyed the command even when he was on the death-bed. So far was this carried that the use of meat, of eggs, of milk, of everything, in short, which was the result of animal propagation, was inhibited, except fish, which by a strange inconsistency seems to have been regarded as having some different origin. The condemnation of marriage and the rejection of meat constituted, with the prohibition of oaths, the chief external characteristics of Catharism, by which the sectaries were marked and known. In 1229 two leading Tuscan Cathari, Pietro and Andrea, performed public abjuration before Gregory IX. in Perugia, and two days later, June 26th, they gave solemn assurance of the sincerity of their conversion by eating flesh in the presence of a number of prelates, which was duly recorded in an instrument drawn up for the purpose.[72]{98}

It was inevitable that, in process of time, diversities should spring up in a sect so widely scattered, and accordingly we find among the Italian Cathari two minor divisions known as Concorrezenses (from Concorrezo, near Monza, in Lombardy) and Bajolenses (from Bagnolo in Piedmont), who held a modified form of Dualism in which Satan was inferior to God, by whose permission he created and ruled the world, and formed man. The Concorrezenses taught that Satan infused in Adam an angel who had sinned a little, and they revived the old Traducian heresy in maintaining that all human souls are derived from that spirit. The Bajolenses differed from this in saying that all human souls were created by God before the world was formed, and that even then they had sinned. These speculations were expanded into a myth relating that Satan was the steward of heaven, charged with the duty of collecting the daily amount of praise and psalmody due by the angels to God. Desiring to become like the Highest, he abstracted and retained for himself a portion of the praise, when God, detecting the fraud, replaced him by Michael and ejected him and his accomplices. Satan thereupon uncovered the earth from water and created Adam and Eve, but labored in vain for thirty years to infuse souls into them, until he procured from heaven two angels who favored him, and who subsequently passed through the bodies of Enoch, Noah, Abraham, and all the patriarchs and prophets, wandering and vainly seeking salvation until, as Simeon and Anna, at the advent of Christ (Luke iii. 25-38), they accomplished their redemption and were permitted to return to heaven. Human souls are similarly all fallen spirits passing through probation, and this was very generally the belief of all the sects of Cathari, leading to a theory of transmigration very similar to that of Buddhism, though modified by the belief that Christ's earthly mission was the redemption of these fallen spirits.{99} Until the perfected soul could return to its Creator, as in the *moksha* or absorption in Brahma of the Hindu, it was forced to undergo repeated existence. As it could be still further punished for evil deeds by transmission into the lower animal forms, there naturally followed the Buddhistic and Brahmanical prohibition of slaying any created thing, except reptiles and fish. The Cathari who were hanged at Goslar in 1052 refused to kill a pullet, even with the gallows before their eyes, and in the thirteenth century this test was regarded as a ready means of identifying them.[73]

There were a few philosophic spirits in the sect, moreover, who emerged from these vain speculations and curiously anticipated the theories of modern Rationalism. With these Nature took the place of Satan; God, after forming the universe, abandoned its conduct to Nature, which has the power of creating all things and regulating them. Even the production of individual species is not the act of divine Providence, but is a process of nature—in fact, of evolution, in modern parlance. These Naturalists, as they called themselves, denied the existence of miracles; they explained, by an exegesis not much more strained than that of orthodoxy, all those in the Gospels; and they held that it was useless to pray to God for good weather, for Nature alone controlled the elements. They wrote much, and a Catholic antagonist admits the attraction of their writings, especially the work known as "Perpendiculum Scientiarum," or the "Plummet of Science," which he says was well adapted to make a deep impression on the reader through its array of philosophy and happily-chosen texts of Scripture.[74]{100}

There was nothing in such a faith to attract the sensual and carnal-minded. In fact, it was far more repellant than attractive, and nothing but the discontent excited by the pervading corruption and oppression of the Church can explain its rapid diffusion and the deep hold which it obtained upon the veneration of its converts. Although the asceticism which it inculcated was beyond the reach of average humanity, its ethical teachings were{101} admirable. As a rule they were reasonably obeyed, and the orthodox admitted with regret and shame the contrast between the heretics and the faithful. It is true that the exaggerated condemnation of marriage expressed in the formula, that relations with a wife were as sinful as incest with mother or sister, was naturally enough perverted into the statement that such incest was permissible and was practised. Wild stories, moreover, were told of the nightly orgies in which the lights were extinguished and promiscuous intercourse took place; and the stubbornness of heresy was explained by telling how, when a child was born of these foul excesses, it was tossed from hand to hand through a fire until it expired; and that from its body was made an infernal eucharist of such power that whoever partook of it was thereafter incapable of abandoning the sect. There is ample store of such tales, but however useful they might be in exciting a wholesome popular detestation of heresy, the candid and intelligent inquisitors who had the best means of knowing the truth admit that they have no foundation in fact; and in the many hundreds of examinations and sentences which I have read there is no allusion to anything of the kind, except in some proceedings of Frà Antonio Secco among the Alpine valleys in 1387. As a rule, the inquisitors wasted no time in searching for what they knew was non-existent. As St. Bernard says, "If you interrogate them, nothing can be more Christian; as to their conversation, nothing can be less reprehensible, and what they speak they prove by deeds. As for the morals of the heretic, he cheats no one, he oppresses no one, he strikes no one; his cheeks are pale with fasting, he eats not the bread of idleness, his hands labor for his livelihood." This last assertion is especially true, for they were mostly simple folk, industrious peasants and mechanics, who felt the evils around them and welcomed any change. The theologians who combated them ridiculed them as ignorant churls, and in France they were popularly known by the name of Texerant (Tisserands), on account of the prevalence of the heresy among the weavers, whose monotonous occupation doubtless gave ample opportunity for thought. Rude and ignorant they might be for the most part, but they had skilled theologians for teachers, and an extensive popular literature which has utterly perished, saving a Catharan version of the New Testament in Romance and a book of ritual.{102} Their familiarity with Scripture is vouched for by the warning of Lucas, Bishop of Tuy, that the Christian should dread their conversation as he would a tempest, unless he is deeply skilled in the law of God, so that he can overcome them in argument. Their strict morality was never corrupted, and a hundred years after St. Bernard the same testimony is rendered to the virtues of those who were persecuted in Florence in the middle of the thirteenth century. In fact the formula of confession used in their assemblies shows how strict a guard was maintained over every idle thought and careless word.[75]

Their proselyting zeal was especially dreaded. No labor was too severe, no risks too great, to deter them from spreading the faith which they deemed essential to salvation. Missionaries wandered over Europe through strange lands to carry the glad tidings to benighted populations, regardless of hardship, and undeterred by the fate of their brethren, whom they saw expiate at the stake the hardihood of their revolt. Externally they professed to be Catholics, and were exemplary in the performance of their religious duties till they had won the confidence of their new neighbors, and could venture on the attempt of secret conversion whenever they saw opportunity. They scattered by the wayside writings in which the poison of their doctrine was skilfully conveyed{103} without being obtrusive, and sometimes they had no scruple in calling to their aid the superstitions of orthodoxy, as when such writings would promise indulgences to those who would read them carefully and circulate them among their neighbors, or when they purported to come from Jesus Christ and be conveyed by angels. It does not say much for the intelligence of the clergy when we are told that many priests were corrupted by such papers, picked up by shepherds and carried to them to be deciphered. Even more reprehensible was the device of the Cathari of Moncoul in France, who made an image of the Virgin, deformed and ugly and one-eyed, saying that Christ, to show his humility, had selected such a woman for a mother. Then they proceeded to work miracles with it, feigning to be sick and to be cured by it, until it acquired such reputation that many similar ones were made and placed in churches or oratories, until the heretics divulged the secret, to the great confusion of the faithful. The same device was carried out with a crucifix having no upper arm, the feet of Christ crossed, and only three nails—an unconventional form which was, imitated and caused great scandal when the mockery was discovered. Even bolder frauds were attempted in Leon, and not without success, as we shall see hereafter.[76]

The zeal for the faith, which prompted these eccentric missionary efforts, manifested itself in a resolute adherence to the precepts enjoined on the neophyte when admitted into the circle of the Perfects. As in the case of the Waldenses, while the Inquisition complained bitterly of the difficulty of obtaining an avowal from the simple "credens," whose rustic astuteness eluded the practised skill of the interrogator, it was the general testimony that the perfected heretic refused to lie, or to take an oath; and one member of the Holy Office warns his brethren not to begin by asking "Are you truly a Catharan?" for the answer will simply be "Yes," and then nothing more can be extracted; but if the Perfect is exhorted by the God in whom he believes to tell all about his life, he will faithfully detail it without falsehood. When we consider that this frankness led inevitably to the torture of death by burning,{104} it is curious to observe that the inquisitor seems utterly unconscious of the emphatic testimony which he renders to the super-human conscientiousness of his victims.[77]

It is not easy for us to realize what there was in the faith of the Cathari to inspire men with the enthusiastic zeal of martyrdom, but no religion can show a more unbroken roll of those who unshrinkingly and joyfully sought death in its most abhorrent form in preference to apostasy. If the blood of the martyrs were really the seed of the Church, Manichæism would now be the dominant religion of Europe. It may be partially explained by the belief that a painful death for the faith insured the return of the soul to God; but human weakness does not often permit such habitual triumph of the spirit over the flesh as that which rendered the Cathari a proverb in their thirst for martyrdom. The hostile testimony to this effect is virtually unanimous. In the earliest persecution on record, at Orleans, about 1017, out of fifteen, thirteen remained steadfast in the face of the fire kindled for their destruction; they refused to recant though pardon was offered, and their constancy was the wonderment of the spectators. When, about 1040, the heretics of Monforte were discovered, and Eriberto, Archbishop of Milan, sent for Gherardo, their leader, he came at once and voluntarily set forth his belief, rejoicing in the opportunity of sealing his faith with torment. Those who were burned at Cologne in 1163 produced a profound impression by the cheerful alacrity with which they endured their fearful punishment; and while they were in their agony it is related that their leader, Arnold, half roasted to death, placed a liberated arm on the heads of his disciples, calmly saying, "Be ye constant in your faith, for this day shall ye be with Lawrence!" Among this group of heretics was a beautiful girl whose modesty moved the compassion of even the brutal executioners. She was withdrawn from the flames and promises were made to find her a husband or place her in a convent. Seeming to assent, she remained quiet till the rest were dead, and then asked her guards to show her the seducer of souls. In pointing out the body of Arnold they loosened their hold, when she suddenly broke from them, and, covering her face with her ⸤105⸥ dress, threw herself upon the remains of her teacher, and, burning to death, descended with him into hell for eternity. Those who about the same time were detected at Oxford, rejected all offers of mercy, with the words of Christ, "Blessed are they which are persecuted for righteousness' sake, for theirs is the kingdom of heaven;" and when they were led forth after a sentence which virtually consigned them to a shameful and lingering death, they went rejoicing to the punishment, their leader Gerhard preceding them, singing "Blessed are ye when men shall revile you." In the Albigensian Crusade, at the capture of the Castle of Minerve, the Crusaders piously offered their prisoners the alternative of recantation or the stake, and a hundred and eighty preferred the stake, when, as the monkish chronicler quietly remarks, "no doubt all these martyrs of the devil passed from temporal to eternal flames." An experienced inquisitor of the fourteenth century tells us that the Cathari usually were either truly converted by the efforts of the Holy Office or else were ready to die for their faith; while the Waldenses were apt to feign conversion in order to escape. This obdurate zeal, we are assured by the orthodox writers, had in it nothing of the constancy of Christian martyrdom, but was simply hardness of heart inspired by Satan; and Frederic II. enumerated among their evil traits the obstinacy which led the survivors to be in no way dismayed or deterred by the ruthless example made of those who were punished.[78]

It was, perhaps, natural that these Manichæans should be accused of worshipping the devil. To men bred in the current orthodox practices of purchasing by prayer, or money, or other good works whatever blessings they desired, and expecting nothing ⸤106⸥ without such payment, it seemed inevitable that the Manichæan, regarding all matter to be the work of Satan, should invoke him for worldly prosperity. The husbandman, for instance, could not pray to God for a plentiful harvest, but must do so to Satan, who was the creator of corn. It is true that there was a sect, known as Luciferani, who were said to worship Satan, regarding him as the brother of God, unjustly banished from heaven, and the dispenser of worldly good, but these, as we shall see hereafter, were a branch of the Brethren of the Free Spirit, probably descended from the Ortlibenses, and there is absolutely no evidence that the Cathari ever wavered in their trust in Christ or diverted their aspirations from the hope of reunion with God.[79]

Such was the faith whose rapid spread throughout the south of Europe filled the Church with well-grounded dismay; and, however much we may deprecate the means used for its suppression and commiserate those who suffered for conscience' sake, we cannot but admit that the cause of orthodoxy was in this case the cause of progress and civilization. Had Catharism become dominant, or even had it been allowed to exist on equal terms, its influence could not have failed to prove disastrous. Its asceticism with regard to commerce between the sexes, if strictly enforced, could only have led to the extinction of the race, and as this involves a contradiction of nature, it would have probably resulted in lawless concubinage and the destruction of the institution of the family, rather than in the disappearance of the human race and the return of exiled souls to their Creator, which was the *summum bonum* of the true Catharan. Its condemnation of the visible universe and of matter in general as the work of Satan rendered sinful all striving after material improvement, and the conscientious belief in such a creed could only lead man back, in time, to his original condition of savagism. It was not only a revolt against the Church, but a renunciation of man's domination over nature. As such it was doomed from the start, and our only wonder must be that it maintained itself so long and so stubbornly even against a Church which had earned so much of popular detestation. Yet though ⸤107⸥ the exaltation caused by persecution might keep it alive among the enthusiastic and the discontented, had it obtained the upper hand and maintained its purity it must surely have perished through its fundamental errors. Had it become a dominant faith, moreover, it would have bred a sacerdotal class as privileged as the Catholic priesthood, for the "veneration" offered to the consecrated ministers as the tabernacles of the Holy Ghost shows us what vantage ground they would have had when persecution had given place to power, and carnal human nature had asserted itself in the ambitious men who would have sought its high places.

The soil was probably prepared for its reception by remains of the older Manichæism which, with strange pertinacity, long maintained itself in secret after its public manifestation had been completely suppressed.

Muratori has printed a Latin anathema of its doctrines, probably dating about the year 800, which shows that even so late as the ninth century it was still an object of persecution. It was about 970 that John Zimiski transplanted the Paulicians to Thrace, whence they spread with great rapidity through the Balkan peninsula. When the Crusaders under Bohemond of Tarento, in 1097, arrived in Macedonia they learned that the city of Pelagonia was inhabited wholly by heretics, whereupon they paused in their pilgrimage to the Holy Sepulchre long enough to capture the town, to raze it to the earth, and to put all the citizens to the sword. In Dalmatia the Paulicians founded the seaport of Dugunthia (Trau), which became the seat of one of their leading episcopates; and in the time of Innocent III. we find them in great numbers throughout the whole Slav territory, making extensive conversions with their customary missionary zeal, and giving that pontiff much concern, in unavailing efforts for their suppression. Numerous as the Cathari of Western Europe became, they always looked to the east of the Adriatic as to the headquarters of their sect. It was there that arose the form of modified Dualism known as Concorrezan, under the influence of the Bogomili, and religious questions were wont to be referred thither for solution.[80]{108}

Their missionary activity made itself felt in the West in a marvellously short period after their settlement in Bulgaria. Our materials for an intimate acquaintance with that age are very scanty, and we must content ourselves with occasional vague indications, but when we see that Gerbert of Aurillac, on his election to the archiepiscopate of Reims in 991, was obliged to utter a profession of faith in which he declared his belief that Satan was wicked of free-will, that the Old and New Testaments were of equal authority, and that marriage and the use of meat were allowable, it shows that Paulician opinions were already well understood and dreaded as far north as Champagne. There seems, indeed, to have been a centre of Catharism there, for in 1000 a peasant named Leutard, at Vertus, was convicted of teaching antisacerdotal doctrines which were evidently of Manichæan origin, and he is discreetly said to have drowned himself in a well when overcome in argument by Bishop Liburnius. The Château of Mont Wimer, in the neighborhood of Vertus, retained its evil reputation as a centre of the heresy. About the same period we have a misty account of a Ravennatese grammarian named Vilgardus who, inspired by demons in the shape of Virgil, Horace, and Juvenal, erected the Latin poets into infallible guides and taught much that was contrary to the faith. His heresy was probably Manichæan; it could not have been simply blind worship of classic writers, for culture was too rare in that age for such belief to become popular, and we are told that Vilgardus had numerous disciples in all the cities in Italy, who, after his condemnation by Peter, Archbishop of Ravenna, were put to death by the sword or at the stake. His heresy likewise spread to Sardinia and Spain, where it was ruthlessly exterminated.[81]

Shortly after this Cathari were discovered in Aquitaine, where they made many converts, and their heresy spread secretly throughout southern France in spite of the free use of the fagot. Even as far north as Orleans it was discovered, in 1017, under circumstances which aroused general attention. A female missionary from Italy had carried the infection there, and a number of the most prominent clergy of the city fell victims to it. In their proselyting zeal they sent out emissaries, and were discovered. On{109}hearing of it, King Robert the Pious hastened to Orleans with Queen Constance, and summoned a council of bishops to determine what should be done to meet the novel and threatening danger. The heretics, on being questioned, made no secret of their faith, and boldly declared themselves ready to die rather than to abandon it. The popular feeling was so bitter against them that Robert stationed his queen at the door of the church in which the assembly was held, to preserve them from being torn to pieces by the mob when they were led forth; but Constance shared the passions of her subjects, and as they passed her she smote with a rod one who had been her confessor, and put out his eye. They were taken beyond the walls, and again, in the presence of the blazing pyre, were entreated to recant, but they preferred death, and their unshrinking firmness was the wonder of all spectators. Such converts as they had made elsewhere were diligently hunted up and mercilessly despatched. In 1025 there was a further discovery of the heresy at Liége, but the sectaries proved less stubborn, and were pardoned on professing conversion. About the same time we hear of others, in Lombardy, in the Castle of Monforte, near Asti, who were the objects of active persecution by the neighboring nobles and bishops, and who were burned whenever they could be captured. At length, about 1040, Eriberto, Archbishop of Milan, in visiting his province, came to Asti, and, hearing of these heretics, sent for them. They came willingly enough, including their teacher, Gherardo, and the Countess of Monforte who was of their sect; all boldly professed their faith, and were carried by Eriberto back to Milan, where he hoped to convert them. In place of this, they labored to spread their heresy among those who crowded to see them in prison, until the enraged people, against the will of the archbishop, forcibly dragged them out, and gave them the choice between the cross and the stake. A few of them yielded, but the most part, covering their faces with their hands, boldly leaped into the flames, and sealed their faith with martyrdom. In 1045 we find them in Chalons, when Bishop Roger applied to Bishop Wazo of Liége, asking what he should do with them, and whether the secular arm should be called in to prevent the leaven from corrupting the whole people, to which the good Wazo replied that they should be left to God, "for those whom the world now regards as tares may be garnered by him as wheat when comes the{110} harvest-time. Those whom we deem the adversaries of God he may make superior to us in heaven." Wazo, indeed, had heard that heretics were commonly detected by their pallor, and, under the delusion that those who were pale must necessarily be heretics, many good Catholics had been slain. By the year 1052 the heresy had extended to Germany, where the pious emperor, Henry the Black, caused a number to be hanged at Goslar. During the rest of the century we hear little more of them, though traces of them occur at Toulouse in 1056 and Béziers in 1062, and about the year 1200 they are described as infecting the whole diocese of Agen.[82]

In the twelfth century the evil continued unabated in northern France. Count John of Soissons was noted as a protector of heretics, but, in spite of his favor, Lisiard, the bishop, captured several, and gave the first example of what subsequently became common enough—the use of the ordeal to determine heretical guilt. One, at least, of the accused, floated when thrown into exorcised water, and the bishop, not knowing what to do with them, held them in prison while he went to the Council of Beauvais, in 1114, to consult his episcopal brethren. The populace, however, felt no doubts on the subject, and, fearing that they would be deprived of their prey, broke open the jail and burned them during the bishop's absence—a manifestation of holy zeal which greatly pleased the pious chronicler. About the same time Flanders was the scene of another discovery of Catharism. The heresiarch, on being summoned before the Bishop of Cambrai, made no secret of his{111} crime; he was stubborn, and was shut up in a hut, which was fired, and he died in prayer. The people must, in this case, have been rather favorably inclined to him, for they allowed his friends to collect his remains, and he was found to have many followers, especially among the craft of weavers. When, about the same period, we see Paschal II. advising the Bishop of Constance that converted heretics were to be welcomed back, we may conclude that error had penetrated even into Switzerland.[83]

As the century wore on the manifestations of heresy became more numerous. In 1144 at Liége again; in 1153 again in Artois; in 1157 at Reims; in 1163 at Vezelai, where there was a significant concomitant attempt to throw off the temporal jurisdiction of the Abbey of St. Madelaine; about 1170 at Besançon; and in 1180 at Reims again. This latter case has picturesque features recited for us by one of the actors in the drama, Gervais of Tilbury, at that time a young man and a canon of Reims. Riding out one afternoon as part of the retinue of his archbishop, William, his fancy was caught by a pretty girl laboring alone in a vineyard. He lost no time in pressing his suit, but was repulsed with the assertion that if she listened to his addresses she would be irretrievably damned. Virtue so severe as this was a manifest sign of heresy, and the archbishop, coming up, ordered her at once into custody, for he recognized her as necessarily belonging to the Cathari, whom Philip of Flanders had for some time been mercilessly persecuting. Under examination, she gave the name of her instructress, who was forthwith arrested, and who manifested such thorough familiarity with Scripture and such consummate dexterity in defending her faith, that no doubt was felt of her being inspired by Satan. The defeated theologians respited the pair till the next day, when they obstinately refused to yield to threats or promises, and were unanimously condemned to the stake. At this the elder woman laughed, saying, "Foolish and unjust judges, think you to burn me in your fire? I fear not your sentence, and dread not your stake." With that she pulled from her bosom a ball of thread and tossed it out of the window, retaining one end, and calling out, "Take it!" The ball arose in the air, and the old woman followed it through{112} the window, and was seen no more. The girl was left, and as she was insensible alike to offers of wealth and threats of punishment, she was duly burned, suffering her torment cheerfully and without a groan. Even in distant Britanny Catharism appeared in 1208, at Nantes and St. Malo.[84]

In Flanders the heresy seems to have taken deep root the industrious craftsmen who were already making their cities centres of wealth and progress. In 1162 Henry, Archbishop of Reims, in a visitation of Flanders, which formed part of his province, found Manichæism prevailing there to an alarming extent. In the existing confusion and uncertainty of the canon law as respects the treatment of heresy, he allowed the appeal of those whom he captured to Alexander III., then in Touraine. The pope inclined to mercy, much to the disgust of the archbishop and of his brother, Louis VII., who urged the adoption of rigorous measures, and asserted that the enormous bribe of six hundred marks had been offered for their liberation. If this were so, the heresy must have penetrated to the upper ranks of society. In spite of Alexander's humanity the persecution was sharp enough, however, to drive many of the heretics away, and we shall meet with some of them at Cologne. Twenty years later we find the evil still growing, and Philip I., Count of Flanders, whose zeal for the faith was manifested subsequently by his death in Palestine, busily engaged in persecuting them with the aid of William, Archbishop of Reims. They are described as comprising all classes, nobles and peasants, clerks, soldiers, and mechanics, maids, wives, and widows, and numbers of them were burned without putting an end to the pestilence.[85]

The Teutonic peoples were comparatively free from the infection, although the propinquity of the Rhinelands to France led to occasional visitations. About 1110 we hear of some heretics at Trèves, who seem to have escaped without punishment, though two among them were priests, and in 1200 eight more were found{113} there and burned. In 1145 a number were discovered in Cologne, some of whom were tried; but, during the examination, the impatient populace, fearing to be balked of their spectacle, broke in, carried off the culprits, and burned them out of hand—a fate which they bore not only with patience, but with joyfulness. There must have been a Catharan Church established by this time at Cologne, since one of the sufferers was called their bishop. In 1163 fugitives from the Flemish persecution were found at Cologne—eight men and three women, who had taken refuge in a barn. As they associated with no one, and did not frequent the churches, the Christian neighbors recognized them as heretics, seized them, and took them before the bishop, when they boldly avowed their faith, and suffered burning with the resolute gladness which distinguished the sect. We hear of others, about the same time, burned at Bonn, but this scanty catalogue exhausts the list of

German heresies in the twelfth century. Missionaries penetrated the country from Hungary, Italy, and Flanders; they are found in Switzerland, Bavaria, Suabia, and even as far as Saxony, but they made few converts.[86]

England was likewise little troubled with heresy. It was shortly after the persecutions in Flanders that in 1166 there were discovered thirty rustics—men and women—German in race and speech, probably Flemings, fleeing from the pious zeal of Henry of Reims, who had come and were endeavoring to propagate their errors. They made but one convert, a woman, who deserted them in the hour of trial. The rest stood firm when Henry II., then engaged in his quarrel with Becket, and anxious to prove his fidelity to the Church, called a council of bishops at Oxford, and presided over it, to determine their faith. They openly avowed it, and were condemned to be scourged, branded in the face with a key, and driven forth. The importance which Henry attached to the matter is shown by his devoting, soon after, in the Assizes of Clarendon, an article to the subject, forbidding any one to receive them under penalty of having his house torn down, and{114} requiring all sheriffs to swear to the observance of the law, and to make all stewards of the barons and all knights and franc-tenants swear likewise— the first secular law on the subject in any statute-book since the fall of Rome. I have already mentioned the steadfastness with which the unfortunates endured their martyrdom. Stripped to the waist and soundly scourged, and branded on the forehead, they were sent adrift shelterless in the winter-time, and speedily, one by one, they miserably perished. England was not hospitable to heresy, and we hear little more of it there. Towards the close of the century some heretics were found in the province of York, and early in the next century a few were discovered in London, and one was burned; but practically the orthodoxy of England was unsullied until the rise of Wickliffe.[87]

Italy, as the channel through which the Bulgarian heresy passed to the West, was naturally deeply infected. Milan had the reputation of being its centre, whence missionaries were despatched to other lands, whither pilgrims resorted from the western kingdoms, and where originated the sinister term of Patarins, by which the Cathari became generally known to the people of Europe.[88] Yet the popes, involved in a death-struggle{115} with the empire, and frequently wanderers abroad, paid little attention to them during the first half of the twelfth century, and the indications which have reached us of their existence are but scanty, though sufficient to show that they were numerous and aggressive in the consciousness of growing strength. Thus at Orvieto, in 1125, they actually obtained the mastery for a while, but after a bloody struggle were subdued by the Catholics. In 1150 the effort was resumed by Diotesalvi of Florence and Gherardo of Massano; but the bishop succeeded in expelling them, when they were replaced by two women missionaries—Milita of Monte-Meano, and Giulitta of Florence—whose piety and charity won the esteem of the clergy and sympathy of the people, until the heresy was discovered, in 1163, when many heretics were burned and hanged, and the rest exiled. Yet soon afterwards Peter the Lombard undertook to propagate it again, and formed{116} a numerous community, embracing many nobles, and towards the close of the century San Pietro di Parenzo earned his canonization by his severe measures of repression, in retaliation for which the heretics took his life in 1199. This may be regarded as an example of the struggle which was going on in many Italian cities, showing the stubborn vitality of the heresy. In the political condition of Italy, subdivided into innumerable virtually self-governing communities, torn by mutual quarrels and civic strife, general measures of repression were almost impossible. Heresy, suppressed by spasmodic exertion in one city, was always flourishing elsewhere, and ready to furnish new missionaries and new martyrs as soon as the storm had passed. Through all these vicissitudes its growth was constant. All the northern half of the peninsula, from the Alps to the Patrimony of St. Peter, was honeycombed with it, and even as far south as Calabria it was to be found. When Innocent III., in 1198, ascended the papal throne he at once commenced active proceedings for its extermination, and the obstinacy of the heretics may be estimated by the struggle in Viterbo, a city subject to the temporal as well as spiritual jurisdiction of the papacy. In March, 1199, Innocent, stimulated by the increase of heresy and the audacity of its public display, wrote to the Viterbians, renewing and sharpening the penalties against all who received or favored heretics. Yet, in spite of this, in 1205, the heretics carried the municipal election and elected as chamberlain a heretic under excommunication. Innocent's indignation was boundless. If the elements, he told the citizens, should conspire to destroy them, without sparing age or sex, leaving their memory an eternal shame, the punishment would be inadequate. He ordered obedience to be refused to the newly-elected municipality, which was to be deposed; that the bishop, who had been ejected, should be received back, that the laws against heresy should be enforced, and that if all this was not done within fifteen days the people of the surrounding towns and castles were commanded to take up arms and make active war upon the rebellious city. Even this was insufficient. Two years later, in February, 1207, there were fresh troubles, and it was not until June of that year, when Innocent himself came to Viterbo, and all the Patarins fled at his approach, that he was able to purify the town by tearing down all the houses of the heretics and confiscating all their property. This{117} he followed up in September with a decree addressed to all the faithful in the Patrimony of St. Peter, ordering measures of increasing severity to be inscribed in the local laws of every community, and all podestà, and other officials to be sworn to their enforcement under heavy penalties. Proceedings of more or less rigor commanded in Milan, Ferrara, Verona, Rimini, Florence, Prato, Faenza, Piacenza, and Treviso show the extent of the evil, the difficulty of restraining it, and the encouragement given to heresy by the scandals of the clergy.[89]

It was in southern France, however, that the struggle was deadliest and the battle was fought to its bitter end. There the soil, as we have seen, was the most favorable, and the growth of heresy the rankest. Early in the century we find open resistance at Albi, when the bishop, Sicard, aided by the Abbot of Castres, endeavored to imprison obstinate heretics and was baffled by the people, leading to a dangerous quarrel between the civil and ecclesiastical jurisdictions. About the same time, Amelius of Toulouse tried milder methods by calling in the aid of the celebrated Robert d'Arbrissel, whose preaching, we are told, was rewarded with many conversions. In 1119 Calixtus II. presided over a council at Toulouse which condemned the Manichæan heresy, but was forced to content itself with sentencing the heretics to expulsion from the Church. It is perhaps remarkable that when Innocent II., driven from Rome by the antipope Pier-Leone, was wandering through France and held a great council at Reims in 1131, no measures were taken for the repression of heresy; but when restored to Rome he seems to have awakened to the necessity of action, and in the Second General Lateran Council, in 1139, he issued a decisive decree which is interesting as the earliest example of the interpellation of the secular arm. Not only were the Cathari condemned and expelled from the Church, but the temporal authorities were ordered to coerce them and all those who favored or defended them. This policy was followed up in 1148 by the Council{118} of Reims, which forbade any one to receive or maintain on his lands the heretics dwelling in Gascony, Provence, and elsewhere, and not to afford them shelter in passing or give them a refuge, under pain of excommunication and interdict.[90]

When Alexander III. was exiled from Rome by Frederic Barbarossa and his antipope Victor, and came to France, he called, in 1163, a great council at Tours. It was an imposing assemblage, comprising seventeen cardinals, one hundred and twenty-four bishops (including Thomas Becket) and hundreds of abbots, besides hosts of other ecclesiastics and a vast number of laymen. This august body, after performing its first duty of anathematizing the rival pope, proceeded to deplore the heresy which, arising in the Toulousain, had spread like a cancer throughout Gascony, deeply infecting the faithful everywhere. The prelates of those regions were ordered to be vigilant in suppressing it by anathematizing all who should permit heretics to dwell on their lands or should hold intercourse with them, in buying or selling, so that, being cut off from human society, they might be compelled to abandon their errors. All secular princes moreover were commanded to imprison them and to confiscate their property. By this time, it is evident that heresy was no longer concealed, but displayed itself openly and defiantly; and the futility of the papal commands at Tours to cut heretics off from human intercourse was shown two years later at the council, or rather colloquy, of Lombers near Albi. This was a public disputation between representatives of orthodoxy and the *bos homes, bos Crestias,* or "good men," as they styled themselves, before judges agreed upon by both sides, in the presence of Pons, Archbishop of Narbonne, and sundry bishops, besides the most powerful nobles of the region—Constance, sister of King Louis VII. and wife of Raymond of Toulouse, Trencavel of Béziers, Sicard of Lautrec, and others. Nearly all of the population of Lombers and Albi assembled, and the proceedings were evidently regarded as of the greatest public interest and importance. A full report of the discussion, including the decision against the Cathari, has reached us from several orthodox sources, but the{119} only interest which the affair has is its marked significance in showing that heresy had fairly outgrown all the means of repression at command of the local churches, that reason had to be appealed to in place of force, that heretics had no scruple in manifesting and declaring themselves, and that the Catholic disputants had to submit to their demands in citing only the New Testament as an authority. The powerlessness of the Church was still further exhibited in the fact that the council, after its argumentative triumph, was obliged to content itself with simply ordering the nobles of Lombers no longer to protect the heretics. What satisfaction Pons of Narbonne found the next year in confirming the conclusions of the Council of Lombers, in a council held at Cabestaing, it would be difficult to define. So great was the prevailing demoralization that when some monks of the strict Cistercian order left their monastery of Villemagne near Agde, and publicly took wives, he was unable to punish this gross infraction of their vows, and the interposition of Alexander III. was invoked—probably without result.[91]

Evidently the Church was powerless. When it could condemn the doctrines and not the persons of heretics it confessed to the world that it possessed no machinery capable of dealing with opposition on a scale of such magnitude. The nobles and the people were indisposed to do its bidding, and without their aid the fulmination of its anathema was an empty ceremony. The Cathari saw this plainly, and within two years of the Council of Lombers they dared, in 1167, to hold a council of their own at St. Felix de Caraman near Toulouse. Their highest dignitary, Bishop Nicetas, came from Constantinople to preside, with deputies from Lombardy; the French Church was strengthened against the modified Dualism of the Concorrezan school; bishops were elected for the vacant sees of Toulouse, Val d'Aran, Carcassonne, Albi, and France north of the Loire, the latter being Robert de Sperone, subsequently a refugee in Lombardy, where he gave his name to the sect of the Speronistæ; commissioners were named to settle a disputed boundary between the sees of Toulouse and Carcassonne; in{120} short, the business was that of an established and independent Church, which looked upon itself as destined to supersede the Church of Rome. Based upon the affection and reverence of the people, which Rome had forfeited, it might well look forward to ultimate supremacy.[92]

In fact, its progress during the next ten years was such as to justify the most enthusiastic hopes. Raymond of Toulouse, whose power was virtually that of an independent sovereign, adhered to Frederic Barbarossa, acknowledged the antipope Victor and his successors, and cared nothing for Alexander III., who was received by the rest of France; and the Church, distracted by the schism, could offer little opposition to the development of heresy. In 1177, however, Alexander triumphed and received the submission of Frederic. Raymond necessarily followed his suzerain (a large portion of his territories was subject to the empire) and suddenly awoke to the necessity of arresting the progress of heresy. Powerful as he was, he felt himself unequal to the task. The burgesses of his cities, independent and intractable, were for the most part Cathari. A large portion of his knights and gentlemen were secretly or avowedly protectors of heresy; the common people throughout his dominions despised the clergy and honored the heretics. When a heretic preached they crowded to listen and applaud; when a Catholic assumed the rare function of religious instruction they jeered at him and asked him what he had to do with proclaiming the Word of God. In a state of chronic war with powerful vassals and more powerful neighbors, like the kings of Aragon and England, it was manifestly impossible for Raymond to undertake the extermination of a half or more than half of his subjects. Whether he was sincere in his desire to suppress heresy is doubtful, but in any case his situation is interesting, as an illustration of the difficulties which surrounded his son and grandson, and led to the Crusades and the extinction of his house. Whatever his motives, however, Raymond V. craftily placed himself on the right side. He called upon the king, Louis VII., to come to his assistance, and, remembering how St. Bernard had, in the previous generation, aided to suppress the Henricians, he applied to Bernard's successor, Henry of Clairvaux, head of the great Cistercian{121} order, to support his appeal. He described the condition of religion in his dominions as desperate. The priesthood had allowed itself to be seduced; the churches were abandoned and falling into ruin; the sacraments were despised and no longer in use; Dualism had prevailed over Trinitarianism. Anxious as he was to be the minister of the vengeance of God, he was powerless, for his principal subjects had embraced the false faith, together with the better part of his people. Spiritual punishment no longer had any terror, and force alone would be of service. If the king would come, Raymond promised personally to conduct him through the land and point out the heretics to be chastised, and with their united efforts success could hardly fail to crown the good work.[93]

Henry II. of England, who as Duke of Aquitaine was nearly concerned in the matter, had just concluded a peace with Louis of France, and, free from the preoccupation of mutual war, the monarchs conferred together with the intention of proceeding in person with a heavy force in response to Raymond's appeal. The Abbot of Clairvaux also wrote to Alexander III., with more earnestness than courtesy, stimulating him to do his duty and put down heresy as he had quelled schism; the two kings, he said, were debating as to the measures to be taken, and no remissness of the spiritual power must serve as excuse for lack of energy on the part of the temporal: in Languedoc, priest and people were alike infected, or rather the contagion proceeded from the shepherds to the flock; the least the pope could do was to instruct his legate, Cardinal Peter of St. Chrysogono, to remain longer in France and to attack the heretics. During these preliminaries the zeal of the monarchs had cooled, and in place of marching at the head of armies they contented themselves with sending a mission consisting of the cardinal legate, the archbishops of Narbonne and Bourges, Henry of Clairvaux and other prelates, at the same time urging the Count of Toulouse, the Viscount of Turenne, and other nobles to aid them.[94]

If Raymond was sincere, this was not the assistance he required. The kings had resolved to depend upon the spiritual{122} sword, and he was too shrewd to exhaust his strength in an unaided struggle with his subjects, especially as a menacing league was then forming against him by Alonso II. of Aragon with the nobles of Narbonne, Nimes, Montpellier, and Carcassonne. While, therefore, he protected the missionary prelates, he made no pretence of drawing the carnal sword. When they entered Toulouse the heretics crowded around them jeering and calling them hypocrites, apostates, and other opprobrious names; and Henry of Clairvaux consoles himself for the insignificant positive results of the mission with the reflection that if it had been postponed until three years later, they would not have found a single Catholic in the city. Lists of heretics, interminable in length, were made out for them, at the head of which stood Pierre Mauran, an old man of great wealth and influence, and so universally respected by his co-religionists that he was popularly known as John the Evangelist. He was selected to be made an example. After many tergiversations he was convicted of heresy, when, to save his confiscated property, he agreed to recant and undergo such penance as might be assigned to him. Stripped to the waist, with the Bishop of Toulouse and the Abbot of St. Sernin busily scourging him on either side, he was led through an immense crowd to the high altar of the Cathedral of St. Stephen, where, for the good of his soul, he was ordered to undertake a three years' pilgrimage to the Holy Land, to be daily scourged through the streets of Toulouse until his departure, to make restitution of all Church lands occupied by him and of all moneys acquired by usury, and to pay to the count five hundred pounds of silver in redemption of his forfeited property. This resolute beginning produced the desired effect, and multitudes of Cathari hastened to make their peace with the Church; but how little real result it had is shown by the fact that when Mauran returned from Palestine his fellow-citizens thrice honored him with election to the office of capitoul, and his family remained bitterly anti-Catholic. In 1234 an old man named Mauran was condemned as a "perfected" heretic, and in 1235 another Mauran, one of the capitouls, was excommunicated for impeding the introduction of the Inquisition. The enormous fine for the benefit of the Count of Toulouse was well calculated to excite the religious fervor of that potentate, but even that stimulus failed to arouse him to the decisive action which he doubtless felt to be impracticable.{123} When the legate desired to confute two heresiarchs, Raymond de Baimiac and Bernard Raymond, the Catharan bishops of Val d'Aran and Toulouse, he was obliged to give them a safe-conduct before they would present themselves before him, and to content himself afterwards with excommunicating them; and when proceedings were had against the powerful Roger Trencavel, Viscount of Béziers, for keeping the Bishop of Albi in prison, excommunication was likewise the only penalty, nor do we read that the captured prelate was

40

liberated. The mission so pompously heralded returned to France, and we can readily believe the statement of contemporary chroniclers that it had accomplished little or nothing. It is true that Raymond of Toulouse and his nobles had been induced to issue an edict banishing all heretics, but this remained a dead letter.[95]

It was in September of the same year, 1178, that Alexander III. published the call for the assembling of the Third Council of Lateran, and an ominous allusion in it to the tares which choke the wheat and must be pulled up by the roots shows that he recognized the futility of all measures heretofore adopted to check the daily growing power of heresy. Accordingly, when the council met, in 1179, it bemoaned the damnable perversity of the Patarins, who publicly seduced the faithful throughout Gascony, the Albigeois, and the Toulousain; it commended the employment of force by the secular power to compel men to their own salvation; it anathematized, as usual, the heretics and those who sheltered and protected them, and it included among heretics the Cotereaux, Brabançons, Aragonese, Navarrese, Basques, and Triaverdins, of whom more anon. It then proceeded to take a step of much significance in proclaiming a crusade against all these enemies of the Church—the first experiment of a resort to this weapon against Christians, which afterwards became so common, and gave the Church in its private quarrels the services of a warlike militia in every land, ever ready to be mobilized. Two years' indulgence{124} was promised to all who should take up arms in the holy cause; they were received under the protection of the Church, and those who should fall were assured of eternal salvation. Among the restless and sinful warriors of the time it was not difficult to raise an army, serving without pay, on terms like these.[96]

Immediately on his return from the council Pons, Archbishop of Narbonne, made haste to publish this decree, with all its anathemas and interdicts, and he included in its terms those who exacted new and unaccustomed tolls from travellers—a rapidly growing extortion of the feudal nobles which we shall constantly see reappear, like the Cotereaux, in the Albigensian quarrels. Henry of Clairvaux had refused the troublesome see of Toulouse, which had become vacant shortly after his mission thither in 1178, but had accepted the cardinalate of Albano, and he was forthwith sent as papal legate to preach and lead the crusade. His eloquence enabled him to raise a considerable force of horse and foot, with which, in 1181, he fell upon the territories of the Viscount of Béziers and laid siege to the stronghold of Lavaur where the Viscountess Adelaide, daughter of Raymond of Toulouse, and the leading Patarins had taken refuge. We are told that Lavaur was captured through a miracle, and that in various parts of France consecrated wafers dropping blood announced the success of the Christian arms. Roger of Béziers hastened to make his submission and swear no longer to protect heresy. Raymond de Baimiac and Bernard Raymond, the Catharan bishops, who were taken prisoners, renounced their heresy and were rewarded with prebends in two churches of Toulouse. Many other heretics gave in their submission, but returned to the false faith as soon as the danger was past. The short term for which the Crusaders had enlisted expired; the army disbanded itself, and the next year the cardinal-legate went back to Rome, having accomplished, virtually, nothing except to increase the mutual exasperation by the devastation of the country through which his troops had passed. Raymond of Toulouse, involved in desperate war with the King of Aragon, seems to have preserved complete indifference as to this expedition, taking no part in it on either side.[97]{125}

The Cotereaux and Brabançons, whom we have seen included with the Patarins in the denunciations of the Council of Lateran, are a feature of the period whose significance deserves a passing notice. We shall find them constantly reappearing, and their maintenance was one of the sins which gained for Raymond VI. of Toulouse almost as much hostility from the Church as the support of heresy which was imputed to him. They were freebooters, the precursors of the dreaded Free Companies which, especially during the fourteenth century, were the terror of all peaceable men, inflicting incalculable damage to the advancement of civilization. Their various names of Brabançons, Hainaulters, Catalans, Aragonese, Navarrese, Basques, etc., show how wide-spread was the evil and how every province ascribed the hated bands to its neighbors; while the more familiar terms of Brigandi, Pilardi, Ruptarii, Mainatae (mesnie), etc., express their function and occupation; and the names of Cotarelli, Palearii, Triaverdins, Asperes, Vales, have afforded ample field for fanciful etymology. They consisted of the idle and dissipated, peasants who had been hopelessly ruined in the increasing desolation of war, fugitives from serfdom, outlaws, escaped criminals, worthless ecclesiastics, outcast monks, and in general the scum which society threw upon the surface in its constant turmoil. They preyed upon the community in bands of varying size, and their swords were ever at the service of the nobles who would grant them pay or plunder when a military force was needed for a longer term than the short campaign prescribed as due from the vassal to his feudal lord. The chronicles of the time are full of lamentations over their incessant devastations; and it is significant of the relations between the Church and the community that the ecclesiastical annalists insist that their blows ever fell heavier on church and monastery than on the castle of the seigneur or the cottage of the peasant. They ridiculed the priests as singers, and it was one of their savage sports to beat them to death while mockingly begging their intercession—"Sing for us, you singer, sing for us;" and the culmination of their irreverent sacrilege was seen in their casting out and trampling on the holy wafers whose precious pyxes they{126} eagerly seized. They were popularly classed as heretics, and were accused of openly denying the existence of God. In 1181 Bishop Stephen of Tournay feelingly describes his terror while traversing, on a mission from the king, through the Toulousain, then recently the seat of war between the Count of Toulouse and the King of Aragon, where deserted solitudes revealed nothing but ruined churches and desolated villages, and where he was ever in expectation of attack, from robbers or from the more dreaded bands of Cotereaux. It was probably a result of the crusade decreed against them, in common with the Patarins, that a concerted attack was soon after made upon the bandits in central France. They were driven together, and in July, 1183, at Châteaudun, a signal victory over them was won, the number of the slain brigands being variously estimated at from six thousand to ten thousand five hundred and twenty-five. An immense booty was obtained, among which may perhaps be reckoned fifteen hundred strumpets, who accompanied the robber host. The victors, who had assumed the name of Paciferi in token of their peaceful object, were not merciful. Fifteen days later we hear of the capture of one of the routier captains with fifteen hundred men, who were all summarily hanged; and about the same time of eighty more, who were caught and blinded. In spite of these ruthless measures, the evil continued unabated. The causes which produced it remained as active as ever, and the services of the reckless and Godless mercenaries continued useful to the great feudatories involved in endless war with their neighbors.[98]

The admitted failure of the crusade of 1181 seems to have rendered the Church hopeless, for the time, of making headway against heresy. For a quarter of a century it was allowed to develop in comparative toleration throughout the territories of Gascony, Languedoc, and Provence. It is true that the decree of Lucius III., issued at Verona in 1184, is important as attempting the foundation of an organized Inquisition, but it worked no immediate effect.{127} It is true that in 1195 another papal legate, Michael, held a provincial council at Montpellier, where he commanded the enforcement of the Lateran canons on all heretics and Mainatæ, or brigands, whose property was to be confiscated and whose persons reduced to slavery;[99] but all this fell dead upon the indifference of the nobles, who, involved in perpetual war with each other, preferred to risk the anathemas of the Church rather than to complicate their troubles by attempting the extermination of a majority of their subjects at the behest of a hierarchy which no longer inspired respect or reverence. Perhaps, also, the fall of Jerusalem, in 1186, in arousing an unprecedented fervor of fanaticism, directed it towards Palestine, and left little for the vindication of the faith nearer home. Be this as it may, no effective persecution was undertaken until the vigorous ability of Innocent III., after vainly trying milder measures, organized overwhelming war against heresy. During this interval the Poor Men of Lyons arose, and were forced to make common cause with the Cathari; the proselyting zeal which had been so successful in secrecy and tribulation had free scope for its development, and had no effective antagonism to dread from a negligent and disheartened clergy. The heretics preached and made converts, while the priests were glad if they could save a fraction of their tithes and revenues from rapacious nobles and rebellious or indifferent parishioners. Heresy throve accordingly. Innocent III. admitted the humiliating fact that the heretics were allowed to preach and teach and make converts in public, and that unless speedy measures were taken for their suppression there was danger that the infection would spread to the whole Church. William of Tudela says that the heretics possessed the Albigeois, the Carcasses, and the Lauragais, and that to describe them as numerous throughout the whole district from Béziers to Bordeaux is not saying enough. Walter Mapes asserts that there were none of them in Britanny, but that they abounded in Anjou, while in Aquitaine and Burgundy their number was infinite. William of Puy-Laurens assures us that Satan possessed in peace the greater part of southern France; the clergy were so despised that they were accustomed to conceal the tonsure through very shame, and the bishops were obliged to admit to holy orders whoever was{128} willing to assume them; the whole land, under a curse, produced nothing but thorns and thistles, ravishers and bandits, robbers, murderers, adulterers, and usurers. Cæsarius of Heisterbach declares that the Albigensian errors increased so rapidly that they soon infected a thousand cities, and he believes that if they had not been repressed by the sword of the faithful the whole of Europe would have been corrupted. A German inquisitor informs us that in Lombardy, Provence, and other regions there were more schools of heresy than of orthodox theology, with more scholars; that they disputed publicly, and summoned the people to public debates; that they preached in the market-places, the fields, the houses; and that there were none who dared to interfere with them, owing to the multitude and power of their protectors. As we have seen, they were regularly organized in dioceses; they had their educational establishments for the training of women as well as men; and, at least in one instance, all the nuns of a convent embraced Catharism without quitting the house or the habit of their order.[100] Such was the position to which corruption had reduced the Church. Intent upon the acquisition of temporal power, it had well-nigh abandoned its spiritual duties; and its empire, which rested on spiritual foundations, was crumbling with their decay, and threatening to pass away like an unsubstantial vision. There have been few crises in the history of the Church more dangerous than that which Lothario Conti, when he assumed the triple crown at the early age of thirty-eight, was called upon to meet. In his consecration sermon he announced that one of his principal duties would be the destruction of heresy, and of this he never lost sight to the end, amid his endless conflicts with emperors and princes.[101] It is fortunate for civilization that he possessed the qualifications which enabled him to guide the shattered bark of St. Peter through the tempest and among the rocks—if not always wisely, yet with a resolute spirit, an unswerving purpose, and an unfailing trust that accomplished his mission in the end.{129}

CHAPTER IV.

THE ALBIGENSIAN CRUSADES.

THE Church admitted that it had brought upon itself the dangers which threatened it—that the alarming progress of heresy was caused and fostered by clerical negligence and corruption. In his opening address to the great Lateran Council, Innocent III. had no scruple in declaring to the assembled fathers: "The corruption of the people has its chief source in the clergy. From this arise the evils of Christendom: faith perishes, religion is defaced, liberty is restricted, justice is trodden under foot, the heretics multiply, the schismatics are emboldened, the faithless grow strong, the Saracens are victorious;" and after the futile attempt of the council to strike at the root of the evil, Honorius III., in admitting its failure, repeated the assertion. In fact this was an axiom which none were so hardy as to deny, yet when, in 1204, the legates whom Innocent had sent to oppose the Albigenses appealed to him for aid against prelates whom they had failed to coerce, and whose infamy of life gave scandal to the faithful and an irresistible argument to the heretic, Innocent curtly bade them attend to the object of their mission and not allow themselves to be diverted by less important matters. The reply fairly indicates the policy of the Church. Thoroughly to cleanse the Augean stable was a task from which even Innocent's fearless spirit might well shrink. It seemed an easier and more hopeful plan to crush revolt with fire and sword.[102]

We have seen how promptly and persistently Innocent took in hand the heretics of Italy, nor were his dealings with those{130} beyond the Alps less active and decisive, though they manifest an evident desire to do exact justice, and not to confound the innocent with the guilty. The Nivernois had long been noted as a deeply infected district. The troubles occasioned by Catharism at Vezelai in 1167 have already been alluded to, and the sharp repression of heresy then had put an end to its outward manifestation without destroying its germs. Towards the end of the century Bishop Hugues of Auxerre earned the title of the Hammer of Heretics by his energy and success in persecution; and though he was likewise noted for avarice, usurpation of illegal rights, oppression of his flock, and ferocity in ruining those who had offended him, his zeal for the faith covered the multitude of sins, hardly needing the urgency with which, in 1204, Innocent commanded him to clear his diocese of heresy. By the pitiless employment of confiscation, exile, and the stake he labored to purify it, but the evil was stubborn and constantly reappeared. The chief propagator was an anchorite named Terric who dwelt in a cavern near Corbigny, where he was finally surprised and burned, through the exertions of Foulques de Neuilly, but the infection was not confined to the poor and humble. In 1199 we find the Dean of Nevers and the Abbot of St. Martin of Nevers appealing to Innocent from prosecutions commenced against them, and the answers of the pope show both his anxious desire that they should have full opportunity to prove their innocence, and the uncertainty and cumbrous nature of the ecclesiastical procedure of the time. In 1201 Bishop Hugues was more successful with a criminal of equal importance, the knight, Everard of Châteauneuf, to whom Count Hervey of Nevers had intrusted the stewardship of his territories. In this case, the Legate Octavian called a council in Paris, comprising many bishops and theologians, for his trial; he was convicted principally on the testimony of Bishop Hugues and was handed over to the secular arm and burned, after a respite for the purpose of rendering an account of his office to Count Hervey. His nephew, Thierry, an equally hardened heretic, escaped to Toulouse, where five years later we find him a bishop among the Albigenses, who were gratified in having a Frenchman as an accomplice. La Charité was an especially active centre of heresy in the Nivernois, and from 1202 to 1208 there are frequent appeals to Innocent from its citizens, showing{131} that Rome was regarded as more indulgent than the local courts; and the papal decisions continue to manifest a laudable desire to prevent injustice. All this proved inefficient, and it was one of the first places to which, in 1233, an inquisitor was sent. At Troyes, in 1200, five male and three female Catharans were burned; and at Braisne, in 1204, a number were similarly put to death, among whom was Nicholas, the most renowned painter in France.[103]

In 1199 another danger threatened the Church in Metz, where Waldensian sectaries were found in possession of French translations of the New Testament, the Psalter, Job, and other portions of Scripture, which they contumaciously studied with unwearied perseverance and refused to abandon at the command of their parish priests; nay, they were hardy enough to assert that they knew more of Holy Writ than their pastors, and that they had a right to the consolation which they found in its perusal. The case was somewhat puzzling, since the Church as yet had had no occasion to interdict formally the popular reading of the Bible, and these poor folk were not accused of any definite heretical tenets. Innocent, therefore, when applied to, admitted that there was nothing condemnable in the desire to understand Scripture, but he added that such is its profundity that even the learned and wise are unequal to its comprehension, and consequently it is far beyond the grasp of the simple and illiterate. The people of Metz were therefore exhorted to abandon these reprehensible practices and return to a proper degree of respect for their pastors if they wished pardon for their sins, with a significant threat of compulsion in case of further obstinacy; and when the simple and illiterate folk proved deaf to this command, a commission was sent to the Abbot of Citeaux and two others, to proceed to Metz and put a stop, without appeal, to these unlawful studies—with what success we may infer from the fact that in 1231 the heretics of Trèves were found in possession of German versions of Holy Writ.[104]{132}

It was the stronghold of heresy in southern France, however, which rightly gave rise to chief concern in Rome, and to this Innocent resolutely bent his energies. Raymond VI. of Toulouse, in the full vigor of mature manhood, at the age of thirty-eight, had, in January, 1195, succeeded his father in the possession of territories which rendered him the most powerful feudatory of the monarchy and almost an independent sovereign. Besides the county of Toulouse, the duchy of Narbonne conferred on him the dignity of first lay peer of France. He was likewise suzerain, with more or less direct authority, of the Marquisate of Provence, the Comtat

Venaissin and the counties of St. Gilles, Foix, Comminges, and Rodez, and of the Albigeois, Vivarais, Gévaudan, Velai, Rouergue, Querci, and Agenois. Even in distant Italy he was known as the greatest count on earth, with fourteen counts as his vassals, and his troubadour flatterers assured him that he was the equal of emperors—

Car il val tan qu'en la soa valor
Auri' assatz ad un emperador.

Even after the sacrifice of a major part of the possessions of the house, his son, Raymond VII., at his splendid Christmas court of 1244, conferred the honor of knighthood on no less than two hundred nobles. So far as matrimonial alliances can have weight, Raymond VI. was strengthened with them on every side, for he was of close kindred to the royal houses of Castile, Aragon, Navarre, France, and England. His fourth wife was Joan of England, whom he married in 1196 in pursuance of a favorable treaty with her brother Richard, thus relieving him of the enmity of that redoubtable warrior, who, as Duke of Aquitaine, had pressed his father hard. Yet that treaty with Richard gave secret offence to Philip Augustus, destined to bear bitter fruit thereafter. Almost at the same time he was liberated from another formidable hereditary foe by the death of Alonso II. of Aragon, whose large possessions and still larger pretensions in southern France had at times almost threatened the extinction of the house of Toulouse. With his successor, Pedro II., Raymond's relations were most friendly, cemented in 1200 by his marriage with Pedro's sister Eleanor, and in 1205 by the engagement of his young son, Raymond VII., with Pedro's infant daughter. Though the distant{133} sovereignty of France troubled him but little, yet the friendliness manifested to him on his accession by Philip Augustus was a not unimportant element in the prosperity which on every side seemed to give him assurance of a peaceful and fortunate reign. Thus secured against external aggression and confident of the future, he recked little of an excommunication which had been fulminated against him in 1195 by Celestin III. on account of the invasion of the rights of the Abbey of St. Gilles—an excommunication which Innocent III. removed shortly after his accession, but not without words of reproof and warning which Raymond defiantly disregarded, thus laying the foundation of a quarrel destined to result so disastrously. Though not a heretic, his indifference on religious questions led him to tolerate the heresy of his subjects. Most of his barons were either heretics or favorably inclined to a faith which, by denying the pretensions of the Church, justified its spoliation or, at least, liberated them from its domination. Raymond himself was doubtless influenced by the same motive, and when, in 1195, the Council of Montpellier anathematized all princes who neglected to enforce the Lateran canons against heretics and mercenaries, he paid no attention to its utterances. It would, in fact, have required the most ardent fanaticism to lead a prince so circumstanced to provoke his vassals, to lay waste his territories, to massacre his subjects, and to invite assault from watchful rivals, for the purpose of enforcing uniformity in religion and subjugation to a Church known only by its rapacity and corruption. Toleration had endured for nearly a generation; the land was blessed with peace after almost interminable war, and all the dictates of worldly prudence counselled him to follow in his father's footsteps. Surrounded by one of the gayest and most cultured courts in Christendom, fond of women, a patron of poets, somewhat irresolute of purpose, and enjoying the love of his subjects, nothing could have appeared to him more objectless than a persecution such as Rome held to be the most indispensable of his duties.[105]

The condition of the Church in his dominions might well excite{134} the indignation of a pontiff like Innocent III., who conscientiously believed in the full measure of its awful authority and imprescriptible rights. A chronicler assures us that among many thousands of the people there were but few Catholics to be found; and although this is doubtless an exaggeration, we have seen in the preceding chapter what rapid strides heresy had made. How utterly discredited the Church had become, and how loss of respect for the spirituality had led to spoliation of the temporality is shown by the condition of the episcopate of the capital, Toulouse. Bishop Fulcrand, who died in 1200, is described as living perforce in apostolical poverty like a private citizen. His tithes had been seized by the knights and the monasteries; his first-fruits by the parish priests, and his only revenue was derived from a few farms and from the public baking-oven over which he retained a feudal right. In his extremity he brought suit against his own chapter to compel them to assign to him the income of a single prebend as a means of livelihood. When he visited the parishes, he was obliged to beg an escort from the lords of the lands over which he passed. When Fulcrand's wretched life came to an end, uninviting as the episcopate seemed to be, it was the subject of a bitter and disgraceful contest which ended in the success of Raymond de Rabastens, Archdeacon of Agen, whose career was even more miserable than that of his predecessor. Perhaps his poverty might excuse the unblushing simony with which he sought to augment his revenues; but when he had pledged or parted with all the remaining possessions of his see to defray the expenses of a fruitless litigation with Raymond de Beaupuy, one of his vassals, he was rightly adjudged a wicked and slothful servant, and was deposed with an annual assignment of thirty livres toulousains to keep him from beggary. His successor, Foulques of Marseilles, a distinguished troubadour who had renounced the world and become Abbot of Florèges, used to relate that when he took possession of the see he was obliged to water his mules at home, having no one to send with them to the common watering-place on the Garonne. Foulques was a man of different temper, whose ruthless bigotry in time carried fire and sword throughout his diocese.[106]{135}

The evil was constantly increasing, and unless checked it seemed only a question of time when the Church would disappear throughout all the Mediterranean provinces of France. Yet it must be said for the credit of the heretics that there was no manifestation of a persecuting spirit on their part. The rapacity of the barons, it

44

is true, was rapidly depriving the ecclesiastics of their revenues and possessions; as they neglected their duties, and as the law of the strongest was all-prevailing, the invader of Church property had small scruple in despoiling lazy monks and worldly priests whose numbers were constantly diminishing; but the Cathari, however much they may have deemed themselves the Church of the future, seem never to have thought of extending their faith by force. They reasoned and argued and disputed when they found a Catholic zealous enough to contend with them, and they preached to the people, who had no other source of instruction; but, content with peaceable conversions and zealous missionary work, they dwelt in perfect amity with their orthodox neighbors. To the Church this state of affairs was unbearable. It has always held the toleration of others to be persecution of itself. By the very law of its being it can brook no rivalry in its domination over the human soul; and, in the present case, as toleration was slowly but surely leading to its destruction, it was bound by its sense of duty no less than of self-preservation to put an end to a situation so abhorrent. Yet, before it could resort effectually to force it was compelled to make what efforts{136} it could at persuasion—not of heretics, indeed, but of their protectors.

Innocent was consecrated February 22, 1198, and already by April 1st we find him writing to the Archbishop of Ausch, deploring the spread of heresy and the danger of its becoming universal. The prelate and his brethren are ordered to extirpate it by the utmost rigor of ecclesiastical censures, and if necessary by bringing the secular arm to bear through the assistance of princes and people. Not only are heretics themselves to be punished, but all who have any dealings with them, or who are suspect by reason of undue familiarity with them. In the existing posture of affairs, the prelates to whom these commands were addressed can only have regarded them with mingled derision and despair; and we can readily imagine the replies in which they declared their zeal and lamented their powerlessness. Innocent probably was aware of this in advance and did not await the response. By April 21st he had two commissioners ready to represent the Holy See on the spot—Rainier and Gui—whom he sent armed with letters to all the prelates, princes, nobles, and people of southern France, empowering them to enforce whatever regulations they might see fit to employ to avert the imminent peril to the Church arising from the countless increase of Cathari and Waldenses, who corrupted the people by simulated works of justice and charity. Those heretics who will not return to the true faith are to be banished and their property confiscated; these provisions are to be enforced by the secular authorities under penalty of interdict for refusal or negligence, and with the reward for obedience of the same indulgences as those granted for a pilgrimage to Rome or Compostella; and all who consort or deal with heretics or show them favor or protection are to share their punishment. It was apparently an after-thought when Rainier, six months later, was empowered to remove the source of the evil by reforming the churches and restoring discipline. Rainier's powers evidently proved insufficient, and in July, 1199, they were enlarged, both as a reformer and a persecutor, and he was appointed legate, to be received and obeyed with as much reverence as the pope himself. About this time there appeared to be a gleam of success in the application of William, Lord of Montpellier, for a legate to assist him in suppressing heresy; but though William was a good Catholic{137} this special manifestation of zeal was due to his anxiety to obtain the legitimation of the children of a second wife whom he had married without legally divorcing a previous one, and as Innocent refused to sanction the wrong, no great results were to be anticipated for religion. A vigorous show of reform was also commenced by attacking two high-placed and notorious offenders, the archbishops of Narbonne and Ausch, whose personal wickedness, negligence, and toleration of heresy had reduced the Church in their provinces to a most deplorable state; but as these proceedings dragged on for ten or twelve years before the removal of the sinners could be effected, no immediate purification could be hoped for by the most sanguine.[107]

In fact, for a time at least, these spasmodic efforts at reform only rendered matters worse. Angered and humiliated by the powers conferred on the representatives of Rome, and alarmed at the attempts to punish their evil lives, the local prelates were in no mood to second the exertions put forth for the eradication of heresy, and at one time it would even seem as though they might be driven to make common cause with the heretics, in opposition to the Holy See, in order to protect themselves and their clergy. Rainier had fallen sick in the summer of 1202 and had been replaced by Pierre de Castelnau and Raoul, two Cistercian monks of Fontfroide, who succeeded, after infinite trouble, by threats of the royal vengeance, in persuading the magistracy of Toulouse to swear to abjure heresy and expel heretics, in return for an oath pledging immunity and the preservation of the liberties of the city; but no sooner were their backs turned than heresy was as flagrant as before. Encouraged by this apparent success, they undertook the task of obtaining a similar oath from Count Raymond. This they finally accomplished, with equally slender result, but the process showed what assistance they might expect from the hierarchy. When they summoned the Archbishop of Narbonne to accompany them to the Count of Toulouse for the purpose, he not only refused, but declined to aid them in any way, and it was only after long entreaty that he would even furnish them a horse for the journey. With the Bishop of Béziers their success was no{138} better. He likewise declined to go with them to Raymond; and when they asked his co-operation in summoning the consuls of Béziers to abjure heresy and defend the Church against heretics, he not only withheld it, but impeded their efforts; and though he finally promised to excommunicate the magistrates for contumacy, he never did so, in spite of the fact that heresy so predominated in the town that the viscount was obliged to authorize the cathedral canons to fortify the Church of St. Peter for fear that the heretics would seize it. Possibly he was deterred by the example made of his neighbor, Berenger, Bishop of Carcassonne, who, in consequence

45

of threatening his flock for heresy, was expelled the city and a heavy fine imposed on any one who should have dealings with him.[108]

Evidently pope and legate were of small account in the chaos which reigned in Languedoc. The prelates refused to be reformed, and yet the legates, in their disputations with the heretics, were so continually answered with references to the evil lives of the clergy that they recognized reformation as a condition precedent to any peaceable conversion of the people. The heretics were daily growing bolder, as if to show their scorn of the futile efforts of Innocent. About this very time Esclairmonde, sister of the powerful Count of Foix, with five other ladies of rank, was "hereticated" in a public assemblage of Cathari, where many knights and nobles were present, and it was remarked that the count was the only one who did not give the heretical salute or "veneration" to the ministrants. Even Pedro the Catholic of Aragon presided over a public debate at Carcassonne, between the legates and a number of leading heretics, which had no result. The situation was desperate, and Innocent may be pardoned if he reached the conclusion that a deluge was needed to cleanse the land of sin and prepare it for a new race.[109]

Enough time had been lost in half-measures while the evil was daily increasing in magnitude, and Innocent proceeded to put{139} forth the whole strength of the Church. To the monks of Fontfroide he adjoined as chief legate the "Abbot of abbots," Arnaud of Citeaux, head of the great Cistercian Order, a stern, resolute, and implacable man, full of zeal for the cause and gifted with rare persistency. Since the time of St. Bernard the abbots of Citeaux had seemed to feel a personal responsibility for the suppression of heresy in Languedoc, and Arnaud was better fitted for the work before him than any of his predecessors. To the legation thus constituted, at the end of May, 1204, Innocent issued a fresh commission of extraordinary powers. The prelates of the infected provinces were bitterly reproached for the negligence and timidity which had permitted heresy to assume its alarming proportions. They were ordered to obey humbly whatever the legates might see fit to command, and the vengeance of the Holy See was threatened for slackness or contumacy. Wherever heresy existed, the legates were armed with authority "to destroy, throw down, or pluck up whatever is to be destroyed, thrown down, or plucked up, and to plant and build whatever is to be built or planted." With one blow the independence of the local churches was destroyed and an absolute dictatorship was created. Recognizing, moreover, of how little worth were ecclesiastical censures, Innocent proceeded to appeal to force, which was evidently the only possible cure for the trouble. Not only were the legates directed to deliver all impenitent heretics to the secular arm for perpetual proscription and confiscation of property, but they were empowered to offer complete remission of sins, the same as for a crusade to the Holy Land, to Philip Augustus and his son, Louis Cœur-de-Lion, and to all nobles who should aid in the suppression of heresy. The dangerous classes were also stimulated by the prospect of pardon and plunder, through a special clause authorizing the legates to absolve all under excommunication for crimes of violence who would join in persecuting heretics—an offer which subsequent correspondence shows was not unfruitful. To Philip Augustus, also, Innocent wrote at the same time, earnestly exhorting him to draw the sword and slay the wolves who had thus far found no one to withstand their ravages in the fold of the Lord. If he could not proceed in person, let him send his son, or some experienced leader, and exercise the power conferred on him for the purpose by Heaven. Not only was remission of sins{140} promised him, as for a voyage to Palestine, but he was empowered to seize and add to his dominions the territories of all nobles who might not join in persecution and expel the hated heretic.[110]

Innocent might well feel disheartened at the failure of this vigorous move. He had played his last card and lost. The prelates of the infected provinces, indignant at the usurpation of their rights, were less disposed than ever to second the efforts of the legates. Philip Augustus was unmoved by the dazzling bribes, spiritual and temporal, offered to him. He had already had the benefit of an indulgence for a crusade to the Holy Land, and had probably not found his spiritual estate much benefited thereby; while his recent acquisitions in Normandy, Anjou, Poitou, and Aquitaine, at the expense of John of England, required his whole attention, and might be endangered by creating fresh enmities in too sudden a renewal of conquest. He took no steps, therefore, in response to the impassioned arguments of Innocent, and the legates found the heretics more obdurate than ever. Pierre de Castelnau grew so discouraged that he begged the pope to permit him to return to his abbey; but Innocent refused permission, assuring him that God would reward him according to the labor rather than to the result. A second urgent appeal to Philip in February, 1205, was equally fruitless; and a concession in the following June, to Pedro of Aragon, of all the lands that he could acquire from heretics, and a year later of all their goods, was similarly without result, except that Pedro seized the Castle of Escure, belonging to the papacy, which had been occupied by Cathari. If something appeared to be gained when at Toulouse, in 1205, some dead heretics were prosecuted and their bones exhumed, it was speedily lost, for the municipality promptly adopted a law forbidding trials of the dead who had not been accused during life, unless they had been hereticated on the death-bed.[111]

The work might well seem hopeless, and all three legates were on the point of abandoning it peremptorily in despair, even Arnaud's iron will yielding to the insurmountable passive resistance of a people among whom the heretics would not be converted and{141} the orthodox could not be stimulated to persecution. Bishop Foulques of Toulouse used to relate that in a disputation at which he was present the Cathari were, as usual, vanquished, when he asked Pons de Rodelle, a knight renowned for wisdom and a good Catholic, why he did not drive from his lands those who were so manifestly in error. "How can we do it?" replied the knight. "We have been brought up with these people, we have kindred among them, and we see them live righteously." Dogmatic zeal fell powerless before such kindliness; and we can readily believe the monk of Vaux-Cernay, when he tells us that the barons of the land were nearly all protectors and receivers of heretics, loving them fervently and defending them against God and the Church.[112]

The case seemed desperate, when a new light fell as though from heaven upon those groping blindly in the darkness. About mid-summer in 1206 the three legates met at Montpellier, and the result of their conference was a determination to withdraw from the thankless labor. By chance, a Spanish prelate, Diego de Azevedo, Bishop of Osma, arrived there on his return from Rome, where he had vainly supplicated Innocent to permit his resignation of his bishopric in order that he might devote his life to missionary work among the infidel. On learning the decision of the legates, he earnestly dissuaded them, and suggested their dismissing their splendid retinues and worldly pomp and going among the people, barefooted and poor like the apostles, to preach the Word of God. The idea was so novel that the legates hesitated, but finally assented, if an example were set them by one in authority. Diego offered himself for the purpose and was accepted, whereupon he sent his servitors home, retaining only his sub-prior, Domingo de Guzman, who had already, on the voyage towards Rome, converted a heretic in Toulouse. Arnaud returned to Citeaux to hold a general chapter of the order and to obtain recruits for the missionary work, while the other two legates with Diego and Dominic commenced their experiment at Caraman, where for eight days they disputed with the heresiarchs Baldwin and Thierry, the latter of whom we have seen driven from the Nivernois some years before. We are told that they converted{142} all the simple folk, but that the lord of the castle would not allow the two disputants to be expelled.[113]

Further colloquies of similar character are recorded, occupying the autumn and winter, and, with the opening of spring, in 1207, Arnaud had held his chapter and obtained numerous volunteers for the pious work, among them no less than twelve abbots. Taking boats, they descended the Saone to the Rhone, without horses or retinue, and proceeded to their field of labor, where they separated into twos and threes, wandering barefoot among the towns and villages and seeking to gather in the lost sheep of Israel. For three months they thus labored diligently, like real evangelists, finding thousands of heretics and few orthodox, but the harvest was scanty and conversions rarely rewarded their pains—in fact, the only practical result was to excite the heretics to renewed missionary zeal. It speaks well for the tolerant temper of the Cathari that men who had been invoking the most powerful sovereigns of Christendom to exterminate them with fire and sword, should have incurred no real danger in a task apparently so full of risk. The missionaries had to complain of occasional insult, but never were even threatened with injury, except perhaps, at Béziers, Pierre de Castelnau, who seems to have attracted to himself the special dislike of the sectaries. It shows, moreover, the zealous care with which the Church restricted the office of preaching that the legates, in spite of the extraordinary powers with which they were clothed, felt obliged to apply to Innocent for special authority to confer the license to teach in public on those whom they deemed worthy. The favorable answer of the pope was in reality one of the important events of the century, for it gave the impulsion out of which eventually grew the great Dominican Order.[114]

Pierre de Castelnau left his colleagues and visited Provence to make peace among the nobles, in the hope of uniting them for the expulsion of heretics. Raymond of Toulouse refused to lay down his arms until the intrepid monk excommunicated him and laid his dominions under interdict, finally reproaching him bitterly to his{143} face for his perjuries and other misdeeds. Raymond submitted in patience to this reproof, while Pierre applied to Innocent for confirmation of the sentence. By this time, in fact, Raymond had acquired the special hatred of the papalists, through his obstinate neglect to persecute his heretical subjects, in spite of his readiness to take what oaths were required of him. Notwithstanding his outward conformity to orthodoxy, they accused him of being at heart a heretic, and stories were circulated that he always carried with him "perfected" heretics, disguised in ordinary vestments, together with a New Testament, that he might be "hereticated" in case of sudden death; that he had declared that he would rather be like a certain crippled heretic living in poverty at Castres than be a king or an emperor; that he knew that he would in the end be disinherited for the sake of the "Good Men," but that he was ready to suffer even beheading for them. All this and much more, including exaggerated gossip as to his undoubted frailties, was diligently published in order to render him odious, but there is no proof that his religious indifference ever led him to deviate from the faith, and no accusation that he had ever interfered with the legates in their mission. They were free to make what converts they could by persuasion or argument, but he committed the unpardonable crime of refusing at their bidding to plunge his dominions in blood.[115]

Innocent promptly confirmed the sentence of his legate, May 29, 1207, in an epistle to Raymond which was an unreserved expression of the passions accumulated through long years of zealous effort frustrated in its results. In the harshest vituperation of ecclesiastical rhetoric, Raymond was threatened with the vengeance of God here and hereafter. The excommunication and interdict were to be strictly observed until due satisfaction and obedience were rendered; and he was warned that these must be speedy, or he would be deprived of certain territories which he held of the Church, and if this did not suffice, the princes of Christendom would be summoned to seize and partition his dominions so that the land might be forever freed from heresy. Yet in the recital of misdeeds which were held to justify this rigorous sentence there was nothing that had not been for two generations so universal in{144} Languedoc that it might almost be regarded as a part of the public law of the land. He had continued to wage war when desired by the legates to make peace, and had refused to suspend

47

operations on feast-days or holidays; he had violated his oaths to purge his land of heresy, and had shown such favor to heretics as to render his own faith vehemently suspected; in derision of the Christian religion he had bestowed public office on Jews; he had despoiled the Church and ill-treated certain bishops; he had continued to employ the robber bands of mercenaries and had increased the tolls. Such is the summary of crime alleged against him, which we may reasonably assume to cover everything possibly susceptible of proof.[116]

Innocent waited awhile to prove the effect of this threat and the results of the missionary effort so auspiciously started by Bishop Azevedo. Both were null. Raymond, indeed, made peace with the Provençal nobles, and was released from excommunication, but he showed no signs of awakening from his exasperating indifference on the religious question, while the Cistercian abbots, disheartened by the obstinacy of the heretics, dropped off one by one, and retired to their monasteries. Legate Raoul died, and Arnaud of Citeaux was called elsewhere by important affairs. Bishop Azevedo went to Spain to set his diocese in order and return to devote his life to the work; but he, too, died when on the point of setting out. He had left behind him the saintly Dominic, who was quietly bringing together a few ardent souls, the germs of the great Order of Preachers, and Pierre de Castelnau remained as the sole representative of Rome until Raoul was replaced by the Bishop of Conserans. Everything thus had been tried and had failed, except the appeal to the sword, and to this Innocent again recurred with all the energy of despair. A milder tone towards Philip Augustus with regard to his matrimonial complications between Ingeburga of Denmark and Agnes of Meran might predispose him to vindicate energetically the wrongs of the Church; but, while condescending to this, Innocent now addressed, not only the king, but all the faithful throughout France, and the leading magnates were honored with special missives. November 17, 1207, the letters were sent out, pathetically representing the incessant and{145}alarming growth of heresy and the failure of all endeavors to bring the heretics to reason, to frighten them with threats, or to allure them with blandishments. Nothing was left but an appeal to arms; and to all who would embark in this good work the same indulgences were offered as for a crusade to Palestine. The lands of all engaged in it were taken under the special protection of holy Church, and those of the heretics were abandoned to the spoiler. All creditors of Crusaders were obliged to postpone their claims without interest, and clerks taking part were empowered to pledge their revenues in advance for two years.[117]

Earnest and impassioned as was this appeal, it fell, like the previous one, upon deaf ears. Innocent had for years been invoking the religious martial ardor of Europe in aid of the Latin kingdoms of the East, and that ardor seemed for a time exhausted. Philip Augustus coolly responded that his relations with England did not allow him to let the forces of his kingdom be divided, but that, if he could be assured of a two years' truce, then, if the barons and knights of France wanted to undertake a crusade, he would permit them, and aid it with fifty livres a day for a year. Apparently the present effort was destined to prove as inefficient as the former one had been, when a startling incident suddenly changed the whole aspect of affairs. The murder of the legate Pierre de Castelnau sent a thrill of horror throughout Christendom like that caused by the assassination of Becket thirty-eight years before. Of its details, however, the accounts are so contradictory that it is impossible to speak of it with precision. This much we know, that Pierre had greatly angered Raymond by the bitterness of his personal reproaches; that the count, aroused by the sense of impending danger in the fresh call for a crusade, had invited the legates to an interview at St. Gilles, promising to show himself in all things an obedient son of the Church; that difficulties arose in the conference, the demands of the legates being greater than Raymond was willing to concede. The Romance version of the catastrophe is simply that, during the conference, Pierre became entangled in an angry religious dispute with one of the gentlemen of the court, who drew his dagger and slew him; that the count was greatly concerned at an event so deplorable,{146} and would have taken summary vengeance on the murderer but for his escape and hiding with friends at Beaucaire. The story carried to Rome by the Bishops of Conserans and Toulouse, who hastened thither to inflame Innocent against Raymond, was that, wearied with the count's tergiversations, the legates announced their intentions to withdraw, when he was heard to threaten them with death, saying that he would track them by land and water. That the Abbot of St. Gilles and the citizens, unable to appease his wrath, furnished the legates with an escort, and they reached the Rhone in safety, where they passed the night. While preparing to cross the river in the morning (January 16, 1208), two strangers, who had joined the party, approached the legates, and one of them suddenly thrust his lance through Pierre, who, turning on his murderer, said, "May God forgive thee, for I forgive thee!" and speedily breathed his last; and that Raymond, so far from punishing the crime, protected and rewarded the perpetrator, even honoring him with a seat at his own table. The papal account, it must be owned, is somewhat impaired in effect by the remark that Pierre, as a martyr, would certainly have shone forth in miracles but for the incredulity of the people. It may well be that a proud and powerful prince, exasperated by continued objurgation and menace, may have uttered some angry expression, which an over-zealous servitor hastened to translate into action, and Raymond, certainly, never was able to clear himself of suspicion of complicity; but there are not wanting indications to show that Innocent eventually regarded his exculpation as satisfactory.[118]

The crime gave the Church an enormous advantage, of which Innocent hastened to make the most. On March 10 he issued letters to all the prelates in the infected provinces commanding that, in all churches, on every Sunday and feast-day, the murderers and their abettors, including Raymond, be excommunicated with bell, book, and candle, and every place cursed with their presence was declared under interdict. As no faith was to be kept with him who kept not faith with God, all of Raymond's{147} vassals were released from their oaths of allegiance, and his lands were declared the prey of any Catholic who might assail them, while, if he applied for pardon, his first sign of repentance must be the extermination of heresy throughout his dominions. These letters were likewise sent to Philip Augustus and his chief barons, with eloquent adjurations to assume the cross, and rescue the imperilled Church from the assaults of the emboldened heretics; commissioners were sent to negotiate and enforce a truce for two years between France and England, that nothing might interfere with the projected crusade, and every effort was made to transmute into warlike zeal the horror which the sacrilegious murder was so well fitted to arouse. Arnaud of Citeaux hastened to call a general chapter of his Order, where it was unanimously resolved to devote all its energies to preaching the crusade, and soon multitudes of fiery monks were inflaming the passions of the people, and offering redemption in every church and on every market-place in Europe.[119]

The flame which had been so long kindling burst forth at last. To estimate fully the force of these popular ebullitions in the Middle Ages, we must bear in mind the susceptibility of the people to contagious emotions and enthusiasms of which we know little in our colder day. A trifle might start a movement which the wisest could not explain nor the most powerful restrain. It was during the preaching of this crusade that villages and towns in Germany were filled with women who, unable to expend their religious ardor in taking the cross, stripped themselves naked and ran silently through the roads and streets. Still more symptomatic of the diseased spirituality of the time was the Crusade of the Children, which desolated thousands of homes. From vast districts of territory, incited apparently by a simultaneous and spontaneous impulse, crowds of children set forth, without leaders or guides, in search of the Holy Land; and their only answer, when questioned as to their object, was that they were going to Jerusalem. Vainly did parents lock their children up; they would break loose and disappear; and the few who eventually found their way home again could give no reason for the overmastering longing which had carried{148} them away. Nor must we lose sight of other and less creditable springs of action which brought to all crusades the vile, who came for license and spoil, and the base, who sought the immunity conferred by the quality of Crusader. This is illustrated by the case of a knave who took the cross to evade the payment of a debt contracted at the fair of Lille, and was on the point of escaping when he was arrested and delivered to his creditor. For this invasion of immunity the Archbishop of Reims excommunicated the Countess Matilda of Flanders, and placed her whole land under interdict in order to compel his release. How this principle worked to secure the higher order of recruits was shown when Gui, Count of Auvergne, who had been excommunicated for the unpardonable offence of imprisoning his brother, the Bishop of Clermont, was absolved on condition of joining the Host of the Lord.[120]

Other special motives contributed in this case to render the crusade attractive. There was antagonism of race, jealousy of the wealth and more advanced civilization of the South, and a natural desire to complete the Frankish conquest so often begun and never yet accomplished. More than all, the pardon to be gained was the same as that for the prolonged and dangerous and costly expedition to Palestine, while here the distance was short and the term of service limited to forty days. Paradise, surely, could not be gained on easier terms, and the preachers did not fail to point out that the labor was small and the reward illimitable. With Christendom fairly aroused by the murder of the legate, there could be no doubt, therefore, as to the result. Whether Philip Augustus contributed, in men or money, is more than doubtful, but he made no opposition to the service of his barons, and endeavored to turn his acquiescence to account in the affair of his divorce, while he declined personal participation on the ground of the threatening aspect of his relations with King John and the Emperor Otho. He significantly warned the pope, however, that Raymond's territories could not be exposed to seizure until he had been condemned for heresy, which had not yet been done, and that when such condemnation should be pronounced it would be for the suzerain, and not for the Holy See, to proclaim the penalty. This was strictly{149} in accordance with existing law, for the principle had not yet been introduced into European jurisprudence that suspicion of heresy annulled all rights—a principle which the case of Raymond went far to establish, for the Church without a trial stripped him of his possessions and then decided that he had forfeited them, after which the king could only acquiesce in the decision. Scruples of this kind, however, did not dampen the zeal of those whom the Church summoned to defend the faith. Many great nobles assumed the cross—the Duke of Burgundy and the Counts of Nevers, St. Pol, Auxerre, Montfort, Geneva, Poitiers, Forez, and others, with numerous bishops. With time there came large contingents from Germany, under the Dukes of Austria and Saxony, the Counts of Bar, of Juliers, and of Berg. Recruits were drawn from distant Bremen on the one hand, and Lombardy on the other, and we even hear of Slavonian barons leaving the original home of Catharism to combat it in its seat of latest development. There was salvation to be had for the pious, knightly fame for the warrior, and spoil for the worldly; and the army of the Cross, recruited from the chivalry and the scum of Europe, promised to be strong enough to settle decisively the question which had now for three generations defied all the efforts of the faithful.[121]

All this was, necessarily, a work of time, and Raymond sought in the interval to conjure the coming storm. Roused at last from his dream of security, he recognized the fatal position in which the murder of the legate had placed him, and if he could save his dignities he was ready to sacrifice his honor and his subjects. He hastened to his uncle, Philip Augustus, who received him kindly and counselled submission, but forbade an appeal to his enemy, the Emperor Otho. Raymond, however, in his despair, sought the emperor, whose vassal he was for his territories beyond the Rhone, obtaining no help, and incurring the ill-will of Philip, which was of much greater moment. On his return, learning that Arnaud was about to hold a council at Aubinas, Raymond hurried thither{150}with his nephew, the young Raymond Roger, Viscount of Béziers, and endeavored to prove his innocence and make his peace, but was coldly refused a hearing, and was referred to Rome. Returning much disconcerted, he took counsel with his nephew, who advised resisting the invasion to the death; but Raymond's courage was unequal to the manly part. They quarrelled, whereupon the hot-headed youth commenced to make war on his uncle, while the latter sent envoys to Rome for terms of submission, and asked for new and impartial legates to replace those who were irrevocably prejudiced against him. Innocent demanded that, as security for his good faith, he should place in the hands of the Church his seven most important strongholds, after which he should be heard, and, if he could prove his innocence, be absolved. Raymond gladly ratified the conditions, and earnestly welcomed Milo and Theodisius, the new representatives of the Church, who treated him with such apparent friendliness that, when Milo subsequently died at Arles, he mourned greatly, believing that he had lost a protector who would have saved him from his misfortunes. He did not know that the legates had secret instructions from Innocent to amuse him with fair promises, to detach him from the heretics, and when they should be disposed of by the Crusaders, to deal with him as they should see fit.[122]

He was played with accordingly, skilfully, cruelly, and remorselessly. The seven castles were duly delivered to Master Theodisius, thus fatally crippling him for resistance; the consuls of Avignon, Nîmes, and St. Gilles were sworn to renounce their allegiance to him if he did not obey implicitly the future commands of the pope, and he was reconciled to the Church by the most humiliating of ceremonies. The new legate, Milo, with some twenty archbishops and bishops, went to St. Gilles, the scene of his alleged crime, and there, June 18, 1209, arrayed themselves before the portal of the Church of St. Gilles. Stripped to the waist, Raymond was brought before them as a penitent, and swore on the relics of St. Gilles to obey the Church in all matters whereof he was accused. Then the legate placed a stole around his neck, in the fashion of a halter, and led him into the Church, while he was industriously scourged on his naked back and shoulders up to the altar, where he was absolved. The curious crowd assembled{151} to witness the degradation of their lord was so great that return through the entrance was impossible, and Raymond was carried down to the crypt where the martyred Pierre de Castelnau lay buried, whose spirit was granted the satisfaction of seeing his humbled enemy led past his tomb with shoulders dropping blood. From a churchman's point of view the conditions of absolution laid upon him were not excessive, though well known to be impossible of fulfilment. Besides the extirpation of heresy, he was to dismiss all Jews from office and all his mercenary bands from his service; he was to restore all property of which the churches had been despoiled, to keep the roads safe, to abolish all arbitrary tolls, and to observe strictly the Truce of God.[123]

All that Raymond had gained by these sacrifices was the privilege of joining the crusade and assisting in the subjugation of his country. Four days after the absolution he solemnly assumed the cross at the hands of the legate Milo and took the oath—"In the name of God, I, Raymond, Duke of Narbonne, Count of Toulouse, and Marquis of Provence, swear with hand upon the Holy Gospels of God that when the crusading princes shall reach my territories I will obey their commands in all things, as well as regards security as whatever they may see fit to enjoin for their benefit and that of the whole army." It is true that in July, Innocent, faithful to his prearranged duplicity, wrote to Raymond benignantly congratulating him on his purgation and submission, and promising him that it should redound to his worldly as well as spiritual benefit; but the same courier carried a letter to Milo urging him to continue as he had begun; and Milo, on whom Raymond was basing his hopes, soon after, hearing a report that the count had gone to Rome, warned his master, with superabundant caution, not to spoil the game. "As for the Count of Toulouse," writes the legate, "that enemy of truth and justice, if he has sought your presence to recover the castles in my hands, as he boasts that he can easily do, be not moved by his tongue, skilful only in his slanders, but let him, as he deserves, feel the hand of the Church heavier day by day. After I had received security for his oath on at least fifteen heads, he has perjured himself on them all. Thus he has manifestly forfeited his rights on Melgueil as well as the seven castles which I hold. They are so strong by{152} nature and art that, with the assistance of the barons and people who are devoted to the Church, it will be easy to drive him from the land which he has polluted with his vileness." Already the absolution which had cost so much was withdrawn, and Raymond was again excommunicated and his dominions laid under a fresh interdict, because he had not, within sixty days, during which he was with the Crusaders, performed the impossible task of expelling all heretics, and the city of Toulouse lay under a special anathema because it had not delivered to the Crusaders all the heretics among its citizens. It is true that subsequently a delay until All-Saints' (Nov. 1) was mercifully granted to Raymond to perform all the duties imposed on him; but he was evidently prejudged and foredoomed, and nothing but his destruction would satisfy the implacable legates.[124]

Meanwhile the Crusaders had assembled in numbers such as never before, according to the delighted Abbot of Citeaux, had been gathered together in Christendom; and it is quite possible that there is but slight exaggeration in the enumeration of twenty thousand cavaliers and more than two hundred thousand foot, including villeins and peasants, besides two subsidiary contingents which advanced from the West. The legates had been empowered to levy what sums they saw fit from all the ecclesiastics in the kingdom, and to enforce the payment by excommunication. As for the laity, their revenues were likewise subjected to the legatine discretion, with the proviso that they were not to be coerced into payment without the consent of their seigneurs. With all the wealth of the realm thus under contribution, backed by the exhaustless treasures of salvation, it was not difficult to provide for the motley host whose campaign opened under the spirit-stirring adjuration of the vicegerent of God—"Forward, then, most valiant soldiers of Christ! Go to meet the forerunners of Antichrist and strike down the ministers of the Old Serpent! Perhaps you have hitherto fought for transitory glory; fight now for everlasting glory; you have fought for the world; fight now for God! We do not exhort you to perform this great service to God for any earthly reward, but for the kingdom of Christ, which we most confidently promise you!"[125]{153}

Under this inspiration the Crusaders assembled at Lyons about St. John's day (June 24, 1209), and Raymond hastened from the scene of his humiliation at St. Gilles to complete his infamy by leading them against his countrymen, offering them his son as a hostage in pledge of his good faith. He was welcomed by them at Valence, and, under the supreme command of Legate Arnaud, guided them against his nephew of Béziers. The latter, after a vain attempt at composition with the legate, who sternly refused his submission, had hurriedly placed his strongholds in condition of defence and levied what forces he could to resist the onset.[126]

The war, it should be observed, despite its religious origin, was already assuming a national character. The position taken by Raymond and the rejected submission of the Viscount of Béziers, in fact, deprived the Church of all colorable excuse for further action; but the men of the North were eager to complete the conquest commenced seven centuries before by Clovis, and the men of the South, Catholics as well as heretics, were virtually unanimous in resisting the invasion, notwithstanding the many pledges given by nobles and cities at the commencement. We hear nothing of religious dissensions among them, and comparatively little of assistance rendered to the invaders by the orthodox, who might be presumed to welcome the Crusaders as liberators from the domination or the presence of a hated antagonistic faith. Toleration had become habitual and race-instinct was too strong for religious feeling, presenting almost the solitary example of the kind during the Middle Ages, when nationality had not yet been developed out of feudalism and religious interests were universally regarded as dominant. This explains the remarkable fact that the pusillanimous course of Raymond was distasteful to his own subjects, who were constantly urging him to resistance, and who clung to him and his son with a fidelity that no misfortune or selfishness could shake, until the extinction of the House of Toulouse left them without a leader.

Raymond Roger of Béziers had fortified and garrisoned his capital, and then, to the great discouragement of his people, had withdrawn to the safer stronghold of Carcassonne. Reginald, Bishop of Béziers, was with the crusading forces, and when they{154}arrived before the city, humanely desiring to save it from destruction, he obtained from the legate authority to offer it full exemption if the heretics, of whom he had a list, were delivered up or expelled. Nothing could be more moderate, from the crusading standpoint, but when he entered the town and called the chief inhabitants together the offer was unanimously spurned. Catholic and Catharan were too firmly united in the bonds of common citizenship for one to betray the other. They would, as they magnanimously declared, although abandoned by their lord, rather defend themselves to such extremity that they should be reduced to eat their children. This unexpected answer stirred the legate to such wrath that he swore to destroy the place with fire and sword—to spare neither age nor sex, and not to leave one stone upon another. While the chiefs of the army were debating as to the next step, suddenly the camp-followers, a vile and unarmed folk as the legates reported, inspired by God, made a rush for the walls and carried them, without orders from the leaders and without their knowledge. The army followed, and the legate's oath was fulfilled by a massacre almost without parallel in European history. From infancy in arms to tottering age, not one was spared—seven thousand, it is said, were slaughtered in the Church of Mary Magdalen to which they had fled for asylum—and the total number of slain is set down by the legates at nearly twenty thousand, which is more probable than the sixty thousand or one hundred thousand reported by less trustworthy chroniclers. A fervent Cistercian contemporary informs us that when Arnaud was asked whether the Catholics should be spared, he feared the heretics would escape by feigning orthodoxy, and fiercely replied, "Kill them all, for God knows his own!" In the mad carnage and pillage the town was set on fire, and the sun of that awful July day closed on a mass of smouldering ruins and blackened corpses—a holocaust to a deity of mercy and love whom the Cathari might well be pardoned for regarding as the Principle of Evil. To the orthodox the whole was so manifestly the work of God that the Crusaders did not doubt that the blessing of Heaven attended their arms. Indeed, other miracles were not wanting to encourage them. Although in their senseless havoc they destroyed all the mills within their reach, bread was always miraculously plentiful and cheap in the camp—thirty loaves for a denier was{155}the ordinary price; and during the whole campaign it was noted as an encouragement from heaven that no vulture, or crow, or other bird ever flew over the host.[127]

Similar good-fortune had attended the smaller crusading armies on their way to join the main body. One, under the Viscount of Turenne and Gui d'Auvergne, had captured the almost impregnable castle of Chasseneuil after a short siege. The garrison obtained terms and were allowed to depart, but the inhabitants were left to the discretion of the conquerors. The choice between conversion and the stake was offered them, and, proving obstinate in their errors, they were pitilessly burned—an example which was generally followed. The other force, under the Bishop of Puy, had put to ransom Caussade and St. Antonin, and was generally censured for this misplaced avaricious mercy. Such terror pervaded the land that when a fugitive came to the Castle of Villemur falsely reporting that the Crusaders were coming and would treat it like the rest, the inhabitants abandoned it under cover of the night and themselves set it on fire. Innumerable strongholds, in fact, were surrendered without a blow, or were found vacant, though amply provisioned and strengthened for a siege, and a mountainous region bristling with castles, which would have cost years to conquer if obstinately defended, was occupied in a campaign of a month or two. The populous and mutinous town of Narbonne, to save itself, adopted the severest laws against heresy, raised a large subvention in aid of the crusade, and surrendered sundry castles as security.[128]

Without dallying over the ruins of Béziers, the Crusaders, still under the guidance of Raymond, moved swiftly to Carcassonne, a place regarded as impregnable, where Raymond Roger had elected to make his final stand. The wiser heads among the invaders, looking to a permanent occupation of the country, had no desire to repeat the example already given, and have on their hands a land without defences. Arriving before the walls on August 1st, only nine days after the sack of Béziers, a regular siege was commenced. The outer suburb, which was scarce defensible,{156} was carried and burned after a desperate resistance. The second suburb, strongly fortified, cost a prolonged effort, in which all the resources of the military art of the day were brought into play on both sides, and when it was no longer tenable the besieged evacuated and burned it. There remained the city itself, the capture of which seemed hopeless. Tradition related that Charlemagne had vainly besieged it for seven years and had finally become its master only by a miracle. Terms were offered to the viscount; he was free to depart with eleven of his own choosing, if the city and its people were abandoned to the discretion of the Crusaders, but he rejected the proposal with manly indignation. Still, the situation was becoming insupportable; the town was crowded with refugees from the surrounding country; the summer had been cursed with drought, and the water supply had given out, causing a pestilence under which the wretched people were daily dying by scores. In his anxiety for peace the young viscount allowed himself to be decoyed into the besieging camp, where he was treacherously detained as a prisoner—dying shortly after, it was said, of dysentery, but not without well-grounded suspicions of foul play. Deprived of their chief, the people lost heart; but to avoid the destruction of the city, they were allowed to depart, carrying with them nothing but their sins—the men in their breeches and the women in their chemises—and the place was occupied without further struggle. Curiously enough, we hear nothing of any investigation into their faith, or any burning of heretics.[129]

The siege of Carcassonne brings before us two men, with whom we shall have much to do hereafter, representing so typically the opposing elements in the contest that we may well pause for a moment to give them consideration. These are Pedro II. of Aragon and Simon de Montfort.{157}

Pedro was the suzerain of Béziers, and the young viscount was bound to him with ties of close friendship. Though when appealed to in advance for aid he had declined, yet when he heard of the sack of Béziers he hurried to Carcassonne to mediate if possible for his vassal, though his efforts were fruitless. He was everywhere regarded as a model for the chivalry of the South. Heroic in stature and trained in every knightly accomplishment, he was ever in the front of battle; and on the tremendous day of Las Navas de Tolosa, which broke the Moorish power in Spain, it was he, by common consent, among all the kings and nobles present, who won the loftiest renown. In the bower he was no less dangerous than in the field. His gallantries were countless, and his licentiousness notorious, even in that age of easy morals. He was munificent to prodigality, fond of magnificent display, courteous to all comers, and magnanimous to all enemies. Like his father, Alonso II., moreover, he was a troubadour, and his songs won applause, none the less hearty, perhaps, that he was a liberal patron of rival poets. With all this his religious zeal was ardent, and he gloried in the title of el Catolico. This he manifested not only in the savage edict against the Waldenses, referred to in a previous chapter, but by an extraordinary act of devotion to the Holy See. In 1085 his ancestor, Sancho I., had placed the kingdom of Aragon under the special protection of the popes, from whom his successors were to receive it on their accession and to pay an annual tribute of five hundred mancuses. In 1204 Pedro II. resolved to perform this act of fealty in person. With a splendid retinue he sailed for Rome, where he took an oath of allegiance to Innocent, including a pledge to persecute heresy. He was crowned with a crown of unleavened bread, and received from the pope the sceptre, mantle, and other royal insignia, which he reverently laid upon the altar of St. Peter, to whom he offered his kingdom, taking in lieu his sword from Innocent, subjecting his realm to an annual tribute, and renouncing all rights of patronage over churches and benefices. As an equivalent for all this he was satisfied with the title of First Alferez or Standard-bearer of the Church and the privilege for his successors of being crowned by the Archbishop of Tarragona in his cathedral church. The nobles of Aragon, however, regarded this as an inadequate return for the taxes occasioned by his extravagance and for the loss of Church patronage, and their dissatisfaction{158} was expressed in forming the confederation known as La Union, which for generations was of dangerous import to his successors. Impulsive and generous, Pedro's career reads like a romance of chivalry, and, with such a character, it was impossible for him to avoid participating in the Albigensian wars, in which he had a direct interest, owing to his claims upon Provence, Montpellier, Béarn, Roussillon, Gascony, Comminges, and Béziers.[130]

In marked contrast with this splendid knight-errantry was the solid and earnest character of de Montfort, who had distinguished himself, as was his wont, at the siege of Carcassonne. He was the first to lead in the assault on the outer suburb; and when an attack upon the second had been repulsed and a Crusader was left writhing in the ditch with a broken thigh, de Montfort with a single squire leaped back into it, under a shower of missiles, and bore him off in safety. The younger son of the Count of Evreux, a descendant of Rollo the Norman, he was Earl of Leicester by right of his mother the heiress, and had won a distinguished name for prowess in the field and wisdom and eloquence in the council. Religious to bigotry, he never passed a day without hearing mass; and the true-hearted affection which his wife, Alice of Montmorency, bore him, shows that his reputation for chastity—a rare virtue in those days—was probably not undeserved. In 1201 he had joined the crusade of Baldwin of Flanders; and when, during the long detention in Venice, the Crusaders sold their services to the Venetians for the destruction of Zara, de Montfort alone refused, saying that he had come to fight the infidel and not to make war on Christians. He left the host in consequence, made his way to Apulia, and with a few friends took ship to Palestine, where he served the cross with honor. It is curious to speculate what change there might have been in the destiny of both France and England had he remained with the crusade to the capture of Constantinople, when he, and his yet greater son, Simon of Leicester, might have founded principalities in Greece or Thessaly and have worn out their lives in obscure and forgotten conflicts. When the Albigensian{159} crusade was preached, one of the Cistercian abbots who devoted himself most earnestly to the work was Gui of Vaux-Cernay, who had been a Crusader with de Montfort at Venice. It was owing to his persuasion that the Duke of Burgundy took the cross on the present occasion, and he was the bearer of letters from the duke to de Montfort making him splendid offers if he would likewise take up arms. At de Montfort's castle of Rochefort, Gui found the pious count in his oratory, and set forth the object of his mission. De Montfort hesitated, and then, taking up a psalter, opened it at random and placed his finger on a verse which he asked the abbot to translate for him. It read:

"For he shall give his angels charge over thee, to keep thee in all thy ways. They shall bear thee in their hands, that thou hurt not thy foot against a stone" (Ps. XCI. 11, 12).

The divine encouragement was manifest. De Montfort took the cross, which was to be his life's work, and the brilliant valor of the Catalan knight proved no match for the deep earnestness of the Norman, who felt himself an instrument in the hand of God.[131]

With the capture of Carcassonne the Crusaders seem to have felt that their mission was accomplished; at least, the brief service of forty days which sufficed to earn the pardon was rendered, and they were eager to return home. The legate naturally held that the conquered territory was to be so occupied and organized that heresy should have no further foothold there, and it was offered first to the Duke of Burgundy and then successively to the Counts of Nevers and St. Pol, but all were too wary to be tempted, and alleged in refusal that the Viscount of Béziers had already been sufficiently punished. Then two bishops and four knights, with Arnaud at their head, were appointed to select the one on whom the confiscated land should be bestowed; and these seven, under the manifest influence of the Holy Ghost, unanimously selected de Montfort. We may well believe, from his reputation for sagacity, that his unwillingness to accept the offer was unfeigned, and that after prayers had proved unavailing, he yielded only to the absolute commands of the legate, speaking with all the authority of{160} the Holy See. He made it a condition, however, that the continued and efficient support which he foresaw would be requisite should be given him. This was duly promised, with little intention of fulfilment. The Count of Nevers, between whom and the Duke of Burgundy a mortal quarrel had arisen, withdrew almost immediately after the capture of Carcassonne, and with him the great body of the Crusaders. The duke remained for a short time, when he likewise turned his face homewards, and de Montfort was left with but about forty-five hundred men, mostly Burgundians and Germans, for whose services he was obliged to offer double pay.[132]

De Montfort's position was perilous in the extreme. It mattered little that in August, during the full flush of success, the legates had held a council in Avignon which ordered all bishops to swear every knight, noble, and magistrate in their dioceses to exterminate heresy, or that such an oath had already been forced upon Montpellier and other cities which were trembling before the wrath to come. Such oaths, extorted by fear, were but an empty form, and the homage which de Montfort received from his new vassals was equally hollow. It is true that he regulated his boundaries with Raymond, who promised to marry his son with de Montfort's daughter, and he styled himself Viscount of Béziers and Carcassonne, but Pedro of Aragon refused to receive his homage, and secretly comforted the castellans who still held out with promises of early assistance, while others who had submitted revolted, and castles which had been occupied were recaptured. The country was recovering from its terror. An annoying partisan warfare sprang up; small parties of his men were cut off, and his rule extended no farther than the reach of his lance. At one time it was with difficulty that he restrained those who were with him in Carcassonne from flight; and when he set forth to besiege Termes it was almost impossible to find a knight willing to assume command of Carcassonne, so dangerous was the post considered. Yet with all this he succeeded in subduing additional strongholds, and extended his dominion over the Albigeois and into the territory{161} of the Count of Foix. He hastened, moreover, to acquire the good graces of Innocent, whose confirmation of his new dignity was requisite, and whose influence for further succor he earnestly implored. All tithes and first-fruits were to be rigorously paid to the churches; any one remaining under excommunication for forty days was to be heavily fined according to his station; Rome, in return for the treasures of salvation so lavishly expended, was to receive from a devastated land an annual tax of three deniers on every hearth, while a yearly tribute from the count himself was vaguely promised. To this, in November, Innocent replied, full of joy at the wonderful success which had wrested five hundred cities and castles from the grasp of heretics. He graciously accepted the offered tribute, and confirmed de Montfort's title to both Béziers and Albi, with an adjuration to be sleepless in the extirpation of heresy; but he could scarce have appreciated the Crusader's perilous position, for he excused himself from efficient aid on the score of complaints which reached him from Palestine that the succor sorely needed there had been diverted to subdue heretics nearer home. He therefore only called upon the Emperor Otho, the Kings of Aragon and Castile, and sundry cities and nobles from whom no real aid could be expected. The archbishops of the whole infected region were directed to persuade their clergy to contribute to him a portion of their revenues, and his troops were exhorted to be patient and to ask no pay until the following Easter; neither of which requests were likely to yield results. Somewhat more fruitful was the release of all Crusaders from any obligations which they might have assumed to pay interest on sums borrowed; but the most practical measure was one which forcibly illustrates the friendly and confidential intercourse which had existed between the heretics and the clergy in southern France, for all abbots and prelates throughout Narbonne, Béziers, Toulouse, and Albi were directed to confiscate for de Montfort's benefit all deposits placed by obstinate heretics for safe-keeping in their hands, the amount of which was said to be considerable.[133]{162}

After losing most of his conquests, de Montfort's position became more hopeful towards the spring of 1210, as his forces were swelled by the arrival of successive bands of "pilgrims"—as these peaceful folk were accustomed to style themselves—and his ambitious views expanded. The short term for which the cross was assumed rendered it necessary to turn the new-comers to immediate account, and de Montfort was unceasingly active in recovering his ground and in reducing the castles which still held out. It is not worth our while to follow in detail these exploits of military religious ardor, which, when successful, were usually crowned by putting the garrison to the sword and offering the non-combatants the choice between obedience to Rome and the stake—a choice which gave occasion to zealous martyrdom on the part of hundreds of obscure and forgotten enthusiasts. Lavaur, Minerve, Casser, Termes, are names which suggest all that man can inflict and man can suffer for the glory of God. The spirit of the respective parties was well exhibited at the capitulation of Minerve, where Robert Mauvoisin, de Montfort's most faithful follower, objected to the clause which spared the heretics who should recant, and was told by Legate Arnaud that he need not fear the conversion of many, as ample experience had shown their prevailing obstinacy. Arnaud was right; for, with the exception of three women, they unanimously refused to secure safety by apostasy, and saved their captors the trouble of casting them on the blazing pyre by leaping exultingly into the flames. If the playful zeal of the pilgrims sometimes manifested itself in eccentric fashion, as when they blinded the monks of Bolbonne and cut off their noses and ears till there was scarce a trace of the human visage left, we must remember the sources whence the Church drew her recruits, and the immunity which she secured for them, here and hereafter.[134]

If Raymond had fancied that he had skilfully saved himself at the expense of his nephew of Béziers, he had at last discovered his{163} mistake. Arnaud of Citeaux had fully resolved upon his ruin, and de Montfort was eager to extend his lordship and the purity of the faith. Already, in the autumn of 1209, the citizens of Toulouse had been startled by a demand from the legate to surrender all whom his envoys might select as heretics, under pain of excommunication and interdict. They protested that there were no heretics among them; that all who were named were ready to purge themselves of heresy; that Raymond V. had, at their instance, passed laws against heretics, under which they had burned many and were burning all who could be found. Therefore they appealed to the pope, naming January 29, 1210, as the day for the hearing. At the same time de Montfort had notified Raymond that unless the legate's demands were conceded he would assail him and enforce obedience. Raymond replied that he would settle the matter with the pope, and lost no time in appealing in person to Philip Augustus and the Emperor Otho, from whom he received only fair words. On reaching Rome he was apparently more fortunate. He had a strong case. He had never been convicted, or even tried, for the crimes whereof he was accused; he had always professed obedience to the Church and readiness to prove his innocence, according to the legal methods of the age, by canonical purgation; he had undergone cruel penance as though convicted, and had been absolved as though forgiven, since when he had rendered faithful and valuable service against his friends and had made what reparation he could to the churches which he had despoiled. He boldly asserted his innocence, demanded a trial, and claimed the restoration of his castles. Innocent seems at first to have been touched by the wrongs inflicted on him and the ruin impending over him; but if so the impression was but momentary, and he returned to the duplicity which thus far had worked so well. The citizens of Toulouse he pronounced to have justified themselves, and ordered their excommunication removed. As regards Raymond, he instructed the Archbishops of Narbonne and Arles to assemble a council of prelates and nobles for the trial which Raymond so earnestly demanded. If there an accuser should assert his heresy and responsibility for the murder of Pierre de Castelnau, both sides should be heard and judgment be rendered and sent to Rome for final decision; if no formal accuser appeared, then fitting purgation should be assigned to him, on performance{164} of which he should be declared a good Catholic and his castles be restored. All this was fair seeming enough, yet it is impossible not to see the purposed deceit in an accompanying letter to the legate Arnaud, praising him warmly for what had been done and explaining that the conduct of the matter had been ostensibly intrusted to the new commissioner, Master Theodisius, merely as a lure for Raymond; or, to use the pope's own words, that the legate was to be the hook of which Theodisius was the bait. Instructions were also given as to some minor matters, and to lull Raymond to a more complete sense of security, on his final audience Innocent presented him with a rich mantle and with a ring which he drew from his own finger.[135]

Joy reigned in Toulouse when the count returned, bringing with him the removal of the interdict and the promise of a speedy settlement of the troubles. Legate Arnaud entered fully into the spirit of his instructions and suddenly became friendly and affectionate. We even hear of a visit paid by him and de Montfort to Raymond in Toulouse, where they were magnificently received; and Raymond, it is said, was persuaded to give the citadel of the town, known as the Château Narbonnois, as a residence to the legate, from whose hands it passed into those of de Montfort, costing eventually the lives of a thousand men for its recapture. Arnaud, moreover, exacted a promise of one thousand livres toulousains from the citizens before he would give effect to the papal letters removing the interdict; when one half was paid, he gave them his benediction, but a delay in raising the other half caused him to renew the interdict, which cost them much trouble to remove.[136]

Master Theodisius joined the legate at Toulouse, as we are told by a fiercely orthodox eye-witness, for the purpose of consulting with him as to the most plausible excuse for eluding Innocent's promise to Raymond of an opportunity of purgation, for they foresaw that he would purge himself and that the destruction of the faith would follow. The readiest method of attaining this pious object lay in Raymond's failure to perform the impossible task assigned him of clearing his lands of heresy; but in order to avoid{165} the appearance of premeditated unfairness, the solemn mockery was arranged of assigning him a day three months distant, to appear at St. Gilles and offer his purgation as to heresy and the murder of the legate—a warning being added about his slackness in persecution. At the appointed time, in September, 1210, a number of prelates and nobles were assembled at St. Gilles, and Raymond presented himself with his compurgators in the full confidence of a final reconciliation with the Church. He was coolly informed that his purgation would not be received; that he was manifestly a perjurer in not having executed the promises to which he had repeatedly sworn, and his oath being worthless in minor matters, it could not be accepted in charges so weighty as those of heresy and legate-murder, nor were those of his accomplices any better. A man of stronger character would have been roused to fiery indignation at this contemptuous revelation of the deception practised on him; but Raymond, overwhelmed with the sudden destruction of his illusions, simply burst into tears—which was duly recorded by his judges as an additional proof of his innate depravity, and he was promptly again placed under the excommunication which it had cost him such infinite pains to remove. For form's sake, however, he was told that when he should clear the land of heresy and otherwise show himself worthy of mercy, the papal commands in his favor would be fulfilled. The Provençal was evidently no match for the wily Italians; and Innocent's approbation of this cruel comedy is seen in a letter addressed by him to Raymond, in December, 1210, expressing his grief that the count had not yet performed his promises as to the extermination of heretics, and warning him that if he did not do so his lands would be delivered to the Crusaders. Another epistle by the same courier to de Montfort, complaining of the scanty returns of the three-denier hearth-tax, shows that even Innocent kept an eye on the profitable side of persecution; while exhortations addressed to the Counts of Toulouse, Comminges, and Foix, and Gaston of Béarn, requiring them to help de Montfort, with threats of holding them to be fautors of heresy in case they resisted him, showed how completely all questions were prejudged and that they were doomed to be delivered up to the spoiler.[137]{166}

Raymond at length began to see what all clear-visioned men must long before have recognized, that his ruin was the deliberate purpose of the legates. Had the nobles of Languedoc been united at the beginning, they could probably have offered successful resistance to the spasmodic attacks of the Crusaders, but they were being devoured one by one, while Raymond, their natural leader, was kept idle with delusive hopes of reconciliation. The restoration of his castles was hopeless, and it was time for him to prepare himself as best he could for the inevitable war. With this object, to unite his subjects, he circulated a list of conditions which he said had been proposed to him at a conference in Arles, in February, 1211—conditions which were onerous and degrading to the last degree to the people as well as to himself—which would have placed the whole territory and its population under the control of the legates and of de Montfort, would have branded every inhabitant, Catholic as well as heretic, noble as well as villein, with the mark of servitude, and would have banished Raymond to the Holy Land virtually for life. Whether such demands were really made or not, their effect was great upon the people, who rallied around their sovereign and were ready for any self-sacrifice.[138]

That the list of conditions was supposititious is rendered probable by other negotiations in which Raymond desperately strove to avert the inevitable rupture. In December, 1210, we find him at Narbonne in conference with the legates, de Montfort, and Pedro of Aragon, where impracticable terms were offered him, and where Pedro finally consented to receive de Montfort's homage for Béziers. Shortly afterwards another meeting was held at Montpellier, equally fruitless, except for de Montfort, who made a treaty with Pedro and received from him his infant son Jayme, to be held as a hostage. Even in the spring of 1211 Raymond again visited de Montfort at the siege of Lavaur and allowed provisions to be supplied for a while to the Crusaders from Toulouse, although he had fruitlessly endeavored to prevent the marching of a contingent{167} which the Toulousains furnished to the besiegers. Almost as soon as Lavaur was taken, May 3, 1211, de Montfort fell upon his territories and captured some of his castles, apparently without defiance or declaration of war, when he made a last miserable effort of submission by offering his whole possessions except the city of Toulouse, to be held by the legate and de Montfort as security for the performance of what might be demanded of him, reserving only his life and his son's right of inheritance. Even these terms were contemptuously rejected. He had so abased himself that he seems to have been regarded as no longer an element of weight in the situation. Besides, the Count of Bar was speedily expected with a large force of Crusaders, whose forty-days' term was to be utilized to the utmost, and the siege of Toulouse was resolved on.[139]

As soon as the citizens heard of this design they sent an embassy to the Crusaders to deprecate it. They had been reconciled to the Church, and had assisted at the siege of Lavaur, but they were sternly told that they would not be spared unless they would eject Raymond from the city and renounce their allegiance to him. This they refused unanimously. All the old civic quarrels were forgotten, and as one man they prepared for resistance. It is a noteworthy illustration of the strength of the republican institution of the civic commune, that the siege of Toulouse was the first considerable check received by the Crusaders. The town was well fortified and garrisoned; the Counts of Foix and Comminges had come at the summons of their suzerain, and the citizens were earnest in defence. They not only kept their gates open, but made breaches in the walls to facilitate the furious sallies which cost the besiegers heavily. The latter retired, June 29th, under cover of the night, so hastily that they abandoned their sick and wounded, having accomplished nothing except the complete devastation of the land—dwellings, vineyards, orchards, women and children were alike indiscriminately destroyed in their wrath—and de Montfort turned from the scene of his defeat to carry the same ravage into Foix. This final effort of self-defence was naturally construed as fautorship of heresy and drew from Innocent a fresh excommunication{168} of Raymond and of the city for "persecuting" de Montfort and the Crusaders.[140]

Encouraged by his escape, Raymond now took the offensive, but with little result. The siege of Castelnaudary was a failure, and a good deal of desultory fighting occurred, mostly to the advantage of de Montfort, whose military skill was exhibited to the best advantage in his difficult position. The crusade was still industriously preached throughout Christendom, and his forces were irregularly renewed with fresh swarms of "pilgrims" for forty-days' service, so that he would frequently find himself at the head of a considerable army, which again would soon melt away to a handful. To utilize this varying stream of strangers of all nationalities in a difficult country which was bitterly hostile required capacity of a high order, and de Montfort proved himself thoroughly equal to it. His opponents, though frequently greatly superior in numbers, never ventured on a pitched battle, and the war was one of sieges and devastations, conducted on both sides with savage ferocity. Prisoners were frequently hanged, or less mercifully blinded or mutilated, and mutual hate grew stronger and fiercer as de Montfort gradually extended his boundaries and Raymond's territories grew less and less. The defection of his natural brother Baldwin, whom he had always treated with suspicion, and who had been won over by de Montfort when captured at Montferrand, before the siege of Toulouse, had been a severe blow to the national cause; how deeply felt was seen when, in 1214, he was treacherously given up and Raymond hanged him, with difficulty granting his last prayer for the consolations of religion.[141]

Early in 1212 the Abbot of Vaux-Cernay received in the bishopric of Carcassonne the reward of his zeal in furthering the crusade, and Legate Arnaud obtained the great archbishopric of Narbonne on the death or degradation of the negligent Berenger. Not content with the ecclesiastical dignity, Arnaud claimed to be likewise duke, giving rise to a vigorous quarrel with de Montfort, who, notwithstanding his devotion to the Church, had no intention of surrendering to it his temporal possessions. Possibly it was the{169} commencement of coolness between them that induced Arnaud to favor the crusade preached at the request of Alonso IX. of Castile, at that time threatened by a desperate effort of the Moors, largely reinforced from Africa, to regain their Spanish possessions. Much as de Montfort needed every man, the new Archbishop of Narbonne marched into Spain at the head of a large force of Crusaders to swell the army with which the kings of Aragon, Castile, and Navarre advanced against the Saracen. It is characteristic of the tenacity of the man that, when the French contingent grew weary of the service and refused to advance after the capture of Calatrava, returning ingloriously home, Arnaud remained with those whom he could persuade to stay, and shared in the glory of Las Navas de Tolosa, where a cross in the sky encouraged the Christians, and two hundred thousand Moors were slain.[142]

The spring and summer of 1212 saw an almost unbroken series of successes for de Montfort, until Raymond's territories were reduced to Montauban and Toulouse, and the latter city, crowded with refugees from the neighboring districts, was virtually beleaguered, as the Crusaders from their surrounding strongholds made forays up to the very gates. De Montfort desired the papal confirmation of his new acquisitions, and for this application was made to Rome by the legates. Innocent seems to have been aroused to a sense of the scandal created by the faithful carrying out of his policy, for Raymond, though constantly claiming a trial, had never been heard or convicted, and yet had been punished by the seizure of nearly all his dominions. Innocent accordingly assumed a tone of grave surprise. It is true, he said, that the count had been found guilty of many offences against the Church, for which he had been excommunicated and his lands exposed to the first comer; but the loss of most of them had served as a punishment, and it must be remembered that, although suspected of heresy and of the murder of the legate, he had never been convicted, nor did the pope know why his commands to afford him an opportunity of purging himself had never been carried out. In the absence of a formal trial and conviction his lands could not be adjudged to another. The proper forms must be observed, or the Church{170} might be deemed guilty of fraud in continuing to hold the castles made over to it in pledge. Innocent evidently felt that his representatives, involved in the passions and ambitions of the strife, had done

56

what could not be justified, and he wound up by ordering them to report to him the full and simple truth. Another letter, in the same sense, to Master Theodisius and the Bishop of Riez, cautioned them not to be remiss in their duty, as they were said to have thus far been, which undoubtedly refers to their withholding from Raymond the opportunity of justification. At the same time, a prolonged correspondence on the subject of the hearth-tax, and the acceptance of an opportune donation of a thousand marks from de Montfort, place Innocent in an unfortunate light as an upright and impartial judge.[143]

To this Theodisius and the Bishop of Riez replied with the transparent falsehood that they had not been remiss, but had repeatedly summoned Raymond to justify himself, and that Raymond had neglected to make reparation to certain prelates and churches, which was quite likely, seeing that de Montfort had been giving him ample occupation. They proceeded, however, to make a bustling show of activity in compliance with Innocent's present commands, and they called a council at Avignon to give a colorable pretext for pushing Raymond to the wall. Avignon, however, was fortunately unhealthy, so that many prelates refused to attend, and Theodisius had a timely sickness, rendering a postponement necessary. Another council was therefore summoned to convene at Lavaur, a castle not far from Toulouse, in the hands of de Montfort, who, at the request of Pedro of Aragon, graciously granted an eight days' suspension of hostilities for the purpose.[144]

The matter, in fact, had assumed a shape which could no longer be eluded. Pedro of Aragon, fresh from the triumph of Las Navas, was a champion of the faith who was not to be treated with contempt, and he had finally come forward as the protector of Raymond and of his own vassals. As overlord he could not passively see the latter stripped of their lands, and his interests in the whole region were too great for him to view with indifference the establishment of so overmastering a power as de Montfort was rapidly{171} consolidating. The conquered fiefs were being filled with Frenchmen; a parliament had just been held at Pamiers to organize the institutions of the country on a French basis, and everything looked to an overturning of the old order. It was full time for him to act. He had already sent a mission to Innocent to complain of the proceedings of the legates as arbitrary, unjust, and subversive of the true interests of religion, and he came to Toulouse for the avowed purpose of interceding for his ruined brother-in-law. By assuming this position he was assuring the supremacy of the House of Aragon over that of Toulouse, with which it had had so many fruitless struggles in the past.[145]

Pedro's envoys drew from Innocent a command to de Montfort to give up all lands seized from those who were not heretics, and instructions to Arnaud not to interfere with the crusade against the Saracens by using indulgences to prolong the war in the Toulousain. This action of Innocent, coupled with the powerful intercession of Pedro, created a profound impression, and all the ecclesiastical organization of Languedoc was summoned to meet the crisis. When the council assembled at Lavaur, in January, 1213, a petition was presented by King Pedro, humbly asking mercy rather than justice for the despoiled nobles. He produced a formal cession executed by Raymond and his son and confirmed by the city of Toulouse, together with similar cessions made by the Counts of Foix and Comminges and by Gaston of Béarn, of all their lands, rights, and jurisdictions to him, to do with as he might see fit in compelling them to obey the commands of the pope in case they should prove recalcitrant. He asked restitution of the lands conquered from them, on their rendering due satisfaction to the Church for all misdeeds; and if Raymond could not be heard, the proposal was made that he should retire in favor of his young son—the father serving with his knights against the infidel in Spain or Palestine, and the youth being retained in careful guardianship until he should show himself worthy of the confidence of the Church. All this, in fact, was virtually the same as the offers already transmitted by Pedro to Innocent.[146]

No submission could be more complete; no guarantees more{172} absolute could be demanded. There was no pretence of shielding heretics, who could, under such a settlement, be securely exterminated; but the prelates assembled at Lavaur were under the domination of passions and ambitions and hatreds, the memory of wrongs suffered and inflicted, and the dread of reprisals, which rendered them deaf to everything that might interfere with the predetermined purpose. The ruin of the house of Toulouse was essential to their comfort— they might well believe even to their personal safety—and it was pressed unswervingly. As legates, Master Theodisius and the Bishop of Riez presided, while the assembled prelates of the land were led by the intractable Arnaud of Narbonne. All forms were duly observed. The legates, as judges, asked the opinion of the prelates as assessors, whether Raymond should be admitted to purgation. A written answer was returned in the negative, not only for the reason previously alleged, that he was too notorious a perjurer to be listened to, but also because of fresh offences committed during the war, the slaying of Crusaders who were attacking him being seriously included among his sins. As a further subterfuge it was agreed that the excommunication under which he lay could only be removed by the pope. Shielding themselves behind this answer, the legates notified Raymond that they could proceed no further without special license from the pope—a repetition of the eternal shifting of responsibility, like a shuttlecock from one player in the game to another—and when Raymond implored for mercy and begged an interview, he was coldly told that it would be useless trouble and expense for both parties. There remained the appeal of King Pedro to be disposed of, and this was treated with the same disingenuous evasion. The prelates undertook to answer this without the legates, so as to be able to say that Raymond's affairs were out of their hands, as he had himself committed them to the legates; and, besides, his excesses had rendered him unworthy of all mercy or kindness. As for the other three nobles, their crimes were recited, especially their self-defence against the Crusaders, and it was added that if they would satisfy the Church

57

and obtain absolution, their complaints would be listened to; but no method was indicated by which absolution could be obtained, and no notice was deigned to the guarantees offered in Pedro's petition. Indeed, Arnaud of Narbonne, in his capacity of legate, wrote to{173} him in violent terms, threatening him with excommunication for consorting with excommunicants and accused heretics, and his request for a truce until Pentecost, or at least until Easter, was refused on the ground that it would interfere with the success of the crusade, which was still preached in France with a vigor justifying doubts of the sincerity of Innocent's orders to the contrary.[147]

The whole proceedings were so defiant a mockery of justice that there was a very manifest alarm lest Innocent should repudiate them and yield to the powerful intercession of King Pedro. Master Theodisius and several bishops were despatched to Rome with the documents so as to bring personal influence to bear. The prelates of the council addressed him, adjuring him by the bowels of the mercy of God not to draw back from the good work which he had commenced, but to lay his axe to the root of the tree and cut it down forever. Raymond was painted in the blackest colors. The effort he had made to obtain succor from the Emperor Otho, and the assistance at one time rendered him by Savary de Mauleon, lieutenant of King John in Aquitaine, were skilfully used to excite odium, as both these monarchs were hostile to Rome; and he was even accused of having implored help from the Emperor of Morocco, to the subversion of Christianity itself. Fearing that this might be insufficient, letters were showered on Innocent by bishops from every part of the troubled region, assuring him that peace and prosperity had followed on the footsteps of the Crusaders, that the land which had been ravaged by heretics and bandits was restored to religion and safety, that if but one more supreme effort were made and the city of Toulouse were wiped out, with its villainous brood, wicked as the children of Sodom and Gomorrah, the faithful could enjoy the Land of Promise; but that if Raymond were allowed to raise his head, chaos would come again, and it would be better for the Church to take refuge among the barbarians. Yet in all this nothing was said to the pope of the guarantees offered through King Pedro, who was obliged, in March, 1213, to transmit to Rome copies of the cessions executed by the inculpated nobles, duly authenticated by the Archbishop of Tarragona and his suffragans.[148]{174}

Master Theodisius and his colleagues found the task harder than they had anticipated. Innocent had solemnly declared that Raymond should have the opportunity of vindication, and that condemnation should only follow trial. He was now required to eat his words, while the persistent refusal to allow a trial must have shown him that the charges so industriously made were destitute of proof. The struggle was hard for a proud man, but he finally yielded to the pressure, though the delay of the decision until May 21, 1213, shows what effort it cost. When the decree came, however, its decisiveness proved that pride and consistency had been overcome. Innocent's letters to his legates have not reached us—perhaps a prudent reticence kept them out of the Regesta—but to Pedro he wrote sternly, commanding him to abandon the protection of heretics unless he was ready to be included in the objects of the new crusade which was threatened if further resistance was attempted. The orders which Pedro had obtained for the restoration of non-heretical lands were withdrawn as granted through misrepresentation, and the lords of Foix, Comminges, and Navarre were remitted to the discretion of Arnaud of Narbonne. The city of Toulouse could obtain reconciliation by banishment and confiscation inflicted on all whom Foulques, its fanatic bishop, might point out, and no peace or truce or other engagement entered into with heretics was to be observed. As to Raymond, the complete silence preserved with respect to him was more significant than could have been the severest animadversions. He was simply ignored, as though no further account was to be taken of him.[149]

Meanwhile both parties had proceeded without waiting the event in Rome. In France the crusade had been vigorously preached; Louis Cœur-de-Lion, son of Philip Augustus, had taken the cross with many barons, and great hopes were entertained of the overwhelming force which would put an end to further resistance, when Philip's preparations for the invasion of England caused him to intervene and stop the movement which threatened seriously to interfere with his designs. On the other hand, King Pedro entered into still closer alliance with Raymond and the excommunicated nobles, and received an oath of fidelity from the{175} magistracy of Toulouse. When the papal mandate was received, he made a pretence of obeying it, but continued, nevertheless, his preparations for the war, among which the one which best illustrates the man and the age was his procuring from Innocent the renewal of Urban's bull of 1095, placing his kingdom under the special protection of the Holy See, with the privilege that it should not be subjected to interdict except by the pope himself. A *sirvente* by an anonymous troubadour shows how anxiously he was expected in Languedoc. He is reproached with his delays, and urged to come to collect his revenues from the Carcassès like a good king, and to suppress the insolence of the French, whom may God confound.[150]

The rupture came with a formal declaration of war from Pedro, accepted by de Montfort, though he had but few troops and the hoped-for reinforcements from France were not forthcoming; indeed, a legate sent by Innocent to preach the crusade for the Holy Land had turned in that direction all the effort which Philip would permit to be made. Pedro had left in Toulouse his representatives and had gone to his own dominions to raise forces, with which he recrossed the Pyrenees and was received enthusiastically by all those who had submitted to de Montfort. He advanced to the castle of Muret, within ten miles of Toulouse, where de Montfort had left a slender garrison, and was joined by the Counts of Toulouse, Foix, and Comminges, their united forces amounting to a considerable army, though far from the hundred thousand men represented by the eulogists of de Montfort. Pedro had brought about a thousand horsemen with him; the three counts, stripped of most of their dominions, can scarce have furnished a larger force of cavaliers, and the great mass of their array consisted of the militia of Toulouse, on foot and untrained in arms.[151]

The siege of Muret commenced September 10, 1213. Word was immediately carried to de Montfort, who lay about twenty-five miles distant at Fanjeaux, with a small force, including seven bishops and three abbots sent by Arnaud of Narbonne to treat{176} with Pedro. Notwithstanding the disparity of numbers, he did not hesitate a moment to advance and succor his people. Sending back the Countess Alice, who was with him, to Carcassonne, where she persuaded some retiring Crusaders to return to his aid, he set forth at once, hastily collecting such troops as were within reach. At Bolbonne, near Saverdun, where he halted to hear mass, Maurin, the sacristan, afterwards Abbot of Pamiers, expressed wonder at his risking with a mere handful of men an encounter with a warrior so renowned as the King of Aragon. De Montfort in reply drew from his pouch an intercepted letter to a lady in Toulouse, in which Pedro assured her that he was coming out of love for her to drive the Frenchman from her land, and when Maurin asked him what he meant by it, he exclaimed, "What do I mean? God help me as much as I little fear him who comes for the sake of a woman to undo the work of God!" It was the God-trusting Norman against the chivalrous Catalan gallant, and he never doubted the result.

The next day de Montfort entered Muret, which was besieged only on one side, the enemy interposing no obstacle, as they hoped to capture the chief of the Crusaders. The bishops sought to negotiate with Pedro, but no terms could be reached, and the following morning, Thursday, September 13, the Crusaders, numbering perhaps a thousand cavaliers, sallied forth for the attack. As they passed, the Bishop of Comminges comforted them greatly by assuring them that on the Day of Judgment he would be their witness, and that none who might be slain would have to undergo the fires of purgatory for any sins which they had confessed or might intend to confess after the battle. The holy men then gathered in the church, praying fervently to God for the success of his warriors; and here we get a traditional glimpse of Dominic, who is said to have been one of the little band; indeed, we are gravely told by his followers that the ensuing victory was due to the devotion of the Rosary, which he invented and assiduously practised.

As de Montfort drew away in the opposite direction, the besiegers at first thought that he was abandoning the town, and they were only undeceived when he wheeled and they saw he had made a circuit to obtain a level field for the attack. Count Raymond counselled awaiting the onset behind the rampart of wagons{177} and exhausting the Crusaders with missiles, but the fiery Catalan rejected the advice as pusillanimous. Then armor was donned in hot haste, and the horsemen rushed forth in a confused mass, leaving the footmen to continue the labors of the siege. Emulous rather of the fame of a good knight than of a general, Pedro was immediately behind the vanguard, as two squadrons of the Crusaders came on in solid order, and was readily found by two renowned French knights, Alain de Roucy and Florent de Ville, who had concerted to set upon him. He was speedily thrown from his horse and slain. The confusion into which his followers were thrown was converted into a panic as de Montfort, at the head of a third squadron, charged them in flank. They turned and fled, followed by the Frenchmen, who slew them without mercy, and then, returning from the pursuit, fell upon the camp where the infantry had remained unconscious of the evil-fortune of the field. Here the slaughter was tremendous, until the flying wretches succeeded in crossing the Garonne, in which many were drowned. The loss of the Crusaders was less than twenty, that of the allies from fifteen to twenty thousand, and no one was hardy enough to doubt that the hand of God was visible in a triumph so miraculous, especially as on the last Sunday in August a great procession had been held in Rome with solemn ceremonies, followed by a two days' fast, for the success of the Catholic arms. Yet King Jayme tells us that his father's death, and the consequent loss of the battle, arose from his prevailing vice. The Albigensian nobles, to ingratiate themselves with him, had placed their wives and daughters at his disposal, and he was so exhausted by his excesses that on the morning of the battle he could not stand at the celebration of the mass.[152]{178}

With the few men at his command de Montfort was unable to follow up his advantage, and the immediate effect of the miraculous victory was scarcely perceptible. The citizens of Toulouse professed a desire for reconciliation, but when their bishop, Foulques, demanded two hundred hostages as security, they refused to give more than sixty, and when the bishop assented to this, they withdrew the offer. De Montfort made a foray into Foix, carrying desolation in his track, and showed himself before Toulouse, but was soon put on the defensive. When he came peaceably to the city of Narbonne, of which he claimed the overlordship, he was refused entrance; the same thing happened to him at Montpellier, and he was obliged to digest these affronts in silence. His condition, indeed, was almost desperate in the winter of 1214, when affairs suddenly took a different turn. The prohibition to preach the crusade in France was removed, and news came that an army of one hundred thousand fresh pilgrims might be expected after Easter. Besides this a new legate, Cardinal Peter of Benevento, arrived with full powers from the pope, and at Narbonne received the unqualified submission of the Counts of Toulouse, Foix, and Comminges, of Aimeric, Viscount of Narbonne, and of the city of Toulouse. All these agreed to expel heretics and to comply explicitly with all demands of the Church, furnishing whatever security might be demanded. Raymond, moreover, placed his dominions in the hands of the legate, at whose command he engaged to absent himself, either at the English court or elsewhere, until he could go to Rome; and in effect, on his return to Toulouse he and his son lived as private citizens with their wives, in the house of David de Roaix. Rome having thus obtained everything that she had ever demanded, the legate absolved all the penitents and reconciled them to the Church.

If the land expected peace with submission it was cruelly deceived. The whole affair had been but another act in the comedy which Innocent and his agents had so long played, another juggle with the despair of whole populations. The legate had merely desired to tide de Montfort over the time during which in his weakness he might have been overwhelmed, and to amuse the threatened provinces until the arrival of the fresh swarm of pilgrims. The trick was perfectly successful, and the monkish chronicler is delighted with the pious fraud so astutely conceived and{179} so dexterously managed. His admiring ejaculation, "O pious fraud of the legate! O fraudulent piety!" is the key which unlocks to us the secrets of Italian diplomacy with the Albigenses.[153]

In spite of King Philip's war with John of England and the Emperor Otho, the expected hordes of Crusaders, eager to win pardon so easily, poured down upon the unhappy southern provinces. Their initial exploit was the capture of Maurillac, notable to us as conveying the first distinct reference to the Waldenses in the history of the war. Of these sectaries, seven were found among the captives; they boldly affirmed their faith before the legate, and were burned, as we are told, with immense rejoicings by the soldiers of Christ. With his wonted ability de Montfort made use of his reinforcements to extend his authority over the Agenois, Quercy, Limousin, Rouergue, and Périgord. Resistance being now at an end, the legate, in January, 1215, assembled a council of prelates at Montpellier. The jealous citizens would not allow de Montfort to enter the town, though he directed the deliberations from the house of the Templars beyond the walls; and once, when he had been secretly introduced to attend a session, the people discovered it, and would have set upon him, had he not been conveyed away through back streets. The council fulfilled its functions by deposing Raymond and electing de Montfort as lord over the whole land; and, as the confirmation of Innocent was required, an embassy was sent to Rome, which obtained his assent. He declared that Raymond, who had never yet had the trial so often demanded, was deposed on account of heresy; his wife was to have her dower, and one hundred and fifty marks were assigned to her, secured by the Castle of Beaucaire. The final disposition of the territory was postponed for the decision of the general council of Lateran, called for the ensuing November; and meanwhile it was confided to the custody of de Montfort, whom the bishops were exhorted to assist and the inhabitants to obey, while from its revenues some provision was contemptuously ordered to be made for the support of Raymond. Bishop Foulques returned to his city of Toulouse, of which he was virtually master, under the legate{180} who continued to hold it and Narbonne, to keep them out of the hands of Louis Cœur-de-Lion, who was shortly expected in fulfilment of his Crusader's vow, taken three years previously; and the "faidits," as the dispossessed knights and gentlemen were called, were graciously permitted to seek a livelihood throughout the country, provided they never entered castles or walled towns, and travelled on ponies, with but one spur, and without arms.[154]

The battle of Bouvines had released France from the dangers which had been so threatening, and the heir-apparent could be spared for the performance of his vow. Louis came with a noble and gallant company, who earned the pardon of their sins by a peaceful pilgrimage of forty days. The fears which had been felt as to his intentions proved groundless. He showed no disposition to demand for the crown the acquisitions made by previous crusades, and advantage was taken of his presence to obtain temporary investiture for de Montfort, and to order the dismantling of the two chief centres of discontent—Toulouse and Narbonne. De Montfort's brother Gui took possession of the former city, and saw to the levelling of its walls. As for Narbonne, Archbishop Arnaud, mindful rather of his pretensions as duke than of the interests of religion, vainly protested against its being rendered defenceless. In making over Raymond's territories to de Montfort, however, Innocent had excepted the county of Melgueil, over which the Church had a sort of claim, and this he sold to the Bishop of Maguelonne, costing the latter, including gratifications to the creatures of the papal camera, no less a sum than thirty-three thousand marks. The transaction held good, in spite of the claims of the crown as the eventual heir of the Count of Toulouse, and, until the Revolution, the Bishops of Maguelonne or Montpellier had the satisfaction of styling themselves Counts of Melgueil. It was but a small share of the gigantic plunder, and Innocent would have best consulted his dignity by abstention.[155]

Meanwhile the two Raymonds had withdrawn—possibly to the English court, where King John is said to have given them{181} ten thousand marks for the rendering of a worthless homage, to which is perhaps attributable the permission given by Philip Augustus to his son to perform the crusade and grant investiture to de Montfort of the lands thus transferred to English sovereignty.[156] Foreign humiliations and domestic revolt, however, rendered John useless as an ally or a suzerain, and Raymond awaited, with what patience he might, the assembling of the great council to which the final decision of his fate had been referred. Here, at least, he would have a last chance of being heard, and of appealing for the justice so long and so steadily denied him.

In April, 1213, had gone forth the call for the Parliament of Christendom, the Twelfth General Council, where the assembled wisdom and piety of the Church were to deliberate on the recovery of the Holy Land, the reformation of the Church, the correction of excesses, the rehabilitation of morals, the extirpation of heresy, the strengthening of faith, and the quieting of discord. All these were specified as the objects of the convocation, and two years and a half had been allowed for preparation. By the appointed day, November 1, 1215, the prelates had gathered together, and Innocent's pardonable ambition was gratified in opening and presiding over the most august assemblage that Latin Christianity had ever seen. The Frankish occupation of Constantinople gave opportunity for the reunion, nominal at least, of the Eastern and the Western churches, and Patriarchs of

Constantinople and Jerusalem were there in humble obedience to St. Peter. All that was foremost in Church and State had come, in person or by representative. Every monarch had his ambassador there, to see that his interests suffered no detriment from a body which, acting under the direct inspiration of the Holy Ghost, and under the principle that temporal concerns were wholly subordinate to spiritual, might have little respect for the rights of sovereigns. The most learned theologians and doctors were at hand to give counsel as to points of faith and intricate questions of canon law. The princes of the Church were present in numbers wholly unprecedented. Besides patriarchs, there were seventy-one primates and metropolitans, four hundred and twelve bishops, more than eight hundred abbots and priors, and the countless delegates of those prelates who were unable{182} to attend in person.[157] Two centuries were to pass away before Europe was again to show its collective strength in a body such as now crowded the ample dimensions of the Basilica of Constantine; and it is a weighty illustration of the service which the Church has rendered in counteracting the centrifugal tendencies of the nations, that such a federative council of Christendom, attainable in no other way, was brought together at the summons of the Roman pontiff. Without some such cohesive power modern civilization would have worn a very different aspect.

The Counts of Toulouse, Foix, and Comminges had reached Rome in advance, where they were joined by the younger Raymond, coming through France from England disguised as the servitor of a merchant, to escape the emissaries of de Montfort. In repeated interviews with Innocent they pleaded their cause, and produced no little impression on him. Arnaud of Narbonne, embittered by his quarrel with de Montfort, is said to have aided them, but the other prelates, to whom it was almost a question of life or death, were so violent in their denunciations of Raymond, and drew so fearful a picture of the destruction impending over religion, that Innocent, after a short period of irresolution, was deterred from action. De Montfort had sent his brother Gui to represent him, and when the council met both parties pressed their claims before it. Its decision was prompt, and, as might be expected, was in favor of the champion of the Church. The verdict, as promulgated by Innocent, December 15, 1215, recited the labors of the Church to free the province of Narbonne from heresy, and the peace and tranquillity with which its success had been crowned. It assumed that Raymond had been found guilty of heresy and spoliation, and therefore deprived him of the dominion which he had abused, and sentenced him to dwell elsewhere in penance for his sins, promising him four hundred marks a year so long as he proved obedient. His wife was to retain the lands of her dower, or to receive a competent equivalent for them. All the territories won by the Crusaders, together with Toulouse, the centre of heresy, and Montauban, were granted to de Montfort, who was extolled as the chief instrument in the triumph of the faith. The other possessions of Raymond, not as yet conquered, were to be{183} held by the Church for the benefit of the younger Raymond, to be delivered to him when he should reach the proper age, in whole or in part, as might be found expedient, provided he should manifest himself worthy. So far as Count Raymond was concerned, the verdict was final; thereafter the Church always spoke of him as "the former count," "*quondam comes.*" Subsequent decisions as to Foix and Comminges at least arrested the arms of de Montfort in that direction, although they proved far less favorable to the native nobles than they appeared on the surface.[158]

The highest tribunal of the Church Universal had spoken, and in no uncertain tone; and we may see a significant illustration of the forfeiture of its hold on popular veneration in the fact that this, in place of meeting with acquiescence, was the signal of revolt. Apparently the decision had been awaited in the confidence that it would repair the long course of wrong and injustice perpetrated in the name of religion; and, with the frustration of that hope, there was no hesitation in resorting to resistance, with the national spirit inflamed to the highest pitch of enthusiasm. If de Montfort thought that his conquests were secured by the voice of the Lateran fathers, and by King Philip's reception of the homage which he lost no time in rendering, he only showed how little he had learned of the temper of the race with which he had to deal. Yet in France he was naturally the hero of the hour, and the journey on his way to tender allegiance was a triumphal progress. Crowds flocked to see the champion of the Church; the clergy marched forth in solemn procession to welcome him to every town, and those thought themselves happy who could touch the hem of his garment.[159]

The younger Raymond, at this time a youth of eighteen, hardened by years of adversity, was winning in manner, and is said to have made a most favorable impression on Innocent, who dismissed him with a benediction and good advice; not to take what belonged to another, but to defend his own—"res de l'autrui non pregas; lo teu, se degun lo te vol hostar, deffendas"—and he made{184} haste to follow the counsel, according to his own interpretation. The part of his inheritance which had been reserved for him under custody of the Church lay to the east of the Rhone, and thither, on their return from Italy, early in 1216, father and son took their way, to find a basis of operations. The outlook was encouraging, and after a short stay the elder Raymond proceeded to Spain to raise what troops he could. Marseilles, Avignon, Tarascon—the whole country, in fact—rose as one man to welcome their lord, and demanded to be led against the Frenchmen, reckless of the fulminations of the Church, and placing life and property at his disposal. The part which the cities and the people play in the conflict becomes henceforth even more noticeable than heretofore—the semi-republican communes fighting for life against the rigid feudalism of the North. How subordinated was the religious question, and how confused were religious notions, is manifested by the fact that, while thus warring against the Church, at the siege of the castle of Beaucaire, when entrenchments were necessary against the relieving army of de Montfort, Raymond's chaplain offered salvation to any one who would labor on the ramparts, and the townsfolk set eagerly to work to obtain the promised pardons. The people apparently reasoned little as to the source from whence indulgences came, nor the object for which they were granted.[160]

De Montfort met this unexpected turn of fortune with his wonted activity, but his hour of prosperity was past, and one might almost say, with the Church historians, that he was weighed down by the excommunication launched at him by the implacable Arnaud of Narbonne, whom he had treated harshly in their quarrel over the dukedom—an excommunication which he wholly disregarded, not even intermitting his attendance at mass, though he had looked upon the censures of the Church with such veneration when they were directed against his antagonists. Obliged, after hard fighting, to leave Beaucaire to its fate, he marched in angry mood to Toulouse, which was preparing to recall its old lord. He set fire to the town in several places, but the citizens barricaded the streets, and resisted his troops step by step, till accommodation was made, and he agreed to spare the city for the immense{185} sum of thirty thousand marks; but he destroyed what was left of the fortifications, filled up the ditches, rendered the place as defenceless as possible, and disarmed the inhabitants. Despite his excommunication, he still had the earnest support of the Church. Innocent died July 20, 1216, but his successor, Honorius III., inherited his policy, and a new legate, Cardinal Bertrand of St. John, and St. Paul, was, if possible, more bitter than his predecessors in the determination to suppress the revolt against Rome. The preaching of the crusade had been resumed, and in the beginning of 1217, with fresh reinforcements of Crusaders and a small contingent furnished by Philip Augustus, de Montfort crossed the Rhone, and made rapid progress in subduing the territories left to young Raymond.

He was suddenly recalled by the news that Toulouse was in rebellion; that Raymond VI. had been received there with rejoicings, bringing with him auxiliaries from Spain; that Foix and Comminges, and all the nobles of the land, had flocked thither to welcome their lord, and that the Countess of Montfort was in peril in the Château Narbonnais, the citadel outside of the town, which he had left to bridle the citizens. Abandoning his conquests, he hastened back. In September, 1217, commenced the second siege of the heroic city, in which the burghers displayed unflinching resolve to preserve themselves from the yoke of the stranger—or perhaps, rather, the courage of desperation, if the account is to be believed that the cardinal-legate ordered the Crusaders to slay all the inhabitants, without distinction of age or sex. In spite of the defenceless condition of the town, which men and women unitedly worked night and day to repair; in spite of the threatening and beseeching letters which Honorius wrote to the Kings of Aragon and France, to the younger Raymond, the Count of Foix, the citizens of Toulouse, Avignon, Marseilles, and all whom he thought to deter or excite; in spite of heavy reinforcements brought by a vigorous renewal of preaching the crusade, for nine weary months the siege dragged on, in furious assaults and yet more furious sallies, with intervals of suspended operations as the crusading army swelled or decreased. De Montfort's brother Gui and his eldest son Amauri were seriously wounded. The baffled chieftain's troubles were rendered sorer by the legate, who taunted him with his ill-success, and accused him of ignorance or slackness in his{186} work. Sick at heart, and praying for death as a welcome release, on the morrow of St. John's day, 1218, he was superintending the reconstruction of his machines, after repelling a sally, when a stone from a mangonel, worked, as Toulousain tradition says, by women, went straight to the right spot—"E venc tot dret la peira lai on era mestiers"—it crushed in his helmet, and he never more spoke word. Great was the sorrow of the faithful through all the lands of Europe when the tidings spread that the glorious champion of Christ, the new Maccabee, the bulwark of the faith, had fallen as a martyr in the cause of religion. He was buried at Haute-Bruyère, a cell of the Monastery of Dol, and the miracles worked at his tomb showed how acceptable to God had been his life and death, though there were not wanting those who drew the moral that his sudden downfall, just as his success seemed to be firmly established, was the punishment of neglecting the persecution of heresy in his eagerness to gratify his ambition.[161]

If proof were lacking of de Montfort's pre-eminent capacity it would be furnished by the rapid undoing of all that he had accomplished, in the hands of his son and successor Amauri. Even during the siege his prestige was yet such that, December 18, 1217, the powerful Jourdain de l'Isle-Jourdain made submission to him as Duke of Narbonne and Count of Toulouse and furnished as securities Géraud, Count of Armagnac and Fézensac, Roger, Viscount of Fézenzaquet, and other nobles; and in February, 1218, the citizens of Narbonne abandoned their rebellious attitude. His death was regarded as the signal of liberation, and wherever the French garrisons were not too strong, the people arose, massacred the invaders, and gave themselves back to their ancient lords. Vainly did Honorius recognize Amauri as the successor to his father's lordships, put the two Raymonds to the ban, and grant Philip Augustus a twentieth of ecclesiastical revenues as an incentive to another crusade,{187} while plenary indulgence was offered to all who would serve. Vainly did Louis Cœur-de-Lion, with his father's sanction, and accompanied by the Cardinal-Legate Bertrand, lead a gallant army of pilgrims which numbered in its ranks no less than thirty-three counts and twenty bishops. They penetrated, indeed, to Toulouse, but the third siege of the unyielding city was no more successful than its predecessors, and Louis was obliged to withdraw ingloriously, having accomplished nothing but the massacre of Marmande, where five thousand souls were put to the sword, without distinction of age or sex. Indeed, the pitiless cruelty and brutal licentiousness habitual among the Crusaders, who spared no man in their wrath, and no woman in their lust, aided no little in inflaming the resistance to foreign domination. One by one the strongholds still held by the French were wrested from their grasp, and but very few of the invaders founded families who kept their place among the gentry of the land. In 1220 a new legate, Conrad, tried the experiment of founding a military order under the name of the Knights of the Faith of Jesus Christ, but it proved useless. Equally vain was the papal sentence of excommunication and exheredation fulminated in 1221; and when, in the same year, Louis undertook a new crusade and received from Honorius a twentieth of the Church revenues to defray the expenses, he turned the army thus raised against the English possessions and captured La Rochelle, in spite of the protests of king and pope.[162]

Early in 1222, Amauri, reduced to desperation, offered to Philip Augustus all his possessions and claims, urging Honorius to support the proposal. The pope welcomed it as the only feasible mode of accomplishing the result for which years of effort had been fruitlessly spent, and he wrote to the king, May 14, representing that in this way alone could the Church be saved. The heretics who had hid themselves in caverns and mountain fastnesses where French{188} domination prevailed, came forth again as soon as the invaders were driven out, and their unceasing missionary efforts were aided by the common detestation in which the foreigner was held by all. The Church had made itself the national enemy, and we can easily believe the description which Honorius gives of the lamentable condition of orthodoxy in Languedoc. Heresy was openly practised and taught; the heretic bishops set themselves up defiantly against the Catholic prelates, and there was danger that the pestilence would spread throughout the land. In spite of all this, however, and of an offer of a twentieth of the church revenues and unlimited indulgences for a crusade, Philip turned a deaf ear to the entreaty; and when Amauri's offer was transferred to Thibaut of Champagne, and the latter applied to the king for encouragement, he was coldly told that if, after due consideration, he resolved on the undertaking, the king wished him all success, but could render him no aid nor release him from his obligations of service in view of the threatening relations with England. Possibly encouraged by this, the younger Raymond in June appealed to Philip as his lord, and, if he dared so to call him, as his kinsman, imploring his pity, and begging in the humblest terms his intervention to procure his reconciliation to the Church, and thus remove the incapacity of inheritance to which he was subjected.[163]

This must have been suggested by the expectation of the death of Raymond VI., which occurred shortly after, in August, 1222. It made no change in the political or religious situation, but is not without interest in view of the charge of heresy so persistently made and used as an excuse for his destruction. In 1218 he had executed his will, in which he left pious legacies to the Templars and Hospitallers of Toulouse, declared his intention of entering the latter order, and desired to be buried with them. On the morning of his sudden death he had twice visited for prayer the church of la Daurade, but his agony was short and he was speechless when the Abbot of St. Sernin, who had been hurriedly sent for, reached his bedside, to administer to him the consolations of religion. A Hospitaller who was present cast over him his cloak with the cross, to secure the burial of the body for his house; but a zealous parishioner{189} of St. Sernin pulled it off, and a disgraceful squabble arose over the dying man, for the abbot claimed the sepulture, as the death chanced to take place in his parish, and he summoned the people not to allow the corpse to be removed beyond its precincts. This ghastly struggle over the remains has its ludicrous aspect, from the fact that the Church would never permit the inhumation of its enemy, and the body remained unburied in spite of the reiterated pious efforts of Raymond VII., after his reconciliation, to secure the repose of his father's soul. It was in vain that the inquest ordered by Innocent IV., in 1247, gathered evidence from a hundred and twenty witnesses to prove that Raymond VI. had been the most pious and charitable of men and most obedient to the Church. His remains lay for a century and a half the sport of rats in the house of the Hospitallers, and when they disappeared piece-meal, the skull was still kept as an object of curiosity, at least until the end of the seventeenth century.[164]

After his father's death Raymond VII. pursued his advantage, and in December Amauri was reduced to offering again his claims to Philip Augustus, only to be exposed to another refusal. In May, 1223, there seem to have been hopes that Philip would undertake a crusade, and the Legate Conrad of Porto, with the bishops of Nîmes, Agde, and Lodève wrote to him urgently from Béziers describing the deplorable state of the land in which the cities and castles were daily opening their gates to the heretics and inviting them to take possession. Negotiations with Raymond followed, and matters went so far that we find Honorius writing to his legate to look after the interest of the Bishop of Viviers in the expected settlement. There was fresh urgency felt for the pacification in the absence of any hope of assistance from the king, since the progress of the Catharan heresy was ever more alarming. Additional energy had been infused into it by the activity of its Bulgarian antipope. Heretics from Languedoc were resorting to him in increasing numbers and returning with freshened zeal; and his representative, Bartholomew, Bishop of Carcassonne, who styled himself, in imitation of the popes, Servant of the servants of the Holy Faith, was making successful efforts to{190} spread the belief. Truces between Amauri and Raymond were therefore made and conferences held, and finally the legate called a council to assemble at Sens, July 6, 1223, where a final pacification was expected. It was transferred to Paris, because Philip Augustus desired to be present, and its importance in his eyes must have been great, since he set out on his journey thither in spite of a raging fever, to which he succumbed on the road, at Meudon, July 14. Raymond's well-grounded hopes were shattered on the eve of realization, for Philip's death rendered the council useless and changed in a moment the whole face of affairs.[165]

Though Philip showed his practical sympathy with de Montfort by leaving him a legacy of thirty thousand livres to assist him in his Albigensian troubles, his prudence had avoided all entanglements, and he had steadily rejected the proffer of the de Montfort claims. Yet his sagacity led him to prophesy truly that after his death the clergy would use every effort to involve Louis, whose feeble health would prove unequal to the strain, and the kingdom would be left in the hands of a woman and a child. It was probably the desire to avert this by a settlement which led him to make the fatal effort to attend the council, and his prediction did not long await its fulfilment. Louis, on the very day of his coronation, promised the legate that he would undertake the matter; Honorius urged it with vehemence, and in February, 1224, Louis accepted a conditional cession from Amauri of all his rights over Languedoc. Raymond thus found himself confronted by the King of France as his adversary.[166]

The situation was full of new and unexpected peril. But a month before, Amauri, in utter penury, had been obliged to surrender what few strongholds he yet retained, and had quitted forever the land which he and his father had cursed, a portion of Philip's legacy being used to extricate his garrisons. The triumph, so long hoped for and won by so many years of persistent struggle, was a Dead-Sea apple, full of ashes and bitterness. The discomfited adversary was now replaced by one who was rash and enterprising,{191}who wielded all the power gained by Philip's long and fortunate reign, and whose pride was enlisted in avenging the check which he had received five years before under the walls of Toulouse. Already in February he wrote to the citizens of Narbonne, praising their loyalty and promising to lead a crusade three weeks after Easter, which should restore to the crown all the lands forfeited by the house of Toulouse. Zealous as he was, however, he felt that the eagerness of the Church warranted him in driving the best bargain he could for his services to the faith, and he demanded as conditions of taking up arms that peace abroad and at home should be assured to him, that a crusade should be preached with the same indulgences as for the Holy Land, that all his vassals not joining in it should be excommunicated, that the Archbishop of Bourges should be legate in place of the Cardinal of Porto, that all the lands of Raymond, of his allies, and of all who resisted the crusade should be his prize, that he should have a subsidy of sixty thousand livres parisis a year from the Church, and that he should be free to return as soon or remain as long as he might see fit.[167]

Louis asserted that these conditions were accepted, and went on with his preparations, while Raymond made desperate efforts to conjure the coming storm. Henry III. of England used his good offices with Honorius, and Raymond was encouraged to make offers of obedience through envoys to Rome, whose liberalities among the officials of the curia are said to have produced a most favorable impression. Honorius replied in a most gracious letter, promising to send Romano, Cardinal of Sant' Angelo, as legate to arrange a settlement, and he followed this by informing Louis that the offers of Frederic II. to recover the Holy Land were so favorable that everything else must be postponed to that great object, and all indulgences must be used solely for that purpose; but that if he will continue to threaten Raymond, that prince will be forced to submit. Instructions were at the same time sent to Arnaud of Narbonne to act with other prelates in leading Raymond to offer acceptable terms. Louis, justly indignant at being thus played with, made public protestation that he washed his hands of the whole business, and told the pope the curia might come to what terms it pleased with Raymond, that he had nothing{192}to do with points of faith, but that his rights must be respected and no new tributes be imposed. At a parliament held in Paris, May 5, 1224, the legate withdrew the indulgences granted against the Albigenses and approved of Raymond as a good Catholic, while Louis made a statement of the whole transaction in terms which showed how completely he felt himself to be duped. He turned his military preparations to account, however, by wrenching from Henry III. a considerable portion of the remaining English possessions in France.[168]

The storm seemed to be successfully conjured. Nothing remained but to settle the terms, and Raymond's escape had been too narrow for him to raise difficulties on this score. At Pentecost (June 2) with his chief vassals, he met Arnaud and the bishops at Montpellier, where he agreed to observe and maintain the Catholic faith throughout his dominions, and expel all heretics pointed out by the Church, confiscate their property and punish their bodies, to maintain peace and dismiss the bandit mercenaries, to restore all rights and privileges to the churches, to pay twenty thousand marks for reparation of ecclesiastical losses and for Amauri's compensation, on condition that the pope would cause Amauri to renounce his claims and deliver up all documents attesting them. If this would not suffice, he would submit himself entirely to the Church, saving his allegiance to the king. His signature to this was accompanied by those of the Count of Foix and the Viscount of Béziers. As an evidence of good faith he reinstated his father's old enemy, Theodisius, in the bishopric of Agde, which the quondam legate had obtained and from which he had been driven, and in addition he restored various other church properties. These conditions were transmitted to Rome for approbation with notice that a council would be held August 20 for their ratification, and Honorius returned an equivocal answer which might be construed as accepting them. On the appointed day the council met at Montpellier. Amauri sent a protest begging the bishops desperately not to throw away the fruits of victory within their grasp. The King of France, he said,{193} was on the point of making the cause his own, and to abandon it now would be a scandal and a humiliation to the Church Universal. Notwithstanding this, the bishops received the oaths of Raymond and his vassals to the conditions previously agreed, with the addition that the decision of the pope should be followed as to the composition with Amauri, and that any further commands of the Church should be obeyed, saving the supremacy of the king and the emperor, for all of which satisfactory security was offered.[169]

What more the Church could ask it is hard to see. Raymond had triumphed over it and all the Crusaders whom it could muster, and yet he offered submission as complete as could reasonably have been exacted of his

64

father in the hour of his deepest abasement. At this very time, moreover, a public disputation held at Castel-Sarrasin between some Catholic priests and Catharan ministers shows the growing confidence of heresy and the necessity of an accommodation if its progress was to be checked. Not less significant was a Catharan council held not long after at Pieussan, where, with the consent of Guillabert of Castres, heretic bishop of Toulouse, the new episcopate of Rasez was carved out of his see and that of Carcassès. Yet the vicissitudes and surprises in this business were not yet exhausted. In October, when Raymond's envoys reached Rome to obtain the papal confirmation of the settlement, they were opposed by Gui de Montfort, sent by Louis to prevent it. There were not wanting Languedocian bishops who feared that with peace they would be forced to restore possessions usurped during the troubles, and who consequently busied themselves with proving that Raymond was at heart a heretic. Honorius shuffled with the negotiation until the commencement of 1225, when he sent Cardinal Romano again to France with full powers as legate, and with instructions to threaten Raymond and to bring about a truce between France and England so as to free Louis's hands. He wrote to Louis in the same sense, while to Amauri he sent money and words of encouragement. His description of Languedoc, as a land of iron and brass{194} of which the rust could only be removed by fire, shows the side which he had finally determined to take.[170]

After several conferences with Louis and the leading bishops and nobles, the legate convened a national council at Bourges in November, 1225, for the final settlement of the question. Raymond appeared before it, humbly seeking absolution and reconciliation; he offered his purgation and whatever amends might be required by the churches, promising to render his lands peaceful and secure and obedient to Rome. As for heresy, he not only engaged to suppress it, but urged the legate to visit every city in his dominions and make inquisition into the faith of the people, pledging himself to punish rigorously all delinquents and to coerce any town offering opposition. For himself, he was ready to render full satisfaction for any derelictions, and to undergo an examination as to his faith. On the other hand, Amauri exhibited the decrees of Innocent condemning Raymond VI. and bestowing his lands on Simon, and Philip's recognition of the latter. There was much wrangling in the council until the legate ordered each archbishop to deliberate separately with his suffragans and deliver to him the result in writing, to be submitted to the king and pope, under the seal of secrecy, enforced by excommunication.[171]

There is an episode in the proceedings of this council worth attention as an illustration of the relations between Rome and the local churches and the character of the establishment to which the heretics were invited to return with the gentle inducements of the stake and gibbet. After the ostensible business of the assemblage was over, the legate craftily gave to the delegates of{195} the chapters permission to depart, while retaining the bishops. The delegates thus dismissed were keen to scent some mischief in the wind; they consulted together and sent to the legate a committee from all the metropolitan chapters to say that they understood him to have special letters from the Roman curia demanding for the pope in perpetuity the fruits of two prebends in every episcopal and abbatial chapter and one in every conventual church. They adjured him, for the sake of God, not to cause so great a scandal, assuring him that the king and the barons would be ready to resist at the peril of life and dignity, and that it would cause a general subversion of the Church. Under this pressure the legate exhibited the letters and argued that the grant would relieve the Roman Church of the scandal of concupiscence, as it would put an end to the necessity of demanding and receiving presents. On this the delegate from Lyons quietly observed that they did not wish to be without friends in the Roman court, and were perfectly willing to bribe them; others represented that the fountain of cupidity never would run dry, and that the added wealth would only render the Romans more madly eager, leading to mutual quarrels which would end in the destruction of the city; others, again, pointed out that the revenues thus accruing to the curia, computed to be greater than those of the crown, would render its members so rich that justice would be more costly than ever; moreover, it was evident that the host of officials in each church, whom the pope would be entitled to appoint to look after the collections, would not only lead to infinite additional exactions, but would be used to control the elections of the chapters, and end by bringing them all under subjection to Rome. They wound up by assuring him that it was for the interest of Rome itself to abandon the project, for if oppression thus became universal it would be followed by universal revolt. The legate, unable to face the storm, agreed to suppress the letters, saying that he disapproved of them, but had had no opportunity of remonstrance, as they had only reached him after his arrival in France. An equally audacious proposition, by which the curia hoped to obtain control over all the abbeys in the kingdom, was frustrated by the active opposition of the archbishops. Heresy might well hold itself justifiable in keeping aloof from such a Church as this.[172]{196}

What were really the conclusions reached in the Albigensian matter by the archiepiscopal caucuses no one might reveal, but with pope and king resolved on intervention there could be little doubt as to the practical result. Moreover, the stars in their courses had fought against Raymond, for in this critical juncture death had carried off Archbishop Arnaud of Narbonne, who had become his vigorous friend, and who was succeeded by Pierre Amiel, his bitter enemy. There could be no effective resistance to royal and papal wishes; it was announced that no peace honorable to the Church could be reached with Raymond, and that a tithe of ecclesiastical revenues for five years was offered to Louis if he would undertake the holy war. Reckless as was Louis, however, and eager to clutch at the tempting prize, he shrank from the encounter with the obstinate patriotism of the South while involved in hostilities with England. He demanded therefore that Honorius should prohibit Henry III. from disturbing the French territories during the crusade. When Henry received the papal letters he was eagerly preparing an expedition to relieve his brother, Richard of Cornwall, but his counsellors urged him not to prevent Louis from entangling himself in so difficult and costly an enterprise, and one of them, William Pierrepont, a skilled astrologer, confidently predicted that Louis would either lose his life or be overwhelmed with misfortune. In the nick of time, news arrived from Richard giving good accounts of his success; Henry's anxieties were calmed, and he gave the required assurances, in spite of an alliance into which he had shortly before entered with Raymond. As a further precaution to insure the success of the crusade, all private wars were forbidden during its continuance.[173]{197}

The question of religion had practically disappeared by this time, except as an excuse for indulgences and ecclesiastical subsidies and as a cloak for dynastic expansion. If Raymond had not yet actively persecuted his heretic subjects it was merely because of the impolicy, under constant threats of foreign aggression, of alienating so large a portion of the population on which he relied for support. He had shown himself quite ready to do so in exchange for reconciliation to the Church, and he had urged the legate to establish an organized inquisition throughout his dominions. Amid all the troubles the Dominicans had been allowed to grow and establish themselves in his territories; and when their rivals in persecution, the Franciscans, had come to Toulouse, he had welcomed them and assisted them in taking root. In this very year, 1225, St. Antony of Padua, who stands next to St. Francis in the veneration of the order, came to France to preach against heresy, and in the Toulousain his eloquence excited such a storm of persecution as to earn for him the honorable title of the Tireless Hammer of Heretics. The coming struggle thus, even more than its predecessors, was to be a war of races, with the whole power of the North, led by the king and the Church, against the exhausted provinces which clung to Raymond as their suzerain. We cannot wonder that he was willing to submit to any terms to avert it, for he was left to breast the tempest alone. His greatest vassal, the Count of Foix, it is true, stood by him, but the next in importance, the Count of Comminges, made his peace, and is found acting for the king; the Count of Provence entered into the alliance against him, while, at a warning from Louis, Jayme of Aragon and Nuñez Sancho of Roussillon forbade their subjects from lending aid to the heretic.[174]

Meanwhile the crusade was organized on the largest scale. At a great parliament held in Paris, January 28, 1226, the nobles presented an address urging the king to undertake it and pledging their assistance to the end. He assumed the cross under condition that he should lay it aside when he pleased, and his example was followed by nearly all the bishops and barons, though we are told that many did so unwillingly, holding it an abuse to assail a faithful{198} Christian who, at the Council of Bourges, had offered all possible satisfaction. Amauri and his uncle Gui executed a renunciation of all their claims in favor of the crown; the cross was diligently preached throughout the kingdom, with the customary offer of indulgences, and the legate guaranteed that the ecclesiastical tithe granted for five years should amount to at least one hundred thousand livres per annum. The only cloud to mar the prospect was the discovery that Honorius had sent letters and legates to the barons of Poitou and Aquitaine, ordering them within a month to return to their allegiance to England in spite of any oaths taken to the contrary. This curious piece of treachery can only be explained by persuasive bribes from Raymond or from Henry III., and Louis promptly met it with liberal payments to the pope, by which he procured the suspension of the letters. This being got out of the way, another council was held March 29, where Louis commanded his lieges to assemble on May 17, at Bourges, fully equipped and prepared to remain with him as long as he should stay in the South. The forty day's service which had so repeatedly snatched from de Montfort the fruits of his victories was no longer to arrest the tide of a permanent conquest.[175]

On the appointed day the chivalry of the kingdom gathered around their monarch at Bourges, but before setting forth there was much to be done. Innumerable abbots and delegates from chapters besieged the king, imploring him not to reduce the national Church to servitude by exacting the tithe bestowed on him, and promising to make ample provision for his needs; but he was unrelenting, and they departed, secretly cursing both crusade and king. The legate was busy dismissing the boys, women, old men, paupers, and cripples who had assumed the cross. These he forced to swear as to the amount of money which they possessed; of this he took the major part and let them go after granting them absolution from the vow—an indirect way of selling indulgences which became habitual and produced large sums. Louis drove a thriving trade of the same kind from a higher class of Crusaders by accepting heavy payments from those who owed him service and were not ambitious of the glory or the perils of the expedition.{199} He also forced the Count of La Marche to send back to Raymond his young daughter Jeanne, betrothed to La Marche's son, and reserved, as we shall see, for loftier nuptials. To Bourges likewise flocked many of the nobles of Narbonne, eager to show their loyalty by doing homage to the king and to advise him not to advance through their district, which was devastated by war, but to march by way of the Rhone to Avignon—disinterested counsel which he adopted.[176]

Louis set forth from Lyons with a magnificent army consisting, it is said, of fifty thousand horse and innumerable foot. The terror of his coming preceded him; many of Raymond's vassals and cities made haste to offer their submission—Nîmes, Narbonne, Carcassonne, Albi, Béziers, Marseilles, Castres, Puylaurens, Avignon—and he seemed reduced to the last extremity. When the host reached Avignon, however, and Louis proposed to march through the city, the inhabitants, with sudden fear, shut their gates in his face, and though they offered him unmolested passage around it, he resolved on a siege, in spite of its being a fief of the empire. It had lain for ten years under excommunication, and was noted as a nest of Waldenses, so the Cardinal-Legate

Romano ordered the Crusaders to purge it of heresy by force of arms. The task proved no easy one. From June 10 till about September 10 the citizens resisted desperately, inflicting heavy loss upon the besiegers. Raymond had devastated the surrounding country and was ever on the watch to cut off foraging-parties, so that supplies were scanty. An epidemic set in, and a plague of flies carried infection from the dead to the living. Disaffection in the camp aggravated the trouble. Pierre Mauclerc of Britanny was offended with Louis for traversing his plot of marriage with Jeanne of Flanders, whose divorce from her husband he had procured from the pope, and he entered into a league with Thibaut of Champagne and the Count of La Marche, who were all suspected of entertaining secret relations with the enemy. Thibaut even left the army without leave, after forty days of service, returned home and commenced strengthening his castles. The crusade, so brilliantly begun, was on the point of abandoning its first serious enterprise, when the Avignonese, reduced to the utmost straits, unexpectedly offered to capitulate.{200} Considering the customs of the age, the terms were not hard. They agreed to satisfy the king and Church, they paid a considerable ransom, their walls were thrown down and three hundred fortified houses in the town were dismantled, and they received as bishop, at the hands of the legate, Nicholas de Corbie, who instituted laws for the suppression of heresy. It was fortunate for Louis that the submission came when it did, for a few days later there occurred an inundation of the Durance which would have drowned his camp.[177]

From Avignon Louis marched westward, everywhere receiving the submission of nobles and cities until within a few leagues of Toulouse. The reduction of that obstinate focus of heresy was apparently all that remained to complete the ruin of Raymond and the success of the crusade, when Louis suddenly turned his face homeward. No explanation of this unlooked-for termination of the campaign is furnished by any of the chroniclers, but it is probably to be sought in the sickness which pursued the Crusaders, and possibly in the commencement of the disease which terminated the march and the life of the king at Montpensier on November 8—fulfilling the prophecy of Merlin, "In ventris monte morietur leo pacificus"—and not without suspicion of poisoning by Thibaut of Champagne. Throughout Europe, however, the retreat was regarded as the result of serious military reverses. Louis had designed to return the following year, and had left garrisons in the places which had submitted to him, with Humbert de Beaujeu, a renowned captain, in supreme command, and Gui de Montfort under him, but their feats of arms were few, though the burning of heretics was not neglected, when occasion offered, if only to maintain the sacred character of the war.[178]

Saved as by a miracle from the ruin which had seemed inevitable, Raymond lost no time in recovering a portion of his dominions. The death of Louis had worked a complete revolution in the situation,{201} and, for a time at least, he had little to fear. It is true that Louis IX., a child of thirteen, was crowned without delay at Reims, and the regency was confided to his mother, Blanche of Castile, but the great barons were restive, and the conspiracy, hatched before the walls of Avignon, was yet in existence. Britanny, Champagne, and La Marche ostentatiously kept away from the coronation, delayed offering their homage, and intrigued with England. Early in 1227, however, they quarrelled, when a show of force and favorable terms brought them in one by one; short truces were made with Henry III. and the Viscount of Thouars, and a temporary respite was obtained. Gregory IX., who mounted the papal throne March 19, 1227, took the regent and the boy-king under the papal protection, on the ground of their being engaged in war against heresy; but the succors which they sent from time to time to de Beaujeu were probably only enough to give color to a continuance of the ecclesiastical tithe, which the four great provinces of Reims, Rouen, Sens, and Tours resisted till the legate authorized the regent to seize church property and compel the payment. Raymond thus was enabled to continue the struggle with varying fortune. The Council of Narbonne, held during Lent, 1227, in excommunicating those who had proved faithless to the oaths given to Louis shows that the people had returned to their ancient allegiance where they safely could; and in commanding a strict perquisition of heretics by the bishops and their punishment by the secular authorities, it indicates that even in territories held by the French the duties of persecution were slackly performed.[179]

The war dragged on through 1227 with varying result. De Beaujeu, assisted by Pierre Amiel of Narbonne and Foulques of Toulouse, captured, after a desperate siege, the castle of Bécède, when the garrison was slaughtered and the heretic deacon Géraud de Motte and his comrades were burned, the castellan, Pagan de{202} Bécède, becoming a "faidit" and a leader among the proscribed heretics, to be burned at last in 1233. Raymond recovered Castel-Sarrasin, but could not prevent the Crusaders from devastating the land up to the walls of Toulouse. The following year found both parties inclined for peace. We have seen that Raymond was eager to make sacrifices for it, even before the last crusade had stripped him of most of his possessions. The regent Blanche had ample motives to come to terms. With all her firmness and capacity the task before her was no easy one. The nobles of Aquitaine were corresponding with Henry III. who always cherished the hope of reconquering the ample territories wrenched from the English crown by Philip Augustus. The great barons, despising the rule of a woman, were quarrelling between themselves and involving a large portion of the kingdom in war. The hope of completing the conquest of the South could scarce repay the constant drain on the royal resources, while chronic warfare there was highly dangerous in the explosive condition of the realm. The difficulty of collecting the tithe from the recalcitrant churches was increasing, and it could not be continued permanently. Every motive of policy would therefore incline Queen Blanche to listen to the humble prayers for reconciliation which Raymond and his father had never ceased to utter, and a way of securing for the royal line the rich inheritance of the house of Toulouse seemed to offer itself in the fact that Raymond had but one child,

Jeanne, still unmarried. A union between her and one of the younger brothers of St. Louis, with a reversion of the territories to them and to their heirs, would attain peaceably all the political advantages of the crusade, while, as to its religious objects, Raymond had left no doubts of his willingness to secure them.

Gregory IX. was quite content thus to close the war which Innocent had commenced twenty years before. Already, in March, 1228, he wrote to Louis IX., urging him to make peace according to the judgment of the legate, Cardinal Romano, who had full powers in the premises, and it was in the name of the legate that the first overtures were made to Raymond through the Abbot of Grandselve. That the marriage was the pivot upon which from the beginning the negotiations turned is shown by another letter of June 25, authorizing Romano to dispense with the impediment of consanguinity if the union between Jeanne and one of{203} the king's brothers would lead to peace. Another epistle of October 21, announcing to all the prelates of France that he had renewed the indulgences for a crusade against the Albigenses, would seem to show that the terms offered to Raymond were hard of acceptance, and that renewed pressure on him was necessary. This was enforced by extensive devastations in his territories, and in December, 1228, he gave the abbot full power to assent to whatever might be agreed upon by Thibaut of Champagne, who acted as mediator for him. A conference was held at Meaux, where we find the consuls of Toulouse also represented, and preliminaries were signed in January, 1229. Finally, on Holy Thursday, April 12, 1229, the long war came to an end. Before the portal of Nôtre Dame de Paris Raymond humbly approached the legate and begged for reconciliation to the Church; barefooted and in his shirt he was conducted to the altar as a penitent, received absolution in the presence of the dignitaries of Church and State, and his followers were relieved from excommunication. After this he constituted himself a prisoner in the Louvre until his daughter and five of his castles should be in the hands of the king, and five hundred toises of the walls of Toulouse should be demolished.[180]

The terms to which he had agreed were hard and humiliating. In the royal proclamation of the treaty, he is represented as acting at the command of the legate, and humbly praying Church and king for mercy and not for justice. He swore to persecute heresy with his whole strength, including heretics and believers, their protectors and receivers, and not sparing his nearest kindred, friends, and vassals. On all these speedy punishment was to be inflicted, and an inquisition for their detection was to be instituted in such form as the legate might dictate, while in its aid Raymond agreed to offer the large reward of two marks per head for every manifest ("perfected") heretic captured during two years, and one mark forever thereafter. As for other heretics, believers, receivers, and defenders, he agreed to do whatever the legate or pope should command. His *baillis*, or local officers,{204} moreover, were to be good Catholics, free of all suspicion. He was to defend the Church and all its members and privileges; to enforce its censures by seizing the property of all who should remain for a year under excommunication; to restore all church lands and lands of ecclesiastics occupied since the commencement of the troubles, and to pay as damages for personal property taken the sum of ten thousand silver marks; to enforce for the future the payment of tithes, and, as a special fine, to pay five thousand marks to five religious houses named, besides six thousand marks to be expended in fortifying certain strongholds to be held by the king as security for the Church, and between three thousand and four thousand marks to support for ten years at Toulouse two masters in theology, two decretalists, and six masters in grammar and the liberal arts. Moreover, as penance, he agreed to assume the cross immediately on receiving absolution, and to proceed within two years to Palestine, to serve there for five years—a penance which he never performed, though repeatedly summoned to do so, until in 1247 he made preparations for a departure which was arrested by death. An oath was further to be administered to his people, renewable every five years, binding them to make active war upon all heretics, their believers, receivers, and fautors, and to help the Church and king in subduing heresy.

The interests of the Church and of religion being thus provided for, the marriage of Jeanne with one of the king's brothers was treated as a favor bestowed on Raymond. It was tacitly assumed that all his dominions had been forfeited, and the king graciously granted him all the lands comprised within the ancient bishopric of Toulouse, subject to their reversion after his death to his daughter and her husband, in such wise that whether there was issue of the marriage or not, or whether she survived her husband or not, they passed irrevocably to the royal family. Agen, Rouergue, Quercy, except Cahors, and part of Albi were likewise granted to Raymond, with reversion to his daughter in default of lawful heirs; but the king retained the extensive territories comprised within the duchy of Narbonne and the counties of Velay, Gévaudan, Viviers, and Lodève. The marquisate of Provence, beyond the Rhone, a dependency of the empire, was given to the Church. Raymond thus lost two thirds of his vast dominions.{205} In addition to this he was obliged to destroy the fortifications of Toulouse and of thirty other strongholds, and was prohibited from strengthening any in their stead; he was to deliver to the king eight other specified places for ten years, and to pay fifteen hundred marks per annum for five years for their maintenance; and he was to take active measures to reduce to subjection any recalcitrant vassals, especially the Count of Foix, who, being thus abandoned, came in the same year and made a humiliating peace. A general amnesty was proclaimed, and the "faidits," or ejected knights and gentlemen, were restored, excluding, of course, all who were heretics. Raymond, moreover, engaged to maintain peace throughout the land, and the *routiers*, or bandit mercenaries, who for fifty years had been the special objects of animadversion by the Church, were to be expelled forever. To all these conditions his vassals and people were to be sworn, obligating themselves to assist him in the performance; and if, after forty days' notice, he continued derelict on any point, all the lands granted him reverted to the king, his subjects' allegiance was transferred, and he fell back into his present condition of an excommunicate.[181]

The king's assumed right to the territories thus disposed of arose partly from the conquests of his father, and partly from Amauri, who a few days later executed a third cession of all his claims without reserve or consideration, other than what the king in his bounty might see fit to grant. The reward he obtained was the reversion of the dignity of Constable of France, which fell in the next year on the death of Matthieu de Montmorency. In 1237 he foolishly revived his claims, again styled himself Duke of Narbonne, made an unsuccessful effort to seize Dauphiné in right of his wife, and invaded the county of Melgueil, thereby incurring the wrath of Gregory IX., who ordered him as a penance to join the crusade then preparing to start for the Holy Land. In effect he did so, and Gregory generously granted him, to be paid after he was beyond seas, the large sum of three thousand marks out of the fund arising from the redemption of their vows by Crusaders staying at home—by this time a customary mode of selling{206}indulgences, and one exceedingly lucrative, for this payment was assigned simply on the province of Sens and the lands of Amauri himself. In 1238 he sailed, and his customary ill-luck pursued him, for in 1241 we hear of him as a prisoner of the Saracens, and Gregory again came to his aid by contributing to his ransom four thousand marks from the same redemption fund. His death occurred the same year at Otranto, on his return from Palestine, thus closing a life of strange vicissitudes and almost uninterrupted misfortune.[182]

The house of Toulouse was thus reduced from the position of the most powerful feudatory, with possessions greater than those of the crown, to a condition in which it was to be no longer dreaded, though Gregory IX. and Frederic II., in 1234, at the reiterated request of Louis IX., restored to it the Marquisate of Provence, probably as a reward for increased zeal in persecution. Raymond no longer, as Duke of Narbonne, held the first rank among the six lay peers of France, but was relegated to the fourth place. The treaty resulted as its framers intended. In 1229 Jeanne of Toulouse and her destined husband Alphonse, brother of Louis, were children in their ninth year. Their marriage was deferred until 1237, and when Raymond, in 1249, closed his unquiet career, they succeeded to his territories. They both died without issue in 1271, when Philip III. took possession, not only of the county of Toulouse, as provided for in the settlement, but also of the other possessions which Jeanne had vainly attempted to dispose of by will, thus rendering the crown supreme throughout southern France, and preparing it for the rude shocks of the wars with Edward III. and Henry V. It is fairly questionable, indeed, whether, during those convulsions, the house of Toulouse might not have become independently royal, governing a well-defined territory of homogeneous population, had not the religious enthusiasm excited by heresy enabled the Capets, with{207} the assistance of the papacy, to destroy it in the thirteenth century.

That a monarchy so distracted and weakened as that of France during the minority of Louis IX. could demand and exact terms so humiliating as those which Raymond was glad to accept, shows the helpless isolation to which the religious question had reduced him, despite the fidelity of his subjects and the repeated failure of the assaults upon him. Those assaults he had met with the courage of a gallant knight and the resources of a skilful leader, but his neglect to persecute heresy deprived him of sympathy and of allies, and the anathema of the Church hung over him as an ever-present curse. To the public law of the period he was an outlaw, without even the right of self-defence against the first-comer, for his very self-defence was rated among his crimes; in the popular faith of the age he was an accursed thing, without hope, here or hereafter. The only way of readmission into human fellowship, the only hope of salvation, lay in reconciliation with the Church through the removal of the awful ban which had formed part of his inheritance. To obtain this he had repeatedly offered to sacrifice his honor and his subjects, and the offer had been contemptuously spurned. Now that the necessities of the royal court had rendered the regent and her counsellors unwilling to risk the drain and the dangers of prolonged war, he was too eager to escape from his cruel position to hesitate long in accepting the hard conditions which were exacted of him, although, as Bernard Gui says, the single provision which assured the reversion of Toulouse to the royal house would have been sufficiently hard if the king had captured Count Raymond on a stricken field.[183]

There was much that he could allege in justification, had he imagined that justification was needed. Born in 1197, he was yet a child when the storm had broken over his father's head. Ever since he could observe and reason he had seen his land the prey of the ruthless chivalry of the North, at the head of vagabond hordes, as eager for spoil as for the redemption of their sins. As soon as one host had melted away it had been succeeded by another, and for twenty years the wretched people who clung to him had known no peace. He and they had barely escaped as by{208} a miracle from destruction in the last crusade, and there was no prospect of better days in the future, so long as Rome's implacable enmity to heresy, acting upon the ambition of the restless Franks, could always call forth fresh swarms of marauders and dignify them with the Cross. Though he could not be a fervent disciple of a Church which had been to him so stern a stepmother, he was yet no Catharan; and while perfectly ready to tolerate the heresy of a large portion of his subjects, he might well ask himself whether their toleration was to be purchased at the cost of the whole population, who could never look for peace so long as heresy was endured among them. The choice lay between sacrificing one side or both sides; and what well might seem the lesser evil coincided with his own selfish instincts of self-preservation. He never hesitated as to the choice; and, after he had accomplished his object, he faithfully adhered to his promise of uprooting heresy, though more than once he interfered when the excessive rigor of the Inquisition threatened trouble. Perhaps the task at first was a distasteful one, but he had no alternative. He was but a man of his time; had he been more he might have played a martyr's part without better securing the happiness of his people.

The battle of toleration against persecution had been fought and lost; nor, with such a warning as the fate of the two Raymonds, was there risk that other potentates would disregard the public opinion of Christendom by ill-advised mercy to the heretic. Calling upon the state for its assured support, the Church made haste to reap the fruits of victory, and the Inquisition was soon at work among those who had so long bidden her defiance. That this was unanimously regarded by Europe as necessary and righteous, in spite of the vices and corruption of the ecclesiastical body, is so strange a development of the religion of Christ as to render the process of its evolution an indispensable subject for our consideration. {209}

CHAPTER V.

PERSECUTION.

THE Church had not always been an organization which considered its highest duty to be the forcible suppression of dissidence at any cost. In the simplicity of apostolic times its members were held together by the bond of love, and the spirit with which discipline was enforced is expressed in St. Paul's precept to the Galatians (VI. 1, 2)—

"Brethren, if a man be overtaken in a fault, ye which are spiritual, restore such an one in the spirit of meekness; considering thyself, lest thou also be tempted.

"Bear ye one another's burdens, and so fulfil the law of Christ."

Christ had commanded his disciples to forgive their brethren seventy times seven, and as yet his teachings had been too recent to be buried beneath a mass of observances and doctrines in which the letter which kills overpowered the spirit which saves. The great primal principles of Christianity were enough for the fervor of the faithful. Dogmatic theology, with its endless complexities and metaphysical subtleties, as yet was not. Even its vocabulary had still to be created and its innumerable points of faith to be evolved out of the chance expressions of writers on other topics, and by the literal interpretation of the imagery of poetical diction.

It is an inexpressible relief to turn from the heated wranglings over questions scarce appreciable by the average human intellect to St. Paul's reproof to the Ephesians for giving heed to fables and endless genealogies, and questions which had in them little of godly edification, for "the end of the commandment is charity out of a pure heart, and of a good conscience, and of faith unfeigned" (I. Tim. I. 4, 5). Those who indulged in these vain janglings he denounces as men "desiring to be teachers of the law, understanding neither what they say nor whereof they affirm" (Ib.{210} 7), and he commands his chosen disciple, "But foolish and unlearned questions avoid, knowing that they engender strife" (II. Tim. II. 23). The Ebionitic section of the Church agreed with the Pauline branch in this simplicity of teaching—"Pure religion and undefiled before God and the Father is this, To visit the fatherless and widows in their affliction, and to keep himself unspotted from the world" (James, I. 27).

Yet already was the seed scattered which was to bear so abounding a harvest of wrong and misery. St. Paul will listen to no deviation from the strictness of his teachings—"But though we, or an angel from heaven, preach any other gospel unto you than that which we have preached, let him be accursed" (Galat. I. 8); and he boasts of delivering unto Satan Hymenæus and Alexander "that they may learn not to blaspheme" (I. Tim. I. 20). How this spirit increased as time wore on may be seen in the apocalyptic threats with which the backsliders and heretics of the seven churches are assailed (Rev. II., III.). The process went on with accelerating rapidity. Theology could not form itself without starting a cloud of questions unsettled by the gospel: earnest disputants arose who, in the heat of controversy, magnified the points at issue till they assumed an importance rendering them the vital tests of Christianity, and men believed with the most fervid conviction that their adversaries were not Christians because they differed on some unimportant fragment of ritual or discipline, or on some infinitesimal dogma which only the mind trained in the dialectics of the schools could comprehend. When Quintilla taught that water was not necessary in baptism, Tertullian shrieks to her that there is nothing in common between them, not even the same God or the same Christ. The Donatist heresy with its deplorable results arose on the question of the eligibility of an individual bishop. When Eutyches, in his zeal against the doctrines of Nestorius, was led to confuse in some degree the double nature of Christ, thinking that he was only defending the dogmas of his friend St. Cyril, he suddenly found himself convicted of a heresy as damnable as Nestorianism; while his defence against the practised rhetoric of Eusebius of Dorylæum shows that he was not able to grasp the subtle distinction between *substantia* and *subsistentia*—a fatal failing which proved the ruin of thousands. Thus, during the first six centuries, as men explored the infinite problems of{211} existence here and hereafter, new questions constantly arose and were disputed with merciless vehemence. Those who held commanding positions in the Church and could enforce their opinions were necessarily orthodox; those who were weaker became heterodox, and the distinction between the faithful and the heretic became year by year more marked.[184]

Nor was it merely the *odium theologicum* that raised these passions; not only pride of opinion and zeal for the purity of faith. Wealth and power have charms even for bishop and priest, and in the Church, as it grew

70

through the centuries, wealth and power depended upon the obedience of the flock. A hardy disputant who questioned the dogmatic accuracy of his ecclesiastical superior was a mutineer of the worst kind; and if he succeeded in attracting followers they became the nucleus of a rebellion which threatened revolution, and every motive, good or evil, prompted the suppression of such sedition at all hazards and by every available means. If the sectaries became sufficiently numerous to form a community of their own, cutting them off from the communion of the Church was of no avail; the keenest shafts of ecclesiastical censure rebounded harmless from their armor of conscientious belief. This naturally led to an animosity against them greater than that visited on the worst of criminals. No matter how trivial may have been the original cause of schism, nor how pure and fervent might be the faith of the schismatics, the fact that they had refused to bend to authority, and had thus sought to divide the seamless garment of Christ, became an offence in comparison with which all other sins dwindled into insignificance, neutralizing all the virtues and all the devotion which men could possess. Even Augustin could see nothing to soften his heart in the enthusiastic ardor with which the Donatists endured, and even courted, martyrdom. Had they carried Christ in their hearts their self-abnegation might have merited praise, but as it was they acted only under the promptings of Satan, like the swine who were driven into the sea by the unclean spirit. Martyrdom, even for Christ's sake, could not save heretic or schismatic from sharing eternal fire with Satan and his angels.[185]{212}

Yet the spirit of persecution was too repugnant to the spirit of Christ for its triumph to come without a struggle, which can be traced in the writings of the early fathers. Tertullian warmly defends the freedom of conscience; it is irreligious to enforce religion; no one wishes to be venerated unwillingly, so that God may be assumed to desire only the worship which comes from the heart. Still, when the combative energy of the man was aroused in disputation with the Gnostics, it was not difficult for him to find in Deuteronomy and Numbers ample warrant for the maxim that obstinacy is to be conquered, not persuaded. Cyprian says that it is for us to endeavor to become wheat, leaving the tares to God, and he qualifies as sacrilegious presumption the spirit which assumes the function of God in seeking to separate and destroy the tares; yet Cyprian had no hesitation in cutting off from the Church all who differed from him, and consigning them to perdition, which was the only form of persecution at that time within reach. It was, indeed, natural that a persecuted Church should plead for toleration, and the fact that, even in this early period, there should be these flashes of intolerance gives ample warning of what was to come with the power of enforcing dogma on the recalcitrant. Lactantius was the last of the fathers of the persecuted Church, and he could feelingly argue that belief is not to be enjoined by force, that slaughter and piety are in no sense connected, and he boasts that none are coerced into remaining in the Church, for he who lacks piety is useless to God.[186]

The triumph of intolerance was inevitable when Christianity became the religion of the State, yet the slowness of its progress shows the difficulty of overcoming the incongruity between persecution and the gospel. Hardly had orthodoxy been defined by the Council of Nicæa when Constantine brought the power of the State to bear to enforce uniformity. All heretic and schismatic priests were deprived of the privileges and immunities bestowed on the clergy and were subjected to the burdens of the State; their meeting-places were confiscated for the benefit of the Church, and their assemblies, whether public or private, were prohibited.{213} There is an instructive illustration of theological perversity in the watchful energy with which these provisions were enforced to the suppression of heresy while yet the pagan temples and ceremonies remained undisturbed. Yet while the churchmen might feel it to be a duty thus to obstruct the development and dissemination of teachings which they regarded as destructive to religion, they still shrank from pushing intolerance to extremity and enforcing uniformity with blood, although the Emperor Julian declared that he had found no wild beasts so cruel to men as most of the Christians were to each other. Constantine, it is true, commanded the surrender of all copies of the writings of Arius under penalty of death, but it does not appear that any executions actually took place in consequence; and at last, tired of the endless strife, he ordered Athanasius to admit all Christians to the churches without distinction. No effort of the sovereign, however, could soothe the bitterness of doctrinal strife, which grew fiercer and fiercer. In 370 Valens is said to have put to death eighty orthodox ecclesiastics who had complained to him of the violence of the Arians, but this was not a judicial execution, but in pursuance of a secret order to the Prefect Modestus, who decoyed them on board of a vessel and caused it to be burned at sea.[187]

It was in 385 that the first instance was given of judicial capital punishment for heresy, and the horror which it excited shows that it was regarded everywhere as a hideous innovation. The Gnostic and Manichæan speculations of Priscillian were looked upon with the peculiar detestation which that group of heresies ever called forth; but when he was tried by the tyrant Maximus, at Trèves, with the use of torture, and was put to death with six of his disciples, while others were banished to a barbarous island beyond Britain, there was a most righteous burst of indignation. Of the two prosecuting bishops, Ithacius and Idacius, one was expelled from the episcopate and the other resigned. The saintly Martin of Tours, who had done all in his power to prevent the atrocity, refused to join in communion with them, or with any who communed with them. If he finally yielded, in order to save the lives of some men for whom he had come to Maximus to beg{214} mercy, and also to prevent the tyrant from persecuting the Priscillianists of Spain (where, like the subsequent Cathari, they were detected by their pallor), yet, in spite of the consoling visit of an angel, he was overcome with grief at what he had done, and he found that he had lost for some time the power to expel devils and heal the sick.[188]

If the Church thus still shrank from shedding blood, it had by this time reached the point of using all other means without scruple to enforce conformity. Early in the fifth century we find Chrysostom teaching that heresy must be suppressed, heretics silenced and prevented from ensnaring others, and their conventicles broken up, but that the death-penalty is unlawful. About the same time St. Augustin entreats the Prefect of Africa not to put any Donatists to death because, if he does so, no ecclesiastic can make complaint of them, for they will prefer to suffer death themselves rather than be the cause of it to others. Yet Augustin approved of the imperial laws which banished and fined them and deprived them of their churches and of testamentary power, and he consoled them by telling them that God did not wish them to perish in antagonism to Catholic unity. To constrain any one from evil to good, he argued, was not oppression, but charity; and when the unlucky schismatics urged that no one ought to be coerced in his faith, he freely admitted it as a general principle, but added that sin and infidelity must be punished.[189]

Step by step the inevitable progress was made, and men easily found specious arguments to justify the indulgence of their passions. The fiery Jerome, when his wrath was excited by Vigilantius forbidding the adoration of relics, expressed his wonder that the bishop of the hardy heretic had not destroyed him in the flesh for the benefit of his soul, and argued that piety and zeal for God{215} could not be cruelty; rigor, in fact, he argues in another place, is the most genuine mercy, since temporal punishment may avert eternal perdition. It was only sixty-two years after the slaughter of Priscillian and his followers had excited so much horror, that Leo. I., when the heresy seemed to be reviving, in 447, not only justified the act, but declared that if the followers of heresy so damnable were allowed to live there would be an end of human and divine law. The final step had been taken, and the Church was definitely pledged to the suppression of heresy at whatever cost. It is impossible not to attribute to ecclesiastical influence the successive edicts by which, from the time of Theodosius the Great, persistence in heresy was punished with death.[190]

A powerful impulse to this development is to be found in the responsibility which grew upon the Church from its connection with the State. When it could influence the monarch and procure from him edicts condemning heretics to exile, deportation, to the mines, and even to death, it felt that God had put into its hands powers to be exercised and not to be neglected. At the same time, with natural human inconsistency, it could argue that it was not responsible for the execution of the laws, and that its own hands were unstained with blood. Even Ithacius, in the case of Priscillian, had shrunk from the function of prosecutor and had put forward a layman in his place. Similar devices, as we shall see, were practised by the Inquisition, and in either case they were transparently false. In the vast body of imperial edicts inflicting upon heretics every variety of disability and punishment, the most ardent churchmen might find conviction that the State recognized the preservation of the purity of the faith as its first duty. Yet whenever the State or any of its officials lagged in the enforcement of these laws, the churchman was at hand to goad them on. Thus the African Church repeatedly asked the intervention of the secular power to suppress the Donatists; Leo the Great insisted with the Empress Pulcheria that the destruction of the Eutychians should be her highest care; and Pelagius I., in{216} urging Narses to suppress heresy by force, sought to quiet the scruples of the soldier by assuring him that to prevent or to punish evil was not persecution, but love. It became the general doctrine of the Church, as expressed by St. Isidor of Seville, that princes are bound not only to be orthodox themselves, but to preserve the purity of the faith by the fullest exercise of their power against heretics. How abundantly these assiduous teachings bore their bitter fruit is shown in the deplorable history of the Church during those centuries, consisting as it does of heresy after heresy relentlessly exterminated, until the Council of Constantinople, under the Patriarch Michael Oxista, introduced the penalty of burning alive as the punishment of the Bogomili. Nor were the heretics always behindhand, when they gained opportunity, in improving the lesson which had been taught them so effectually. The persecution of the Catholics by the Arian Vandals in Africa under Genseric was quite worthy of orthodoxy; and when Hunneric succeeded his father, and his proposition to the Emperor Zeno of mutual toleration was refused, his barbarous zeal was inflamed to pitiless wrath. Under King Euric the Wisigoth, also, there was a spasmodic persecution in Aquitaine. Yet, as a rule, the Arian Goths and Burgundians set an example of toleration worthy of imitation, and their conversion to Catholicism was attended with but little cruelty on either side, except a passing ebullition in Spain at the crisis under Leuvigild, about 585, followed by disturbances which were rather political than religious. Later Catholic monarchs, however, enacted laws punishing with exile and confiscation any deviations from orthodoxy, which are notable as the only examples of the kind under the Barbarians. The Catholic Merovingians in France seem never to have troubled their Arian subjects, who were numerous in Burgundy and Aquitaine. The conversion of these latter was gradual and apparently peaceful.[191]{217}

The Latin Church through all this had taken little part in actual persecution, for the Western mind lacked the perverse ingenuity of the East in originating and adopting heresy. With the downfall of the Western Empire it commenced the great task which absorbed its energies and by which it earned the thanks of all succeeding generations—the conversion and civilization of the Barbarians. Its new converts were not likely to indulge in abstruse speculations; they accepted the faith which was taught them, acquiesced for the most part in the established discipline, and while oft unruly and turbulent, gave little trouble on the score of orthodoxy. Under these influences the persecuting spirit died out. Claudius of Turin, whose iconoclastic zeal destroyed all the images in his diocese, escaped without punishment. Felix of Urgel was forgiven his Adoptianism, and was welcomed back into the Church in spite of his repeated tergiversations, and though not restored to his see, his residence for fifteen or twenty years at Lyons does not seem to have been an imprisonment, for he secretly maintained his doctrines, and an heretical declaration was found among his papers after his death. No force is alluded to when Archbishop Leidrad converted twenty thousand of the Catalan followers of Felix, whose principal disciple, Elipandus, Archbishop of Toledo, retained his primatial seat although there is no evidence that he ever recanted his errors. In the case of the monk Gottschalc, who disseminated his predestinarian heresy in extensive wanderings throughout Italy, Dalmatia, Austria, and Bavaria, apparently without opposition, Rabanus of Mainz finally summoned a council which condemned his doctrine in the presence of Louis le Germanique. Yet it did not venture to punish him, but sent him to his prelate, Hincmar of Reims, who, with the authority of Charles le Chauve, declared him an incorrigible heretic in the Council of Chiersy in 849. So little disposition was there to inflict penalties for heresy, though his theories struck at the root of the mediatory power of the Church, that the scourging ordered for him was carefully stated to be merely the discipline provided by the Council of Agde for the infraction of the Benedictine rule prohibiting monks from travelling without commendatory letters from their bishops; and if he was imprisoned, we are told that this was simply to prevent him from continuing to contaminate others. The Carlovingian{218} legislation was exceedingly moderate as to heretics, merely classing them with Pagans, Jews, and infamous persons, and subjecting them to certain disabilities.[192]

The stupor of the tenth century was too profound for heresy, which presupposes a certain amount of healthy mental activity. The Church, ruling unquestioned over the slumbering consciences of men, laid aside the rusted weapons of persecution and forgot their use. When, about 1018, Bishop Burchard compiled his collection of canon law he made no reference to heretical opinions or their punishment save a couple of regulations exhumed from the forgotten Council of Elvira in 305, respecting the treatment of apostates to idolatry. Even the introduction of the doctrine of transubstantiation was received submissively until, two centuries after Gottschalc, Berenger of Tours called it in question; but he had not in him the stuff of martyrdom, and yielded to moderate pressure. The warmer faith of the Cathari, who commenced to disturb the stagnation of orthodoxy in the eleventh century, called for energetic measures, but even with those abhorred sectaries the Church was wonderfully slow to resort to extremities. It hesitated before the unaccustomed task; it shrank from contradicting its teachings of charity and was driven forward by popular fanaticism. The persecution of Orleans in 1017 was the work of King Robert the Pious; the burning at Milan soon after was done by the people against the will of the archbishop. So unfamiliar was the Church with its duty that when, about 1045, some Manichæans were discovered at Chalons, Bishop Roger applied to Bishop Wazo of Liége for advice as to what he should do with them, and whether he should hand them over to the secular arm for punishment; to which the good Wazo replied, urging that their lives should not be forfeited{219} to the secular sword, as God, their Creator and Redeemer, showed them patience and mercy; and Canon Anselm, Wazo's biographer, strongly condemns the executions under Henry III., at Goslar, in 1052, saying that if our Wazo had been there he would have acted as did St. Martin in the case of Priscillian. The same lenity was manifested by St. Anno of Cologne about 1060, when some of his flock refused, after repeated commands, to abandon the use of milk, eggs, and cheese during Lent, and the archbishop at length allowed them to have their own way, saying that those who were firm in the faith could not be much harmed by a difference in food. Even as late as 1144 the Church of Liége congratulated itself on having, by the mercy of God, saved the greater part of a number of confessed and convicted Cathari from the turbulent mob which strove to burn them. Those who were thus preserved were distributed among the religious houses while awaiting the response of Lucius II., to whom application was made for advice as to what should be done with them.[193]

It is not worth while to repeat in detail the cases related in a former chapter which show how uncertain was the position of the Church towards heresy at this period. There was no definite policy, no fixed rule, and heretics continued to be treated with rigor or with mercy according to the temper of the prelate concerned. Theodwin, Wazo's successor in the see of Liége, writes in 1050 to King Henry I. of France, urging him to punish the followers of Berenger of Tours without even giving them a hearing. This uncertainty is well reflected by St. Bernard in his remarks on the occurrence at Cologne in 1145, when the zealous populace seized the Cathari and burned them despite the resistance of the ecclesiastical authorities. He argues that heretics should be won over by reason rather than by coercion, and if they will not be converted they are to be avoided; he approves the zeal of the people, but not of their action, for faith is to be spread by persuasion and not by force; yet he assumes the duty of the secular power to avenge the wrong done to God by heresy, and, blind to the danger of man's assuming himself to be the minister of the wrath of God, he quotes St. Paul, "For he beareth not the sword{220} in vain; for he is the minister of God, and revenger to execute wrath upon him that doeth evil" (Rom. XIII. 4). Alexander III. leaned decidedly to the side of mercy when, in 1162, he refused to pass judgment on the Cathari sent to him by the Archbishop of Reims, saying that it was better to pardon the guilty than to take the lives of the innocent. Even at the close of the century Peter Cantor dared to argue that the apostle ordered the heretic to be avoided, not slain, and he dwelt upon the inconsistency of the severity shown to the slightest deviation from faith, while the grossest sins and immoralities were allowed to go unpunished.[194]

73

This hesitation and uncertainty extended to the punishment appropriate to heresy. We have seen numerous cases of burning alive interspersed with sentences of imprisonment, and it was long before a definite formula was reached. Even when Alexander III., at the Council of Tours, in 1163, sought to check the alarming progress of Manichæism in Languedoc, he only commanded the secular princes to imprison the heretics and confiscate their property; though in the same year the Cathari detected in Cologne were sentenced to be burned by judges appointed for the purpose. In 1157 the punishment inflicted by the Council of Reims was branding in the face; and the same expedient was resorted to by that of Oxford in 1166. Even as late as 1199, the first measures of Innocent III. against the Albigenses only threaten exile and confiscation; there is no allusion to any duty on the part of the secular power beyond enforcing these penalties, and their enforcement is rewarded by the same indulgences as those to be gained by pilgrimage to Rome or to Compostella. As the struggle increased in bitterness, we have seen how stronger measures were adopted; yet even Simon de Montfort, in the code promulgated at Pamiers, December 1, 1212, while stimulating persecution to the utmost, and rendering it the duty of every man, does not formally adjudge the heretic to the stake, although in this very year eighty heretics were burned in Strassburg. This form of punishment had been enacted for the first time in positive law, as already stated, by Pedro II. of Aragon, in his edict of 1197, but the example was not speedily followed. Otho IV., in his constitution{221} of 1210, simply places heretics under the imperial ban, orders their property confiscated and their houses torn down. Frederic II., in his famous statute of November 22, 1220, which made the persecution of heresy a part of the public law of Europe, only threatened confiscation and outlawry, although this, it must be added, placed their lives at the mercy of the first comer. In his constitution of March, 1224, he went farther and decreed death by fire or loss of the tongue, at the discretion of the judge; and the contemporary practice in Germany left the penalty to be similarly decided. It was not until 1231, in the Sicilian Constitutions, that Frederic rendered the punishment by cremation absolute. This was in force merely in his Neapolitan dominions, and the edict of Ravenna, in March, 1232, while inflicting the death penalty does not prescribe the method; but that of Cremona, in May, 1238, embodied the Sicilian law and thus rendered the fagot and stake the recognized punishment for heresy throughout the empire, as we find it subsequently embodied in both the Sachsenspiegel and the Schwabenspiegel, or municipal laws of northern and southern Germany. In Venice, after 1249, the ducal oath of office contained a pledge to burn all heretics. In 1255 Alonso the Wise of Castile decreed the stake for all Christians who apostatized to Islam or to Judaism. In France the legislation adopted by both Louis IX. and Raymond of Toulouse, for carrying out the provisions of the settlement of 1229, is discreetly silent with regard to the penalty of heresy, though under it the use of the stake was universal, and it is not until Louis issued his *Établissements*, in 1270, that we find the heretic formally condemned to be burned alive, thus rendering it part of the recognized law of the land, although the terms in which Beaumanoir alludes to it show that it had long been a settled custom. England, which was free from heresy, was even later in adopting it, and it was not until the rise of the Lollards caused fear in both Church and State that the writ "*de hæretico comburendo*" was created by statute in 1401.[195]{222}

The practice of burning the heretic alive was thus not the creature of positive law, but arose generally and spontaneously, and its adoption by the legislator was only the recognition of a popular custom. We have seen numerous instances of this in a former chapter, and even as late as 1219, at Troyes, an insane enthusiast who maintained that he was the Holy Ghost was seized by the people, placed in a wicker crate surrounded by combustibles, and promptly reduced to ashes. The origin of this punishment is not easily traced, unless it is to the pagan legislation of Diocletian, who decreed this penalty for Manichæism. The torturing deaths to which the martyrs were exposed in times of persecution seem to suggest, and in some sort to justify, a similar infliction on heretics; sorcerers were sometimes burned under the imperial jurisprudence, and Gregory the Great mentions a case in which one was thus put to death by the Christian zeal of the people. As heresy was regarded as the greatest of crimes, the desire which was felt alike by laity and clergy to render its punishment as severe and as impressive as possible found in the stake its appropriate instrument. With the system of exegesis then in vogue, it was not difficult to discover an emphatic command to this effect in John, XV. 6. "If a man abide not in me, he is cast forth as a branch and is withered; and men gather them and cast them into the fire and they are burned." The literal interpretation of Scriptural metaphor has{223} been too frequent a source of error for us to wonder at this application of the text. An authoritative commentary on the decree of Lucius III. in 1184, ordering heretics to be delivered to the secular arm for due punishment, quotes the text of John and the imperial jurisprudence, and thence triumphantly concludes that death by fire is the penalty due to heretics, not only by divine but also by human law and by universal custom. Nor was the heretic mercifully strangled in advance; the authorities of the Inquisition assure us that he must be burned alive before the people, nay, even a whole city may be burned if heretics dwell there.[196]

Whatever scruples the Church had, during the eleventh and twelfth centuries, as to its duty towards heresy, it had none as to that of the secular power, though it kept its own hands free from blood. A decent usage from early times forbade any ecclesiastic from being concerned in judgments involving death or mutilation, and even from being present in the torture-chamber where criminals were placed on the rack. This sensitiveness continued, and even was exaggerated in the time of the bloodiest persecution. While thousands were being slaughtered in Languedoc the Council of Lateran, in 1215, revived the ancient canons prohibiting clerks from uttering a judgment of blood or being present at an execution. In 1255 the Council of Bordeaux added to this a prohibition of dictating or writing letters connected with such judgments; and that of Buda, in 1279, in repeating this canon, appended to it a clause forbidding clerks to practise any surgery requiring burning or cutting. The pollution of blood was so seriously felt that a church or cemetery in which blood chanced to be shed could not be used until it had been reconciled, and this was carried so far that priests were forbidden to allow judges to administer justice in churches, because cases involving corporal punishment might be tried before them. Had this shrinking from participation in the infliction of human suffering{224} been genuine, it would have been worthy of all respect; but it was merely a device to avoid responsibility for its own acts. In prosecutions for heresy the ecclesiastical tribunal passed no judgments of blood. It merely found the defendant to be a heretic and "relaxed" him, or relinquished him to the secular authorities with the hypocritical adjuration to be merciful to him, to spare his life and not to spill his blood. What was the real import of this plea for mercy is easily seen from the theory of the Church as to the duty of the temporal power, when inquisitors enforced as a legal rule that the mere belief that persecution for conscience' sake was sinful was in itself a heresy, to be visited with the full penalties of that unpardonable crime.[197]

The early teachings of Leo and Pelagius were revived as soon as heresy became alarming. Early in the twelfth century Honorius of Autun proclaimed that the rebels against God who were obdurate to the voice of the Church must be coerced with the material sword. In the compilations of canon law by Ivo and Gratian the allusions to the treatment of heretics by the Church are singularly few, but there are abundant citations to show the duty of the sovereign to extirpate heresy and to obey the mandates of the Church to that end. Frederic Barbarossa gave the imperial sanction to the theory that the sword had been intrusted to him for the purpose of smiting the enemies of Christ, when he alleged this in 1159 as a reason for persecuting Alexander III. and supporting his antipope, Victor IV. The second Lateran Council, in 1139, orders all potentates to coerce heretics into obedience; the third, in 1179, sanctimoniously says that the Church does not seek blood, but it is helped by the secular laws, for men will seek the salutary remedy to escape bodily punishment. We have seen how inefficacious all this proved; and in despair of voluntary assistance from the temporal princes the Church took a further step by which it assumed for itself the responsibility for the material as well as the spiritual punishment of heretics. The decree of Lucius III. at the so-called Council of Verona, in 1184, commanded that all potentates{225} should take an oath before their bishops to enforce the ecclesiastical and secular laws against heresy fully and efficaciously. Any refusal or neglect was to be punished by excommunication, deprivation of rank, and incapacity to hold other station, while in the case of cities they were to be segregated and debarred from all commerce with other places.[198]

The Church thus undertook to coerce the sovereign to persecution. It would not listen to mercy, it would not hear of expediency. The monarch held his crown by the tenure of extirpating heresy, of seeing that the laws were sharp and were pitilessly enforced. Any hesitation was visited with excommunication, and if this proved inefficacious, his dominions were thrown open to the first hardy adventurer whom the Church would supply with an army for his overthrow. Whether this new feature in the public law of Europe could establish itself was the question at issue in the Albigensian crusades. Raymond's lands were forfeited simply because he would not punish heretics, and those which his son retained were treated as a fresh gift from the crown. The triumph of the new principle was complete, and it never was subsequently questioned.

It was applied from the highest to the lowest, and the Church made every dignitary feel that his station was an office in a universal theocracy wherein all interests were subordinate to the great duty of maintaining the purity of the faith. The hegemony of Europe was vested in the Holy Roman Empire, and its coronation was a strangely solemn religious ceremony in which the emperor was admitted to the lower orders of the priesthood, and was made to anathematize all heresy raising itself against the holy Catholic Church. In handing him the ring, the pope told him that it was a symbol that he was to destroy heresy; and in girding him with the sword, that with it he was to strike down the enemies of the Church. Frederic II. declared that he had received the imperial dignity for the maintenance and propagation of the faith. In the bull of Clement VI. recognizing Charles{226} IV. the first named of the imperial duties enumerated are the extension of the faith and the extirpation of heretics; and the neglect of the Emperor Wenceslas to suppress Wickliffitism was regarded as a satisfactory reason for his deposition. In fact, according to the high churchmen, the only reason of the transfer of the empire from the Greeks to the Germans was that the Church might have an efficient agent. The principles applied to Raymond of Toulouse were embodied in the canon law, and every prince and noble was made to understand that his lands would be exposed to the spoiler if, after due notice, he hesitated in trampling out heresy. Minor officials were subjected to the same discipline. According to the Council of Toulouse in 1229, any bailli not diligent in persecuting heresy forfeited his property and was ineligible to public employment, while by the Council of Narbonne in 1244, any one holding temporal jurisdiction who delayed in exterminating heretics was held guilty of fautorship of heresy, became an accomplice of heretics, and thus was subjected to the penalties of heresy; this was extended to all who should neglect a favorable opportunity of capturing a heretic, or of helping those seeking to capture him. From the emperor to the meanest peasant the duty of persecution was enforced with all the sanctions, spiritual and temporal, which the Church could command. Not only must the ruler enact rigorous laws to punish heretics, but he and his subjects must see them strenuously executed, for any slackness of persecution was, in the canon law, construed as fautorship of heresy, putting a man on his purgation.[199]

These principles were tacitly or explicitly received into the{227} public law of Europe. Frederic II. accepted them in his cruel edicts against heresy, whence they passed into the general compilations of civil and feudal law, and even into bodies of local jurisprudence. Thus we see in the statutes of Verona, in 1228, the Podestà swearing, on taking office, to expel all heretics from the city; and in the Schwabenspiegel, or code in force throughout southern Germany, it is laid down that a ruler who neglects to persecute heresy is to be stripped of all possessions, and if he does not burn those who are delivered to him as heretics by the ecclesiastical courts he is to be punished as a heretic himself. The Church took care that this legislation should not remain a dead letter. Frederic's decrees in all their atrocity were required to be read and taught in the great law-school of Bologna as a fundamental portion of jurisprudence, and were even embodied in the canon law itself. We shall see that they were repeatedly ordered by the popes to be inscribed irrevocably among the laws of all the cities and states which they could control, and the inquisitor was commanded to coerce all officials to their rigid enforcement, by excommunicating those who were negligent in the good work. Even excommunication, which rendered a magistrate incompetent to perform his official functions, did not relieve him from the duty of punishing heretics when called upon by bishop or inquisitor. In view of this earnestness to embody in the statute-books the sharpest laws for the extermination of heretics and to oblige the secular officials to execute those laws, under the alternative of being themselves condemned and punished as heretics, the adjuration for mercy with which the inquisitors handed over their victims to be burned was evidently, as we shall see hereafter, a mere technical formula to avoid the "irregularity" of being concerned in judgments of blood. In process of time the moral responsibility was freely admitted, as when in February, 1418, the Council of Constance decreed that all who should defend Hussitism, or regard Huss or Jerome of Prague as holy men, should be treated as relapsed heretics and be punished with fire—*"puniantur ad ignem."* It is altogether a modern perversion of history to assume, as apologists do, that the request for mercy was sincere, and that the secular magistrate and not the Inquisition was responsible for the death of the heretic. We can imagine the smile of amused surprise with which Gregory IX. or Gregory XI. would have{228} listened to the dialectics with which the Comte Joseph de Maistre proves that it is an error to suppose, and much more to assert, that Catholic priests can in any manner be instrumental in compassing the death of a fellow-creature.[200]

Not only were all Christians thus made to feel that it was their highest duty to aid in the extermination of heretics, but they were taught that they must denounce them to the authorities regardless of all considerations, human or divine. No tie of kindred served as an excuse for concealing heresy. The son must denounce the father, and the husband was guilty if he did not deliver his wife to a frightful death. Every human bond was severed by the guilt of heresy; children were taught to desert their parents, and even the sacrament of matrimony could not unite an orthodox wife to a misbelieving husband. No pledge was to remain unbroken. It was an old rule that faith was not to be kept with heretics—as Innocent III. emphatically phrased it, "according to the canons, faith is not to be kept with him who keeps not faith with God." No oath of secrecy, therefore, was binding in a matter of heresy, for if one is faithful to a heretic he is unfaithful to{229} God. Apostasy from the faith is the greatest of all sins, says Bishop Lucas of Tuy; therefore if any one has bound himself by oath to keep the secret of such inexplicable wickedness, he must reveal the heresy and perform penance for the perjury, with the comfortable assurance that, as charity covereth a multitude of sins, he will be gently dealt with in consideration of his zeal.[201]

Thus the hesitation as to the treatment of heretics which marked the eleventh and twelfth centuries disappeared in the thirteenth, when the Church was involved in mortal struggle with the sectaries. There was no pretence of moderation, and, save in the technical adjuration for mercy, no attempt to evade the responsibility. St. Raymond of Pennaforte, the compiler of the decretals of Gregory IX., who was the highest authority in his generation, lays it down as a principle of ecclesiastical law that the heretic is to be coerced by excommunication and confiscation, and if they fail, by the extreme exercise of the secular power. The man who was doubtful in faith was to be held a heretic, and so also was the schismatic who, while believing all the articles of religion, refused the obedience due to the Roman Church. All alike were to be forced into the Roman fold, and the fate of Korah, Dathan, and Abiram was invoked for the destruction of the obstinate.[202]

St. Thomas Aquinas, whose overshadowing authority superseded all his predecessors, and who brought canon and dogma into a permanent system still in force, lays down the rules with merciless precision. Heretics, he tells us, are not to be tolerated. The tenderness of the Church allows them to have two warnings, after which, if pertinacious, they are to be abandoned to the secular power, to be removed from the world by death. This, he argues, shows the abounding charity of the Church, for it is much more{230} wicked to corrupt the faith on which depends the life of the soul than to debase the coinage which provides merely for temporal life; wherefore, if coiners and other malefactors are justly doomed at once to death, much more may heretics be justly slain as soon as they are convicted. Yet in its mercy the Church will always receive the heretic back into its bosom, no matter how often he may have relapsed, and will kindly give him penance whereby he may win eternal life; but charity to one must not be allowed to work evil to others. Therefore for once the heretic who repents and recants will be received and his life be spared; but if he relapses, though he may be received to penance for his soul's salvation, he will not be released from the death-penalty. This is the definite expression of the policy of the Church, which, as we shall see, became its unalterable rule of practice.[203]

Nor was the Church content to exercise its power over the living only; the dead must feel its chastening hand. It seemed intolerable that one who had successfully concealed his iniquity and had died in communion should be left to lie in consecrated ground and should be remembered in the prayers of the faithful. Not only had he escaped the penalty due to his sins, but his property, which was forfeit to Church and State, had unlawfully descended to his heirs, and must be recovered from them. Ample reason therefore existed for the trial of those who had passed to the judgment-seat of God. It had been a debatable question in the earlier Church whether excommunication, with all its tremendous penalties, here and hereafter, could be directed against departed souls. As early as the time of Cyprian the custom of excommunicating the dead had come into fashion; and about 382 St. John Chrysostom had denounced the frequency of such sentences as an interference attempted with the judgment of God. Leo I., in 432, took the same position, and it was confirmed by Gelasius I. and a council of Rome towards the end of the century. At the fifth general council, however, held in Constantinople in 553, the question came up as to the power of the Church to anathematize Theodoret of Cyrus, Ibas of Edessa, and Theodore of Mopsuestia, who had been dead for a hundred years. Many of the fathers of the council doubted it, when Eutychius, a man well versed in Scripture, pointed out that the{231} pious King Josiah had not only put to death the priests of pagandom, but had dug up the remains of those who were deceased. The argument was irrefragable, and the anathema was pronounced in spite of the protests of Pope Vigilius, who stubbornly refused to be convinced. The ingenuity of Eutychius, till then an obscure man, was rewarded with the patriarchate of Constantinople, and Vigilius was compelled, by means not the most gentle, to subscribe to the anathema. In 618 the Council of Seville denied the power of condemning the dead; but in 680 the sixth general council, held at Constantinople, exercised the largest liberty in anathematizing all whom it regarded as heretical, both living and dead. In 897 Stephen VII. accordingly held himself authorized to dig up the body of his predecessor, Pope Formosus, then seven months in the tomb, drag it by the feet and seat it in the synod which he had assembled in judgment, and, after condemning it, to cut off two fingers of the right hand and throw it into the Tiber, whence it chanced to be rescued and buried. The next year, however, a new pope, John IX., annulled these proceedings and caused a synod to declare that no one should be condemned after death, for the accused must have the opportunity of defence. This did not prevent Sergius III., in 905, from again exhuming the body, when it was clothed in pontifical robes, seated on a throne, and once more solemnly condemned, beheaded, three more fingers cut off, and thrown in the Tiber. Yet the iniquity of these proceedings was proved when the restless remains were dragged from the river by some fishermen, and, on being carried to the church of St. Peter, the images of saints there bowed before them and saluted them reverently. About the year 1100, St. Ivo of Chartres, the foremost canonist of his day, pronounced unhesitatingly that the power of the Church to bind and to loose was confined to things on earth; that the dead had passed beyond human judgment, they could not be condemned, and burial must not be refused to those who had not been tried while living. Yet as heresy multiplied and its obstinacy seemed to justify the passionate hatred which it excited, the churchman might well feel himself unable to endure the thought that the bones of heretics polluted the sacred precincts of church and cemetery, and that unconsciously he was including them in his prayers for the dead. It was easy to find a method of reaching them. The Council of Verona in 1184, and subsequent popes and{232} councils, repeatedly and formally excommunicated all heretics. It was an old rule of the Church that all excommunicates who did not within a year apply for absolution were condemned. All heretics who died without confession or recantation were thus self-condemned, and were ineligible to sepulture in consecrated ground. Though they could not be excommunicated, being already under *ipso facto* excommunication, they could be anathematized. If mistakenly they had received Christian burial, as soon as the fact was discovered they were to be dug up and burned; the inquisition which established their guilt was merely an examination into the facts, not a condemnation, and the penalties followed of themselves. That it required some effort to establish the rule is shown by an epistle of Innocent III., in 1207, to the abbot and monks of St. Hippolytus of Faenza, who had refused, at the order of a legate, to exhume the body of Otto of damnable memory, a heretic buried in their cemetery, or to observe the interdict pronounced against them in consequence, and Innocent is obliged to threaten the most energetic measures to compel them to obedience. With time, however, the principle became firmly established; it was recognized as a grievous offence knowingly to bury the body of a heretic or a fautor of heretics—an offence only to be pardoned on condition of the offender exhuming the remains with his own hands, while the grave was accursed forever. We shall see that the business of investigating the record of the dead became no small or unimportant part of the duties of the Inquisition.[204]

The influence which these teachings and practices had in guiding the actions and policy of the age is well exemplified in the career of Frederic II. Half Italian in blood, and wholly Italian{233} in training, he was a philosophical free-thinker. The accusations of Gregory IX., that he was secretly a disciple of Mahomet, and the tradition that he was privately in the habit of calling Moses, Christ, and Mahomet the three impostors, contradict each other, but show what ground he gave for such imputations. Yet this man, whom Gregory declared to take the sacrament only to show his contempt for excommunication, was too sagacious not to recognize that he could only reign over a Christian people by at least pretending zeal in the work of exterminating heresy. He obtained his coronation in St. Peter's, November 22, 1220, by issuing the edict which is memorable in the history of persecution; and, as part of the solemnities, Honorius paused in the ineffable mysteries of the mass to fulminate an anathema in the name of Almighty God against all heresies and heretics, including those rulers whose laws interfered with their extermination. To the function thus assumed Frederic was ever true, perhaps even more so because, in his recognition of the necessity of ecclesiastical reform, he indulged in dreams of a caliphate in which he would wield both the temporal and spiritual swords. However this may be, his lifelong quarrel with the papacy only rendered him the more merciless in his extirpation of heresy; and just when Gregory IX. was engrossed in laying the foundation of the Inquisition we find Frederic audaciously urging him to greater zeal in defence of the faith, and suggesting his own example as one which the pope would do well to follow.[205]

The cruel ferocity of barbarous zeal which, through so many centuries, wrought misery on mankind in the name of Christ, has been explained in many ways. Fanatics on the other side have denounced it as mere bloodthirstiness or selfish lust of power. Philosophers have traced it to the doctrine of exclusive salvation, through which it seemed the duty of those in authority to coerce the recalcitrant for their own benefit, and prevent them from leading other souls to perdition. Another school has taught that it{234}arose from the survival of the atavistic notion of tribal solidarity, expanded into that of Christendom, making all share the guilt of sin offensive to God which they neglected to exterminate. Human impulses and motives, however, are too complex to be analyzed by a single solvent, even in the case of an individual, while here we have to deal with the whole Church, in its broadest acceptation, embracing the laity as well as the clergy. There is no doubt that the people were as eager as their pastors to send the heretic to the stake. There is no doubt that men of the kindliest tempers, the profoundest intelligence, the noblest aspirations, the purest zeal for righteousness, professing a religion founded on love and charity, were ruthless when heresy was concerned, and were ready to trample it out at the cost of any suffering. Dominic and Francis, Bonaventura and Thomas Aquinas, Innocent III. and St. Louis, were types, in their several ways, of which humanity, in any age, might well feel proud, and yet they were as unsparing of the heretic as Ezzelin da Romano was of his enemies. With such men it was not hope of gain or lust of blood or pride of opinion or wanton exercise of power, but sense of duty, and they but represented what was universal public opinion from the thirteenth to the seventeenth century.

To comprehend it, we must picture to ourselves a stage of civilization in many respects wholly unlike our own. Passions were fiercer, convictions stronger, virtues and vices more exaggerated, than in our colder and more self-contained time. The age, moreover, was a cruel one. The military spirit was everywhere dominant; men were accustomed to rely upon force rather than on persuasion, and habitually looked on human suffering with indifference. The industrial spirit, which has so softened modern manners and modes of thought, was as yet hardly known.[206] We have only to look upon the atrocities of the criminal law of the Middle Ages to see how pitiless men were in their dealings with each other. The wheel, the caldron of boiling oil, burning alive, burying alive,{235} flaying alive, tearing apart with wild horses, were the ordinary expedients by which the criminal jurist sought to deter crime by frightful examples which would make a profound impression on a not over-sensitive population. An Anglo-Saxon law punishes a female slave convicted of theft by making eighty other female slaves each bring three pieces of wood and burn her to death, while each contributes a fine besides; and in mediæval England burning was the customary penalty for attempts on the life of the feudal lord. In the Customs of Arques, granted by the Abbey of St. Bertin in 1231, there is a provision that, if a thief have a concubine who is his accomplice, she is to be buried alive; though, if pregnant, a respite is given till after childbirth. Frederic II., the most enlightened prince of his time, burned captive rebels to death in his presence, and is even said to have encased them in lead in order to roast them slowly. In 1261 St. Louis humanely abolished a custom of Touraine by which the theft of a loaf of bread or a pot of wine by a servant from his master was punished by the loss of a limb. In Frisia arson committed at night was visited with burning alive; and, by the old German law, the penalty of both murder and arson was breaking on the wheel. In France women were customarily burned or buried alive for simple felonies, while Jews were hung by the feet between two savage dogs, while men were boiled to death for coining. In Milan Italian ingenuity exhausted itself in devising deaths of lingering torture for criminals of all descriptions. The *Carolina*, or criminal code of Charles V., issued in 1530, is a hideous catalogue of blinding, mutilation, tearing with hot pincers, burning alive, and breaking on the wheel. In England poisoners were boiled to death even as lately as 1542, as in the cases of Rouse and Margaret Davie; the barbarous penalty for high treason—of hanging, drawing, and quartering—is well known, while that for petty treason was enforced no longer ago than 1726, on Catharine Hayes, who was burned at Tyburn for murdering her husband. By the laws of Christian V. of Denmark, in 1683, blasphemers were beheaded after having the tongue cut out. As recently as 1706, in Hanover, a pastor named Zacharie Georg Flagge was burned alive for coining. Modern tenderness for the criminal is evidently a matter of very recent date. So careless were legislators of human suffering in general that, in England, to cut out a man's tongue, or to pluck out his eyes with{236}malice prepense, was not made a felony until the fifteenth century, in a criminal law so severe that, even in the reign of Elizabeth, the robbing of a hawk's nest was similarly a felony; and as recently as 1833 a child of nine was sentenced to be hanged for breaking a patched pane of glass and stealing twopence worth of paint.[207]

The nations thus habituated to the most savage cruelty, moreover, regarded the propagation of heresy with peculiar detestation, as not merely a sin, but as the worst of crimes. Heresy itself, says Bishop Lucas of Tuy,

78

justifies, by comparison, the infidelity of the Jews; its pollution cleanses the filthy madness of Mahomet; its vileness renders pure even Sodom and Gomorrah. Whatever is worst in other sin becomes holy in comparison with the turpitude of heresy. Less rhetorical, but equally emphatic, is Thomas Aquinas, when his merciless logic demonstrates that the sin of heresy separates man from God more than all other sins, and therefore it is the worst of sins, and is to be punished more severely. Of all kinds of infidelity, that of heresy is the worst. So sensitive did the clerical mind become on the subject that Stephen Palecz of Prague declared, in a sermon before the Council of Constance, that if a belief was Catholic in a thousand points, and false in one, the whole was heretical. The heretic, therefore, who labored, as all earnest heretics necessarily did, to convert others to his way of{237} thinking, was inevitably regarded as a demon, striving to win souls to share his own damnation, and none of the orthodox doubted that he was the direct and efficient instrument of Satan in his warfare with God. The intensity of the abhorrence thus awakened can only be realized by those who recognize the vividness of mediæval eschatology, the living horror which all men felt as to the possibilities of the dread hereafter.[208]

That this view of heresy and of the duty of its suppression was not reached at once by the mediæval Church and peoples we have seen in the hesitation and vacillation which characterized the proceedings of the eleventh and twelfth centuries; and this shows that the idea of solidarity in the responsibility before God, while it undoubtedly had a share in exaggerating the persecuting spirit, cannot by any means wholly account for it. It stimulated the masses, who snatched the sectaries from the hands of protecting priests, but had less influence on the educated clergy. As heresies increased and grew more threatening, and milder means seemed only to aggravate the evil, the minds of earnest and enlightened men brooding over it, and contemplating the awful possibilities of the future, when the Church of God might be overthrown by the conventicles of Satan, grew inflamed, and fanaticism inevitably followed. When this point was reached, when people and pastor alike felt that the Church Militant must strike without pity if it would prevail against the legions of hell, no firm believer in the doctrine of exclusive salvation could doubt that the truest mercy lay in sweeping away the emissaries of Satan with fire and sword. God had wonderfully raised the Church to fight his battle. It had become supreme over temporal princes, and could command their implicit obedience. It had full power over the sword of the flesh, and with that power came responsibility. It was responsible not only in the present, but also for the souls of the faithful yet unborn through countless generations, and, if weakly untrue to its trust, it could not plead inability in extenuation. In view of the awful possibilities of neglected duty, what were the sufferings of a few thousand hardened wretches who, deaf to the solicitations of{238} repentance, were hurried, but a few years before their time, to their master the Devil?

We must also bear in mind the character which Christianity had assumed in the gradual development of its theology, and its consequent influence on those who guided the policy of the Church. They knew that Christ had said "I am not come to destroy the law but to fulfil" (Matt. v. 17). They also knew from Holy Writ that Jehovah was a God delighting in the extermination of his enemies. They read how Saul, the chosen King of Israel, had been divinely punished for sparing Agag of Amalek, and how the prophet Samuel had hewn him in pieces; how the wholesale slaughter of the unbelieving Canaanites had been ruthlessly commanded and enforced; how Elijah had been commended for slaying four hundred and fifty priests of Baal; and they could not conceive how mercy to those who rejected the true faith could be aught but disobedience to God. Moreover, Jehovah was a God who was only to be placated by the continual sacrifice of victims. The very doctrine of the Atonement assumed that the human race could only be rendered eligible to salvation by the most awful sacrifice that the human mind could conceive—that of one of the members of the Trinity. The Christian worshipped a God who had subjected himself to the most painful and humiliating of sacrifices, and the salvation of souls was dependent on the daily repetition of this sacrifice in the mass, throughout Christendom. To minds moulded in such a belief, it might well seem that the extremity of punishment inflicted on the enemies of the Church of God was nothing in itself, and that it was an acceptable offering to him who had commanded that neither age nor sex should be spared in the land of Canaan.

These tendencies had been fostered and exaggerated by the growth of asceticism. That mortal life was a thing to be despised and that heaven was to be purchased by shunning the pleasures of existence and extinguishing all human affections, was a lesson taught broadly throughout the hagiology of the Church. Maceration and mortification were the surest roads to Paradise, and sin was to be redeemed by self-inflicted penance. This theory worked in a double sense. On the one hand, the practices of the zealot—strict celibacy, fasting, solitude, are direct incentives to insanity, as is shown by the epidemics of diabolical possession and{239} suicide which were so frequent in the stricter monastic establishments;[209] and without assuming that such a man as St. Peter Martyr was mad, it is impossible to read the extremity of ascetic maceration which he habitually practised—fasts, vigils, scourgings, and every device which perverse ingenuity could suggest— without recognizing morbid mental conditions which could readily render him a monomaniac on any subject which greatly engrossed his feelings. On the other hand, the men who thus tamed their own strong passions and mastered the rebellious flesh by these means, were not likely to feel for the suffering of those who had abandoned themselves to Satan, and who might be saved by temporal fire from eternal flame. Or if, perchance, they had softer hearts and compassionated the agonies of their victims, they might well regard the repression of their own emotions at the spectacle as part of the penance which they were called upon to endure. In any case, life was but an infinitesimal point in eternity, and all human interests shrank into nothingness in comparison with the one overmastering duty of keeping the flock from straying and of preventing an infected sheep from communicating his poison to his fellows. Charity itself could not hesitate over whatever methods might be requisite to accomplish this.

That the men who conducted the Inquisition and who toiled sedulously in its arduous, repulsive, and often dangerous labor, were thoroughly convinced that they were furthering the kingdom of God, is shown by the habitual practice of encouraging them with the remission of sins, similar to that offered for a pilgrimage to the Holy Land. Besides the consciousness of duty performed, it was the only recognized reward of their joyless lives, and it was considered enough.[210] How, moreover, cruelty to the heretic could be conjoined with boundless love and good-will to men is well exemplified in the career of the Dominican, Frà Giovanni Schio{240} da Vicenza. Profoundly moved by the condition of northern Italy, filled with dissensions which raged, not only between city and city, and burgher and noble, but which divided families in the factions of Guelf and Ghibelline, he devoted himself to the mission of an Apostle of Peace. In 1233 his eloquence at Bologna induced the opposing parties to lay aside their arms, and led enemies to swear mutual forgiveness in a delirium of joyful reconciliation. So great was the enthusiasm which he excited that the magistrates submitted to him the statutes of the city and allowed him to revise them at discretion. The same success attended him at Padua, Treviso, Feltro, and Belluno. The lords of Camino, Romano, Conigliano, and San Bonifacio, and the republics of Brescia, Vicenza, Verona, and Mantua made him the arbiter of their differences and urged him to alter their political organization as he saw fit. On the plain of Paquara, near Verona, he called a great assembly of the Lombard peoples, and that innumerable multitude, swayed by his fervor as by a voice from heaven, proclaimed a general pacification. Yet this man, so worthy a disciple of the Great Teacher of divine love, when installed in power in Verona, proceeded to burn in the public square sixty men and women of the principal families of the town, whom he had condemned as heretics; and twenty years later he reappears as the leader of a Bolognese contingent in the crusade preached by Alexander IV. against Ezzelin de Romano.[211]

In fact the zealot, however loving and charitable he might otherwise be, was taught and believed that compassion for the sufferings of the heretic was not only a weakness but a sin. As well might he sympathize with Satan and his demons writhing in the endless torment of hell. If a just and omnipotent God wreaked divine vengeance on those of his creatures who offended him, it was not for man to question the righteousness of his ways, but humbly to imitate his example and rejoice when the opportunity to do so was vouchsafed to him. The stern moralists of the age held it to be a Christian duty to find pleasure in contemplating the anguish of the sinner. Gregory the Great, five centuries before, had argued that the bliss of the elect in heaven would not{241} be perfect unless they were able to look across the abyss and enjoy the agonies of their brethren in eternal fire. This idea was a popular one and was not allowed to grow obsolete. Peter Lombard, the great "Master of Sentences," whose "Sentences," produced about the middle of the twelfth century, was the leading authority in the schools, quotes St. Gregory with approbation, and enlarges upon the satisfaction which the just will feel in the ineffable misery of the damned. Even the mystic tenderness of Bonaventura does not prevent him from echoing the same terrible exultation. When such were the sentiments in which all thinking men were trained, and such were the views which they disseminated among the people, it is not to be supposed that any feelings of compassion for the sufferers would deter the most charitable from the rigid exercise of justice. The ruthless extermination of heresy was a work which could only be pleasing to the righteous, whether simply as spectators or whether they were called by conscience or by station to the higher duties of active persecution. If, notwithstanding this, any scruple remained, the schoolmen easily removed it by proving that persecution was a work of charity, for the benefit of the persecuted.[212]

It is true that all popes were not like Innocent III. nor all inquisitors like Frà Giovanni. Selfish and interested motives were at work, as they are in all human institutions, and the actions even of the best may doubtless have unconsciously been stimulated by pride of opinion and by ambition as well as by a sense of duty to God and man. The religious revolt threatened the temporal possessions of the Church and the privileges of its members, and the desire to preserve these had its share in the resistance which was organized against innovation. Selfish as this desire may have been, we must not forget that, in the thirteenth century, the power and wealth of the hierarchy, however much abused, had yet long been recognized by the public law of Europe. The rulers of the Church could only regard as a sacred duty the maintenance of{242} rights which they had inherited, against audacious assailants whose doctrines threatened the overthrow of what they regarded as the basis of social order. Sympathize as we must with the Waldenses and the Cathari in their hideous martyrdom, we cannot but feel that the treatment which they endured was inevitable, and we should pity the blindness of the persecutor as well as the sufferings of the persecuted.

Man is seldom wholly consistent in the practical application of his principles, and the persecutors of the thirteenth century made one concession to humanity and common-sense which was fatal to the completeness of the theory on which they acted. To carry it out fully, they should have proselyted with the sword among all non-Christians whom fate threw in their power; but from this they abstained. Infidels who had never received the faith, such as Jews and Saracens, were not to be compelled to Christianity. Even their children were not to be baptized without parental consent, as this would be contrary to natural justice, as well as dangerous to the purity of the faith. It was necessary that the misbeliever should have been united with the Church by baptism in order to give her jurisdiction over him.[213]{243}

80

CHAPTER VI.

THE MENDICANT ORDERS.

IN the struggle which the Church was making to regain its forfeited hold upon the veneration of Christendom its most efficient instrument was not force. It is true that the dignitaries at its head relied solely on persecution, and by skilful use of popular superstition and princely ambition they succeeded in crushing the open revolt which threatened its supremacy. Something more was required to render that success permanent by arousing anew the trust and confidence of the people, and that something could not be supplied by a worldly and ambitious prelacy. Far down in the ranks of the Church, however, were men with truer insight and nobler aspirations, who saw its fatal omissions and who sought in their humble spheres to do the work which lay immediately around them. They builded better than they knew, and to them rather than to the Innocents and the de Montforts did the hierarchy owe the restoration of the tottering edifice. The response which they met showed how deep was the popular longing for a church which should in some degree fitly reflect the precepts of its Founder.

It is not to be supposed that the corruption of the ecclesiastical body was allowed to pass unnoticed and unreproved by the pious among the orthodox, and that occasional efforts at reform were not made by those who would have shrunk with horror from open opposition or even secret dissidence. The free speaking of St. Bernard, Geroch of Reichersberg, and Peter Cantor show how deeply the offences of priest and prelate were felt and how sharply they were criticised. The self-imposed mission of Peter Waldo was an effort to evangelize the Church, which in its inception had no thought of antagonizing the existing order, and was forced into schism by the obstinacy of the disciples in recurring to Scripture, and the natural dread which conservatism feels of all enthusiasm{244}that may become dangerous. As the twelfth century drew to an end there appeared another apostle whose brief career for a space seemed to give assurance that both clergy and people might be aroused to a practical sense of the changes requisite to enable the Church to fulfil its bright promises to mankind.

Foulques de Neuilly was an obscure priest, with little education or training and with profound contempt for the dialectics of the schools, but whose conviction of the sins of Church and people led him to abandon the cure of souls for the more arduous duties of a missionary. Moved by his enthusiasm, Peter Cantor procured for him from Innocent III. a license to preach, but at first his success was disheartening. He had not discovered the secret of reaching the hearts of his hearers, but the experience gained by earnest work acquired it for him, and his legend explains it in the customary shape of a special revelation from God, accompanied with the gift of working miracles. He caused, it is said, the deaf to hear, the blind to see, and the crippled to walk, but he selected his subjects and ofttimes refused to work cures, telling the applicant that his time had not yet come, and that health would but give him fresh opportunity to sin. Though popularly known as "*le sainct homme*," he was no ascetic, and at a time when maceration was popularly deemed an indispensable accompaniment of holiness, it was remarked with wonder that he would eat thankfully whatever was set before him, and that he was not observant of vigils. Yet he was irascible, and was wont to give over to Satan those who refused to listen to him, when it was observed that they would shortly perish through the divine vengeance. Thousands of sinners flocked to hear him and were converted to repentance, though few of them persevered in the path of righteousness, and he was so successful in reclaiming women of evil life who became nuns that the Convent of St. Antoine in Paris was founded to receive them. Many Cathari, also, were won over by him to the faith, and it was through his exertions that Terric, the heresiarch of the Nivernois, was discovered in his cave at Corbigny and was burned. He was especially severe on the licentiousness of the clergy, and at Lisieux he so angered them with his invectives that they seized and threw him in a dungeon and loaded him with chains, when his miraculous powers stood him in good stead and he walked forth without difficulty. The same thing occurred at Caen, when the officials of{245} Richard of England imprisoned him, thinking to gratify their master, who was supposed to be offended by the preacher's plain speaking. Foulques warned him to marry off his three daughters lest worse should befall him; and when the king retorted that Foulques was a hypocrite who knew that he had no daughters, the monitor rejoined that the first daughter was pride, the second avarice, and the third lust. Richard, however, was too keen-witted to be overcome in a war of words; he assembled his court, and solemnly repeating what Foulques had said, added, "My pride I give to the Templars, my avarice to the Cistercians, and my lust to the prelates in general."

Foulques suffered somewhat in public estimation from the backsliding of Pierre de Roissi, whom he had taken as an associate, and who in preaching poverty amassed wealth and obtained a canonry at Chartres, where he rose to be chancellor. Yet he might have accomplished much had not Innocent III., who thought more of the recovery of the Holy Land than of the spiritual awakening of souls, sent him, in 1198, an urgent request to preach the crusade. Into this work Foulques threw himself with all his enthusiasm. It was owing to his eloquence that Baldwin of Flanders and other magnates undertook the crusade; he is said with his own hand to have imposed the cross upon two hundred thousand pilgrims, taking the poor by preference, as he deemed the rich unworthy of it, and the Latin Empire of Constantinople, which was the outcome of the crusade, was his work. Scandal said that of the immense sum which he raised he kept a portion, but this may be safely set to the account of malice; certain it is that never was money more joyfully received by the struggling Christians in Palestine than the large remittances from him which enabled them to rebuild the walls of Tyre and Ptolemais, recently overthrown by an earthquake. As the crusade was about to set out, which he proposed to accompany, he died at Neuilly, in May, 1202, leaving whatever he possessed to the pilgrims. Had his life been lengthened and had he not been diverted from his true career, he might possibly have accomplished permanent results.[214]{246}

Wholly different from Foulques was Durán de Huesca the Catalan. Despite the persecuting edicts of Alonso and Pedro, the Waldensian heresy had taken deep root in Aragon. Durán was one of its leaders, who took part in the disputation held at Pamiers about 1207 between the Waldenses and the Bishops of Osma, Toulouse, and Conserans, in the presence of the Count of Foix. It is probable that Dominic also took part in it, and as the two men had so much in common, one is tempted to believe that to Dominic's eloquence was due the conversion of Durán, which was the only substantial result of the colloquy. Durán was too earnest a man to remain satisfied with assuring his own salvation, and sought thenceforth to win over other erring souls. He not only wrote various tracts against his recent heresy, but he conceived the idea of founding an order which should serve as a model of poverty and self-abnegation, and be devoted to preaching and missionary work, thus fighting the heretics with the very weapons which they had found so efficacious in obtaining converts from the wealthy and worldly Church. Filled with this inspiration, he labored among his brethren and brought many of them over to his way of thinking, from Spain to Italy. In Milan a hundred of them agreed to return to the Church if a building erected by them for a school, which the archbishop had torn down, were restored to them. Durán, with three companions, presented himself before Innocent, who was satisfied with his profession of faith and approved of his plan. Most of the associates were clerks, who had already given away all their possessions in charity. Renouncing the world, they proposed to live in the strictest chastity, to sleep on boards, except in case of sickness, praying seven times a day and observing specified fasts in addition to those prescribed by the Church. Absolute poverty was to be enforced; no thought was to be taken of the morrow, all gifts of gold and silver were to be refused, and only the necessaries of food and clothing were to be accepted. A habit of white or gray was adopted, with sandals to distinguish them from the Waldenses. Those of them who were learned and fit for the work were to devote themselves to preaching{247} to the faithful and converting the heretic, pledging themselves not to attack the vices of the clergy. Laymen unable to serve in this capacity were to live in houses and labor with their hands, giving due tithes, oblations, and first-fruits to the Church. The care of the poor, moreover, was to be a special duty, and a rich layman in the diocese of Elne proposed to build for them a hospital with fifty beds, to erect a church, and to distribute garments to the naked. They were to elect their own superior, but were to be in no wise exempt from the regular jurisdiction of the prelates.[215]

In this institution of the "Pauperes Catholici," or Poor Catholics—as they called themselves in contradistinction to the "Pauperes de Lugduno" or Waldenses—there lay the possibilities of all that Dominic and Francis afterwards conceived and executed. It was the origin, or at least the precursor, of the great Mendicant Orders, the germ of the great fructifying idea which accomplished results so marvellous; and while it is not likely that Francis in Italy borrowed his conception from Durán, it is more than probable that Dominic in France, where he must have been familiar with the movement, was led by the plan of the Poor Catholics to that of the Preaching Friars, which was so closely modelled on it. Yet though at the start Durán had apparently far better prospects of success than either Dominic or Francis, his project was foredoomed from the beginning. Already in 1209 he had communities planted in Aragon, Narbonne, Béziers, Usez, Carcassonne, and Nîmes, but the prelates of Languedoc were universally suspicious of the project and secretly or actively hostile. Cavils were raised as to the reconciliation of converted heretics; complaints were made that the conversions were feigned and that the converts were lacking in respect for the Church and its observances. The crusade was on foot; it seemed easier to crush than to persuade, and in the tumultuous passions of that fierce time the humble methods of Durán and his brethren were laughed to scorn. In vain he appealed to Innocent. In vain Innocent, who viewed the project with the intuition of a Christian statesman, assured him of the papal protection, and wrote again and again to the prelates commanding them to favor the Poor Catholics, reminding them that wandering sheep{248} were to be welcomed back to the fold, that souls were to be won by gentleness and mercy, and commanding them not to insist on trifles. In vain he even conceded to Durán that secular members of his society should not be required to join in war against Christians, or to take oaths in secular matters, in so far as was compatible with justice and with the rights of their suzerains. The passions and the prejudices which he had unchained in Languedoc had grown beyond his control, and the Poor Catholics disappeared in the tumult. After 1212 we hear little more of them. We find Gregory IX., in 1237, ordering the Dominican Provincial of Tarragona to reform them and let them select one of the approved Rules under which to live. A mandate of Innocent IV., in 1247, to the Archbishop of Narbonne and Bishop of Elne to restrain them from preaching shows that when they attempted to perform the function for which the order had been established they were promptly silenced. It was left to other hands to develop the enormous possibilities of the scheme which Durán had devised.[216]

Far different were the results achieved by Domingo de Guzman, whom the Latin Church reverences as the greatest and most successful of its champions.

"Della fede Christiana santo atleta,
Benigno a' suoi, et a' nemici crudo—
—E negli sterpi eretici percosse

82

L'impeto suo più vivamente quivi
Dove le resistenze eran più grosse."
—PARADISO, XII.

Born at Calaruega, in Old Castile, in 1170, of a stock which his brethren love to connect with the royal house, his saintliness was so penetrating that it reflected back upon his mother, who is reverenced as St. Juana de Aga, and at one time there was danger that even his father might be drawn into the saintly circle. Both parents were buried in the convent of San Pedro de Gumiel, until, about 1320, the Infante Juan Manuel of Castile obtained the body of Juana to enrich the Dominican convent of San Pablo de Peñafiel which he had founded; when Fray Geronymo Orozco, the Abbot of Gumiel, prudently transferred the remains of Don Felix de[249] Guzman to an unknown spot in order to preserve it from an extension of acquisitive veneration. Even the font of white stone, fashioned like a shell, in which Dominic was baptized could not escape. In 1605 Philip III. transported it with much pomp from Calaruega to Valladolid. Thence it was translated to the royal Convent of San Domingo in Madrid, where it has since been used for the baptism of the royal children.[217]

Ten years of training in the University of Palencia made of Dominic an accomplished theologian and equipped him thoroughly for the missionary work to which his life was devoted. Entering the Chapter of Osma, he was speedily made sub-prior, and in this capacity we have seen him accompany his bishop, who from 1203 onward for some years was employed on missions that carried him through Languedoc. Dominic's biographers relate that his career was determined by an incident in this first voyage, when he chanced to lodge in the house of a heretic of Toulouse and spent the night in converting him. This success, and the sight of the wide extent of heresy, led him to devote his life to its extirpation. When in 1206 Bishop Diego dismissed his retinue and remained to evangelize the land, Dominic alone was retained; when Diego returned to Spain to die, Dominic remained behind and continued to make Languedoc the scene of his activity.[218]

The legend which has grown around Dominic represents him as one of the chief causes of the overthrow of the Albigensian heresies. Doubtless he did all that an earnest and single-hearted man could do in a cause to which he had surrendered himself, but historically his influence was imperceptible. The monk of Vaux-Cernay alludes to him but once, as a follower of Bishop Diego, and the epithet there applied to him of "*vir totius sanctitatis*" is but one of the customary meaningless civilities of the day. That he was one of the preachers licensed by the legates under the authority granted by Innocent, in 1207, is shown by an absolution issued by him which has chanced to be preserved, in which he styles himself canon of Osma and "*prædicator minimus*;" but his subordinate[250] position is indicated by the absolution being subject to the pleasure of Legate Arnaud, from whom his authority was derived. This and a dispensation to a burgher of Toulouse to lodge a heretic in his house are the only extant evidences of his activity as a missionary. Yet already his talent for organization had been shown by his founding the Monastery of Prouille. One of the most efficient means by which the heretics propagated their belief was by establishments in which poor girls of gentle blood could obtain gratuitous education. To meet them on their own ground, Dominic, about 1206, conceived the idea of a similar foundation for Catholics, and with the aid of Bishop Foulques of Toulouse he carried it out. Prouille became a large and wealthy convent, which boasted of being the germ of the great Dominican Order.[219]

For the next eight years the life of Dominic is a blank. That he labored strenuously in his self-imposed mission we cannot doubt, gaining, if not souls, at least skill in disputation, knowledge of men, and the force which comes from the concentration of energies on a task of conscience; but of results there is not a trace in the wild tumult of the crusades. We may safely dismiss as a fable the tradition that he refused successively the bishoprics of Béziers, Conserans, and Comminges, and the legends of the miracles which he wrought in vain among hard-hearted Cathari. He emerges again to view after the battle of Muret had destroyed the hopes of Count Raymond, when the cause of orthodoxy seemed triumphant and the field was unobstructed for conversions. In 1214 he was in his forty-fifth year, in the full strength of mature manhood, yet having thus far accomplished nothing that gave promise of what was to follow. Divested of their supernatural adornments, the accounts which we have of him show him to us as a man of earnest, resolute purpose, deep and unalterable convictions, full of burning zeal for the propagation of the faith, yet kindly in heart, cheerful in temper, and winning in manner. It is significant of the impression produced on his contemporaries that with scarce an exception the miracles related of him are beneficent ones—raising the dead, healing[251] the sick and converting heretics, not by punishment, but by showing that he spoke by command of the Almighty. The accounts of his habitual austerities may be exaggerated, but no one who is familiar with the self-inflicted macerations of the hagiology need hesitate to believe that Dominic was as severe with himself as with his fellows, even though we may not place faith in the legend that his constant falling out of bed when an infant was caused by an early ascetic development which led him to prefer mortifying the flesh on a hard floor to the luxury of a soft couch. His endless scourgings, his tireless vigils, and, when exhausted nature could bear them no longer, his short repose on a board, or in the corner of a church where he had passed the night, his almost uninterrupted prayer, his super-human fasts, are probably only harmless exaggerations of the truth. So, too, may be the legends which tell of his boundless charity and his love for his fellows; how, when a student, in a time of dearth he sold all his books to relieve the distress around him, and would, unless divinely prevented, have sold himself to redeem from the Moors a captive whose sister he saw overwhelmed with grief. Whether these stories be true or not, they at least show us the ideal which his immediate disciples thought to realize in him.[220]

The brief remaining years of Dominic's life witnessed the rapid garnering of the harvest sowed in the period of humble but zealous obscurity. In 1214 Pierre Cella, a rich citizen of Toulouse, moved by his earnestness, resolved to join him in his mission-work, and gave for the purpose a stately house near the Château Narbonnais, which for more than a hundred years remained the home of the Inquisition. A few other zealous souls gathered around him, and the little fraternity commenced to live like monks. Foulques, the fanatic Bishop of Toulouse, assigned to them a sixth of the {252} tithes, to provide them with books and other necessaries, that they might not lack the means of training themselves and others for the work of preaching, which was the main object of the community. By this time Durán de Huesca's attempt had proved a failure, and Dominic, who must have been familiar with it, doubtless saw the causes of its ill-success and the means to avoid them. Yet it is noteworthy that in the inception of the plan there was no thought of employing force. The heretics of Languedoc lay defenceless at the feet of de Montfort, an easy prey to the spoiler, but Dominic's project only looked to their peaceful conversion and to performing the duties of instruction and exhortation of which the Church had been so wholly neglectful.[221]

All eyes were now bent on the Lateran Council which was to decide the fate of the land. Foulques of Toulouse on his voyage thither took with him Dominic to obtain from the pope his approval of the new community. Tradition relates that Innocent hesitated; his experience with Durán de Huesca had not taught him to expect much from the irregular action of enthusiasts; the council had forbidden the formation of new orders of monkhood, and had commanded that zeal for the future should satisfy itself with those already established. Yet Innocent's doubts were removed by a dream in which he saw the Lateran Basilica tottering and ready to fall, and a man in whom he recognized the humble Dominic supporting it on his shoulders. Thus divinely warned that the crumbling church edifice was to be restored by the man whose zeal he had despised, he approved the project on condition that Dominic and his brethren should adopt the Rule of some established order.[222]

Dominic returned and assembled his brethren at Prouille. They were by this time sixteen in number, and it is a curious illustration of the denationalizing influence of the Church to observe in this little gathering of earnest men in that remote spot that Castile, Navarre, Normandy, France, Languedoc, England, and Germany were represented. This self-devoted band adopted the rule of the Canons Regular of St. Augustin, which was Dominic's own,{253} and elected Matthieu le Gaulois as their abbot. He was the first and last who bore this title, for as the Order grew its organization was modified to secure greater unity and at the same time greater freedom of action. It was divided into provinces, the head of each being a provincial prior. Supreme over all was the general master. These offices were filled by election, with tenure during good behavior, and provisions were made for stated assemblies, or chapters, both provincial and general. Each brother, or friar, was held to implicit obedience. Like a soldier on duty, he was liable at any moment to be despatched on any mission that the interest of religion or of the Order might demand. They deemed themselves, in fact, soldiers of Christ, not devoted, like the monks, to a life of contemplation, but trained to mix with the world, exercised in all the arts of persuasion, skilled in theology and rhetoric, and ready to dare and suffer all things in the interest of the Church Militant. The name of Preaching Friars, which acquired such world-wide significance, was the result of accident. During the Lateran Council, while Dominic was in Rome, Innocent had occasion to address a note to him and ordered his secretary to begin, "To brother Dominic and his companions;" then, correcting himself, he said, "To brother Dominic and the preachers with him," and finally, considering further, "to Master Dominic and the brethren preachers." This greatly pleased them, and they at once commenced calling themselves Friar Preachers.[223]

Curiously enough, poverty formed no part of the original design. The impulse to found the order was given by Cella's donation of his property and the share of the tithes offered by Bishop Foulques; and, as soon as it was organized, Dominic had no scruple in accepting three churches from Foulques—one in Toulouse, one in Pamiers, and one in Puylaurens. The historians of the Order endeavor to explain this by saying that its founders desired to make poverty a feature of the Rule, but were deterred for fear that so novel an idea would prevent the papal confirmation. As Innocent had already approved of poverty in Durán de Huesca's scheme, the futility of this excuse is apparent, and we may well doubt the {254} legends about Dominic's rigidity in requiring his brethren to dispense absolutely with the use of money. Certain it is that as early as 1217 we find the friars quarrelling with the agents of Bishop Foulques over the grant of tithes, and demanding that churches with only half a dozen communicants should be reckoned as parish churches and subject to their claim on the tithes. It was not until the success of the Franciscans had shown the attractive power of poverty that it was adopted by the Dominicans in the General Chapter of 1220. It was finally embodied in the constitution adopted by the Chapter of 1228, which prohibited that lands or revenues should be acquired, ordered preachers not to solicit money, and classed among the graver offences the retention by a brother of any of the things forbidden to be received. The Order speedily outgrew these restrictions, but Dominic himself set an example of the utmost rigidity in this respect, and when he died in Bologna, in 1221, it was in the bed of Friar Moneta, as he had none of his own, and in Moneta's gown, for his own was worn out and he had not another to replace it; and when the Rule was adopted in 1220 such property as was not essential for the needs of the Order was made over to the Convent of Prouille.[224]

All that now was lacking was the papal confirmation of the Order and its statutes. Before Dominic could reach Rome on the errand to obtain this, Innocent had died, but his successor, Honorius III., entered fully into his views, and the sanction of the Holy See was given on December 21, 1216. Returning to Toulouse in 1217,

Dominic lost no time in dispersing his followers. It was not for them to practise the strenuous idleness of conventual life, in a ceaseless round of barren liturgies. They were the leaven which was to leaven Christianity, the soldiers of Christ who were to carry the banner of salvation to the farthest corners of the earth, and for them there was no pause or rest. The little band seemed absurdly inadequate for the task, but Dominic never hesitated. Some were sent to Spain, others to Paris, others again to Bologna, while{255} Dominic himself went to Rome, where, under the favor of the papal court, his enthusiasm was rewarded with an abundance of disciples. Those who went to Paris were warmly received, and were granted the house of St. Jacques, where they founded the famous convent of the Jacobins, which endured until the Order was swept away in the Revolution. The state of mental exaltation in which laymen and ecclesiastics of all ranks hastened to join the new Order is shown by the persecutions which the early brethren of St. Jacques endured from Satan. Frightful or sensual visions were constant with them, so that they were obliged by turns to keep watch at night over each other. Many of them were diabolically possessed and became mad. Their only refuge was the Virgin, and to the gracious assistance which she rendered them in their trials is attributed the Dominican custom of singing "Salve Regina" after complins, during which pious exercise she was frequently seen hovering over them in a sphere of light. Men in such a frame of mind were ready to suffer and to inflict all things for the sake of salvation.[225]

It is not worth while to follow further in detail the marvellous growth of the Order in all the lands of Europe. Already in 1221, when Dominic as General Master held the second General Chapter in Bologna, four years after the sixteen disciples had parted in Toulouse, the Order already had sixty convents, and was organized into eight provinces—Spain, Provence, France, England, Germany, Hungary, Lombardy, and Romagnuola. The same year witnessed the death of Dominic, but his work was done and his removal from the scene made no change in the mighty machine which he had built and set in motion. Everywhere the strongest intellects of the age were donning the Dominican scapular, and everywhere they were earning the respect and veneration of the people. Their services to the papacy were fully recognized, and they are speedily found filling important offices in the curia. In 1243 the learned Hugh of Vienne became the first Dominican cardinal, and in 1276 the Dominicans rejoiced to see Brother Peter of Tarentaise raised{256} to the chair of St. Peter as Innocent V. Yet the delay in Dominic's canonization would seem to show that personally he made less impression on his contemporaries than his followers would have us believe. Dying in 1221, the bull enrolling him in the calendar of saints only bears date July 3, 1234. His great colleague, or rival, Francis, who died in 1226, was canonized within two years, in 1228; the young Franciscan, Antony of Padua, who died in 1231, was recognized as a saint in 1233; and when the great Dominican martyr, St. Peter Martyr, was slain, April 12, 1252, proceedings for his canonization were commenced August 31 of the same year and were completed by March 25, 1253, less than a twelvemonth after his death. That thirteen years should have elapsed in the case of Dominic shows that his merits were recognized but slowly.[226]

If the Franciscans were in the end closely assimilated to the Dominicans, it was through the overmastering demands of the work to be accomplished by both, for in their origin the Orders were destined to objects as diverse as the characters of their founders. If St. Dominic was the type of the active practical missionary, St. Francis was the ideal of the contemplative ascetic, modified by boundless love and charity for his fellows.

Born in 1182, Giovanni Bernardone was the son of a prosperous trader of Assisi, who trained him in his business. Accompanying his father on a voyage to France, he came back with the accomplishment of speaking French, which gained for him among his companions the nickname of Francesco, a name which he adopted as his own. A dissipated youth was brought to a sudden close in his twentieth year by a dangerous illness which resulted in his conversion, and thereafter he devoted himself to works of mercy and charity, earning for himself with no little verisimilitude the reputation of insanity. In order to restore the dilapidated church of St. Damiani he stole a quantity of his father'{257}s cloths, which he sold at Foligno, together with the horse that carried them. Finding him irrevocably bent on following his own devices, the exasperated parent took him before the bishop to make him renounce all claim on his inheritance, which Francis willingly did, and to render the renunciation more complete stripped off all his clothes, save a hair shirt worn to mortify the flesh, when the bishop, to cover his nakedness, gave him the worn-out cloak of a peasant serving-man.[227]

Francis was now fairly embarked on a life of wandering beggary, which he used to so good an account that he was able to restore four churches which were sinking to ruin. He had no thought other than to work out his own salvation in poverty and acts of loving charity, especially to lepers; but the fame of his holiness spread, and the Blessed Bernard of Quintavalle asked to be associated with him. The solitary ascetic at first was indisposed to companionship, but to learn the will of God he thrice opened the Gospels at random, and his finger lit on the three texts on which the great Franciscan order was founded:

"And Jesus said unto him, If thou wilt be perfect, go and sell that thou hast and give to the poor, and thou shalt have treasure in heaven: and come and follow me" (Matt. XIX. 21).

"Be not ye therefore like unto them, for your Father knoweth what things ye have need of before ye ask him" (Matt. VI. 8).

"Then said Jesus unto his disciples, If any man will come after me, let him deny himself, and take up his cross and follow me" (Matt. XVI. 24).

The command was obeyed and the recruit accepted. Others joined from time to time, till the little band numbered eight. Then Francis announced that the time had come for them to evangelize the world, and dispersed them in pairs to the four points of the compass. On their reuniting, four more volunteers were added, when Francis drew up a Rule for their governance, and the twelve proceeded to Rome, according to the Franciscan legend, at the time of the Lateran Council, to procure the papal confirmation. When Francis presented himself to the pope in the aspect of a beggar the pontiff indignantly ordered him away, but tradition relates that a vision that night induced him to send for the mendicant. There was much hesitation among the papal advisers, but the earnestness{258} and eloquence of Francis won the day, and finally the Rule was approved and the brethren were authorized to preach the Word of God.[228]

Even yet were they undecided whether to abandon themselves to the contemplative life of anchorites or to undertake the great work of evangelization which lay before them in its immensity. They withdrew to Spoleto and counselled earnestly together without being able to reach a conclusion, until a revelation from God, which we can readily believe as actual to a mind such as that of Francis, turned the scale, and the Franciscan Order, in place of dying out in a few scattered hermitages, became one of the most powerful organizations of Christendom, though the abandoned hovel to which they resorted on their return to Assisi gave little promise of future splendor. The rapidity of the growth of the Order may be measured by the fact that when Francis called together his first General Chapter in 1221, it was attended by brethren variously reported as from three thousand to five thousand, including a cardinal and several bishops; and when, in the General Chapter of 1260, under Bonaventura, the Order was redistributed to accord with its growth, it was partitioned into thirty-three provinces and three vicariates, comprehending in all one hundred and eighty-two guardianships. This organization can be understood by the example of England, which formed a province divided into seven guardianships, containing, as we learn from another source, in 1256, forty-nine houses with twelve hundred and forty-two friars. The Order then extended into every corner of what was regarded as the civilized world and its contiguous regions.[229]

The Minorites, as in humility they called themselves, were so different in their inception from any existing organization of the{259} Church that when, in 1219, St. Francis made the first dispersion and sent his disciples to evangelize Europe, those who went to Germany and Hungary were regarded as heretics, and were roughly handled and expelled. In France they were taken for Cathari, to whose wandering perfected missionaries their austerity doubtless gave them close resemblance. They were asked if they were Albigenses, and, not knowing the meaning of the term, knew not what to say, and it was only after the authorities had consulted Honorius III. that they were relieved from suspicion. In Spain five of them endured martyrdom. Innocent had only given a verbal approbation of the Rule; he was dead, and something more formal was requisite to protect the brethren from persecution. Francis accordingly drew up a second Rule, more concise and less rigid than the first, which he submitted to Honorius. The pope approved it, though not without objecting to some of the clauses; but Francis refused to modify them, saying that it was not his but Christ's, and that he could not change the words of Christ. From this his followers assumed that the Rule had been divinely revealed to him. This belief passed into the traditions of the Order, and the Rule has been maintained unaltered in letter, though, as we shall see, its spirit has been more than once explained away by ingenious papal casuists.[230]

It is simple enough, amounting hardly to more than a gloss on the entrance-oath required of each friar, to live according to the gospel, in obedience, chastity, and without possessing property. The applicant for admission was required to sell all he had and give it to the poor, and if this were impossible the will so to do sufficed. Each one was permitted to have two gowns, but they must be vile in texture, and were to be patched and repaired as long as they could be made to hang together. Shoes were allowed to those who found it impossible to forego them. All were to go on foot, except in case of sickness or necessity. No one was to receive money, either directly or through a third party, except{260} that the ministers (as the provincial superiors were called) could do so for the care of the sick and for provision of clothing, especially in rigorous climates. Labor was strenuously enjoined on all those able to perform it, but wages were not to be in money, but in necessaries for themselves and their brethren. The clause requiring absolute poverty caused, as we shall see, a schism in the order, and therefore is worth giving textually: "The brethren shall appropriate to themselves nothing, neither house, nor place, nor other thing, but shall live in the world as strangers and pilgrims, and shall go confidently after alms. In this they shall feel no shame, since the Lord for our sake made himself poor in the world. It is this perfection of poverty which has made you, dearest brethren, heirs and kings of the kingdom of heaven. Having this, you should wish to have naught else under heaven." The head of the Order, or General Minister, was chosen by the Provincial Ministers, who could at any time depose him when the general good required it. Faculties for preaching were to be issued by the General, but no brother was to preach in any diocese without the assent of the bishop.[231]

This is all; and there is nothing in it to give promise of the immense results achieved under it. What gave it an enduring hold on the affections of the world was the spirit which the founder infused in it and in his brethren. No human creature since Christ has more fully incarnated the ideal of Christianity than Francis. Amid the extravagance, amounting at times almost to insanity, of his asceticism, there shines forth the Christian love and humility with which he devoted himself to the wretched and neglected—the outcasts for whom, in that rude time, there were few indeed to care. The Church, absorbed in worldliness, had outgrown the duties on which was founded its control over the souls and hearts of men, and there was need of the exaggeration of self-sacrifice taught by Francis to recall humanity to a sense of its obligations. Thus, of all the miseries of that age of misery, the hardest lot was that of the leper—the being afflicted by God with a loathsome, incurable, and contagious disease, who was cut off from all intercourse with fellow-men, and who, when he wandered abroad for alms from the lazar-house in which he was herded,{261} was obliged, by clattering sticks, to give notice of his approach, that all might shun his pestiferous neighborhood. It was to these, the most helpless and hopeless and abhorred of mankind, that the boundless charity and love of Francis was especially directed. The example which he set in his own person he required to be followed by his brethren; and when noble or simple applied for admission to the Order he was told that prominent among the obligations which he assumed was that of humbly serving the lepers in their hospitals. Francis did not hesitate to sleep in the lazar-houses, to handle the dangerous sores of the afflicted, to apply medicaments, and to minister to the sufferings of the body as well as of the soul. For the sake of the leper he relaxed the rule as to receiving alms in money. Yet his humility led him to forbid his disciples from leading in public the "Christian brethren," as he called them. Once, when Friar James had taken with him to church a leper who was shockingly eaten by disease, Francis reproved him; then, reproaching himself for what the sufferer might regard as a slight, he asked Friar Peter of Catania, at that time the minister-general of the Order, to confirm the penance which he had appointed for himself, and when Peter, who looked upon him with too much reverence to deny him anything, had assented, he announced that he would eat out of the same dish as the sick man. At the next simple meal, therefore, the leper was seated among them, and the brethren were terrified to see a single dish set between the two, and the leper dipping his fingers, dripping with blood and purulent discharge, into the food common to both.[232]

It would perhaps be too much to assert one's faith in the absolute veracity of such stories, but that makes little difference. If they be but legendary, the very growth of the legend shows the impression which Francis left on those who followed him; and the value of such an ideal on an age so hard and cruel can scarce be exaggerated. We know as a fact that the Franciscans were ever foremost in the cure of the sick, that they tended the hospitals in the midst of pestilence, and that to their intelligent devotion is due whatever progress the science of healing made in the dark ages. We are told, moreover, that the tender love of{262} Francis lavished itself on the brute creation as well as on man—on insects, birds, and beasts, whom he was wont to call his brethren and sisters, and for whom he was never weary in caring. All the stories related of him and his immediate disciples, in fact, are instinct with infinite love and self-sacrifice, with the perfection of humility and patience and long-suffering, with the control of the passions, and with endless striving to subdue all that renders human nature imperfect, and to realize the standard which Christ had erected for the guidance of man. Viewed in this aspect, even the semi-blasphemy of the "Book of Conformities of Christ and Francis" loses its grotesqueness. We may, indeed, smile at the absurdity of some of its parallels, and they may seem shocking enough when cleverly presented, stripped of all that softens them, in the "Alcoran des Cordeliers." We may doubt the verity of the Stigmata which it took so long and so many miracles, and repetition of papal bulls, to impose upon the incredulity of a hard-hearted generation. We may think that Satan showed less than his usual shrewdness when he so repeatedly wasted his energies in seeking to tempt or to terrify the saint in the crude form of a lion or of a dragon. Yet, in spite of all the absurdities of the cult of St. Francis, we recognize the profound impression which his virtues made on his followers in the vision which showed the heavenly throne of Lucifer, next to the Highest, kept vacant to be filled by Francis.[233]

To the pride and cruelty of the age he opposed patience and humility. "The perfection of gladness," he says, "consists not in working miracles, in curing the sick, expelling devils, or raising{263} the dead; nor in learning and knowledge of all things; nor in eloquence to convert the world, but in bearing all ills and injuries and injustice and despiteful treatment with patience and humility." So far from valuing himself on his virtues, he humbly confesses that he had himself not lived up to the Rule, and apologizes for it through his infirmity and ignorance. To what extravagant lengths his disciples carried this striving for humility is shown by Giacomo Benedettone, better known as Jacopone da Todi, the author of the Stabat Mater, an active and successful lawyer, who, crushed by the death of a lovely wife, entered the Order, and for ten years feigned idiocy in order to revel in the abuse and ill-treatment that were showered upon him.[234]

Obedience was taught and enforced to the utter renunciation of the will, and many are the stories related to show how completely the earlier disciples subjected themselves to each other and to their superiors. When, in 1224, the Franciscans were first sent to England, Gregory, the Provincial Minister of France, asked Friar William of Esseby if he wished to go. William replied that he did not know whether he wished it or not, because his will was not his own, but the minister's, and therefore he wished whatever the minister wished him to wish. Somewhat similar is a story told of two brethren of Salzburg in 1222. This blindness of obedience produced a discipline in the Order which increased incalculably its importance to the Church when it grew to be an instrument in the hands of the papacy. St. Francis was especially emphatic in urging upon the brethren the most implicit devotion to Rome, and the Franciscans became an army which played in the thirteenth century the part filled by the Jesuits in the sixteenth.[235]

It was no part of Francis's design that the friars should live by idle mendicancy, and we have seen that the Rule expresses the obligation to labor. This was obeyed by the stricter members. Thus his third disciple, the blessed Giles, earned his subsistence by the rudest work, such as that of carrying wood, and he always{264} adhered to the precept not to take wages in money, but in necessaries for his support. When he had earned more than enough for the scanty subsistence of the day, he would give away the surplus in charity, and trust to God for the morrow. It was well that, in an age of class distinctions so rigid, there should be some to teach practically the dignity of labor as a Christian doctrine. When St. Bonaventura was elevated to the cardinalate, in 1273, he had for seventeen years been the head of what by that time was the most powerful organization in Christendom, yet the messengers sent to announce to him his promotion arrived while he was engaged in his daily task of washing the dishes used in the frugal dinner of his convent. He refused to see them till his work was finished, and meanwhile the hat which they had brought was hung upon the branch of a tree.[236]

Thus the aim of St. Francis and his followers was to realize the simplicity of Christ and the apostles, and in nothing was this manifested with so much fervor as in their seeking after poverty. They argued that Jesus and his disciples owned nothing, and that the perfect Christian must likewise divest himself of all property. Of food and clothing and shelter he might have the use, as likewise of books requisite for his religious needs, but property of all kinds was absolutely prohibited, and the Christian's trust in God rendered forethought for the morrow a sin. As a protest against the avarice and worldliness of the Church, this was of exceeding value, but it was pushed to an extravagance which idealized poverty as an intrinsic good, and the greatest of all goods. "Brethren," said St. Francis, "know that poverty is the special path to salvation, the inciter to humility, and the root of perfection.... He who seeks to attain the height of poverty must, in a sense, renounce not only worldly prudence, but the knowledge of letters, so that, divesting himself of these possessions, he may offer himself naked to the arms of the Crucified.... Wherefore, like beggars, build little hovels in which to live, not as in your own, but as strangers and pilgrims in the houses of others." His prayer to Christ for poverty is a curiously earnest rhapsody. She is Lady Poverty, the Queen of virtues, for whose sake Christ descended unto earth, to marry her and beget on her all the children of perfection.{265} She clung to him with inseparable fidelity, and in her arms he died upon the cross. She alone possesses the seal with which to mark the elect who choose the way of perfection. "Grant me, O Jesus, that I may never possess under heaven anything of my own, and sustain the flesh sparely by the use of the things of others!" This exaggerated lust of poverty he carried out to the last, and on his death-bed stripped himself naked that he might die possessing absolutely nothing. Poverty thus was the corner-stone on which he founded the Order, and, as we shall see, the effort to maintain this super-human perfection led to a schism and gave to the Inquisition an ample store of victims whose heresy consisted in fidelity to the precepts of their founder.[237]

With all this there was too much kindliness in his nature for gloom, and cheerfulness was a virtue which he constantly inculcated. Sadness he held to be one of the most deadly weapons of Satan, while cheerfulness was the Christian's thankful acknowledgment of the blessings bestowed by God upon his creatures. This was consequently a distinguishing characteristic of the Friars in the early days of the Order. In Eccleston's simple and quiet narration of their advent to England, in 1224, when nine of them crossed to Dover without knowing what their fate might be from day to day, there is something singularly beautiful in the picture of their zeal, their trustfulness, their patience, their unfailing cheerfulness under privation and disappointment, and in their tireless activity in ministering to the spiritual and corporeal wants of the neglected children of the Church. Such men were real apostles, and had the Order continued to follow the lines laid down by its founder its services to humanity would have been incalculable.[238]

The Mendicant Orders were a startling innovation upon the monastic theory. In its essence monachism was the selfish effort of the individual to secure his own salvation by repudiating all the duties and responsibilities of life. It is true that at one time it had earned the gratitude of the world by leaving its retreats and carrying civilization and Christianity into barbarous regions,{266} under such men as St. Columba, St. Gall, and St. Willibrod, but that time had long past, and for ages it had sunk into worse than its primitive selfishness. The Mendicants came upon Christendom like a revelation—men who had abandoned all that was enticing in life to imitate the apostles, to convert the sinner and unbeliever, to arouse the slumbering moral sense of mankind, to instruct the ignorant, to offer salvation to all; in short, to do what the Church was paid so enormously in wealth and privileges and power for neglecting. Wandering on foot over the face of Europe, under burning suns or chilling blasts, rejecting alms in money but receiving thankfully whatever coarse food might be set before the wayfarer, or enduring hunger in silent resignation, taking no thought for the morrow, but busied eternally in the work of snatching souls from Satan, and lifting men up from the sordid cares of daily life, of ministering to their infirmities and of bringing to their darkened souls a glimpse of heavenly light—such was the aspect in which the earliest Dominicans and Franciscans presented themselves to the eyes of men who had been accustomed to see in the ecclesiastic only the sensual worldling intent solely upon the indulgence of his appetites. It is no wonder that such an apparition accomplished much in restoring to the populations the faith in Christianity which had begun to be so sorely shaken, or that it spread through Christendom the hope of an approaching regeneration in the Church which greatly lessened popular impatience under its exactions, and doubtless staved off a rebellion which would have altered the aspect of modern civilization.

It is no wonder, moreover, that the love and veneration of the people followed the Mendicants; that the charitable showered their gifts upon them, to the destruction of the primal obligation of poverty; that the men

88

of earnest convictions pressed forward to join their ranks. The purest and noblest intellects might well see in such a career the realization of their loftiest aspirations; and whenever in the thirteenth century we find a man towering above his fellows, we are almost sure to trace him to one of the Mendicant Orders. Raymond of Pennaforte, Alexander Hales, Albertus Magnus, Thomas Aquinas, Bonaventura, Roger Bacon, Duns Scotus, are names which show how irresistibly the men of highest gifts were led to seek among the Dominicans or Franciscans their ideal of life. That they failed to find it goes without{267} saying, but their presence in the Orders is at once an evidence of the impression which the Mendicants made upon all that was worthiest in the age, and an explanation of the enormous influence which the Orders obtained with such marvellous rapidity. Even Dante cannot refuse to them the tribute of his admiration—

"L'un fu tutto serafico in ardore,
L'altro per sapienza in terra fue
Di cherubica luce uno splendore."
(PARADISO, XI.)

There was another instrumentality of vast importance, in utilizing which both Francis and Dominic manifested their organizing ability—the Tertiary Orders through which laymen, without abandoning the world, were assimilated to the respective brotherhoods, aided in their labors, shared in their glory, and added to their influence, thus stimulating and utilizing the zeal of the community at large. There is a trace of an order of Crucigeri or Cross-bearers, laymen organized for the defence of the Church, claiming to date back to the time of Helena, mother of Constantine, and revived in 1215 by the Lateran Council, but there is no evidence of its activity or usefulness. Francis, however, who, though unlearned in scholastic theology and untrained in rhetoric, excelled his contemporaries in insight into the gospel and possessed a simple, earnest eloquence which carried the hearts of his hearers, on one occasion produced by his preaching so profound an impression that all the inhabitants of the town, men, women, and children, begged admission to his Order. This was manifestly impossible, and he bethought him of framing a Rule by which persons of both sexes, while remaining in the world, could be subjected to wholesome discipline and be connected with the fraternity, which in turn promised them its protection. Of the restrictions placed on them perhaps the most significant was that they should carry no weapons of offence except for the defence of the Roman Church, the Christian faith, and their own lands. The project and the Rule were approved by the pope in 1221, and the official name of the organization was "The Brothers and Sisters of Penitence," though it became popularly known as the Tertiary Order of Minorites, or Franciscans. Under the more aggressive name of "Militia Jesu Christi," or Soldiery of Christ, Dominic founded a{268} similar association of laymen connected with his Order. The idea proved a most fruitful one. It reorganized to some degree the Church by removing a portion of the barrier which separated the layman from the ecclesiastic. It brought immense support to the Mendicant Orders by enlisting with them multitudes of the earnest and zealous, as well as those who from less worthy motives sought to share their protection and enjoy the benefit of their influence. Types of both classes may be found in the royal house of France, for both St. Louis and Catherine de Medicis were Tertiaries of St. Francis.[239]

To comprehend fully the magnitude and influence of these movements we must bear in mind the impressionable character of the populations and their readiness to yield to contagious emotion. When we are told that the Franciscan Berthold of Ratisbon frequently preached to crowds of sixty thousand souls we realize what power was lodged in the hands of those who could reach masses so easily swayed and so full of blind yearnings to escape from the ignoble life to which they were condemned. How the slumbering souls were awakened is shown by the successive waves of excitement which swept over one portion of Europe after another about the middle of the century. The dumb, untutored minds began to ask whether an existence of hopeless and brutal misery was all that was to be realized from the promises of the gospel. The Church had made no real effort at internal reform; it was still grasping, covetous, licentious, and a strange desire for something—they knew not exactly what—began to take possession of men's hearts and spread like an epidemic from village to village and from land to land. In Germany and France there is another Crusade of the Children, earning from Gregory IX. the declaration that they gave a fitting rebuke to their elders, who were basely abandoning the birth-place of humanity.[240]

But the most formidable and significant manifestation of this universal restlessness and gregarious enthusiasm is seen in the uprising of the peasantry—the first of the wandering bands known{269} as Pastoureaux. The helpless and hopeless state of the lower classes of society in those dreary ages has probably never been exceeded in any period of the world's history. The terrible maxim of the feudal law, that the villein's only appeal from his lord was to God—"Mès par notre usage n'a-il entre toi et ton vilein juge fors Deu"— condenses in a word the abject defencelessness of the major part of the population, and human degradation has never, perhaps, been more forcibly expressed than in the infamous *jus primæ noctis* or "droit de marquette." The bitter humor of the trouvère Rutebœuf describes how Satan considered the soul of the villein too despicable to be received in hell; there was no place for it in heaven, so that, after a life of misery on earth, it had no refuge in the hereafter. It is noteworthy in many ways that the Church, which should have been the mediator between the villein and his lord, and which, in teaching the common brotherhood of man, should have earned the gratitude of the miserable serf, was always the special object of aversion and attack in the brief saturnalia of the self-enfranchised wretches.[241]

Suddenly, about Easter, 1251, there appeared a mysterious preacher, known as the Hungarian, advanced in years, and clothed with the attributes which most excite popular awe and veneration. In his clenched hand, which never was opened, he carried a paper given to him by the Virgin Mary herself, which was his mandate and commission. Yet men said that he had from his youth been an apostate from Christ to Mahomet, that he had drunk deeply of the poisonous wells of magic flowing at Toledo, and that he had received from Satan the mission of carrying the unarmed populations of Europe to the East, so that the Soldan of Babylon should find Christendom an easy prey. Remembering the Crusade of the Children, people leaped to the conclusion that it was he who had devastated so many houses with his magic arts, leading forth the tender youth to perish of starvation and exposure. Tall and pale, gifted with eloquence to win the hearts of the multitude, speaking like a native in French and German and Latin, he set forth, preaching from town to town the supineness of the rich and powerful{270} who allowed the Holy Land to remain in the grasp of the Infidel and the good King Louis to languish in his Egyptian dungeon. God had tired of the selfishness and ambition of the nobles, and he called the poor and humble, without arms and captains, to rescue the Holy Places and the Good King. All this found ready response, but even greater applause followed his attacks upon the clergy. The Mendicant Orders were vagrants and hypocrites; the Cistercians were greedy of money and lands; the Benedictines proud and gluttonous; the canons wholly given to secular aims and the lusts of the flesh; the bishops and their officials were money-seekers, who shrank from no trickery to accomplish their aims. As for Rome, no terms of objurgation were too strong for the papal court. The people, whose hate and contempt for the clergy were unbounded, listened to this rhetoric with delight, and eagerly joined a movement which promised a reform in some unseen way. Shepherds left their sheep, husbandmen their ploughs, deaf to the commands of their lords, and followed him unarmed, taking no thought of the morrow, nor asking how they were to be fed.

There were not lacking those high in station who, carried away with the general enthusiasm, imagined that God was about to work miracles with the poor and helpless after the great ones of the earth had failed. Even Queen Blanche, eager for any means that promised to liberate her son, looked upon the movement for a while with favor, and lent it her countenance. It swelled and grew till the wandering multitudes amounted to more than a hundred thousand men, bearing fifty banners as an emblem of victory. It was impossible, of course, to confine such an uprising to the peaceful and humble. No sooner did it assume proportions promising immunity than it inevitably drew to itself all the disorderly elements inseparable from the society of the time—the "ruptarii" and "ribaldi," whom we have seen figure so largely in the Albigensian troubles. These flocked to it from all sides, bringing knife and dagger, sword and axe, and giving to the immense procession a still more menacing aspect. That outrages were committed we can well believe, for the wrongs of class against class were too flagrant to remain unavenged when opportunity offered for reprisals.

On June 11, 1251, they entered Orleans, against the commands of the bishop, but welcomed by the people, though the{271} richer citizens prudently locked their doors. All might have passed peaceably there as elsewhere but for a hot-headed student of the flourishing university of the city, who interrupted the preaching of the Hungarian to denounce him as a liar, and was promptly brained by a zealous follower. A tumult followed, in which the Pastoureaux made short work of the Orleans clergy, breaking into their houses, burning their books, and slaying many, or tossing them into the Loire; and, what is most significant, the people are described as looking on approvingly. The bishop, and all who could hide themselves from the fury of the mob, escaped during the night, and valiantly laid the city under interdict for the guilty complicity of the citizens.

On hearing this the Regent Blanche said, "God knows I thought they would recover the Holy Land in simplicity and holiness. But since they are deceivers, let them be excommunicated and destroyed." Accordingly they were excommunicated, but before the anathema could be published they had reached Bourges, where, in a tumult, the Hungarian was slain, and they broke up into bands. The authorities, recovering from their stupor, pursued the luckless wretches everywhere, who were slain like mad dogs. Some emissaries who penetrated to England, and succeeded in raising a revolt of some five hundred peasants, met the same fate; and it was reported that the second in command under the Hungarian was captured in a vessel on the Garonne, while endeavoring to escape, and on his person were found magic powders and strange letters in Arabic and Chaldee characters from the Soldan of Babylon promising his co-operation.

The quasi-religious nature of the uprising is shown in the functions exercised by the leaders, who acted the part of bishops, blessing the people, sprinkling holy water, and even celebrating marriages. The favor which the people everywhere showed them was attributed principally to their spoiling, beating, and slaying the clergy, thus indicating the deep-seated popular antagonism to the Church, and justifying the declaration made by prelates high in station that so great a danger had never threatened Christendom since the time of Mahomet.[242]{272}

Even more remarkable, as a manifestation of popular emotion, was the first apparition of the Flagellants. Suddenly, in 1259, in Perugia, no one knew why, the population was seized with a fury of devotional penitence, without incitement by friar or priest. The contagion spread, and soon the whole of upper Italy was filled with tens of thousands of penitents. Nobles and peasants, old and young, even to children five years of age, walked solemnly in procession, two by two, naked except a loin-cloth, weeping and praying God for mercy, and scourging themselves with leather thongs to the drawing of blood. The women decently inflicted the penance on themselves in their chambers, but the men marched through the cities by day and night, in the sharpest winter, preceded by priests with crosses and banners, to the churches, where they prostrated themselves before the altars. A contemporary tells us that the fields and mountains echoed with the voices of the sinners calling to God, while music and love-songs were heard no more. A general fever of repentance and amendment seized the people. Usurers and robbers restored their ill-gotten gain; criminals confessed their sins and renounced their vices; the prison doors were thrown open, and the captives walked forth; homicides offered themselves on their knees, with drawn swords, to the kindred of their victims, and were embraced with tears; old enmities were forgiven, and exiles were permitted to return to their homes. Everywhere was seen the operation of divine grace, and men seemed to be consumed with heavenly fire. The movement even spread to the Rhinelands and throughout Germany and Bohemia; but whatever hopes were aroused of the regeneration of man vanished with the subsidence of the excitement, which disappeared as rapidly as it came, and was even denounced as a heresy. Uberto Pallavicino took effectual means of keeping the Flagellants out of his city of Milan; for when he heard of their approach he erected three hundred gibbets by the roadside, at sight of which they abruptly retraced their steps.[243]{273}

It was in a population subject to such tempests of emotion, and groping thus blindly for something higher and better than the hopeless degradation around them, that the Mendicant Orders came to gather to themselves the potential religious exaltation of the time. That they should develop with unexampled rapidity was inevitable.

Everything favored them. The papal court early recognized in them an instrument more efficient than had yet been devised to bring the power of the Holy See to bear directly upon the Church and the people in every corner of Christendom; to break down the independence of the local prelates; to combat the temporal enemies of the papacy, and to lead the people into direct relations with the successor of St. Peter. Privileges and exemptions of all kinds were showered upon them, until, by a series of bulls issued, between 1240 and 1244, by Gregory IX. and Innocent IV., they were rendered completely independent of the regular ecclesiastical organization. A time-honored rule of the Church required that any excommunication or anathema could only be removed by him who had pronounced it, but this was revolutionized in their favor. Not only were the bishops required to give absolution to any Dominican or Franciscan who should apply for it, except in cases of such enormity that the Holy See alone could act, but the Mendicant priors and ministers were authorized to absolve their friars from any censures inflicted on them. These extraordinary measures removed them entirely from the regular jurisdiction of the establishment; the members of each Order became responsible only to their own superiors, and in their all-pervading activity throughout Europe they could secretly undermine the power and influence of the local hierarchy, and replace it with that of Rome, which they so directly represented. This independent position, however, had only been reached by degrees. Papal briefs of 1229 and 1234, enjoining them to show proper respect and obedience to the bishops, and empowering the bishops to condemn any friars who abuse their privileges of preaching for purposes of gain, show that complaints of their aggressions had commenced thus early, and that Rome was not yet prepared to render them independent of the hierarchy; but when the policy had once been adopted it was carried to its fullest development, and the cycle of legislation was completed by Boniface VIII., in 1295 and 1296, by a series of{274} bulls in which, following his predecessors, the Mendicants were formally released from all episcopal jurisdiction, and the statutes of the Orders were declared to be the only laws by which they were to be judged, all provisions of the canon law to the contrary notwithstanding. At the same time, by a new issue of the bull *Virtute conspicuos*, commonly known as the *Mare Magnum*, he codified and confirmed all the privileges conferred by his predecessors.[244]

The Holy See was thus provided with a militia, recruited and sustained at the expense of the faithful, panoplied in invulnerability, and devoted to its exclusive service. In order that its usefulness might suffer no limitation, in 1241 Gregory IX. granted to the friars the privilege of freely living in the lands of excommunicates, and of asking and receiving assistance and food from them. They could, therefore, penetrate everywhere, and serve as secret emissaries in the dominions of those hostile to Rome. Human ingenuity could have devised no more efficient army, for, not only were they full of zeal and inspired with profound convictions, but the reputation for superior sanctity which they everywhere acquired{275} secured for them popular sympathy and support, and gave them an enormous advantage in any contest with local churches.[245]

Their efficiency, when directed against temporal opponents, was thoroughly tried in the long and mortal struggle of the papacy with Frederic II., the most powerful and dangerous enemy whom Rome has ever had. As early as the year 1229 we hear of the banishment of all the Franciscans from the kingdom of Naples, as papal emissaries seeking to withdraw from the emperor the allegiance of his subjects. In 1234 we find them raising money in England to enable the pope to carry on the struggle, and using every device of persuasion and menace with a success which realized immense sums and reduced numbers to beggary. When, in the solemnities of Easter, 1239, Gregory fulminated an excommunication against the emperor, it was to the Franciscan priors that he communicated it, with a full recital of the imperial misdeeds, and ordered them to publish it with ringing of bells on every Sunday and feast-day. It was the most effective method that could be devised to create public opinion against his adversary, and Frederic retorted with another edict of expulsion. When Frederic was deposed by the Council of Lyons, in 1244, it was the Dominicans who were selected to announce the sentence in all accessible public places, with an indulgence of forty days for all who would gather to listen to them, and plenary remission of sins to the friars who might suffer persecution in consequence. Soon afterwards we find them playing the part, which the Jesuits filled in Jacobean England, of secret emissaries engaged in hidden plots and fomenting disturbances. Frederic always declared that the conspiracy against his life in 1244 was the work of Franciscans who had been commissioned to preach a secret crusade against him in his own dominions, and who encouraged his enemies with prophecies of his speedy death. When, as the result of papal intrigues, Henry Raspe of Thuringia was elected, in 1246, as King of the Romans,{276} to supersede Frederic, Innocent IV. sent a circular brief of instructions to the Franciscans to use every opportunity, public or secret, to advocate his cause, and to promise remission of sins to those who should aid him. Again, in 1248, we find friars of both orders sent as secret emissaries to stir up disaffection in Frederic's territories. He complained bitterly of it, as he had always cherished and protected the Mendicants, and he met the attempt with savage ferocity. The Dominican Simon de Montesarculo, who was caught, was subjected to eighteen successive tortures; and Frederic instructed his son-in-law, the Count of Caserta, that all friars showing signs of disaffection, or contravening the strict regulations which he prescribes, shall not be exiled as heretofore, but shall be promptly burned. The shrewd and experienced prince evidently recognized them as the most dangerous enemies to whom he was exposed. They continued to earn his hostility by the zeal with which they preached the crusade against him, and, after his death, against his son Conrad; and we can regard as not improbable the statement that Ezzelin da Romano, his vicar in the March of Treviso, put to death no less than sixty Franciscans during his thirty years of power.[246]

The Mendicants gradually superseded the bishops, when papal commands were to be communicated to the people or papal mandates enforced. Even when fugitives were to be tracked, they formed an invisible network of police, spread over Europe and available in a thousand ways. Formerly, when a complaint reached Rome of an abuse to be rectified or of a prelate whose conduct required investigation or trial, a commission would be issued to two or three neighboring bishops or abbots to make an examination and report, or to reform churches and monasteries neglectful of discipline. Gradually this changed, and the Mendicants alone were charged with these duties, which made the papal power felt so directly in every episcopal palace and every abbey in Europe. They complained repeatedly of the amount of this extra work thrown upon them, and they were promised relief, but{277} they were too useful to be dispensed with in thus subjecting the Church to the Apostolic See. How disagreeable and even dangerous these duties might be is visible in a case which shows how little the condition of the Church in the middle of the thirteenth century had changed from what we had seen it in the previous age. The great electoral archiepiscopate of Trèves, in 1259, was claimed by two rivals who litigated with each other for two years in Rome, to the great profit of the curia, till Alexander IV. set them both aside. The Dean of Metz, Henry of Fistigen, went on some pretext to Rome, where, by promising to pay the enormous debts left behind by the two litigants, he obtained the appointment from Alexander. On his return the pallium was withheld as security for the debts which he had incurred, but without waiting for it he assumed archiepiscopal functions, consecrated his suffragan Bishop of Metz, and commenced a series of military enterprises, in the course of which he devastated the Abbey of St. Matthias and nearly burned to death the unhappy monks. These misdeeds, and his neglect to pay his debts, led Urban IV., in 1261, to commission the Bishops of Worms and Spires and the Abbot of Rodenkirk to investigate the charges against him of simony, perjury, homicide, sacrilege, and other sins, but the archbishop bribed them, and they did nothing. Then, in 1262, Urban sent another commission to William and Roric, two Franciscans of the province of Trèves, ordering them to investigate and report under pain of excommunication. This frightened all the Mendicants of the province. The Franciscan guardian and the Dominican prior, more worldly-wise than righteous, forbade them under pain of dungeon from exercising the functions imposed on them, and the two unlucky commissioners were glad to escape with their lives by flying from Trèves to Metz. The Franciscan provincial had the effrontery to send envoys to Rome asking that the investigation be postponed or committed to others. They were heard in full consistory, in presence of Urban himself and of Bonaventura, the general of the Order, when Urban bitterly retorted, "If I had sent bishoprics to two of your brethren they would have been accepted with avidity. You shall not refuse to do what is necessary for the honor of God and the Church." It is not worth while to pursue the intricate details of the dreary quarrel, which lasted until 1272 and presented in its successive phases every variety of fraud,{278} forgery, robbery, and outrage. It is sufficient to say that when William and Roric were forced to work, they seem to have performed their duty with independence and fidelity, and that the Roman curia, in the course of the proceedings, managed to extort from the unfortunate diocese the enormous sum of thirty-three thousand sterling marks—in spite of which Archbishop Henry attended the coronation of Rodolph of Hapsburg, in 1273, with a splendid retinue of eighteen hundred armed men.[247]

It is easy to imagine that such functions as these produced antagonism between the new orders and the old organization which they were undermining and supplanting. Yet this was, perhaps, the least of the causes of bitterness between them. A far more fruitful source of discord was the intrusion of the Mendicants in the office of preaching and hearing confessions. We have seen how jealously the former had always been reserved by the bishops and how utterly it had been neglected until the primary object of St. Dominic had been to supply the deficiency, which Honorius III. lamented as one of the pressing wants of the age. The Church was scarce better prepared to discharge the duty of the confessional, which the Lateran Council had rendered obligatory and had confined to the priesthood. Lazy and sensual priests, intent only on maintaining their revenues, neglected the souls of their flocks and permitted no intrusion which might diminish their gains. In the populous town of

Montpellier there was only one church in which the sacrament of penitence could be administered, and the consuls, in 1213, petitioned Innocent III., in view of the multitude of perishing souls, to empower four or five of the other churches of the town to divide the duty. As late as 1247, Ypres, with two hundred thousand inhabitants, had but four parish churches. If the Church Militant was to perform its duty, and if it was to regain the veneration of the people, these deficiencies must be supplied.[248]

The first efforts of Dominic had been based on the power{279} granted to the legates of Languedoc to issue licenses for preaching, and these were, of course, at the time independent of episcopal permission, but in the Rule of 1228 it was especially provided that no friar should preach in a diocese without first obtaining permission of the bishop, and in no case was he to declaim against the vices of the secular priesthood. Francis professed the humblest reverence for the established clergy; he declared that if he were to meet simultaneously a priest and an angel, he would first turn to kiss the hands of the priest, saying to the angel, "Wait, for these hands handle the Word of Life and possess something more than human;" and in his Rule it was also provided that no friar should preach in any diocese against the will of the bishop. The bishops were not particularly disposed to welcome the intruders, and Honorius III. condescended to entreaty in asking them to permit the Dominicans to preach, while he also took steps to provide preachers from among the secular clergy by stimulating their study of theology. The intrusion of the Mendicants on the functions of the parish priests was gradual, and was commenced with the privilege granted them of celebrating mass everywhere on portable altars. Some resistance was made to this, but it was broken down; and when Gregory IX., in 1227, signalized his accession by empowering both Orders to preach, hear confessions, and grant absolution everywhere, the wandering friars, in spite of the prohibitions of the Rules, gradually invaded every parish and performed all the duties of the cure of souls, to the immense discomfort of the local priesthood, who had always guarded with extreme jealousy the rights which were the main source of their influence and revenue. Complaints were loud and reiterated, and were sometimes listened to, but were more frequently answered by an emphatic confirmation of the innovation.[249]{280}

The matter was made worse by the fact that everywhere the laity welcomed the intruders and preferred them to their own curates. The fervor of their preaching and their reputation for superior sanctity brought crowds to the sermon and the confessional. Training and experience rendered them far more skilful directors of conscience than the indolent incumbents, and there arose a natural popular feeling that the penance which they imposed was more holy and their absolution more efficacious. If the beneficed clergy complained that this was because they soothed and indulged their penitents, they were able to retort with justice that the laymen preferred them for themselves and their wives rather than the drunken and unchaste priests who filled most of the parishes. A friar would come and set up his portable altar, as he said, for a day. His preaching was attractive; penitents aroused to a sense of their sins would hasten to confess; his stay was prolonged and he became a fixture. If the place was populous, he would be joined by others. The gifts of the charitable would flow in. A modest chapel and cloisters would be provided, which grew till it overshadowed the parish church and was filled at its expense. Worse than all, the dying sinner would assume the robe of the Mendicant on his death-bed, bequeath his body to the friars, and make them the recipient of his legacies, leading to a prolonged and embittered renewal of the old ghoul-like quarrels over corpses. In 1247, at Pamplona, some bodies long lay unburied owing to a fierce contention between the canons and the Franciscans; and a division of the spoils, by which a share varying from a half to a quarter, was allotted to the parish priests, only gave rise to new disputes. Whenever an open conflict arose, however much the pope might deprecate scandal, the decision would be almost certainly in favor of the friars, and the clergy saw with dismay and hatred that the upstarts were supplanting them in all their functions, in the veneration of the people, and in the profitable results of that veneration. When, in 1268, a popular uprising against tyranny occurred in Holland and Guelderland, and, encouraged by success, the rebels formulated a policy for the reformation of society, they proposed{281} to slay all nobles and prelates and monks, but to spare the Mendicants and such few parish priests as might be necessary to administer the sacraments. Some feeble efforts were made by the clergy to emulate the services and activity of the new-comers, but the sloth and self-indulgence of ages could not be overcome. It was inevitable that the strongest antagonism between the old order and the new should spring up, heightened by the duty which the friars felt of denouncing publicly the vices and corruption of the clergy. Already in the previous century the secular priesthood had complained bitterly of the impulse given to monachism by the founding and development of the Cistercians. They had even dared to make vigorous representations to the third Council of Lateran, in 1179, alleging that they were threatened with pauperization. Here was a new and vastly more dangerous inroad, and it was impossible that they should submit without an effort of self-preservation. There must be a struggle for supremacy between the local churches on the one hand and the papacy with its new militia on the other, and the conservatives manifested skill in their selection of the field of battle.[250]

The University of Paris was the centre of scholastic theology. Cosmopolitan in its character, a long line of great teachers had lectured to immense masses of students from every land, until its reputation was European and it was looked upon as the bulwark of orthodoxy. In every episcopate it could count its graduates{282} and the holders of its degrees, who looked back upon it with filial affection as to their *alma mater*. It had welcomed Dominic's first missionaries when they came to Paris to found a house of the Order, and it had admitted Dominicans to its corps of teachers. Suddenly there arose a quarrel, the insignificance of its cause showing the tension which existed and the eagerness of all classes of the clergy to repress the growing influence of the Mendicants. The University had always been jealous of its privileges, among which not the least was the jurisdiction which it enjoyed over its students. One of these was slain and several were wounded by the Paris watch in a disturbance, and the reparation tendered for the offence was deemed insufficient. The University closed its doors, but the Dominican teachers, Bonushomo and Elias, continued their lectures. To punish this contumacy they were ordered to be silent, and students were forbidden to listen to them. They appealed to the pope, but their appeal was disregarded; and when the University resumed its functions, they were required to take an oath to observe its statutes, provided there was nothing therein to conflict with the Rule of the Order. This they refused unless they were allowed two teachers of theology, and after a delay of a fortnight they were expelled. The provincials of both Orders at Paris took up the quarrel and appealed to Rome, and Innocent IV. demanded the repeal of the obnoxious rules.[251]

The gage of battle was thrown and the university was resolved on no half-measures. It would reduce the Mendicants to the condition of the other religious orders and earn the gratitude of all the prelates and clergy by stripping them of the privileges which rendered them so dangerous. For this purpose it was necessary to win the favor of Rome, and the students enthusiastically assessed themselves, economizing in their expenses that they might contribute to the fund which was necessary if anything was to be done with the curia. The leader of the faculty in the quarrel was William of St. Amour, noted both as a preacher and a teacher,{283} learned, eloquent, and inflexible of purpose. He was sent to the Holy See, where he found Innocent IV. in a frame of mind adapted to listen to his arguments that the Mendicant Rules were fitted only to lead souls to perdition. The pope had been the friend of the Orders, and had confirmed and enlarged their privileges, but just now was out of humor. The Dominicans asserted that this arose from their having secretly received into the Order one of his cousins whom he loved greatly and intended to advance in the world; and also from the malevolence of another cousin, who proposed to build at Genoa a fortress-palace to dominate the city, and had been prevented by the Dominicans refusing to sell a piece of ground essential to his purpose. Innocent's mind must indeed have been receptive of William of St. Amour's arguments. In July and August, 1254, he had issued repeated briefs in favor of the Mendicants and against the University. On November 21 he promulgated the bull *Etsi Animarum*, known among the Mendicants as the "terrible" bull, by which the members of all religious orders were forbidden to receive in their churches on Sundays and feast-days the parishioners of others; they were not to hear confessions without the special license of the parish priests, they were not to preach in their own churches before mass, so that parishioners should not be drawn away from their parish churches, nor were they to preach in the parish churches, nor when bishops preached or caused preaching to be done.[252]

The bull was in reality a terrible one, for it shattered at a blow the edifice erected with such infinite labor and self-sacrifice. To meet it, the Dominicans not only summoned their greatest and wisest members, but appealed to Heaven. Every friar was ordered daily after matins to recite seven psalms and the litanies of the Virgin and St. Dominic. A brother, during this exercise, was encouraged with a vision of the Virgin pleading with the Son and saying "Listen to them, my Son, listen to them!" He did listen{284}to them, for though we may doubt the Dominican story that Innocent was stricken with paralysis the very day that he signed the "*crudelissimum edictum*" he certainly did die on December 7, within sixteen days after it, and a pious Roman had a vision of his soul handed over to the two wrathful saints, Dominic and Francis. Moreover the Cardinal of Albano, whose hostility to the Orders had led him to take an active part in advising Innocent to the measure, was imprudent enough to boast that he had caused the subjugation of the Mendicants to the bishops and would place them under the feet of the lowest priests. The same day a beam in his house gave way; he fell and broke his neck. It would perhaps be unjust to accuse the Dominicans of having assisted nature in these catastrophes; but, strange as it seems to hear them boast of having prayed a pope to death, they certainly do relate with pride that "Beware of the Dominican litanies, for they work miracles," became a common phrase.[253]

The death of Innocent saved the Mendicant Orders. That his successor was elected after an interval of only fourteen days was due to the provident care of the Prefect of Rome, who, distrusting the operation of the Holy Ghost, put the fathers of the Conclave on short rations, resulting in the election of Alexander IV. The new pope was specially favorable to the Mendicants. When John of Parma, the Franciscan general, came to him with the customary request that he would appoint a cardinal as "Protector" of the Order, he refused, saying that so long as he lived it should need no other protector than himself; and his selection of the Dominican Raymond of Pennaforte and the Franciscan Ruffino as papal chaplains showed how willingly he subjected himself to their influence. On December 31, ten days after his elevation, he addressed letters to both Orders asking their suffrages and intercession with God, and the same day he issued an encyclical, revoking the terrible bull of Innocent and pronouncing it void.[254]

Before such a judge the case of the University was evidently lost. On April 14, 1255, appeared the bull *Quasi lignum vitæ*, deciding the quarrel in favor of the Dominicans. Yet William of{285} St. Amour returned to Paris resolved to carry on the war. In the pulpit he and his friends thundered forth against the Mendicants. They were not specifically named, but there was no mistaking the ingenious application to them of the signs foretold by the prophets of those who should usher in the days of Antichrist, nor the description of the Pharisees and Publicans made to fit them. New and unimagined perils threatened the Church in the last times. The devil has found that he gained nothing in sending heretics who were easily confuted, so now he has sent the

Pale Horse of the Apocalypse—the hypocrites and false brethren who, under an external guise of sanctity, convulse the Church. The persecution of the hypocrites will be more disastrous than all previous persecutions. Another weapon which lay to his hand was eagerly grasped. In 1254 there appeared a work under the name of "Introduction to the Everlasting Gospel," of which the authorship was ascribed to John of Parma, the Franciscan general. We shall have occasion to recur to this, and need only say here that a section of the Franciscans were strongly inclined to the mysticism which now began to show itself, and that the writings of Abbot Joachim of Fiore, now revived and hardily developed, predicted the downfall, in 1260, of the existing order of things in Church and State, the substitution of a new evangel for that of Christ, and the replacement of the hierarchy by mendicant monachism. The "Introduction to the Everlasting Gospel" attracted universal attention and offered too tempting an opening for attack to be neglected.

The University sullenly held out, while Alexander fulminated bull after bull against the recalcitrants, threatening them with varied penalties, and finally calling in the assistance of the secular arm by an appeal to St. Louis. The clergy of Paris, delighted with the opportunity afforded by the temporary unpopularity of the Mendicants, reviled them from the pulpit, and even attacked them personally with blows and threats of worse treatment, till they scarce ventured to appear in the streets and beg their daily bread. The controversy raged wilder as the indomitable St. Amour, undeterred by Alexander's request to the king to throw him into jail, issued a tract entitled *"De Periculis novissimorum Temporum,"* in which he boldly set forth all the arguments of his discourses against the Mendicants. He proved that the pope had no right to contravene the commands of the prophets and apostles, and that{286} they were convicted of error when they upturned the established order of the Church in permitting these wandering hypocrites and false prophets to preach and hear confessions. Those who live by beggary are flatterers and liars and detractors and thieves and avoiders of justice. Whoever asserts that Christ was a beggar denies that he was the Messiah, and thus is a heresiarch who destroys the foundation of all Christian faith. An able-bodied man commits sacrilege if he receives the alms of the poor for his own use, and if the Church has permitted this for the monks it has been in error and should be corrected. It rests with the bishops to purge their dioceses of these hypocrites; they have the power, and if they neglect their duty the blood of those who perish will be upon their heads. This was answered by Aquinas and Bonaventura. The former, in his tract *"Contra Impugnantes Religionem,"* proved in the most finished style of scholastic logic that the friars have a right to teach, to preach and hear confessions, and to live without labor; in the same mode he rebutted the charges as to their morals and influence, showing that they were not precursors of Antichrist. He also demonstrated the more suggestive theorems that they had a right to resist their defamers, to use the courts in their defence, to secure their safety if necessary by resort to arms, and to punish their persecutors. That his dialectics were equal to bringing out any desired conclusion when once his premises were granted is well known, and they did not fail him on this occasion. Bonaventura also replied in several treatises—*"De Paupertate Christi,"* in which he earnestly pleaded the example of Christ as an argument for poverty and mendicancy; the *"Libellus Apologeticus"* and the *"Tractatus quia Fratres Minores prædicent,"* in which he carried the war into the enemy's territory with a vigorous and plain-spoken onslaught on the shortcomings and defects and sins and corruption and vileness of the clergy. Heretics might well feel justified in seeing the two parties into which the Church was divided thus expose each other; and the faithful might well doubt whether salvation was assured with either.

Yet this wordy war was mere surplusage. On the appearance of St. Amour's book, St. Louis had hastened to send copies to Alexander for judgment. The University likewise sent St. Amour at the head of a delegation to demand the condemnation of the Everlasting Gospel. Albertus Magnus and Bonaventura came{287} to defend their Orders, and a hot disputation was held before the consistory. The Everlasting Gospel and its Introduction were condemned with decent reserve by a special commission assembled at Anagni, in July, 1255, but St. Amour's book was declared by the bull *Romanus Pontifex*, October 5, 1256, to be lying, scandalous, deceptive, wicked, and execrable. It was ordered to be burned before the curia and the University; every copy was to be surrendered within eight days to be burned, and any one presuming to defend it was pronounced a rebel. The envoys of St. Louis and the University were obliged to subscribe to a declaration assenting to this and to the right of the Mendicants to preach and hear confessions and to live on alms without labor, William of St. Amour alone resolutely refusing. Alexander moreover ordered all teachers and preachers to abstain from reviling the Mendicants and to retract the abuse they had uttered under pain of loss of preferment—a command which was but slackly obeyed.[255]

The victory was won for the Mendicants. The University submitted ungraciously to the irresistible power of the papacy, and the unconquerable William of St. Amour alone held out. He would make no acknowledgments, no concessions. He had sworn to abide by the mandates of the Church, but he refused to recant like his comrades. When about to return, in August, 1257, Alexander forbade him to go to France and perpetually interdicted him from teaching, and so great was the dread which he inspired that the pope wrote to St. Louis asking him to prevent the inflexible theologian from entering his kingdom. Yet from abroad he maintained an active correspondence with his old colleagues, and the University continued in a state of disquiet. It was in vain that Alexander prohibited all intercourse with him. Though the Mendicants were allowed to teach, they were ridiculed in indecent rhymes and lampoons, which were eagerly circulated; and, on Palm Sunday of 1259 the beadle of the University, Guillot of Picardy, interrupted the preaching of Thomas Aquinas by publishing{288} a scandalous and libellous book against the Mendicants. Yet this gradually died out, and the final act of the quarrel is seen in an epistle of Alexander's, December 3, 1260, authorizing the Bishop of Paris to absolve those who had incurred excommunication by keeping copies of St. Amour's book, on their surrendering them to be burned, the number of these "rebels" apparently being quite large. Still St. Amour remained steadfast in exile. He was allowed to return to Paris by Clement IV. who ascended the papal throne in 1264, and in 1266 he sent to the pontiff another book on the same theme. Clement had hastened, in 1265, to proclaim his good-will to the Mendicant Orders by a bull in which he confirmed in the amplest manner their independence of the bishops, and, as was inevitable, he rejected St. Amour's new book as filled with the old virus. William died in 1272, obstinate and unrepentant, and was honorably buried in his native village of St. Amour, though he is reputed as a heretic by all good Dominicans and Franciscans.[256]

The embers of the controversy had been rekindled in 1269 by an anonymous Franciscan who assailed St. Amour's book. Gerald of Abbeville, who is ranked with Aquinas, Bonaventura, and Robert of Sorbonne, as one of the four chief theologians of the age, replied with an attack on the doctrine of poverty and a defence of the ownership of property. Bonaventura rejoined with his "*Apologia Pauperum*," an eloquent defence of poverty, and the Franciscan annalists relate with natural glee how Gerard was so overcome by his adversary's logic that, under the vengeance of God, he lost the {289} faculty of reasoning, sank into paralysis, and ended with a horrible death by leprosy.[257]

Though an occasional outbreak like this might occur, the victory was won. The aggressions of the Mendicants had raised a deep and wide-spread hostility against them in all ranks of the clergy, who recognized not only that their privileges and wealth were impaired, that the reverence of the people was intercepted, but, what was even more important, that this new papal militia was subjecting them to Rome with a force that would deprive them of what little independence had been left by former encroachments. When, therefore, the upstarts had dared a combat with the honored and powerful University of Paris—the shining sun, to use the words of Alexander IV., which pours the light of pure doctrine through the whole world, the body from which, as from the bosom of a parent, are born the noble race of doctors who enlighten Christendom and uphold the Catholic faith—it might well be thought that the rash interlopers had provoked their fate. Everything had been tried—learning and wit, reverence for established institutions, popular favor, the long-enjoyed right of the governing faculty to regulate its internal affairs—yet everything had failed against the steadfastness of the Mendicants supported by the unwavering favor of Alexander. When the University of Paris had been worsted in the struggle, though aided with the sympathy of all the prelates of Christendom, there was little hope in further opposition to those whom the pope, in forbidding the prelates to side with the University, described as "Golden vials filled with sweet odors."[258]

Yet spasmodic resistance, however hopeless, still continued. A bull of Clement IV., in 1268, forbidding the archbishops and bishops from even interpreting the privileges conferred on the Mendicants, shows that the hostility was as bitter as ever. The clergy would also still occasionally endeavor to prevent the establishment of new Mendicant houses, or seek to drive them away by ill-treatment, with the inevitable result of calling forth the papal vengeance. They had a gleam of hope when the wise and learned John XXI. ascended the papal throne, but his antagonism to the Mendicants, {290} like that of Innocent IV., was not conducive to longevity. The roof of his palace fell in upon him after a pontificate of but eight months, and the pious chroniclers of the Orders handed down his memory as that of a heretic and magician. About 1284 the interpretation put on some fresh concessions by Martin IV. aroused the antagonism anew. The whole Gallican Church uprose. In 1287 the Archbishop of Reims called a provincial council to consider the subject. He pathetically described his futile efforts to reach a peaceful solution, the unbearable encroachments of the friars, the intolerable injuries inflicted on both clergy and laity, and the necessity of an appeal to Rome. The expenses of such an appeal were known to be heavy, and all the bishops agreed to contribute five per cent. of their revenues, while a levy of one per cent. was made on all abbots, priors, deans, chapters, and parochial churches of the province. The pious Franciscan Salimbene informs us that a hundred thousand livres tournois were raised and Honorius IV. was won over. On Good Friday of 1287 he was to issue a bull depriving the Mendicants of the right to preach and hear confessions. They were in despair, but this time it was the prayers of the Franciscans which prevailed, as those of the Dominicans had done in the case of Innocent IV. The hand of God fell upon Honorius in the night of Wednesday, he died on Thursday, and the Orders were saved. Yet the struggle continued till the bull of Martin IV. was withdrawn in 1298 by Boniface VIII., who in vain attempted to put an end to the quarrel which distracted the Church. Benedict XI. was no more successful, and complained that the trouble was a hydra, putting forth seven heads for every one which was cut off. In 1323 John XXII. pronounced heretical the doctrine of Jean de Poilly, who held that confession to the friars was void and that every one must confess to his parish priest. In 1351 the clergy again took heart for another attack. Possibly the devotion shown by the Mendicants during the Black Death, when twenty-five million human beings were swept away, when the priests abandoned their posts, and the friars alone were found to tend the sick and console the dying, may have led to fresh progress by them and have enkindled antagonism anew. Be this as it may, a vast deputation, embracing cardinals, bishops, and minor clergy, waited on Clement VI. and petitioned for the abolition of the Orders, or at least the prohibition of their preaching and hearing {291} confessions, and enjoying the burial profits, by which they were enormously enriched at the expense of the parish priests. The Mendicants deigned no reply, but Clement spoke for them, denying the allegation of the petition that they were useless to the Church, and asserting that, on the contrary, they were most valuable. "And if," he continued, "their preaching be stopped, about what can you preach to the people? If on humility, you yourselves are the proudest of the world, arrogant and given to pomp. If on poverty, you are the most grasping and most covetous, so that all the benefices in the world will not satisfy you. If on chastity—but we will be silent on this, for God knoweth what each man does and how many of you satisfy your lusts. You hate the Mendicants and shut your doors on them lest they should see your mode of life, while you waste your temporal wealth on pimps and swindlers. You should not complain if the Mendicants receive some temporal possessions from the dying to whom they minister when you have fled, nor that they spend it in buildings where everything is ordered for the honor of God and the Church, in place of wasting it in pleasure and licentiousness. And because you do not likewise, you accuse the Mendicants, for most of you give yourselves up to vain and worldly lives." Under this fierce rebuke, even though uttered by a pope whom St. Birgitta denounced as himself a follower of the lusts of the flesh, there was evidently nothing practicable but submission. Yet the prelates were not silenced, for a few years later Richard, Archbishop of Armagh, preached in London some sermons against the Mendicants, for which they accused him of heresy before Innocent VI. In 1357 he defended himself in a discourse wherein he handled them unsparingly, but his case dragged on, and he died in Avignon, in 1360, before it reached an end. This was not reassuring for the secular clergy, but still the quarrel went on. Thus in 1373 the Franciscan Guardian of Syracuse applied to Gregory XI. for an authentic copy of the bull of John XXII. against the errors of Jean de Poilly, showing that in Sicily the secular clergy were contesting the right of the Mendicants to hear confessions. In 1386 the Council of Salzburg forcibly described the scandals wrought by the intrusion in all parishes, uninvited and irrepressible, of those licentious wandering friars, who kindled discord and set an example of evil, and it proceeded to decree that in future they should not be allowed{292} to preach and hear confessions without the license of the bishop and the invitation of the pastor. In 1393 Conrad II., Archbishop of Mainz, varied his persecution of the Waldenses by an edict in which he described the Mendicants as wolves in sheep's clothing, and prohibited them from hearing confessions. On the other hand, Maître Jean de Gorelle, a Franciscan, in 1408, publicly argued that curates were not competent to preach and hear confessions, which was the business of the friars—a proposition which the University of Paris promptly compelled him to retract.[259]

The quarrel seemed endless. In 1409 the Mendicants complained that the clergy stigmatized them as robbers and wolves, and insisted that all sins confessed to them must be confessed again to the parish curates, thus reviving the error of Jean de Poilly condemned by John XXII. Alexander V., himself a Franciscan, responded to their request by issuing the bull *Regnans in exelsis*, which threatened with the pains of heresy all who should uphold such doctrines, or that the consent of the priest was requisite before the parishioner could confess to the friars. During the great schism the papacy was no longer an object of terror. The University of Paris boldly took up the quarrel, and under the leadership of John Gerson refused to receive this bull, compelling the Dominicans and Carmelites publicly to renounce it, and expelling{293} the Franciscans and Augustinians, who refused to do likewise. Gerson did not hesitate to preach publicly against it in a sermon, in which he enumerated the four persecutions of the Church in the order of their severity—tyrants, heretics, the Mendicants, and Antichrist. This unflattering collocation was not likely to promote harmony, but the matter seems to have slept for a while in the greater questions raised by the councils of Constance and Basle, though the latter assembly took occasion to decide against the Mendicants on the points at issue, as well as to condemn the wide-spread popular belief that any one dying in a Franciscan habit would not spend more than a year at most in purgatory, since St. Francis made an annual visit there and carried off all his followers to heaven. When the papacy regained its strength it renewed the struggle for its favorites. In 1446 Eugenius IV. put forth a new bull, *Gregis nobis crediti*, condemning the doctrines of Jean de Poilly, which attracted little attention, and was followed in 1453 by Nicholas V. with another, *Provisionis nostræ*, of similar import. This was brought in 1456 to the notice of the University, which denounced it as surreptitious, destructive to peace, and subversive of hierarchial subordination. Calixtus III. continued the struggle, and, finding the University unyielding, appealed to Louis XI. for secular interposition, but in vain; the University refused to admit into its body any friars who would not pledge themselves not to make use of these bulls. It is true that in 1458 a priest of Valladolid who denied the authority of the Mendicants to supersede the parish priests was forced to recant publicly in his own church; but the trouble continued, leading in Germany to such scandals that the archbishops of Mainz and Trèves, with other bishops, and the Duke of Bavaria, were obliged to appeal to the Holy See. A commission of two cardinals and two bishops was appointed to determine upon a compromise, which was accepted by both parties and approved by Sixtus IV. about 1480. The priests were not to teach that the Orders were fruitful of heresies, the friars were not to teach that parishioners need not hear mass on Sundays and feast days in their parish churches, or confess to their curates at Easter, though they were not to be deprived of hearing confessions and granting absolutions. Neither priests nor friars were to endeavor to get the laity to choose sepulture with either; and neither party was to assail or detract from the other in their sermons. The insertion{294} of this compromise in the canon law shows the importance attached to it, and that it was regarded as a lasting settlement, applicable throughout Latin Christendom. Its effect is seen in the inclusion, among the heresies of Jean Lallier condemned in Paris in 1484, of those which revived the doctrine of Jean de Poilly and declared that John XXII. had no power to pronounce it heretical. Yet, at the Lateran Council, in 1515, a determined effort was made by the bishops to obtain the revocation of the special privileges of the

97

Mendicants. By refusing to vote for any measures they obtained a promise of this, but skilful delay enabled Leo X. to elude performance till the following year, when a compromise was effected, which merely shows by what it forbade to the Mendicants how contemptuous had been their defiance of episcopal authority. They lost little by this, for in 1519 Erasmus complains in a letter to Albert, Cardinal-Archbishop of Mainz, "The world is overburdened with the tyranny of the Mendicants, who, though they are the satellites of the Roman See, are yet so numerous and powerful that they are formidable to the pope himself and even to kings. To them, when the pope aids them, he is more than God, when he displeases them he is worthless as a dream."[260]

It must be confessed that both Dominicans and Franciscans had greatly fallen away from the virtues of their founders. Scarce had the Orders commenced to spread when false brethren were found who, contrary to their vow of poverty, made use of their faculty of preaching for purposes of filthy gain; and as early as 1233 we find Gregory IX. sharply reminding the Dominican chapter-general that the poverty professed by the Order should be genuine and not fictitious. The wide employment of the friars by the popes as political emissaries necessarily diverted them from their spiritual functions, attracted ambitious and restless men into their ranks, and gave the institutions a worldly character thoroughly{295} in opposition to their original design. Their members, moreover, were peculiarly subject to temptation. Wanderers by profession, they were relieved from supervision, and were subject only to the jurisdiction of their own superiors and to the laws of their own Orders, thus intensifying and rendering peculiarly dangerous the immunity common to all ecclesiastics.[261]

The "Seraphic Religion" of the Franciscans, as it was based on a lofty ideal, was especially subject to the reaction of human imperfection. This was manifest even in the lifetime of St. Francis, who resigned the generalate on account of the abuses which were creeping in, and offered to resume it if the brethren would walk according to his will. It was inevitable that trouble should come between those who conscientiously adhered to the Rule in all its strictness and the worldlings who saw in the Order the instrument of their ambition; and it did not need the prophetic spirit to lead Francis to predict on his death-bed future scandals and divisions and the persecution of those who would not consent to error—a forecast which we will see abundantly verified, as well as that in which he foretold that the Order would become so defamed that it would be ashamed to be seen in public. His successor in the mastership, Elias, gave the Order a powerful impetus on its downward path. Reckoned the shrewdest and most skilful political manager in Italy, he greatly increased its influence and public activity, till his relaxation of the strictness of the Rule gave such offence to the more rigid brethren that, after a hard struggle, they compelled Gregory IX. to remove him, whereupon he went over to the party of Frederic II., and was duly excommunicated. As the Order spread it was not in human nature to reject the wealth which came pouring in upon it from all sides, and ingenious dialectics were resorted to to reconcile its ample possessions with the absolute rejection of property prescribed by the Rule. The humble hovels which Francis had enjoined became stately palaces, which arose in every city, rivalling or putting to shame the loftiest cathedrals and most sumptuous abbeys. In 1257 St. Bonaventura, who had just succeeded John of Parma as General of the Order, varied his controversy with William of St. Amour by an encyclical to his provincials in which he bewailed the contempt{296} and dislike felt universally for the Order, caused by its greedy seeking after money; the idleness of so many of its members, leading them into all manner of vices; the excesses of the vagabond friars, who oppress those who receive them and leave behind them the memory of scandals rather than examples of virtue; the importunate beggary which renders the friar more terrible than a robber to the wayfarer; the construction of magnificent palaces, which oppress friends and give occasion to attacks from enemies; the intrusting of preaching and confession to those wholly unfit; the greedy grasping after legacies and burial fees, to the great disturbance of the clergy, and in general the extravagance which would inevitably cause the chilling of charity. Evidently the assaults of St. Amour and the complaints of the clergy were not without foundation; but this vigorous rebuke was ineffective, and ten years later Bonaventura was obliged to repeat it in even stronger terms. This time he expressed his special horror at the shameless audacity of those brethren who, in their sermons to the laity, attacked the vices of the clergy, and gave rise to scandals, quarrels, and hatreds; and he wound up by declaring, "It is a foul and profane lie to assert one's self the voluntary professor of absolute poverty and then refuse to submit to the lack of anything; to beg abroad like a pauper and to roll in wealth at home." Bonaventura's declamations were in vain, and the struggle in the Order continued, until it ejected its stricter members as heretics, as we shall see when we come to consider the Spiritual Franciscans and the Fraticelli. In the succeeding century both Orders gave free rein to their worldly propensities. St. Birgitta, in her Revelations, which were sanctioned by the Church as inspired, declares that "although founded upon vows of poverty they have amassed riches, place their whole aim in increasing their wealth, dress as richly as bishops, and many of them are more extravagant in their jewelry and ornaments than laymen who are reputed wealthy."[262]

Such was the development of the Mendicant Orders and their{297} complicated relations with the Church. Yet their activity was too great to be confined to the defence of the Holy See and to the religious revival by which they, for a time, reacquired for Rome the veneration of the people. One of the collateral objects to which they devoted a portion of their energies was missionary work, and in this they set a worthy example to their successors, the Jesuits of the sixteenth and seventeenth centuries. Among the incessant labors of St. Francis his efforts to convert the infidel were conspicuous. He proposed to visit Morocco, in the hope of converting

King Miramolin, and had reached Spain on his voyage thither, when compelled by sickness to return. In the thirteenth year of his conversion he travelled to Syria for the purpose of bringing over the Soldan of Babylon to the Christian faith, although war was then raging with the Saracens. Captured between the hostile lines, he was carried with his companion in chains to the soldan, when he offered to undergo the ordeal of fire to prove the truth of his faith; he was offered magnificent presents, but spurned them, and was allowed to depart. His followers were true to his example. No distance and no danger deterred them from the task of winning souls to Christianity, and in these arduous labors there was a noble emulation between them and the Dominicans, for Dominic had likewise proposed an extended scheme of missions in which to close his life's work. As early as 1225 we find missionaries of both orders laboring in Morocco. In 1233 Franciscans were despatched to convert Miramolin, the Sultan of Damascus, the caliph, and Asia in general. In 1237 the Eastern Jacobites were brought back to Catholic unity by the zeal of Dominicans, and they were at work among Nestorians, Georgians, Greeks, and other Eastern schismatics. Indulgences, the same as for a crusade, were offered to all who engaged in these enterprises, which were perilous enough, for soon after we hear of ninety Dominicans suffering martyrdom among the Cumans in eastern Hungary, when the hordes of Genghis Khan swept over the land. After the retirement of the Tartars they returned and converted the Cumans by wholesale, besides laboring among the Cathari of Bosnia and Dalmatia, where several of them were slain and two of their convents were burned by the heretics. The extent of the Franciscan missions may be judged by a bull of Alexander IV., in 1258, addressed to all the brethren in the lands of the Saracens,{298}Pagans, Greeks, Bulgarians, Cumans, Ethiopians, Syrians, Iberians, Alans, Cathari, Goths, Zichori, Russians, Jacobites, Nubians, Nestorians, Georgians, Armenians, Indians, Muscovites, Tartars, Hungarians, and the missionaries to the Christian captives among the Turks; and however hazy may be the geography of this enumeration, the extent of the ground sought to be covered shows the activity and self-sacrificing energy of the good brethren. Among the Tartars their success was for a while encouraging. The great khan himself was baptized, and the converts were so numerous that a bishop became necessary for their organization; but the khan apostatized and the missionaries paid with their lives the forfeit of their zeal, nor were they by any means the only martyrs who suffered in the cause. The efficacy of their Armenian mission may be seen in the renunciation of King Haito of Armenia, who entered the Order and assumed the name of Friar John, though the vicissitudes of his subsequent career were not encouraging to future imitators. He was not, however, the only royal Franciscan, for St. Louis of Toulouse, son of Charles the Lame of Naples and Provence, resisted his father's offer of a crown to become a Franciscan. Less authentic, perhaps, are the Dominican accounts of eight missionaries of their Order who, in 1316, penetrated to the empire of Prester John in Abyssinia, where they founded so durable a Church that in half a century they had the Inquisition organized there, with Friar Philip, son of one of Prester John's subject kings, as inquisitor-general. His zeal led him to attack with both spiritual and fleshly weapons another king who indulged in bigamy, and by whom he was treacherously seized and put to death, November 4, 1366, his martyrdom and sanctity being attested by numerous miracles. Be this as it may, the Franciscans record with pardonable pride that members of their Order accompanied Columbus on his second voyage to America, eager to commence the conversion of the New World.[263]{299}

The special field of activity of the Mendicants, however, which more particularly concerns us, was that of the conversion and persecution of heretics—of the Inquisition, which they made their own. It was inevitable that this should fall into their hands as soon as the inadequacy of the ancient episcopal courts required the organization of a new system. The discovery and conviction of the heretic was no easy task. It required special training, and that training was exactly what the Orders sought to give their neophytes to fit them for the work of preaching and conversion. With no ties of locality, soldiers of the Cross ready to march to any point at the word of command, they could be despatched at a moment's notice whenever their services were required. Moreover, their peculiar devotion to the Holy See rendered them specially useful in organizing the papal Inquisition which was to supersede by degrees the episcopal jurisdiction, and prove so efficient an instrument in reducing the local churches to subjection.

That Dominic was the founder of the Inquisition and the first inquisitor-general has become a part of Roman tradition. It is affirmed by all the historians of the Order, and by all the panegyrists of the Inquisition; it has the sanction of infallibility in the bull*Invictarum* of Sixtus V., and it is confirmed by quoting a bull of Innocent III. appointing him inquisitor-general. Yet it is safe to say that no tradition of the Church rests on a slenderer basis. That Dominic devoted the best years of his life to combating heresy there is no doubt, and as little that, when a heretic was deaf to argument or persuasion, he would cheerfully stand by the pyre and see him burned, like any other zealous missionary of the time; but in this he was no more prominent than hundreds of others, and of organized work in this direction he was utterly guiltless. Indeed, from the year 1215, when he laid the foundation of his Order, he was engrossed in it to the exclusion of all other objects, and was obliged to forego his cherished design of ending his days as a missionary to Persia. We shall see that it{300} was not until more than ten years after his death, in 1221, that such an institution as the papal Inquisition can be said to have existed. The prominent part assigned in it to his successors easily explains the legend which has grown around his name, a legend which may safely be classed with the enthusiastic declaration of an historian of the Order that more than a hundred thousand heretics had been converted by his teaching, his merits, and his miracles.[264]

A similar legendary halo exaggerates the exclusive glory, claimed by the Order, of organizing and perfecting the Inquisition. The bulls of Gregory IX. alleged in support of the assertion are simply special orders to individual Dominican provincials to depute brethren fitted for the purpose to the duty of preaching against heresy and examining heretics, and prosecuting their defenders. Sometimes Dominicans are sent to special districts to proceed against heretics, with an apology to the bishops and an explanation that the friars are skilful in convincing heretics, and that the other episcopal duties are too engrossing to enable the prelates to give proper attention to this. The fact simply is that there was no formal confiding of the Inquisition to the Dominicans any more than there was any formal founding of the Inquisition itself. As the institution gradually assumed shape and organization in the effort to find some effectual means to ferret out concealed heretics, the Dominicans were the readiest instrument{301} at hand, especially as they professed the function of preaching and converting as their primary business. As conversion became less the object, and persecution the main business of the Inquisition, the Franciscans were equally useful, and the honors of the organization were divided between them. Indeed, there was no hesitation in confiding inquisitorial functions to clerics of any denomination when occasion required. As early as 1258 we find two canons of Lodève acting under papal commissions as inquisitors of Albi, and we shall meet hereafter, at the close of the fourteenth century, Peter the Celestinian discharging the duties of papal inquisitor with abundant energy from the Baltic to Styria.[265]

Yet the earliest inquisitors, properly so called, were unquestionably Dominicans. When, after the settlement between Raymond of Toulouse and St. Louis, the extirpation of heresy in the Albigensian territories was seriously undertaken, and the episcopal organization proved unequal to the task, it was Dominicans who were sent thither to work under the direction of the bishops. In northern France the business gradually fell almost exclusively into the hands of Dominicans. In Aragon, as early as 1232, they are recommended to the Archbishop of Tarragona as fitting instruments, and in 1249 the institution was confided to them. Eventually southern France was divided between them and the Franciscans, the western portion being given to the Dominicans, while the Comtat Venaissin, Provence, Forcalquier, and the states of the empire in the provinces of Arles, Aix, and Embrun were under charge of the Franciscans. As for Italy, after some confusion arising from the conflicting pretensions of the two Orders, it was, in 1254, formally divided between them by Innocent IV., the Dominicans being assigned to Lombardy, Romagnola, Tarvesina, and Genoa, while the central portion of the peninsula fell to the Franciscans; Naples, as yet, being free from the institution. This division, however, was not always strictly observed, for at times we find Franciscan inquisitors in Milan, Romagnola, and Tarvesina. In Germany and Austria the Inquisition, as we shall see, never took deep root, but, in so far as it was organized there, it{302} was in Dominican hands, while Bohemia and Dalmatia were under the care of Franciscans.[266]

Sometimes the two orders were conjoined. In 1237 the Franciscan Étienne de Saint Thibéry was associated with the Dominican Guillem Arnaud in Toulouse, in hopes that the reputation of his Order for greater mildness might diminish the popular aversion for the new institution. In April, 1238, Gregory IX. appointed the provincials of the two Orders in Aragon as inquisitors for that kingdom, and in the same year the same policy was pursued in Navarre. In 1255 the Franciscan Guardian of Paris was associated with the Dominican prior as the heads of the Inquisition in France; in 1267 we find both Orders furnishing inquisitors for Burgundy and Lorraine; and in 1311 we hear of two Dominicans and one Franciscan as inquisitors in the province of Ravenna. It was found the wisest course, however, to define sharply the boundaries of their respective jurisdictions, for the active and incessant jealousy between the two bodies rendered any concurrence or competition between them an explosive mine liable to be started by a spark. Their mutual hatreds began early, and the unscrupulous means by which they were gratified were a perpetual scandal and danger to the Church. In 1266, for instance, a lively quarrel arose between the Dominicans of Marseilles and the Franciscan inquisitor of that city. The dissension spread until the two Orders were embroiled throughout Provence, Forcalquier, Avignon, Arles, Beaucaire, Montpellier, and Carcassonne, and everywhere they were preaching against and insulting each other in public. Several briefs of Clement IV. show that the pope was obliged to intervene, and his command that in future inquisitors shall forbear to use their powers to prosecute each other, no matter how guilty the offending party may apparently be, indicates that the sharpest weapons of the Holy Office had been used in the strife. When, as late as 1479, Sixtus IV. forbade inquisitors{303} of either Order to sit in judgment on brethren of the other, it would indicate that the intervening two centuries had not diminished the tendency. The jealousy with which their respective limits were defended is illustrated by troubles which occurred in 1290 about the Tarvesina. This was Dominican territory, but for many years the office of inquisitor at Treviso was filled by the Franciscan Filippo Bonaccorso. When, in 1289, he accepted the episcopate of Trent, the Dominicans expected the office to be restored to them, and were indignant at seeing it given to another Franciscan, Frà Bonajuncta. The Dominican inquisitor of Lombardy Frà Pagano, and his vicar, Frà Viviano, went so far in their resistance that serious disturbances were excited in Verona, and it became necessary for Nicholas IV. to intervene in 1291, when he punished the recalcitrants by perpetual deprivation of their functions. To the heretics it must have offered excusable delight to see their persecutors persecuting each other. So ineradicable was the hostility between the two Orders that Clement IV. established the rule that there should be a distance of at least three thousand feet between their respective possessions—a regulation which only led to new and more intricate disputes. They even quarrelled as to the right of precedence in processions and funerals, which was claimed by the Dominicans, and settled in their favor by Martin V. in 1423. We shall see hereafter how important in the development of the mediæval Church was this implacable rivalry.[267]{304}

In the busy world of the thirteenth century there was thus no agency more active than that of the Mendicant Orders, for good and for evil. On the whole perhaps the good preponderated, for they undoubtedly aided in postponing a revolution for which the world was not yet ready. Though the self-abnegation of their earlier days was a quality too rare and perishable to be long preserved, and though they soon sank to the level of the social order around them, yet had their work not been altogether lost. They had brought afresh to men's minds some of the forgotten truths of the gospel, and had taught them to view their duties to their fellows from a higher plane. How well they recognized and appreciated their own services is shown by the story, common to the legend of both Orders, which tells that while Dominic and Francis were waiting the approval of Innocent III. a holy man had a vision in which he saw Christ brandishing three darts with which to destroy the world, and the Virgin inquiring his purpose. Then said Christ, "The world is full of pride, avarice, and lust; I have borne with it too long, and with these darts will I consume it." The Virgin fell on her knees and interceded for man, but in vain, until she revealed to him that she had two faithful servants who would reduce it to his dominion. Then Christ desired to see the champions; she showed him Dominic and Francis, and he was content. The pious author of the story could hardly have foreseen that in 1627 Urban VIII. would be obliged to deprive the Mendicant Friars of Cordova of their dearly prized immunity, and to subject them to episcopal jurisdiction, in the hope of restraining them from seducing their spiritual daughters in the confessional.[268]{305}

CHAPTER VII.

THE INQUISITION FOUNDED.

THE gradual organization of the Inquisition was simply a process of evolution arising from the mutual reaction of the social forces which we have described. The Albigensian Crusades had put an end to open resistance, yet the heretics were none the less numerous, and, if less defiant, were only the more difficult to discover. The triumph of force had increased the responsibility of the Church, while the imperfection of its means of discharging that responsibility was self-confessed in the enormous spread of heresy during the twelfth century. We have seen the confused and uncertain manner in which the local prelates had sought to meet the new demands upon them. When the existence of hidden crime is suspected there are three stages in the process of its suppression—the discovery of the criminal, the proof of his guilt, and finally his punishment. Of all others the crime of heresy was the most difficult to discover and to prove, and when its progress became threatening the ecclesiastics on whom fell the responsibility of its eradication were equally at a loss in each of the three steps to be taken for its extermination.

Immersed, for the most part, in the multiplied troubles connected with the overgrown temporalities of their sees, the bishops would await popular rumor to designate some man or group of men as heretical. On seizing the suspected persons, there was rarely any external evidence to prove their guilt, for except where numbers rendered repression impossible, the sectaries were assiduous in outward conformity to orthodox observance, and the slender theological training of episcopal officials was generally unequal to the task of extracting confessions from thoughtful and keen-witted men, or of convicting them out of their own mouths. The judicial use of torture was as yet happily unknown, and the current substitute of a barbarous age, the Ordeal, was resorted to{306} with a frequency which shows how ludicrously helpless were the ecclesiastics called upon to perform functions so novel. Even St. Bernard approved of this expedient, and in 1157 the Council of Reims prescribed it as the rule in all cases of suspected heresy. More enlightened churchmen viewed its results with well-grounded disbelief, and Peter Cantor mentions several cases to prove its injustice. A poor woman accused of Catharism was abandoned to die of hunger, till in confession to a religious dean she protested her innocence and was advised by him to offer the hot-iron ordeal in proof, which she did with the result of being burned first by the iron and then at the stake. A good Catholic, against whom the only suspicious evidence was his poverty and his pallor, was ordered by an assembly of bishops to undergo the same ordeal, which he refused to do unless the prelates would prove to him that this would not be a mortal sin in tempting God. This tenderness of conscience was sufficient, so without further parley they unanimously handed him over to the secular authorities, and he was promptly burned. With the study of the Roman law, however, this mode of procedure gradually fell into disfavor with the Church, and the enlightenment of Innocent III. peremptorily forbade its use in 1212, when it was extensively employed by Henry of Vehringen, Bishop of Strassburg, to convict a number of heretics; while in 1215 the Council of Lateran, following the example of Alexander III. and Lucius III., formally prohibited all ecclesiastics from taking part in the administration of ordeals of any kind. How great was the perplexity of ignorant prelates, debarred from this ready method of seeking the judgment of God, may be guessed by the expedient which had, in 1170, been adopted by the good Bishop of Besançon, when the religious repose of his diocese was troubled by some miracle-working heretics. He is described as a learned man, and yet to solve his doubts as to whether the strangers were saints or heretics, he summoned the assistance of an ecclesiastic deeply skilled in necromancy and ordered him to ascertain the truth by consulting Satan. The cunning clerk deceived the devil into a confidential mood and learned that the strangers were his servants; they were deprived of the satanic amulets which were their protection, and the populace, which had previously sustained them, cast them pitilessly into the flames.[269]{307}

When supernatural means were not resorted to, the proceedings were far too cumbrous and uncertain to be efficient against an evil so widely spread and against malefactors so numerous. In 1204 Gui, Archbishop of Reims, summoned Count Robert, cousin of Philip Augustus, the Countess Yolande, and many other laymen and ecclesiastics to sit in judgment on some heretics discovered at Brienne, with the result of burning the unfortunate wretches. In 1201, when the Knight Everard of Châteauneuf was accused of Catharism by Bishop Hugues of Nevers, the Legate Octavian summoned for his trial at Paris a council composed of archbishops, bishops, and masters of the university, who condemned him. All this was complicated by the supreme universal jurisdiction of Rome, which enabled those who were skilful and rich to protract indefinitely the proceedings and perhaps at last to escape. Thus in 1211 a canon of Langres, accused of heresy, was summoned by his bishop to appear before a council of theologians assembled to examine him. Though he had sworn to do so and had given bail, he failed to come forward, and was, after three days' waiting, condemned in default. His absence was accounted for when he turned up in Rome and asserted to Innocent that he had been forced to take the oath and give security after he had appealed to the Holy See. The pope sent him back to the Archbishop of Sens, to the Bishop of Nevers, and Master Robert de Corzon, with instructions to examine into his orthodoxy. Two years later, in 1213, he is again seen in Rome, explaining that he had feared to come before his judges at the appointed time, because the popular feeling against heresy was so strong that not only were all heretics burned, but all who were even suspected, wherefore he craved papal protection and permission to perform due purgation at Rome. Innocent again sent him back with orders to the prelates to give him a safe-conduct and protection until his case should be decided. Whether he was innocent or guilty, whether absolved or condemned, is of little moment. The case sufficiently shows the impossibility{308} of efficient suppression of heresy under the existing system.[270]

Even after conviction had been obtained there was the same uncertainty as to penalties. In the case of the Cathari who confessed at Liége in 1144, and were with difficulty rescued from the mob who sought to burn them, the church authorities applied to Lucius II. for instructions as to what disposition should be made of them. Those who were captured in Flanders in 1162 were sent to Alexander III., then in France, for judgment, and he sent them back to the Archbishop of Reims. William Abbot of Vezelai possessed full jurisdiction, but when, in 1167, he had some confessed heretics on his hands, in his embarrassment he asked the assembled crowd what he should do with them, and the ready sentence was found in the unanimous shout, "Burn them! burn them!" which was duly executed, although one who recanted and was yet condemned by the water ordeal was publicly scourged and banished by the abbot in spite of a popular demand for concremation. In 1114 the Bishop of Soissons, after convicting some heretics by the water ordeal, went to the Council of Beauvais to consult as to their punishment; but during his absence the people, fearing the lenity of the bishops, broke into the jail and burned them.[271]

It was not that the Church was absolutely devoid of the machinery for discharging its admitted function of suppressing heresy. It is true that in the early days of the Carlovingian revival, Zachary's instructions to St. Boniface show that the only recognized method at that time of disposing of heretics was by summoning a council, and sending the convicted culprits to Rome for final judgment. Charlemagne's civilizing policy, however, made efficient use of all instrumentalities capable of maintaining order and security in his empire, and the bishops assumed an important position in his system. They were ordered, in conjunction with the secular officials, zealously to prohibit all superstitious observances and remnants of paganism; to travel assiduously throughout their{309} dioceses making strict inquiry as to all sins abhorred of God, and thus a considerable jurisdiction was placed in their hands, although strictly subordinated to the State. During the troubles which followed the division of the empire, as the feudal system arose on the ruins of the monarchy, gradually the bishops threw off not only dependence on the crown, but acquired extensive rights and powers in the administration of the canon law, which now no longer depended on the civil or municipal law, but assumed to be its superior. Thus came to be founded the spiritual courts which were attached to every episcopate and which exercised exclusive jurisdiction of a constantly widening field of jurisprudence. Of course all errors of faith necessarily came within their purview.[272]

The organization and functions of these courts received a powerful impetus through the study of the Roman law after the middle of the twelfth century. Ecclesiastics, in fact, monopolized to such an extent the educated intelligence of the age that at first there were few besides themselves to penetrate into the mysteries of the Code and Digest. Even in the second half of the thirteenth century Roger Bacon complains that a civil lawyer, even if wholly untrained in canon law and theology, had a much better chance of high preferment than a theologian, and he exclaims in bitterness that the Church is governed by lawyers to the great injury of all Christian folk. Thus long before the feudal and seignorial courts felt the influence of the imperial jurisprudence, it had profoundly modified the principles and practice of ecclesiastical procedure. The old archdeacon gave way, not without vituperation, before the formal episcopal judge, known as the Official or Ordinary, who was usually a doctor of both laws—an LL.D. in fact—learned in both civil and canon law; and the effect of this was soon seen in a systematizing of ecclesiastical jurisprudence which gave it an immense advantage over the rude processes of the feudal and customary law. These episcopal courts, moreover, were soon surrounded{310} by a crowd of clerkly advocates, whose zeal for their clients often outran their discretion, furnishing the first mediæval representatives of the legal profession.[273]

Following in the traces of the civil law, there were three forms of action in criminal cases—*accusatio, denunciatio,* and *inquisitio.* In *accusatio* there was an accuser who formally inscribed himself as responsible and was subject to the *talio* in case of failure. *Denunciatio* was the official act of the public officer, such as the *testis synodalis* or archdeacon, who summoned the court to take action against offenders coming within his official knowledge. In *inquisitio* the Ordinary cited the suspected criminal, imprisoning him if necessary; the indictment, or *capitula inquisitionis,* was communicated to him, and he was interrogated thereupon, with the proviso that nothing extraneous to the indictment could be subsequently brought into the case to aggravate it. If the defendant could not be made to confess, the Ordinary proceeded to take testimony, and though the examination of witnesses was not conducted in the defendant's presence, their names and evidence were communicated to him, he could summon witnesses in rebuttal, and his advocate had full opportunity to defend him by argument, exception, and appeal. The Ordinary finally gave the verdict; if uncertain as to guilt, he prescribed the *purgatio canonica,* or oath of denial shared by a given number of peers of the accused, more or less, according to the nature of the charge and degree of suspicion. In all cases of conviction by the inquisitorial process, the penalty inflicted was lighter than in accusation or denunciation. The danger was recognized of a procedure in which the judge was also the accuser; a man must be popularly reputed as guilty before the Ordinary could commence inquisition against him, and this not by merely a few men or by his enemies, or those unworthy of belief. There must be ample ground for esteeming him guilty before this extraordinary power vested in the judge could be exercised. It is important to bear in mind the equitable provisions of all this episcopal jurisdiction when we come to consider the{311} methods of what we call the Inquisition, erected on these foundations.[274]

Theoretically there also existed a thorough system of general inquisition or inquest for the detection of all offences, including heresy; and as it was only an application of this which gave rise to the Inquisition, it is worth our brief attention. The idea of a systematic investigation into infractions of the law was familiar to secular as well as to ecclesiastical jurisprudence. In the Roman law, although there was no public prosecutor, it was part of the duty of the ruler or proconsul to make perquisition after all criminals with a view to their detection and punishment, and Septimius Severus, in the year 202, had made the persecution of Christians an especial feature of this official inquisition. The Missi Dominici of Charlemagne were officials commissioned to traverse the empire, making diligent inquisition into all cases of disorder, crime, and injustice, with jurisdiction over clerk and layman alike. They held their assizes four times a year, listened to all complaints and accusations, and were empowered to redress all wrongs and to punish all offenders of whatever rank. The institution was maintained by the successors of Charlemagne so long as the royal power could assert itself; and after the Capetian revolution, as soon as the new dynasty found itself established with a jurisdiction that could be enforced beyond the narrow bounds set by feudalism, it adopted a similar expedient of "inquisitors," with a view of keeping the royal officials under control and insuring a due enforcement of the law. The same device is seen in the itinerant justiciaries of England, at least as early as the Assizes of Clarendon in 1166, when, utilizing the Anglo-Saxon organization, they made an inquest in every hundred and tithing by the lawful men of the vicinage to try and punish all who were publicly suspected of crime, giving rise to the time-honored system of the grand-jury—in itself a prototype of the incipient papal Inquisition. Similar in character were the "Inquisitors and Manifestors" whom we find in Verona in 1228, employed by the State for the detection and punishment of blasphemy; and a still stronger resemblance is seen in the *Jurados* of Sardinia in the fourteenth century—inhabitants{312} selected in each district and sworn to investigate all cases of crime, to capture the malefactor, and to bring him before court for trial.[275]

The Church naturally fell into the same system. We have just seen that Charlemagne ordered his bishops to make diligent visitations throughout their dioceses, investigating all offences; and with the growth of ecclesiastical jurisdiction this inquisitorial duty was, nominally at least, perfected and organized. Already at the commencement of the tenth century we find in use a method (falsely attributed to Pope Eutychianus) which was subsequently imitated by the Inquisition. As the bishop reached each parish in his visitation, the whole body of the people was assembled in a local synod. From among these he selected seven men of mature age and approved integrity who were then sworn on relics to reveal without fear or favor whatever they might know or hear, then or subsequently, of any offence requiring investigation. These *testes synodales,* or synodal witnesses, became an institution established, theoretically at least, in the Church, and long lists of interrogatories were drawn up to guide the bishops in examining them so that no possible sin or immorality might escape the searching inquisition. Yet how completely these well-devised measures fell into desuetude, under the negligence of the bishops, is seen in the surprise awakened when, in 1246, Robert Grosseteste, the reforming Bishop of Lincoln, ordered, at the suggestion of the Franciscans, such a general inquisition into the morals of the people throughout his extensive diocese. His archdeacons and deans summoned both noble and commoner before them and examined them under oath, as required by the canons; but the proceeding was so unusual and brought to light so many scandals that Henry{313} III. was induced to interfere and ordered the sheriffs to put an end to it.[276]

The Church thus possessed an organization well adapted for the discovery and investigation of heretics. All that it lacked were the men who should put that organization to its destined use; and the progress of heresy up to the date of the Albigensian Crusades manifests how utterly neglectful were the ignorant prelates of the day, immersed in worldly cares, for the most part, and thinking only of the methods by which their temporalities could be defended and their revenues increased. Successive popes made fruitless efforts to arouse them to a sense of duty and induce them to use the means at their disposal for a systematic and vigorous onslaught on the sectaries, who daily grew more alarming. From the assembly of prelates who attended, in 1184, the meeting at Verona between Lucius III. and Frederic Barbarossa, the pope issued a decretal at the instance of the emperor and with the assent of the bishops, which if strictly and energetically obeyed might have established an episcopal instead of a papal Inquisition. In addition to the oath—referred to in a previous chapter—prescribed to every ruler, to assist the Church in persecuting heresy, all archbishops and bishops were ordered, either personally or by their archdeacons or other fitting persons, once or twice a year to visit every parish where there was suspicion of heresy, and compel two or three men of good character, or the whole vicinage if necessary, to swear to reveal any reputed heretic, or any person holding secret conventicles, or in any way differing in mode of life from the faithful in general. The prelate was to summon to his presence those designated, who, unless they could purge themselves at his discretion, or in accordance with local custom, were to be punished as the bishop might see fit. Similarly, any who refused to swear, through superstition, were to be condemned and punished as heretics *ipso facto*. Obstinate heretics, refusing to abjure and return to the Church with due penance, and those who after abjuration relapsed, were to be abandoned to the secular arm for fitting punishment. There was nothing organically new in all this—only a{314} utilizing of existing institutions and an endeavor to recall the bishops to a sense of their duties; but a further important step was taken in removing all exemptions from episcopal jurisdiction in the matter of heresy and subjecting to their bishops the privileged monastic orders which depended directly on Rome. Fautors of heresy were, moreover, declared incapable of acting as advocates or witnesses or of filling any public office.[277]

We have already seen how utterly this effort failed to arouse the hierarchy from their sloth. The weapons rusted in the careless hands of the bishops, and the heretics became ever more numerous and more enterprising, until their gathering strength showed clearly that if Rome would retain her domination she must summon the faithful to the arbitrament of arms. She did not shrink from the alternative, but she recognized that even the triumph of her crusading hosts would be comparatively a barren victory in the absence of an organized system of persecution. Thus while de Montfort and his bands were slaying the abettors of heresy who dared to resist in the field, a council assembled in Avignon, in 1209, under the presidency of the papal legate, Hugues, and enacted a series of regulations which are little more than a repetition of those so fruitlessly promulgated twenty-five years before by Lucius III., the principal change being that in every parish a priest should be adjoined to the laymen who were to act as synodal witnesses or local inquisitors of heresy. Under this arrangement, repeated by the Council of Montpellier in 1215, there was considerable persecution and not a few burnings. In the same spirit, when the Council of Lateran met in 1215 to consolidate the conquests which then seemed secure to the Church, it again repeated the orders of Lucius. No other device suggested itself, no further means seemed either available or requisite, if only this could be carried out, and its enforcement was sought by decreeing the deposition of any bishop neglecting this paramount duty, and his replacement by one willing and able to confound heresy.[278]

This utterance of the supreme council of Christendom was as{315} ineffectual as its predecessors. An occasional earnest fanatic was found, like Foulques of Toulouse or Henry of Strassburg, who labored vigorously in the suppression of heresy, but for the most part the prelates were as negligent as ever, and there is no trace of any sustained and systematic endeavor to put in practice the periodical inquisition so strenuously enjoined. The Council of Narbonne, in 1227, imperatively commanded all bishops to institute in every parish *testes synodales* who should investigate heresy and other offences, and report them to the episcopal officials, but the good prelates who composed the assembly, satisfied with this exhibition of vigor, separated and allowed matters to run on their usual course. We hardly need the assurance of the contemporary Lucas of Tuy, that bishops for the most part were indifferent as to the matter of heresy, while some even protected heretics for filthy gain, saying, when reproached, "How can we condemn those who are neither convicted nor confessed?" No better success followed the device of the Council of Béziers in 1234, which earnestly ordered the parish priests to make out lists of all suspected of heresy and keep a strict watch upon them.[279]

The popes had endeavored to overcome this episcopal indifference by a sort of irregular and spasmodic Legatine Inquisition. As the papal jurisdiction extended itself under the system of Gregory VII. the legate had become a very useful instrument to bring the papal power to bear upon the internal affairs of the dioceses. As the direct representatives and plenipotentiaries of the vicegerent of God the legates carried and exercised the supreme authority of the Holy See into the remotest corners of Christendom. That they should be employed in stimulating languid persecution was inevitable. We have already seen the part they played in the affairs of the Albigenses, from the time of Henry of Citeaux to that of Cardinal Romano. In the absence of any systematic method of procedure they were even used in special cases to supplement the ignorance of local prelates, as when, in 1224, Honorius III. ordered Conrad, Bishop of Hildesheim, to bring before the Legate Cinthio, Cardinal of Porto, for judgment Henry Minneke, Provost of St. Maria of Goslar, whom he held in prison{316} on suspicion of heresy. It was, however, in Toulouse, after the treaty of Paris, in 1229, that we find the most noteworthy case of the concurrence of legatine and episcopal action, showing how crude as yet were the conceptions of the nascent Inquisition. After Count Raymond had been reconciled to the Church, he returned in July to his dominions, followed by the Cardinal-Legate Romano, to see to the execution of the treaty and to turn back the armed "pilgrims" who were swarming to fight for the Cross, and who revenged themselves for their disappointment by wantonly destroying the harvests and creating a famine in the land. In September a council was assembled at Toulouse, consisting of all the prelates of Languedoc, and most of the leading barons. This adopted a canon ordering anew all archbishops, bishops, and exempted abbots to put in force the device of the synodal witnesses, who were charged with the duty of making constant inquisition for heretics and examining all suspected houses, subterranean rooms, and other hiding-places; but there is no trace of any obedience to this command or of any results arising from it. Under the impulsion of the legate and of Foulques of Toulouse, however, the council itself was turned into an inquisition. A converted "perfected" Catharan, named Guillem de Solier, was found and was restored to his legal rights in order to enable him to give evidence against his former brethren, while Bishop Foulques industriously hunted up other witnesses. Each bishop present took his share in examining these, sending to Foulques the evidence reduced to writing, and thus, we are told, a vast amount of business was accomplished in a short time. It was found that the heretics had mostly pledged each other to secrecy, and that it was virtually impossible to extract anything from them, but a few of the more timid came forward voluntarily and confessed, and of course each one of these, under the rules in force, was obliged to tell all he knew about others, as the condition of reconciliation. A vast amount of evidence was thus collected, which was taken by the legate for the purpose of deciding the fate of the accused, and with it he left Toulouse for Montpellier. A few of the more hardy offenders endeavored to defend themselves judicially, and demanded to see the names of the witnesses, even following the legate to Montpellier for that purpose; but he, under the pretext that this demand was for the purpose of slaying those who had testified{317}against them, adroitly eluded it by exhibiting a combined list of all the witnesses, so that the culprits were forced to submit without defence. He then held another council at Orange, and sent to Foulques the sentences, which were duly communicated to the accused assembled for the purpose in the church of St. Jacques. All the papers of the inquisition were carried to Rome by the legate for fear that if they should fall into the hands of the evil-minded they would be the cause of many murders—and, in fact, a number of the witnesses were slain on simple suspicion.[280]

All this shows how crude and cumbrous an implement was the episcopal and legatine Inquisition even in the most energetic hands, and how formless and tentative was its procedure. A few instances of the use of synodal witnesses are subsequently to be found, as in the Council of Arles, in 1234, that of Tours, in 1239, that of Béziers, in 1246, of Albi, in 1254, and in a letter of Alphonse of Poitiers in 1257, urging his bishops to appoint them as required by the Council of Toulouse. An occasional example of the legatine Inquisition may also be met with. In 1237 the inquisitors of Toulouse were acting under legatine powers, as sub-delegates to the Legate Jean de Vienne; and in the same year, when the people of Montpellier asked the pope for assistance to suppress the growth of heresy, their bishop apparently being supine, he sent Jean de Vienne there with instructions to act vigorously. The episcopal office was similarly disregarded in 1239, when Gregory IX. sent orders to the inquisitors of Toulouse to obey the instructions of his legate. Yet this legatine function in time passed so completely out of remembrance that in 1351 the Signiory of Florence asked the papal legate to desist from a charge of heresy on which he had cited the Camaldulensian abbot, because the republic had never permitted its citizens to be judged for such an offence except by the inquisitors; and as early as 1257, when the inquisitors of Languedoc complained of the zeal of the Legate Zoen, Bishop of Avignon, in carrying on inquisitorial work, Alexander IV. promptly decided that he had no such power outside of his own diocese.[281]{318}

The public opinion of the ruling classes of Europe demanded that heresy should be exterminated at whatever cost, and yet with the suppression of open resistance the desired end seemed as far off as ever. Bishop and legate were alike unequal to the task of discovering those who carefully shrouded themselves under the cloak of the most orthodox observance; and when by chance a nest of heretics was brought to light, the learning and skill of the average Ordinary failed to elicit a confession from those who professed the most entire accord with the teachings of Rome. In the absence of overt acts it was difficult to reach the secret thoughts of the sectary. Trained experts were needed whose sole business it should be to unearth the offenders and extort a confession of their guilt. As this necessity became more and more apparent two new factors contributed to the solution of the long-vexed problem.

The first of these was the organization of the Mendicant Orders, whose peculiar fitness for the work which had outgrown the capacity of the episcopal courts might well make their establishment seem a providential interposition to supply the Church of Christ with what it most sorely needed. As the necessity grew apparent of special and permanent tribunals devoted exclusively to the wide-spread sin of heresy, there was every reason why they should be wholly free from the local jealousies and enmities which might tend to the prejudice of the innocent, or the local favoritism which might connive at the escape of the guilty. If, in addition to this freedom from local partialities, the examiners and judges were men specially trained to the detection and conversion of the heretic; if, also, they had by irrevocable vows renounced the world; if they could acquire no wealth and were dead to the enticements of pleasure, every guarantee seemed to be afforded that their momentous duties would be fulfilled with the strictest justice—that while the purity of the faith would be protected, there would be no unnecessary oppression or cruelty or persecution dictated by private interests and personal revenge. Their unlimited popularity was also a warrant that they would receive far more efficient assistance in their arduous labors than could be expected by the{319} bishops, whose position was generally that of antagonism to their flocks and to the petty seigneurs and powerful barons whose aid was indispensable. That the Mendicant Orders, to which this duty thus naturally fell, were peculiarly devoted to the papacy, and that they made the Inquisition a powerful instrument to extend the influence of Rome and destroy what little independence was left to the local churches, became subsequently doubtless an additional reason for their employment, but could scarce have been a motive in the early tentative efforts. Thus to the public of the thirteenth century the organization of the Inquisition and its commitment to the children of St. Dominic and St. Francis appeared a perfectly natural or rather inevitable development arising from the admitted necessities of the time and the instrumentalities at hand.

The other factor which promised success to the Church, in an organized effort to discharge the duty of persecution, was the secular legislation against heresy which at this period took form and shape. We have seen the spasmodic edicts of England and Aragon in the twelfth century, which have interest only as showing the absence of anterior penal laws. Frederic Barbarossa took no effective steps to give validity to the regulations which Lucius III. issued from Verona in 1184, though they purported to be drawn up with the emperor's sanction. The body of customary law which de Montfort adopted at Pamiers in 1212 of course disappeared with his short-lived domination. There had been, it is true, some fragmentary attempts at legislation, as when the Emperor Henry VI., in 1194, prescribed confiscation of property, severe personal punishment, and destruction of houses for heretics, and heavy fines for persons or communities omitting to arrest them; and this was virtually repeated in 1210 by Otho IV., showing how soon it had been forgotten. How little uniformity, indeed, there was in the treatment of heresy is proved by such stray edicts of the period as chance to have reached us. Thus in 1217 Nuñez Sancho of Rosellon decreed outlawry for heretics, and in 1228 Jayme I. of Aragon followed his example, showing that this could not have previously been customary. On the other hand, the statutes of Pignerol in 1220 only inflict a fine of ten sols for knowingly giving shelter to Vaudois. Louis VIII. of France, just before his death, issued an *ordonnance* punishing this same crime with confiscation and deprivation of all legal rights, while the royal officials were{320} ordered to inflict proper and immediate punishment on all who were convicted of heresy by the ecclesiastical judges. The statutes in force in Florence in 1227 required the bishop to act in conjunction with the podestà in all prosecutions for heresy, which was a serious limitation on the episcopal courts. In 1228 we hear of new laws adopted in Milan, at the instance of the papal legate, Goffredo, by which all heretics were banished from the territory of the republic, their houses torn down, the contents confiscated, their persons outlawed, with graduated fines for harboring them. A mixed secular and ecclesiastical inquisition was established for the discovery of heretics, and the archbishop and podestà were to co-operate in their examination and sentence; while the latter was bound to put to death within ten days all convicts. In Germany, as late as 1231, it required the decision of King Henry VII. to determine the disposition of property confiscated on heretics, and allodial lands were allowed to descend to the heirs, in contradiction, as we shall see, to all subsequent ruling.[282]

To put in action any comprehensive system of persecution, it evidently was requisite to overcome the centrifugal tendency of mediæval legislation, which finds its ultimate expression in free Navarre, where every town of importance had its special *fuero*, and almost every house its individual custom. Innocent III. endeavored, at the Lateran Council of 1215, to secure uniformity by a series of severe regulations defining the attitude of the Church to heretics, and the duties which the secular power owed to exterminate them under pain of forfeiture, and this became a recognized part of canon law; but in the absence of active secular co-operation its provisions for a while remained practically a dead letter. It was reserved for the arch-enemy of the Church, Frederic II., to break down, throughout the greater part of Europe, the particularism of local statutes, and place the population at the mercy of such emissaries as the popes might send to represent them. It was requisite for him to acquire the favor of Honorius III. to secure his coronation in 1220; and when the inevitable rupture took place, it was still necessary for him to meet the charge of heresy so freely brought against{321} him by manifesting special zeal in the persecution of heretics, though doubtless, if left to himself, philosophic indifference would have led him to tolerate any form of belief that did not threaten disobedience to the ruler.[283]

In a series of edicts dating from 1220 to 1239 he thus enacted a complete and pitiless code of persecution, based upon the Lateran canons. Those who were merely suspected of heresy were required to purge themselves at command of the Church, under penalty of being deprived of civil rights and placed under the imperial ban; while, if they remained in this condition for a year, they were to be condemned as heretics. Heretics of all sects were outlawed; and when condemned as such by the Church they were to be delivered to the secular arm to be burned. If, through fear of death, they recanted, they were to be thrust in prison for life, there to perform penance. If they relapsed into error, thus showing that their conversion had been fictitious, they were to be put to death. All the property of the heretic was confiscated and his heirs disinherited. His children, to the second generation, were declared ineligible to any positions of emolument or dignity, unless they should win mercy by betraying their father or some other heretic. All "credentes," fautors, defenders, receivers, or advocates of heretics were banished forever, their property confiscated, and their descendants subjected to the same disabilities as those of heretics. Those who defended the errors of heretics were to be treated as heretics unless, on admonition, they mended their ways. The houses of heretics and their receivers were to be destroyed, never to be rebuilt. Although the evidence of a heretic was not receivable in court, yet an exception was made in favor of the faith, and it was to be held good against another heretic. All rulers and magistrates,

106

present or future, were required to swear to exterminate with their utmost ability all whom the Church might designate as heretics, under pain of forfeiture of office. The lands of any temporal lord who neglected, for a year after summons by the Church, to clear them of heresy, were exposed to the occupancy of any Catholics who, after extirpating the heretics, were to possess them in peace without prejudice to the rights of{322} the suzerain, provided he had offered no opposition. When the papal Inquisition was commenced, Frederic hastened, in 1232, to place the whole machinery of the State at the command of the inquisitors, who were authorized to call upon any official to capture whomsoever they might designate as a heretic, and hold him in prison until the Church should condemn him, when he was to be put to death.[284]

This fiendish legislation was hailed by the Church with acclamation, and was not allowed to remain, like its predecessors, a dead letter. The coronation-edict of 1220 was sent by Honorius to the University of Bologna to be read and taught as a part of practical law. It was consequently embodied in the authoritative compilation of the feudal customs, and its most stringent enactments were incorporated in the Civil Code. The whole series of edicts was subsequently promulgated by successive popes in repeated bulls, commanding all states and cities to inscribe these laws irrevocably in their local statute-books. It became the duty of the inquisitors to see that this was done, to swear all magistrates and officials to enforce them, and to compel their obedience by the free use of excommunication. In 1222, when the magistrates of Rieti adopted laws conflicting with them, Honorius at once ordered the offenders removed from office; in 1227 the people of Rimini resisted, but were coerced to submission; in 1253, when some of the Lombard cities demurred, Innocent IV. promptly ordered the inquisitors to subdue them; in 1254 Asti peacefully accepted them as part of its local laws; Como followed the example,{323} September 10, 1255; and in the recension of the laws of Florence made as late as 1355, they still appear as an integral part. Finally, they were incorporated in the latest additions to the Corpus Juris as part of the canon law itself, and, technically speaking, they may be regarded as in force to the present day.[285]

This virtually provided for a very large portion of Europe, extending from Sicily to the North Sea. The western regions made haste to follow the pious example. Coincident with the Treaty of Paris, in 1229, was an *ordonnance* issued in the name of the boy-king, Louis IX., giving efficient assistance by the royal officials to the Church in its efforts to purge the land of heresy. In the territories which remained to Count Raymond his vacillating course gave rise to much dissatisfaction, until, in 1234, he was compelled to enact, with the consent of his prelates and barons, a statute drawn up by the fanatic Raymond du Fauga of Toulouse, which embodied all the practical points of Frederic's legislation, and decreed confiscation against every one who failed, when called upon, to aid the Church in the capture and detention of heretics. In the compilations and law books of the latter half of the century we see the system thoroughly established as the law of the whole land, and in 1315 Louis Hutin formally adopted the edicts of Frederic and made them valid throughout France.[286]

In Aragon Don Jayme I., in 1226, issued an edict prohibiting all heretics from entering his dominions, probably on account of the fugitives driven out of Languedoc by the crusade of Louis VIII. In 1234, in conjunction with his prelates, he drew up a{324} series of laws instituting an episcopal Inquisition of the severest character, to be supported by the royal officials; in this appears for the first time a secular prohibition of the Bible in the vernacular. All possessing any books of the Old or New Testament, "in Romancio," are summoned to deliver them within eight days to their bishops to be burned, under pain of being held suspect of heresy. Thus, with the exception of farther Spain and the Northern nations, where heresy had never taken root, throughout Christendom the State was rendered completely subservient to the Church in the great task of exterminating heresy. And, when the Inquisition had been established, the enforcing of this legislation was the peculiar privilege of the inquisitors, whose ceaseless vigilance and unlimited powers gave full assurance that it would be relentlessly carried into effect.[287]

Meanwhile zeal or jealousy led, in the confusion and uncertainty of this transition period, to the experiment, in several parts of Italy, of a secular Inquisition. In Rome, in 1231, Gregory IX. drew up a series of regulations which was issued by the Senator Annibaldo in the name of the Roman people. Under this the senator was bound to capture all who were designated to him as heretics, whether by inquisitors appointed by the Church or other good Catholics, and to punish them within eight days after condemnation. Of their confiscated property one third went to the detector, one third to the senator, and one third to repairing the city walls. Any house in which a heretic was received was to be destroyed, and converted forever into a receptacle of filth. "Credentes" were treated as heretics, while fautors, receivers, etc., forfeited one third of their possessions, applicable to the city walls. A fine of twenty lire was imposed on any one cognizant of heresy and not denouncing it; while the senator who neglected to enforce the law was subject to a mulct of two hundred marks and perpetual disability to office. To appreciate the magnitude of these fines we must consider the rude poverty of the Italy of the period as described by a contemporary—the squalor of daily life{325} and the scarcity of the precious metals, as indicated by the absence of gold and silver ornaments in the dress of the period. Not satisfied with the local enforcement of these regulations, Gregory sent them to the archbishops and princes throughout Europe, with orders to put them in execution in their respective territories, and for some time they formed the basis of inquisitorial proceedings. In Rome the perquisition was successful, and the faithful were rewarded with the spectacle of a considerable number of burnings; while Gregory, encouraged by success, proceeded to issue a decretal, forming the basis of all subsequent inquisitorial legislation, by which condemned heretics were to be abandoned to the secular arm for exemplary punishment, those who returned to the Church were to be perpetually imprisoned, and every one cognizant of heresy was bound to denounce it to the ecclesiastical authorities under pain of excommunication.[288]

At the same time Frederic II., who desired to give Rome as little foothold as possible in his Neapolitan dominions, placed the business of persecution there in the hands of the royal officials. In his Sicilian Constitutions, issued in 1231, he ordered his representatives to make diligent inquisition into the heretics who walk in darkness. All, however slightly suspected, are to be arrested and subjected to examination by ecclesiastics, and those who deviate ever so little from the faith, if obstinate, are to be gratified with the fiery martyrdom to which they aspire, while any one daring to intercede for them shall feel the full weight of the imperial displeasure. As the legislation of a free-thinker, this shows the irresistible weight of public opinion, to which Frederic dared not run counter. Nor did he allow this to remain a dead letter. A number of executions under it took place forthwith, and two years later we find him writing to Gregory deploring that this had not been sufficient, for heresy was reviving, and that he therefore had ordered the justiciary of each district, in conjunction with some prelate, to renew the inquisition with all activity; the bishops were required to traverse their dioceses thoroughly, in company, when necessary, of judges delegated for the purpose; in{326} each province the General Court held two assizes a year, when heresy was punished like any other crime. Yet, so far from praising this systematized persecution, Gregory replied that Frederic was using pretended zeal to punish his personal enemies, and was burning good Catholics rather than heretics.[289]

In this confused and irregular striving to accomplish the extirpation of heresy, it was inevitable that the Holy See should intervene, and through the exercise of its supreme apostolic authority seek to provide some general system for the efficient performance of the indispensable duty. The only wonder, indeed, is that this should have been postponed so long and have been at last commenced so tentatively and apologetically.

In 1226 an effort was made to check the rapid spread of Catharism in Florence by the arrest of the heretic bishop Filippo Paternon, whose diocese extended from Pisa to Arezzo. He was tried, in accordance with the existing Florentine statutes, by the bishop and podestà conjointly, when he cut short the proceedings by abjuration, and was released; but he speedily relapsed, and became more odious than ever to the orthodox. In 1227 a converted heretic complained of this backsliding to Gregory IX., and the pontiff, who had just ascended the papal throne, made haste to remedy the evil by issuing a commission, which may be regarded as the foundation of the papal Inquisition. Yet it was exceedingly unobtrusive, though the church of Florence was so directly under papal control. Bearing date June 20, 1227, it simply authorizes Giovanni di Salerno, prior of the Dominican house of Santa Maria Novella, with one of his frati and Canon Bernardo, to proceed judicially against Paternon and his followers and force them to abjuration; acting, in case of obstinacy, under the canons of the Lateran Council, and, if necessary, calling upon the clerks and laymen of the sees of Fiesole and Fiesole for aid. Thus, while there was no scruple in invading the jurisdiction of the Bishop of Florence, there was no legislation other than the Lateran canons to guide the proceedings. What the commissioners{327} accomplished with regard to the inferior heretics is not known. They succeeded in capturing Bishop Paternon and cast him in prison, but he was forcibly rescued by his friends and disappeared, leaving his episcopate to his successor, Torsello.[290]

Frà Giovanni retained his commission until his death in 1230, when a successor was appointed in the person of another Dominican, Aldobrandino Cavalcanti. Still, their jurisdiction was as yet wholly undetermined, for in June, 1229, we hear of the Abbot of San Miniato carrying to Gregory IX., in Perugia, two leading heretics, Andrea and Pietro, who were forced to a public abjuration in presence of the papal court; and in several cases in 1234 we find Gregory IX. intervening, taking bail of the accused and sending special instructions to the inquisitor in charge. Yet the Inquisition was gradually taking shape, for shortly afterwards there were numerous heretics discovered, some of whom were burned, their trials being still preserved in the archives of Santa Maria Novella. Yet how little thought there could have been of founding a permanent institution is shown, in 1233, by the persecuting statutes drawn up by Bishop Ardingho, approved by Gregory, and ordered by him to be irrevocably inscribed in the statute-book of Florence. In these the bishop is still the persecuting representative of the Church, and there is no allusion to inquisitors. The podestà is bound to arrest any one pointed out to him by the bishop, and to punish him within eight days after the episcopal condemnation, with other provisions borrowed from the edicts of Frederic II. Frà Aldobrandino seems to have relied rather on preaching than on persecution; in fact he nowhere in the documents signed by him qualifies himself as inquisitor, and neither his efforts nor those of Bishop Ardingho were able to prevent the rapid growth of heresy. In 1235, when the project of an organized Inquisition throughout Europe was taking shape, Gregory appointed the Dominican Provincial of Rome inquisitor throughout his extensive province, which embraced both Sicily and Tuscany; but this seems to have proved too large a district, and about 1240 we find the city of Florence under the charge of Frà Ruggieri Calcagni. He was of a temper well fitted to extend the prerogatives of his office and to render it effective; but it was not until 1243 that{328} he qualified himself as "*Inquisitor Domini Papæ in Tuscia*," and in a sentence rendered in 1245 he is careful to call himself inquisitor of Bishop Ardingho as well as of the pope, and recites the episcopal commission given him as authority to act. In the proceedings of this period the rudimentary character of the Inquisition is evident. One confession in 1244 bears only the names of two frati, the inquisitor not being even present. In 1245 there are sentences signed by Ruggieri alone, while other proceedings show him to be acting conjointly with Ardingho. He may be said, indeed, to have given the Inquisition in Florence form and shape when, about 1243, he opened for the first time his independent tribunal in Santa Maria Novella, taking as assessors two or three prominent friars of the convent and employing public notaries to make record of his proceedings.[291]

This is a fair illustration of the gradual development of the Inquisition. It was not an institution definitely projected and founded, but was moulded step by step out of the materials which lay nearest to hand fitted for the object to be attained. In fact, when Gregory, recognizing the futility of further dependence on episcopal zeal, sought to take advantage of the favorable secular legislation against heresy, the preaching friars were the readiest instruments within reach for the accomplishment of his object. We shall see hereafter how, as in Florence, the experiment was tried in Aragon and Languedoc and Germany, and the success which on the whole attended it and led to an extended and permanent organization.

The Inquisition has sometimes been said to have been founded April 20, 1233, the day on which Gregory issued two bulls making the persecution of heresy the special function of the Dominicans; but the apologetic tone in which he addresses the prelates shows how uncertain he felt as to their enduring this invasion of their jurisdiction, while the character of his instructions proves that he had no conception of what the innovation was to lead to. In fact, his immediate object seems rather the punishment of priests and other ecclesiastics, concerning whom there was a standing{329} complaint that they favored heretics by instructing them how to evade examination by concealing their beliefs and feigning orthodoxy. After reciting the necessity of subduing heresy and the raising up by God of the preaching friars, who devote themselves in voluntary poverty to spreading the Word and extirpating misbelief, Gregory proceeds to tell the bishops: "We, seeing you engrossed in the whirlwind of cares and scarce able to breathe in the pressure of overwhelming anxieties, think it well to divide your burdens that they may be more easily borne. We have therefore determined to send preaching friars against the heretics of France and the adjoining provinces, and we beg, warn, and exhort you, ordering you as you reverence the Holy See, to receive them kindly and treat them well, giving them in this, as in all else, favor, counsel, and aid, that they may fulfil their office." The other bull is addressed "to the Priors and Friars of the Order of Preachers, Inquisitors," and after alluding to the sons of perdition who defend heresy, it proceeds: "Therefore you, or any of you, wherever you may happen to preach, are empowered, unless they desist from such defence (of heretics) on monition, to deprive clerks of their benefices forever, and to proceed against them and all others, without appeal, calling in the aid of the secular arm, if necessary, and coercing opposition, if requisite, with the censures of the Church, without appeal."[292]

This experiment of investing all the Dominican preachers with legatine authority to condemn without appeal was inconsiderate. It could only lead to exasperation, as we shall see hereafter in Germany, and Gregory soon adopted a more practical expedient. Shortly after the issue of the above bulls we find him ordering the Provincial Prior of Toulouse to select some learned friars who should be commissioned to preach the cross in the diocese, and to proceed against heretics in accordance with the recent statutes. Though here there is still some incongruous mingling of duties, yet Gregory had finally hit upon the device which remained the permanent basis of the Inquisition—the selection by the provincial of certain fitting brethren, who exercised within their province{330} the delegated authority of the Holy See in searching out and examining heretics with a view to the ascertainment of their guilt. Under this bull the provincial appointed Friars Pierre Cella and Guillem Arnaud, whose labors will be detailed in a subsequent chapter. Thus the Inquisition, as an organized system, may be considered as fairly commenced, though it is noteworthy that these early inquisitors in their official papers qualify themselves as acting under legatine and not under papal authority. How little idea there was as yet of creating a general and permanent institution is seen when the Archbishop of Sens complained of the intrusion of inquisitors in his province, and Gregory, by a brief of February 4, 1234, apologetically revoked all commissions issued for it, adding a suggestion that the archbishop should call in the assistance of the Dominicans if he thought that their superior skill in confuting heretics was likely to prove useful.[293]

As yet there was no idea of superseding the episcopal functions. About this time we find Gregory writing to the bishops of the province of Narbonne, threatening them if they shall not inflict due chastisement on heretics, and making no allusion to the new expedient; and as late as October 1, 1234, Pierre Amiel, Archbishop of Narbonne, exacted an oath from his people to denounce all heretics to him or to his officials, apparently in ignorance of the existence of special inquisitors. Even where the latter were commissioned, their duties and functions, their powers and responsibilities, were wholly undefined and remained to be determined. As they were regarded simply in the light of assistants to the bishops in the exercise of the immemorial episcopal jurisdiction over heresy, it was naturally to the bishops that were referred the questions which immediately arose. Many points as to the treatment of heretics had been settled, not only by Gregory's Roman{331} statutes of 1231, but by the Council of Toulouse in 1229, and those of Béziers and Arles in 1234, which were solely occupied with stimulating and organizing the episcopal Inquisition, yet matters of detail constantly suggested themselves in practice, and a new code of some kind was evidently required to render persecution effective. The suspension of the Inquisition for some years at the request of Count Raymond postponed this, but when the Holy Office resumed its functions in 1241 the necessity became pressing, and the bishops were looked to as the authority from which such a code should emanate. Sentences rendered in 1241 by Guillem Arnaud recite not only that Bishop Raymond of Toulouse acted as assessor, but that the special advice of the Archbishop of

Narbonne had been asked. It was evident that general principles for the guidance of the Inquisition must be laid down, and accordingly a great council of the three provinces of Narbonne, Arles, and Aix was assembled at Narbonne in 1243 or 1244, where an elaborate series of canons were framed, which remained the basis of inquisitorial action. These were addressed to "Our cherished and faithful children in Christ the Preaching Friars Inquisitors;" and though the bishops discreetly say, "We write this to you, not that we wish to bind you down by our counsels, as it would not be fitting to limit the liberty accorded to your discretion by other forms and rules than those of the Holy See, to the prejudice of the business; but we wish to help your devotion as we are commanded to do by the Holy See, since you, who bear our burdens, ought to be, through mutual charity, assisted with help and advice in our own business," yet the tone of the whole is that of absolute command, both in the definition of jurisdiction and the instructions as to dealing with heretics. It is highly significant that, in surrendering control over the bodies of their flocks, these good shepherds strictly reserved to themselves the profits to be expected from persecution, for they straitly enjoined upon the new officials, "You are to abstain from these pecuniary penances and exactions, both for the sake of the honor of your Order, and because you will have fully enough other work to attend to." While thus carefully preserving their financial interests, they abandoned what was vastly more important, the right of passing judgment and imposing sentence. Sentences of this period are rendered in the name of the inquisitors, though if the bishop or other notable person {332} took part, as was frequently the case, he is mentioned as an assessor.[294]

The transfer of the old episcopal jurisdiction over heresy to the Inquisition naturally rendered the connection between bishop and inquisitor a matter of exceeding delicacy, and the new institution could not establish itself without considerable friction, revealed in the varying and contradictory policy adopted at successive periods in adjusting their mutual relations. This renders itself especially noticeable in the development of the Inquisition in the different lands of Europe. In Italy the independence of the episcopate had long since been broken down, and it could offer no efficient opposition to the encroachment on its jurisdiction. In Germany, on the other hand, the lordly prince-bishops looked with jealous eyes on the intruder, and, as we shall see hereafter, never allowed it to obtain a permanent foothold. In France, and more especially in Languedoc, although the prelates were far more independent than those of Italy, the prevalence of heresy required for its suppression a vigilance and an activity far beyond their ability, and they found themselves obliged to sacrifice a portion of their prerogatives in order to escape the more painful sacrifice of performing their long-neglected duties. Yet they did not submit to this without a struggle which may be dimly traced in the successive efforts to establish a *modus vivendi* between the respective tribunals.

We have just seen that at an early period the inquisitors assumed to render sentences in their own names, without reference to the bishops. This invasion of the latter's jurisdiction was evidently too great an innovation to be permanent; indeed, almost immediately we find the Cardinal Legate of Albano instructing the Archbishop of Narbonne to order the inquisitors not to condemn heretics or impose penances without the concurrence of the bishops. This order had to be repeated and rendered more absolute; and the question was settled in this sense by the Council of Béziers in 1246, where the bishops, on the other hand, surrendered the fines to be used for the expenses of the Inquisition, and drew {333} up another elaborate series of instructions for the inquisitors, "willingly yielding to your devout requests which you have humbly made to us." For a while the popes continued to treat the bishops as responsible for the suppression of heresy in their respective dioceses, and consequently as the real source of jurisdiction. In 1245 Innocent IV., in permitting inquisitors to modify or commute previous sentences, specified that this must be done with the advice of the bishop. In 1246 he orders the Bishop of Agen to make diligent inquisition against heresy under the rules prescribed by the Cardinal Legate of Albano, and with the same power as the inquisitor to grant indulgences. In 1247 he treats the bishops as the real judges of heresy in instructing them to labor sedulously for the conversion of the convict, before passing sentence involving death, perpetual imprisonment, or pilgrimages beyond seas; even with obstinate heretics they are to consult diligently with the inquisitor or other discreet persons whether to pass sentence or to postpone it, as may best subserve the salvation of the sinner and the interest of the faith. Still, in spite of all this, the sentences of Bernard de Caux, from 1246 to 1248, bear no trace of episcopal concurrence. There evidently was jealousy and antagonism. In 1248 the Council of Valence was obliged to coerce the bishops into publishing and observing the sentences of the inquisitors, by interdicting the entry into their own churches to those who refused to do so, showing that the bishops were not consulted as to the sentences and were indisposed to enforce them. In 1249 we find the Archbishop of Narbonne complaining to the pope that the inquisitor Pierre Durant and his colleagues had, without his knowledge, absolved the Chevalier Pierre de Cugunham, who had been convicted of heresy, whereupon Innocent forthwith annulled their proceedings. In fact the pardoning power seems to have been considered as specially vested in the Holy See, and about this period we find several instances in which it is conferred by Innocent on bishops, sometimes with and sometimes without injunctions to confer with the inquisitors. Finally this question of practice was settled by adopting the habit of reserving in every sentence the right to modify, increase, diminish, or abrogate it.[295]{334}

Inasmuch as the inquisitors in 1246 still expected the bishops to defray their expenses, they recognized themselves, at least in theory, as merely an adjunct to the episcopal tribunals. The bishops, moreover, were expected to build the prisons for the confinement of converts, and though they eluded this and the king was obliged to do it, the Council of Albi, held in 1254 by the papal legate, Zoen of Avignon, assumes that the prisons are under episcopal control. The same council drew up an elaborate series of instructions for the treatment of heretics, which marks the termination of episcopal control of such matters, for all subsequent regulations were issued by the Holy See. Even so experienced a persecutor as Bernard de Caux, notwithstanding his neglect of episcopal jurisdiction in his sentences, admitted in 1248 his subordination to the episcopate by applying for advice to Guillem of Narbonne, and the archbishop replied, not only with directions as to special cases, but with general instructions. Indeed, in 1250 and 1251 the archbishop was actively employed in making an inquisition of his own and in punishing heretics without the intervention of papal inquisitors; and a brief of Innocent IV. in 1251 alludes to a previous intention, subsequently abandoned, of restoring the whole business to the bishops. In spite of these indications of reaction the intruders continued to win their way, with struggles, bitter enough, no doubt, in many places, and intensified by the hostility between the secular clergy and the Mendicants, but only to be conjectured from the scattered indications visible in the fragmentary remains of the period. There is an effort to retain vanishing authority in the offer made in 1252 by the bishops of Toulouse, Albi, Agen, and Carpentras to give full authority as inquisitors to any Dominicans who might be selected by the commissioners of Alphonse of Poitiers, only stipulating that their assent must be asked to all sentences,{335} and promising to observe in all cases the rules established by the Inquisition. This question of episcopal concurrence in condemnations evidently excited strong feeling and was long contested with varying success. If previous orders requiring it had not been treated with contempt, Innocent IV. would not have been obliged, in 1254, to reiterate the instructions that no condemnations to death or life-imprisonment should be uttered without consulting the bishops; and in 1255 he conjoined bishop and inquisitor to interpret in consultation any obscurities in the laws against heresy and to administer the lighter penalties of deprivation of office and preferment. This recognition of episcopal jurisdiction was annulled by Alexander IV., who, after some vacillation, in 1257 rendered the Inquisition independent by releasing it from the necessity of consulting with the bishops even in cases of obstinate and confessed heretics, and this he repeated in 1260. Then there was a reaction. In 1262 Urban IV., in an elaborate code of instructions, formally revived the consultation in all cases involving the death-penalty or perpetual imprisonment; and this was repeated by Clement IV. in 1265. Either these instructions, however, were revoked in some subsequent enactment or they soon fell into desuetude, for in 1273 Gregory X., after alluding to the action of Alexander IV. in annulling consultation, proceeds to direct that inquisitors in deciding upon sentences shall proceed in accordance with the counsel of the bishops or their delegates, so that the episcopal authority may share in decisions of such moment. Up to this period the Inquisition seems to have been regarded as merely a temporary expedient to meet a special exigency, and every pope on his accession had issued a series of bulls renewing its provisions. Heresy, however, was apparently ineradicable; the populations had accepted the new institution, and its usefulness had been proved in many ways besides that of preserving the purity of the faith. Henceforth it was considered a permanent part of the machinery of the Church, and its rules were definitely settled. Gregory's decision in favor of concurrent episcopal and inquisitorial action in all cases of condemnation consequently remained unaltered, and we shall see hereafter that when Clement V. endeavored to check the more scandalous abuses of inquisitorial power, he sought the remedy, insufficient enough, in some slight increase of episcopal supervision and responsibility, following in this an effort in the same direction{336} which had been essayed by Philippe le Bel. Yet when bishop and inquisitor chanced to be on good terms, the slender safeguard thus afforded for the accused was eluded by one of them giving to the other power to act for him, and cases are on record in which the bishop acts as the inquisitor's deputy, or the inquisitor as the bishop's. The question as to whether either of them could render without the other a valid sentence of absolution was one which greatly vexed the canonists, and names of high repute are ranged on either side, with the weight of authority inclining to the affirmative.[296]

The control of the bishops was vastly increased, at least in Italy, over the vital question of expenditures, when Nicholas IV., in 1288, ordered that all moneys arising from fines and confiscations should be deposited with men selected jointly by the inquisitor and bishop, to be expended only with the advice of the latter, to whom accounts were to be rendered regularly. This was a serious limitation of inquisitorial independence, and it was not of long duration. The bishops soon made use of their supervisory power to demand a share of the spoils under pretext of conducting inquisitions of their own. The quarrel was an unseemly one, and Benedict XI., in 1304, put an end to it by annulling the regulations of his predecessor. The bishops were prohibited from requiring accounts, and these were ordered to be rendered to the papal camera or to special papal deputies.[297]

If there was this not unnatural vacillation in regulating the delicate relations of these competing jurisdictions, there was none whatever in regard to those between the Inquisition and society at large. Even in its early years of tentative existence and uncertain{337} organization it developed such abundant promise of usefulness in bringing the secular laws to bear upon heresy that means were sought to give it a fixed organization which should render it still more efficient in its functions both of detection and punishment. The death of Frederic II., in 1250, in removing the principal antagonist of the papacy, offered the opportunity of giving practical enforcement to his edicts, and accordingly, May 15, 1252, Innocent IV. issued to all the potentates and rulers of Italy his famous bull, *Ad extirpanda*, a carefully considered and elaborate law which should establish machinery for systematic persecution as an integral part of the social edifice in every city and every state, though the uncertain way in which bishop, inquisitor, and friar are alternately referred to in it shows how indefinite were still their respective relations and duties in the matter. All rulers were ordered in public assembly to put heretics to the ban, as though they were sorcerers. Any one finding a heretic could seize him, and take possession of his goods. Each chief magistrate, within three days after assuming office, was to appoint, on the nomination of his bishop and of two friars of each of the Mendicant Orders, twelve good Catholics with two notaries and two or more servitors whose sole business was to arrest heretics, seize their goods, and deliver them to the bishop or his vicars. Their wages and expenses were to be defrayed by the State, their evidence was receivable without oaths, and no testimony was good against the concurrent statement of any three of them. They held office for six months, to be reappointed or replaced then, or at any time, on demand of the bishop and friars; they were entitled to one third of the proceeds of all fines and confiscations inflicted on heretics; they were exempt from all public duties and services incompatible with their functions, and no statutes were to be passed interfering with their actions. The ruler was bound when required to send his assessor or a knight to aid them, and every inhabitant when called upon was obliged to assist them, under a heavy penalty. When the inquisitors visited any portion of the jurisdiction they were accompanied by a deputy of the ruler elected by themselves or by the bishop. In each place visited, this official was to summon under oath three men of good repute, or even the whole vicinage, to reveal any heretics within their knowledge, or the property of such, or of any persons holding secret conventicles or differing in life or{338} manners from the ordinary faithful. The State was bound to arrest all accused, to hold them in prison, to deliver them to the bishop or inquisitor under safe escort, and to execute within fifteen days, in accordance with Frederic's decrees, all judgments pronounced against them. The ruler was further required, when called upon, to inflict torture on those who would not confess and betray all the heretics of their acquaintance. If resistance was made to an arrest, the community where it occurred was liable to an enormous fine unless it delivered up to justice within three days all who were implicated. The ruler was required to have four lists made out of all who were defamed or banned for heresy; this was to be read in public thrice a year and a copy given to the bishop, one to the Dominicans and one to the Franciscans; he was likewise to execute the destruction of houses within ten days of sentence, and the exaction of fines within three months, throwing in prison those who could not pay and keeping them until they should pay. The proceeds of fines, commutations, and confiscations were divisible into three parts, one enuring to the city, one to those concerned in the business, and the remainder to the bishop and inquisitors to be expended in persecuting heresy.

The enforcement of this stupendous measure was provided for with equally careful elaboration. It was to be inscribed ineffaceably in all the local statute-books, together with all subsequent laws which the popes might issue, under penalty of excommunication for recalcitrant officials, and interdict upon the city. Any attempt to alter these laws consigned the offender to perpetual infamy and fine, enforced by the ban. The rulers and their officials were to swear to their observance under pain of loss of office; and any neglect in their enforcement was punishable as perjury with perpetual infamy, a fine of two hundred marks, and suspicion of heresy involving loss of office and disability for all official position in future. Every ruler, within ten days after assuming office, was required to appoint, on the nomination of the bishop or the Mendicants, three good Catholics, who under oath were to investigate the acts of his predecessor and prosecute him for any failure of obedience. Moreover each podestà at the beginning and end of his term was required to have the bull read in all places that might be designated by the bishop and inquisitors, and to erase from the statute-books all laws in conflict with them. At the same time{339} Innocent issued instructions to the inquisitors to enforce by excommunication the embodiment of this and of the edicts of Frederic in the statutes of all cities and states, and he soon after conferred on them the dangerous power of interpreting, in conjunction with the bishops, all doubtful points in local laws on the subject of heresy.

These provisions are not the wild imaginings of a nightmare, but sober matter-of-fact legislation shrewdly and carefully devised to accomplish a settled policy, and it affords us a valuable insight into the public opinion of the day to find that there was no effective resistance to its acceptance. Before the death of Innocent IV., in 1254., he made one or two slight modifications suggested by experience in its working. In 1255, 1256, and 1257 Alexander IV. revised the bull, explaining some doubts which had arisen, and providing for the enforcement in all cases of the appointment of examiners of rulers going out of office, and in 1259 he reissued the bull as a whole. In 1265 Clement IV. again went over it carefully, making some changes, principally in adding the words "inquisitors" in passages where Innocent had only designated the bishops and friars, thus showing that the Inquisition had during the interval established itself as the recognized instrumentality in the persecution of heresy; and the next year he repeated Innocent's emphatic order to the inquisitors to enforce the insertion of his legislation and that of his predecessors upon the statute-books everywhere, with the free use of excommunication and interdict. This shows that it had not been universally accepted with alacrity, but the few instances which we find recorded of refusal show how generally it was submitted to. Thus in 1256 Alexander IV. learned that the authorities of Genoa were recalcitrant, and he promptly ordered the censure and interdict if they did not comply within fifteen days; and in 1258 a similar course was observed with those of Mantua; while the retention of the bull in the statutes of Florence as late as the recension of 1355, even in the midst of incongruous legislation, shows how literally the papal mandates had been obeyed for a century.[298]{340}

In Italy this furnished the Inquisition with a completely organized *personnel* paid and sustained by the State, rendering it a substantive institution armed with all the means and appliances necessary for the thorough performance of its work. Whether the popes ever endeavored to render the bulls operative elsewhere does not appear, but if they did so they failed, for the measure was not recognized as in force beyond the Alps. Yet this was scarce necessary so long as public law and the conservative spirit of the ruling class everywhere rendered it the highest duty of the citizen of every degree to aid in every way the business of the inquisitor, and pious monarchs hastened to enforce the obligation of their subjects. By the terms of the Treaty of Paris all public officials were obliged to aid in the inquisition and capture of heretics, and all inhabitants, males over fourteen years of age and females over twelve, were to be sworn to reveal all offenders to the bishops. The Council of Narbonne in 1229 put these provisions in force; that of Albi in 1254 included inquisitors among those to whom the heretic was to be denounced, and it freely threatened with the censures of the Church all temporal seigneurs who neglected the duty of aiding the Inquisition and of executing its sentences of death or confiscation. The aid demanded was freely given, and every inquisitor was armed with royal letters empowering him to call upon all officials for safe-conduct, escort, and assistance in the discharge of his functions. In a memorial dated about 1317 Bernard Gui says that the inquisitors make under these letters full use of the baillis, sergeants, and other officials, both of the king and of the seigneurs, without which they would accomplish little. This was not confined to France, for Eymerich, writing in Aragon, informs{341} us that the first act of the inquisitor on receiving his commission was to exhibit it to the king or ruler, and ask and exhort him for these letters, explaining to him that he is bound by the canons to give them if he desires to avoid the numerous penalties decreed in the bulls *Ad abolendam* and *Ut inquisionis*. His next step is to exhibit these letters to the officials and swear them to obey him in his official duties to the utmost of their power. Thus the whole force of the State was unreservedly at command of the Holy Office. Not only this, indeed, but every individual was bound to lend his aid when called upon, and any slackness of zeal exposed him to excommunication as a fautor of heresy, leading after twelve months, if neglected, to conviction as a heretic, with all its tremendous penalties.[299]

The right to abrogate any laws which impeded the freest exercise of the powers of the Inquisition was likewise arrogated on both sides of the Alps. When, in 1257, Alexander IV. heard with indignant emotion that Mantua had adopted certain damnable statutes interfering with the absolutism of the Inquisition, he straightway ordered the Bishop of Mantua to investigate the matter, and to annul anything which should impede or delay its operations, enforcing his action by excommunicating the authorities and laying an interdict on the city. This was simply in furtherance of the bull *Ad extirpanda*, but in 1265 Urban IV. repeated the order and made it universally applicable, and it was carried into the canon law as the expression of the undoubted rights of the Church. This rendered the Inquisition virtually supreme in all lands, and it became an accepted maxim of law that all statutes interfering with the free action of the Inquisition were void, and those who enacted them were to be punished; where such laws existed the inquisitor{342} was instructed to have them submitted to him, and if he found them objectionable the authorities were obliged to repeal or modify them. It was not the fault of the Church if a bold monarch like Philippe le Bel occasionally ventured to incur divine vengeance by protecting his subjects.[300]

Beyond the Alps there was no legal responsibility admitted, as in Italy, to defray the expenses of the Inquisition by the State. This is a subject which will be treated more fully hereafter, and meanwhile I may briefly state that royal generosity was amply sufficient to keep the organization in effective condition. Its necessary expenses were exceedingly small. The Dominican convents furnished buildings in which to hold its tribunals. The public officials were bound under royal order and the tremendous penalties involved in suspicion of heresy to render service whenever called upon. If the bishops had neglected the duty of establishing and maintaining prisons, the royal zeal had stepped in, had built them and had kept them up. In 1317 we learn that during the past eight years the king had spent the large sum of six hundred and thirty livres tournois on that of Toulouse alone, and he also regularly paid the jailers. Besides this, the inquisitors, whenever they needed aid and counsel, were empowered to summon experts to attend them and to enforce obedience to the summons. There was no exception of dignity or station. All the learning and wisdom of the land were made subservient to the supreme duty of suppressing heresy and were placed gratuitously at the service of the Inquisition; and any prelate who hesitated to render assistance of any kind when called upon was threatened in no gentle terms with the full force of the papal vengeance.[301]

That the powers thus conferred on the inquisitors were real and not merely theoretical we see in 1260 in the case of Capello di Chia, a powerful noble of the Roman province, who incurred the suspicion of heresy, was condemned, proscribed, and his lands confiscated. He refused to submit, when Frà Andrea, the inquisitor, called for assistance on the citizens of the neighboring town of{343} Viterbo, and they obeyed him by raising an army with which he marched to besiege Capello in his castle of Colle-Casale. Capello had craftily conveyed his lands to a Roman noble named Pietro Giacomo Surdi, and the pious enterprise of the Viterbians was arrested by a command from the senator of Rome forbidding violence to the property of a good Catholic Roman citizen. Then Alexander IV. intervened, ordering Surdi to withdraw from the quarrel, as his claim to the castle was null and void. He likewise commanded the senator to abandon his indefensible position, and warmly thanked the Viterbians for the zeal and alacrity with which they had obeyed the summons of Frà Andrea. Frà Andrea, in fact, had only exercised the power which Zanghino declares to be inherent in the office of inquisitor, of levying open war against heretics and heresy.[302]

113

In the exercise of this almost limitless authority, inquisitors were practically relieved from all supervision and responsibility. Even a papal legate was not to interfere with them or inquire into heresy within their inquisitorial districts. They were not liable to excommunication while in discharge of their duties, nor could they be suspended by any delegate of the Holy See. If such a thing were attempted, the excommunication or suspension was pronounced void, unless, indeed, it was issued by special command of the pope. Already, in 1245, they were empowered to absolve their familiars for any excesses, and in 1261 they were authorized to absolve each other from excommunication for any cause; which, as each inquisitor usually had a subordinate associate ready to perform this office for him, rendered them virtually invulnerable. Moreover, they were released from all obedience to their provincials and generals, whom they were even forbidden to obey in anything relating to the business of their office, and they were secured from any attempt to undermine them with the curia by the enormous privilege of being able to go to Rome at any time and to stay there as long as they might see fit, even in spite of prohibition by provincial or general chapters. At first their commissions were thought to expire with the death of the pope who issued them, but in 1267 they were declared to be continuously valid.[303]{344}

The question of the removability of inquisitors was one which bore directly upon their subordination or independence, and was the subject of much conflicting legislation. When the power of appointment was first conferred upon the provincials it carried with it authority to remove and replace them after consultation with discreet brethren; and in 1244 Innocent IV. declared that the provincials and generals of the Mendicant Orders had full power to remove, revoke, supersede, and transfer all members of their orders serving as inquisitors, even when commissioned by the pope. Some ten years later the vacillating policy of Alexander IV. indicates an earnest effort on the part of the inquisitors to obtain independence. In 1256 he asserted the removing power of the provincials; July 5, 1257, he withdrew their power, and December 9, of the same year, he reaffirmed it in his bull *Quod super nonnullis*, which was repeatedly reissued by himself and his successors. Later popes issued conflicting orders, until at length Boniface VIII. decided in favor of the removing power; but the inquisitors claimed that it could only be exercised for cause and after due trial, which practically reduced it to a nullity. It is true that in the reformatory effort of Clement V. *ipso facto* excommunication, removable only by the pope, was provided for three crimes of inquisitors—falsely prosecuting or neglecting to prosecute for favor, enmity, or profit, for extorting money, and for confiscating church property for the offence of a clerk—but these provisions, although they called forth the earnest protest of Bernard Gui, only amounted to a declaration of what was desirable, and were of no practical effect.[304]{345}

The Franciscans endeavored to reduce their inquisitors to subjection by the expedient of issuing commissions for a limited term. Thus in 1320 the General Michele da Cesena adopted the term of five years, which seems to have long continued the rule, for in 1375 we see Gregory XI. requesting the Franciscan general to keep in office as inquisitor of Rome Frà Gabriele da Viterbo on account of his eminent merits. In 1439 a commission as inquisitor of Florence, issued to Frà Francesco da Michele, to take effect on the expiration of the term of the incumbent, Frà Jacopo della Biada, indicates that appointments were still for specified times, although in 1432 Eugenius IV. had conferred on the Franciscan general, Guglielmo di Casale, full power of appointment and removal. The Dominicans do not seem to have adopted this expedient, and no precautions of any kind were available to enforce subordination and discipline in view of the constant interference of the Holy See, which doubtless could always be obtained by those who knew how to approach it. Commissions were continually issued directly by the pope, and those who held them seem not to have been removable by any one else. Even when this was not done, it mattered little that the popes admitted the power of the provincials to remove, when they interposed to nullify its exercise. In 1323 John XXII. gave to Frà Piero da Perugia, inquisitor of Assisi, letters which protected him from suspension and removal. In 1339 we happen to hear of Giovanni di Borgo removed by the Franciscan general and replaced by Benedict XII. Even more subversive of discipline was the case of Francisco de Sala, appointed by the provincial of Aragon, removed by his successor, and reinstated by Martin V. in 1419, with a provision of inamovability by any superior of his Order. Yet in 1439 Eugenius IV., and in 1474 Sixtus IV. renewed the provisions of Clement IV. rendering inquisitors removable at will by both generals and provincials; and in 1479, Sixtus IV., to impress them with some sense of responsibility, adopted the expedient of requiring all complaints against them to be brought before the general of the Order to{346} which they belonged, to whom was confided power of punishment up to removal.[305]

The natural result of this conflicting legislation was that the inquisitors held themselves accountable to their superiors only for their actions as friars and not as inquisitors; in the latter capacity they acknowledged responsibility only to the pope, and they asserted that the power of removal could only be exercised in cases of inability to act through sickness, age, or ignorance. Their vicars and commissioners they held to be completely beyond any jurisdiction but their own, and any attempt on the part of a provincial to remove such a subordinate was to be met with a prosecution for suspicion of heresy, as an impeding of the Inquisition, to be followed by excommunication, when, if this was endured for a year, it was to be ended by condemnation for heresy. Men armed with these tremendous powers, and animated with this resolute spirit, were not lightly to be meddled with. The warmth with which Eymerich argues the subject suggests the character of the struggle continually going on between the provincials and their appointees, and the conclusions to which he arrives indicate the temper in which the latter vindicated their independence. The grave abuses and disorders to which this led obliged John XXIII. to intervene and declare that the inquisitors should in all things be subject and obedient to their superiors. The Great Schism, however, had weakened the papal authority, and this injunction met with scant respect, so that one of the first utterances of Martin V., in 1418, when the Church was reunited at Constance, was to repeat the order, and to prescribe implicit obedience to it. Yet, as in the matter of removals, the insatiable greed of the curia was a fatal obstacle to the enforcement of subordination, for those who were commissioned directly by the pope could not be expected to endure subjection to the officials of their Orders.[306]

From Eymerich's remarks we see that an inquisitor was bound{347} to have little hesitation in prosecuting his superior. His jurisdiction, in fact, was almost unlimited, for the dread suspicion of heresy brought, with few exceptions, all mankind to a common level, and suspicion of heresy was to be technically inferred from anything which affected the dignity or crossed the purposes of those who carried on the Inquisition. Even the jealously-guarded right of asylum in the churches was waived in its favor, and the immunities of the Mendicant Orders gave them no exemption from its jurisdiction. Kings, themselves, were subject to this jurisdiction, though Eymerich discreetly observes that in their case it is more prudent to inform the pope and await his instructions. Yet one exception there was. The episcopal office still retained enough of its earlier dignity to render its possessor exempt unless the inquisitor was furnished with special papal letters. It was his duty, however, in case a bishop was suspected of vacillating in the faith, to collect with diligence all the evidence procurable, and to forward it to Rome for examination and decision—a duty in the exercise of which he could render himself abundantly disagreeable, and even dangerous. The choleric John XXII., in 1327, introduced another exemption when provoked by the arrogance of the Sicilian inquisitor, Matthieu de Pontigny, who dared to excommunicate Guillaume de Balet, archdeacon of Fréjus, papal chaplain and representative of the Avignonese papacy in the Campagna and Maritima. The angry pope issued a decretal forbidding all judges and inquisitors to attack in any way the officials and nuncios of the Holy See without special letters of authority— but the mere audacity of the attempt shows the height of presumption to which the members of the Holy Office had attained. That laymen learned to address them as "your religious majesty" shows the impression made on the popular mind by their irresponsible supremacy.[307]

If bishops were exempt from judgment by the Inquisition they were not released from obedience to the inquisitors. In the ordinary papal commission issued to the latter, archbishops, bishops,{348} abbots, and other prelates are commanded to obey them in all concerning their office, under pain of excommunication, suspension, and interdict. That this was not a mere idle form is manifest by the tone of arrogant domination in which the inquisitors issued their commands to episcopal officials. Though the papal superscription to the bishop was "venerable brother" and to the inquisitor "cherished son," yet the inquisitors held that they were superior to the bishops, as being direct delegates of the Holy See, and that if any one were cited simultaneously by a bishop and an inquisitor he must first attend to the summons of the latter. The inquisitor was to be obeyed as the pope himself, and this supremacy included the bishop. This formed part of the papal policy, for the inquisitor was a convenient instrument to reduce the episcopate to subjection. Thus in 1296 Boniface VIII., in giving directions to the bishops to suppress certain irregular and unauthorized hermits and mendicants, enclosed copies of the bull to the inquisitors with instructions to stimulate the bishops to their duty and to report to him all who showed themselves negligent. In spite of the assumed superiority of the inquisitor, however, the Inquisition was very commonly used as a stepping-stone to the episcopate. It is not easy to set bounds to the sources of influence which the office placed within reach of an ambitious man, and this influence was constantly employed to procure promotion into the ranks of the hierarchy. Instances of this are too frequent to be specified, commencing with the earliest inquisitors, Frà Aldobrandino Cavalcanti of Florence, who became Bishop of Viterbo, while his successor, Frà Ruggieri Calcagni, in 1245, was rewarded with the bishopric of Castro in the Maremma. I need only refer to the case of Florence, in 1343, where the inquisitor, Frà Andrea da Perugia was advanced to the episcopate and was succeeded by Frà Pietro di Aquila, who in 1346 was made Bishop of Santangelo dei Lombardi. His successor was Frà Michele di Lapo, and in 1350 we find the Signiory writing to the pope with the request that he be placed in the bishopric of Florence, which had become vacant. The office also afforded opportunities of promotion within the Orders which were not neglected. Thus in a list of Dominican provincials of Saxony in the latter half of the fourteenth century, three who occupied that post in succession from 1369 to 1382, Walther Kerlinger, Hermann Helstede, and Heinrich{349} von Albrecht, are all described as having been previously inquisitors.[308]

It is not to be imagined that this gigantic structure which overshadowed Christendom was allowed to establish itself wholly without opposition, despite the favor of popes and kings. When we come to consider the details of its history we shall find numerous cases of popular resistance, desperate and isolated struggles, crushed remorselessly before revolt could so extend as to become dangerous. It required, indeed, courage to foolhardiness for any one to raise hand or voice against an inquisitor, no matter how cruel or nefarious were his actions. Under the canon law, any one, from the meanest to the highest, who opposed or impeded in any way the functions of an inquisitor, or gave aid or counsel to those who did so, became at once *ipso facto* excommunicate. After the lapse of a year in this condition he was legally a heretic to be handed over without further ceremony to the secular arm for burning, without trial and without forgiveness. The awful authority which thus shrouded the inquisitor was rendered yet more terrible by the elasticity of definition given to the crime of impeding the Holy Office and the tireless tenacity with which those guilty of it were pursued. If friendly death came to shield them, the Inquisition attacked their memories, and visited their offences upon their children and grandchildren.[309]

All unorganized efforts of insubordination were easily repressed. Had the bishops united in resistance, they could readily have prevented the serious encroachment on their jurisdiction and influence, and have saved their flocks from the horrors in store for them. There was no unity of action, however, among the prelates. Some {350} of them were honest fanatics who welcomed the Holy Office and assisted it in every way. Others were indifferent. Multitudes, engrossed in worldly cares and quarrels, were rather glad to be relieved of duties which were onerous and for which they had neither learning nor leisure. If any foresaw the end from the humble beginning, none dared to raise a voice against what was everywhere regarded by pious souls as supplying the most urgent need of the time. Still, that the episcopate at large looked with disfavor on these new functions and activities of the upstart Mendicants there can be no doubt, although jealousy could only manifest itself through a futile pretence to discharge the neglected duties in which the Mendicants had been summoned to replace them. Accordingly we find a certain bustling show of activity in ordering perquisition against heretics by the old device of the synodal witnesses, in the Council of Tours in 1239, that of Béziers in 1246, that of Albi in 1254; while that of Lille (Venaissin) in 1251 made a bolder effort to recover lost ground by not only ordering the bishops to make searching inquisition in their dioceses, but by demanding from the Inquisition the surrender of all its records to the Ordinaries; and when this failed the Council of Albi, in 1254, made a fruitless effort to obtain duplicate copies. The spirit in which the rival tribunals regarded each other is seen in the complaint of an inquisitor, not long after 1250, that heretics were encouraged and rendered audacious by the constant attacks and detraction to which the inquisitors were exposed, as being fools, and negligent and slow, and incapable of bringing any affair to a termination, as punishing the innocent and allowing the guilty to escape. These slanders, he says, proceed from judges, both secular and ecclesiastical, who profess great zeal for the extermination of heresy, but who are really impelled by covetousness for bribes, or who are secretly inclined to heresy, or have friends or relatives who are heretics or suspected of heresy. Evidently there was little love lost between the old organization and the new.[310]

If any thought existed of combined opposition, outside of Germany, {351} it might well be thrown aside as impracticable after the spectacle of the defeat of the University of Paris on its own ground by the Mendicants. The jealousy perpetually fed by the constant encroachments of the inquisitors could only find vent in obscure squabbles wherein the final decision of the Holy See could always be confidently reckoned upon as against the episcopate. In 1330 we see the inquisitor, Henri de Chamay, complaining to John XXII. that the Bishop of Maguelonne was interfering with the free exercise of his office in Montpellier, on the ground of certain papal privileges granted him, when the pope at once instructs him to proceed without hesitation and to disregard the bishop's pretensions. Such a decision was a foregone conclusion, as the Archbishop of Narbonne and all his suffragans found in 1441, when they united in addressing Eugenius IV., complaining of the exorbitant pretensions of the Inquisition, and asking him to delay action till they should send him full details. Without waiting to hear their specific charges, he replied that the inquisitor had already accused them of impeding him in his office and with vexing him with proceedings and suits at law. There is no business, he added, of greater importance to the Church than the destruction of heresy, and no way to win his favor more efficacious than by aiding the Inquisition. It had been organized for the purpose of relieving bishops of a portion of their cares, and any interference with it would be visited with his displeasure. In the present case, for the sake of concord, the inquisitor would revoke the grievances complained of, and the pope pronounced all suits against him quashed and extinguished. Evidently in any contest the odds were too great against the episcopate, and the danger of systematic opposition too real, to render any organized antagonism feasible. How completely the papacy regarded the Inquisition as an instrumentality for furthering its schemes of aggrandizement is seen when, on the outbreak of the Great Schism, inquisitors were required to take a formal feudal oath of fidelity to the pope appointing him and to his successors.[311]

With so little to check and so much to stimulate, the spread of {352} the Inquisition was rapid throughout most of the lands of Christendom. I shall have occasion hereafter to trace its vicissitudes in the principal centres of its activity, and need here only indicate the limits of its extension.

The northern nations were too far removed from the focus of heresy to be exposed to aberrations from the faith at the time when papal supremacy found its most useful instruments in the Mendicant inquisitors. Consequently the papal Inquisition cannot be said to have had an existence in the British Islands, Denmark, or Scandinavia. The edicts of Frederic II. had no currency there; and when, in 1277, Robert Kilwarby, Archbishop of Canterbury, and the masters of Oxford denounced certain errors springing from the Averrhoist doctrines; when, in 1286, Archbishop Peckham condemned the heresy of Friar Richard Crapewell, and in 1368 Archbishop Langham denounced as heretical thirty articles of scholastic speculation, even had there been martyrs ready there were no laws under which to punish them, although lawyers had sought to introduce the penalty of the stake, and it had once been inflicted by a council of Oxford, in 1222, on a clerk who had apostatized to Judaism. We shall see hereafter that in the affair of the Templars the papal Inquisition was found necessary to procure condemnation, but even then it was so opposed to the character of English institutions that it worked defectively and disappeared as soon as the occasion for its temporary introduction passed away. When Wickliff came and was followed by Lollardry, the English conceptions of the relations between Church and State had already become such that there was no thought of applying to Rome for a special tribunal with which to meet the threatened danger. The statute of May 25, 1382, directs the king to issue to his sheriffs commissions to arrest Wickliff's travelling preachers, and aiders and abettors of heresy, and to hold them till they justify themselves *"selonc reson et la ley de seinte esglise;"* and, in the following July, royal letters ordered the authorities of Oxford to make inquisition for heresy throughout the university. The weakness of Richard II. allowed the Lollards to become a powerful political as well as religious party, but their chances disappeared with the revolution which placed Henry IV. on the throne. The support of the Church was a necessity to the new dynasty, which lost no time in earning its gratitude. After the burning of Sawtré by a⌊353⌋ royal warrant confirmed by Parliament, in 1400, the statute *"de hæretico comburendo"* for the first time inflicted in England the death-penalty as a settled punishment for heresy. It restricted preaching to the beneficed curates and those *ex officio* privileged, it forbade the dissemination of heretical opinions and books, empowered the bishops to seize all offenders and hold them in prison until they should purge themselves or abjure, and ordered the bishops to proceed against them within three months after arrest. For minor offences the bishops were empowered to imprison during pleasure and fine at discretion—the fine enuring to the royal exchequer. For obstinate heresy or relapse, involving under the canon law abandonment to the secular arm, the bishops and their commissioners were the sole judges, and, on their delivery of such convicts, the sheriff of the county or the mayor and bailiffs of the nearest town were obliged to burn them before the people on an eminence. Henry V. followed this up, and the statute of 1414 established throughout the kingdom a sort of mixed secular and ecclesiastical inquisition for which the English system of grand inquests gave especial facilities. Under this legislation burning for heresy became a not unfamiliar sight to English eyes, and Lollardry was readily suppressed. In 1533 Henry VIII. repealed the statute of 1400, while retaining those of 1382 and 1414, and also the penalty of burning alive for contumacious heresy and relapse, and the dangerous admixture of politics and religion rendered the stake a favorite instrument of statecraft. One of the earliest measures of the reign of Edward VI. was the repeal of this law, as well as of those of 1382 and 1414, together with all the atrocious legislation of the Six Articles. With the reaction under Philip and Mary came a revival of the sharp laws against heresy. Scarce had the Spanish marriage been concluded when an obedient Parliament reenacted the legislation of 1382, 1400, and 1414, which afforded ample machinery for the numerous burnings which followed. The earliest act of the first Parliament of Elizabeth was the repeal of the legislation of Philip and Mary and of the old statutes which it had revived; but the writ *de hæretico comburendo* had become an integral part of English law and survived until the desire of Charles II. for Catholic toleration caused him, in 1676, to procure its abrogation and the restraint of the ecclesiastical courts "in cases of atheism, blasphemy, heresy, and schism and other damnable doctrines⌊354⌋ and opinions" to the ecclesiastical remedies of "excommunication, deprivation, degradation, and other ecclesiastical censures not extending to death." Scotland was more tardy than England in humanitarian development, but the last execution for heresy in the British Islands was that of a youth of eighteen, a medical student named Aikenhead, who was hanged in Edinburgh in 1696.[312]

In Ireland the fiery temper of the Franciscan, Richard Ledred, Bishop of Ossory, led him into a prolonged struggle with presumed heretics—the Lady Alice Kyteler, accused of sorcery, and her accomplices. So little was known in Ireland of the laws concerning heresy that at first the secular officials refused contemptuously to take the oath prescribed by the canons to aid inquisitors in their persecuting duties, but Ledred finally obliged them to do so and had the satisfaction of burning some of the accused in 1325. He incurred, however, the enmity of the chief personages of the island, leading to a counter-charge of heresy against himself. For years he was obliged to live in exile, and it was not till 1354 that he was able to reside quietly in his diocese, though in 1335 we find Benedict XII. writing to Edward III., deploring the absence in England of so useful an institution as the Inquisition, and urging him to order the secular officials to lend efficient aid to the pious Bishop of Ossory in his struggles with the heretics, of whom the most exaggerated description is given. Even Alexander, Archbishop of Dublin, in 1347, was declared to have been a fautor of heresy because he interfered with Ledred's violent proceedings; and, in 1351, his successor, Archbishop John, was directed to take active measures to punish those who had escaped from Ossory and had taken refuge in his see.[313]

It is true that when the Hussite troubles became alarming and⌊355⌋ there was danger that the disaffection might spread to the North, Martin V., in 1421, authorized the Bishop of Sleswick to appoint a Franciscan, Friar Nicholas John, as inquisitor for Denmark, Norway, and Sweden, but there is no trace of his activity in those regions, and the Inquisition may be considered as non-existent there.[314]

As the mediæval missions for the conversion of schismatics and heathen were exclusively Dominican and Franciscan, the churches which they built up, however slender in membership, were nevertheless completely equipped with apparatus for preserving the orthodoxy of converts, and thus we read of Inquisitions in Africa and Asia. Friar Raymond Martius is honored as the founder of the Inquisition in Tunis and Morocco. About 1370 Gregory XI. appointed the Dominican Friar John Gallus as inquisitor in the East, who in conjunction with Friar Elias Petit planted the institution, as we are told, in Armenia, Russia, Georgia, and Wallachia, while Upper Armenia was similarly provided by Friar Bartolomeo Ponco. On the death of Friar Gallus, Urban VI., about

1378, applied to the Dominican general to select three brethren to serve as inquisitors, one in Armenia and Georgia, one in Greece and Tartary, and one in Russia and the two Wallachias; and in 1389 one of these, Friar Andreas of Caffa, obtained the privilege of appointing an associate in his extensive province of Greece and Tartary. In the fourteenth century an inquisitor seems to have been regarded as a necessary portion of the missionary outfit. Even in the fabled Ethiopian empire of Prester John we hear of an Inquisition founded in Abyssinia by the Dominican Friar, St. Pantaleone, and another in Nubia by Friar Bartolomeo de Tybuli, who was also honored as a saint in those regions. Grotesque as all this sounds, one cannot help honoring the unselfish zeal of the men who thus devoted themselves to the diffusion of the gospel among barbarous Gentiles, and one can find comfort in the conviction that their Inquisitions were comparatively harmless so long as they were not backed by the terrible laws of a Frederic II. or of a St. Louis.[315]

Even the decaying fragments of the Kingdom of Jerusalem{356} could not be allowed burial without an inquisitor to attend the obsequies. The misfortunes of war, according to Nicholas IV., the first Franciscan pope, gave opportunity for the growth of heresy and Judaism. Therefore, in 1290, he granted full powers to his legate, Nicholas, Patriarch of Jerusalem, to appoint inquisitors, with the advice of the Mendicant provincials. This was accordingly done, but the fatherly care of Nicholas was a trifle tardy. The capture of Acre, May 19, 1291, drove the Christians finally from the Holy Land, and the career of the Syrian Inquisition was therefore of the briefest. It was revived, however, in 1375, by Gregory XI., who empowered the Franciscan provincial of the Holy Land to act as inquisitor in Palestine, Syria, and Egypt, to check the too prevalent apostasy of the Christian pilgrims who continued to flock to those regions.[316]

It is not to be supposed that the triumph of the Inquisition over the bishops gave to it a monopoly of persecution. The ordinary episcopal jurisdiction remained intact. About 1240 we see the Bishop of Toulouse and his provost conducting, without the aid of an inquisitor, an inquest for heresy upon the powerful seigneurs de Niort. Bishops who were zealous were frequently seen co-operating with inquisitors in the examination of heretics, as well as holding their own inquisitions. Thus, in a number of cases occurring at Albi in 1299, we find the trials held in the episcopal palace before the bishop, assisted sometimes by Nicholas d'Abbeville, inquisitor of Carcassonne, and sometimes by Bertrand de Clermont, inquisitor of Toulouse, and sometimes by both. At first, as we have seen, the inquisitor was only the assistant of the bishop, and the latter was by no means relieved of his duties and responsibilities in the extermination of heresy. In fact the bishops themselves sometimes appointed inquisitors of their own in order to operate more efficiently; and the names of such functionaries acting for the archbishops of Narbonne appear in documents of 1251 and 1325. There was nothing, moreover, to prevent a zealous{357} prelate, who thought less of the dignity of his order than the suppression of heresy, from accepting a commission as inquisitor from the pope, as was the case with Guillem Arnaud, Bishop of Carcassonne, who, during his episcopate, lasting from 1249 to 1255, presided over the tribunal of Carcassonne with an energy that Dominicans might have envied.[317]

Yet, as the Inquisition achieved its independence of the episcopate, two concurrent jurisdictions could hardly coexist without jarring, even when both were animated by the desire of harmony: when jealousy and rivalry were strong, quarrels were inevitable. It was even hinted that bishops, desiring to preserve friends from the zeal of the inquisitors, would prosecute them in their own courts to save them from the rigorous impartiality of the Holy Office. To settle the questions which thus were constantly arising, Urban IV., in 1262, empowered the inquisitors to proceed in all cases at their discretion, whether or not these were also under examination by the bishops; and this was repeated in 1265 and 1266 by Clement IV., with strong injunctions to the inquisitors that they were not to allow their processes to be impeded by concurrent action of the bishops. In 1273 Gregory X. laid down the same rule; and it became the settled practice of the Church, embodied in the canon law, that both courts could simultaneously try the same case, communicating at intervals their proceedings to each other. Mutual conference, moreover, was necessary at the final sentence, and when they could not agree a full statement had to be submitted to the pope for decision. Even when proceeding alone and by his ordinary authority, the bishop was obliged to call in the concurrence of an inquisitor when he rendered sentence.[318]{358}

During this period, at one time, it became a question whether the episcopal jurisdiction over heresy was not completely superseded by the papal commission given to an inquisitor to act in his diocese. Gui Foucoix, the foremost jurist of his day, in his "*Quæstiones*," which long remained an authority in the inquisitorial tribunals, answered this question in the affirmative, and argued that the bishop was debarred from action by the special delegation of papal powers to the inquisitor. Yet, when Gui became pope, under the name of Clement IV., his bulls of 1265 and 1266, quoted above, show that he abandoned this position, and Gregory X. also expressly declared that the diocesan jurisdiction was not interfered with. Still the question was regarded as doubtful by canon lawyers, and for a period the episcopal jurisdiction sank almost into abeyance. There were few more active prelates in his day than Simon, Archbishop of Bourges, who, from 1284 to 1291, made repeated visitations of his southern dioceses, such as Albi, Rodez, Cahors, etc. Yet, in the records of these visitations, there is no allusion to his taking any cognizance of heresy, unless, indeed, his forcing, in 1285, a number of usurers of Gourdon to abjure be assumed as such, though usury was not justiciable by the Inquisition unless it became heresy by the assertion of its legality. About 1298, however, Boniface VIII. reasserted the jurisdiction of the episcopate, and we see Bernard de Castanet, Bishop of Albi, stirring up a revolt among his flock by the energy with which he scourged the heretics of Albi. Soon afterwards Clement V. enlarged the functions of the episcopate as a means of curbing the atrocities of the Inquisition, and the glossators argued that the appointment of inquisitors in no way relieved the bishop from the duty of investigating and suppressing heresy in his diocese—indeed, he was liable to deposition by the pope for negligence in this respect, though he was shielded by his position from prosecution by the inquisitor. Yet, even after the Clementines, Bernard Gui asserts it to be improper for the episcopal ordinary to cite any one who is already before the Inquisition. Still, if the power of the bishop had been limited by requiring him to consult with the inquisitor before rendering sentence, it had been enlarged in another direction by authorizing him to summon witnesses as well as offenders who had fled to other dioceses. There was one discrimination, however, against the bishop which handicapped him{359} heavily. His attempts to get a share of the proceeds of fines and confiscations to meet the expenses of prosecution were ineffectual. He was told that he and his officials had revenues for the functions of the Church, and these must suffice to pay him for the service. Ingenious dialecticians reasoned this away as far as regards the bishop when he acted personally, but it held good against his officials. To the latter it was not encouraging to be urged to work and pay their own costs, while the inquisitor, at least in Italy, had control of the confiscations, without accountability to the bishop.[319]

Under the legislation of Boniface VIII. and Clement V. it was natural that the first quarter of the fourteenth century should witness a revival of the episcopal Inquisition. Even in Italy the provincial Council of Milan, held at Bergamo in 1311 under the Archbishop Gastone Torriani, organized a thorough system of inquisition on the model of the papal institution. The growing{360} power of the Visconti, hostile to the papacy, had greatly crippled the Dominicans, and a vigorous effort was made to replace them. In every town the arch-priest or provost was instructed to raise an armed guard, whose duty was the ceaseless perquisition of heresy, and whose privileges and immunities were the same as those of the familiars of the Dominican inquisitors; and all citizens, from the noble to the peasant, were summoned to lend assistance, when called upon, under significant threats. In France some proceedings, in 1319 and 1320, at Béziers, Pamiers, and Montpellier show the episcopal courts in full activity, with the occasional appearance of an inquisitor in a subordinate capacity as assistant, or of an episcopal inquisitor as a colleague of equal rank with those who acted under papal authority. In fact we find one such, in 1322, representing the see of Ausch, contending with the great Bernard Gui himself over a prisoner whom they both claimed. When, also, in 1319, the great opponent of the Inquisition, Friar Bernard Délicieux, was to be tried for impeding it, John XXII. appointed a special commission for the work, consisting of the Archbishop of Toulouse and the Bishops of Pamiers and St. Papoul, while one of the most experienced inquisitors of the time, Jean de Beaune of Carcassonne, acted as prosecutor, and not as judge.[320]

In Germany, about the same time, there was a sudden development of episcopal activity in the prosecutions of the Beghards by the Bishop of Strassburg and the Archbishop of Cologne, leading to a fair trial of strength between the hierarchy and the Dominicans in the case of Master Eckhart, the teacher of Suso and Tauler and the founder of the German mystics. He was looked upon with pride by the whole Order as one of its most prominent members. He had taught theology with applause in the great University of Paris; in 1303, when Germany was divided into two provinces, he had been made the first provincial Prior of Saxony; in 1307 the general had appointed him Vicar of Bohemia. In 1326 we find him, as teacher of theology in the Dominican school of Cologne, falling under suspicion of complicity with the heresy of the Beghards, against whom a sharp persecution was raging. His{361} lofty mysticism trenched dangerously on their pantheism, and possibly they may have sought to shelter themselves behind his great name. At the general chapter of 1325 complaints had been made that in Germany members of the Order preached to the people in the vulgar tongue doctrines that might lead to error, and Gervaise, Prior of Angers, was ordered to investigate them; while, about the same time, John XXII., in concurrence with the wishes of the Order, appointed Nicholas of Strassburg, lector or teacher of the Cologne Dominicans, as his inquisitor for the province of Germany, to inquire into the faith and life of the brethren. Thus far everything had been kept within the precincts of the Order, but the archbishop was growing hot in his pursuit of the Beghards. He evidently was dissatisfied with what was on foot, and he appointed two episcopal commissioners or inquisitors to look after Master Eckhart. Nicholas of Strassburg was himself inclined to mysticism; every motive conspired to lead him to deal tenderly with the accused, and Eckhart was accordingly acquitted, in July, 1326. The episcopal inquisitors were not content with this (one of them was a Franciscan), and proceeded to take evidence against Eckhart. After six months, on January 14, 1327, they summoned Nicholas, as was their right, to communicate to them his proceedings. He came, accompanied by ten friars, not to obey the command, but to enter a solemn protest against the whole business, demanding his "Apostoli," or letters of appeal to the pope, on the ground that Dominicans were not subject to the episcopal Inquisition, and that he in especial was an inquisitor appointed by the pope with full jurisdiction. As early as 1184 Lucius III. had abolished all immunities of monastic orders in cases of heresy, but the Dominicans were of later origin, they had been strengthened with special privileges, and they claimed this exemption although they could not prove it. The episcopal inquisitors promptly answered this by commencing the same day an action against Nicholas himself, who on the morrow interjected an appeal to the Holy See. They further summoned Master Eckhart to appear before them on January 31, but on the 24th he came with numerous supporters and filed an indignant protest, in

119

which he complained bitterly of their protracting the proceedings for the purpose of ruining his reputation, in place of pushing them to an end, as they could readily have done six months before; besides,[362] they were using for the same purpose certain vile Dominicans who were notorious for their crimes. He demanded his "Apostoli," and named May 4 as the term for prosecuting the appeal in the Roman court. To this the archiepiscopal inquisitors had by law thirty days to reply, and during the interval, on February 13, he took an extra-judicial step, which seems to show how greatly his reputation had suffered by these proceedings, and which has given rise to the assertion that he recanted his errors. After preaching in the Dominican church he caused a paper to be read in which he exculpated himself to the people from the erroneous doctrines attributed to him—denying that he had said that his little finger had created all things, or that there was in the soul something uncreated and uncreatable. At the expiration of the thirty days, on February 22, the archiepiscopal inquisitors rejected Eckhart's appeal as frivolous. Worn out with the controversy, he died soon after, but his Order had sufficient influence with John XXII. to obtain an evocation of the case to Avignon. There the regularity of the archbishop's action was recognized, and on March 27, 1329, judgment was rendered, defining in Eckhart's teachings seventeen heretical articles and eleven suspect of heresy. Although his assumed recantation saved his bones from exhumation and incremation, the result was none the less a full justification of the archbishop's proceedings. For once the old order had triumphed over the new. The episcopal jurisdiction was confirmed, for Eckhart's heresy was declared to have been proved both by the inquisition held by the archbishop under his ordinary authority, and by the investigation subsequently made in Avignon by papal command, and the decision was the more emphatic, since John XXII. had at the moment every motive to soothe the Dominicans, involved as he was in mortal struggle at once with Louis of Bavaria and with the whole puritanic section of the Franciscans.[321][363]

The episcopal Inquisition was thus fairly re-established as part of the recognized organization of the Church. The Council of Paris in 1350 treats of the persecution of heresy as part of the recognized duties of the bishop, and instructs the Ordinaries as to their powers of arrest and authority to call upon the secular officials for assistance in precisely the same terms as the Inquisition might do. A brief of Urban V. in 1363 refers to a knight and five gentlemen suspected of heresy, then in the custody of the Bishop of Carcassonne, and orders their trial by the bishop or inquisitor, or by both conjointly, the result to be referred to the papal court. When a bishop had spirit to resist the invasion of his rights by an inquisitor, he was able to make them respected. In 1423 the Inquisitor of Carcassonne had gone to Albi, where he swore in two notaries and some other officials to act for him; he had then taken certain evidence relating to a case before him, and had sworn the witnesses to secrecy in order that the accused might not receive warning. Of all this the Bishop of Albi complained as an invasion of his jurisdiction. The swearing in of the officials he claimed should only have been done in presence of his ordinary or of a deputy; the secrecy imposed on the witnesses was an impediment to his own inquisitorial procedure, as depriving him of evidence in the event of his prosecuting the case. The points were somewhat nice, and illustrate the friction and jealousy inseparable from the concurrent and competing jurisdictions; but in the present case, to avoid unseemly strife, the Bishop of Carcassonne was chosen as arbitrator, the inquisitor acknowledged himself in the wrong and annulled his acts, and a public instrument was drawn up in attestation[364] of the settlement. Yet in spite of these inevitable quarrels a *modus vivendi* was practically established. Eymerich, writing about 1375, almost always represents the bishop and inquisitor as co-operating together, not only in the final sentence, but in the preliminary proceedings; he evidently seeks to represent the two powers as working harmoniously for a common end, and that the Inquisition in no way superseded the episcopal jurisdiction or relieved the bishop from the responsibility inherent in his office. A century later Sprenger, in discussing the jurisdiction of the Inquisition from the standpoint of an inquisitor, takes virtually the same position; and the commissions issued to inquisitors usually contained a clause to the effect that no prejudice was intended to the inquisitorial jurisdiction of the Ordinaries. In the habitual negligence of the episcopal officials, however, the inquisitors found little difficulty in trespassing upon their functions, and complaints of this interference continued until the eve of the Reformation.[322]

Technically there was no difference between the episcopal and papal Inquisitions. The equitable system of procedure borrowed from the Roman law by the courts of the Ordinaries was cast aside, and the bishops were permitted and even instructed to follow the inquisitorial system, which was a standing mockery of justice— perhaps the most iniquitous that the arbitrary cruelty of man has ever devised. In tracing the history of the institution, therefore, there is no distinction to be drawn between its two branches, and the exploits of both are to be recorded as springing from the same impulses, using the same methods, and leading to the same ends.[323]

Yet the papal Inquisition was an instrument of infinitely greater efficiency for the work in hand. However zealous an episcopal official might be, his efforts were necessarily isolated, temporary, and spasmodic. The papal Inquisition, on the other hand, constituted[365] a chain of tribunals throughout Continental Europe perpetually manned by those who had no other work to attend to. Not only, therefore, did persecution in their hands assume the aspect of part of the endless and inevitable operations of nature, which was necessary to accomplish its end, and which rendered the heretic hopeless that time would bring relief, but by constant interchange of documents and mutual co-operation they covered Christendom with a network rendering escape almost hopeless. This, combined with the most careful preservation and indexing of records, produced a system of police singularly perfect for a period when international communication was so imperfect. The Inquisition had a long arm, a sleepless memory, and we can well understand the mysterious terror inspired by the secrecy of its operations and its almost supernatural vigilance. If public proclamation was desired, it summoned all the faithful, with promises of eternal life and reasonable temporal reward, to seize some designated heresiarch, and every parish priest where he was suspected to be in hiding was bound to spread the call before the whole population. If secret information was required, there were spies and familiars trained to the work. The record of every heretical family for generations could be traced out from the papers of one tribunal or another. A single lucky capture and extorted confession would put the sleuth-hounds on the track of hundreds who deemed themselves secure, and each new victim added his circle of denunciations. The heretic lived over a volcano which might burst forth at any moment. During the fierce persecution of the Spiritual Franciscans in 1317 and 1318 a number of pitying souls had assisted fugitives, had stood by the pyres of their martyrs and had comforted them in various ways. Some had been suspected, had fled and changed their names: others had remained in favoring obscurity; all might well have fancied that the affair was forgotten. Suddenly, in 1325, some chance—probably the confession of a prisoner—placed the Inquisition on their track. Twenty or more were traced out and seized. Kept in prison for a year or two, their resolution broke down one by one; they successively confessed their half-forgotten guilt and were duly penanced. Even more significant was the case of Guillelma Maza of Castres, who lost her husband in 1302. In the first grief of her widowhood she was induced to listen to the teachings of two Waldensian missionaries whose exhortations brought her{366} comfort. They visited her but twice, in the darkness of the night; she never saw their faces nor those of others. After twenty-five years of orthodox observance, in 1327, she is brought before the Inquisition of Carcassonne, confesses this single aberration from the faith, and repents. Unforgiving and unforgetting, no trifle was beneath the minute vigilance of the Holy Office. Thus in the case of Manenta Rosa, who, in 1325, was called before it at Carcassonne on the mortal charge of relapse, the prosecution was because, after having abjured the heresy of the Spirituals, she had been seen talking with a man who was under suspicion and had sent by him two sols to a sick woman likewise suspect.[324]

Flight was of little avail. Descriptions of heretics who disappeared were sent throughout Europe, to every spot where they could be supposed to seek refuge, putting the authorities on the alert to search for every stranger who wore the air of one differing in life and conversation from the ordinary run of the faithful. News of captures was transmitted from one tribunal to another, evidence of guilt was furnished, or the hapless victim was returned to the spot where his extorted evidence would be most effective in implicating others. In 1287 an arrest of heretics at Treviso included some from France. Immediately the French inquisitors request that they be sent to them, especially one who ranked as bishop among the Cathari, for they may be induced to reveal the names of many others; and Nicholas IV. forthwith sends instructions to Friar Philip of Treviso to deliver them, after extracting all he can from them, to the messenger of the French Inquisition. Well might the orthodox imagine that only the hand of God, the heretic that only the inspiration of Satan, could produce such results as would follow the return of these poor wretches. To human apprehension the papal Inquisition was well-nigh ubiquitous, omniscient, and omnipotent.[325]

Occasionally, it is true, the efficiency of the organization was marred with quarrels. Antagonisms could not always be avoided, and the jealousy and mutual dislike of the Dominican and Franciscan Orders would sometimes interfere with the harmony essential to mutual co-operation. I have already alluded to the troubles arising from this cause at Marseilles in 1266 and at Verona in 1291.{367} A further symptom of lack of unity is seen in 1327, when Pierre Trencavel, a noted Spiritual, who had escaped from the prison of Carcassonne, was captured in Provence with his daughter Andrée, likewise a fugitive. There could be no question as to their belonging to those from whom they had fled, yet Friar Michel, the Franciscan inquisitor of Provence, refused to surrender them, and the Carcassonne tribunal was obliged to appeal to John XXII., who intervened with a peremptory command to Friar Michel to lay aside all opposition and surrender the prisoners at once. Yet, considering the imperfections of human nature, these quarrels seem to have been few.[326]

Properly to govern and direct an engine of such infinite power, dealing with the life and happiness of countless thousands, would require more than human wisdom and virtue; and it may be worth a moment's attention to see what was the ideal of those to whom the practical working of the Holy Office was confided. Bernard Gui, the most experienced inquisitor of his day, concludes his elaborate instructions as to procedure with some general directions as to conduct and character. The inquisitor, he tells us, should be diligent and fervent in his zeal for the truth of religion, for the salvation of souls, and for the extirpation of heresy. Amid troubles and opposing accidents he should grow earnest, without allowing himself to be inflamed with the fury of wrath and indignation. He must not be sluggish of body, for sloth destroys the vigor of action. He must be intrepid, persisting through danger to death, laboring for religious truth, neither precipitating peril by audacity nor shrinking from it through timidity. He must be unmoved by the prayers and blandishments of those who seek to influence him, yet not be, through hardness of heart, so obstinate that he will yield nothing to entreaty, whether in granting delays or in mitigating punishment, according to place and circumstance, for this implies stubbornness; nor must he be weak and yielding through too great a desire to please, for this will destroy the vigor and value of his work—he who is weak in his work is brother to him who destroys his work. In doubtful matters he must be circumspect and not readily yield credence to what seems probable, for such is not always true; nor should he obstinately reject the opposite, for{368} that which seems improbable often turns out to be

121

fact. He must listen, discuss, and examine with all zeal, that the truth may be reached at the end. Like a just judge let him so bear himself in passing sentence of corporal punishment that his face may show compassion, while his inward purpose remains unshaken, and thus will he avoid the appearance of indignation and wrath leading to the charge of cruelty. In imposing pecuniary penalties, let his face preserve the severity of justice as though he were compelled by necessity and not allured by cupidity. Let truth and mercy, which should never leave the heart of a judge, shine forth from his countenance, that his decisions may be free from all suspicion of covetousness or cruelty.[327]

To appreciate rightly the career and influence of the Inquisition will require a somewhat minute examination into its methods and procedure. In no other way can we fully understand its action; and the lessons to be drawn from such an investigation are perhaps the most important that it has to teach.{369}

CHAPTER VIII.

ORGANIZATION.

WE have seen how the Church had found persuasion powerless to arrest the spread of heresy. St. Bernard, Foulques de Neuilly, Durán de Huesca, St. Dominic, St. Francis, had successively tried the rarest eloquence to convince, and the example of the sublimest self-abnegation to convert. Only force remained, and it had been pitilessly employed. It had subjected the populations, only to render heresy hidden in place of public; and, in order to reap the fruits of victory, it became apparent that organized, ceaseless persecution continued to perpetuity was the only hope of preserving Catholic unity, and of preventing the garment of the Lord from being permanently rent. To this end the Inquisition was developed into a settled institution manned by the Mendicant Orders, which had been formed to persuade by argument and example, and which now were utilized to suppress by force.

The organization of the Inquisition was simple, yet effective. It did not care to impress the minds of men with magnificence, but rather to paralyze them with terror. To the secular prelacy it left the gorgeous vestments and the imposing splendors of worship, the picturesque processions and the showy retinues of retainers. The inquisitor wore the simple habits of his Order. When he appeared abroad he was at most accompanied by a few armed familiars, partly as a guard, partly to execute his orders. His principal scene of activity was in the recesses of the dreaded Holy Office, whence he issued his commands and decided the fate of whole populations in a silence and secrecy which impressed upon the people a mysterious awe a thousand times more potent than the external magnificence of the bishop. Every detail in the Inquisition was intended for work and not for show. It was built up by resolute, earnest men of one idea who knew what they{370} wanted, who rendered everything subservient to the one object, and who sternly rejected all that might embarrass with superfluities the unerring and ruthless justice which it was their mission to enforce.

The previous chapter has shown us the simplicity which marked the beginnings of the institution, consisting virtually of the individual friars selected to hunt up heretics and determine their guilt. Their districts were naturally coterminous with the provinces of the Mendicant Orders, whose provincials were charged with the duty of appointment, and these provinces each comprised many bishoprics. Though the chief town of each province came to be regarded as the seat of the Inquisition, with its building and prisons, yet it was the duty of the inquisitor to go in pursuit of the heretics, to visit all places where heresy might be suspected to exist, and to summon the people to assemble, exactly as the bishops formerly did in their visitations, with the added inducement of an indulgence of twenty or forty days for all who attended. It is true that at first the inquisitors of Toulouse established themselves in that city and cited before them all whom they wished to appear, but such complaints arose as to the intolerable hardship of this that, in 1237, the Legate Jean de Vienne ordered them to transport themselves to the places where they wished to make inquest. In obedience to this we see them going to Castelnaudari, where they were baffled by the people, who had entered into a common understanding not to betray each other, so they turned unexpectedly to Puy Laurens, where they took the population by surprise and gathered an ample harvest. The murders of Avignonet, in 1242, gave warning that these itinerant inquests were not without risk, yet they continued to be prescribed by the Cardinal of Albano, about 1244, and by the Council of Béziers, in 1246. Although, in 1247, Innocent IV. authorized inquisitors, when there was danger, to summon heretics and witnesses to some place of safety, yet the theory of personal visitation remained unchanged. In Italy we see it in the bulls *Ad extirpanda*; a contemporary German inquisitor describes it as the customary practice; in northern France we have the formulas used in 1278 by Friar Simon Duval for summoning the people on such occasions; about 1330 Bernard Gui alludes to it as one of the special privileges of the Inquisition; and, about 1375, Eymerich describes{371} the method of conducting these inquests as part of the established routine.[328]

Nothing could well be devised more effective than these visitations, and though they may have become neglected when the machinery of spies and familiars was perfected, or when the heretics had been nearly weeded out, during the busy times of the Inquisition they must have formed an important portion of its functions. A few days in advance of his visit to a city, the inquisitor would send notice to the ecclesiastical authorities requiring them to summon the people to assemble at a specified time, with an announcement of the indulgence given to all who should attend. To the populace thus brought together he preached on the faith, urging them to its defence with such eloquence as he could command, summoning every one within a certain radius to come forward within six or twelve days and reveal to him whatever they may have known or heard of any one leading to the belief or suspicion that he might be a heretic, or defamed for heresy, or that he had spoken against any article of faith, or that he differed in life and morals from the common conversation of the faithful. Neglect to comply with this command incurred *ipso facto* excommunication, removable only by the inquisitor himself; compliance with it was rewarded with an indulgence of three years. At the same time he proclaimed a "time of grace," varying from fifteen to thirty days, during which any heretic coming forward spontaneously, confessing his guilt, abjuring, and giving full information about his fellow-sectaries, was promised mercy. This mercy varied at different times from complete immunity to exemption from the severer penalties of death, imprisonment, exile, or confiscation. The latter is the grace promised in the earliest allusion to the practice in {372} 1235, and in a sentence of 1237 on such an occasion the offender escaped with a penance consisting of two of the shorter pilgrimages, the finding of a beggar daily during life, and a fine of ten livres Morlaas given "for the love of God" to the Inquisition. After the expiration of the term they were told that no mercy would be shown; while it lasted, the inquisitor was instructed to keep himself housed, so as to be ready at any moment to receive denunciations and confessions; and long series of interrogatories, most searching and suggestive, were drawn up to prompt him in the examination of those who should present themselves. Even as late as 1387 when Frà Antonio Secco attacked the heretics of the Waldensian valleys, he commenced by publishing in the church of Pignerol a summons giving a week of grace during which all who should confess as to themselves and others should escape public punishment except for perjury committed before the Inquisition, and all who did not come forward were denounced as excommunicates.[329]

Bernard Gui assures us that this device was exceedingly fruitful, not only in causing numerous happy conversions, but also in furnishing information of many heretics who would not otherwise have been thought of, as each penitent was forced to denounce all whom he knew or suspected; and he particularly dwells upon its utility in securing the capture of the "perfected" Catharans who habitually lay in hiding and who thus were betrayed by those in whom they trusted. It is easy, in fact, to imagine the terror into which a community would be thrown when an inquisitor suddenly descended upon it and made his proclamation. No one could know what stories might be circulating about himself which zealous fanaticism or personal enmity might exaggerate and carry to the inquisitor, and in this the orthodox and the heretic would suffer alike. All scandals passing from mouth to mouth would be brought to light. All confidence between man and man would disappear. {373} Old grudges would be gratified in safety. To him who had been heretically inclined the terrible suspense would grow day by day more insupportable, with the thought that some careless word might have been treasured up to be now revealed by those who ought to be nearest and dearest to him, until at last he would yield and betray others rather than be betrayed himself. Gregory IX. boasted that, on at least one such occasion, parents were led to denounce their children, and children their parents, husbands their wives, and wives their husbands. We may well believe Bernard Gui when he says that each revelation led to others, until the invisible net extended far and wide, and that not the least of the benefits thence arising were the extensive confiscations which were sure to follow.[330]

These preliminary proceedings were commonly held in the convent of the Order to which the inquisitor belonged, if such there were, or in the episcopal palace if it were a cathedral town. In other cases the church or municipal buildings would afford the necessary accommodation, for the authorities, both lay and clerical, were bound to afford all assistance demanded. Each inquisitor, however, necessarily had his headquarters to which he would return after these forays, carrying with him the depositions of accusers and confessions of accused, and such prisoners as he deemed it important to secure, the secular authorities being bound to furnish him the necessary transportation and guards. Others he would cite to appear before him at a specified time, taking sufficient bail to secure their punctuality. In the earlier period, the seat of his tribunal was the Mendicant convent, while the episcopal or public prison was at his disposal for the detention of his captives; but in time special buildings were provided, amply furnished with the necessary appliances and dungeons—cells built along the walls and thence known as "*murus*," in contradistinction to the "*carcer*" or prison—where the unfortunates awaiting sentence were under the immediate supervision of their judge. It was here, for the most part, that the judicial proceedings were carried on, though we occasionally hear of the episcopal palace being used, especially when the bishop was zealous and co-operated with the Inquisition.

During the earlier period there was no limitation as to the age {374} of the inquisitor; the provincial who held the appointing power could select any member of his Order. That this frequently led to the nomination of young and inexperienced men is presumable from the language in which Clement V., when reforming the Holy Office, prescribed forty years as the minimum age in future. Bernard Gui remonstrated against this, not only because younger men were often thoroughly capable of the duties, but also because bishops and their ordinaries who exercised inquisitorial power were not required to be so old. The rule, however, held good. In 1422 the Provincial of Toulouse appointed an inquisitor of Carcassonne, Friar Raymond du Tille, who was only thirty-two years of age. Though he was confirmed by the general of the Order, it was held that the office was vacant until an appeal was made to Martin V., who ordered the Official of Alet to investigate his fitness, and, if found worthy, the Clementine canon might be suspended in his favor.[331]

The trials were usually conducted by a single inquisitor, though sometimes two would work together. One, however, sufficed, but he generally had subordinate assistants, who prepared the cases for him, and took the preliminary examinations. He had a right to call upon the provincial to assign to him as many of these assistants as he deemed necessary, but he could not select them for himself. Sometimes, when the bishop was eager for persecution and careless of the episcopal dignity, he would accept the position; and it was frequently filled by the Dominican prior of the local convent. When the state defrayed the expenses of the Inquisition, it seems to have exercised some control over the number of officials. Thus in Naples Charles of Anjou, in 1269, only provides for one assistant.[332]

These assistants represented the inquisitor during his absence, and thus were closely assimilated to the commissioners who came{375} to be a permanent feature of the Holy Office. Even in the twelfth century it was determined that a judicial delegate of the Holy See could delegate his powers; and in 1246 the Council of Béziers authorized the inquisitor to appoint a deputy whenever he wished to have an inquest made in any place to which he could not himself proceed. Special commissions were sometimes issued, as when, in 1276, Pons de Pornac, Inquisitor of Toulouse, authorized the Dominican Prior of Montauban to take testimony against Bernard de Solhac and forward it to him under seal. In the extensive districts of the Inquisition the work must necessarily have been divided in this manner, especially during the earlier period, when the harvest of heresy was abundant and numerous laborers were requisite. Yet the formal authority to appoint commissioners with full powers does not seem to have been granted to inquisitors until 1262 by Urban IV., and this had to be confirmed by Boniface VIII. towards the close of the century. These commissioners, or vicars, differed from the assistants, inasmuch as they were appointed and discharged at the discretion of the inquisitor. They became a permanent feature of the institution, and conducted its business in places remote from the main tribunal; or, in case of the absence or incapacity of the inquisitor, one of them might be summoned to replace him temporarily, or the inquisitor could appoint a vicar-general. Like their principal, they had, after the Clementine reforms in 1317, to be at least forty years of age, and they wielded full inquisitorial powers, in the citation, arrest, and examination of witnesses and prisoners, even to the infliction of torture and condemnation to imprisonment. Whether they could proceed to final sentence in capital cases was a disputed question, and Eymerich recommends that such authority should always be reserved to the inquisitor himself; but, as we shall see, the cases of Joan of Arc and of the Vaudois of Arras show that this reservation was rarely observed. A further limitation on their powers was the inability to appoint deputies.[333]{376}

In the later period there seems to have been occasionally another official with the title of "counsellor." In 1370 the Inquisition of Carcassonne claimed the right to appoint three, who should be exempt from all local taxation. In a document of 1423 the person filling this position is not a Dominican, but is qualified as a licentiate in law; and doubtless such a functionary was a useful and usual member of the tribunal, though with no precise official status. Zanghino informs us that in general inquisitors were utterly ignorant of law. In most cases this made no difference, for, as we shall see, they enjoyed the widest latitude of arbitrary procedure, with little danger that any one would dare to complain, but occasionally they had to deal with victims not entirely unresisting, and then some adviser as to their legal duties and responsibilities was desirable. Eymerich, in fact, recommends that a commissioner should always associate with himself some discreet lawyer to save him from mistakes which may redound to the disadvantage of the Inquisition, call for papal interposition, and perhaps cost him his place.[334]

As absolute secrecy became a main feature of all the proceedings of the Inquisition after its earlier tentative period, it was a universal rule that testimony, whether of witnesses or of accused, should only be taken in the presence of two impartial men, not connected with the institution, but sworn to silence. The inquisitor was empowered to compel the attendance of any one whom he might summon to perform this duty. These representatives of the public were preferably clerics, and usually Dominicans, "discreet and religious men," who were expected to sign with the notary the written report of the testimony in attestation of its fidelity. Though not alluded to in the instructions of the Council of Béziers in 1246, a deposition taken in 1244 shows that already the practice had become customary; and the frequent repetitions of the rule by successive popes and its embodiment in the canon law show what importance was attached to it as a means of preventing{377} injustice, and giving at least a color of impartiality to the proceedings. Yet in this, as in everything else, the inquisitors were a law unto themselves, and disregarded at pleasure the very slender restrictions imposed on them. One of the rare cases in which the Inquisition lost a victim turned upon the neglect of this rule. In 1325 a priest named Pierre de Tornamire, accused of Spiritual Franciscanism, was brought to the Inquisition of Carcassonne in a dying state. The inquisitor was absent. His deputy and notary took the deposition in the presence of three laymen who chanced to be present, and the priest died before it was well concluded. Two Dominicans came, after he was speechless, and, without making any inquiry as to its correctness, signed their names to the deposition in attestation. On this irregular evidence a prosecution against Pierre's memory was based, and was contested by his heirs to save his property from confiscation. Thirty-two years the struggle lasted, and when the inquisitor came, in 1357, to ask assent to his sentence of condemnation in the customary assembly of experts, twenty-five jurists unanimously voted against it on the ground of irregularity, and only two, both Dominicans, ventured to uphold it. It was not long after this that Eymerich instructed his brethren how the rule could be evaded, when it was inconvenient, by at least having two honest persons present at the close of the examination, when the testimony was read over to the deponent. No one else was allowed to be present at the trial, except at Avignon for a brief period, about the middle of the thirteenth century, when the magistrates temporarily secured the right of attendance for themselves and a certain number of seigneurs. With this exception, the unfortunates who were wrestling for their lives with their judges were wholly at the discretion of the inquisitor and his creatures.[335]

The *personnel* of the tribunal was completed by the notary—an official of considerable standing and dignity in the Middle Ages. All the proceedings of the Inquisition were taken down in writing—{378}every question and every answer—each witness and each defendant being obliged to confirm his testimony when read over to him at the close of the interrogatory, and judgment was finally rendered on an inspection of the evidence thus recorded. The function of the notary was no light one, and occasionally scriveners were called in to his assistance, but he formally attested every document. Not only was there the fearful multiplication of papers accumulating in the current business of the tribunal, and their careful transcription for preservation, but the several Inquisitions were continually furnishing each other with copies of their records, so that a considerable force must have been necessarily employed. As in everything else, the inquisitor was empowered to call for gratuitous service on the part of any one whom he might summon, but the continuous business of the office required undivided attention, and its proper despatch rendered desirable the peculiar training acquired by experience. In the earlier periods, the authorization to impress any notary to serve, and the advice to select if possible Dominicans who had been notaries, with the power, if none such could be had, to replace him with two discreet persons, shows that the itinerant tribunals depended for the most part on this chance conscription; but in the permanent seats of the Inquisition the notary was a regular official, in receipt of a salary. In the attempted reform of Clement V. it was provided that he should take his official oath before the bishop as well as before the inquisitor, and to this Bernard Gui objected on the ground that the exigencies of business sometimes required the force to be suddenly increased to two or three or four, and that in places where no public notaries were to be had, other competent persons were necessarily employed on the spur of the moment, as it often happens that the guilty will confess when in the mood, and if their confession is not promptly taken they draw back, and they are always more given to concealment than to truth. Curiously enough, the power to appoint notaries was regarded with so much jealousy that it was denied to the inquisitor. He may if he choose, says Eymerich, send three or four names to the pope, who will appoint them for him, but this leads to such bad feeling on the part of the local authorities that he had better content himself with the notaries of the bishops or of the secular rulers.[336]{379}

The enormous mass of documents produced by these innumerable busy hands was the object of well-deserved solicitude. At the very inception of the work its value was recognized. In 1235 we hear of the confessions of penitents being sedulously recorded in books kept for the purpose. This speedily became the universal custom, and the inquisitors were instructed to preserve careful records of all their proceedings, from the first summons to the final sentence in every case, together with lists of all who took the oath enforced on every one to defend the faith and persecute heresy. The importance attached to this is shown by the frequent iteration of the command, and by the further precaution that all the papers should be duplicated, and a copy lodged in a safe place or with the bishop. With what elaborate care they were rendered practically useful is shown by the Book of Sentences of the Inquisition of Toulouse, from 1308 to 1323, printed by Limborch, where at the end there is an index of the 636 culprits sentenced, grouped under their places of residence alphabetically arranged, with reference to the pages on which their names occur and brief mention of the several punishments inflicted on each, and of any subsequent modifications of the penalty, thus enabling the official who wished information as to the people of any hamlet to see at a glance who among them had been suspected and what had been done. One case in the same book will illustrate the completeness and the exactitude of the previous records. In 1316 an old woman was brought before the tribunal; on examination it was found that in 1268, nearly fifty years before, she had confessed and abjured heresy and had been reconciled, and as this aggravated her guilt the miserable wretch was condemned to perpetual imprisonment in chains. Thus in process of time the Inquisition accumulated {380} a store of information which not only increased greatly its efficiency, but which rendered it an object of terror to every man. The confiscations and disabilities which, as we shall see hereafter, were inflicted on descendants, rendered the secrets of family history so carefully preserved in its archives the means by which a crushing blow might at any moment fall on the head of any one; and the Inquisition had an awkward way of discovering disagreeable facts about the ancestry of those who provoked its ill-will, and possibly its cupidity. Thus, in 1306, during the troubles at Albi, when the royal *viguier*, or governor, supported the cause of the people, the inquisitor, Geoffroi d'Ablis, issued letters declaring that he had found among the records that the grandfather of the *viguier* had been a heretic, and his grandson consequently was incapable of holding office. The whole population was thus at the mercy of the Holy Office.[337]

The temptation to falsify the records when an enemy was to be struck down was exceedingly strong, and the opponents of the Inquisition had no hesitation in declaring that it was freely yielded to. Friar Bernard Délicieux, speaking for the whole Franciscan Order of Languedoc, in a formal document of the year 1300, not only declared that the records were unworthy of trust, but that they were generally believed to be so. We shall see hereafter facts which fully justified this assertion, and the popular mistrust was intensified by the jealous secrecy which rendered it an offence punishable with excommunication for any one to possess any papers relating to the proceedings of the Inquisition or to prosecutions against heretics. On the other hand, the temptation on the part of those who were endangered to destroy the archives was equally strong, and the attempts to effect this show the importance attached to their possession. As early as 1235 we find the citizens of

Narbonne, in an insurrection against the Inquisition, carefully destroying all the books and records. The order of the Council of Albi in 1254, to make duplicates and lodge them in some safe place was doubtless caused by another successful[381] effort made in 1248 by the heretics of Narbonne. On the occasion of an assembly of bishops in that city a clerk and a messenger bearing records with the names of heretics were slain and the books burned, giving rise to a good many troublesome questions with regard to existing and future prosecutions. About 1285, at Carcassonne, a plot was entered into by the consuls of the town and several of its leading ecclesiastics to destroy the inquisitorial records. They bribed one of the familiars, Bernard Garric, to burn them, but the conspiracy was discovered and its authors punished. One of these, a lawyer named Guillem Garric, languished in prison for about thirty years before his final sentence in 1321.[338]

Not the least important among the functionaries of the Inquisition were the lowest class—the apparitors, messengers, spies, and bravos, known generally by the name of familiars, which came to have so ill-omened a significance in the popular ear. The service was not without risk, and it had few attractions for the honest and peaceable, but it was full of promise for the reckless and evil-minded. Not only did they enjoy the immunity from secular jurisdiction attaching to all in the service of the Church, but the special authority granted by Innocent IV., in 1245, to the inquisitors to absolve their familiars for acts of violence rendered them independent even of the ecclesiastical tribunals. Besides, as any molestation of the servants of the Inquisition was qualified as impeding its operations and thus savoring of heresy, any one who dared to resist aggression rendered himself liable to prosecution before the tribunal of the aggressor. Thus panoplied, they could tyrannize at will over the defenceless population, and it is easy to imagine the amount of extortion which they could practise with virtual impunity by threatening arrest or accusation at a time when falling into the hands of the Inquisition was about the heaviest misfortune which could befall any man, whether orthodox or heretic.[339] [382]

All that was needed to render this social scourge complete was devised when the familiars were authorized to carry arms. The murders at Avignonet, in 1242, with that of Peter Martyr, and other similar events, seemed to justify the inquisitors in desiring an armed guard; and the service of tracking and capturing heretics was frequently one of peril, yet the privilege was a dangerous one to bestow on such men as could be got for the work, while releasing them from the restraints of law. In the turbulence of the age the carrying of weapons was rigidly repressed in all peace-loving communities. As early as the eleventh century we find it prohibited in the city of Pistoja, and in 1228 in Verona. In Bologna knights and doctors only were allowed to bear arms, and to have one armed servant. In Milan, a statute of Gian-Galeazzo, in 1386, forbids the carrying of weapons, but allows the bishops to arm the retainers living under their roofs. In Paris an *ordonnance* of 1288 inhibits the citizens from carrying pointed knives, swords, bucklers, or other similar weapons. In Beaucaire, an edict of 1320 prescribes various penalties, including the loss of a hand, for bearing arms, except in the case of travellers, who are restricted simply to swords and knives. Such regulations were of inestimable value in the progress of civilization, but they amounted to little when the inquisitor could arm any one he pleased, and invest him with the privileges and immunities of the Holy Office.[340]

As early as 1249 the scandals and abuses arising from the unlimited employment of scriveners and familiars who oppressed the people with their extortions called forth the indignant rebuke of Innocent IV., who commanded that their numbers should be reduced to correspond with the bare exigencies of duty. In those countries in which the Inquisition was supported by the State there was not much opportunity for the development of overgrown abuses of this nature. Thus, in Naples, Charles of Anjou, in permitting the carrying of arms, specifies three as the number of familiars for each inquisitor; and when Bernard Gui protested[383] against the reforms of Clement V. he pointed out the contrast between France, where the inquisitors relied upon the secular officials, and were forced to be content with few retainers, and Italy, where they had almost unlimited opportunities. There, in fact, as we shall see, the Inquisition was self-supporting and independent by reason of its share in the fines and confiscations, and restraint of any kind was difficult. Clement V. forbade the useless multiplication of officials and the abuse of the right to bear arms, but his well-meant efforts availed little. In 1321 we find John XXII. reproving the inquisitors of Lombardy for creating scandals and tumults in Bologna by their armed familiars of depraved character and perverse habits, who committed murders and other outrages. In 1337 the papal nuncio, Bertrand, Archbishop of Embrun, seeing by personal observation the troubles which existed in Florence, owing to the practice of the inquisitor issuing licenses to carry arms, which was abused to the frequent injury of defenceless citizens, restricted him to twelve armed familiars, informing him that the secular authorities would furnish whatever additional armed assistance might be necessary for the capture of heretics. Yet within nine years one of the accusations brought against a new inquisitor, Frà Piero di Aquila, was that he had sold licenses to carry arms to more than two hundred and fifty men, bringing him in an annual revenue of about one thousand gold florins, and proving sadly detrimental to the peace of the city. Accordingly a law was passed restricting the inquisitor to six familiars bearing arms, the Bishop of Florence to twelve, and the Bishop of Fiesole to six, all of whom were required to wear the insignia of their masters. Still, the profit arising from the sale of such licenses was too great a temptation, and in the Florentine code of 1355 we find general regulations intended to check it in another way. Any one caught bearing arms and pleading a license was deported beyond the territory of the republic, to a distance of at least fifty miles from the city, and had to give a bond to remain there for a year. Even the podestà was prohibited from issuing such licenses under the penalties of perjury and a fine of five hundred lire. All this was an infraction of the liberties of the Church, and formed the substance of one of the complaints of Gregory XI., when, in 1376, he excommunicated the republic; and when, in 1378, Florence was forced to submit, one{384} of the conditions was that a papal commissioner should expunge from the statute-book all the obnoxious laws. Yet the excesses of these brawling ruffians were too great to be long submitted to, and in 1386 another device was tried. The two bishops and the inquisitor were forbidden to have armed familiars who were taxable or inscribed on the roll of citizens; those to whom they issued licenses had to be declared their familiars by the priors of the arts, and this declaration had to be renewed yearly by a public instrument delivered to them. Some restraint thus was exercised, and this provision was retained in the recension of the code in 1415. This same struggle was doubtless going on in all the Italian cities which had independence enough to seek a remedy for the daily outrages inflicted by these licensed bravos, though the record of the troubles may not be accessible to history. Even in Venice, which kept the Inquisition in so subordinate a position, and wisely maintained its rights by defraying the expenses of the institution—even Venice felt the necessity of restraining the multiplication of pretended armed retainers. In August, 1450, the Great Council, by a vote of fourteen to two, denounced the abuse by which the inquisitor had sold to twelve persons the license to bear arms; such a force, it is said, was wholly unnecessary, as he could always invoke the assistance of the secular power, and therefore he should, in accordance with ancient custom, be restricted to four armed familiars. Six months later, in February, 1451, at the earnest request of the Franciscan general minister, this regulation was rescinded; the inquisitor was allowed to increase the number to twelve, but the police were directed to observe and report whether they were really engaged in the duties of the Inquisition. Yet Eymerich assures us that all such interference is unlawful, and that any secular ruler who endeavors to prevent the familiars of the Holy Office from bearing arms is impeding the Inquisition and is a fautor of heresy, while Bernard Gui characterizes in similar terms any limitation of the number of officials below what the inquisitor may deem requisite, all of which, according to Zanghino, is punishable at the discretion of the inquisitor.[341]{385}

In the preceding chapter I have alluded to the power claimed and often exercised of abrogating all local statutes obnoxious to the Holy Office, and of the duty of every secular official to lend aid whenever called upon. This duty was recognized and enforced so that the organization of the Inquisition may be said to have embraced that of the State, whose whole resources were placed at its disposition. The oath of obedience which the inquisitor was empowered and directed to exact of all holding official station was no mere form. Refusal to take it was visited with excommunication, leading to prosecution for heresy in case of obduracy, and humiliating penance on submission. At times it was neglected by careless inquisitors, but the earnest ones made a point of it. Bernard Gui, at all his *autos de fé*, solemnly administered it to all the royal officials and local magistrates, and when, in May, 1309, Jean de Maucochin, the royal seneschal of the Tolosain and Albigeois declined to take it, he was speedily brought to see his error, and submitted within a month. Bernard himself, as we have seen, admits that the help thus promised was efficiently rendered, and when, in 1329, Henri de Chamay, Inquisitor of Carcassonne, applied to Philippe de Valois for a reaffirmation of the privileges of the Inquisition, the monarch promptly responded in an edict in which he proclaimed that "each and all, dukes, counts, barons, seneschals, baillis, provosts, viguiers, castellans, sergeants, and other justiciaries of the kingdom of France are bound to obey the inquisitors and their commissioners in seizing, holding, guarding, and taking to prison all heretics and suspects of heresy, and to execute diligently the sentences of the inquisitors, and to give to the inquisitors, their commissioners and messengers, safe-conduct, prompt help and favor, through all the lands of their jurisdictions, in all that concerns the business of the Inquisition, whenever and how often soever they may be called upon." Any{386} hesitation on the part of public officials to grant assistance when summoned was promptly punished. Thus, in 1303, when Bonrico di Busca, vicar of the podestà of Mandrisio, refused to furnish men to the representatives of the Milanese Inquisition, he was forthwith condemned to a fine of a hundred imperial solidi, to be paid within five days. Even the condition of an excommunicate, which rendered an official incapable of performing any other function, did not relieve him from this duty; he could be called upon to execute the commands of the inquisitor, but he was warned that he must not imagine himself competent therefore to do anything else.[342]

In addition to this the Inquisition had, to a greater or less extent, at its service the whole orthodox population, and especially the clergy. It was the duty of every man to give information as to all cases of heresy with which he might become acquainted under pain of incurring the guilt of fautorship. It was further his duty to arrest all heretics, as Bernard de St. Genais found in 1242, when he was tried by the Inquisition of Toulouse for the offence of not capturing certain heretics when it was in his power to do so, and was condemned to the penance of pilgrimages to the shrines of Puy, St. Gilles, and Compostella. The parish priests, moreover, were required, whenever called upon, to cite their parishioners for appearance, either publicly from the pulpit or secretly as the case might require, and to publish all sentences of excommunication. They were likewise held to the duty of surveillance over penitents to see that the penances enjoined were duly performed, and to report any cases of neglect. A very thorough system of local police, framed upon the model of the old synodal witnesses, was devised by the Council of Béziers in 1246, under which the inquisitor was{387} empowered to appoint in every parish a priest and one or two laymen, whose duty it should be to search for heretics, examining all houses, inside and out, and especially all secret hiding-places. In addition to this they were instructed to watch over penitents and enforce the faithful observance of the sentences of the Inquisition, and a manual of practice of the period instructs inquisitors to see that this system is thoroughly carried out. In fact, the whole resources of the land, public and private, were freely placed at the disposal of the Holy Office, so that nothing should be wanting in its sacred mission of extirpating heresy.[343]

An important feature in the organization of the Inquisition was the assembly in which the fate of the accused was finally determined. The inquisitor had technically no power to pass sentence by himself. We have seen how, after various fluctuations of policy, the co-operation of the bishops was established as indispensable. As in everything else, the inquisitors contemptuously neglected this limitation on their powers, and when Clement V. endeavored to reform abuses he pronounced null and void any sentences rendered independently, yet to avert delays he permitted consent to be expressed in writing if after eight days a meeting could not be arranged. If, indeed, we may judge from some specimens of these written consultations which have reached us, they were perfunctory to the last degree and placed no real check upon the discretion of the inquisitor. Still Bernard Gui complained bitterly even of this restriction in terms which show how little respect had previously been paid to the rule, and he adds, in justification, that one bishop kept the trials of some persons of his diocese from being finished for two years and more, while another delayed the celebration of an *auto de fé* for six months. He himself observed the regulation scrupulously, both before and after the publication of the Clementines, and in the reports of the *autos* held by him in Toulouse the participation of the bishops of the prisoners, or of episcopal delegates, is always carefully specified. Yet how easy was the evasion of this, as of all other regulations for the protection{388} of the accused, is seen when even Bernard Gui accepted commissions from three bishops—those of Cahors, St. Papoul, and Montauban—to act for them in the *auto* of September 30, 1319. This device became frequent, and inquisitors constantly rendered sentence on their individual responsibility under power granted them by the bishops, as in the persecutions of the Waldenses of Piedmont in 1387, and that of the witches of Canavese in 1474. Sometimes, however, the bishops were not altogether free agents, as when, in the early persecution of the Spiritual Franciscans, about 1318, those of the province of Narbonne were coerced to consent to the burning of some unfortunates by the inquisitor threatening them with the pope, who was known to have the prosecutions much at heart.[344]

This episcopal concurrence in the sentence was reached in consultation with the assembly of experts. As the inquisitors from the beginning were chosen rather with regard to zeal than learning, and as they maintained a reputation for ignorance, it was soon found requisite to associate with them in the rendering of sentences men versed in the civil and canon law, which had by this time become an intricate study requiring the devotion of a lifetime. Accordingly they were empowered to call in experts to deliberate with them over the evidence and advise with them on the sentence to be rendered, and those who were thus summoned could not refuse to serve gratuitously, though it is intimated that the inquisitor can pay them if he feels so inclined. At first it would seem as though notables were assembled at the condemnation of prominent heretics rather to give solemnity to the occasion than for actual consultation, as when, in 1237, at the sentence passed on Alaman de Roaix in Toulouse, the presence is recorded of the Bishop of Toulouse, the Abbot of Moissac, the Dominican and Franciscan provincials, and a number of other notables. The amount of work, in fact, performed by the Inquisition of Languedoc in the early years of its existence would seem to preclude the idea of any serious deliberation by counsellors thus called in, who would have to consider the interminable reports of examinations and interrogations;{389} especially as, at a comparatively early date, the practice was adopted of allowing a number of culprits to accumulate whose fate was determined and announced in a solemn "*Sermo*" or *auto de fé*. Still, the form was kept up, and in 1247 a sentence rendered by Bernard de Caux and Jean de St. Pierre on seven relapsed heretics is specified as being "with the counsel of many prelates and other good men." In the final shape which the assembly of counsellors assumed, we find it summoned to meet on Fridays, the "*Sermo*" always taking place on Sundays. When the number of criminals was large there was thus not much time for deliberation on special cases. The assessors were always to be jurists and Mendicant friars, selected by the inquisitor in such numbers as he saw fit. They were severally sworn on the Gospels to secrecy, and to give good and wise counsel, each one according to his conscience and the knowledge vouchsafed him by God. The inquisitor then read over to them his summary of each case, sometimes withholding the name of the accused, and they voted the sentence— "Penance at the discretion of the inquisitor"—"That person is to be imprisoned, or abandoned to the secular arm," while the Gospels lay on the table in their midst, "so that our judgment may come from the face of God and our eyes may see justice."[345]

As a rule it is safe to assume that these proceedings were scarcely more than formal. Not only was the inquisitor at liberty to present each case in such aspect as he saw fit, but it became the custom to call in such numbers of experts that in the press of business deliberation was scarce possible. Thus the Inquisitor of Carcassonne, Henri de Chamay, assembled at Narbonne, December 10, 1328, besides himself and the episcopal Ordinary, forty-two counsellors, consisting of canons, jurisconsults, and lay experts. In the two days allotted to them this unwieldly assemblage despatched thirty-four cases, which would show that little consideration could have been given to each. In only two cases, indeed, was there any difference{390} of opinion expressed, and these were of no special importance. On September 8, 1329, he held another assembly at Carcassonne, attended by forty-seven experts, which in its two days' session acted upon forty cases. Yet these assemblies were not always so expeditious and self-effacing. From Narbonne Henri de Chamay passed to Pamiers, where, January 7, 1329, he called together thirty-five experts besides the Bishop of Toulouse. On the first day several cases were postponed for greater deliberation, and of these some were acted upon and others were not. Considerable debate took place, each individual expressing his opinion, and the result was apparently settled by the majority vote. They evidently felt and assumed the responsibility of the decision; and yet the impossibility of deliberate action by so cumbrous a body is seen in their bunching together all the cases of "believing" heretics, condemning them *en masse* to prison, and leaving it with the inquisitor to determine the character of the imprisonment for each individual. Curiously enough, this assembly also assumed legislative functions in laying down general rules of punishment for false-witness. A still more notable instance of deliberation occurred at an assembly convoked by Henri de Chamay at Béziers, May 19, 1329, where there were thirty-five experts present. In the case of a Franciscan friar, Pierre Julien, all agreed that, strictly speaking, he was a "relapsed," but many were anxious to show him mercy. After long debate, the inquisitor told them to meet again in the evening, and in the meanwhile consider whether they could devise some means of grace. At the evening session there was again earnest discussion, and postponement was agreed to on the excuse that no bishop could be had in time for his degradation. The experts were finally summoned, under pain of excommunication, to give their opinions, which were taken down in writing and ranged from simple purgation to abandonment to the secular arm. The assembly then was dismissed and consultation was held with some of the more prominent members, when it was agreed either to send to Avignon, Toulouse, or Montpellier for advice or to await an *auto de fé* at Carcassonne for further counsel.[346]

Yet, while the forms were thus preserved, the inquisitors, with their customary arbitrary disregard of all that limited their discretion,{391} paid attention or not to the decisions of the experts, as best suited them. In the sentences which follow the reports of these assemblies it is by no means unusual to find names which had never been laid before them. After the assembly of Pamiers, for instance, which showed so much disposition to act for itself, there is a sentence condemning five defuncts, only two of whom are named in the proceedings. On the same occasion, another culprit, Ermessende, daughter of Raymond Monier, was condemned by the assembly for false-witness to the "*murus largus*," or simple prison, and was sentenced by the inquisitor to "*murus strictus*," or imprisonment in chains, which was a very different penalty. In fact, it was a disputed point whether the inquisitor was bound to obey the counsel of the assembly, and though Eymerich decides in the affirmative, Bernardo di Como positively asserts the negative.[347]

From the necessity of these consultations with bishops and experts it is easy to understand the origin of the "*Sermo generalis*," or *auto de fé*. It was evidently impossible to bring all parties together to consult over each individual case, and convenience was not only served by allowing the cases to accumulate, but opportunity was also afforded of arranging an impressive solemnity which should strike terror on the heretic and comfort the hearts of the faithful. In the rudimentary Inquisition of Florence, in 1245, where the inquisitor Ruggieri Calcagni and Bishop Ardingho were zealously co-operating, and no assembly of experts was required, we find the heretics sentenced and executed day by day, singly or in twos or threes, but the form was already adopted of assembling the people in the cathedral and reading the sentence to them, when doubtless the occasion was improved of delivering a discourse upon the wickedness of dissent and the duty of all citizens to persecute the children of Satan. In Toulouse the fragment of the register of sentences of Bernard de Caux and Jean de Saint-Pierre, from March, 1246, to June, 1248, shows a similar disregard of form. The *autos* or *Sermones* are sometimes held every few days—there are five in May, 1246—and often there are only one or two heretics to be sentenced, rendering it exceedingly probable{392} that the co-operation of the bishop was not asked for, especially as he is never mentioned as joining in the condemnation. There are always present, however, a certain number of local magistrates, civil and ecclesiastical, and the ceremony is usually performed in the cloister of the church of St. Sernin, though other places are sometimes mentioned, and among them the Hotel-de-Ville twice, showing that divine service as yet formed no part of the solemnity.[348]

With time the ceremony grew in stateliness and impressiveness. Sunday became prescribed for it, and as no other sermons were allowed on that day in the city, it was forbidden to be held on Quadragesima or Advent Sunday, or any other of the principal feast-days. Notice was given in advance from all the pulpits summoning all the people to be present and obtain the indulgence of forty days. A staging was erected in the centre of the church, on which the "penitents" were placed, surrounded by the secular and clerical officials. The sermon was delivered by the inquisitor, after which the oath of obedience was administered to the representatives of the civil power, and a solemn decree of excommunication was fulminated against all who should in any manner impede the operations of the Holy Office. Then the notary commenced reading the confessions one by one in the vulgar tongue, and as each was finished the culprit was asked if he acknowledged it to be true—care being taken, however, only to do this when he was known to be truly penitent and not likely to create scandal by a denial. On his replying in the affirmative he was asked whether he would repent, or lose body and soul by persevering in heresy; and on his expressing a desire to abjure, the form of abjuration was read and he repeated it, sentence by sentence. Then the inquisitor absolved him from the *ipso facto* excommunication which he had incurred by heresy, and promised him mercy if he behaved well under the sentence about to be imposed. The sentence

129

followed, and thus the penitents were brought forward successively, commencing with the least guilty and proceeding with those incurring severer penalties. Those who were to be "relaxed," or abandoned to the secular arm, were reserved to the last, and for them the ceremony was adjourned to the public{393} square, where a platform had been constructed for the purpose, in order that the holy precincts of the church might not be polluted by a sentence leading to blood. For the same reason it was not to be performed on a holy day. The execution, however, was not to take place on the same day, but on the following, so as to afford the convicts time for conversion, that their souls might not pass from temporal to eternal flame, and care was enjoined not to permit them to address the people, lest sympathy should be aroused by their assertions of innocence.[349]

We can readily picture to ourselves the effect produced on the popular mind by these awful celebrations, when, at the bidding of the Inquisition, all that was great and powerful in the land was called together humbly to take the oath of obedience and witness its exercise of the highest expression of human authority, regulating the destinies of fellow-creatures here and hereafter. In the great *auto de fé* held by Bernard Gui at Toulouse, in April, 1310, the solemnities lasted from Sunday the 5th until Thursday the 9th. After the preliminary work of mitigating the penances of some deserving penitents, twenty persons were condemned to wear crosses and perform pilgrimages, sixty-five were consigned to perpetual imprisonment, three of them in chains, and eighteen were delivered to the secular justice and were duly burned. In that of April, 1312, fifty-one were sentenced to crosses, eighty-six to imprisonment, ten defunct persons were pronounced worthy of prison and their estates confiscated, the bones of thirty-six were ordered to be exhumed and burned, five living ones were handed over to the secular court to be burned, and five more condemned for contumacy in absenting themselves. The faith which could thus vindicate itself might certainly inspire the respect of fear if not the attraction of love. Sometimes, however, a godless heretic would interfere with the prescribed order of solemnities, as when, in October, 1309, Amiel de Perles, a noted Catharan teacher, who defiantly avowed his heterodoxy, immediately on his capture commenced the *endura* and refused all food and drink. Unwilling thus to be robbed of his victim, Bernard hastened the usual dilatory{394} proceedings, and gave to Amiel the honor of a special *auto* in which he was the only victim. A similar case occurred in 1313, when a certain Pierre Raymond, who as a Catharan "*credens*" had been led to abjure and seek reconciliation in the *auto* of 1310, and had been condemned to imprisonment, repented of his weakness in his solitary cell. The mental tortures of the poor wretch grew so strong that at last he defiantly proclaimed his relapse into heresy, in which he declared he would live and die, only regretting that he could not have access to some minister of his faith in order to be "perfected" or "hereticated." He likewise placed himself in *endura*, and after six days of starvation, as he was evidently nearing the end which he so resolutely sought, he was hurriedly sentenced, and a small *auto* was arranged with a few other culprits in order that the stake might not be cheated of its prey.[350]

With such an organization as this, in the hands of able, vigorous, and earnest men, it shows the marvellous constancy of the heretics that the Cathari for a hundred years opposed to it the simple resistance of inertia, and that the Waldenses were never trampled out. The effectiveness of the organization was unhampered by any limits of jurisdiction, and was multiplied by the co-operation of the tribunals everywhere, so that there was no resting-place, no harbor of refuge for the heretic in any land where the Inquisition existed. Vainly might he change his abode, it was ever on his track. A suspicious stranger would be observed and arrested; his birthplace would be ascertained, and as soon as swift messengers could traverse the intervening distance, full official documents as to his antecedents would be received from the Holy Office of his former home. It was a mere matter of convenience whether he should be tried where he was caught or sent back, for every tribunal had full jurisdiction over all offences committed within its district, and over all such offenders wherever they should stray. When Jacopo della Chiusa, one of the assassins of St. Peter Martyr, discreetly absented himself, notices commanding his capture were sent as far as the Inquisition of Carcassonne. Of course, questions sometimes arose which seemed likely to give trouble. Before the Inquisition was thoroughly organized, Jayme I. of Aragon,{395} in 1248, complained of the Tolosan inquisitor, Bernard de Caux, for citing his subjects to appear, and Innocent IV. commanded that the abuse should cease, an order which received but slack obedience; and with the growth of the Holy Office such reclamations were not likely to be repeated. Cases, of course, occurred, in which two tribunals would claim the same culprit, and in this the rule of the Council of Narbonne, in 1244, was generally observed, that he should be tried by the inquisitor who had first commenced prosecution. Considering, indeed, the abundant causes of jealousy, and especially the bitter rivalry between the Dominican and Franciscan Orders, the cases of quarrel seem to have been singularly few. Whatever there were, they were hushed up with prudent reserve, and with occasional exceptions we find a hearty and zealous co-operation in the holy work to which all were alike devoted.[351]

The implacable energy with which the resources of this organization were employed may be understood from one or two instances. Under the Hohenstaufens the two Sicilies had served as a refuge for many heretics self-exiled by the rigor of the Inquisition of Languedoc, and merciless as was Frederic when it suited him, his system was by no means so searching and unintermittent as that of the Holy Office. After his death, the active warfare between Manfred and the papacy doubtless left the heretics in comparative peace, but when Charles of Anjou conquered the kingdom as the vassal of Rome, it was at once thrown open and the French inquisitors made haste to pursue those who had eluded them. But seven months after the execution of Conradin, Charles issued his letters-patent, May 31, 1269, to all the nobles and magistrates of the realm, setting forth that the inquisitors of France were about coming or sending agents to track and seize the fugitive heretics who had sought refuge in Italy, and ordering his subjects to give them safe-conduct and assistance whenever they might require it. In {396} fact, the inquisitor's jurisdiction was personal as well as local, and it accompanied him. When, in 1359, some renegade converted Jews escaped from Provence to Spain, Innocent VI. authorized the Provençal inquisitor, Bernard du Puy, to follow them, arrest, try, condemn, and punish them wherever he might find them, with power to coerce the aid of the secular authorities everywhere; and he wrote at the same time to the kings of Aragon and Castile, instructing them to give to Bernard all necessary assistance.[352]

How the same tireless and unforgiving zeal was habitually brought to bear upon the humblest objects is seen in the case of Arnaud Ysarn, who, when a youth of fifteen, was condemned at Toulouse in 1309, after an imprisonment of two years, to wear crosses and perform certain pilgrimages, his sole offence being that he had once "adored" a heretic at the command of his father. He wore the insignia of his shame for more than a year, when, finding that they prevented him from earning a livelihood, he threw them off and obtained employment as a boatman on the Garonne between Moissac and Bordeaux. In his obscurity he might well fancy himself safe; but the inquisitorial police was too well organized, and he was discovered. Cited in 1312 to appear, he was afraid to do so, though urged by his father to take the chance of mercy. In 1315 he was excommunicated for contumacy, and, remaining under the censure for a year, he was finally declared a heretic, and was condemned as such in the *auto de fé* of 1319. In June, 1321, by command of Bernard Gui, he was captured at Moissac, but escaped on the road to be recaptured and taken to Toulouse. He had been guilty of no act of heresy during the interval, but his contumacious rejection of the parental chastisement of the Inquisition was an offence worthy of death, and he was mercifully treated in being condemned, in 1322, to imprisonment for life on bread and water. The net of the Inquisition extended everywhere, and no prey was too small to elude its meshes.[353]

The whole organization of the Church was at its service. In 1255 a Dominican of Alessandria, Frà Niccolò da Vercelli, confessed voluntarily some heretical beliefs to his sub-prior, who thereupon {397} promptly ejected him. He entered a neighboring Cistercian convent, and then, fearing the pursuit of the Inquisition, quietly disappeared to some other convent beyond the Alps. There would not seem much to be feared from a heretic who would bury himself in the rigid Cistercian Order, and yet at once Alexander IV. issued letters to all Cistercian abbots and to all archbishops and bishops everywhere, commanding them to seize him and send him to Rainerio Saccone, the Lombard inquisitor.[354]

To render it an instrumentality perfect for the work assigned to it, all that was wanting to the Inquisition was its subjection to a chief who should command the implicit obedience of its members and weld the organization into an organic whole. This function the pope could perform but imperfectly amid the overwhelming diversity of his cares, and he needed a minister who, as inquisitor-general, could devote his undivided attention to the innumerable questions arising from the conflict between orthodoxy and heresy, and between papal supremacy and local episcopal independence. The importance of such a measure seems to have made itself felt at a comparatively early period, and in 1262 Urban IV. created a virtual inquisitor-general when he ordered all inquisitors to report, either in person or by letter, to Caietano Orsini, Cardinal of S. Niccolò in carcere Tulliano, all impediments to the due performance of their functions, and to obey the instructions which he might give. Cardinal Orsini speaks of himself as inquisitor-general, and he labored to bring the several tribunals into the closest relations with each other and subjection to himself. May 19, 1273, we find him ordering the Italian inquisitors to furnish to the inquisitors of France facilities for the transcription of all the depositions of witnesses already on record in their archives, as well as of all future ones. The perpetual migration of Catharans and Waldenses between France and Italy rendered this information most valuable, and the French inquisitors had requested it of him, but the excessive diffuseness of the inquisitorial documents made the task appalling in magnitude and cost, and the terms of the cardinal's missive show that it was not expected to be welcome. Whether any further attempt was made to carry out this gigantic {398} plan, which would have so greatly multiplied the effectiveness of the Inquisition, does not appear, but its conception shows the view entertained by Orsini of the powers of his office and of the possibilities of what the Inquisition might become under energetic supervision. Another letter of his, dated May 24, 1273, to the inquisitors of France, indicates that for a time at least the general instructions to the functionaries of the Holy Office were issued through him.[355]

We have no further evidence of his activity, but his elevation to the papacy in 1277, as Nicholas III., may possibly indicate that the position was one which afforded abundant opportunities of influence, perhaps rendering its possessor disagreeably, if not dangerously powerful, and when Nicholas appointed his nephew, Cardinal Latino Malebranca, as his successor in the office vacated by his elevation, he may have felt it necessary to secure himself by keeping the position in his family. Malebranca was Dean of the Sacred College, and his influence was shown when, in 1294, he ended the weary conflict of the conclave by procuring the election of the hermit, Pietro Morrone, as pope, under the name of Celestin V. He did not survive the short pontificate of Celestin, and the proud and vigorous Boniface VIII. regarded it as impolitic or unnecessary to continue the office. It remained in abeyance under the Avignonese popes, until Clement VI. revived it for William, Cardinal of S. Stefano in Monte Celio, who signalized his zeal by burning several heretics, and in other ways. After his death the post remained vacant, and at no time does it appear to have exercised any special influence over the development and activity of the Inquisition.[356] {399}

CHAPTER IX.

THE INQUISITORIAL PROCESS.

THE procedure of the episcopal courts, as described in a former chapter, was based on the principles of the Roman law, and whatever may have been its abuses in practice, it was equitable in theory, and its processes were limited by strictly defined rules. In the Inquisition all this was changed, and if we would rightly appreciate its methods we must understand the relations which the inquisitor conceived to exist between himself and the offenders brought before his tribunal. As a judge, he was vindicating the faith and avenging God for the wrongs inflicted on him by misbelief. He was more than a judge, however, he was a father-confessor striving for the salvation of the wretched souls perversely bent on perdition. In both capacities he acted with an authority far higher than that of an earthly judge. If his sacred mission was accomplished, it mattered little what methods were used. If the offender asked mercy for his unpardonable crime it must be through the most unreserved submission to the spiritual father who was seeking to save him from the endless torment of hell. The first thing demanded of him when he appeared before the tribunal was an oath to stand to the mandates of the Church, to answer truly all questions asked of him, to betray all heretics known to him, and to perform whatever penance might be imposed on him; and refusal to take this oath was to proclaim himself at once a defiant and obstinate heretic.[357] {400}

The duty of the inquisitor, moreover, was distinguished from that of the ordinary judge by the fact that the task assigned to him was the impossible one of ascertaining the secret thoughts and opinions of the prisoner. External acts were to him only of value as indications of belief, to be accepted or rejected as he might deem them conclusive or illusory. The crime he sought to suppress by punishment was purely a mental one—acts, however criminal, were beyond his jurisdiction. The murderers of St. Peter Martyr were prosecuted, not as assassins, but as fautors of heresy and impeders of the Inquisition. The usurer only came within his purview when he asserted or showed by his acts that he considered usury no sin; the sorcerer when his incantations proved that he preferred to rely on the powers of demons rather than those of God, or that he entertained wrongful notions upon the sacraments. Zanghino tells us that he witnessed the condemnation of a concubinary priest by the Inquisition, who was punished not for his licentiousness, but because while thus polluted he celebrated daily mass and urged in excuse that he considered himself purified by putting on the sacred vestments. Then, too, even doubt was heresy; the believer must have fixed and unwavering faith, and it was the inquisitor's business to ascertain this condition of his mind.[358] External acts and verbal professions were as naught. The accused might be regular in his attendance at mass; he might be liberal in his oblations, punctual in confession and communion, and yet be a heretic at heart. When brought before the tribunal he might profess the most unbounded submission to the decisions of the Holy See, the strictest adherence to orthodox doctrine, the freest readiness to subscribe to whatever was demanded of him, {401} and yet be secretly a Catharan or a Vaudois, fit only for the stake. Few, indeed, were there who courageously admitted their heresy when brought before the tribunal, and to the conscientious judge, eager to destroy the foxes which ravaged the vineyard of the Lord, the task of exploring the secret heart of man was no easy one. We cannot wonder that he speedily emancipated himself from the trammels of recognized judicial procedure which, in preventing him from committing injustice, would have rendered his labors futile. Still less can we be surprised that fanatic zeal, arbitrary cruelty, and insatiable cupidity rivalled each other in building up a system unspeakably atrocious. Omniscience alone was capable of solving with justice the problems which were the daily routine of the inquisitor; human frailty, resolved to accomplish a predetermined end, inevitably reached the practical conclusion that the sacrifice of a hundred innocent men were better than the escape of one guilty.

Thus of the three forms of criminal actions, accusation, denunciation, and inquisition, the latter necessarily became, in place of an exception, the invariable rule, and at the same time it was stripped of the safeguards by which its dangerous tendencies had been in some degree neutralized. If a formal accuser presented himself, the inquisitor was instructed to discourage him by pointing out the danger of the *talio* to which he was exposed by inscribing himself; and by general consent this form of action was rejected in consequence of its being "litigious"—that is, because it afforded the accused some opportunities of defence. That there was danger to the accuser, and that the Inquisition practically discouraged the process, was shown in 1304, when an inquisitor, Frà Landulfo, imposed a fine of one hundred and fifty ounces of gold on the town of Theate because it had officially accused a man of heresy and had failed in the proof. The action by denunciation was less objectionable, because in it the inquisitor acted *ex officio*; but it was unusual, and the inquisitorial process at an early period became substantially the only one followed.[359] {402}

Not only, as we shall see, were its safeguards withdrawn, but virtually the presumption of guilt was assumed in advance. About 1278 an experienced inquisitor lays down the rule as one generally received, that in places much suspected of heresy every inhabitant must be cited to appear, must be forced to abjure heresy and to tell the truth, and be subjected to a detailed interrogatory about himself and others, in which any lack of frankness will subject him hereafter to the dreadful penalties of relapse. That this was not a mere theoretical proposition appears from the great inquests held by Bernard de Caux and Jean de Saint-Pierre in 1245 and 1246, when there are recorded two hundred and thirty interrogatories of inhabitants of the little town of Avignonet, one hundred of those of Fanjeaux, and four hundred and twenty of Mas-Saintes-Puelles.[360]

From this responsibility there was no escape for any one who had reached the age at which the Church held him able to answer for his own acts. What this age was, however, was a subject of dispute. The Councils of Toulouse, Béziers, and Albi assumed it to be fourteen for males and twelve for females, when they prescribed the oath of abjuration to be taken by the whole population, and{403} this rule was adopted by some authorities. Others contented themselves with the definition that the child must be old enough to understand the purport of an oath, while there were not wanting high authorities who reduced the age of responsibility to seven years, and those who more charitably fixed it at nine and a half for girls and ten and a half for boys. It is true that in Latin countries, where minority did not cease until the age of twenty-five, no one beneath that age had a standing in court, but this was readily evaded by appointing for him a "curator," under whose shadow he could be tortured and condemned; and when we are told that no one below the age of fourteen should be tortured, we are left to conjecture the minimum age of responsibility for heresy.[361]

Nor could the offender escape by absenting himself. Absence was contumacy and only increased his guilt, by adding a fresh and unpardonable offence, besides being technically tantamount to confession. In fact, before the Inquisition was thought of, the inquisitorial process was rendered absolute in ecclesiastical jurisprudence precisely to meet such cases, as when Innocent III. degraded the Bishop of Coire on evidence taken *ex parte* by his commissioners, after the bishop had repeatedly refused to appear before them; and the importance of this decision is shown by the fact that Raymond of Pennaforte embodied it in the canon law to prove that in cases of contumacy the testimony taken in an *inquisitio* was valid ground for condemnation without a *litis contestatio* or contest between the prosecution and the defence. Accordingly, when a party failed to appear, after due citation published in his parish church and proper delay, there was no hesitation in proceeding against him to conviction *in absentia*—the absence of the culprit being piously supplied by "the presence of God and the Gospels" when the sentence was rendered. Contumacious absence, in fact, was in itself enough. Frederic II. in his earliest edict, in 1220, following the Lateran Council of 1215, had declared that the suspect who{404} did not clear himself within twelve months was to be condemned as a heretic, and this was applied to the absent, who were ordered to be sentenced after a year's excommunication, whether anything was proved against them or not. Enduring excommunication for a year without seeking its removal was evidence of heresy as to the sacraments and the power of the keys, if as to nothing else; and some authorities were so rigid with regard to this that the Council of Béziers denounced the punishment of heresy for all who remained excommunicate for forty days. Even the delay of a twelvemonth, however, was evaded, for inquisitors were instructed when citing the absent to summon them, not only to appear, but to purge themselves within a given time, and then as soon as it had elapsed the accused was held to be convicted. Yet the extreme penalty of relaxation was rarely enforced in such cases, and the Inquisition contented itself generally with imprisoning for life those against whom no offence was proved save contumacy, unless, indeed, when caught they refused to submit and abjure.[362]

As little was there any escape by death. It mattered not that the sinner had been called to the judgment-seat of God, the faith must be vindicated by his condemnation and the faithful be edified by his punishment. If he had incurred only imprisonment or the lighter penalties, his bones were simply dug up and cast out. If his heresy had deserved the stake, they were solemnly burned. A simulacrum of defence was allowed to heirs and descendants, on whom were visited the heavy penalties of confiscation and personal disabilities. How unflagging was the zeal with which these mortuary prosecutions were sometimes carried on is visible in the case of Armanno Pongilupo of Ferrara, over whose remains war was waged between the Bishop and the Inquisitor of Ferrara for{405} thirty-two years after his death, in 1269, ending with the triumph of the Inquisition in 1301. No prescription of time barred the Church in these matters, as the heirs and descendants of Gherardo of Florence found when, in 1313, Frà Grimaldo the inquisitor commenced a successful prosecution against their ancestor who had died prior to 1250.[363]

At best the inquisitorial process was a dangerous one in its conjunction of prosecutor with judge, and when it was first introduced in ecclesiastical jurisprudence careful limitations to prevent abuse were felt to be absolutely essential. The danger was doubled when the prosecuting judge was an earnest zealot bent on upholding the faith and predetermined on seeing in every prisoner before him a heretic to be convicted at any cost; nor was the danger lessened when he was merely rapacious and eager for fines and confiscations. Yet the theory of the Church was that the inquisitor was an impartial spiritual father whose functions in the salvation of souls should be fettered by no rules. All the safeguards which human experience had shown to be necessary in judicial proceedings of the most trivial character were deliberately cast aside in these cases, where life and reputation and property through three generations were involved. Every doubtful point was decided "in favor of the faith." The inquisitor, with endless iteration, was empowered and instructed to proceed summarily, to disregard forms, to permit no impediments arising from judicial rules or the wrangling of advocates, to shorten the proceedings as much as possible by depriving the accused of the ordinary facilities of defence, and by rejecting all appeals and dilatory exceptions. The validity of the result was not to be vitiated by the omission at any stage of the trial of the forms which had been devised to prevent injustice and subject the judge to responsibility.[364]{406}

133

Had the proceedings been public, there might have been some check upon this hideous system, but the Inquisition shrouded itself in the awful mystery of secrecy until after sentence had been awarded and it was ready to impress the multitude with the fearful solemnities of the *auto de fé*. Unless proclamation were to be made for an absentee, the citation of a suspected heretic was made in secret. All knowledge of what took place after he presented himself was confined to the few discreet men selected by his judge, who were sworn to inviolable silence, and even the experts assembled to consult over his fate were subjected to similar oaths. The secrets of that dismal tribunal were guarded with the same caution, and we are told by Bernard Gui that extracts from the records were to be furnished rarely and only with the most careful discretion. Paramo, in the quaint pedantry with which he ingeniously proves that God was the first inquisitor and the condemnation of Adam and Eve the first model of the inquisitorial process, triumphantly points out that he judged them in secret, thus setting the example which the Inquisition is bound to follow, and avoiding the subtleties which the criminals would have raised in their defence, especially at the suggestion of the crafty serpent. That he called no witnesses is explained by the confession of the accused, and ample legal authority is cited to show that these confessions were sufficient to justify the conviction and punishment. If this blasphemous absurdity raises a smile, it has also its melancholy side, for it reveals to us the view which the inquisitors themselves took of their functions, assimilating themselves to God and wielding an irresponsible power which nothing short of divine wisdom could prevent from being turned by human passions into an engine of the most deadly injustice. Released from all the restraint of publicity and unrestricted by the formalities of law, the procedure of the Inquisition, as Zanghino tells us, was purely arbitrary. How the inquisitors construed their powers and what use they made of their discretion we shall have abundant opportunity of seeing hereafter.[365] {407}

The ordinary course of a trial by the Inquisition was this. A man would be reported to the inquisitor as of ill-repute for heresy, or his name would occur in the confessions of other prisoners. A secret inquisition would be made and all accessible evidence against him would be collected. He would then be secretly cited to appear at a given time, and bail taken to secure his obedience, or if he were suspected of flight, he would be suddenly arrested and confined until the tribunal was ready to give him a hearing. Legally there required to be three citations, but this was eluded by making the summons "one for three;" when the prosecution was based on common report the witnesses were called apparently at random, making a sort of drag-net, and when the mass of surmises and gossip, exaggerated and distorted by the natural fear of the witnesses, eager to save themselves from suspicion of favoring heretics, grew sufficient for action, the blow would fall. The accused was thus prejudged. He was assumed to be guilty, or he would not have been put on trial, and virtually his only mode of escape was by confessing the charges made against him, abjuring heresy, and accepting whatever punishment might be imposed on him in the shape of penance. Persistent denial of guilt and assertion of orthodoxy, when there was evidence against him, rendered him an impenitent, obstinate heretic, to be abandoned to the secular arm and consigned to the stake. The process thus was an exceedingly simple one, and is aptly summarized by an inquisitor of the fifteenth century in an argument against admitting the accused to bail. If one is caught in heresy, by his own confession, and is impenitent, he is to be delivered to the secular arm to be put to death; if penitent, he is to be thrust in prison for life, and therefore is not to be let loose on bail; if he denies, and is legitimately convicted by witnesses, he is, as an impenitent, to be delivered to the secular court to be executed.[366] {408}

Yet many reasons led the inquisitor earnestly to desire to secure confession. In numerous cases—indeed, no doubt in a majority—the evidence, while possibly justifying suspicion, was of too loose and undefined a character to justify condemnation, for every idle rumor was taken up, and any flimsy pretext which led to prosecution assumed importance when the inquisitor found himself bound to show that he had not acted unadvisedly, or when he had in prospect fines and confiscations for the benefit of the faith. Even when the evidence was sufficient, there were motives equally strong to induce the inquisitor to labor with his prisoner in the hope of leading him to withdraw his denial and throw himself upon the mercy of the tribunal. Except in the somewhat rare cases of defiant heretics, confession was always accompanied with professions of conversion and repentance. Not only thus was a soul snatched from Satan, but the new convert was bound to prove his sincerity by denouncing all whom he knew or might suspect to be heretic, thus opening fresh avenues for the extirpation of heresy.

Bernard Gui, copying an earlier inquisitor, tells us eloquently that when the external evidence was insufficient for conviction, the mind of the inquisitor was torn with anxious cares. On the one side, his conscience pained him if he punished one who was neither confessed nor convicted; but he suffered still more, knowing by constant experience the falsity and cunning and malice of these men, if he allowed them to escape through their vulpine astuteness, to the damage of the faith. In such case they were strengthened and multiplied, and rendered keener than ever, while the laity were scandalized at seeing the inefficiency of the Inquisition, baffled in its undertakings, and its most learned men played with and defied by rude and illiterate persons, for they believed the inquisitors to have all the proofs and arguments of the faith so ready at hand that no heretic could elude them or prevent their converting him. From this it is easy to see how the self-conceit of the inquisitor led him inevitably to conviction. In another passage he points out {409} how greatly profitable to the faith was the conversion of such persons, because not only were they obliged to betray their fellows and the hiding-places and conventicles of darkness, but those whom they had influenced were more ready to acknowledge their errors and seek in turn to be converted. As early as 1246 the Council of Béziers had pointed out the utility of such conversions, and had instructed the inquisitors to spare no pains in procuring them, and all subsequent authorities evidently regarded this as the first of their duties. They all agree, moreover, in holding delation of accomplices as the indispensable evidence of true conversion. Without this the repentant heretic in vain might ask for reconciliation and mercy; his refusal to betray his friends and kindred was proof that he was unrepentant, and he was forthwith handed over to the secular arm, exactly as in the Roman law a converted Manichæan who consorted with Manichæans without denouncing them to the authorities was punishable with death. How useful this was is seen in the case of Saurine Rigaud, whose confession is recorded at Toulouse in 1254, where it is followed by a list of one hundred and sixty-nine persons incriminated by her, their names being carefully tabulated with their places of residence for immediate action. How strictly, moreover, the duty of the reconciled heretic was construed is seen in the fate of Guillem Sicrède at Toulouse in 1312. He had abjured and been reconciled in 1262. Fifty years afterwards, in 1311, he had been present at the death-bed of his brother, where hereticated had been performed, and he had failed to betray it, though he had vainly objected to it. When asked for his reasons, he simply said that he had not wished to injure his nephews, and for this, in 1312, he was imprisoned for life. Delation was so indispensable to the Inquisition that it was to be secured by rewards as well as by punishments. Bernard Gui tells us that those who voluntarily come forward and prove their zeal by confession and by betraying all their associates are not only to be pardoned, but their livelihood must be secured at the hands of princes and prelates; while betraying a single "perfected" heretic insured immunity and perhaps additional reward.[367]{410}

The inquisitor's anxiety to secure confession was well grounded, not only through the advantages thus secured, but to satisfy his own conscience. In ordinary crimes, a judge was usually certain that an offence had been committed before he undertook to prosecute a prisoner accused of murder or theft. In many cases, however, the inquisitor could have no assurance that there had been any crime. A man might be reasonably suspected, he might have been seen conversing with those subsequently proved to be heretics, he might have given them alms or other assistance, he might even have attended a meeting of heretics, and yet be thoroughly orthodox at heart; or he might be a bitter heretic and yet have given no outward sign. His own assertion of orthodoxy, his willingness to subscribe to the faith of Rome, went for nothing, for experience had proved that most heretics were willing to subscribe to anything, and that they had been trained by persecution to conceal their beliefs under the mask of rigid orthodoxy. Confession of heresy thus became a matter of vital importance, and no effort was deemed too great, no means too repulsive, to secure it. This became the centre of the inquisitorial process, and it is deserving of detailed consideration, not only because it formed the basis of procedure in the Holy Office, but also because of the vast and deplorable influence which it exercised for five centuries on the whole judicial system of Continental Europe.

The first and readiest means was, of course, the examination of the accused. For this the inquisitor prepared himself by collecting and studying all the adverse evidence that could be procured, while the prisoner was kept in sedulous ignorance of the charges against him. Skill in interrogation was the one pre-eminent requisite of the inquisitor, and manuals prepared by experienced brethren for the benefit of the younger officials are full of details with regard to it and of carefully prepared forms of interrogations suited for every heretical sect. Constant training developed a class of acute and subtle minds, practised to read the thoughts of the accused, skilled to lay pitfalls for the incautious, versed in every art to confuse, prompt to detect ambiguities, and quick to take advantage{411} of hesitation or contradiction. Even in the infancy of the institution the consuls of Narbonne complained to those of Nimes that the inquisitors, in their efforts to entrap the unwary, did not hesitate to make use of dialectics as sophistical as those with which students encountered each other in scholastic diversion. Nothing more ludicrous can well be imagined than the complaints of these veteran examiners, restricted by no rules, of the shrewd duplicity of their victims, who struggled, occasionally with success, to avoid criminating themselves, and they sought to explain it by asserting that wicked and shameless priests instructed them how to equivocate on points of faith.[368]

An experienced inquisitor drew up for the guidance of his successors a specimen examination of a heretic, to show them the quibbles and tergiversations for which they must be prepared when dealing with those who shrank from boldly denying their faith. Its fidelity is attested by Bernard Gui reproducing it fifty years later in his "Practica," and it is too characteristic an illustration of the encounter between the trained intellect of the inquisitor and the untutored shrewdness of the peasant struggling to save his life and his conscience, to be omitted.

"When a heretic is first brought up for examination, he assumes a confident air, as though secure in his innocence. I ask him why he has been brought before me. He replies, smiling and courteous, 'Sir, I would be glad to learn the cause from you.'

"I. 'You are accused as a heretic, and that you believe and teach otherwise than Holy Church believes.'

"A. (Raising his eyes to heaven, with an air of the greatest faith) 'Lord, thou knowest that I am innocent of this, and that I never held any faith other than that of true Christianity.'

"I. 'You call your faith Christian, for you consider ours as false and heretical. But I ask whether you have ever believed as true another faith than that which the Roman Church holds to be true.{412}

"A. 'I believe the true faith which the Roman Church believes, and which you openly preach to us.'

"I. 'Perhaps you have some of your sect at Rome whom you call the Roman Church. I, when I preach, say many things, some of which are common to us both, as that God liveth, and you believe some of what I preach. Nevertheless you may be a heretic in not believing other matters which are to be believed.'

"A. 'I believe all things that a Christian should believe.'

"I. 'I know your tricks. What the members of your sect believe you hold to be that which a Christian should believe. But we waste time in this fencing. Say simply, Do you believe in one God the Father, and the Son, and the Holy Ghost?'

"A. 'I believe.'

"I. 'Do you believe in Christ born of the Virgin, suffered, risen, and ascended to heaven?'

"A. (Briskly) 'I believe.'

"I. 'Do you believe the bread and wine in the mass performed by the priests to be changed into the body and blood of Christ by divine virtue?'

"A. 'Ought I not to believe this?'

"I. 'I don't ask if you ought to believe, but if you do believe.'

"A. 'I believe whatever you and other good doctors order me to believe.'

"I. 'Those good doctors are the masters of your sect; if I accord with them you believe with me; if not, not.'

"A. 'I willingly believe with you if you teach what is good to me.'

"I. 'You consider it good to you if I teach what your other masters teach. Say, then, do you believe the body of our Lord Jesus Christ to be in the altar?'

"A. (Promptly) 'I believe.'

"I. 'You know that a body is there, and that all bodies are of our Lord. I ask whether the body there is of the Lord who was born of the Virgin, hung on the cross, arose from the dead, ascended, etc.?'

"A. 'And you, sir, do you not believe it?'

"I. 'I believe it wholly.'

"A. 'I believe likewise.'{415}

"I. 'You believe that I believe it, which is not what I ask, but whether you believe it.'

"A. 'If you wish to interpret all that I say otherwise than simply and plainly, then I don't know what to say. I am a simple and ignorant man. Pray don't catch me in my words.'

"I. 'If you are simple, answer simply, without evasions.'

"A. 'Willingly.'

"I. 'Will you then swear that you have never learned anything contrary to the faith which we hold to be true?'

"A. (Growing pale) 'If I ought to swear, I will willingly swear.'

"I. 'I don't ask whether you ought, but whether you will swear.'

"A. 'If you order me to swear, I will swear.'

"I. 'I don't force you to swear, because as you believe oaths to be unlawful, you will transfer the sin to me who forced you; but if you will swear, I will hear it.'

"A. 'Why should I swear if you do not order me to?'

"I. 'So that you may remove the suspicion of being a heretic.'

"A. 'Sir, I do not know how unless you teach me.'

"I. 'If I had to swear, I would raise my hand and spread my fingers and say, "So help me God, I have never learned heresy or believed what is contrary to the true faith."'

"Then trembling as if he cannot repeat the form, he will stumble along as though speaking for himself or for another, so that there is not an absolute form of oath and yet he may be thought to have sworn. If the words are there, they are so turned around that he does not swear and yet appears to have sworn. Or he converts the oath into a form of prayer, as 'God help me that I am not a heretic or the like;' and when asked whether he had sworn, he will say: 'Did you not hear me swear' And when further hard pressed he will appeal, saying 'Sir, if I have done amiss in aught, I will willingly bear the penance, only help me to avoid the infamy of which I am accused through malice and without fault of mine.' But a vigorous inquisitor must not allow himself to be worked upon in this way, but proceed firmly till he makes these people confess their error, or at least publicly abjure heresy, so that if they are subsequently found to have sworn falsely, he can, without{414} further hearing, abandon them to the secular arm. If one consents to swear that he is not a heretic, I say to him, 'If you wish to swear so as to escape the stake, one oath will not suffice for me, nor ten, nor a hundred, nor a thousand, because you dispense each other for a certain number of oaths taken under necessity, but I will require a countless number. Moreover, if I have, as I presume, adverse witnesses against you, your oaths will not save you from being burned. You will only stain your conscience without escaping death. But if you will simply confess your error, you may find mercy.' Under this anxiety, I have seen some confess."[369]

The same inquisitor illustrates the ease with which the cunning of these simple folk fenced and played with the best-trained men of the Holy Office by a case in which he saw a serving-wench elude the questions of picked examiners for several days together, and she would have escaped had there not by chance been found in her chest the fragment of a bone of a heretic recently burned, which she had preserved as a relic, according to one of her companions who had collected the bones with her. But the inquisitor does not tell us how many thousand good Catholics, confused by the awful game which they were playing, mystified with the intricacies of scholastic theology, ignorant how to answer the dangerous questions put to them so searchingly, and terrified with the threats of burning for persistent denial, despairingly confessed the crime of which they were so confidently assumed to be guilty, and ratified their conversion by inventing tales about their neighbors, while expiating the wrong by suffering confiscation and lifelong imprisonment.

Yet the inquisitor was frequently baffled in this intellectual digladiation by the innocence or astuteness of the accused. His resources, however, were by no means exhausted, and here we approach one of the darkest and most repulsive aspects of our theme. Human inconsistency, in its manifold development, has never exhibited itself in more deplorable fashion than in the instructions on this subject transmitted to their younger brethren by the veterans of the Holy Office—instructions intended for none but official eyes, and therefore framed with the utmost unreserve. Trained through long experience in an accurate knowledge of all that can move{415} the human breast; skilled not only to detect the subtle evasions of the intellect, but to seek and find the tenderest point through which to assail the conscience and the heart; relentless in inflicting agony on body and brain, whether through the mouldering wretchedness of the hopeless dungeon protracted through uncounted years, the sharper pain of the torture-chamber, or by coldly playing on the affections; using without scruple the most violent alternatives of hope and fear; employing with cynical openness every resource of guile and fraud on wretches purposely starved to render them incapable of self-defence, the counsels which these men utter might well seem the promptings of fiends exulting in the unlimited power to wreak their evil passions on helpless mortals. Yet through all this there shines the evident conviction that they are doing the work of God. No labor is too great if they can win a soul from perdition; no toil too repulsive if they can bring a fellow-creature to an acknowledgment of his wrong-doing and a genuine repentance that will wipe out his sins; no patience too prolonged if it will avoid the unjust conviction of the innocent. All the cunning fence between judge and culprit, all the fraud, all the torture of body and mind so ruthlessly employed to extort unwilling confessions, were not necessarily used for the mere purpose of securing a victim, for the inquisitor was taught to be as earnest with the recalcitrants against whom he had sufficient testimony as with the cases in which evidence was deficient. With the former he was seeking to save a soul from immolating itself in the pride of obstinacy; with the latter he was laboring to preserve the sheep by not liberating an infected one to spread pestilence among the flock. It mattered little to the victim what were the motives actuating his persecutor, for conscientious cruelty is apt to be more cold-blooded and calculating, more relentless and effective, than passionate wrath, but the impartial student must needs recognize that while many inquisitors were doubtless dullards who followed unthinkingly a prescribed routine as a vocation, and others were covetous or sanguinary tyrants actuated only by self-interest or ambition, yet among them were not a few who believed themselves to be discharging a high and holy duty, whether they abandoned the impenitent to the flames, or by methods of unspeakable baseness rescued from Satan a soul which he had reckoned as his own. They were instructed that{416} it was better to let the guilty escape than to condemn the innocent, and, therefore, that they must have either clear proofs or confession. In the absence of absolute evidence, therefore, the very conscientiousness of the judge, under such a system, led him to resort to any means to satisfy himself by wringing an acknowledgment from his victim.[370]

The resources for procuring unwilling confession, at command of the inquisitor, may be roughly divided into two classes—deceit and torture, the latter comprehending both mental and physical pain, however administered. Both classes were resorted to freely and without scruple, and there was ample variety to suit the idiosyncrasies of all judges and prisoners.

Perhaps the mildest form of the devices to entrap an unwary prisoner was the recommendation that the examiner should always assume the fact of which he was in quest and ask about the details, as, for instance, "How often have you confessed as a heretic?" "In what chamber of yours did they lie?" Going a step further, the inquisitor is advised during the examination to turn over the pages of evidence as though referring to it, and then boldly inform the prisoner that he is not telling the truth, for it is thus and thus; or to pick up a paper and pretend to read from it whatever is necessary to deceive him; or he can be told circumstantially that some of the masters of the sect have incriminated him in their revelations. To render these devices more effective, the jailer was instructed to worm himself into the confidence of the prisoners, with feigned interest and compassion, and urge them to confess at once, because the inquisitor is a merciful man who will take pity on them. Then the inquisitor was to pretend that he had conclusive evidence, and that if the accused would confess and point out those who had led him astray, he should be allowed to go home forthwith, with any other blandishments likely to prove effective. A more elaborate trap was that of treating the prisoner with kindness in place of rigor; sending trusty agents to his cell to gain his confidence, and then urge him to confess, with promises of mercy and that they would intercede for him. When everything was ripe, the inquisitor himself would appear and confirm these promises, with the mental reservation{417} that all which is done for the conversion of heretics is merciful, that penances are mercies and spiritual remedies, so that when the unlucky wretch was prevailed upon to ask for mercy in return for his revelations, he was to be led on with the general expression that more would be done for him than he asked.[371]

That spies should play a prominent part in such a system was inevitable. The trusty agents who were admitted to the prisoner's cell were instructed to lead him gradually on from one confession to another until they should gain sufficient evidence to incriminate him, without his realizing it. Converted heretics, we are told, were very useful in this business. One would be sent to visit him and say that he had only pretended conversion through fear, and after repeated visits overstay his time and be locked up. Confidential talk would follow in the darkness, while witnesses with a notary were crouching within earshot to take down all that might fall from the lips of the unconscious victim. Fellow-prisoners were utilized whenever possible, and were duly rewarded for treachery. In the sentence of a Carmelite monk, January 17, 1329, guilty of the most infamous sorceries, it is recorded in extenuation of his black catalogue of guilt, that while in prison with sundry heretics he had aided greatly in making them confess and had revealed many important matters which they had confided to him, from which the Inquisition had derived great advantage and hoped to gain more.[372]

These artifices were diversified with appeals to force. The heretic, whether acknowledged or suspected, had no rights. His body was at the mercy of the Church, and if through tribulation of the flesh he could be led to see the error of his ways, there was no hesitation in employing whatever means were readiest to save his soul and advance the faith. Among the miracles for which St. Francis was canonized it is related that a certain Pietro of Assisi was captured in Rome on an accusation of heresy, and confided for conversion to the Bishop of Todi, who loaded him with chains and fed him on measured quantities of bread and water in a dark dungeon. Thus brought through suffering to repentance, on the{418} vigil of St. Francis he invoked the saint for help with passionate tears. Moved by his zeal, St. Francis appeared to him and ordered him forth. His chains fell off and the doors flew open, but the poor wretch was so crazed by the sudden answer to his prayer that he clung to the doorpost with cries which brought the jailers running to him. The pious bishop hastened to the prison, and reverently acknowledging the power of God, sent the shivered fetters to the pope in token of the miracle. Even more illustrative and better authenticated is a case related with much gratulation by Nider as occurring when he was teaching in the University of Vienna. A heretic priest, thrown into prison by his bishop, proved obstinate, and the most eminent theologians who labored for his conversion found him their match in disputation. Believing that vexation brings understanding, they at length ordered him to be bound tightly to a pillar. The cords eating into the swelling flesh caused such exquisite torture that when they visited him the next day he begged piteously to be taken out and burned. Coldly refusing, they left him for another twenty-four hours, by which time physical pain and exhaustion had broken his spirit. He humbly recanted, retired to a Paulite monastery, and lived an exemplary life.[373]

It will readily be believed that there was scant hesitation in employing any methods likely to crush the obduracy of the prisoner who refused the confession and recantation demanded of him. If he were likely to be reached through the affections, his wife and children were admitted to his cell in hopes that their tears and pleadings might work on his feelings and overcome his convictions. Alternate threats and blandishments were tried; he would be removed from his foul and dismal dungeon to commodious quarters, with liberal diet and a show of kindness, to see if his resolution would be weakened by alternations of hope and despair. Master of the art of playing upon the human heart, the trained inquisitor left no method untried which promised victory in the struggle between him and the helpless wretch abandoned to his experiments. Among these, one of the most efficient was the slow torture of delay. The prisoner who refused to confess, or whose confession was deemed imperfect, was remanded to his cell, and left to ponder{419} in solitude and darkness. Except in rare cases time was no object with the Inquisition, and it could afford to wait. Perhaps in a few weeks his resolution might break down, and he might ask to be heard. If not, six months might elapse before he was again called up for hearing. If still obstinate he would be again sent back. Months would lengthen into years, perhaps years into decades, and find him still unconvicted and still a prisoner, hopeless and despairing. Should friendly death not intervene, the terrible patience of the Inquisition was nearly certain to triumph in the end, and the authorities all agree upon the effectiveness of delay. This explains what otherwise would be hard to understand—the immense protraction of so many of the inquisitorial trials whose records have reached us. Three, five, or ten years are common enough as intervals between the first audience of a prisoner and his final conviction, nor are instances wanting of even greater delays. Bernalde, wife of Guillem de Montaigu, was imprisoned at Toulouse in 1297, and made a confession the same year, yet she was not formally sentenced to imprisonment until the *auto* of 1310. I have already alluded to the case of Guillem Garric, brought to confess at Carcassonne in 1321 after a detention of nearly thirty years. In the *auto de fé* of 1319, at Toulouse, Guillem Salavert was sentenced, who had made an unsatisfactory confession in 1299 and another in 1316; to the latter he had unwaveringly adhered, and at last Bernard Gui, overcome by his obstinacy, let him off with the penance of wearing crosses, in consideration of his twenty years' imprisonment without conviction. At the same *auto* were sentenced six wretches who had recently died in prison, two of whom had made their first confession in 1305, one in 1306, two in 1311, and one in 1315. Nor was this hideous torture of suspense peculiar to any special tribunal. Guillem Salavert was one of those implicated in the troubles of Albi in 1299, when many of the accused were speedily tried and sentenced by the bishop, Bernard de Castenet, and Nicholas d'Abbeville, inquisitor of Carcassonne, but some were reserved for the harder fate of detention without trial. The intervention of the pope was sought, and in 1310 Clement V. wrote to the bishop and the inquisitor, giving the names of ten of them, including some of the most respectable citizens of Albi, who had lain for eight years or more in jail awaiting judgment, many of them in{420} chains and all in narrow, dark cells. His order for their immediate trial was disobeyed, and in a subsequent letter he speaks of several of them having died before his previous epistle, and reiterated his command for the prompt disposal of the survivors. The Inquisition was a law unto itself, however, and again his mandate was disregarded. In 1319, besides Guillem Salavert, two others, Guillem Calverie and Isarn Colli, were brought from their dungeon and retracted their confessions which had been extorted from them by torture. Calverie figured with Salavert in the *auto* of Toulouse in the same year. When Colli was sentenced we do not know, but in the accounts of Arnaud Assalit, royal steward of confiscations, for 1322-3, there appears the property of "Isarnus Colli condemnatus," showing his ultimate fate. In the *auto* of 1319, moreover, occur the names of two citizens of Cordes, Durand Boissa and Bernard Ouvrier (then deceased), whose confessions date respectively from 1301 and 1300, doubtless belonging to the same unfortunate group, who had eaten their hearts in despair and misery for a score of years.[374]

When it was desired to hasten this slow torture, the object was easily accomplished by rendering the imprisonment unendurably harsh. As we shall see hereafter, the dungeons of the Inquisition at best were abodes of fearful misery, but when there was reason for increasing their terrors there was no difficulty in increasing the hardships. The "*durus career et arcta vita*"—chains and starvation in a stifling hole—was a favorite device for extracting confession from unwilling lips. We shall meet hereafter an atrocious instance of this inflicted on a witness, as early as 1263, when the ruin of the great house of Foix was sought. It was pointed out that judicious restriction of diet not only reduced the body but weakened the will, and rendered the prisoner less able{421} to resist alternate threats of death and promises of mercy. Starvation, in fact, was reckoned as one of the regular and most efficient methods to subdue unwilling witnesses and defendants. In 1306 Clement V. declared, after an official investigation, that at Carcassonne prisoners were habitually constrained to confession by the harshness of the prison, the lack of beds, and the deficiency of food, as well as by torture.[375]

With all these resources at their command, it might seem superfluous for inquisitors to have recourse to the vulgar and ruder implements of the torture-chamber. The rack and strappado, in fact, were in such violent antagonism, not only with the principles of Christianity, but with the practices of the Church, that their use by the Inquisition, as a means of furthering the faith, is one of the saddest anomalies of that dismal period. I have elsewhere shown how consistently the Church opposed the use of torture, so that, in the barbarism of the twelfth century, Gratian lays it down as an accepted rule of the canon law that no confession is to be extorted by torment. Torture, moreover, except among the Wisigoths, had been unknown among the barbarians who founded the commonwealths of Europe, and their system of jurisprudence had grown up free from its contamination. It was not until the study of the revived Roman law, and the prohibition of ordeals by the Lateran Council of 1215, which was gradually enforced during the first half of the thirteenth century, that jurists began to feel the need of torture and accustom themselves to the idea of its introduction. The earliest instances with which I have met occur in the Veronese Code of 1228 and the Sicilian Constitutions of Frederic II. in 1231, and in both of these the references to it show how sparingly and hesitatingly it was employed. Even Frederic, in his ruthless edicts, from 1220 to 1239, makes no allusion to it, but, in accordance with the Verona decree of Lucius III., prescribes the recognized form of canonical purgation for the trial of all suspected heretics. Yet it rapidly won its way in Italy, and when Innocent IV., in 1252, published his bull *Ad extirpanda*, he adopted it, and authorized its use for the discovery of{422} heresy. A decent respect for the old-time prejudices of the Church, however, forbade him to allow its administration by the inquisitors themselves or their servitors. It was the secular authorities who were ordered to force all captured heretics to confess and accuse their accomplices, by torture which should not imperil life or injure limb, "just as thieves and robbers are forced to confess their crimes and accuse their accomplices." The unrepealed canons of the Church, in fact, prohibited all ecclesiastics from being concerned in such acts, and even from being present where torture was administered, so that the inquisitor whose zeal should lead him to take part in it was thereby rendered "irregular" and unfit for sacred functions until he could be "dispensed" or purified. This did not suit the policy of the institution. Possibly outside of Italy, where torture was as yet virtually unknown, it found difficulty in securing the co-operation of the public officials; everywhere it complained that this cumbrous mode of administration interfered with the profound secrecy which was an essential characteristic of its operations. But four years after the bull of Innocent IV., Alexander IV., in 1256, removed the difficulty with characteristic indirection by authorizing inquisitors and their associates to absolve each other, and mutually grant dispensations for irregularities—a permission which was repeatedly reiterated, and which was held to remove all impediment to the use of torture under the direct supervision of the inquisitor and his ministers. In Naples, where the Inquisition was but slenderly organized, we find the public officials used by it as torturers until the end of the century, but elsewhere it speedily arrogated the administration of torment to its own officials. Even in Naples, however, Frà Tomaso d'Aversa is seen, in 1305, personally inflicting the most brutal tortures on the Spiritual Franciscans; and when he found it impossible in this manner to make them convict themselves, he employed the ingenious expedient of starving for a few days one of the younger brethren, and then giving him strong wine to drink; when the poor wretch was fuddled there was no difficulty in getting him to admit that he and his twoscore comrades were all heretics.[376]{423}

Torture saved the trouble and expense of prolonged imprisonment; it was a speedy and effective method of obtaining what revelations might be desired, and it grew rapidly in favor with the Inquisition, while its extension throughout secular jurisprudence was remarkably slow. In 1260 the charter granted by Alphonse of Poitiers to the town of Auzon specially exempts the accused from torture, no matter what the crime involved. This shows that its use was gradually spreading, and already, in 1291, Philippe le Bel felt himself called upon to restrain its abuses; in letters to the seneschal of Carcassonne he alludes to the newly-introduced methods of torture in the Inquisition, whereby the innocent were convicted and scandal and desolation pervaded the land. He could not interfere with the internal management of the Holy Office, but he sought a corrective in forbidding indiscriminate arrests at the sole bidding of the inquisitors. As might be expected, this was only a palliative; callous indifference to human suffering grows by habit, and the misuse of this terrible method of coercion continued to increase. When the despairing cry of the population induced Clement V. to order an investigation into the iniquities of the Inquisition of Carcassonne, the commission issued to the cardinals sent thither in 1306 recites that confessions were extorted by torture so severe that the unfortunates subjected to it had only the alternative of death; and in the proceedings before the commissioners the use of torture is so frequently alluded to as to leave no doubt of its habitual employment. It is a noteworthy fact, however, that in the fragmentary documents of inquisitorial proceedings which have reached us the references to torture are singularly few. Apparently it was felt that to record its use[424] would in some sort invalidate the force of the testimony. Thus, in the cases of Isarn Colli and Guillem Calverie, mentioned above, it happens to be stated that they retracted their confessions made under torture, but in the confessions themselves there is nothing to indicate that it had been used. In the six hundred and thirty-six sentences borne upon the register of Toulouse from 1309 to 1323 the only allusion to torture is in the recital of the case of Calverie, but there are numerous instances in which the information wrung from the convicts who had no hope of escape could scarce have been procured in any other manner. Bernard Gui, who conducted the Inquisition of Toulouse during this period, has too emphatically expressed his sense of the utility of torture on both principals and witnesses for us to doubt his readiness in its employment.[377]

The result of Clement's investigation in 1306 led to an effort at reform which was agreed to in the Council of Vienne in 1311, but with customary indecision Clement delayed the publication of the considerable body of legislation adopted by the council until his death, and it was not issued till October, 1317, by his successor John XXII. Among the abuses which he sought to limit was that of torture, and to this end he ordered that it should not be administered without the concurrent action of bishop and inquisitor if this could be had within the space of eight days. Bernard Gui emphatically remonstrated against this as seriously crippling the efficiency of the Inquisition, and he proposed to substitute for it the meaningless phrase that torture should only be used with mature and careful deliberation, but his suggestion was unheeded, and the Clementine regulation remained the law of the Church.[378]

The inquisitors, however, were too little accustomed to restraint in any form to submit long to this infringement on their privileges. It is true that disobedience rendered the proceedings void, and the unhappy wretch who was unlawfully tortured without episcopal[425] consultation could appeal to the pope, but this did not undo the work; Rome was distant, and the victims of the Inquisition for the most part were too friendless and too helpless to protect themselves in such illusory fashion. In Bernard Gui's "Practica," written probably about 1328 or 1330, he only speaks of consultation with experts, making no allusions to bishops; Eymerich adheres to the Clementines, but his instructions as to what is to be done in case of their disregard shows how frequent was such action; while Zanghino boldly affirms that the canon is to be construed as permitting torture by either bishop or inquisitor. In some proceedings against the Waldenses of Piedmont in 1387, if the accused did not confess freely on a first examination an entry was made that the inquisitor was not content, and twenty-four hours were given the prisoner to amend his statements; he would be tortured and brought back next morning in a more complying frame of mind, when a careful record would be made that his confession was without torture and aloof from the torture-chamber. Cunning casuists, moreover, discovered that Clement had only spoken of torture in general and had not specifically alluded to witnesses, whence they concluded that one of the most shocking abuses of the system, the torture of witnesses, was left to the sole discretion of the inquisitor, and this became the accepted rule. It only required an additional step to show that after the accused had been convicted by evidence or had confessed as to himself, he became a witness as to the guilt of his friends and thus could be arbitrarily tortured to betray them. Even when the Clementines were observed, the limit of eight days enabled the inquisitor to proceed independently after waiting for that length of time.[379]

While witnesses who were supposed to be concealing the truth[426] could be tortured as a matter of course, there was some discussion among jurists as to the amount of adverse evidence that would justify placing the accused on the rack. Unless there was some colorable reason to believe that the crime of heresy had been committed, evidently there was no excuse for the employment of such means of investigation. Eymerich tells us that when there are two incriminating witnesses, a man of good reputation can be tortured to ascertain the truth, while if he is of evil repute he can be condemned without it or can be tortured on the evidence of a single witness. Zanghino, on the other hand, asserts that the evidence of a single witness of good character is sufficient for the authorization of torture, without distinction of persons, while Bernardo di Como says that common report is enough. In time elaborate instructions were drawn up for the guidance of inquisitors in this matter, but their uselessness was confessed in the admission that, after all, the decision was to be left to the discretion of the judge. How little sufficed to justify the exercise of this discretion is seen when jurists held it to be sufficient if the accused, on examination, was frightened and stammered and varied in his answers, without any external evidence against him.[380]

In the administration of torture the rules adopted by the Inquisition became those of the secular courts of Christendom at large, and therefore are worth brief attention. Eymerich, whose instructions on the subject are the fullest we have, admits the grave difficulties which surrounded the question, and the notorious uncertainty of the result. Torture should be moderate, and effusion of blood be scrupulously avoided, but then, what was moderation? Some prisoners were so weak that at the first turn of the pulleys they would concede anything asked them; others so obstinate that they would endure all things rather than confess the truth. Those who had previously undergone the experience might be either the stronger or the weaker for it, for with some the arms were hardened, while with others they were permanently weakened. In short, the discretion of the judge was the only rule.

Both bishop and inquisitor ought rightfully to be present. The prisoner was shown the implements of torment and urged to confess.{427} On his refusal he was stripped and bound by the executioners and again entreated to speak, with promises of mercy in all cases in which mercy could be shown. This frequently produced the desired result, and we may be assured that the efficacy of torture lay not so much in what was extracted by its use as in the innumerable cases in which its dread, near or remote, paralyzed the resolution with agonizing expectations. If this proved ineffectual, the torture was applied with gradually increased severity. In the case of continued obstinacy additional implements of torment were exhibited and the sufferer was told that he would be subjected to them all in turn. If still undaunted, he was unbound, and the next or third day was appointed for renewal of the infliction. According to rule, torture could be applied but once, but this, like all other rules for the protection of the accused, was easily eluded. It was only necessary to order, not a repetition, but a "continuance" of the torture, and no matter how long the interval, the holy casuists were able to continue it indefinitely; or a further excuse would be found in alleging that additional evidence had been discovered, which required a second torturing to purge it away. During the interval fresh solicitations were made to elicit confession, and these being unavailing, the accused was again subjected to torment either of the same kind as before or to others likely to prove more efficacious. If he remained silent after torture, deemed sufficient by his judges, some authorities say that he should be discharged and that a declaration was to be given him that nothing had been proved against him; others, however, order that he should be remanded to prison and be kept there. The trial of Bernard Délicieux, in 1319, reveals another device to elude the prohibition of repeated torture, for the examiners could at any moment order the torture to satisfy their curiosity about a single point, and thus could go on indefinitely with others.

Any confession made under torture required to be confirmed after removal from the torture-chamber. Usually the procedure appears to be that the torture was continued until the accused signified his readiness to confess, when he was unbound and carried into another room where his confession was made. If, however, the confession was extracted during the torture, it was read over subsequently to the prisoner and he was asked if it were true: there was, indeed, a rule that there should be an interval of twenty-four{428} hours between the torture and the confession, or its confirmation, but this was commonly disregarded. Silence indicated assent, and the length of silence to be allowed for was, as usual, left to the discretion of the judge, with warning to consider the condition of the prisoner, whether young or old, male or female, simple or learned. In any case the record was carefully made that the confession was free and spontaneous, without the pressure of force or fear. If the confession was retracted, the accused could be taken back for a continuance of the torture—not, as we are carefully told, for a repetition—provided always that he had not been "sufficiently" tortured before.[381]

The question as to the retraction of confession was one which exercised to no small degree the inquisitorial jurists, and practice was not wholly uniform. It placed the inquisitor in a disagreeable position, and, in view of the methods adopted to secure confession, it was so likely to occur that naturally stringent measures were adopted to prevent it. Some authorities draw a distinction between confessions made "spontaneously" and those extorted by torture or its threat, but in practice the difference was disregarded. The most merciful view taken of revocation is that of Eymerich, who says that if the torture had been sufficient, the accused who persistently revokes is entitled to a discharge. In this Eymerich is alone. Some authorities recommend that the accused be forced to withdraw his revocation by repetition of torture. Others content themselves with regarding it as impeding the Inquisition, and as such including it in the excommunication regularly published by parish priests and at the opening of every *auto de fé*, and this excommunication included notaries who might wickedly aid in drawing up such revocations. The general presumption of law, however,{429} was that the confession was true and the retraction a perjury, and the view taken of such cases was that the retraction proved the accused to be an impenitent heretic, who had relapsed after confession and asking for penance. As such there was nothing to be done with him but to hand him over to the secular arm for punishment without a hearing. It is true, that in the case of Guillem Calverie, thus condemned in 1319 by Bernard Gui for withdrawing his confession, the culprit was mercifully allowed fifteen days in which to revoke his revocation, but this was a mere exercise of the discretion customarily lodged with the inquisitor. How strictly the rule was construed which regarded revocation as relapse is seen in the remark of Zanghino, that if a man had confessed and abjured and been set free under penance, and if he subsequently remarked in public that he had confessed under fear of expense or to avoid heavier punishment, he was to be regarded as an impenitent heretic, liable to be burned as a relapsed. We shall see hereafter the full significance of this point in its application to the Templars. There was an additional question of some nicety which arose when the retracted confession incriminated others besides the accused; in this case the most merciful view taken was that, if it was not to be held good against them, the one who confessed was liable to punishment for false-witness. As no confession was sufficient which did not reveal the names of partners in guilt, those inquisitors who did not regard revocation as relapse could at least imprison the accused for life as a false witness.[382]

The inquisitorial process as thus perfected was sure of its victim. No one whom a judge wished to condemn could escape. The form in which it became naturalized in secular jurisprudence was less arbitrary and effective, yet Sir John Fortescue, the chancellor of Henry VI., who in his exile had ample opportunity to observe its working, declares that it placed every man's life or limb at the mercy of any enemy who could suborn two unknown witnesses to swear against him.[383]{430}

CHAPTER X.

EVIDENCE.

WE have seen in the foregoing chapter the inevitable tendency of the inquisitorial process to assume the character of a duel between the judge and the accused with the former as the assailant. This deplorable result was the necessary outcome of the system and of the task imposed upon the inquisitor. He was required to penetrate the inscrutable heart of man, and professional pride perhaps contributed as much as zeal for the faith in stimulating him to prove that he was not to be baffled by the unfortunates brought before him in judgment.

In such a struggle as this the testimony of witnesses, for the most part, counted for little except as a basis for arrest and prosecution, and for threatening the accused with the unknown mass of evidence against him, and for this the slightest breath of scandal, even from a single person notoriously foul-mouthed, sufficed, without calling witnesses.[384] The real battlefield was the prisoner's conscience, and his confession the prize of victory. Yet the subject of evidence as treated by the Inquisition is not wholly to be passed over, for it affords fresh illustration of the manner in which the practice of construing everything "in favor of the faith" led to the development of the worst body of jurisprudence invented by man, and to the habitual perpetration of the foulest injustice. The matter-of-course way in which rules destructive of every principle of fairness are laid down by men presumably correct in the ordinary affairs of life affords a wholesome lesson as to the power of fanaticism to warp the intellect of the most acute.

This did not arise from any peculiar laxity of practice in the ordinary ecclesiastical courts. Their procedure, based upon the civil law, accepted and enforced its rules as to the admission of{431} evidence, and the onus of proof lay upon the assertor of a fact. Innocent III., in his instructions as to the Cathari of La Charité, reminded the local authorities that even violent presumptions were not proof, and were insufficient for condemnation in a matter so heinous—a rule which was embodied in the canon law, where it became for the inquisitors merely an excuse for obtaining certitude by extorting confession. How completely they felt themselves emancipated from all wholesome restraint is shown by the remarks of Bernard Gui—"The accused are not to be condemned unless they confess or are convicted by witnesses, though not according to the ordinary laws, as in other crimes, but according to the private laws or privileges conceded to the inquisitors by the Holy See, for there is much that is peculiar to the Inquisition."[385]

From almost the inception of the Holy Office there was an effort to lay down rules as to what constituted evidence of heresy; but the Council of Narbonne, in 1244, winds up an enumeration of the various indications by saying that it is sufficient if the accused can be shown to have manifested by any word or sign that he had faith or belief in heretics or considered them to be "good men" (*bos homes*). The kind of testimony received was as flimsy and impalpable as the facts, or supposed facts, sought to be proved. In the voluminous examinations and depositions which have reached us from the archives of the Inquisition we find the witnesses allowed and encouraged to say everything that may occur to them. Great weight was attached to popular report or belief, and to ascertain this the opinion of the witness was freely received, whether based on knowledge or prejudice, hearsay evidence, vague rumors, general impressions, or idle gossip. Everything, in fact, that could affect the accused injuriously was eagerly sought and scrupulously written down. In the determined effort to ruin the seigneurs de Niort, in 1240, of the one hundred and eight witnesses examined scarce one was able to speak of his own knowledge as to any act of the accused. In 1254 Arnaud Baud of Montréal was qualified as "suspect" of heresy because he continued to visit his mother and aided her in her need after she had been hereticated, though there was absolutely nothing else against him; only delivering her{432} up to be burned would have cleared him. It became, in fact, a settled principle of law that either husband or wife knowing the other to be a heretic and not giving information within a twelvemonth was held to be a consenting party without further evidence, and was punishable as a heretic.[386]

Naturally the conscientious inquisitor recognized the vicious circle in which he moved and sought to satisfy himself that he could designate infallible signs which would justify the conclusion of heresy. There is ample store of such enumerated. Thus for the Cathari it sufficed to show that the accused had venerated one of the perfected, had asked a blessing, had eaten of the blessed bread or had kept it, had been voluntarily present at an heretication, had entered into the *covenansa* to be hereticated on the death-bed, etc. For the Waldenses such indications were considered to be the confessing of sins to and accepting penance from those known not to be regularly ordained by an orthodox bishop, praying with them according to their rites by bending the knees with them on a bench or other inclined object, being present with them when they pretended to make the Host, receiving "peace" from them, or blessed bread. All this was easily catalogued, but beyond it lay a region of doubt concerning which authorities differed. The Council of Albi, in 1254, declared that entering a house, in which a heretic was known to be, converted simple suspicion into vehement; and Bernard Gui mentions that some inquisitors held that visiting heretics, giving them alms, guiding them in their journeys, and the like was sufficient for condemnation, but he agrees with Gui Foucoix in not so considering it, as all this might be done through carnal affection or for hire. The heart of man, he adds, is deep and inscrutable, but he seeks to satisfy himself for attempting the impossible by arguing that all which cannot be explained favorably must be admitted as adverse proof. It is a noteworthy fact that in long series of interrogations there will frequently be not a single question as to the belief of the party making confession. The whole energy of the inquisitor was directed to obtaining statements of external acts. The upshot of it all necessarily was that almost{433} everything was left to the discretion of the inquisitor, whose temper had more to do with the result than the proof of guilt or its absence. How insignificant were the tokens on which a man's fate might depend may be understood by a single instance. In 1234 Accursio Aldobrandini, a Florentine merchant in Paris, made the acquaintance of some strangers with whom he conversed several times, giving their servant on one occasion ten sols, and bowing to them when they met, out of politeness. This latter act was equivalent to the "veneration" which was the crucial test of heresy, and when he chanced to learn that his new acquaintances were heretics he felt himself lost. Hastening to Rome, he laid the matter before Gregory IX., who exacted bail of him and sent a commission to the Bishop of Florence to investigate the antecedents of Accursio. The report was examined by the cardinals of Ostia and Preneste and found to be emphatic in commending his orthodoxy, so he escaped with a penance prescribed by Raymond of Pennaforte, the papal penitentiary, and Gregory wrote to the inquisitors of Paris not to molest him. Under such a system the most devout Catholic could never feel safe for a moment.[387]

Yet in spite of all these efforts to define the indefinable, it was in the very nature of things that absolute certitude could not, in a vast range of cases, be reached except through confession. In order, therefore, to avert the misfortune of acquitting those who could not be brought to confess, it became necessary to invent a new crime—that known as "suspicion of heresy." This opened a wide field for the endless subtleties and refinements in which the jurists of the schools delighted, rendering their so-called science of law a worthy rival of scholastic theology. Suspicion thus was primarily divided into three grades, designated as light, vehement, and violent, and the glossators revel in defining the amount and quality of evidence which renders the accused guilty of either of these, with the usual result that practically the matter was left to the discretion of the tribunal. That a man against whom nothing substantial was proved should be punished merely because he was suspected of guilt may seem to modern eyes a scant measure of justice;{434} but to the inquisitor it appeared a wrong to God and man that any one should escape against whose orthodoxy there rested a shadow of a doubt. Like much else taught by the Inquisition, this found its way into general criminal law, which it perverted for centuries.[388]

Two witnesses were usually assumed to be necessary for the condemnation of a man of good repute, though some authorities demanded more. Yet when a case threatened to fail for lack of testimony, the discretion of the inquisitor was the ultimate arbitrator; and it was agreed that if two witnesses to the same fact could not be had, single witnesses to two separate facts of the same general character would suffice. When there was only one witness in all, the accused was still put on his purgation. With the same determination to remove all obstacles in the way of conviction, if a witness revoked his testimony it was held that if his evidence had been favorable to the accused, the revocation annulled it; if adverse, the revocation was null.[389]

The same disposition to construe everything in favor of the faith governed the admissibility of witnesses of evil character. The Roman law rejected the evidence of accomplices, and the Church had adopted the rule. In the False Decretals it had ordered that no one should be admitted as an accuser who was a heretic or suspected of heresy, was excommunicate, a homicide, a thief, a sorcerer, a diviner, a ravisher, an adulterer, a bearer of false witness, or a consulter of diviners and soothsayers. Yet when it came to prosecuting heresy all these prohibitions were thrown to the winds. As early as the time of Gratian, infamous and heretical witnesses were receivable against heretics. The edicts of Frederic II. rendered heretics incapable of giving testimony, but this disability was removed when they testified against heretics.{435} That there was some hesitation on this point we see in the Legatine Inquisition held in Toulouse in 1229, where it is recorded that Guillem Solier, a converted heretic, was restored in fame in order to enable him to bear witness against his former associates, and even as late as 1260 Alexander IV. was obliged to reassure the French inquisitors that they could safely use the evidence of heretics; but the principle became a settled one, adopted in the canon law, and constantly enforced in practice. Without it, in fact, the Inquisition would have been deprived of its most fruitful means of tracking heretics. It was the same with excommunicates, perjurers, infamous persons, usurers, harlots, and all those who, in the ordinary criminal jurisprudence of the age, were regarded as incapable of bearing witness, yet whose evidence was receivable against heretics. All legal exceptions were declared inoperative except that of mortal enmity.[390]

In the ordinary criminal law of Italy no evidence was received from a witness under twenty, but in cases of heresy such testimony was taken, and, though not legal, it sufficed to justify torture. In France the distinction seems to have been less rigidly defined, and the matter probably was left, like so much else, to the discretion of the inquisitors. As the Council of Albi specifies seven years as the period at which all children were ordered to be made to attend church and learn the Creed, Paternoster, and Salutation to the Virgin, it may be safely assumed that below that age they would hardly be admitted to give testimony. In the records of the Inquisition the age of the witness is rarely stated, but I have met with one case, in 1244, after the capture of the pestilent nest of heretics at Montségur, where the Inquisition gathered so goodly a{436} harvest, when the age of a witness, Arnaud Olivier, happens to be mentioned as ten years. He admitted having been a Catharan "believer" since he had reached the age of discretion, and thus was responsible for himself and others. His evidence is gravely recorded against his father, his sister, and nearly seventy others; and in it he is made to give the names of sixty-six persons who were present about a year before at the sermon of a Catharan bishop. The wonderful exercise of so young a memory does not seem to have excited any doubts as to the validity of his testimony, which must have been held conclusive against the unfortunates enumerated, as he stated that they all "venerated" their prelate.[391]

Wives and children and servants were not admitted to give evidence in favor of the accused, but their testimony if adverse to him was welcomed, and was considered peculiarly strong. It was the same with the heretic, who, as we have seen, was freely admitted as an adverse witness, but who was rejected if appearing for the defence. In short, the only exception which could be taken to an accusing witness was malignity. If he was a mortal enemy of the prisoner it was presumed that his testimony was rather the prompting of hate than zeal for the faith, and it was required to be thrown out. In the case of the dead, the evidence of a priest that he had shriven the defunct and administered the *viaticum* went for nothing; but if he testified that the departed had confessed to being a heretic, had recanted, and had received absolution, then his bones were not exhumed and burned, but the heirs had to endure such penance of fine or confiscation as would have been inflicted on him if alive.[392]

Of course no witness could refuse to give evidence. No privilege or vow or oath released him from the duty. If he was unwilling and paltered or prevaricated and equivocated, there was the gentle persuasion of the torture-chamber, which, as we have seen,{437} was even more freely used on witnesses than on principals. It was the ready instrument by which any doubts as to the testimony could be cleared up; and it is fair to attribute to the sanction of this terrible abuse by the Inquisition the currency which it so long enjoyed in European criminal law. Even the secrecy of the confessional was not respected in the frenzied effort to obtain all possible information against heretics. All priests were enjoined to make strict inquiries of their penitents as to their knowledge of heretics and fautors of heresy. The seal of sacramental confession could not be openly and habitually violated, but the result was reached by indirection. When the confessor succeeded in learning anything he was told to write it down and then endeavor to induce his penitent to reveal it to the proper authorities. Failing in this, he was, without mentioning names, to consult God-fearing experts as to what he ought to do— with what effect can readily be conjectured, since the very fact of consulting as to his duty shows that the obligation of secrecy was not to be deemed absolute.[393]

After this glimpse at the inquisitorial system of evidence, we hardly need the assurance of the legists that less was required for conviction in heresy than in any other crime, and inquisitors were instructed that slender testimony was sufficient to prove it—"*probatur quis hæreticus ex levi causa.*" Yet evil as was all this, the crowning infamy of the Inquisition in its treatment of testimony was withholding from the accused all knowledge of the names of the witnesses against him. In the ordinary courts, even in the inquisitorial process, their names were communicated to him along with the evidence which they had given, and it will be remembered that when the Legate Romano held his inquest at Toulouse, in 1229, the accused followed him to Montpellier with demands{438} to see the names of those who had testified against them, when the cardinal recognized their right to this, but eluded it by showing merely a long list of all the witnesses who had appeared during the whole inquest, giving as an excuse the danger to which they were exposed from the malevolence of those who had suffered by their evidence. That there was some risk incurred by those who destroyed their neighbors is true; the inquisitors and chroniclers mention that assassinations from this cause sometimes occurred—six being reported in Toulouse between 1301 and 1310. It would have been strange had this not been the case, nor was the chance of such wild justice altogether an unwholesome check upon the security of malevolence. Yet that so flimsy an excuse should have been systematically put forward shows merely that the Church recognized and was ashamed of its plain denial of justice, since no such precaution was deemed necessary in other criminal affairs. Already in 1244 and 1246 the councils of Narbonne and Béziers order the inquisitors not to indicate in any manner the names of the witnesses, alleging as a reason the "prudent wish" of the Holy See, although in the instructions of the Cardinal of Albano the saving clause of risk is expressed. When Innocent IV. and his successors regulated the inquisitorial procedure, the same limitation to cases in which divulging the names would expose the witnesses to danger was sometimes omitted and sometimes repeated, and when Boniface VIII. embodied in the canon law the rule of withholding the names he expressly cautioned bishops and inquisitors to act with pure intentions, not to withhold the names when there was no peril in communicating them, and if the peril ceased they were to be revealed. Yet it is impossible to regard all this as more than a decent veil of hypocrisy to cover recognized injustice, for it was a flagrant fact that inquisitors everywhere treated these exhortations as the councils of Narbonne and Béziers had treated the limitations prescribed by the Cardinal of Albano. Although in the inquisitorial manuals the limitation of risk is usually mentioned, the instructions with regard to the conduct of the trials always assume as a matter of course that the prisoner is kept in ignorance of the names of the witnesses against him. As early as the time of Gui Foucoix that jurist treats it as the universal practice; a nearly contemporary MS. manual lays it down as an invariable rule; and in the later periods we are coolly{439} informed by both Eymerich and Bernardo di Como that cases were rare in which risk did not exist; that it was great when the accused was rich and powerful, but greater still when he was poor and had friends who had nothing to lose. Eymerich evidently considers it much more decent to refuse the names than to adopt the expedients of some over-conscientious inquisitors who furnished, like Cardinal Romano, the names written on a different piece of paper and so arranged that their identification with their evidence was impossible, or who mixed up other names with those of the witnesses so as to confuse hopelessly the defence. Occasionally a less disreputable but almost equally confusing plan was adopted, in swearing a portion of the witnesses in the presence of the accused, while examining them in his absence. Thus in the trial of Bernard Délicieux, in 1319, out of forty-eight witnesses whose depositions are recorded, sixteen were sworn in his presence; in that of Huss, in 1414, it is mentioned that fifteen witnesses at one time were taken to his cell that he might see them sworn.[394]

From this withholding of names it was but a step to withholding the evidence altogether, and that step was sometimes taken. In truth the whole process was so completely at the arbitrary discretion of the inquisitor, and the accused was so wholly without rights, that whatever seemed good in the eyes of the former was allowable in the interest of the faith. Thus we are told that if a witness retracted his evidence, the fact should not be made known to the defendant lest it should encourage him in his defence, but the judge is recommended to bear it in mind when rendering{440} judgment. The tender care for the safety of witnesses even went so far that it was left to the conscience of the inquisitor whether or not to give the accused a copy of the evidence itself if there appeared to be danger to be apprehended from doing so. Relieved from all supervision, and practically not subject to appeals, it may be said that there were no rules which the inquisitor might not suspend or abrogate at pleasure when the exigencies of the faith seemed to require it.[395]

Among the many evils springing from this concealment, which released witnesses and accusers from all responsibility, not the least was the stimulus which it afforded to delation and the temptation created to gratify malice by reckless perjury. Even without any special desire to do mischief, an unfortunate, whose resolution had been broken down by suffering and torture, when brought at last to confess, might readily be led to make his story as satisfactory as possible to his tormentors by mentioning all names that might occur to him as being present at conventicles and heretications. There can be no question that the business of the Inquisition was greatly increased by the protection which it thus afforded to informers and enemies, and that it was made the instrument of an immense amount of false-witness. The inquisitors felt this danger and frequently took such precautions as they could without trouble, by warning a witness of the penalties incurred by perjury, making him obligate himself in advance to endure them, and rigidly questioning him as to whether he had been suborned. Occasionally, also, we find a conscientious judge like Bernard Gui carefully sifting evidence, comparing the testimony of different witnesses, and tracing out incompatibilities which proved that one at least was false. He accomplished this twice, once in 1312 and again in 1316, the earlier case presenting some peculiar features. A man named Pons Arnaud came forward spontaneously and accused his son Pierre of having endeavored to have him hereticated when laboring under apparently mortal sickness. The son denied it. Bernard, on investigation, found that Pons had not been sick at the date specified, and that there had been no heretics at the place named. Armed with this information{441} he speedily forced the accuser to confess that he had fabricated the story to injure his son. Creditable as is this case to the inquisitor, it is hideously suggestive of the pitfalls which lay around the feet of every man; and no less so is an instance in which Henri de Chamay, Inquisitor of Carcassonne, in 1329, resolutely traced out a conspiracy to ruin an innocent man, and had the satisfaction of forcing five false-witnesses to confess their guilt. Rare instances such as these, however, offered but a feeble palliation for the inherent vices of the system, and in spite of the severe punishment meted out to those who were discovered, the crime was of very frequent occurrence. The security with which it could be committed renders it safe to assume that detection occurred in a very small proportion of the cases; so when among the scanty documents that have reached us we see six false-witnesses (of whom two were priests and one a clerk), sentenced at an *auto de fé* held at Pamiers in 1323; four at Narbonne in December, 1328; one, a few weeks after, at Pamiers; four more at Pamiers in January, 1329, and seven (one of whom was a notary) at Carcassonne in September, 1329, we may conclude that if the full records of the Inquisition were accessible, the list would be a frightful one, and would suggest an incalculable amount of injustice which remained undiscovered. We do not need the admission of Eymerich that witnesses are found frequently to conspire together to ruin an innocent man, and we may well doubt his assurance that persistent scrutiny by the inquisitor will detect the wrong. There is, perhaps, only a consistent exhibition of inquisitorial logic in the dictum of Zanghino, that a witness who withdraws testimony adverse to a prisoner is to be punished for false-witness, while his testimony is to stand, and to receive full weight in rendering judgment.[396]

A false-witness, when detected, was treated with as little mercy as a heretic. As a symbol of his crime two pieces of red cloth in the shape of tongues were affixed to his breast and two to his back, to be worn through life. He was exhibited at the church-doors on a scaffolding during divine service on Sundays, and was{442} usually imprisoned for life. The symbol was changed to that of a letter in the case of Guillem Maurs, condemned in 1322 for conspiring with others to forge letters of the Inquisition whereby some parties were to be cited for heresy with the view of extorting hush-money from them. As the degree of criminality varied, so there were differences in the severity of punishment. Those condemned in Pamiers in 1323 were let off without incarceration. The four at Narbonne, in 1328, were regarded as peculiarly culpable, having been suborned by enemies of the accused, and they were accordingly condemned to the severest form of imprisonment, on bread and water, with chains on hands and feet. The assembly of experts held at Pamiers for the *auto* of January, 1329, decided that, in addition to imprisonment, either lenient or harsh, according to the gravity of the offence, the offenders should make good any damage accruing to the accused. This was an approach to the *talio*, and the principle was fully carried out in 1518 by Leo X. in a rescript to the Spanish Inquisition, authorizing the abandonment to the secular arm of false witnesses who had succeeded in inflicting any notable injury on their victims. The expressions used by the pope justify the conclusion that the crime was still frequent. Zanghino tells us that in his time there was no defined legal penalty, and that the false witness was to be punished at the discretion of the inquisitor—another instance of the tendency which pervades the whole inquisitorial jurisprudence, to fetter the tribunals with as few rules as possible, to clothe them with arbitrary power, and trust to God, in whose name and for whose glory they professed to act, to inspire them with the wisdom necessary for the discharge of their irresponsible trust.[397] {443}

CHAPTER XI.

THE DEFENCE.

FROM the preceding sketch of the inquisitorial process it may readily be inferred that scant opportunities for defence were allowed by the Holy Office. It was in the very nature of the process that all the preliminary proceedings were taken in secrecy and without the knowledge of the accused. The case against him was made up before his arrest, and he was examined, urged to confess, and perhaps imprisoned for years and tortured, before he was allowed to know what were the charges against him. It was only after a confession had been extorted from him, or the inquisitor despaired of extorting one, that he was furnished with the evidence against him, and even then the names of the witnesses were habitually suppressed. All this is in cruel contrast with the righteous care to avoid injustice prescribed for the ordinary episcopal courts. In them the Council of Lateran orders that the accused shall be present at the inquisition against him, unless he contumaciously absents himself; the charges are to be explained to him, that he may have the opportunity of defending himself; the witnesses' names, with their respective evidence, are to be made public, and all legitimate exceptions and answers be admitted, for suppression of names would invite slander, and rejection of exceptions would admit false testimony.[398] The suspected heretic, however, was prejudged. The effort of the inquisitor was not to avoid injustice, but to force him to admit his guilt and seek reconciliation with the Church. To accomplish this effectually the facilities for defence were systematically reduced to a minimum. {444}

It is true that, in 1246, the Council of Béziers lays down the rule that the accused shall have proper opportunities for defence, including necessary delays and the admission of exceptions and legitimate replies; but if this were intended as a check on the arbitrary operations which already characterized the Inquisition, it was wholly disregarded. In the first place, the secrecy of the tribunal enabled the judge to do as he might think best. In the second place, the only possible remaining check to arbitrary action was removed by denying to the accused the advantage of counsel. Then, as now, the intricacy of legal forms rendered the trained advocate a necessity to every man on trial; the layman, ignorant of his rights, and of the method of enforcing them, was utterly helpless. So thoroughly was this understood that in the ecclesiastical courts it was frequently a custom to furnish advocates gratuitously to poor men unable to employ them, and in the charter granted by Simon de Montfort, in 1212, to his newly-acquired territories, it was provided that justice should always be gratuitous, and that counsel should be provided by the court for pleaders too poor to retain them. When this right thus was recognized in the most trifling cases, to refuse it to those who were battling for their lives before a tribunal in which the judge was also prosecutor, was more than the Church at first dared openly to do, but it practically reached the result by indirection. Innocent III., in a decretal embodied in the canon law, had ordered advocates and scriveners to lend no aid or counsel to heretics and their defenders, or to undertake their causes in litigation. This, which was presumably intended as one of the disabilities inflicted on defiant and acknowledged heretics, was readily applied to the suspect who were not yet convicted, and who were struggling to prove their innocence, for their guilt was always assumed in advance. The councils of Valence and Albi, in 1248 and 1254, while ordering inquisitors not to embarrass themselves with the vain jangling of lawyers in the conduct of the prosecution, significantly make reference to this provision of the canon law as applicable to counsel who might be so hardy as to aid the defence. That this became a settled and recognized principle is shown by Bernard Gui's assertion that advocates who excuse and defend heretics are to be held guilty of fautorship of heresy—a crime which became heresy itself if satisfaction at the discretion of the {445} inquisitor was not rendered within a twelvemonth. When to this we add the perpetually reiterated commands to the inquisitors to proceed without regard to legal forms or the wrangling of advocates, and the notice to notaries that he who drew up the revocation of a confession was excommunicated as an impeder of the Inquisition, it will readily be seen that there was no need of formally refusing counsel to the accused, and that there was no practical benefit permitted from the admission of the barren generality that one who believed a heretic to be innocent and endeavored to prove him so was not on that account liable to punishment. Eymerich is careful to specify that the accused has the right to employ counsel, and that a denial of this justifies an appeal, but then he likewise states that the inquisitor can prosecute any advocate or notary who undertakes the cause of heretics; and a century earlier a manuscript manual for inquisitors directs them to prosecute as defenders of heresy any advocates who take such cases, with the addition that if they are clerks they are to be perpetually deprived of their benefices. It is no wonder, therefore, that finally inquisitors adopted the rule that advocates were not to be allowed in inquisitorial trials. This injustice had its compensation, however, for the employment of counsel, in fact, was likely to prove as dangerous to the defendant as to his advocate, for the Inquisition was entitled to all accessible information, and could summon the latter as a witness, force him to surrender any papers in his hands, and reveal what had passed between him and his client. Such considerations, however, are rather theoretical than practical, for it may well be doubted whether, in the ordinary course of the Inquisition, counsel for the defence ever appeared before it. The terror that it inspired is well illustrated by the circumstance that when, in 1300, Friar Bernard Délicieux was commissioned by his Franciscan provincial to defend the memory of Castel Fabri, and Nicholas d'Abbeville, the Inquisitor of Carcassonne, rudely refused him even an audience, he could find no notary in the city who dared to assist him in drawing up a legal protest; every one feared arrest and prosecution if he took the least part in an opposition to the dreaded inquisitor, and Bernard had to wait ten or twelve days until he could bring a notary from a distance to perform the simplest formality. The local officials might well hesitate to incur the wrath of Nicholas, for a few years before he had{446} cast in jail a notary who had ventured to draw up an appeal of the inhabitants of Carcassonne to the king.[399]

All this is interesting as an illustration of the spirit which pervaded every act of the Inquisition, but in reality no advocate could be of material service to the accused, save in the most exceptional cases. The men who organized the Holy Office knew too well what they wanted to leave open any possibilities of which even the shrewdest advocate could take advantage, and it was admitted on all hands as a recognized fact that there was no method of defence save disabling the witnesses for the prosecution. It has been seen that enmity was the only source of disability in a witness, and this had to be mortal—there must have been bloodshed between the parties, or other cause sufficient to induce one to seek the life of the other. If, therefore, the case rested on witnesses of this kind, their testimony had to be rejected and the prosecution fell. As this was the only possible mode of escape, the cruelty of withholding from the prisoner the names of the adverse witnesses becomes doubly conspicuous. He was forced to grope around in the dark and blindly name such persons as he imagined might have a hand in his misfortunes. If he failed to hit upon any who appeared in the case, the evidence against him was conclusive, as far as it went. If he chanced to name some of the witnesses, he was interrogated as to the causes of enmity; the inquisitor examined into the facts of the alleged quarrel, and decided as he saw fit as to the retention or the rejection of their testimony. Conscientious jurists like Gui Foucoix and inquisitors like Eymerich warned their brethren that as the accused had so slender a chance of guessing the sources of evidence, the judge ought to investigate for himself and discard any that seemed to be the product of malice; but there were others who sought rather to deprive the poor wretch of every straw that might postpone his sinking. One device was to ask him, as though{447} casually, at the end of his examination, whether he had any enemies who would so disregard the fear of God as to accuse him falsely, and if, thus taken unawares, he replied in the negative, he debarred himself from any subsequent defence; or the most damaging witness would be selected and the prisoner be asked if he knew him, when a denial would estop him from claiming enmity. It is easy to imagine other tricks by which shrewd and experienced inquisitors could save themselves the trouble of admitting the accused to even the nugatory form of defence to which alone he was entitled. As to allowing him to call witnesses in his favor, except to prove enmity of the accusers, it was never thought of in ordinary cases. By a legal fiction, the inquisitor was supposed to look at both sides of the case, and to take care of the defence as well as of the prosecution. If the accused failed to guess the names of enemies among the witnesses and to disable their testimony, he was condemned.[400]

In England, under the barbarous custom of the *peine forte et dure*, a prisoner who refused to plead either guilty or not guilty was pressed to death, because the trial could not go on without either confession or defence. Cruel as was this expedient, it was the outcome of a manly sense of justice, which based its procedure on the rule that the worst felon should have a fair opportunity to prove his innocence. Far worse was the system of the Inquisition, which was equally resolved that its culprits should have no such easy method of escape as a refusal to plead. It had no scruples as to proceeding in such cases, and the obstinacy of the accused only simplified matters. The refusal was an act of contumacy, equivalent to disobeying a summons to appear, or it was held to be tantamount to a confession, and the obdurate prisoner was forthwith handed over to the secular arm as an impenitent heretic, fit only for the stake. The use of torture, however, rendered such cases rare.[401]{448}

The enviable simplicity which the inquisitorial process thus assumed in the absence of counsel and of all practical opportunities for defence can perhaps best be illustrated by one or two cases. Thus in the Inquisition of Carcassonne, June 19, 1252, P. Morret is called up and asked if he wishes to defend himself against the matters found in the *instructio* or indictment against him. He has nothing to allege except that he has enemies, of whom he names five. Apparently he did not happen to guess any of the witnesses, for the case proceeded by reading the evidence to him, after which he is again asked thrice if he has anything further to say. To this he replies in the negative, and the case ends by assigning January 29 for the rendering of sentence. Two years later, in 1254, at Carcassonne, a certain Bernard Pons was more lucky, for he happened to guess aright in naming his wife as an inimical witness, and we have the proceedings of the inquest held to determine whether the enmity was mortal.

147

Three witnesses are examined, all of whom swear that she is a woman of loose character; one deposes that she had been taken in adultery by her husband; another that he had beaten her for it, and the third that he had recently heard her say that she wished her husband dead that she might marry a certain Pug Oler, and that she would willingly become a leper if that would bring it about. This would certainly seem sufficient, but Pons appears nevertheless not to have escaped. So thoroughly hopeless, indeed, was the prospect of any effort at defence, that it frequently was not even attempted, and the accused, like Arnaud Fabri at Carcassonne, August 20, 1252, when asked if he wished a copy of the evidence against him, would despairingly decline it. It was a customary formula in a sentence to state that the convict had been offered opportunity for defence and had not availed himself of it, showing how frequently this was the case.[402]

In the case of prosecution of the dead, the children or the heirs were scrupulously cited to appear and defend his memory, as they were necessarily parties to the case through the disabilities and confiscation following upon condemnation. Proclamation was also{449} made publicly in the churches inviting any one else who chose to appear or who had any interest in the matter by reason of holding property of the deceased; and then a third public notice was given that if no one came forward on the day named, definitive sentence would be rendered. Thus in a case occurring in 1327, Jean Duprat, Inquisitor of Carcassonne, orders the priests of all the churches in the dioceses of Carcassonne, Narbonne, and Alet to publish the notice during divine service on every Sunday and feast-day till the day of hearing, and to send him a notarial attestation of their action. The sentences in these cases are careful to recite these notices so sedulously served on all concerned; but notwithstanding this display of a desire to do exact justice, the proceedings were quite as hollow a mockery as those against the living. That it was so recognized is seen at the *auto* of 1309 at Toulouse, where there were four dead persons sentenced, and it is stated that in one case no one appeared, and in the other three the heirs obeyed the citation but renounced all defence. In the case of Castel Fabri, before alluded to, at Carcassonne, in 1300, where the estate was very large, the heirs appeared, but were denied all opportunity of defence by Nicholas d'Abbeville, the inquisitor; and in that of Pierre de Tornamire, though the heirs, as we have seen, succeeded in reversing the judgment through the gross informality of the proceedings, it was not until after a struggle which lasted for thirty-two years, during which time the estate must have been sequestrated. Sometimes, when death-bed heretications had occurred, the children put in the plea of *non compos*, which was admitted to be good, but as none of the family were allowed to testify, and only disinterested witnesses of approved orthodoxy were received, instances of success must have been rare indeed.[403]

Practically every avenue of escape was closed to those who fell into the hands of the inquisitor. Technically the accused had a right, as in other cases, to recuse his judge, but this was a dangerous experiment, and we hardly need the assurance of Bernardo di{450}Como that it was virtually unknown. Ignorance was no defence, and its mere assertion, according to Bernard Gui, only rendered a man worthy of condemnation along with his master, the father of lies. Persistent denial of the offence charged, even when accompanied with profession of faith and readiness to submit to the mandates of the Church, was obstinacy and impenitence which precluded all hope of mercy. Even suicide in prison was equivalent to confession of guilt without repentance. It is true that insanity or drunkenness might be urged in extenuation of the utterance of heretical words, and this might mitigate the sentence, if there were due contrition and seeking for reconciliation, but admission of the conclusion at which the inquisitor had arrived from his *ex parte* inquest was the predetermined result, and the only alternative to this was abandonment to the secular arm.[404]

That plain-spoken friar, Bernard Délicieux, uttered the literal truth when he declared, in the presence of Philippe le Bel and all his court, that if St. Peter and St. Paul were accused of "adoring" heretics and were prosecuted after the fashion of the Inquisition, there would be no defence open for them. Questioned as to their faith, they would answer like masters in theology and doctors of the Church, but when told that they had adored heretics, and they asked what heretics, some names, common in those parts, would be mentioned, but no particulars would be given. When they would ask for statements as to time and place, no facts would be furnished, and when they would demand the names of the witnesses these would be withheld. How, then, asked Bernard, could the holy apostles defend themselves, especially when any one who wished to aid them would himself be attacked as a fautor of heresy. It was so. The victim was enveloped in a net from which there was no escape, and his frantic struggles only twisted it more tightly around him.[405]

Theoretically, indeed, an appeal lay to the pope from the Holy Office, and to the metropolitan from the bishop, for denial of justice{451} or irregularity of procedure, but it had to be made before sentence was rendered, as condemnation was final. Possibly this may have held out some prospect of benefit in the case of bishops exercising their inquisitorial jurisdiction. In that of inquisitors, when "*apostoli*," or letters remanding the case to the Holy See, were demanded, it rested with them to grant affirmative ("reverential") ones, or negative ones. The former admitted the transfer of the case; the latter kept it in the inquisitor's hands unless it was formally taken from him by the pope. This, it is safe to say, could rarely happen, and, as the proceeding was an intricate one, it could only be resorted to by experts. A man like Master Eckart, supported by the whole Dominican Order, could undertake it, even though in the end he fared no better at the hands of John XXII. than he would have done at those of the Archbishop of Cologne. So when, in 1323, the Sire de Partenay, one of the most powerful nobles of Poitou, was cited for heresy by Friar Maurice, the Inquisitor of Paris, and was thrown into the Temple by Charles le Bel, he appealed from Maurice as a judge prejudiced by personal hatred.

Charles sent him under guard to John XXII. at Avignon, who at first refused to entertain the appeal, but at length, by the influential intercession of Partenay's friends, was induced to appoint several bishops as assessors to the inquisitor, and after long-protracted proceedings the interest of Partenay was sufficient to obtain his liberation. Cases like these, however, are wholly exceptional and have no bearing upon the thousands of humble folk and "*petite noblesse*" who filled the prisons of the Inquisition and figured in its *autos de fé*. The manuals for inquisitors, indeed, make no scruple in instructing them as to the devices and deceits by which they can elude all attempts to appeal when through disregard of rules they have exposed themselves to it.[406]

There was another class of cases, however, in which the interference of the pope occasionally gave relief, for the Holy See was autocratic and could set aside all rules. The curia was always greedy for money, and, outside of Italy, had no share in the confiscations. It can, therefore, readily be imagined that men of {452} wealth whose whole property was at stake might well consent to divide it with the papal court, whose all-powerful intervention would thereby be secured. As early as 1245 the bishops of Languedoc are found complaining to Innocent IV. of the number of heretics who thus obtain exemption. Not only those undergoing trial, but those fearing to be cited, those excommunicated for contumacy, or legitimately sentenced, escape the jurisdiction of the Inquisition and enjoy immunity on the strength of letters granted by the papal penitentiaries. I have met with a number of special cases of this interference of the Holy See with the Holy Office, one at least of which indicates the means of persuasion employed. In letters of December 28, 1248, the papal penitentiary Algisius orders the release, without confiscation, of six prisoners of the Inquisition who had confessed to heresy, one of the reasons assigned being the liberal contributions which they had made to the cause of the Holy Land. It is no wonder that the inquisitors sometimes grew mutinous under this aggravating interference, of which they could so readily guess the motive, and, on one occasion at least, they gave the curia a lesson. Some inhabitants of Limoux, in 1249, condemned to wear crosses and perform heavy penances, obtained from Innocent IV. an order for their mitigation, whereupon the inquisitors, in their irritation, went a step further and absolved the penitents without reserve. Accepting this rebuke, Innocent commanded the original sentence to be reimposed, and the unlucky culprits gained nothing by their effort. Less questionable was the interference, in 1255, of Alexander IV. in the case of Aimeric de Bressols of Castel-Sarrazin, who had been condemned for heretical acts committed thirty years before. He represented that he had performed most of the penance enjoined on him and that he was unable, through old age and poverty, to accomplish the rest, whereupon the pope mercifully authorized the Inquisitors to commute it into other pious works. A somewhat remarkable case occurred in 1371, when Gregory XI. authorized the Inquisitor of Carcassonne to release Bidon de Puy-Guillem, condemned to perpetual imprisonment, and repentant, the reason given for papal intervention being that there existed no other power to commute the sentence.[407] {453}

This kind of papal intervention, however, was in contravention of the law and not in its fulfilment, and need not be weighed in considering the results of the inquisitorial process. That result, as might be expected, was condemnation in some form or other so uniformly that it may be regarded as inevitable. In the register of Carcassonne from 1249 to 1258, comprising about two hundred cases, there does not occur a single instance of a prisoner discharged as innocent. It is true that the interrogatory of Alizaïs Debax, March 27, 1249, is followed by the note "she was not heard a second time because she was considered innocent," but this apparent exception is nullified by a second memorandum "*crucesignata est*"—she was condemned to the public infamy of wearing crosses, probably to confirm the popular impression that the Inquisition never missed its mark. A man against whom there was no evidence to justify conviction and who yet would not confess himself guilty, was kept in prison indefinitely at the discretion of the inquisitor; at length, if the proof against him was only incidental and not direct, and the suspicion was light, he might be mercifully discharged under bail, with orders to stand at the door of the Inquisition from breakfast-time until dinner, and from dinner until supper, until some further testimony should turn up against him, and the inquisitor be able to prove the guilt so confidently assumed. On this side of the Alps it was a recognized rule that no one should be acquitted. The utmost stretch of justice, when the accusation failed entirely, was a sentence of not proven. The charges were simply declared not to be substantiated, and the inquisitors were carefully warned never to pronounce a man innocent, so that there might be no bar to subsequent proceedings in case of further evidence. Possibly in Italy, in the fourteenth century, this rule may have been neglected, for Zanghino gives a formula of acquittal, based, significantly enough, on the evidence being proved to be malicious.[408]

Clement V. recognized the injustice wrought under this system when he embodied in the canon law a declaration that inquisitors abused to the injury of the faithful the wise provisions made for the defence of the faith; when he forbade them from falsely convicting {454} any one, or acting either for or against the accused through love, hate, or the hopes of gain, under penalty of *ipso facto* excommunication, removable only by the Holy See. Bernard Gui hotly denied these assertions, which he declared to be precisely those with which the heretics defamed the Holy Office to its great damage. To impute heresy to the innocent, he said, is worthy of damnation, but none the less so is it to slander the Inquisition. In spite, he adds, of the refutation of the accusations brought against it, this canon assumes their truth and the heretics exult over its disgrace. If the heretics exulted, their rejoicings were premature. The Inquisition went its way in the accustomed paths, and Clement's well-meant effort at reform proved wholly unavailing.[409]

149

The erection of suspicion into a crime gave ample opportunity for the habitual avoidance of acquittal. This took its origin in the customs of the barbarian and mediæval codes, which required the accused, against whom a probable case was made out, to demonstrate his innocence either by the ordeal, or by the form of purgation known in England as the Wager of Law, in which he produced a prescribed number of his friends to share with him the oath of denial. In the coronation-edict of Frederic II. those who were suspected of heresy were required to purge themselves in this manner, as the Church might demand, under pain of being outlawed, and, if they remained so for a year, of being condemned as heretics. This gave a peculiar and sinister significance to suspicion of heresy which was carefully elaborated and turned to account. Suspicion might arise from many causes, the chief of which was popular rumor and belief. Omission to take the oath abjuring heresy imposed on all the inhabitants of Languedoc, within the term prescribed, was sufficient, or neglect to reveal heretics, or the possession of heretical books. The intricate questions to which this extension of criminality gave rise are fairly illustrated in the discussion of an inquisitor whether those who listened to the instructions of the Waldenses, "Do not lie, nor swear, nor commit fornication, but give to every man his due; go to church, pay your tithes, and the perquisites of the priests," and, knowing this to be good advice, conclude the utterers to be good men— whether such{455} are to be considered suspect of heresy; and he tells us that after diligent consideration he must decide in the affirmative, and order them to purgation. The difficulty of reducing to practice these intangible speculations was realized by Chancellor Gerson, who admits that due allowance should be made for variations of habits and manners in different places and times, but the ordinary inquisitor was troubled with few such scruples. It was easier to treat the suspect as criminals; to classify suspicion into its three grades of light, vehement, and violent; to prescribe punishment for it, and to inflict the disabilities of heresy on the suspect and their descendants. Even the definition of the three grades of suspicion was abandoned as impossible, and it was left to the arbitrary discretion of the inquisitor to classify each individual case which came before him. Nothing more condemnatory of the whole system can well be imagined than the explanation of Eymerich that suspects are not heretics; that they are not to be condemned for heresy, and that therefore their punishment should be lighter, except in the case of violent suspicion. Against this there was no defence possible, and no evidence to be admitted. The culprit might not be a heretic or entertain any error of belief, but if he would not abjure and give satisfaction (and abjuration included confession), he was to be handed over to the secular arm; if he confessed and sought reconciliation, he was to be imprisoned for life.[410]

For light and vehement suspicion the accused was ordered to furnish conjurators in his oath of denial. These were to be men{456} of his own rank in life, who knew him personally and who swore to their belief in his orthodoxy and in the truth of his exculpatory oath. Their number varied, at the discretion of the inquisitor, with the degree of suspicion to be purged away, from three to twenty or thirty, and even more. In the case of strangers, however, who had no acquaintances, the inquisitor was advised to be moderate. It was no mere idle ceremony, and, as usual, all the chances were thrown against the defendant. If he was unable to procure the required number of compurgators, or neglected to do so within a year, the law of Frederic II. was enforced, and he was usually condemned as a heretic to burning alive; although some inquisitors argued that this was only presumptive, not absolute, proof, and that he could escape the stake by confessing and abjuring—of course being subject to the penance of perpetual prison. If he succeeded and performed his purgation duly, he was by no means acquitted. If the suspicion against him was vehement he could still be punished; even if it was light the fact that he had been suspected was an ineradicable blot. With the curious logical inconsequence characteristic of inquisitorial procedure, in addition to the purgation, he was obliged to abjure the heresy of which he had cleared himself; this abjuration remained of record against him, and in case of a second accusation his escape from the previous one was not reckoned as having proved his innocence, but as an evidence of guilt. If the purgation had been for light suspicion, his punishment now was increased; and if it had been for vehement suspicion, he was now regarded as a relapsed, to whom no mercy could be shown, but who was handed over to the secular arm without a hearing. Practically, however, this injustice is important chiefly as a manifestation of the spirit of the Inquisition; its methods were too thorough to render frequent a recourse to purgation, and Zanghino, when he treats of it, feels obliged to explain it as a custom little known. One case, however, at least, is on record at Angermünde, where the inquisitor Friar Jordan, in 1336, tried by this method a number of persons accused of the mysterious Luciferan heresy, when fourteen men and women who were unable to procure the requisite number of compurgators were duly burned.[411]{457}

An indispensable formality in all cases in which the culprit was admitted to reconciliation with the Church was abjuration of heresy. Of this there were various forms adapted to the different occasions of its use— whether for suspicion, light, vehement, or violent, or after confession and repentance. It was performed in public, at the *autos de fé*, except in rare cases, such as those of ecclesiastics likely to cause scandal, and it frequently embodied a pecuniary penalty for infraction of its promises, and security for their performance. The principal point to be observed in all was to see that the penitent abjured heresy in general as well as the special heresy with which he had been charged. If this were duly attended to, he could always be handed over to the secular arm without a hearing in case of relapse, except when the abjuration had been for light suspicion. If it were neglected, and he had, for instance, abjured Catharism only, he might subsequently indulge in some other form of heresy, such as Waldensianism or usury, and have the benefit of another chance. The case was one not likely to occur, but the point is interesting as showing how the Inquisition could manifest the most scrupulous attention to form, while discarding in its practice all that entitles the administration of justice to respect. The importance attached to the abjuration is illustrated by a case in the Inquisition of Toulouse in 1310. Sibylla, wife of Bernard Borell, had been forced to confession and abjuration in 1305. Continuing her heretical practices, she was arrested in 1309 and again obliged to confess. As a relapsed heretic she was doomed irrevocably to the stake, but, luckily for her, the abjuration could not be found among the papers of the Holy Office, and though the rest of the record seems to have been accessible, she could only be prosecuted as though for a first offence, and she escaped with imprisonment for life.[412]

In the case of suspects of heresy who cleared themselves by compurgation, abjuration, of course, did not include confession.{458} In accusations of heresy, supported by evidence, however, no one could be admitted to abjuration who did not confess that of which he was accused. Denial, as we have seen, was obduracy, punished by the stake, and confession was a condition precedent to admission to abjuration. In ordinary cases, where torture was freely used, confession was almost a matter of course. There were extraordinary cases, however, like that of Huss at Constance, where torture was spared and where the accused denied the doctrines attributed to him. In such cases the necessity of confession prior to abjuration must be borne in mind if we are to understand the inevitable consequences.{459}

CHAPTER XII.

THE SENTENCE.

THE penal functions of the Inquisition were based upon a fiction which must be comprehended in order rightly to appreciate much of its action. Theoretically it had no power to inflict punishment. Its mission was to save men's souls; to recall them to the way of salvation, and to assign salutary penance to those who sought it, like a father-confessor with his penitents. Its sentences, therefore, were not, like those of an earthly judge, the retaliation of society on the wrong-doer, or deterrent examples to prevent the spread of crime; they were simply imposed for the benefit of the erring soul, to wash away its sin. The inquisitors themselves habitually speak of their ministrations in this sense. When they condemned a poor wretch to lifelong imprisonment, the formula in use, after the procedure of the Holy Office had become systematized, was a simple injunction on him to betake himself to the jail and confine himself there, performing penance on bread and water, with a warning that he was not to leave it under pain of excommunication, and of being regarded as a perjured and impenitent heretic. If he broke jail and escaped, the requisition for his recapture under a foreign jurisdiction describes him, with a singular lack of humor, as one insanely led to reject the salutary medicine offered for his cure, and to spurn the wine and oil which were soothing his wounds.[413]

Technically, therefore, the list of penalties available to the inquisitor{460} was limited. He never condemned to death, but merely withdrew the protection of the Church from the hardened and impenitent sinner who afforded no hope of conversion, or from him who showed by relapse that there was no trust to be placed in his pretended repentance. Except in Italy, he never confiscated the heretic's property; he merely declared the existence of a crime which, under the secular law, rendered the culprit incapable of possession. At most he could impose a fine, as a penance, to be expended in good works. His tribunal was a spiritual one, and dealt only with the sins and remedies of the spirit, under the inspiration of the Gospels, which always lay open before it. Such, at least, was the theory of the Church, and this must be borne in mind if we would understand what may occasionally seem to be inconsistencies and incongruities—especially in view of the arbitrary discretion which left to the individual inquisitor such opportunity to display his personal characteristics in dealing with the penitents before him. He was a judge in the forum of conscience, bound by no statutes and limited by no rules, with his penitents at his mercy, and no power save that of the Holy See itself could alter one jot of his decrees.[414]

This sometimes led to a lenity which would be otherwise inexplicable, as in the case of the murderers of St. Peter Martyr. Pietro Balsamo, known as Carino, one of the hired assassins, was caught red-handed, and his escape by bribery from prison created a popular excitement leading to a revolution in Milan. Yet, when recaptured, he repented, was forgiven, and allowed to enter the Dominican Order, in which he peacefully died, with the repute of a "*beato*;" and though the Church never formally recognized his right to the public worship paid to him in some places, still, in one of the stalls of the martyr's own great church of Sant' Eustorgio, he appears, with the title of the blessed Acerinus, in a chiaroscuro of 1505, among the Dominican saints. Not one, indeed, of those concerned in the assassination appears to have been put to death, and the leading instigator of the crime, Stefano Confaloniere{461} of Aliate, a notorious heretic and fautor of heretics, after repeated abjurations, releases, and relapses, was not fairly imprisoned until 1295, forty-three years after the murder. It was the same when, soon afterwards, the Franciscan inquisitor, Pier da Bracciano, was assassinated, and Manfredo di Sesto, who had hired the assassins, was brought before Rainerio Saccone, the Inquisitor of Milan. He confessed the crime and other offences in aid of heresy, but was only ordered to present himself to the pope and receive penance. Contumaciously neglecting to do this, Innocent IV. merely ordered the magistrates of Italy to arrest and detain him if he should be found.[415]

Yet the theory which held the Church to be a loving mother unwillingly inflicting wholesome chastisement on her unruly children only lent a sharper rigor to most of the operations of the Inquisition. Those who were obdurate to its kindly efforts were ungrateful and disobedient when ingratitude and disobedience were offences of the most heinous nature. They were parricides whom it was mercy to reduce to subjection, and whose sin only the severest suffering could expiate. We have seen how little the inquisitor recked of human misery in his efforts to detect and convert the heretic, and it is not to be supposed that he would be more tender in his ministrations to the diseased souls asking for absolution and penance—and it was only the penitent who had confessed and abjured his sin who came before the judgment-seat for punishment. All others were left to the secular arm.

The flimsiness of this theory, however, is manifest from the fact that it was not only heretics—those who consciously erred in matters of faith—who were subjected to the jurisdiction and chastisement of the Inquisition. Fautors, receivers, and defenders—those who showed hospitality, gave alms, or sheltered or assisted heretics in any way, or neglected to denounce them to the authorities, or to capture them when occasion offered, also rulers who omitted to execute the laws against heresy, however orthodox themselves, incurred suspicion of heresy, simple, vehement, or violent. If violent, it was tantamount to heresy; if simple or vehement, {462} we have seen how readily it might, by failure of purgation, or by repetition, grow into technical heresy and relapse, incurring the gravest penalties, including relaxation to the secular arm. Not less conclusive to the real import of the inquisitorial organization is the argument of Zanghino, that if a heretic repents, confesses to his priest, accepts and performs penance and receives absolution, however he may be relieved from hell and pardoned in the sight of God, he is not released from temporal punishment, and is still subject to prosecution by the Inquisition. It would not abandon its prey, while yet it could not impugn the efficacy of the sacrament of penitence, and such difficulties were eluded by forbidding priests to take cognizance of heresy, which was reserved for bishops and inquisitors.[416]

The penances customarily imposed by the Inquisition were comparatively few in number. They consisted, firstly, of pious observances—recitation of prayers, frequenting of churches, the discipline, fasting, pilgrimages, and fines nominally for pious uses, such as a confessor might impose on his ordinary penitents. These were for offences of trifling import. Next in grade are the "*pœnæ confusibiles*"—the humiliating and degrading penances, of which the most important was the wearing of yellow crosses sewed upon the garments; and, finally, the severest punishment among those strictly within the competence of the Holy Office, the "*murus*," or prison. Confiscation, as I have said, was an incident, and the stake, like it, was the affair of the secular power; and though both were really controlled by the inquisitor, they will be more conveniently considered separately. The Councils of Narbonne and Béziers, in addition, prescribe a purely temporal punishment—banishment, either temporary or perpetual—but this would appear to have been so rarely employed that it may be disregarded, although in the earlier period it occasionally occurs in sentences, or is found among the penances to which repentant heretics pledged themselves to submit.[417] {463}

The sin of heresy was too grave to be expiated simply by contrition and amendment. While the Church professed to welcome back to her bosom all her erring and repentant children, the way of the transgressor was made hard, and his offence could only be washed away by penances severe enough to prove the robustness of his convictions. Before the Inquisition was founded, about 1208, St. Dominic, while acting under the authority of the Legate Arnaud, converted a Catharan named Pons Roger, and prescribed for him a penance which has chanced to be preserved. It will give us an insight into what were considered reasonable terms of readmission to the Church, at a time when it was straining every nerve to win the heretics back, and before it had fairly resorted to the use of force. On three Sundays the penitent is to be stripped to the waist and scourged by the priest from the entrance of the town of Tréville to the church-door. He is to abstain forever from meat and eggs and cheese, except on Easter, Pentecost, and Christmas, when he is to eat of them in sign of his abnegation of his Manichæan errors. For twoscore days, twice a year, he is to forego the use of fish, and for three days in each week that of fish, wine, and oil, fasting, if his health and labors will permit. He is to wear monastic vestments, with a small cross sewed on each breast. If possible, he is to hear mass daily, and on feast-days to attend church at vespers. Seven times a day he is to recite the canonical hours, and, in addition, the Paternoster ten times each day and twenty times each night. He is to observe the strictest chastity. Every month he is to show this paper to the priest, who is to watch its observance closely, and this mode of life is to be maintained until the legate shall see fit to alter it, while for infraction of the penance he is to be held as a perjurer and a heretic, and be segregated from the society of the faithful.[418]

This shows how the various forms of penance were mingled together at the discretion of the ghostly father. The same is seen in an exceedingly lenient sentence imposed in 1258 by the inquisitors of Carcassonne on Raymond Maria, who had confessed to various acts of heresy committed twenty or thirty years before, and who, for other reasons, had strong claims for merciful treatment. It further illustrates the practice of compounding pious {464} observances for money. Raymond is ordered to fast from the Friday after Michaelmas until Easter, and to eat no meat on Saturdays, but he can redeem the fast by giving a denier to a poor man. Every day he is to recite seven times the Paternoster and Ave Maria. Within three years he is to visit the shrines of St. Mary of Roche-amour, St. Rufus of Aliscamp, St. Gilles of Vauverte, St. William of the Desert, and Santiago de Compostella, bringing home testimonial letters from the rector of each church; and in lieu of other penances he is to give six livres Tournois to the Bishop of Albi to aid in building a chapel. He is to hear mass at least every Sunday and feast-day, and to abstain from all work on those days. Another penance belonging to the same general category is that inflicted on a Carthusian monk of la Loubatière who was guilty of Spiritual Franciscanism. He was ordered not to leave the abbey for three years, and during that time not to speak except in extreme necessity. For a year he was to confess daily in the presence of his brethren that John XXII. was the true pope and entitled to obedience; and, in addition, he was to undergo certain fasts and perform certain recitations of the liturgy and psalter. Penances of this character could be varied *ad infinitum* at the caprice of the inquisitor.[419]

In all this there is no mention of flagellation, but that was so general a feature of penance that it is frequently taken for granted in prescribing pilgrimages and attendance at church. We have seen Raymond of Toulouse submitting to it, and however abhorrent it may be to our modern ideas, it did not carry with it that sense of humiliation which to us appears inseparable from it. In the lightest penalties provided for voluntary converts, coming forward within the time of grace, the Councils of Narbonne and Béziers, in 1244 and 1246, and that of Tarragona, in 1242, order the discipline. It was no light matter. Stripped as much as decency and the inclemency of the weather would permit, the penitent presented himself every Sunday, between the Epistle and the Gospel, with a rod in his hand, to the priest engaged in celebrating mass, who soundly scourged him in the presence of the congregation, as a fitting interlude in the mysteries of divine service. On the first Sunday in every month, after mass, he was to visit, similarly{465} equipped, every house in which he had seen heretics, and receive the same infliction; and on the occasion of every solemn procession he was to accompany it in the same guise, to be beaten at every station and at the end. Even when the town happened to be placed under interdict, or himself to be excommunicated, there was to be no cessation of the penance, and apparently it lasted as long as the wretched life of the penitent, or at least until it pleased the inquisitor to remember him and liberate him. That this was no idle threat is shown by these precise details occurring in a formula given by Bernard Gui, about 1330, for the release from prison of penitents who by patience and humility in their captivity have earned a mitigation of their punishment, and virtually the same formula was employed immediately after the organization of the Inquisition.[420]

The pilgrimages, which were regarded as among the lightest of penances, were also mercies only by comparison. Performed on foot, the number commonly enjoined might well consume several years of a man's life, during which his family might perish. A frequent injunction by Pierre Cella, one of the most moderate of inquisitors, comprehended Compostella and Canterbury, with perhaps several intermediate shrines, and in one case a man over ninety years of age was ordered to perform the weary tramp to Compostella simply for having consorted with heretics. These pilgrimages were not without peril and hardship, although the hospitality exercised by the numerous convents on the road enabled the poorest pilgrim to sustain life. Still, pilgrimages were so habitual a feature of mediæval habits, and entered so frequently into ordinary penance, that their use by the Inquisition was inevitable. When the yearning for salvation was so strong that two hundred thousand pilgrims arriving in Rome in a single day is said to have been no uncommon occurrence during the Jubilee of 1300, the penitent who escaped with the performance of such pious observances might well regard himself as mercifully treated.[421]

The penitential pilgrimages of the Inquisition were divided{466} into two classes—the greater and the less. In Languedoc the greater pilgrimages were customarily four—to Rome, Compostella, St. Thomas of Canterbury, and the Three Kings of Cologne. The smaller were nineteen in number, extending from shrines of local celebrity to Paris and Boulogne-sur-mer. The cases in which they were employed may be estimated by the sentence passed by Bernard Gui, in 1322, on three culprits whose only offence was that, some fifteen or twenty years before, they had seen Waldensian teachers in their fathers' houses without knowing what they were. Commencing within three months, the penitents were required to perform seventeen of the minor pilgrimages, reaching from Bordeaux to Vienne, bringing back, as usual, from each shrine testimonial letters of the visit. In this case it is specified that they were not obliged to wear the crosses, and I think it probable that this exempted them from scourging at each of the shrines, to which penitents with crosses would naturally be subjected. In one case, occurring in 1308, a culprit was excused from pilgrimages on account of his age and weakness, and was only required to make two visitations a year in the city of Toulouse. Considerate humanity such as this is not sufficiently common in the annals of the Inquisition for an example of it to be passed in silence.[422]

At the inception of the Inquisition the pilgrimage universally ordered for men was that to Palestine, as a crusader. Indeed, the legate, Cardinal Romano, commanded this for all who were suspect of heresy. It seems to have been felt that the best use to which a heretic could be put, if he was to escape the fagot, was to make him aid in the defence of the Holy Land—a service of infinite hardship and peril. In the wholesale persecutions in Languedoc the numbers of these unwilling crusaders were so great that alarm was excited lest they should pervert the faith in the land of its origin, and about 1242 or 1243 a papal prohibition was issued, forbidding it for the future. The Council of Béziers, in 1246, commits to the discretion of the inquisitors whether penitents shall serve beyond seas, or send a man-at-arms to represent them, or fight the battles of the faith nearer home, against heretics or Saracens. The term of service was also left to the inquisitors, but{467} was usually for two or three years, though sometimes for seven or eight, and those who went to Palestine, if they were so fortunate as to return, were obliged to bring back testimonial letters from the Patriarch of Jerusalem or Acre. When Count Raymond was preparing to fulfil his long-delayed vow of a crusade, in his eagerness for recruits he procured in 1247, from Innocent IV., a bull empowering the Archbishop of Ausch and Bishop of Agen, within Raymond's dominions, to commute into a pilgrimage beyond seas the penance of temporary crosses and prison, and even when these were perpetual, if the consent could be had of the inquisitor who had uttered the sentence; and the following year this was extended to those in the territories of the Counts of Montfort. Under this impulsion, the penance of crusading became common again. There is extant a notice given by the inquisitors of Carcassonne, October 5, 1251, in the church of St. Michael, to those wearing crosses and those relieved from them, that they must without fail sail for the Holy Land, as they had pledged themselves to do, in the next fleet; and in the Register of Carcassonne the injunction of the crusade is of frequent occurrence. With the disastrous result of the ventures of St. Louis and the fall of the Kingdom of Jerusalem this form of penance gradually diminished, but it continued to be occasionally prescribed. As late as 1321 we find Guillem Garric condemned to go beyond seas with the next convoy and remain until recalled by the inquisitor; if legitimately impeded (which was likely, as he was an old man who had rotted in a dungeon for thirty years) he could replace himself with a competent fighting-man, and if he neglected to do so, he was condemned to perpetual prison. This sentence, moreover, affords one of the rare instances of banishment, for Guillem, besides furnishing a substitute, is ordered to expatriate himself to such place as shall be designated, during the pleasure of the inquisitor.[423]

These penances did not interfere with the social position and self-respect of the penitent. Far heavier was the apparently simple {468} penalty of wearing the crosses, which was known as a *pœna confusibilis*, or humiliating punishment. We have seen that already, in 1208, St. Dominic orders his converted heretic to wear two small crosses on the breast in sign of his sin and repentance. It seems a contradiction that the emblem of the Redemption, so proudly worn by the crusader and the military orders, should be to the convert an infliction almost unbearable, but when it became the sign of his sin and disgrace there were few inflictions which might not more readily be borne. The two little crosses of St. Dominic grew to conspicuous pieces of saffron-colored cloth, of which the arms were two and a half fingers in breadth, two and a half palms in height, and two palms in width, one sewed on the breast and the other on the back, though occasionally one on the breast sufficed. If the convert during his trial had committed perjury, a second transverse arm was added at the top; and if he had been a "perfected" heretic, a third cross was placed upon the cap. Another form was that of a hammer, worn by prisoners temporarily liberated on bail; and we have seen the red tongues fastened on false-witnesses, and the symbol of a letter inflicted on a forger, while other emblematical forms were prescribed, as the fancy of the inquisitor might dictate. They were never to be laid aside, in doors or out, and when worn out the penitent was obliged to renew them. During the latter half of the thirteenth century those who went beyond seas might abandon their crosses during their crusade, but were obliged to reassume them on returning. In the earlier days of the Inquisition a term ranging from one year to seven or eight was usually prescribed, but in the later period it was always for life, unless the inquisitor saw fit, as a reward of good behavior, to remit it. Thus in the *auto de fé* of 1309 Bernard Gui permitted Raymonde, wife of Étienne Got, to remove the crosses which she had been condemned to wear, some forty years before, by Pons de Poyet and Étienne de Gâtine.[424] {469}

The Council of Narbonne, in 1229, prescribed the wearing of these crosses by all converts who voluntarily abandoned heresy and returned to the faith of their own free will, as an evidence of their detestation of their former errors. Apparently the penance was found hard to bear, and efforts were made to escape it, for the statutes of Raymond, in 1234, and the Council of Béziers of the same year, threaten confiscation for all who refuse to wear them, or endeavor to conceal them. Subsequent councils renewed and extended the obligation on all who were reconciled to the Church; and that of Valence, in 1248, decreed that all who disobeyed should be forced without mercy to resume them, and that abandoning them after due monition should be visited, like jail-breaking, with the full penalties of impenitent heresy. In a case recorded in 1251, a penitent preparing for a crusade seems to have thought himself authorized to abandon the crosses before starting, and was sentenced to come to Carcassonne on the first Sunday of every month until his departure, barefooted and in shirt and drawers, and visit every church in the city, with a rod, to undergo scourging.[425]

Though this penance was regarded as merciful in comparison with imprisonment, it was not easily endurable, and we can readily understand the sharp penalties required to enforce obedience. In the sentences of Pierre Cella it is only prescribed in aggravated cases, and then merely for from one to five years, though subsequently it grew to be universal, and without a limit of time. The unfortunate penitent was exposed to the ridicule and derision of all whom he met, and was heavily handicapped in every effort to earn a livelihood. Even in the earlier time, when a majority of the population of Languedoc were heretics, and the cross-wearers were so numerous that their presence in Palestine was dreaded, the Council of Béziers, in 1246, feels obliged to warn the people that penitents should be welcomed and their cheerful endurance of penance should be a subject of gratulation for all the faithful, and therefore it strictly forbids ridicule of those who wear crosses, or refusal to transact business with them. Though penitents were {470} under the special protection of the Church, it had too zealously preached detestation of heresy to be able to control the feelings of the population towards those whom it thus saw fit to stigmatize. A slight indication of this is seen in the case of Raymonde Manifacier, who, in 1252, was cited before the Inquisition of Carcassone for abandoning the crosses, when she urged in extenuation that the one on her cloak had been torn and she was too poor to replace it, while as regards that on her cape, her mistress, whom she served as nurse, had forbidden her to wear it and had given her a cape without one. A stronger case is that already cited of Arnaud Isarn, who found, after year's experience, that he could not earn a living while thus bearing the marks of his degradation.[426]

154

The Inquisition recognized the intolerable hardships to which its penitents were exposed, and sometimes in mercy mitigated them. Thus, in 1250, at Carcassonne, Pierre Pelha receives permission to lay aside the crosses temporarily during a voyage which he is obliged to make to France. Bernard Gui assures us that young women were frequently excused from wearing them, because with them they would be unable to find husbands; and among the formulas of his "*Practica*" one which exempts the penitent from crosses enumerates the various reasons usually assigned, such as the age or infirmity of the wearer (presumably rendering him a safe object of insult) or on account of his children, whom he may not otherwise be able to support, or for the sake of his daughters, whom he cannot marry. Still more suggestive are formulas of proclamations threatening to prosecute as impeders of the Inquisition and to impose crosses on those who ridicule such penitents or drive them away or prevent them from following their callings; and the insufficiency of this is shown by still other formulas of orders addressed to the secular officials, who are required to see that no such outrages are perpetrated. Sometimes monitions of this kind formed part of the regular proceedings of the *autos de fé*. The wearing of the symbol of Christianity was evidently a punishment of no slight character. The well-known *sanbenito* of the modern Spanish Inquisition was derived{471} from the scapular with saffron-colored crosses which was worn by those condemned to imprisonment, when on certain feast-days they were exposed at the church doors, that their misery and humiliation might serve as a warning to the people.[427]

It will be remembered that at the outset there was some discussion as to whether it should be competent for the inquisitors to inflict the pecuniary penance of fines. The voluntary poverty and renunciation of money of the Mendicants, to whom the Holy Office was confided, had not yet become so obsolete that the incongruity could be overlooked of their using their almost limitless discretion in levying fines and handling the money thence accruing. That they commenced it early is shown by a sentence of 1237, already quoted, in which Pons Grimoardi, a voluntary convert, is required to pay to the order of the inquisitor ten livres Morlaas, while in 1245, in Florence, one rendered by the indefatigable inquisitor, Ruggieri Calcagni, shows that already fines were habitual there. It was not without cause, therefore, that the Council of Narbonne, in 1244, in its instructions to inquisitors, ordered them to abstain from pecuniary penances both for the sake of the honor of their Order and because they would have ample other work to do. The Order itself felt this to be the case, and as inquisitors were not yet, at least in theory, emancipated from the control of their superiors, already, in 1242, the Provincial Chapter of Montpellier had endeavored to enforce the rules of the Order by strictly prohibiting them from inflicting pecuniary penances for the future, or from collecting those which had already been imposed. How little respect was shown to these injunctions is visible from a bull of Innocent IV., in 1245, in which, to preserve the reputation of the inquisitors, he orders all fines paid over to two persons selected by the bishop and inquisitor, to be expended in building prisons and in supporting prisoners, in compliance with which the Council of Béziers, in 1246, abandoned the position taken by the Council of Narbonne, and agreed that the fines should be employed on the prisons, and in defraying the necessary{472} expenses of the Inquisition, possibly because the good bishops found that they themselves were expected to meet these demands as appertaining to the episcopal jurisdiction. In an inquisitorial manual of the period this is specified as the destination of the fines, but the power was speedily abused, and in 1249 Innocent IV. sternly rebuked the inquisitors in general for the heavy exactions which they wrung from their converts, to the disgrace of the Holy See and the scandal of the faithful at large. This apparently had no effect, and in 1251 he prohibited them wholly from levying fines if any other form of penance could be employed. Yet the inquisitors finally triumphed and won the right to inflict pecuniary penances at discretion. These were understood to be for pious uses, in which term were included the expenses of the Inquisition; and as they were payable to the inquisitors themselves, they doubtless were so expended—it is to be hoped in accordance with the caution of Eymerich, "decently and without scandal to the laity." In the sentences of Frà Antonio Secco on the peasants of the Waldensian valleys in 1387, the penance of crosses is usually accompanied with a fine of five or ten florins of pure gold, payable to the Inquisition, nominally to defray the expenses of the trial. An attempt of the State to secure a share was defeated by a council of experts assembled at Piacenza in 1276 by the Lombard inquisitors, Frà Niccolò da Cremona and Frà Daniele da Giussano. A more decent use of the power to inflict money payments was one which Pierre Cella, the first inquisitor of Toulouse, frequently employed, by adding to the pilgrimages or other penances imposed the obligation of maintaining a priest or a poor man for a term of years or for life.[428]

In the later period of the Inquisition it was argued that fines were inadmissible, because if the accused were a heretic all his property disappeared in confiscation, while if he were not he{473} should not be punished, but the inquisitors responded that, although this was true, there were fautors and defenders of heresy, and those whose heresy consisted merely in a thoughtless word, all of whom could legitimately be fined; and the profitable abuse went on.[429]

Scarcely separable from the practice of fines was that of commuting penances for money. When we remember how extensive and lucrative was the custom of commuting the vows of crusaders, it was inevitable that a similar abuse should flourish in the Church's dealings with the penitents whom the Inquisition had placed within its power. A ready excuse was found in the proviso that the sums thence arising should be spent in pious uses—and no use could be more pious than that of ministering to the wants of those who were zealously laboring for the purity of the faith. In this the Holy See set the example. We have seen how, in 1248, Algisius, the papal penitentiary, ordered the release, by authority of Innocent IV., of six prisoners who had confessed heresy, alleging as a reason the satisfactory contributions which they had made to the Holy Land. The same year Innocent formally authorized Algisius to commute the penalties of certain heretics, without regard to the inquisitors, and he further empowered the Archbishop of Ausch to transmute into subsidies the penances imposed on reconciled heretics. Raymond was preparing for his crusade, and the excuse was a good one. The heretics were eager to escape by sacrificing their substance, and the project promised to be profitable. In 1249, accordingly, Algisius was sent to Languedoc armed with power to commute all inquisitorial penances into fines to be devoted to the needs of the Church and of the Holy Land, and to issue all necessary dispensations notwithstanding the privileges of the Inquisition. It is not to be supposed that the example was lost upon the inquisitors. Naturally enough, the cases which have reached us usually specify some pious work to which the funds were to be devoted, as when, in 1255, the inquisitors of Toulouse allowed twelve of the principal citizens of Lavaur to commute their penances into money to be contributed to building the church which was afterwards the Cathedral of Lavaur; and in 1258 they assisted the church of Najac in the same way by {474} allowing a number of the inhabitants to redeem their penalties for its benefit. The public utility of bridges caused them to be included in the somewhat elastic term of pious uses. Thus, in 1310, at Toulouse, Mathieu Aychard is released from wearing crosses and performing certain pilgrimages on condition of contributing forty livres Tournois to a new bridge then under construction at Tonneins; and in a formula for such transactions given by Bernard Gui, absolution and dispensation from pilgrimages and other penances are said to be granted in consideration of the payment of fifty livres for the building of a certain bridge, or of a certain church, or "to be spent in pious uses at our discretion." This last clause shows that commutations were by no means always thus liberally disposed of, and in fact they often inured to the benefit of those imposing them. We have a specimen of this in letters of the Inquisitor of Narbonne in 1264, granting absolution to Guillem du Puy in consideration of his giving one hundred and fifty livres Tournois to the Inquisition. The magnitude of these sums shows the eagerness of the penitents to escape, and the enormous power of extortion wielded by the inquisitor. If he was a man of integrity he could doubtless resist the temptation, but to the covetous and self-indulgent the opportunity of oppressing the helpless was almost unlimited. The system was kept up to the end. Under Nicholas V. Fray Miguel, the Inquisitor of Aragon, gave mortal offence to some high dignitaries in following certain papal instructions, whereupon they maltreated him and kept him in prison for nine months. It was a flagrant case of impeding the Inquisition, and in 1458 Pius II. ordered the Archbishop of Tarragona to dig up the bones of one of the offenders who had died, and to send the rest to the Holy See for judgment—but he added that the archbishop might, at his discretion, substitute a mulct for the war against the Turks, to be transmitted to the papal camera. It goes without saying that the death-penalty could never legally be commuted.[430]{475}

Penitents who died before fulfilling their penance afforded a specially favorable opportunity for such transactions as these. Death, as we have seen, afforded no immunity from the jurisdiction of the Inquisition and in no wise abated its energy of prosecution. There might be a distinction drawn in practice between those who were taken off while humbly performing the penance assigned to them, but before its completion, and those who had wilfully neglected its commencement; but legally the non-fulfilment of penance entailed condemnation for heresy whether in the dead or living. In 1329, for instance, the Inquisition of Carcassonne ordered the exhumation and cremation of the bones of seven persons declared to have died in heresy for not having fulfilled the penance enjoined on them, which of course carried with it the confiscation of their property and the subjection of their descendants to the usual disabilities. The Councils of Narbonne and Albi directed the inquisitors to exact satisfaction at discretion from the heirs of those who had died before judgment, if they would have been condemned to wear crosses, as well as those who had confessed and been sentenced, and who had not lived, whether to commence or to complete their penance. Gui Foucoix expresses his belief that in these cases the penitent is admitted to purgatory, and he decides that nothing should be demanded from his heirs; but even his authority did not overcome the more palatable doctrine of the councils, and a contemporary manual directs the inquisitor to exact a "congruous satisfaction." There is something peculiarly repulsive in the rapacity which followed beyond the grave those who had humbly confessed and repented and were received into the bosom of the Church, but the Inquisition was unrelenting and exacted the last penny. For instance, the Inquisitor of Carcassonne had prescribed five years' pilgrimage to the Holy Land for Jean Vidal, who died before performing it. March 21, 1252, his heirs, under citation, swore that his whole estate was worth twenty livres, and gave security to obey the decision of the inquisitor, which was announced the following August, and proved to be a demand for twenty livres—the entire value of his property. In another case, Raymonde Barbaira had died before accomplishing some pilgrimages with crosses to which she had been sentenced. An inventory of her property showed it to consist of some bedding, clothing, a chest, a few cattle, and four sous in {476} money, which had been divided up among her kindred, and from this pitiful inheritance the inquisitor, on March 7, 1256 demanded forty sous, for the payment of which by Easter the heirs had to give security. Such petty and vulgar details as these give us a clearer insight into the spirit and working of the Inquisition, and of the grinding oppression which it exercised on the subject populations. Even in the case of fautors who were not heretics, the heirs were obliged to perform any pecuniary penance which had been inflicted upon them.[431]

A more legitimate source of income, but yet one which opened the door to grave abuses, was the custom of taking bail, which of course was liable to forfeiture, serving, in such cases, as an irregular form of commutation. This custom dated from the inception of the Inquisition, and was practised at every stage of the proceedings, from the first citation to the final sentence, and even afterwards, when prisoners were sometimes liberated temporarily on giving security for their return. The convert who was absolved on abjuring was also required to give security that he would not relapse. Thus, in 1234, we see Lantelmo, a Milanese noble, ordered to give bail in two thousand lire, and two Florentine merchants bailed by their friends in two thousand silver marks. So, in 1244, the Baroni, of Florence, gave bail in one thousand lire to obey the mandates of the Church; and in 1252 a certain Guillem Roger pledged one hundred livres that he would go beyond seas by the next fleet and serve there for two years. The security was always to be pecuniary, and the inquisitor was warned not to take it of heretics, for their offence implied confiscation, but this was not strictly observed, as in special cases friends were found who furnished the necessary pledges. Forfeited bail was payable to the inquisitor, sometimes directly, and sometimes through the hands of the bishops, and was to be used for the expenses of the Inquisition. The usual form of bond pledged all the property of the principal and that of two sureties, jointly and severally; and as a general rule bail may be said to have been universal, except{477} in cases where the offence was regarded as too serious to admit of it, or when the offender could not procure it.[432]

It was impossible that these methods of converting the sentences of the Inquisition into current coin could flourish without introducing wide-spread corruption. Admission to bail might be the result of favoritism or degenerate into covert bribery. The discretion of the inquisitor was so wide that bribery itself could be safely indulged in. A crime necessarily so secret as this form of extortion cannot be expected to leave traces behind it, except in those cases in which it proved a failure, but sufficient instances of the latter are on record to show that the tribunals were surrounded by men who made a trade of their influence, real or presumed, with the judges. When these were incorruptible the business was suppressed with more or less success, but when they were acquisitive, they had ample field for unhallowed gain, to be wrung without stint or check from the subject populations both by bribery and extortion. Considering that every one above the age of seven was liable to the indelible suspicion of heresy by the mere fact of citation, it will be seen what an opportunity lay before the inquisitor and his spies and familiars to practise upon the fears of all, to sell exemptions from arrest, as well as to bargain for liberation. That these fruitful sources of gain were not abundantly worked would be incredible even in the absence of proof, but proof sufficient exists. In 1302 Boniface VIII. wrote to the Dominican Provincial of Lombardy that the papal ears had been lacerated with complaints of the Franciscan inquisitors of Padua and Vicenza, whose malicious cupidity had wronged many men and women by exacting from them immense sums and inflicting on them all manner of injuries. When the pope naïvely adduces in cumulation of their{478} villainy that these wrong-doers had not employed the illicit gains for the benefit of the Holy Office, or of the Roman Church, or even of their own Order, he affords ground for the suspicion that a judicious distribution of the spoils secured silent condonation of such offences in many cases. He had sent Gui, Bishop of Saintes, to investigate these complaints, who reported them well founded, and he orders the provincial to replace the delinquents with Dominicans. The change brought little relief, for the very next year Mascate de' Mosceri, a jurist of Padua, appealed to Benedict from the new Dominican inquisitor, Frà Benigno, who was vexing him with prosecutions in order to extort money from him; and in 1304 Benedict was obliged to address to the inquisitors of Padua and Vicenza a grave warning as to the official complaints which still arose about their fraudulent prosecution of good Catholics by means of false witnesses. It is easy to understand the complaint made by the stricter Franciscans that the inquisitors of their Order rode abroad in state in place of walking barefoot as was prescribed by the rule. At this very time, moreover, the Dominicans of Languedoc were the subject of precisely similar arraignment on the part of the communities subjected to them. Redress in this case was long in coming, but at last the investigation set on foot by Clement V. convinced him of the truth of the facts alleged, and at the Council of Vienne, in 1311, he caused the adoption of canons, embodied in the Corpus Juris, which placed on record conspicuously his conviction that the inquisitorial office was frequently abused by the extortion of money from the innocent and the escape of the guilty through bribery. The remedy which he devised, of *ipso facto* excommunication in such cases, was complained of by Bernard Gui on the ground that it would invalidate the rightful acts, as well as the evil ones, of the wrong-doer; which only serves to show the vicious circle in which the whole business moved. Yet neither the hopes of Clement nor the fears of Bernard were justified by the result. The inquisitors continued to enrich themselves and the people to suffer untold miseries. In 1338 a papal investigation was made of a transaction by which the city of Albi purchased, by the payment of a sum of money to the Inquisitor of Carcassonne, the liberation of some citizens accused of heresy. In 1337 Benedict XII. ordered his nuncio in Italy, Bertrand, Archbishop of Embrun, to investigate the complaints which{479} came from all parts of Italy that the inquisitors extorted money, received presents, allowed the guilty to escape, and punished the innocent, through hatred or avarice, and empowered him to make removals in consequence; and the exercise of this power shows that the complaints were well founded. The effects of the measure, however, were evanescent. In 1346 the whole republic of Florence rose against their inquisitor, Piero di Aquila, for various abuses, among which figured extortion. He fled and refused to return during the investigation which followed, in spite of the offer of a safe-conduct. A single witness swore to sixty-six cases of extortion, and in a partial list of them which has been preserved the sums exacted vary from twenty-five to seventeen hundred gold florins, showing how unlimited were the profits which tempted the unscrupulous. Villani tells us that in two years he had thus amassed more than seven thousand florins, an enormous sum in those days; that there were no heretics in Florence at the time, and that the offences which thus proved so lucrative to him consisted of usury and thoughtless blasphemy. As for usury, Alvaro Pelayo tells us that at that time the bishops of Tuscany set the example by habitually so employing the church funds, but the inquisitors did not meddle with the prelates. As for blasphemy, the subtle refinements which converted simple blasphemous expressions into heresy, as set forth by Eymerich, show how readily a skilful inquisitor could speculate on idle oaths. Boccaccio doubtless had Frà Piero in memory when he described the recent inquisitor of Florence who, like all his brethren, had an eye as keen to discover a rich man as a heretic, and who extracted a heavy *douceur* from a citizen for boasting in his cups that he had wine so good that Christ would drink it. The keenness which thus made profitable business for the Holy Office, when heresy was declining, is illustrated by the case of Marie du Canech, a money-changer of Cambrai, in 1403. In a case before the Ordinary she incautiously expressed the opinion that when under oath she was not bound to give evidence against her own honor and interest. For this the deputy inquisitor, Frère Nicholas de Péronne, prosecuted her and condemned her to various penances, including nine years' abstention from business and eighty gold crowns for expenses.[433]{480}

These abuses continued to the last. Cornelius Agrippa tells us that it was customary for inquisitors to convert corporal punishments into pecuniary ones and even to exact annual payments as the price of forbearance. When he was in the Milanese, about 1515, there was a disturbance caused by their secretly extorting large sums from women of noble birth, whose husbands at length discovered it, and the inquisitors were glad to escape with their lives.[434]

I have dwelt at some length upon this feature of the Inquisition because it is one which has rarely received attention, although it inflicted misery and wrong to an almost unlimited extent. The stake consumed comparatively few victims. While the horrors of the crowded dungeon can scarce be exaggerated, yet more effective for evil and more widely exasperating was the sleepless watchfulness which was ever on the alert to plunder the rich and to wrench from the poor the hard-earned gains on which a family{481}depended for support. It was only in rare cases that the victims dared to raise a cry, and rarer still were those in which that cry was heard; but sufficient instances have reached us to prove what a scourge was the institution, in this aspect alone, on all the populations cursed by its presence. At a very early period the wealthy already recognized that well-timed liberality was advisable towards those who held such power in the hollow of their hands. In 1244 the Dominican Chapter of Cahors lifted a warning voice and ordered inquisitors not to allow their brethren to receive presents which would expose the whole Order to disrepute; but this scrupulousness wore off, and even a man of high character like Eymerich could argue that inquisitors may properly be the recipients of gifts, though he dubiously adds that they ought to be refused from those under trial, except in special circumstances. As the accounts of the Inquisition were rendered only to the papal camera, it will be seen how little the officials had to dread investigation and exposure. As little had they to fear the divine wrath, for their very functions, while thus engaged, insured them plenary indulgence for all sins confessed and repented. Thus secure, here and hereafter, they were virtually relieved from all restraint.[435]

There was one purely temporal penalty which came within the competence of the Inquisition—the designation of the houses which were to be destroyed in consequence of the contamination of heresy. The origin of this curious practice is not readily traced. Under the Roman law, buildings in which heretics held their conventicles with the owner's consent were not torn down, but were forfeited to the Church. Yet as soon as heresy began to be formidable we find their destruction commanded by secular rulers with singular unanimity. The earliest provision I have met with occurs in the assizes of Clarendon in 1166, which order the razing of all houses in which heretics were received. The example was followed by the Emperor Henry VI. in the edict of Prato, in 1194, by Otho IV. in 1210, and by Frederic II. in the edict of Ravenna, in 1232, as an addition to his coronation-edict of 1220, from which it had been omitted. It had already been adopted in the code of Verona in 1228 in all cases in which the owner, after eight days' notice,{482} neglected to expel heretic occupants; it is found in the statutes of Florence a few years later, and is included in the papal bulls defining the procedure of the Inquisition. In France the Council of Toulouse, in 1229, decreed that any house in which a heretic was found was to be destroyed, and this was given the force of secular law by Count Raymond in 1234. It naturally forms a feature of the legislation of the succeeding councils which regulated the inquisitorial proceedings, and was adopted by St. Louis. Castile, in fact, seems to be the only land in which the regulation was not observed, owing doubtless to the direct derivation of its legislation from the Roman law, for, in the Partidas, houses in which heretics were sheltered are ordered to be given to the Church. Elsewhere such dwellings were razed to the ground, and the site, as accursed, was to remain forever a receptacle for filth and unfit for human habitation; yet the materials could be employed for pious uses unless they were ordered to be burned by the inquisitor who rendered the sentence. This sentence was addressed to the parish priest, with directions to publish it for three successive Sundays during divine service.[436]

In France the royal officials in charge of the confiscations came at length to object to this destruction of property, which was sometimes considerable, as the castle of the seigneur was as liable to it as the cabin of the peasant. In 1329 it forms one of the points for which the Inquisitor of Carcassonne, Henri de Chamay, asked and obtained the confirmation of Philippe de Valois, and the same year he had the satisfaction, in an *auto* held in

158

September, to order the destruction of four houses, and a farm, whose owners had been hereticated in them on their death-beds. Some fifty years later, however, a quarrel on the subject between the king's representatives and the inquisitors of Dauphiné resulted differently. Charles le Sage, after consulting with the pope, issued letters of{483}October 19, 1378, ordering that the penalty should no longer be enforced. The independent spirit of northern Germany manifested itself in the same manner, and in the Sachsenspiegel there is a peremptory command that no houses shall be destroyed except for rape committed within them. In Italy the custom continued, as there the confiscations did not inure to the sovereign, but it was held that if the owner had no guilty knowledge of the use made of his house he was entitled to keep it. Lawyers disputed, however, as to the perpetuity of the prohibition to build on the spot, some holding that possession by a Catholic for forty years conferred a right to erect a new house, which others denied, arguing that a perpetual and imprescriptible servitude had been created. The inquisitors, in process of time, arrogated to themselves the power to issue licenses to build anew on these sites, and this right they exercised, doubtless, to their own profit, though they might not have found it easy to cite authority for it.[437]

Another temporal penalty may be alluded to as illustrating the unlimited discretion enjoyed by the inquisitors in imposing penance. When, in 1321, the town of Cordes made humble submission for its long-continued insubordination to its bishop and inquisitor, the penance assigned to the community by Bernard Gui and Jean de Beaune was the construction of a chapel of such size as might be ordered, in honor of St. Peter Martyr, St. Cecilia, St. Louis, and St. Dominic, with the statues of those saints in wood or stone above the altar; and, to complete the humiliation of the community, the portal was to be adorned with statues of the bishop and of the two inquisitors, the whole to be finished within two years, under a penalty of five hundred livres Tournois, which was to be doubled for a delay of another two years. Doubtless the people of Cordes built the chapel without delay, but they hesitated at this glorifying of their oppressors, for, twenty-seven years afterwards, in 1348, we find the municipal authorities summoned before the Inquisition of Toulouse and compelled to give pledges that the portal forthwith be completed and the inquisitorial effigies be erected.[438]{484}

The severest penance the inquisitor could impose was incarceration. It was, according to the theory of the inquisitors, not a punishment, but a means by which the penitent could obtain, on the bread of tribulation and water of affliction, pardon from God for his sins, while at the same time he was closely supervised to see that he persevered in the right path and was segregated from the rest of the flock, thus removing all danger of infection. Of course it was only used for converts. The defiant heretic who persisted in disobedience, or who pertinaciously refused to confess his heresy and asserted his innocence, could not be admitted to penance, and was handed over to the secular arm.[439]

In the bull *Excommunicamus* of Gregory IX., in 1229, all who after arrest were converted to the faith through fear of death were ordered to be incarcerated for life, thus to perform appropriate penance. The Council of Toulouse almost simultaneously made the same regulation, and manifested its sense of the real value of the involuntary conversions by adding the caution that they be prevented from corrupting others. The Ravenna decree of Frederic II., in 1332, adopted the same rule and made it settled legal practice. The Council of Arles, in 1234, called attention to the perpetual backsliding of those converted by force, and ordered the bishops to enforce strictly the penance of perpetual prison in all such cases. As yet the relapsed were not considered as hopeless, and were not abandoned to the secular court, or "relaxed," but were similarly imprisoned for life.[440]

The Inquisition at its inception thus found the rule established, and enforced it with the relentless vigor which it manifested in all its functions. It was represented as a special mercy shown to those who had forfeited all claims on human compassion. There were to be no exemptions. The Council of Narbonne, in 1244,{485} specifically declared that, except when special indulgence could be procured from the Holy See, no husband was to be spared on account of his wife, or wife on account of her husband, or parent in consideration of helpless children; neither sickness nor old age should claim mitigation. Every one who did not come forward within the time of grace and confess and denounce his acquaintances was liable to this penance, which in all cases was to be lifelong; but the prevalence of heresy in Languedoc was so great, and the terror inspired by the activity of the inquisitors grew so strong, that those who had allowed the allotted period to elapse flocked in, begging for reconciliation, in such multitudes that the good bishops declare not only that funds for the support of such crowds of prisoners were lacking, but even that it would be impossible to find stones and mortar sufficient to build prisons for them. The inquisitors are therefore instructed to delay incarceration in these cases, unless impenitence, relapse, or flight, is to be apprehended, until the pleasure of the pope can be learned. Apparently Innocent IV. was not disposed to leniency, for in 1246 the Council of Béziers sternly orders the imprisonment of all who have overstayed the time of grace, while counselling commutation when it would entail evident peril of death on parents or children. Imprisonment thus became the usual punishment, except of obstinate heretics, who were burned. In a single sentence of February 19, 1237, at Toulouse, some twenty or thirty penitents are thus condemned, and are ordered to confine themselves in a house until prisons can be built. In a fragment which has been preserved of the register of sentences in the Inquisition of Toulouse from 1246 to 1248, comprising one hundred and ninety-two cases, with the exception of forty-three contumacious absentees, the sentence is invariably imprisonment. Of these, one hundred and twenty-seven are perpetual, six are for ten years, and sixteen for an indefinite period, as may seem expedient to the Church. It apparently was not till a later period that the order of the Council of Narbonne was obeyed, and the sentence always was for life. In the later periods this proportion will not hold good, for all inquisitors were not like the fierce Bernard de Caux, who then ruled the Holy Office in Toulouse; but perpetual imprisonment remained to the last the principal penance inflicted on penitents, although the decrees of Frederic and the canons of the councils of Toulouse and Narbonne{486} were not held to apply to those who abjured heartily after arrest.[441]

In the later sentences which have reached us it is often not easy to guess why one prisoner is incarcerated and another let off with crosses, when the offences enumerated as to each would seem to be indistinguishable. The test between the two probably was one which does not appear on the record. All alike were converts, but he whose conversion appeared to be hearty and spontaneous was considered to be entitled to the easier penance, while the harsher one was inflicted when the conversion seemed to be enforced and the result of fear. Yet how relentlessly a man like Bernard Gui, who represents the better class of inquisitors, could enforce the strict measure of the law is seen in the case of Pierre Raymond Dominique, who had been cited to appear in 1309, had fled and incurred excommunication, had consequently, in 1315, been condemned as a contumacious heretic, and in 1321 had voluntarily come forward and surrendered himself on a promise that his life should be spared. His acts of heresy had not been flagrant, and he pleaded as an excuse for his contumacy his wife and seven children, who would have starved had they been deprived of his labor, but in spite of this he was incarcerated for life. Even the stern Bernard de Caux was not always so merciless. In 1246, we find him, in sentencing Bernard Sabbatier, a relapsed heretic, to perpetual imprisonment, adding that as the culprit's father is a good Catholic and old and sick, the son may remain with him and support him as long as he lives, meanwhile wearing the crosses.[442]

There were two kinds of imprisonment, the milder, or "*murus largus,*" and the harsher, known as "*murus strictus*" or "*durus*" or "*arctus.*" All were on bread and water, and the confinement, according to rule, was solitary, each penitent in a separate cell, with no access allowed to him, to prevent his being corrupted or corrupting others; but this could not be strictly enforced, and about 1306 Geoffroi d'Ablis stigmatizes as an abuse the visits of{487} clergy, and laity of both sexes, permitted to prisoners. Husband and wife, however, were allowed access to each other if either or both were imprisoned; and late in the fourteenth century Eymerich agrees that zealous Catholics may be admitted to visit prisoners, but not women and simple folk who might be perverted, for converted prisoners, he adds, are very liable to relapse, and to infect others, and usually end with the stake.[443]

In the milder form, or "*murus largus,*" the prisoners apparently were, if well behaved, allowed to take exercise in the corridors, where sometimes they had opportunities of converse with each other and with the outside world. This privilege was ordered to be given to the aged and infirm by the cardinals who investigated the prison of Carcassonne and took measures to alleviate its rigors. In the harsher confinement, or "*murus strictus,*" the prisoner was thrust into the smallest, darkest, and most noisome of cells, with chains on his feet—in some cases chained to the wall. This penance was inflicted on those whose offences had been conspicuous, or who had perjured themselves by making incomplete confessions, the matter being wholly at the discretion of the inquisitor. I have met with one case, in 1328, of aggravated false-witness, condemned to "*murus strictissimus,*" with chains on both hands and feet. When the culprits were members of a religious order, to avoid scandal the proceedings were usually held in private, and the imprisonment would be ordered to take place in a convent of their own Order. As these buildings, however, usually were provided with cells for the punishment of offenders, this was probably of no great advantage to the victim. In the case of Jeanne, widow of B. de la Tour, a nun of Lespenasse, in 1246, who had committed acts of both Catharan and Waldensian heresy, and had prevaricated in her confession, the sentence was confinement in a separate cell in her own convent, where no one was to enter or see her, her food being pushed in through an opening left for the purpose—in fact, the living tomb known as the "*in pace.*"[444]{488}

I have already alluded to the varying treatment designedly practised in the detentive imprisonment of those who were under trial. When there was no special object to be attained by cruelty, this probably was as mild as could reasonably be expected. From occasional indications in the trials, it would seem that considerable intercourse was allowed with the outside world, as well as between the prisoners themselves, though watchful care was enjoined to prevent communication of any kind which might tend to harden the prisoner against a full confession of his sins.[445]

The prisons themselves were not designed to lighten the penance of confinement. At best the jails of the Middle Ages were frightful abodes of misery. The seigneurs-justiciers and cities obliged to maintain them looked upon the support of prisoners as a heavy charge of which they would gladly relieve themselves. If a debtor was thrust into a dungeon, although the law limited his confinement to forty days and ordered him to be comfortably fed, these prescriptions were customarily eluded, for the worse he was treated the greater effort he would make to release himself. As for criminals, bread and water were their sole diet, and if they perished through neglect and starvation it was a saving of expense. The prisoner who had money and friends could naturally obtain better treatment by liberal payment; but this alleviation was not often to be looked for in the case of heretics whose property had been confiscated, and with whom sympathy was dangerous.[446]{489}

The enormous number of captives resulting from the vigorous operations of the Inquisition in Languedoc had rendered the question as to the duty of building and maintaining prisons one of no little magnitude. It unquestionably rested with the bishops, whose laches in persecuting heresy were only made good by the inquisitors, and the bishops, at the Council of Toulouse, in 1229, had admitted this, only excepting that when the heretic had property those to whom the confiscations inured should provide for him. The burden, however, proved unexpectedly large, and we find them, in the Council of Narbonne, in 1244, trying to shift their responsibility by suggesting that the penitents who, but for the recent papal command, would be sent on crusades, should be utilized in building prisons and furnishing them with necessaries, "lest the prelates be overburdened with the poor converts, and be unable to provide for them on account of their multitude." Two years later, at Béziers, they declared that provision for both construction and maintenance ought to be made by those who profited by the confiscations, to which might be added the fines imposed by the inquisitors, which was not unreasonable; but in 1249 Innocent IV. still asserted that it was their business, and scolded them for not attending to it, and ordered that they be compelled to do it. At length, in 1254, the Council of Albi definitely decided that the holders of confiscated property should make provision for the imprisonment and maintenance of its former owners, and that, when heretics had nothing to confiscate, the cities or lords on whose lands they were captured should be responsible for them, and should be compelled by excommunication to attend to it. Still, the responsibility of the bishops was so self-evident that some zealous inquisitors talked of prosecuting them as fautors of heresy for neglecting to provide prisons, but Gui Foucoix discreetly advises against this, and recommends that such cases should be referred to the Holy See.[447] [490]

The fate of the unfortunate captives was evidently most precarious while their oppressors and despoilers were thus squabbling as to the cost of keeping them in jail and providing them with bread and water. There was evident fitness that those who profited by the enormous confiscations resulting from persecution should at least provide prisons and maintenance for the unhappy victims of fanaticism and greed; and St. Louis, to whom the chief profits came as suzerain of the territories ceded at the Treaty of Paris, recognized in part his responsibility. In 1233 he undertook to provide prisons in Toulouse, Carcassonne, and Béziers. In 1246 he ordered his seneschal to provide for the inquisitors competent prisons in Carcassonne and Béziers, and to furnish daily bread and water for the prisoners. In 1258 we find him ordering his seneschal of Carcassonne to bring to speedy completion those which had been commenced; he assumes that the prelates and barons on whose lands heretics are captured should provide for their maintenance; but, in order to avoid trouble, he is willing that expenditures for this purpose shall be made from the royal funds, to be subsequently collected from the seigneurs. With the death of Alfonse and Jeanne of Toulouse, in 1272, all the territories lapsed to the crown, and, with insignificant exceptions, all the confiscations fell to the king. Henceforth the maintenance of prisons and prisoners, and the wages of jailers and attendants, were defrayed by the crown, except perhaps at Albi, where the bishop shared in the spoils, and seems to have been held to a portion of the expenses. Among the requests of Henri de Chamay, granted in 1329 by Philippe de Valois, is that the inquisitorial prison at Carcassonne shall be repaired by the king, and that all who have shared in the confiscations shall be made to contribute *pro rata*. Thereupon the seneschal assessed the Count of Foix to the extent of three hundred and two livres eleven sols nine deniers, which the latter refused to pay, and appealed to the king, with what result is not known. From a decision of the Parlement of Paris in 1304 it appears that the royal allowance for maintenance was three deniers per diem for each convicted prisoner, which would seem liberal enough, though Jacques de Polignac,[491] who had charge of the prison at Carcassonne, and who was punished for his frauds, made out his accounts at the rate of eight deniers. This extravagance was not a precedent, and in 1337 we find the accounts still made out at the old rate of three deniers. For the accused detained and awaiting trial the Inquisition itself presumably had to provide. In Italy, where the confiscations, as we shall see, were divided into thirds, the Inquisition was self-supporting. In Naples the royal prisons were employed, and a royal order was required for incarceration.[448]

While the penance prescribed was a diet of bread and water, the Inquisition, with unwonted kindness, did not object to its prisoners receiving from their friends contributions of food, wine, money, and garments, and among its documents are such frequent allusions to this that it may be regarded as an established custom. Collections were made among those secretly inclined to heresy to alleviate the condition of their incarcerated brethren, and it argues much in favor of the disinterested zeal of the persecuted that they were willing to incur the risk attendant on this benevolence, for any interest shown towards these poor wretches exposed them to accusation to fautorship.[449]

The prisons were naturally built with a view to economy of construction and space rather than to the health and comfort of the captives. In fact the papal orders were that they should be constructed of small, dark cells for solitary confinement, only taking care that the "*enormis rigor*" of the incarceration should not extinguish life. M. Molinier's description of the Tour de l'Inquisition at Carcassonne, which was used as the inquisitorial prison, shows how literally these instructions were obeyed. It was a horrible place, consisting of small cells, deprived of all light and ventilation, where through long years the miserable inmates endured [492] a living death far worse than the short agony of the stake. In these abodes of despair they were completely at the mercy of the jailers and their servants. Complaints were not listened to; if a prisoner alleged violence or ill-treatment his oath was contemptuously refused, while that of the prison officials was received. A glimpse into the discipline of these establishments is afforded by the instructions given, in 1282, by Frère Jean Galande, Inquisitor of Carcassonne, to the jailer Raoul and his wife Bertrande, whose management had been rather lax. Under pain of irrevocable dismissal he is prohibited in future from keeping scriveners or horses in the prison; from borrowing money or accepting gifts from the prisoners; from retaining the money or effects of those who die; from releasing prisoners or allowing them to go beyond the first door, or to eat with him; from employing the servants on any other work or sending them anywhere, or gambling with them, or permitting them to gamble with each other.[450]

Evidently a prisoner who had money could obtain illicit favors from the honest Raoul; but these injunctions make no allusion to one of the most crying abuses which disgraced the establishments—the retention by the jailers of the moneys and provisions placed in their hands by the friends of the imprisoned. Frauds of all kinds naturally grew up among all who were concerned in dealing with these helpless creatures. In 1304 Hugolin de Polignac, the custodian of the royal prison at Carcassonne, was tried on charges of embezzling a part of the king's allowance, of carrying the names of prisoners on the rolls for years after their death, and of retaining the moneys contributed for them by their friends; but the evidence was insufficient to convict him. The cardinals whom Clement V. commissioned soon after to investigate the abuses of the Inquisition of Languedoc intimate broadly the nature of the frauds habitually practised, when they required the new jailers whom they appointed to swear to deliver to each captive without diminution the provisions supplied by the king, as well as those furnished by friends—an intimation confirmed by the decretals of Clement V. Their report shows that they were horror-struck with what they saw. At Carcassonne they took the control of{493} the prison wholly from the inquisitor, Geoffroi d'Ablis, and placed it in the hands of the bishop, ordering the upper cells to be repaired at once, in order that the aged and sick should be transferred to them; at Albi they struck the chains off the prisoners, commanded the cells to be lighted and new and better ones built within a month; at Toulouse things were equally bad. Everywhere there was complaint of lack of food and of beds, as well as of frequent torture. Their measures for reformation consisted in dividing the responsibility between bishop and inquisitor, whose concurrence was requisite to a sentence of imprisonment, and each of whom should appoint a jailer, while each jailer should have a key to each cell, and swear never to speak to a prisoner except in presence of his colleague. This insufficient remedy was adopted by Clement, and can hardly be imagined to have worked much improvement. Bernard Gui bitterly complained of the infamy cast on the Inquisition by the papal assertion of fraud and ill-treatment in the management of its prisons, and he pronounced the new regulations impracticable. Slender as was the restraint which they imposed on the inquisitors, we may feel sure that it was not long submitted to. In a few years Bernard Gui, in his Practica, assumes that the power of imprisoning lies wholly with the inquisitor; he contemptuously cites the Clementine canon by its title only, and proceeds to quote a bull of Clement IV. as if still in force, giving the authority to the inquisitor, and making no mention of the bishop. In fact, before the century was out, Eymerich considered the Clementine canons on this subject not worth inserting in his work, because, as he tells us, they were nowhere observed in consequence of their cost and inconvenience. About 1500, however, Bernardo di Como admits that the Clementine rule may be observed in punitive confinement after sentence, but holds that the inquisitor has sole control of the detentive prisons used before and during trial.[451]{494}

With such jailers it is probably rather to their corruption than to any lack of strength in the buildings that we may attribute the occasional escape of the inmates, which appears to have been by no means an infrequent occurrence. Even those who were confined in chains sometimes effected their liberation. More sufficient, however, as a means of release from the horrors of these foul dungeons was the excessive mortality caused by their filthy and unventilated squalor. Occasionally, as we have seen, the unfortunate were unlucky enough to live through protracted confinement, and there is one case in which a woman was graciously discharged, with crosses, in view of her having been for thirty-three years in the prison of Toulouse. As a rule, however, we may conclude that the expectation of life was very short. No records remain, if any were kept, to show the average term of those condemned to lifelong penance; but in the *autos de fé* there occur sentences pronounced upon prisoners who had died before their cases were ended, which show how large was the death-rate. These cases were despatched in batches. In the *auto* of 1310, at Toulouse, there are ten, who had died after confessing their heresy and before receiving sentence; in that of 1319 there are eight. The prison of Carcassonne seems to have been almost as deadly. In the *auto* of 1325 we find a lot of four similar cases, and in that of 1328 there are five. It is only under these peculiar circumstances that we have any chance of guessing at the deaths which occurred in prison, and from these scattered indications we can assume that the insanitary condition of the jails worked its inevitable result without human interference.[452]

Imprisonment was naturally the most frequent penance inflicted by the inquisitors. In Bernard Gui's Register of Sentences, comprising his operations between 1308 and 1322, there are six hundred and thirty-six condemnations recorded, which may be thus classified:{495}

Delivered to the secular court and burned	0
Bones exhumed and burned	7
Imprisoned	00
Bones exhumed of those who would have been imprisoned	1
Condemned to wear crosses	

Condemned to perform pilgrimages	6
Banished to Holy Land	
Fugitives	6
Condemnation of the Talmud	
Houses to be destroyed	6
	___
	36

and this may presumably be taken as a fair measure of the comparative frequency of the several punishments in use.

One peculiarity of the inquisitorial sentence remains to be noted. It always ended with a reservation of power to modify, to mitigate, to increase, and to reimpose at discretion. As early as 1244 the Council of Narbonne instructed the inquisitors always to reserve this power, and it became established as an invariable custom. Even without its formal expression, Innocent IV., in 1245, conferred on the inquisitors, acting with the advice and consent of the bishop of the penitent, authority to modify the penance imposed. The bishop, in fact, usually concurred in these alterations of sentences, but Zanchini informs us that though his assent should be asked, it was not essential, except in the case of clerks. The inquisitor, however, had no power to grant absolute pardons, which was reserved exclusively to the pope. The sin of heresy was so indelible that no authority short of the vicegerent of God could wash it out completely.[453]

This power to mitigate sentences was frequently exercised. It served as a stimulus to the penitents to give evidence by their deportment of the sincerity of their conversion, and, perhaps, also, it was occasionally of benefit as a means of depleting overcrowded jails. Thus in Bernard Gui's Register of Sentences there occur one hundred and nineteen cases of release from prison, with the obligation to wear the crosses, and of these fifty-one were subsequently{496} relieved from the crosses. Besides these latter, there are also eighty-seven cases in which those originally condemned to crosses were permitted to lay them aside. This mercy was not peculiar to the Inquisition of Toulouse. In 1328, in a single sentence, twenty-three persons were released from the prison of Carcassone, their penance being commuted to crosses, pilgrimages, and other observances. What the measure of mercy was in such cases may be guessed from another sentence of commutation at Carcassonne in 1329, liberating ten penitents, among them the Baroness of Montréal. They were required to wear the yellow crosses for life and to perform twenty-one pilgrimages, embracing shrines as distant as Rome, Compostella, Canterbury, and Cologne. They were to hear mass every Sunday and feast-day during life, and present themselves with rods to the officiating priest and receive the discipline in the face of the congregation; and also to accompany all processions and be similarly disciplined at the final station. Existence under such conditions might well be regarded as a doubtful blessing.[454]

These mitigatory sentences, moreover, like the original ones, strictly reserved the power of alteration and reimposition, with or without cause. When the Inquisition once laid hands upon a man it never released its hold, and its utmost mercy was merely a ticket-of-leave. Just as no verdict of acquittal ever was issued, so the Council of Béziers, in 1246, and Innocent IV., in 1247, told the inquisitors that when they liberated a prisoner he was to be warned that the slightest cause of suspicion would lead him to be punished without mercy, and that they must retain the right to incarcerate him again without the formality of a fresh trial or sentence if the interest of the faith required. These conditions were observed in the formularies and enjoined in the manuals of practice. The penitent was made to understand fully that whatever liberty he enjoyed was subject to the arbitrary discretion of his judge, who could recall him to dungeon or fetters at any moment, and in his oath of abjuration he pledged his person and all his property to appear at once whenever he might be summoned. If Bernard Gui in his Formulary gives a draft of pardon for person and property and disabilities of heirs, he adds a caution that it is{497} never, or most rarely, to be used. When some great object was to be attained, such as the capture of a prominent heretic teacher, the inquisitors might stretch their authority and hold out promises of this kind to his disciples to induce them to betray him—promises which, it is pleasant to say, were almost universally spurned. If special penances had been imposed, on their fulfilment the inquisitor, if he saw fit, might declare the penitent to be a man of good character, but this did not alter the reservation in the original sentence. The mercy of the Inquisition did not extend to a pardon, but only to a reprieve, *dum bene se gesserit*, and the man who had once undergone a sentence never knew at what moment he might not be summoned to hear of its reimposition or even of a harsher one. Once a delinquent, his fate forever after was in the hands of the silent and mysterious judge who need not hear him nor give any reason for his destruction. He lived forever on the verge of ruin, never knowing when the blow might fall, and utterly powerless to avert it. He was always a subject to be watched by the universal police of the Inquisition—the parish priest, the monks, the clergy, nay, the whole population—who were strictly enjoined to report any neglect of penance or suspicious conduct, when he was at once liable to the awful penalties of relapse. Nothing was easier for a secret enemy than to destroy him, safe that his name would never be mentioned. We may pity the victims of the stake and the dungeon, but their fate was scarce harder than that of the multitudes who were the objects of the Inquisition's apparent mercy, but whose existence from that hour was one of endless, hopeless anxiety.[455]

The same implacability manifested itself after death. Allusion has frequently been made to the exhumation of the bones of those who by opportunely dying had seemed to exchange the vengeance of man for that of God, and it is only necessary to mention here that the fate of the dead was harder than that of the living. If he had died after confession and repentance, it is true, his punishment{498} was only that which he would have received if alive, the digging up replacing imprisonment, and his heirs being forced to perform or compound for any lighter penance; but if he had not confessed and there was evidence of heresy he was classed with the impenitent heretics, his remains were delivered to the secular arm, and his property hopelessly confiscated. This will account for the large number of these executions as shown in the records quoted above. If the secular authorities hesitated to perform the task of exhumation, they were coerced with excommunication.[456]

The same spirit pursued the descendants. In the Roman law the crime of treason was pursued with merciless vindictiveness, and its provisions are constantly quoted by the canon lawyers as precedents for the punishment of heresy, with the addition that treason to God is far more heinous than that to an earthly sovereign. It was, perhaps, natural that the churchman, in his eagerness to defend the kingdom of God, should follow and surpass the example of the emperors, and this will explain, if it may not justify, much that is abhorrent in the inquisitorial procedure. In the Code of Justinian, treason is made especially odious by inflicting on the sons disability to hold office and to succeed to collateral estates. By the Council of Toulouse, in 1229, even spontaneously converted heretics were declared ineligible to public office. It was natural, therefore, that Frederic II. should apply the Roman practice to heresy, and should extend its provision to grandchildren. This, like the rest of his legislation, was eagerly adopted and enforced by the Church. Alexander IV., however, in a bull of 1257, repeatedly reissued by his successors, explained that this did not apply in cases where the culprit had made amends and performed penance, and this was still further lightened by Boniface VIII., who removed the incapacity from grandchildren by the female line of those who had died in heresy. In this form it remained permanently in the canon law.[457]{499}

The Inquisition depended so much upon secular officials for assistance that there was some justification in its seeking to prevent those who might be suspected of sympathizing with heresy from holding office in which they could thwart its plans and aid the offender. Yet as there was no prescription of time as to proceedings against the dead, so was there none in invoking disabilities against their descendants, and the records of the Inquisition were an inexhaustible treasury of torment for those who were in any way connected with heresy. No one, in fact, could feel sure that evidence might not at any moment be discovered or manufactured against some long-deceased parent or grandparent, which would ruin his career, and that some industrious searcher into the archives might not find some blot on his genealogical tree. In 1288 Philippe le Bel writes to the Seneschal of Carcassonne that Raymond Vitalis of Avignon is exercising the office of notary in Carcassonne, though his maternal grandfather, Roger Isarn, is said to have been burned for heresy. If this is the fact, the seneschal is ordered to deprive him of the position. In 1292 Guiraud d'Auterive, a sergeant-at-arms of the king, was proceeded against on the same grounds, and we find Guillem de S. Seine, the Inquisitor of Carcassonne, furnishing to the royal procureur evidence that, in 1256, Guiraud's father and mother had confessed to acts of heresy, and that, in 1276, his uncle, Raymond Carbonnel, had been burned as a perfected heretic. In these cases we see the royal power invoked for the dismissal of the official, but in the perfected theory of the Inquisition the inquisitor had the power to deprive of office any one whose father or grandfather had been a heretic or defender of heretics. In order to avoid questions like these, when a penitent had fulfilled his penance, prudent children would take out letters declaratory of the fact, so as to have evidence of capacity to hold office. In special cases the inquisitor had power to relieve descendants of these disabilities, and this was occasionally done; but, like the remission of penance, this relief was only a suspension, liable at any moment to forfeiture on the slightest manifestation of heretical tendencies.[458]{500}

Underlying all these sentences was another on which they, and, indeed, the whole power of the Inquisition, were based in last resort—the sentence of excommunication. Theoretically the censures of the Inquisition might be the same as those of any other ecclesiastics authorized to cut men off from salvation, but the latter had so habitually abused their functions that the anathema, in the mouth of priests who were neither feared nor respected, lost, at times at least, its awe-inspiring authority. The censures of the Inquisition were in the hands of a smaller body of men, selected for their implacable vigor, and no one ever disregarded them with impunity. The secular authorities, moreover, were bound to put to the ban and confiscate the property of any one whom the inquisitor might excommunicate for heresy or fautorship. In fact, as the inquisitors were fond of boasting, their curse was stronger in four ways than that of the secular clergy. They could coerce the temporal government to outlaw the excommunicate; they could force it to confiscate his property; they could condemn any one remaining under excommunication for a year; and they could inflict the major excommunication upon any one communicating with their excommunicates.[459] Thus they enforced obedience to their citations and submission to their penances. Thus they made the secular power execute their sentences; thus they swept aside the statutes that interfered with their proceedings; thus they proved that the kingdom of God which they represented was superior to the kingdoms of earth. Of all excommunications that of the inquisitor worked the speediest vengeance and inspired the sharpest terror, and the boldest shrank from provoking it. {501}

CHAPTER XIII.

CONFISCATION.

ALTHOUGH, for the most part, as we shall see, confiscation was technically not the work of the Inquisition, the distinction was rather nominal than real. Even in times and places in which the inquisitor did not pronounce the sentence of confiscation, it was the accompaniment of the sentence which he did pronounce. It was, therefore, one of the most serious of the penalties at his disposal, and the largeness of the results effected by it give it an importance worthy a somewhat minute examination.

For the source of this, as of so much else, we must look to the Roman law. It is true that, cruel as were the imperial edicts against heresy, they did not go to the length of thus indirectly punishing the innocent. Even when the detested Manichæans were mercilessly condemned to death, their property was confiscated only when their heirs were likewise heretics. If the children were orthodox they succeeded to the estate of the heretic parent, who could not execute a will and disinherit them. It was otherwise with crime. Any conviction involving deportation or the mines carried with it confiscation, though the wife could reclaim her dower and any gifts made to her before the commission of the offence, and so could children emancipated from the *patria potestas*. All else inured to the fisc. In *majestas* or treason, the offender was liable to condemnation after death, involving the confiscation of his estate, which was held to have lapsed to the fisc at the time when he first conceived the crime. These provisions furnished the armory whence pope and king drew the weapons which rendered the pursuit of heresy attractive and profitable.[460]

King Roger, who occupied the throne of the Two Sicilies during the first half of the twelfth century, seems to have been the {502} first to apply the Roman practice by decreeing confiscation for all who apostatized from the Catholic faith—whether to the Greek Church, to Islam, or to Judaism does not appear. Yet the Church cannot escape the responsibility of naturalizing this penalty in European law as a punishment for spiritual transgressions. The great Council of Tours, held by Alexander III., in 1163, commanded all secular princes to imprison heretics and confiscate their property. Lucius III., in his Verona decretal of 1184, sought to obtain for the Church the benefit of the confiscation which he again declared to be incurred by heresy. One of the earliest acts of Innocent III., in his double capacity of temporal prince and head of Christianity, was to address a decretal to his subjects of Viterbo, in which he says,

"In the lands subject to our temporal jurisdiction we order the property of heretics to be confiscated; in other lands we command this to be done by the temporal princes and powers, who, if they show themselves negligent therein, shall be compelled to do it by ecclesiastical censures. Nor shall the property of heretics who withdraw from heresy revert to them, unless some one pleases to take pity on them. For as, according to the legal sanctions, in addition to capital punishment, the property of those guilty of *majestas* is confiscated, and life simply is allowed to their children through mercy alone, so much the more should those who wander from the faith and offend the Son of God be cut off from Christ and be despoiled of their temporal goods, since it is a far greater crime to assail spiritual than temporal majesty."[461]

This decretal, which was adopted into the canon law, is important as embodying the whole theory of the subject. In imitation of the Roman law of *majestas*, the property of the heretic was forfeited from the moment he became a heretic or committed an act {503} of heresy. If he recanted, it might be restored to him purely in mercy. When the ecclesiastical tribunals declared him to be, or to have been, a heretic, confiscation operated itself; the act of seizing the property was a matter for the secular power to whom it inured, and the mercy which might spare it could only be shown by that power. All this it is requisite to keep in mind if we would correctly appreciate some points which have frequently been misunderstood.

Innocent's decretal further illustrates the fact that at the commencement of the struggle with heresy the chief difficulty encountered by the Church in relation to confiscation was to persuade or coerce the temporal rulers to do what it held to be their duty in taking possession of heretical property. This was one of the principal offences which Raymond VI. of Toulouse expiated so bitterly, as explained to him by Innocent in 1210. His son proclaimed it as the law in his statutes of 1234, and included in its provisions, in accordance with the Ordonnance of Louis VIII., in 1226, and that of Louis IX., in 1229, all who favored heretics in any way or refused to aid in their capture; but his policy did not always comport with its enforcement, and he sometimes had to be sternly rebuked for non-feasance. After all danger of armed resistance had disappeared, however, sovereigns, as a rule, eagerly welcomed the opportunity of recruiting their slender revenues, and the confiscation of the property of heretics and of fautors of heresy was generally recognized in European law, although the Church was occasionally obliged to repeat its injunctions and threats, and though there were some regions in which they were slackly obeyed.[462] {504}

The relation of the Inquisition to confiscation varied essentially with time and place. In France the principle derived from the Roman law was generally recognized, that the title to property devolved to the fisc as soon as the crime had been committed. There was therefore nothing for the inquisitor to do with regard to it. He simply ascertained and announced the guilt of the accused and left the State to take action. Thus Gui

Foucoix treats the subject as one wholly outside of the functions of the inquisitor, who at most can only advise the secular ruler or intercede for mercy; while he holds that those only are legally exempt from forfeiture who come forward spontaneously and confess before any evidence has been taken against them. In accordance with this, there is, as a rule, no allusion to confiscation in the sentences of the French Inquisition, though in one or two instances chance has preserved for us, in the accounts of the *procureurs des encours*, or royal stewards of the confiscations, evidence that estates were sold and covered into the fisc in cases in which the forfeiture is not specified in the sentence. In condemnations of absentees and of the dead, confiscation is occasionally declared, as though in these the State might need some guidance, but even here the practice is not uniform. In a sentence issued by Guillem Arnaud and Étienne de S. Thibery, November 24, 1241, on two absentees, their estates are adjudged to whom it may concern. In the Register of Bernard de Caux (1246-1248), in thirty-two cases of contumacious absentees confiscation is included in the sentence, and in nine similar ones it is omitted, as well as in one hundred and fifty-nine condemnations to prison in which it was undoubtedly operative. In the Inquisition of Carcassonne, a sentence of December 12, 1328, on five deceased persons, who would have been imprisoned had they lived, ends with "*et consequenter bona ipsorum dicimus confiscanda*," while a previous sentence, February 24, 1325, identical in character, on four defunct culprits, has no such corollary appended. In fact, strictly speaking, it was recognized that the inquisitor{505} had no power to remit confiscations without permission from the fisc, and the custom of extending mercy to those who came forward voluntarily and confessed was founded upon a special concession to that effect granted by Raymond of Toulouse to the Inquisition in 1235. As soon as a suspected heretic was cited or arrested the secular officials sequestrated his property and notified his debtors by proclamation. No doubt, when condemnation took place, the inquisitor communicated the result to the proper officials, but as a rule no record of the fact seems to have been kept in the archives of the Holy Office, although an early manual of practice specifies it as part of his duty to see that the confiscation was enforced. At a later period, in 1328, in a record of an assembly of experts held at Pamiers, the presence is specified of Arnaud Assalit, royal *procureur des encours* of Carcassonne, so that probably by this time it had become customary for that official to attend these deliberations and thus obtain early notice of the sentences to be passed.[463]

In Italy it was long before any settled practice was established. In 1252 a bull of Innocent IV. directs the rulers of Lombardy, Tarvisina, and Romagna to confiscate without fail the property of all who were excommunicated as heretics, or as receivers, defenders, or fautors of heretics, thus recognizing confiscation as a matter belonging to the secular power. Yet soon the papal authority succeeded in obtaining a share of the spoils, even beyond the limits of the States of the Church, as is seen in the bulls *Ad extirpanda* of Innocent IV. and Alexander IV., and the matter thus became one in which the Inquisition had a direct interest. The indifference which so well became the French tribunals was therefore not readily maintained, and the share of the inquisitor in the results led him to participate in the process of securing them. Yet there{506} were variations in practice. Zanghino tells us that formerly confiscations were decreed in the States of the Church by the ecclesiastical judges and elsewhere by the secular power, but that in his time (circa 1320) they were everywhere (in Italy) included in the jurisdiction of the episcopal and inquisitorial courts, and the secular authorities had nothing to do with them; but he adds that confiscation is prescribed by law for heresy, and that the inquisitor has no discretion to remit it, except in the case of voluntary converts with the assent of the bishop. Yet though the forfeiture occurs *ipso facto* by the commission of the crime, it requires a declaratory sentence of confiscation. This consequently was expressed in the most formal manner in the condemnation of the accused by the Italian Inquisition, and the secular authorities were told not to interfere unless called upon.[464]

At a very early period in some places the Italian inquisitors seem to have undertaken not only to decree but to control the confiscations. About 1245 we find the Florentine inquisitor, Ruggieri Calcagni, sentencing a Catharan named Diotaiuti, for relapse, with a fine of one hundred lire. Ruggieri acknowledges the receipt of this, to be applied to the pope, or to the furtherance of the faith, and formally concedes the rest of the heretic's estate to his wife Jacoba, thus exercising ownership over the whole. Yet this was not maintained, for in 1283 there is a sentence of the Podestà of Florence, reciting that the inquisitor Frà Salomone da Lucca had notified him that the widow Ruvinosa, lately deceased, had died a heretic, and that her property was to be confiscated; whereupon he orders it to be seized and sold, and the proceeds divided according to the papal constitutions. At length, however, the inquisitors assumed and exercised full control over the handling of the confiscations. In the conveyance of a confiscated house by the municipal authorities of Florence, in 1327, to the Dominicans, the deed is careful to assert that it is made with the assent of the inquisitor. Even in Naples we see King Robert, in 1324, ordering the inquisitors to pay out of the royal share of the confiscations fifty ounces of gold to the Prior of the Church of San Domenico of Naples, to aid in its completion.[465]{507}

In Germany the Diet of Worms, in 1231, indicates the confusion existing in the feudal mind between heresy and treason by allowing the allodial lands and personal property of the condemned to descend to the heirs, while fiefs were confiscated to the suzerain. If he was a serf, his goods inured to his master; but from all personal property was deducted the cost of burning its owner and the *droits de justice* of the seigneur-justicier. Two years later, in 1233, the Council of Mainz protested against the injustice, which quickly showed itself in Germany as elsewhere, of assuming guilt as soon as a man was accused, and treating his property as though he were convicted. It directed that the estates of those on trial should remain untouched until sentence was rendered, and any one who meanwhile should plunder or partition them should be excommunicated until he made restitution and rendered satisfaction. Finally, however, when the Emperor Charles IV. endeavored to introduce the Inquisition into Germany, in 1369, he adopted the Italian custom and ordered one third of the confiscations to be made over to the inquisitors.[466]

The exact degree of criminality which entailed confiscation is not capable of very rigid definition. Even in states where the inquisitor nominally had no control over it, the arbitrary discretion lodged with him as to the fate of the accused placed the matter practically in his hands, and his notification to the secular authorities would be a virtual sentence. It is probable that custom varied with time and with the temper of the inquisitor. We have seen that Innocent III. commanded it for all heretics, but what constituted technical heresy was not so easily determined. The statutes of Raymond decreed it not only for heretics, but for those who showed them favor. The Council of Béziers, in 1233, demanded it for all reconciled converts not condemned to wear crosses, and those of Béziers, in 1246, and Albi, in 1254, prescribed it for all whom the inquisitors should penance with imprisonment. Still, in a sentence of February 19, 1237, in which the inquisitors{508} of Toulouse condemn some twenty or thirty penitents to perpetual imprisonment, confiscation is only threatened as an additional punishment in case they do not perform the penance. Imprisonment, however, finally was admitted by legists as the invariable test; although St. Louis, when in 1259 he mitigated his Ordonnance of 1229, ordered confiscation not only for those who were condemned to prison, but for those who contumaciously refused obedience to citations and those in whose houses heretics were found, his officials being instructed to ascertain from the inquisitors in all cases, while pending, whether the accused deserved imprisonment, and if so, to retain the sequestrated property. When he further provided, as a special grace, that the heirs should be restored to possession in cases where the heretic had offered himself for conversion before citation, had entered a religious order, and had worthily died there, he shows how universal confiscation had previously been and how ruthlessly the principle had been enforced that a single act of heresy forfeited all ownership. In fact, even at the close of the fifteenth century, the rule was laid down that confiscation was a matter of course, while restoration of property to a reconciled penitent required an express declaration.[467]

According to the most lenient construction of the law, therefore, the imprisonment of a reconciled convert carried with it the confiscation of his property, and as imprisonment was the ordinary penance, confiscation was general. There may possibly have been exceptions. The six prisoners released in 1248 by Innocent IV. had been in jail for some time—some of them for four years and more after confessing heresy—and yet the liberal contributions to the Holy Land which purchased their pardon show that they or their friends must have had control of property—unless, indeed, the money was raised on a pledge of the estates to be restored. So when Alaman de Roaix was condemned to imprisonment by Bernard de Caux, in 1248, the sentence provided for an annuity to be paid to a person designated, and for compensation to be made for the rapine which he had committed, which would look as though{509} property were left to him; but as he had for ten years been a contumacious and proscribed fugitive, these fines must have been taken out of his estate in the hands of the State. Apparent exceptions such as these can be accounted for, and the proceedings of the Inquisition as a whole indicate that imprisonment and confiscation were inseparable. Sometimes, even, it is stated in sentences passed upon the dead that they are pronounced worthy of imprisonment in order to deprive the heirs of succession to the estates. At a later date, indeed, Eymerich, who dismisses the whole matter briefly as one with which the inquisitor has no concern, speaks as though confiscation only took place when a heretic did not repent and recant before sentence, but his commentator, Pegna, easily proves this to be an error. Zanghino assumes as a matter of course that property is forfeited by the act of heresy; and he points out that pecuniary penances cannot be imposed because the whole estate is gone, although there may be mercy shown at discretion with the assent of the bishop, and simple suspicion is not subject to confiscation.[468]

In the early zeal of persecution everything was swept away in wholesale seizure, but, in 1237, Gregory IX. assumed that the dowers of Catholic wives ought to be exempt in certain cases, and in 1247 Innocent IV. erected it into a rule that such dowers should be restored to the wives and should not be included in future forfeitures, although heresy would not justify divorce, and, in 1258, St. Louis accepted this rule. It was subject to serious limitations, however, since under the canon law the wife could not claim it if she had been cognizant of the husband's heresy when she married, and, according to some authorities, if she had lived with him after ascertaining it, or even if she had failed to inform against him within forty days after discovering it. As the children were incapable of inheritance, she only held the dower for life, after which it fell into the fisc.[469]{510}

Although in principle confiscation was an affair of the State, the division of the spoils did not follow any invariable rule. Before the organization of the Inquisition, when the Waldenses of Strassburg were burned, it is mentioned that their forfeited property was equally divided between the Church and the secular authorities. Lucius III., as we have just seen, endeavored to turn the forfeitures to the benefit of the Church. In the papal territory there could be little question as to this, and Innocent IV., in his bull *Ad extirpanda* of 1252, showed disinterestedness in devoting the whole proceeds to the stimulation of persecution. One third was given to the local authorities, one third to the officials of the Inquisition, and one third to the bishop and inquisitor, to be expended in the assault on heresy—provisions which were retained in the subsequent recensions of the bull by Alexander IV. and Clement IV., while forfeited bail went exclusively to the inquisitor. Yet this was speedily held to refer only to the independent states of Italy, for, in 1260, we find Alexander IV. ordering the inquisitors of Rome and Spoleto to sell the confiscated estates of heretics and pay over the proceeds to the pope himself; and a transaction of 1261 shows Urban IV. collecting three hundred and twenty lire from some confiscations at Spoleto.[470]

At length, both in the Roman province and elsewhere throughout Italy, the custom settled down to a tripartite division between the local community, the Inquisition, and the papal camera, the reason for the latter, as given by Benedict XI., being that the bishops appropriated to themselves the share intrusted to them for the persecution of heresy. In Florence a transaction of 1283 shows this to be the received regulation; and documents of various dates during the next half-century indicate that it was the custom of the republic to appoint attorneys or trustees to take seisin of confiscated property in the name of the city, which in 1319 liberally granted its share for the next ten years to the construction of the church of Santa Reparata. That the amounts were not small may be guessed from a petition of the inquisitors to the republic in 1299, setting forth that the Holy Office must have funds wherewith{511} to pay its stipendiary officials, and therefore praying leave to invest in real estate the sums accruing to the Inquisition from this source—showing accumulations prudently garnered for the future. The request was granted to the extent of one thousand lire, with the proviso that none of the city's share be taken. This latter precaution would seem to argue no great confidence in the integrity of the inquisitors, nor was the insinuation uncalled for. By this time the money-changers had fairly occupied the Temple, and, as we have seen in the last chapter, it seemed almost impossible to preserve official honesty when persecution had become almost as much a financial speculation as a matter of faith. That plain-spoken Franciscan, Alvaro Pelayo, Bishop of Silva, writing about the year 1335, bitterly reproaches those of his brethren who act as inquisitors with their abuse of the funds accruing to the Holy Office. The papal division into thirds he declares was generally disregarded; the inquisitors monopolized the whole and spent it on themselves or enriched their kindred at their pleasure. Chance has preserved in the Florentine archives some documents confirmatory of this accusation. It seems that in 1343 Clement VI. obtained evidence that the inquisitors of both Florence and Lucca were habitually defrauding the papal camera of its third of the fines and confiscations, and accordingly he sent to Pietro di Vitale, Primicerio of Lucca, authority to collect the sums in arrears and to prosecute the embezzlers. How it fared with them we have no means of knowing, but the camera seems not to have gained much. In filling the vacancies thus occasioned Pietro di Aquila, a Franciscan of high standing, was appointed in Florence, who fell at once into the same evil ways, and within two years was obliged to fly from a prosecution by the primicerio, in addition to the charges of extortion brought against him by the republic.[471]

In Naples, under the Angevines, when the Inquisition was first introduced, Charles of Anjou monopolized the confiscations with the same rapacity that was customary in France. As early as March, 1270, we find him writing to his representatives in the Principato Ultra that three heretics had recently been burned at{512} Benevento, whose estates he orders looked after and accounted for in detail. In 1290, however, Charles II. ordered the fines and confiscations to be divided into thirds, of which one should inure to the royal fisc, one be used for the promotion of the faith, and one be given to the Inquisition. Feudal lands, however, were to revert to the crown or to the immediate lord as the case might require.[472]

In Venice the compromise reached in 1289 between the signiory and Nicholas IV., whereby the republic permitted the introduction of the Inquisition, provided that all receipts of the Holy Office should be for the benefit of the State, and this arrangement seems to have been maintained. In Piedmont the confiscations were divided between the State and the Inquisition until, in the latter half of the fifteenth century, Amedeo IX. took the whole, allowing to the Holy Office only the expenses of the proceedings.[473]

In the other Italian states the papal curia grew dissatisfied with its share, when there was no longer a necessity of purchasing the co-operation of the civil power with a third of the spoils. It is a disputed point with the jurists when and how the change was effected, but in the first quarter of the fourteenth century the Church succeeded in grasping the whole of the confiscations, which were divided equally between the Inquisition and the papal camera. The rapacity with which this source of income was exploited is illustrated in a case occurring at Pisa in 1304. The inquisitor Angelo da Reggio had condemned the memory of a deceased citizen, Loterio Bonamici, and confiscated his property, part of which he then gave away and part he sold at prices which the papal curia esteemed too low. Benedict XI. thereupon ordered the Bishop of Ostia not to punish the inquisitor, but to use freely the censures of the Church in hunting up the assets in the hands of the holders and to take it from them. Finally, in 1438, Eugenius IV. generously handed back to the bishops the share of the papal camera in order to stimulate their slackness in persecution, and, where the bishop was also the temporal lord of his see, the confiscations were to be equally divided between him and the Inquisition. Bernardo di Como, however, writing about the year 1500, asserts that the{513} whole confiscations inure to the inquisitor to be expended at his discretion; but he subsequently admits that the subject is confused and uncertain, owing to contradictory papal decisions and conflicting jurisdictions in different territories.[474]

In Spain the rule was laid down that if the heretic were a clerk, or a lay vassal of the Church, the confiscation went to the Church; if otherwise, to the temporal seigneur.[475]

This greed for the plunder of the wretched victims of persecution is peculiarly repulsive as exhibited by the Church, and may to some extent palliate the similar action by the State in countries where the latter was strong enough to seize and retain it. The threats of coercion, which at first were necessary to induce the temporal princes to confiscate the property of their heretical subjects, soon became superfluous, and history has few displays of man's eagerness to profit by his fellow's misfortunes more deplorable than that of the vultures which followed in the wake of the Inquisition to batten on the ruin which it wrought.

In Languedoc at first the Inquisition endeavored to control the confiscations for the purpose of building prisons and maintaining prisoners, but these pretensions received no attention. Under the feudal system, the confiscations were for the benefit of the seigneur haut-justicier. The rapid extension of the royal jurisdiction, in the second half of the thirteenth century in France, ended by practically placing them in the hands of the king, but during the earlier and more profitable period there were quarrels over the spoils. After the treaty of Paris, in 1229, St. Louis, in granting fiefs in the newly-acquired territories, seems to have endeavored to provide for these questions by reserving the confiscations for heresy. The prudence{514} of this is shown by the suit brought by the Maréchaux de Mirepoix—one of the few families founded by the adventurers who accompanied de Montfort—who claimed the movables of all heretics captured in their lands, even if the goods were in the lands of the king—a demand which was rejected by the Parlement of Paris, in 1269. The bishops put in a claim to the confiscations of all real and personal property of heretics living under their jurisdiction, and at the Council of Lille (Comtat Venaissin) in 1251, they threatened with excommunication any one who should dispute it. The groundlessness of this claim is seen in an agreement made under the auspices of the Legate Romano in December, 1229, between the Bishop of Béziers and the king, in which the royal right to the confiscations is recognized as incontestable, and the bishop only stipulates that in case of fiefs they shall, if granted, be held subject to his seignorial rights, or if the king retains them some compensation shall be made for the loss of the suzerainty. This indicates a source of reasonable complaint, for, in the annexation of fiefs to the crown, the bishops found themselves losing in place of profiting by persecution. Various efforts were made to adjust these conflicting claims over the spoil. By a transaction of 1234 we see that the king had subjected himself to the stipulation of parting with all confiscated property within a year and a day. The Council of Béziers, in 1246, adopted a canon on the subject, but it could not be enforced, and at length, about 1255, St. Louis agreed upon a compromise, whereby all confiscated lands subject to the bishops were equally divided, with a right on the part of the prelates to buy out, within two months, the royal share at a price fixed by arbitration; if this right was not exercised the king was bound, within a year and a day, to pass the lands out of his hands into those of a person of the same condition as the former owner, to be held under the same terms of service or villeinage; but all movables were declared to belong unreservedly to the crown. Under this arrangement the temporalities of the sees grew rapidly. We have seen the apostolic poverty which afflicted the bishops of Toulouse prior to the crusades: during the succeeding century the whole land was impoverished and the cities suffered especially, yet when, in 1317, John XXII. carved six new bishoprics out of the see of Toulouse, his reason was found in the excessive revenues of the bishop, amounting to forty thousand livres Tournois per annum, although{515} it had already been shorn of nearly half of its territory by Boniface VIII. to form the see of Pamiers.[476]

The bishops of Albi were especially active and fortunate in this saturnalia of plunder. During the confusion of the wars and the settlement they assumed rights, including*haute justice* and the confiscations, which led to contests with the representatives of the crown, lasting for thirty years. They were specially active in the pursuit of heretics, which they thus found profitable as well as praiseworthy. In 1247 Bishop Bertrand procured from Innocent IV. a special deputation of inquisitorial power, probably to strengthen his claims, and the next year he drove a thriving business in selling commutations for confiscation to condemned and repentant heretics—an expedient more lucrative than regular, for when Alphonse of Poitiers, in 1253, endeavored to speculate in the confiscations in the same way, he was compelled to desist by the Archbishop of Narbonne and the Bishop of Toulouse, who declared that it would lead to the scandal of the faithful and the destruction of religion. Finally, to settle the claims of the bishop on the confiscations, St. Louis, in December, 1264, made with Bernard de Combret, the incumbent of the see, a convention, promptly confirmed by Urban IV., by which the prelate was entitled to one half of all confiscations of realty and personalty within the diocese, with the further advantage that the king's share of the real estate passed into possession of the bishop if it was not sold within a twelvemonth, and became his absolute property if not sold within{516} three years. Accordingly in the accounts of the royal*procureurs des encours* of Carcassonne we constantly find the confiscations in Albi shared with the bishop. Although between St. John's day 1322 and 1323 this share in money amounted only to one hundred and sixty livres, there were times when it was much greater. About the year 1300 Bishop Bernard de Castanet generously gave to the Dominican Church of Albi his portion of the estates of two citizens, Guillem Aymeric and Jean de Castanet, condemned after death, which amounted to more than one thousand livres. It can readily be imagined that this arrangement with the crown gave rise to constant quarrels. In vain Philippe le Bel, in 1307, ordered the observance of the agreement with restitution for any infractions. In 1316 we find the bishop claiming properties which had not been sold within the three years, and Arnaud Assalit, the*procureur*, arguing that he had been prevented from effecting sales by just and legitimate causes, when the seneschal, Aymeric de Croso, decided that the impediments had been legitimate, and that the rights of the king were not forfeited.[477]

These were not the only questions arising from this wholesale spoliation which afforded an ample harvest to the legal profession. A suit brought by the bishops of Rodez for some lands held by the crown as heretic confiscations dragged on for thirty years until it reached the Parlement of Paris, which coolly annulled all the

169

proceedings on the ground that those who had acted for the crown had lacked the requisite authority. Almost equally protracted and confused was a suit between Eleanor de Montfort, Countess of Vendôme, and the king over the lands of Jean Baudier and Raymond Calverie. The confiscations occurred in 1300; in 1327 the suit was still pursuing its weary way, to be finally compromised in 1335.[478]

All prelates were not as rapacious as those of Albi, one of whom we find still, in 1328, complaining of the evasions resorted to by the victims to save a fragment of their property for their{517} families; but the princes and their representatives were relentless in grasping all that they could lay their hands on. I have mentioned that as soon as a suspect was cited before the Inquisition his property was sequestrated to await the result, and proclamation was made to all his debtors and those who held his effects to bring everything to the king. Charles of Anjou carried this practice to Naples, where a royal order, in 1269, to arrest sixty-nine heretics contains instructions to seize simultaneously their goods, which are to be held for the king. So assured were the officials that condemnation would follow trial that they frequently did not await the result, but carried out the confiscation in advance. This abuse was coeval with the founding of the Inquisition. In 1237 Gregory IX. complained of it and forbade it, but to little purpose, for in 1246 the Council of Béziers again prohibited it, unless, indeed, the offender had knowingly adhered to those who were known to be heretics, in which case, apparently, it was sanctioned. When, in 1259, St. Louis mitigated the rigors of confiscation, he indirectly forbade this wrong by instructing his officials that, when the accused was not condemned to imprisonment, they should give him or his heirs a hearing to reclaim the property; but, if there was any suspicion of heresy, it was not to be restored without taking security that it should be surrendered if anything was proved within five years, during which period it was not to be alienated. Yet still the outrage of confiscation before conviction continued with sufficient frequency to induce Boniface VIII. to embody its prohibition in the canon law. Even this did not put a stop to it. The Inquisition had so habituated men's minds to the belief that no one escaped who had once fallen into its hands, that the officials considered themselves safe in acting upon the presumption. By an unusual coincidence we have the data from various sources in a single case of this kind which is doubtless the type of many others. In the prosecutions at Albi in 1300, a certain Jean Baudier was first examined January 20, when he acknowledged nothing. At a second hearing, February 5, he confessed to acts of heresy, and he was condemned March 7. Yet his confiscated property was sold January 29, not only before his sentence, but before his confession. Guillem Garric, charged with complicity in the plot to destroy the inquisitorial records of Carcassonne in 1284, was not sentenced until 1319, but in 1301 we find the Count of Foix{518} and the royal officials quarrelling over his confiscated castle of Monteirat.[479]

The ferocious rapacity with which this process of confiscation was carried on may be conceived from a report made by Jean d'Arsis, Seneschal of Rouergue, to Alphonse of Poitiers, about 1253, as an evidence of the zeal with which he was guarding the interests of his suzerain. The Bishop of Rodez was conducting a vigorous episcopal inquisition, and at Najac had handed over a certain Hugues Paraire as a heretic, whom the seneschal burned "incontinently" and collected over one thousand livres Tournois from his estate. Hearing, subsequently, that the bishop had cited before him at Rodez six other citizens of Najac, d'Arsis hastened thither to see that no fraud was practised on the count. The bishop told him that these men were all heretics, and that he would make the count gain one hundred thousand sols from their confiscations, but both he and his assessors begged the seneschal to forego a portion to the culprits or their children, which that loyal servitor bluntly refused. Then the bishop, following evil counsel, and in fraud of the rights of the count, endeavored to elude the forfeiture by condemning the heretics to some lighter penance. The seneschal, however, knew his master's rights and seized the property, after which he allowed some pittance to the penitents and their children, reporting that in addition to this he was in possession of about one thousand livres; and he winds up by advising the count, if he wishes not to be defrauded, to appoint some one to watch and supervise the further inquisitions of the bishop. On the other hand the bishops complained that the officials of Alphonse permitted heretics, for a pecuniary consideration, to retain a part or the whole of their confiscated property, or else condemned to the flames those who did not deserve it in order to seize their estates. These frightful abuses grew so unbearable that, in 1254, the officials of Alphonse, including Gui Foucoix, endeavored to reform them by issuing general regulations on the subject, but the matter was one{519} which in its inherent nature scarce admitted of reform. Yet Alphonse, with all his greed, was not unwilling to share the plunder with those who secured it for him, and several of his not wholly disinterested liberalities of this kind are on record. In 1268 we have a letter of his assigning to the Inquisition a revenue of one hundred livres per annum on the confiscated estate of a heretic; and in 1270 another, confirming the foundation of a chapel from a similar source.[480]

Nothing could exceed the minute thoroughness with which every fragment of a confiscated estate was followed up and seized. The account of the collections of confiscated property from 1302 to 1313 by the *procureurs des encours* of Carcassone is extant in MS., and shows how carefully the debts due to the condemned were looked after, even to a few pence for a measure of corn. In the case of one wealthy prisoner, Guillem de Fenasse, the estate was not wound up for eight or ten years, and the whole number of debts collected foots up to eight hundred and fifty-nine, in amounts ranging from five deniers upward. As the collectors never credit themselves with amounts paid in discharge of debts due by these estates, it is evident that the rule that a heretic could give no valid obligations was strictly construed and that creditors were shamelessly cheated. In this seizure of debts the nobles asserted a right to claim any sums due by debtors who were their vassals, but Philippe de

Valois, in 1329, decided that when the debts were payable at the domicile of the heretic they inured to the royal fisc, irrespective of the allegiance of the debtor. Another illustration of the remorseless greed which seized everything is found in a suit decided by the Parlement of Paris in 1302. On the death of the Chevalier Guillem Prunèle and his wife Isabelle, the guardianship of their orphans would legally vest in the next of kin, the Chevalier Bernard de Montesquieu, but he had been burned some years before for heresy, and his estate, of course, confiscated. The Seneschal of Carcassonne insisted that the guardianship which thus subsequently fell in formed part of the assets of the estate, and he accordingly assumed it, but a nephew, an Esquire Bernard de{520} Montesquieu, contested the matter and finally obtained a decision in his favor.[481]

Equal care was exercised in recovering alienated property. As, in obedience to the Roman law of *majestas*, forfeiture occurred *ipso facto* as soon as the crime of heresy was committed, the heretic could convey no legal title, and any assignments which he might have made were void, no matter through how many hands the property might have passed. The holder was forced to surrender it, nor could he demand restitution of what he had paid, unless the money or other consideration were found among the goods of the heretic. The eagerness with which, in such cases, the rigor of the law was enforced may be estimated from one occurring in 1272. Charles of Anjou had written from Naples to his viguier and sous-viguier at Marseilles telling them that a certain Maria Roberta, before condemnation to prison for heresy, had sold a house which was subject to confiscation; this he ordered them to seize, to sell by auction, and to report the proceeds; but they neglected to do so. The viguiers were changed, and now the unforgetful Charles writes to the new officials, repeating his orders and holding them personally responsible for obedience. At the same time he writes to his seneschal with instructions to look after the matter, as it lies very near to his heart.[482]

The cruelty of the process of confiscation was enhanced by the pitiless methods employed. As soon as a man was arrested for suspicion of heresy his property was sequestrated and seized by the officials, to be returned to him in the rare cases in which his guilt might be declared not proven. This rule was enforced in the most rigorous manner, every article of his household gear and provisions being inventoried, as well as his real estate.[483] Thus, whether innocent or guilty, his family were turned out-of-doors to starve or to depend upon the precarious charity of others—a charity{521} chilled by the fact that any manifestation of sympathy was dangerous. It would be difficult to estimate the amount of human misery arising from this source alone.

In this chaos of plunder we may readily imagine that those who were engaged in such work were not over-nice as to securing a share of the spoliations. In 1304 Jacques de Polignac, who had been for twenty years keeper of the inquisitorial jail at Carcassonne, and several of the officials employed on the confiscations, were found to have converted and detained a large amount of valuable property, including a castle, several farms and other lands, vineyards, orchards, and movables, all of which they were compelled to disgorge and to suffer punishment at the king's pleasure.[484]

It is pleasant to turn from this cruel greed to a case which excited much interest in Flanders at a time when in that region the Inquisition had become so nearly dormant that the usages of confiscation were almost forgotten. The Bishop of Tournay and the Vicar of the Inquisition condemned at Lille a number of heretics, who were duly burned. They confiscated the property, claiming the movables for the Church and the inquisitor, and the realty for the fisc. The magistrates of Lille boldly interposed, declaring that among the liberties of their town was the privilege that no burgher could forfeit both body and goods; and, acting for the children of one of the victims, they took out *apostoli* and appealed to the pope. The counsellors of the suzerain, Philippe le Bon of Burgundy, with a clearer perception of the law, claimed that the whole confiscations inured to him, while the ecclesiastics declared the rule to be invariable that the personalty went to the Church and only the real estate to the fisc. The triangular quarrel threatened long and costly litigation, and finally all parties agreed to leave the decision to the duke himself. With rare wisdom, in 1430, he settled the matter, with general consent, by deciding that the sentence of confiscation should be treated as not rendered, and the property be left to the heirs, at the same time expressly declaring that the rights of Church, Inquisition, city, and state, were reserved without prejudice, in any case that might arise in future, which was, he said, not likely to occur. He did not manifest the same disinterestedness in 1460, however, in the terrible persecution{522} of the sorcerers of Arras, when the movables were confiscated to the episcopal treasury, and he seized the landed property in spite of the privileges alleged by the city.[485]

In addition to the misery inflicted by these wholesale confiscations on the thousands of innocent and helpless women and children thus stripped of everything, it would be almost impossible to exaggerate the evil which they entailed upon all classes in the business of daily life. All safeguards were withdrawn from every transaction. No creditor or purchaser could be sure of the orthodoxy of him with whom he was dealing; and, even more than the principle that ownership was forfeited as soon as heresy had been committed by the living, the practice of proceeding against the memory of the dead after an interval virtually unlimited, rendered it impossible for any man to feel secure in the possession of property, whether it had descended in his family for generations, or had been acquired within an ordinary lifetime.

The prescription of time against the Church had to be at least forty years—against the Roman Church, a hundred, and this prescription ran, not from the commission of the crime, but from its detection. Though some legists held that proceedings against the deceased had to be commenced within five years after death, others asserted that there was no limit, and the practice of the Inquisition shows that the latter opinion was followed. The prescription of forty years' possession by good Catholics was further limited by the conditions that they must at no time have had a knowledge that the former owner was a heretic, and, moreover, he must have died with an unsullied reputation for orthodoxy—both points which might cast a grave doubt on titles.[486]{523}

Prosecution of the dead, as we have seen, was a mockery in which virtually defence was impossible and confiscation inevitable. How unexpectedly the blow might fall is seen in the case of Gherardo of Florence. He was rich and powerful, a member of one of the noblest and oldest houses, and was consul of the city in 1218. Secretly a heretic, he was hereticated on his death-bed between 1246 and 1250, but the matter lay dormant until 1313, when Frà Grimaldo, the Inquisitor of Florence, brought a successful prosecution against his memory. In the condemnation were included his children Ugolino, Cante, Nerlo, and Bertuccio, and his grandchildren, Goccia, Coppo, Frà Giovanni, Gherardo, prior of S. Quirico, Goccino, Baldino, and Marco—not that they were heretics, but that they were disinherited and subjected to the disabilities of descendants of heretics. When such proceedings were hailed as pre-eminent exhibitions of holy zeal, no man could feel secure in his possessions, whether derived from descent or purchase.[487]

An instance of a different character, but equally illustrative, is furnished by the case of Géraud de Puy-Germer. His father had been condemned for heresy in the times of Raymond VII. of Toulouse, who generously restored the confiscated estates. Yet, twenty years after the death of the count, in 1268, the zealous agents of Alphonse seized them as still liable to forfeiture. Géraud thereupon{524} appealed to Alphonse, who ordered an investigation, but with what result does not appear.[488]

Not only were all alienations made by heretics set aside and the property wrested from the purchasers, but all debts contracted by them, and all hypothecations and liens given to secure loans, were void. Thus doubt was cast upon every obligation that a man could enter into. Even when St. Louis softened the rigor of confiscation in Languedoc, the utmost concession he would make was that creditors should be paid for debts contracted by culprits before they became heretics, while all claims arising subsequently to an act of heresy were rejected. As no man could be certain of the orthodoxy of another, it will be evident how much distrust must have been thrown upon every bargain and every sale in the commonest transactions of life. The blighting influence of this upon the development of commerce and industry can readily be perceived, coming as it did at a time when the commercial and industrial movement of Europe was beginning to usher in the dawn of modern culture. It was not merely the spiritual striving of the thirteenth century that was repressed by the Inquisition; the progress of material improvement was seriously retarded. It was this, among other incidents of persecution, which arrested the promising civilization of the south of France and transferred to England and the Netherlands, where the Inquisition was comparatively unknown, the predominance in commerce and industry which brought freedom and wealth and power and progress in its train.[489]

The quick-witted Italian commonwealths, then rising into mercantile importance, were keen to recognize the disabilities thus inflicted upon them. In Florence a remedy was sought by requiring the seller of real estate always to give security against possible future sentences of confiscation by the Inquisition—the security in general being that of a third party, although there must have been no little difficulty in obtaining it, and though it might likewise be invalidated at any moment by the same cause.{525} Even in contracts for personalty, security was also often demanded and given. This was, at least, only replacing one evil by another of scarcely less magnitude, and the trouble grew so intolerable that a remedy was sought for one of its worst features. The republic solemnly represented to Martin IV. the scandals which had occurred and the yet greater ones threatened, in consequence of the confiscation of the real estate of heretics in the hands of *bona fide* purchasers, and by a special bull of Nov. 22, 1283, the pontiff graciously ordered the Florentine inquisitors in future not to seize such property.[490]

The princes who enjoyed the results of confiscations recognized that they carried with them the correlative duty of defraying the expenses of the Inquisition; indeed, self-interest alone would have prompted them to maintain in a state of the highest efficiency an instrumentality so profitable. Theoretically, it could not be denied that the bishops were liable for these expenses, and at first the inquisitors of Languedoc sought to obtain funds from them, suggesting that at least pecuniary penances inflicted for pious uses should be devoted to paying their notaries and clerks. This was fruitless, for, as Gui Foucoix (Clement IV.) remarks, their hands were tenacious and their purses constipated, and as it was useless to look to them for resources, he advises that the pecuniary penances be used for the purpose, providing it be done decently and without scandalizing the people. Throughout central and northern Italy, as we have seen, the fines and confiscations rendered the Inquisition fully self-supporting, and the inquisitors were eager to make business out of which they could reap a pecuniary harvest. In Venice the State defrayed all expenses and took all profits. In Naples the same policy was at first pursued by the Angevine monarchs, who took the confiscations and, in addition to maintaining prisoners, paid to each inquisitor one augustale (one quarter ounce of gold) per diem for the expenses of himself and his associate, his notary, and three familiars, with their horses. These stipends were assigned upon the Naples customs on iron, pitch, and salt; the orders for their payment ran usually for six{526} months at a time and had to be renewed; there was considerable delay in the settlements, and the inquisitors had substantial cause of complaint, although the officials were threatened with fines for lack of promptness. In 1272, however, I find a letter issued to the inquisitor, Frà Matteo di Castellamare, providing him with a year's salary, payable six months in advance. When, as mentioned above, Charles II., in 1290, divided the proceeds according to the papal prescription, he liberally continued to contribute to the expenses, though on a somewhat reduced scale. In letters of May 16, 1294, he orders the payment to Frà Bartolomeo di Aquila of four tareni per diem (the tareno was one thirtieth of an ounce of gold), and July 7 of the same year he provides that five ounces per month be paid to him for the expenses of his official family.[491]

In France there was at first some question as to the responsibility for the charges attendant upon persecution. The duty of the bishops to suppress heresy was so plain that they could not refuse to meet the expenses, at least in part. Before the establishment of the Inquisition this consisted almost wholly in the maintenance of imprisoned converts, and at the Council of Toulouse they agreed to defray this in the case of those who had no money, while those who had property to be confiscated they claimed should be supported by the princes who obtained it. This proposition, like the subsequent one of the Council of Albi, in 1254, was altogether too cumbrous to work. The statutes of Raymond, in 1234, while dwelling elaborately on the subject of confiscation, made no provision for meeting the cost of the new Inquisition, and the matter remained unsettled. In 1237 we find Gregory IX. complaining that the royal officials contributed nothing for the support of the prisoners whose property they had confiscated. When, in 1246, the Council of Béziers was assembled, the Cardinal Legate of Albano reminded the bishops that it was their business to provide for it, according to the instructions of the Council of Montpellier, whose proceedings have not reached us. The good bishops were not disposed to do this. As we have seen, they {527} claimed that prisons should be built at the expense of the recipients of the confiscations, and suggested that the fines should be used for their maintenance and for that of the inquisitors. The piety of St. Louis, however, would not see the good work halt for lack of the necessary means; with a more worldly prince we might assume that he recognized the money spent on inquisitors as profitably invested. In 1248 we find him defraying their expenses in all the domains of the crown, and we have shown above how he assumed the cost of prisons and prisoners; in addition to which, in 1246, he ordered his Seneschal of Carcassonne to pay out of the confiscations ten sols per diem to the inquisitors for their expenses. It may fairly be presumed that Count Raymond contributed with a grudging hand to the support of an institution which he had opposed so long as he dared; but when he was succeeded, in 1249, by Jeanne and Alphonse of Poitiers, the latter politic and avaricious prince saw his account in stimulating the zeal of those to whom he owed his harvest of confiscations. Not only did he defray the cost of the fixed tribunals, but his seneschals had orders to pay the expenses of the inquisitors and their familiars in their movements throughout his territories. He paid close attention to detail. In 1268 we find Guillem de Montreuil, Inquisitor of Toulouse, reporting to him the engagement of a notary at six deniers per diem and of a servitor at four, and Alphonse graciously ordering the payment of their wages. Charles of Anjou, who was equally greedy, found time amid his Italian distractions to see that his Seneschal of Provence and Forcalquier kept the Inquisition supplied on the same basis as did the king in the royal dominions.[492]

Large as were the returns to the fisc from the industry of the Inquisition, the inquisitors were sometimes disposed to presume upon their usefulness, and to spend money with a freedom which {528} seemed unnecessary to those who paid the bills. Even in the fresh zeal of 1242 and 1244, before the princes had made provision for the Holy Office, and while the bishops were yet zealously maintaining their claims to the fines, the luxury and extravagance of the inquisitors called down upon them the reproof of their own Order as expressed in the Dominican provincial chapters of Montpellier and Avignon. It would be, of course, unjust to cast such reproach upon all inquisitors, but no doubt many deserved it, and we have seen that there were numerous ways in which they could supply their wants, legitimate or otherwise. It might, indeed, be a curious question to determine the source whence Bernard de Caux, who presided over the tribunal of Toulouse until his death, in 1252, and who, as a Dominican, could have owned no property, obtained the means which enabled him to be a great benefactor to the convent of Agen, founded in 1249. Even Alphonse of Poitiers sometimes grew tired of ministering to the wishes of those who served him so well. In a confidential letter of 1268 he complains of the vast expenditures of Pons de Poyet and Étienne de Gâtine, the inquisitors of Toulouse, and instructs his agent to try to persuade them to remove to Lavaur, where less extravagance might be hoped for. He offered to put at their disposal the castle of Lavaur, or any other that might be fit to serve as a prison; and at the same time he craftily wrote to them direct, explaining that, in order to enable them to extend their operations, he would place an enormous castle in their hands.[493]

Some very curious details as to the expenses of the Inquisition, thus defrayed from the confiscations, from St. John's day, 1322, to 1323, are afforded by the accounts of Arnaud Assalit, *procureur des encours* of Carcassonne and Béziers, which have fortunately been preserved. From the sums thus coming into his hands the *procureur* met the outlays of the Inquisition to the minutest item—the cost of maintaining prisoners, the hunting up of witnesses, the tracking of fugitives, and the charges for an *auto de fé*, including the banquets for the assembly of experts and the saffron-colored cloth for the crosses of the penitents. We learn from this {529} that the wages of the inquisitor himself were one hundred and fifty livres per annum, and also that they were very irregularly paid. Frère Otbert had been appointed in Lent, 1316, and thus far had received nothing of his stipend, but now, in consequence of a special letter from King Charles le Bel, the whole accumulation for six years, amounting to nine hundred livres, is paid in a lump. Although by this time persecution was slackening for lack of material, the confiscations were still quite profitable. Assalit charges himself with two thousand two hundred and nineteen livres seven sols ten deniers collected during the year, while his outlays, including heavy legal expenses and the extraordinary payment to Frère Otbert, amounted to one thousand one hundred and sixty-eight livres eleven sols four deniers, leaving about one thousand and fifty livres of profit to the crown.[494]

Persecution, as a steady and continuous policy, rested, after all, upon confiscation. It was this which supplied the fuel to keep up the fires of zeal, and when it was lacking the business of defending the faith languished lamentably. When Catharism disappeared under the brilliant aggressiveness of Bernard Gui, the culminating point of the Inquisition was passed, and thenceforth it steadily declined, although still there were occasional confiscated estates over which king, prelate, and noble quarrelled for some years to come. The Spirituals, Dulcinists, and Fraticelli were Mendicants, who held property to be an abomination; the Waldenses were poor folk—mountain shepherds and lowland peasants—and the only prizes were an occasional sorcerer or usurer. Still, as late as 1337 the office of bailli of the confiscations for heresy in Toulouse was sufficiently lucrative to be worth purchasing under the prevailing custom of selling all such positions, and the collections for the preceding fiscal year amounted to six hundred and forty livres six sols.[495]

The intimate connection between the activity of persecuting zeal and the material results to be derived from it is well illustrated[530] in the failure of the first attempt to extend the Inquisition into Franche Comté. John, Count of Burgundy, in 1248, represented to Innocent IV. the alarming spread of Waldensianism throughout the province of Besançon and begged for its repression. Apparently the zeal of Count John did not lead him to pay for the purgation of his dominions, and the plunder to be gained was inconsiderable, for, in 1255, Alexander IV. granted the petition of the friars to be relieved from the duty, in which they averred that they had exhausted themselves fruitlessly for lack of money. The same lesson is taught by the want of success which attended all attempts to establish the Inquisition in Portugal. When, in 1376, Gregory XI. ordered the Bishop of Lisbon to appoint a Franciscan inquisitor for the kingdom, recognizing apparently that there would be small receipts from confiscations, he provided that the incumbent should be paid a salary of two hundred gold florins per annum, assessed upon the various sees in the proportion of their forced contributions to the papal camera. The resistance of inertia, which rendered this command resultless, doubtless arose from the objection of the prelates to being thus taxed; and the same may be said of the effort of Boniface IX., when he appointed Fray Vicente de Lisboa as Inquisitor of Spain and ordered his expenses defrayed by the bishops.[496]

Perhaps the most unscrupulous attempt to provide for the maintenance of the Inquisition was that made by the Emperor Charles IV. when, in 1369, he endeavored to establish it in Germany on a permanent basis. Heretics were neither numerous nor rich, and little could be gained from their confiscations to sustain the zeal of Kerlinger and his brethren; and we shall see hereafter how the houses of the orthodox and inoffensive Beghards and Beguines were summarily confiscated in order to provide domiciles and prisons for the inquisitors, while the cities were invited to share in the spoils in order to enlist popular support for the odious measure; we shall see also how it failed in consequence of the steady repugnance of prelates and people for the Holy Office.[497]

Eymerich, writing in Aragon, about 1375, says that the source[531] whence the expenses of the Inquisition should be met is a question which has been long debated and never settled. The most popular view among churchmen was that the burden should fall on the temporal princes, since they obtained the confiscations and should accept the charge with the benefit; but in these times, he sorrowfully adds, there are few obstinate heretics, fewer still relapsed, and scarce any rich ones, so that, as there is little to be gained, the princes are not willing to defray the expenses. Some other means ought to be found, but of all the devices which have been proposed each has its insuperable objection; and he concludes by regretting that an institution so wholesome and so necessary to Christendom should be so badly provided.[498]

It was probably while Eymerich was saddened with these unpalatable truths that the question was raising itself in the most practical shape elsewhere. As late as 1337 in the accounts of the Sénéchaussée of Toulouse there are expenditures for an *auto de fé* and for repairs to the buildings and prison of the Inquisition, the salaries of the inquisitor and his officials, and the maintenance of prisoners, but the confusion and bankruptcy entailed by the English war doubtless soon afterwards caused this duty to be neglected. In 1375 Gregory XI. persuaded King Frederic of Sicily to allow the confiscations to inure to the benefit of the Inquisition, so that funds might not be lacking for the prosecution of the good work. At the same time he made a vigorous effort to exterminate the Waldenses who were multiplying in Dauphiné. There were prisons to be built and crowds of prisoners to be supported, and he directed that the expenses should be defrayed by the prelates whose negligence had given opportunity for the growth of heresy. Although he ordered this to be enforced by excommunication, it would seem that the constipated purses of the bishops could not be relaxed, for soon after we find the inquisitor laying claim to a share in the confiscations, on the reasonable ground of his having no other source whence to defray the necessary expenses of his tribunal. The royal officials insisted on keeping the whole, and a lively contest arose, which was referred to King Charles le Sage. The monarch dutifully conferred with the Holy See, and, in 1378, issued an *Ordonnance* retaining the whole of the confiscations and[532] assigning to the inquisitor a yearly stipend—the same as that paid to the tribunals of Toulouse and Carcassonne—of one hundred and ninety livres Tournois, out of which all the expenses of the Inquisition were to be met; with a proviso that if the allowance was not regularly paid then the inquisitor should be at liberty to detain a portion of the forfeitures. No doubt this agreement was observed for a time, but it lapsed in the terrible disorders which ensued on the insanity of Charles VI. In 1409 Alexander V. left to his legate to decide whether the Inquisitor of Dauphiné should receive three hundred gold florins a year, to be levied on the Jews of Avignon, or ten florins a year from each of the bishops of his extensive district, or whether the bishops should be compelled to support him and his officials in his journeys through the country. These precarious resources disappeared in the confusion of the civil wars and invasion which so nearly wrecked the monarchy. In 1432, when Frère Pierre Fabri, Inquisitor of Embrun, was summoned to attend the Council of Basle, he excused himself on account of his preoccupation with the stubborn Waldenses, and also on the ground of his indescribable poverty, "for never have I had a penny from the Church of God, nor have I a stipend from any other source."[499]

Of course it would be unjust to say that greed and thirst for plunder were the impelling motives of the Inquisition, though, when complaints were made that the fisc was defrauded of its dues by the immunity promised to those who would come in and confess during the time of grace, and when Bernard Gui met this objection by pointing out that these penitents were obliged to betray their associates, and thus, in the long run, the fisc was the gainer, we see how largely the minds of those who urged on persecution were occupied by its profits.[500] We therefore are perfectly safe in asserting that but for the gains to be made out of fines and confiscations its work would have been much less thorough, and that it would have sunk into comparative insignificance{533} as soon as the first frantic zeal of bigotry had exhausted itself. This zeal might have lasted for a generation, to be followed by a period of comparative inaction, until a fresh onslaught would have been excited by the recrudescence of heresy. Under a succession of such spasmodic attacks Catharism might perhaps have never been completely rooted out. By confiscation the heretics were forced to furnish the means for their own destruction. Avarice joined hands with fanaticism, and between them they supplied motive power for a hundred years of fierce, unremitting, unrelenting persecution, which in the end accomplished its main purpose.{534}

CHAPTER XIV.

THE STAKE.

LIKE confiscation, the death-penalty was a matter with which the Inquisition had theoretically no concern. It exhausted every effort to bring the heretic back to the bosom of the Church. If he proved obdurate, or if his conversion was evidently feigned, it could do no more. As a non-Catholic, he was no longer amenable to the spiritual jurisdiction of a Church which he did not recognize, and all that it could do was to declare him a heretic and withdraw its protection. In the earlier periods the sentence thus is simply a condemnation as a heretic, accompanied by excommunication, or it merely states that the offender is no longer considered as subject to the jurisdiction of the Church. Sometimes there is the addition that he is abandoned to secular judgment—"relaxed," according to the terrible euphemism which assumed that he was simply discharged from custody. When the formulas had become more perfected there is frequently the explanatory remark that the Church has nothing left to do to him for his demerits; and the relinquishment to the secular arm is accompanied with the significant addition "*debita animadversione puniendum*"—that he is to be duly punished by it. The adjuration that this punishment, in accordance with the canonical sanctions, shall not imperil life or limb, or shall not cause death or effusion of blood, does not appear in the earlier sentences, and was not universal even at a later period.[501]

That this appeal for mercy was the merest form is admitted by Pegna, who explains that it was used only that the inquisitors might seem not to consent to the effusion of blood, and thus avoid{535} incurring "irregularity." The Church took good care that the nature of the request should not be misapprehended. It taught that in such cases all mercy was misplaced unless the heretic became a convert, and proved his sincerity by denouncing all his fellows. The remorseless logic of St. Thomas Aquinas rendered it self-evident that the secular power could not escape the duty of putting the heretic to death, and that it was only the exceeding kindness of the Church that led it to give the criminal two warnings before handing him over to meet his fate. The inquisitors themselves had no scruples on the subject, and condescended to no subterfuges respecting it, but always held that their condemnation of a heretic was a sentence of death. They showed this in averting the pollution of a Church by not uttering these sentences within the sacred precincts, this portion of the ceremony of an *auto de fé* being performed in the public square. One of their teachers in the thirteenth century, copied by Bernard Gui in the fourteenth, argues: "The object of the Inquisition is the destruction of heresy. Heresy cannot be destroyed unless heretics are destroyed: heretics cannot be destroyed unless their defenders and fautors are destroyed, and this is effected in two ways, viz., when they are converted to the true Catholic faith, or when, on being abandoned to the secular arm, they are corporally burned." In the next century, Fray Alonso de Spina points out that they are not to be delivered up to extermination without warning once and again, unless, indeed, their growth threatens trouble to the Church, when they are to be extirpated without delay or examination. Under these teachings the secular powers naturally recognized that in burning heretics they were only obeying the commands of the Inquisition. In a commission issued by Philippe le Bon of Burgundy, November 9, 1431, ordering his officials to render obedience to Friar Kaleyser, recently appointed Inquisitor of Lille and Cambrai, among the duties enumerated is that of inflicting due punishment on heretics "as he shall decree, and as is customary." In the accounts of the royal *procureurs des encours*, the cost of these executions in Languedoc was charged against the proceeds of the confiscations as part of the expenses of the Inquisition, thus showing that they were not regarded as ordinary incidents of criminal justice, to be defrayed out of the ordinary revenues, but as peculiarly connected with and dependent upon the{536} operations of the Inquisition, of which the royal officials only acted as ministers. The Inquisitor Sprenger had no hesitation in alluding to the victims whom he caused to be burned—"*quas incinerari fecimus.*" In fact, how modern is the pretension that the Church was not responsible for the atrocity is apparent when, as late as the seventeenth century, the learned Cardinal Albizio, in controverting Frà Paolo as to the control of the Inquisition by the State in Venice, had no scruple in asserting that "the inquisitors in conducting the trials, regularly came to the sentence, and if it was one of death it was immediately and necessarily put into execution by the doge and the senate."[502]

We have already seen that the Church was responsible for the enactment of the ferocious laws punishing heresy with death, and that she intervened authoritatively to annul any secular statutes which should interfere with the prompt and effective application of the penalties. In the same way, as we have also seen, she provided against any negligence or laxity on the part of the magistrates in executing the sentences pronounced by the inquisitors. According to the universal belief of the period, this was her plainest and highest duty, and she did not shrink from it. Boniface VIII. only recorded the current practice when he embodied in the canon law the provision whereby the secular authorities were commanded to punish duly and promptly all who were handed over to them by the inquisitors, under pain of excommunication, which became heresy if endured for a twelvemonth, and the inquisitors were rigidly instructed to proceed against all magistrates who proved recalcitrant,{537} while they were at the same time cautioned only to speak of executing the laws without specifically mentioning the penalty, in order to avoid falling into "irregularity," though the only punishment recognized by the Church as sufficient for heresy was burning alive. Even if the ruler was excommunicated and incapable of legally performing any other function, he was not relieved from the obligation of this supreme duty, with which nothing was allowed to interfere. Indeed, authorities were found to argue that if an inquisitor were obliged to execute the sentence himself he would not thereby incur irregularity.[503]

We are not to imagine, however, from these reduplicated commands that the secular power, as a rule, showed itself in the slightest degree disinclined to perform the duty. The teachings of the Church had made too profound an impression for any doubt in the premises to exist. As has been seen above, the laws of all the states of Europe prescribed concremation as the appropriate penalty for heresy, and even the free commonwealths of Italy recognized the Inquisition as the judge whose sentences were to be blindly executed. Raymond of Toulouse himself, in the fit of piety which preceded his death in 1249, caused eighty believers in heresy to be burned at Berlaiges, near Agen, after they had confessed in his presence, apparently without giving them the opportunity of recanting. From the contemporary sentences of Bernard de Caux, it is probable that, had these unfortunates been tried before that ardent champion of the faith, not one of them would have been condemned to the stake as impenitent. Quite as significant was the suit brought by the Maréchal de Mirepoix against the Seneschal of Carcassonne, because the latter had invaded his right to burn for himself all his subjects condemned as heretics by the Inquisition. In 1269 the Parlement of Paris decided the case in his favor, after which, on March 18, 1270, the seneschal acceded to his demand that the bones of seven men and three women of his territories,{538} recently burned at Carcassonne, should be solemnly surrendered to him in recognition of his right; or, if they could not be found and identified, then, as substitutes, ten canvas bags filled with straw—a ghastly symbolic ceremony which was actually performed two days later, and a formal notarial act executed in attestation of it. Yet, though the De Levis of Mirepoix rejoiced in the title of Maréchaux de la Foi, it is not to be assumed that this eagerness arose wholly from bloodthirsty fanaticism, for there was nothing to which the seigneur-justicier clung more jealously than to every detail of his jurisdiction. A similar dispute arose in 1309, when the Count of Foix claimed the right to burn the Catharan heresiarch, Jacques Autier, and a woman named Guillelma Cristola, condemned by Bernard Gui, because they were his subjects, but the royal officials maintained their master's privileges in the premises, and the suit thence arising was still pending in 1326. So at Narbonne, where there was a long-standing dispute between the archbishop and the viscount as to the jurisdiction, and where, in 1319, the former in conjunction with the inquisitor Jean de Beaune relaxed three heretics, he claimed for his court the right to burn them. The commune, as representing the viscount, resisted this, and the hideous quarrel was only settled by the representative of the king stepping in and performing the act. In so doing, however, he carefully specified that it was not to work prejudice to either party, while to the end the archbishop protested against the intrusion upon his rights.[504]

If, however, from any cause, the secular authorities were reluctant to execute the death-sentence, the Church had little ceremony in putting forth its powers to coerce obedience. When, for instance, the first resistance in Toulouse had been broken down and the Holy Office had been reinstated there, the inquisitors, in 1237, condemned six men and women as heretics; but the viguier and consuls refused to receive the convicts, to confiscate their property, and "to do with them what was customary to be done with heretics"—that is, to burn them alive. Thereupon the inquisitors, after counselling with the bishop, the Abbot du Mas, the Provost of St. Étienne, and the Prior of La Daurade, proceeded to{539} excommunicate solemnly the recalcitrant officials in the Cathedral of St. Étienne. In 1288 Nicholas IV. lamented the neglect and covert opposition with which in many places the secular authorities evaded the execution of the inquisitorial sentences, and directed that they should be punished with excommunication and deprivation of office and their communities be subjected to interdict. In 1458, at Strassburg, the Burgermeister, Hans Drachenfels, and his colleagues refused at first to burn the Hussite missionary Frederic Reiser and his servant Anna Weiler, but their resistance was overcome and they were finally forced to execute the sentence. Thirty years later, in 1486, the magistrates of Brescia objected to burning certain witches of both sexes condemned by the Inquisition, unless they should be permitted to examine the proceedings. This was held to be flat rebellion. Civil lawyers, it is true, had endeavored to prove that the secular authorities had a right to see the papers, but the inquisitors had succeeded in having this claim rejected. Innocent VIII. promptly declared the Venetian demands to be a scandal to the faith, and he ordered the excommunication of the magistrates if within six days they did not execute the convicts, any municipal statutes to the contrary being pronounced null and void—a decision which was held to give the secular courts six days in which to carry out the sentence of condemnation. A more stubborn contest arose in 1521, when the Inquisition endeavored to purge the dioceses of both Brescia and Bergamo of the witches who still infested them. The inquisitor and episcopal ordinaries proceeded against them vigorously, but the Signiory of Venice interposed and appealed to Leo X., who appointed his nuncio at Venice to revise the trials. The latter delegated his power to the Bishop of Justinopolis, who proceeded with the inquisitor and ordinaries to the Valcamonica of Brescia, where the so-called heretics were numerous, and condemned some of them to be relaxed to the secular arm. Still dissatisfied, the Venetian Senate ordered the Governor of Brescia not to execute the sentences or to permit them to be executed, or to pay the expenses of the proceedings, but to send the papers to Venice for revision, and to compel the Bishop of Justinopolis to appear before them, which he was obliged to do. This inflamed the papal indignation to the highest pitch. Leo X. warmly assured the inquisitor and the episcopal officials that they had full jurisdiction over the culprits, that their sentences were to{540} be executed without revision or examination, and that they must enforce these rights with the free use of ecclesiastical censures. The spirit of the age, however, was insubordinate, and Venice had always been peculiarly so in all matters connected with the Holy Office. We shall see hereafter how the Council of Ten undauntedly held its position and asserted the superiority of its jurisdiction in a manner previously unexampled.[505]

In view of this unvarying policy of the Church during the three centuries under consideration, and for a century and a half later, there is a typical instance of the manner in which history is written to order, in the quiet assertion of the latest Catholic historian of the Inquisition that "the Church took no part in the corporal punishment of heretics. Those who perished miserably were only chastised for their crimes, sentenced by judges invested with the royal jurisdiction. The record of the excesses committed by the heretics of Bulgaria, by the Gnostics and Manichæans, is historical, and capital punishment was only inflicted on criminals confessing to robbery, assassination, and violence. The Albigenses were treated with equal benignity; ... the Catholic Church deplored all acts of vengeance, however great was the provocation given by the ferocity of those factious masses." So completely, in truth, was the Church convinced of its duty to see that all heretics were burned that, at the Council of Constance, the eighteenth article of heresy charged against John Huss was that, in his treatise *de Ecclesia*, he had taught that no heretic ought to be abandoned to secular judgment to be punished with death. In his defence even Huss admitted that a heretic who could not be mildly led from error ought to suffer bodily punishment; and when a passage was read from his book in which those who deliver an unconvicted heretic to the secular arm are compared to the Scribes and Pharisees who delivered Christ to Pilate, the assembly broke out into a storm of objurgation, during which even the sturdy reformer, Cardinal Pierre d'Ailly, was heard to exclaim,{541} "Verily those who drew up the articles were most moderate, for his writings are much more atrocious."[506]

The continuous teachings of the Church led its best men to regard no act as more self-evidently just than the burning of the heretic, and no heresy less defensible than a demand for toleration. Even Chancellor Gerson himself could see nothing else to be done with those who pertinaciously adhered to error, even in matters not at present explicitly articles necessary to the faith.[507] The fact is, the Church not only defined the guilt and forced its punishment, but created the crime itself. As we shall see, under Nicholas IV. and Celestine V., the strict Franciscans were pre-eminently orthodox; but when John XXII. stigmatized as heretical the belief that Christ lived in absolute poverty, he transformed them into unpardonable criminals whom the temporal officials were bound to send to the stake, under pain of being themselves treated as heretics.

There was thus a universal consensus of opinion that there was nothing to do with a heretic but to burn him. The heretic as known to the laws, both secular and ecclesiastical, was he who not only admitted his heretical belief, but defended it and refused to recant. He was obstinate and impenitent; the Church could do nothing with him, and as soon as the secular lawgivers had provided for his guilt the awful punishment of the stake, there was no hesitation in handing him over to the temporal jurisdiction to endure it. All authorities unite in this, and the annals of the Inquisition can vainly be searched for an exception. Yet this was regarded by the inquisitor as a last resort. To say nothing of the saving of a soul, a convert who would betray his friends was more useful than a roasted corpse, and, as we have seen, no effort was spared to obtain recantation. Experience had shown that such zealots were often eager for martyrdom and desired to be speedily burned, and it was no part of the inquisitor's pleasure to gratify them. He was advised that this ardor frequently gave way under time and suffering, and therefore he was told to keep the obstinate and defiant heretic chained in a dungeon for six{542} months or a year in utter solitude, save when a dozen theologians and legists should be let in upon him to labor for his conversion, or his wife and children be admitted to work upon his heart. It was not until all this had been tried and failed that he was to be relaxed. Even then the execution was postponed for a day to give further opportunity for recantation, which, we are told, rarely happened, for those who went thus far usually persevered to the end; but if his resolution gave way and he professed repentance, his conversion was presumed to be the work of fear rather than of grace, and he was to be strictly imprisoned for life. Even at the stake his offer to abjure ought not to be refused, though there was no absolute rule as to this, and there could be little hope of the genuineness of such conversion. Eymerich relates a case occurring at Barcelona when three heretics were burned, and one of them, a priest, after being scorched on one side, cried out that he would recant. He was removed and abjured, but fourteen years later was found to have persisted in heresy and to have infected many others, when he was despatched without more ado.[508]

The obstinate heretic who preferred martyrdom to apostasy was by no means the sole victim doomed to the stake. The secular lawgiver had provided this punishment for heresy, but had left to the Church its definition, and the definition was enlarged to serve as a gentle persuasive that should supplement all deficiencies in the inquisitorial process. Where testimony deemed sufficient existed, persistent denial only aggravated guilt, and the profession of orthodoxy was of no avail. If two witnesses swore to having seen a man "adore" a perfected heretic it was enough, and no declaration of readiness to subscribe to all the tenets of Rome availed him, without confession, abjuration, recantation, and acceptance of penance. Such a one was a heretic, to be pitilessly burned. It was the same with the contumacious who did not obey the summons to stand trial. Persistent refusal of the oath was likewise technical heresy, condemning the recalcitrant to the stake. Even when there was no proof, simple suspicion became{543} heresy if the suspect failed to purge himself with conjurators and remained so for a year. In violent suspicion, refusal to abjure worked the same result in a twelvemonth. A retracted confession was similarly regarded. In short, the stake supplied all defects. It was the *ultima ratio*, and although not many cases have reached us in which executions actually occurred on these grounds, there is no doubt that such provisions were of the utmost utility in practice, and that the terror which they inspired extorted many a confession, true or false, from unwilling lips.[509]

There was another class of cases, however, which gave the inquisitors much trouble, and in which they were long in settling upon a definite and uniform course of procedure. The innumerable forced conversions wrought by the dungeon and stake filled the prisons and the land with those whose outward conformity left them at heart no less heretics than before. I have elsewhere spoken of the all-pervading police of the Holy Office and of the watchfulness exercised over the converts whose liberation at best was but a ticket-of-leave. That cases of relapse into heresy should be constant was therefore a matter of course. Even in the jails it was impossible to segregate all the prisoners, and complaints are frequent of these wolves in sheep's clothing who infected their more innocent fellow-captives. A man whose solemn conversion had once been proved fraudulent could never again be trusted. He was an incorrigible heretic whom the Church could no longer hope to win over. On him mercy was wasted, and the stake was the only resource. Yet it is creditable to the Inquisition that it was so long in reducing to practice this self-evident proposition.

As early as 1184 the Verona decree of Lucius III. provides that those who, after abjuration, relapse into the abjured heresy shall be delivered to the secular courts, without even the opportunity of being heard. The Ravenna edict of Frederic II., in 1232, prescribed death for all who, by relapse, showed that their conversion had been a pretext to escape the penalty of heresy. In 1244 the Council of Narbonne alludes to the great multitude of such cases, and, following Lucius III., orders them to be relaxed without{544} a hearing. Yet these stern mandates were not enforced. In 1233 we find Gregory IX. contenting himself with prescribing perpetual imprisonment for such cases, which he speaks of as being already numerous. In a single sentence of February 10, 1237, the inquisitors of Toulouse condemn seventeen relapsed heretics to perpetual imprisonment. Raymond de Pennaforte, at the Council of Tarragona, in 1242, alludes to the diversity of opinion on the subject, and pronounces in favor of imprisonment; and, in 1246, the Council of Béziers, in giving similar instructions, speaks of them as being in accordance with the apostolic mandates. Even this degree of severity was not always inflicted. In 1242 Pierre Cella only prescribes pilgrimages and crosses for such offenders, and, in a case occurring in Florence in 1245, Frà Ruggieri Calcagni lets off the culprit with a not extravagant fine.[510]

What to do with these multitudes of false converts was evidently a question which perplexed the Church no little, and, as usual, a solution, at least for the time, was found in leaving the matter to the discretion of the inquisitors. In answer to the inquiries of the Lombard Holy Office, the Cardinal of Albano, about 1245, tells the officials to make use of such penalties as they shall deem appropriate. In 1248 Bernard de Caux asked the same question of the Archbishop of Narbonne, and was told that, according to the "apostolic mandates," those who returned to the Church a second time, humbly and obediently, might be let off with perpetual imprisonment, while those who were disobedient should be abandoned to the secular arm. Under these instructions the practice varied, though it is pleasant to be able to say that, in the vast majority of cases, the inquisitors leaned to the side of mercy. Even the ardent zeal of Bernard de Caux allowed him to use his discretion gently. In his register of sentences, from 1246 to 1248, there are sixty cases of relapse, none of which are punished more severely than by imprisonment, and in some of them the confinement is not perpetual. The same lenity is observable{545} in various sentences rendered during the next ten years, both by him and by other inquisitors. Yet, with one

178

exception, the codes of instruction which date about this period assume that relapse is always to be visited with relaxation, and that the offender is to have no hearing in his defence. In the exceptional instance the compiler illustrates the uncertainty which existed by sometimes treating relapse as punishable with imprisonment and sometimes as entailing the stake. Relapse into usury, however, was let off with the lighter alternative. The fact is that in Languedoc, under the Treaty of Paris, as stated above, an oath of abjuration was administered every two years to all males over fourteen and all females over twelve, and any subsequent act of heresy was technically a relapse. This, perhaps, explains the indecision of the inquisitors of Toulouse. It was impossible to burn all such cases.[511]

Whatever be the cause, there evidently was considerable doubt in the minds of inquisitors as to the penalty of relapse, and it must be recorded to their credit that in this they were more merciful than the current public opinion of the age. Jean de Saint-Pierre, the colleague and successor of Bernard de Caux, followed his example in always condemning the relapsed to imprisonment, and when, after Bernard's death, in 1252, Frère Renaud de Chartres was adjoined to him, the same rule continued to be observed. Frère Renaud found, however, to his horror, that the secular judges disregarded the sentence and mercilessly burned the unhappy victims, and that this had been going on under his predecessors. The civil authorities defended their course by arguing that in no other way could the land be purged of heresy, which was acquiring new force under the mistaken lenity of the inquisitors. Frère Renaud felt that he could not overlook this cruelty in silence as his predecessors had done. He therefore reported the facts to Alphonse of Poitiers, and informed him that he proposed to refer the matter to the pope, pending whose answer he would keep {546} his prisoners secure from the brutal violence of the secular officials.[512]

What was the papal response we can only conjecture, but it doubtless leaned rather to the rigorous zeal of Alphonse's officials than to the milder methods of Frère Renaud, for it was about this time that Rome definitely decided for the unconditional relaxation of all who were guilty of relapsing into heresy which had once been abjured. The precise date of this I have not been able to determine. In 1254 Innocent IV. contents himself, in a very aggravated case of double relapse occurring in Milan, with ordering destruction of houses and public penance, but in 1258 relaxation for relapse is alluded to by Alexander IV. as a matter previously irrevocably settled—possibly by the very appeal of Frère Renaud. It seems to have taken the inquisitors somewhat by surprise, and for several years they continued to trouble the Holy See with the pertinent question of how such a rule was to be reconciled with the universally received maxim that the Church never closes her bosom to her wayward children seeking to return. To this the characteristic explanation was given that the Church was not closed to them, for if they showed signs of penitence they might receive the Eucharist, even at the stake, but without escaping death. In this shape the decision was embodied in the canon law, and made a part of orthodox doctrine in the Summa of St. Thomas Aquinas. The promise of the Eucharist frequently formed part of the sentence in these cases, and the victim was always accompanied to execution by holy men striving to save his soul until the last—though it is shrewdly advised that the inquisitor himself had better not exhibit his zeal in this way, as his appearance will be more likely to excite hardening than softening of the heart.[513]

Although inquisitors continued to assume discretion in these cases and did not by any means invariably send the relapsed to the stake, still relapse became the main cause of capital punishment. Defiant heretics courting martyrdom were comparatively {547} rare, but there were many poor souls who could not abandon conscientiously the errors which they had cherished, and who vainly hoped, after escaping once, to be able to hide their guilt more effectually.[514] All this gave a fresh importance to the question of what legally constituted relapse, and led to endless definitions and subtleties. It became necessary to determine with some precision, when the offender was refused a hearing, the exact amount of criminality in both the first and second offences, which would justify condemnation for impenitent heresy. Where guilt was ofttimes so shadowy and impalpable, this was evidently no easy matter.

There were cases in which a first trial had only developed suspicion without proof, and it seemed hard to condemn a man to death for an assumed second offence when he had not been proved guilty of the first. Hesitating to do so, the inquisitors applied to Alexander IV. to resolve their doubts, and he answered in the most positive manner. When the suspicion had been "violent" he said, it was "by a sort of legal fiction" to be held as legal proof of guilt, and the accused was to be condemned. When it was "light" he was to be punished more heavily than for a first offence, but not with the full penalty of relapse. Moreover, the evidence required to prove the second offence was of the slightest; any communication with or kindness shown to heretics sufficed. This decision was repeated by Alexander and his successors with a frequency which shows how doubtful and puzzling were the points which came up for discussion, but the rule of condemnation was finally carried into the canon law and became the unalterable policy of the Church. The authorities, except Zanghino, agree that in such cases there was no room for mercy.[515]

Besides these enigmas there were others respecting forms of guilt which might reasonably be regarded as less deserving of the last resort. Thus relapse into fautorship gave rise to considerable {548} divergence of views. The Council of Narbonne, in 1244, was of opinion that those guilty of this offence should be sent to the pope for absolution and the imposition of penance—a cumbrous procedure, not likely to find favor. During the middle period of the Inquisition, the authorities, including Bernard Gui, while not prescribing relaxation to the secular arm, suggest that penance be imposed sufficiently severe to inspire wholesome fear in others; while,

179

towards the end of the fourteenth century, Eymerich holds that a relapsed fautor is to be abandoned to secular justice without a hearing. Even those defamed for heresy, if after due purgation they again incur defamation, are strictly liable to the same fate, though this was so hard a measure that Eymerich proposes that such cases should be referred to the pope.[516]

There was another class of offenders who gave the inquisitors endless trouble, and for whom it was difficult to frame rigid and invariable rules—those who escaped from prison or omitted to fulfil the penances assigned to them. According to theory, all penitents were converts to the true faith who eagerly accepted penance as their sole hope of salvation. To reject it subsequently was therefore an evidence that the conversion had been feigned or that the inconstant soul had reverted to its former errors, as otherwise the loving and wholesome discipline of the benignant Mother Church would not be spurned. From the beginning, therefore, these culprits were classed with the relapsed. In 1248 the Council of Valence ordered them to have the benefit of a warning, after which further persistence in disobedience rendered them liable to the full penalty of obstinate heresy; and this was sometimes provided for in the sentence itself, by a clause which warned them that any disregard of the observances enjoined would expose them to the fate of perjured and impenitent heretics. Yet as late as 1260 Alexander IV. seems at a loss what rule to prescribe in such cases, and merely talks vaguely of excommunication and reimposition of the penalties, with the assistance, if necessary, of the secular authorities. Yet about the same period Gui Foucoix pronounced in favor of the death-penalty for these offenders, arguing that the offence proved impenitent heresy; but Bernard Gui held this to {549} be too severe, and advised leaving them to the discretion of the inquisitor—a discretion which he himself had no hesitation in exercising. The two most frequent varieties of the offence were laying aside the yellow crosses and prison-breaking. The former was never, so far as I have seen, punished with death, though visited with penalties sufficiently sharp to serve as a deterrent. The latter, according to the later inquisitors, was capital—the escaped prisoner was a relapsed heretic, to be burned without a hearing. Some jurists argued that a failure fully to betray all heretics of whom the convert had knowledge—a pledge to do so forming a necessary part of the oath of abjuration—constituted relapse, but Bernard Gui regards this as unduly harsh. Absolute refusal to perform the penance enjoined was, of course, evidence of obstinate heresy, leading inevitably to the stake. Such cases were naturally rare, for penance was only prescribed for those who had confessed, had professed conversion, and had asked for reconciliation; but there is one on record of a woman, in the latter half of the fifteenth century, before the Inquisition of Cartagena, who was duly abandoned to the secular arm.[517]

Notwithstanding these extensions of the death-penalty, I am convinced that the number of victims who actually perished at the stake is considerably less than has ordinarily been imagined. The deliberate burning alive of a human being, simply for difference of belief, is an atrocity so dramatic and appeals so strongly to the imagination that it has come to be regarded as the leading feature in the activity of the Inquisition. Yet, frequent as recourse to the stake undoubtedly was, it formed but a comparatively small part of the instrumentalities of repression. The records of those evil days have mostly disappeared, and there is now no possibility of reconstructing {550} their statistics, but if this could be done I have no doubt that the actual executions by fire would excite surprise by falling far short of the popular estimate. Imagination has grown inflamed at the manifold iniquities of the Holy Office, and has been ready to accept without examination exaggerations which have become habitual. No one can suspect the learned Dom Brial of prejudice or of ordinary lack of accuracy, and yet in his Preface to Vol. XXI. of the "Recueil des Historiens des Gaules" (p. xxiii.), he quotes as trustworthy an assertion that Bernard Gui, during his service as Inquisitor of Toulouse from 1308 to 1323, put to death no less than six hundred and thirty-seven heretics. Now that, as we have seen, was the total number of sentences uttered by the tribunal during those years, and of these sentences only forty were capital—in addition to sixty-seven dead heretics condemned to be exhumed and burned, for the most part because they were not alive to recant. Again, no inquisitor left behind him a more enviable record for zeal and activity in the relentless persecution of heresy than Bernard de Caux, who labored in the earlier period when the land was yet full of heresy, and heretics had not yet been cowed into submissiveness. Bernard Gui characterizes him as "a persecutor and hammer of heretics, a holy man and full of God, ... wonderful in his life, wonderful in doctrine, wonderful in extirpating heresy;" he wrought miracles while alive, and in 1281, twenty-eight years after his death, his body was found uncorrupted and perfect, except part of the nose. Such a man is not to be accused of undue tenderness towards heretics, and yet, in his register of sentences from 1246 to 1248, there is not a single case of abandonment to the secular arm, unless we may reckon as such the condemnations of contumacious absentees, who were necessarily declared to be heretics. These, indeed, were liable to be burned by the secular justice, but, in fact, they could always save themselves by submission, and this very register affords a very striking instance in point. There was no more obnoxious heretic in Toulouse than Alaman de Roaix. He belonged to one of the noblest families in the city, and one which furnished many members to the heretic church, of which he himself was suspected of being a bishop. In 1229 the Legate Romano had condemned him and had imposed on him the penance of a crusade to the Holy Land, which he had sworn to perform and never fulfilled. In 1237 the earliest inquisitors, {551} Guillem Arnaud and Étienne de Saint-Thibery, again took up his case, finding him unremittingly active in protecting heretics and disseminating heresy, spoiling, ransoming, wounding, and slaying priests and clerks, and this time they condemned him *in absentia*. He became a *faydit*, or proscribed man, living sword in hand and plundering the orthodox to support himself and his friends. No more aggravated case of obstinate heresy and persistent contumacy can well be imagined, and yet when he acknowledged his errors, January 16, 1248, professed conversion, and asked for penance, a score of years after his first conversion, he was only condemned to imprisonment.[518]

In fact, as we have already seen, the earnest endeavors of the inquisitors were directed much more to obtaining conversions with confiscations and betrayal of friends than to provoking martyrdoms. An occasional burning only was required to maintain a wholesome terror in the minds of the population. With his forty cases of concremation in fifteen years, Bernard Gui managed to crush the last convulsive struggle of Catharism, to keep the Waldenses in check, and repress the zealous ardor of the Spiritual Franciscans. The really effective weapons of the Holy Office, the real curses with which it afflicted the people, can be looked for in its dungeons and its confiscations, in the humiliating penances of the saffron crosses, and in the invisible police with which it benumbed the heart and soul of every man who had once fallen into its hands.

A few words will suffice as to the repulsive subject of the execution itself. When the populace was called together to view the last agonies of the martyrs of heresy, its pious zeal was not mocked by any ill-advised devices of mercy. The culprit was not, as in the later Spanish Inquisition, strangled before the lighting of the fagots; nor had the invention of gunpowder suggested the somewhat less humane expedient of hanging a bag of that explosive around his neck to shorten his torture when the flames should reach it. He was tied living to a post set high enough over a pile {552} of combustibles to enable the faithful to watch every act of the tragedy to its awful end. Holy men accompanied him to the last, to snatch his soul if possible from Satan; and, if he were not a relapsed, he could, as we have seen, save also his body at the last moment. Yet even in these final ministrations we see a fresh illustration of the curious inconsistency with which the Church imagined that it could shirk the responsibility of putting a human creature to death, for the friars who accompanied the victim were strictly warned not to exhort him to meet death promptly or to ascend firmly the ladder leading to the stake, or to submit cheerfully to the manipulations of the executioner, for if they did so they would be hastening his end and thus fall into "irregularity"—a tender scruple, it must be confessed, and one singularly out of place in those who had accomplished the judicial murder. For these occasions a holiday was usually selected, in order that the crowd might be larger and the lesson more effective; while, to prevent scandal, the sufferer was silenced, lest he might provoke the people to pity and sympathy.[519]

As for minor details, we happen to have them preserved in an account by an eye-witness of the execution of John Huss at Constance, in 1415. He was made to stand upon a couple of fagots and tightly bound to a thick post with ropes, around the ankles, below the knee, above the knee, at the groin, the waist, and under the arms. A chain was also secured around the neck. Then it was observed that he faced the east, which was not fitting for a heretic, and he was shifted to the west; fagots mixed with straw were piled around him to the chin. Then the Count Palatine Louis, who superintended the execution, approached with the Marshal of Constance, and asked him for the last time to recant. On his refusal they withdrew and clapped their hands, which was the signal for the executioners to light the pile. After it had burned away there followed the revolting process requisite to utterly destroy the half-burned body—separating it in pieces, breaking up the bones and throwing the fragments and the viscera on a fresh fire of logs. When, as in the cases of Arnaldo of Brescia, some of the Spiritual Franciscans, Huss, Savonarola, and others, it was {553} feared that relics of the martyr would be preserved, especial care was taken, after the fire was extinguished, to gather up the ashes and cast them in a running stream.[520]

There is something grotesquely horrible in the contrast between this crowning exhibition of human perversity and the cool business calculation of the cost of thus sending a human soul through flame to its Creator. In the accounts of Arnaud Assalit we have a statement of the expenses of burning four heretics at Carcassonne, April 24, 1323. It runs thus:

For large wood	55 sols	6 deniers.
For vine-branches	21 sols	3 deniers.
For straw	2 sols	6 deniers.
For four stakes	10 sols	9 deniers.
For ropes to tie the convicts	4 sols	7 deniers.
For the executioner, each 20 sols	80 sols.	
In all	8 livres 14 sols	7 deniers.

or, a little more than two livres apiece.[521]

When the heretic had eluded his tormentors by death and his body or skeleton was dug up and burned, the ceremony was necessarily less impressive, but nevertheless the most was made of it. As early as 1237 Guillem Pelisson, a contemporary, describes how at Toulouse a number of nobles and others were exhumed, when "their bones and stinking corpses" were dragged through the streets, preceded by a trumpeter proclaiming "*Qui aytal fara, aytal perira*"—who does so shall perish so—and at length were duly burned "in honor of God and of the blessed Mary His mother, and the blessed Dominic His servant." This formula was preserved to the end, and it was not economical from a pecuniary point of view. In Assalit's accounts we find that it cost five livres nineteen sols and six deniers, in 1323, for labor to dig up the bones of three dead heretics, a sack and cord in which to stow them, and two horses to drag them to the Grève, where they were burned the next day.[522]

The agency of fire was also invoked by the Inquisition to rid{554} the land of pestilent and heretical writings, a matter not without interest as signalizing the commencement of its activity in what subsequently became the censorship of the press. The burning of books displeasing to the authorities was a custom respectable by its antiquity. Constantine, as we have seen, demanded the surrender of all Arian works under penalty of death. In 435 Theodosius II. and Valentinian III. ordered all Nestorian books to be burned, and another law threatens punishment on all who will not deliver up Manichæan writings for the same fate. Justinian condemned the *secunda editio*, in which the glossators agree in recognizing the Talmud. During the ages of barbarism which followed there was little to call forth this method of repressing the human mind, but with the revival of speculation the ancient measures were speedily again called into use. When, in 1210, the University of Paris was agitated with the heresy of Amaury, the writings of his colleague, David de Dinant, together with the Physics and Metaphysics of Aristotle, to which it was attributed, were ordered to be burned. Allusion has already been made to the burning of Romance versions of the Scriptures by Jayme I. of Aragon and to the commands of the Council of Narbonne, in 1229, against the possession of any portion of Holy Writ by laymen, as well as to the burning of William of St. Amour's book, "*De periculis.*" Jewish books, however, and particularly the Talmud, on account of its blasphemous allusions to the Saviour and the Virgin, were the objects of special detestation, in the suppression of which the Church was unwearying. In the middle of the twelfth century Peter the Venerable contented himself with studying the Talmud and holding up to contempt some of the wild imaginings which abound in that curious compound of the sublime and the ridiculous. His argumentative methods were not suited to the impatience of the thirteenth century, which had committed itself to sterner dealings with misbelievers, and the persecution of Jewish literature followed swiftly on that of Albigenses and Waldenses. It was started by a converted Jew named Nicholas de Rupella, who, about 1236, called the attention of Gregory IX. to the blasphemies with which the Hebrew books were filled, and especially the Talmud. In June, 1239, Gregory issued letters to the Kings of England, France, Navarre, Aragon, Castile, and Portugal, and to the prelates in those kingdoms, ordering that on a Sabbath in{555} the following Lent, when the Jews would be in their synagogues, all their books should be seized and delivered to the Mendicant Friars. A report of the examination which ensued in Paris has been preserved, and shows that there was no difficulty in finding in the Jewish writings abundant matter offensive to pious ears, though the Rabbis who ventured to appear in their defence endeavored to explain away the blasphemous allusions to the Christian Messiah, the Virgin, and the saints. The proceedings dragged on for years, and sentence was not finally rendered until May 13, 1248, after which Paris was edified with the spectacle of the burning of fourteen wagon-loads at one time and of six at another. Like the *luz* or *os coccygis*, which the Rabbis held to be indestructible, the Talmud could not be wiped out of existence, and in 1255, St. Louis, in his instructions to his seneschals in the Narbonnais, again orders all copies to be burned, together with all other books containing blasphemies; while in 1267 Clement IV. (Gui Foucoix) instructed the Archbishop of Tarragona to coerce by excommunication the King of Aragon and his nobles to force the Jews to deliver up their Talmuds and other books to the inquisitors for examination, when, if they contain no blasphemies, they may be returned, but if otherwise they are to be sealed up and securely kept. Alonso the Wise of Castile was wiser, if, as reported, he caused the Talmud to be translated, in order that its errors might be exposed to the public. The passive resistance of the faithful was not to be overcome, and in 1299 Philippe le Bel felt obliged to denounce the persistent multiplication of the Talmud, and to order his judges to aid the Inquisition in its extermination. Ten years later, in 1309, we hear of three large wagon-loads of Jewish books publicly burned in Paris. How fruitless were all these efforts is seen in a formal sentence recited by Bernard Gui in the *auto de fé* of 1319. Under the impulsion of the Inquisition the royal officials had again made diligent perquisition and had collected all the copies of the Talmud on which they could lay their hands. Experts in the Hebrew tongue had then been employed to examine them carefully, and after mature counsel between the inquisitors and the jurists called in to assist, the books were condemned to be carried in two carts through the streets of Toulouse, while the royal officers proclaimed in loud voice that their fate was due to their blasphemies against the Lord Jesus{556} Christ and his mother the most holy Virgin and the Christian name, after which they were to be solemnly burned. This is the only case of execution occurring during Bernard Gui's term of service as inquisitor, and, from two carts being required to accommodate the obnoxious books, it was probable the result of search continued for a considerable time. That he deemed the matter to require constant vigilance is shown by his including in his collection of forms one which orders all priests for three Sundays to publish an injunction commanding the delivery to the Inquisition, for examination, of all Jewish books, including "Talamuz," under pain of excommunication. The warfare against this specially obnoxious work continued. In the very next year, 1320, John XXII. issued orders that all copies of it should be seized and burned. In 1409 Alexander V. paused in his denunciation of rival popes to order its destruction. The contest is well known which arose over it at the revival of letters, with Pfefferkorn and Reuchlin as the rival champions, and not all the efforts of the humanists availed to save it from proscription. Even as late as 1554 Julius III. repeated the command to the Inquisition to burn it without mercy, and all Jews were ordered, under pain of death, to surrender all books blaspheming Christ—a provision which was embodied in the canon law and remains there to this day. The censorship of the Inquisition was not confined to Jewish errors, but its activity in this direction will be more conveniently considered hereafter.[523]{557}

This is not the place for us to consider the influence of the Inquisition in all its breadth, but while yet we have its procedure in view it may not be amiss to glance cursorily at some of the effects immediately resulting from its mode of dealing with those whom it tried and condemned or absolved.

On the Church the processes invented and recommended to respect by the Inquisition had a most unfortunate effect. The ordinary episcopal courts employed them in dealing with heretics, and found their arbitrary violence too efficient not to extend it over other matters coming within their jurisdiction. Thus the spiritual tribunals rapidly came to employ inquisitorial methods. Already, in 1317, Bernard Gui speaks of the use of torture being habitual in them; and in complaining of the Clementine restrictions, he asks why the bishops should be limited in applying torture to heretics, while they could employ it without limit in everything else.[524]

Thus habituated to the harshest measures, the Church grew harder and crueller and more unchristian. The worst popes of the twelfth and thirteenth centuries could scarce have dared to shock the world with such an exhibition as that with which John XXII. glutted his hatred of Hugues Gerold, Bishop of Cahors. John was the son of an humble mechanic of Cahors, and possibly some ancient grudge may have existed between him and Hugues. Certain it is that no sooner did he mount the pontifical throne than he lost no time in assailing his enemy. May 4, 1317, the unfortunate prelate was solemnly degraded at Avignon and condemned to perpetual imprisonment. This was not enough. On a charge of conspiring against the life of the pope he was delivered to the secular arm, and in July of the same year he was partially flayed alive and then dragged to the stake and burned.[525]

This hardening process went on until the quarrels of the loftiest prelates were conducted with a savage ferocity which would have shamed a band of buccaneers. When, in 1385, six cardinals were accused of conspiring against Urban VI. the angry pontiff had them seized as they left the consistory and thrust into an{558} abandoned cistern in the castle of Nocera, where he was staying, so restricted in dimensions that the Cardinal di Sangro, who was tall and portly, could not stretch himself at full length. The methods taught by the inquisitors were brought into play. Subjected to hunger, cold, and vermin, the accused were plied by the creatures of the pope with promises of mercy if they would confess. This failing, torture was used on the Bishop of Aquila and a confession was procured implicating the others. They still refused to admit their guilt, and they were tortured on successive days. All that could be obtained from the Cardinal di Sangro was the despairing self-accusation that he suffered justly in view of the evil which he had wrought on archbishops, bishops, and other prelates at Urban's command. When it came to the turn of the Cardinal of Venice, Urban intrusted the work to an ancient pirate, whom he had created Prior of the Order of St. John in Sicily, with instructions to apply the torture till he could hear the victim howl; the infliction lasted from early morning till the dinner-hour, while the pope paced the garden under the window of the torture-chamber, reading his breviary aloud that the sound of his voice might keep the executioner reminded of the instructions. The strappado and rack were applied by turns, but though the victim was old and sickly, nothing could be wrenched from him save the ejaculation, "Christ suffered for us!" The accused were kept in their foul dungeon until Urban, besieged in Nocera by Charles of Durazzo, managed to escape and dragged them with him. In the flight the Bishop of Aquila, weakened by torture and mounted on a miserable hack, could not keep up with the party, when Urban ordered him despatched and left his corpse unburied by the wayside. The six cardinals, less fortunate, were carried by sea to Genoa, and kept in so vile a dungeon that the authorities were moved to pity and vainly begged mercy for them. Cardinal Adam Aston, an Englishman, was released on the vigorous intercession of Richard II., but the other five were never seen again. Some said that Urban had them beheaded; others that when he sailed for Sicily he carried them to sea and cast them overboard; others, again, that a trench was dug in his stable in which they were buried alive with a quantity of quicklime, to hasten the disappearance of their bodies. Urban's competitor, known as Clement VII., was no less sanguinary. When, as Cardinal Robert of{559} Geneva, he exercised legatine functions for Gregory XI., he led a band of Free Companions to vindicate the papal territorial claims. The terrible cold-blooded massacre of Cesena was his most conspicuous exploit, but equally characteristic of the man was his threat to the citizens of Bologna that he would wash his hands and feet in their blood. Such was the retroactive influence of the inquisitorial methods on the Church which had invented them to plague the heretic. If Bernabo and Galeazzo Visconti caused ecclesiastics to be tortured and burned to death over slow fires, they were merely improving on the lessons which the Church itself had taught.[526]

On secular jurisprudence the example of the Inquisition worked even more deplorably. It came at a time when the old order of things was giving way to the new—when the ancient customs of the barbarians, the ordeal, the wager of law, the wer-gild, were growing obsolete in the increasing intelligence of the age, when a new system was springing into life under the revived study of the Roman law, and when the administration of justice by the local feudal lord was becoming swallowed up in the widening jurisdiction of the crown. The whole judicial system of the European monarchies was undergoing reconstruction, and the happiness of future generations depended on the character of the new institutions. That in this reorganization the worst features of the imperial jurisprudence—the use of torture and the inquisitorial process—should be eagerly, nay, almost exclusively, adopted, should be divested of the safeguards which in Rome had restricted their abuse, should be exaggerated in all their evil tendencies, and should, for five centuries, become the prominent characteristic of the criminal jurisprudence of Europe, may safely be ascribed to the fact that they received the sanction of the Church. Thus recommended, they penetrated everywhere along with the Inquisition; while most of the nations to whom the Holy Office was unknown maintained their ancestral customs, developing into various{560} forms of criminal practice, harsh enough, indeed, to modern eyes, but wholly divested of the more hideous atrocities which characterized the habitual investigation into crime in other regions.[527]

Of all the curses which the Inquisition brought in its train this, perhaps, was the greatest—that, until the closing years of the eighteenth century, throughout the greater part of Europe, the inquisitorial process, as developed for the destruction of heresy, became the customary method of dealing with all who were under accusation; that the accused was treated as one having no rights, whose guilt was assumed in advance, and from whom confession was to be extorted by guile or force. Even witnesses were treated in the same fashion; and the prisoner who acknowledged guilt under torture was tortured again to obtain information about any other evil-doers of whom he perchance might have knowledge. So, also, the crime of "suspicion" was imported from the Inquisition into ordinary practice, and the accused who could not be convicted of the crime laid to his door could be punished for being suspected of it, not with the penalty legally provided for the offence, but with some other, at the fancy and discretion of the judge. It would be impossible to compute the amount of misery and wrong, inflicted on the defenceless up to the present century, which may be directly traced to the arbitrary and unrestricted methods introduced by the Inquisition and adopted by the jurists who fashioned{561} the criminal jurisprudence of the Continent. It was a system which might well seem the invention of demons, and was fitly characterized by Sir John Fortescue as the Road to Hell.[528]

{562}

{563}

APPENDIX.

I.

CATHARAN ARGUMENTS TO JUSTIFY THE ATTRIBUTION OF THE OLD TESTAMENT TO THE EVIL PRINCIPLE.

(Archives de l'Inquisition de Carcassonne.—Doat, XXXVI. 91.)

THE literature of the Cathari has been so successfully exterminated that anything attributable to the sect is of interest. The following, from a controversial tract, dating probably about the close of the thirteenth century, may be regarded as a fair summary of the reasons alleged by the sect to prove that the Creator, Jehovah, was Satan. There is sufficient identity between them and those given by Moneta (adversus Catharos, Lib. II. c. vi.) to show that they are in some sort the official and customary arguments of the heretics. I omit the counter-arguments of the writer, who generally follows Moneta, though he often reasons independently.

Primo igitur objicitur illud, Geneseos tertio: *Ecce Adam quasi unus ex nobis factus est.* Hoc dicit Deus de Adam postquam peccavit, et constat quod dicit verum aut falsum: si verum, ergo Adam factus erat similis ei qui loquebatur et eis cum quibus loquebatur. Sed Adam post peccatum factus erat peccator; ergo malus: si dixit falsum, ergo est mendax, ergo sic dicendo peccavit, et sic fuit malus.

Item ad idem. Deus ille dicit, Geneseos primo: *Videte ne forte sumat de ligno vitæ* etc. Deus autem novi testamenti dicit, Apocalipsis primo: *Vincenti dabo edere de ligno vitæ.* Ille prohibet, iste promittit, ergo contrarii sunt ad invicem.

Item ad idem, Geneseos primo: *Tenebræ erant super facie abyssi, dixitque Deus: Fiat lux.* Ergo Deus veteri testamenti incepit a tenebris et finivit in lucem; ergo est tenebrosus; ergo est malus, qui prius fecit tenebras quam lucem.

Item ad idem, Geneseos tertio: *Inimicitias ponam inter te et mulierem et inter semen tuum et semen mulieris.* Ecce Deus veteris testamenti seminator est discordiæ et inimicitiæ. Deus autem novi testamenti dator est pacis et solutor inimicitiarum, sicut legitur Coloss. primo: *Quoniam in ipso placuit omnem plenitudinem deitatis habitare, et per ipsum reconciliari omnia in ipsum, sive quæ in*{564} *cælis, sive quæ in terris sunt.* Ecce ille seminat inimicitias, iste vult omnia reconciliare et pacificare in se; Ergo sunt contrarii sibi.

Item, Geneseos tertio: *Maledicta terra in opere tuo.* Ecce Deus veteri testamenti maledicit terram quam Deus novi testamenti benedicit, psalmo: *Benedixisti domine terram tuam.* Ergo sunt contrarii.

Item, Genesi: *Omnis anima quæ circumcisa non fuerit peribit de populo suo.* Apostolus autem e contra prohibet Galatis: *si circumcidimini Christo nihil vobis prodest.* Ergo iste contrarius illi.

Item ad idem, Exodi undecimo: *Postulet unusquisque a vicino suo et unaquæque a vicina sua vasa aurea et argentea.* Ecce Deus veteris testamenti præcipit rapinam. Deus autem novi testamenti *non rapinam* arbitratus est, ut dicit Apostolus: Ergo sunt contrarii.

184

Item ad idem, Matthæi quinto: *Dictum est antiquis: Diliges proximum tuum et odio habebis inimicum tuum.* Sed constat quod hoc dictum est a Deo veteris testamenti. Deus autem novi testamenti dicit: *Diligite inimicos vestros.* Igitur contrariantur sibi invicem.

Item ad idem, Matthæi quinto: *Dictum est antiquis: Oculum pro oculo* etc. *Ego autem dico vobis non resistere malo, sed si quis percusserit* etc. Ecce ille Deus vindictam, iste veniam imperat: Ergo sunt contrarii.

Item ad idem, Exodi vicesimo primo dicit Deus veteris testamenti: *Si occiderit quispiam proximum suum dabit animam pro anima.* Deus autem novi testamenti dicit apud Lucam: *Non veni animas perdere sed salvare.*

Item, Joannis primo: *Deum nemo vidit unquam,* et ad Timotheum: *Quem nullus hominum vidit.* At e contra Deus veteris testamenti dicit, Deuteron. tertio: *Si quis fuerit inter vos propheta*etc.; et paulo post: *At non talis est servus meus Moyses* etc.; et infra: *Ore ad os loquitur ei et palam non per ænigmata et figuras Deum vidit.*

Item ad idem, Levitici vicesimo sexto: *Persequimini inimicos vestros;* At e contra, Matthæi quinto: *Beati qui persecutionem patiuntur;* et iterum: *Cum vos persecuti fuerint in unam civitatem, fugite in aliam.* Ille præcipit persequi inimicos, iste fugere: Ergo, etc.

Item, Deus veteris testamenti præcipit sibi immolari animalia, et in illis delectatur sacrificiis; Deus autem novi testamenti, secundum aliam translationem dicit in Psalmo: *hostiam et oblationem noluisti, corpus autem aptasti mihi; holocaustomata pro peccato tibi non placuerunt.* Ille Deus talia præcipit, iste respuit: Ergo, etc.

Item ad idem, Deuteron. decimo tertio: *Si surrexerit de medio tuo prophetes* etc. *et ita interficietur;* et iterum: *si tibi voluerit persuadere frater tuus* etc.; et infra: *non parcet ei oculus tuus ut miserearis et occultes eum, sed statim interficies.* Deus autem novi testamenti e contra dicit: *Estote misericordes* etc. Hie præcipit misereri, ille non miserere: Ergo etc.

Deus veteris testamenti dicit: *Crescite et multiplicamini,* Geneseos octavo. Deus autem novi testamenti dicit, Lucæ decimo octavo: *Væ prægnantibus et nutrientibus in diebus illis;* et in eodem vicesimo: *Beatæ steriles quæ non genuerunt.* Item, Matthæi quinto: *Qui viderit mulierem ad concupiscendam eam* etc.{565} Ecce ille præcipit coitum, iste prohibet omnem coitum, tam uxoris quam mulieris alterius: Igitur sunt sibi contrarii.

Item, Matthæi vicesimo, Lucæ vicesimo secundo: *Scitis quoniam principes gentium dominantur eorum, et qui majores sunt,* etc. *et non ita erit inter vos sicut inter gentes.* Ecce iste reprobat principatus et dominationes, ille probat.[529]

Item, Deuteronomii decimoquinto multis gentibus concedit hic usuram; Deus autem novi testamenti prohibet in Lucæ sexto: *Date mutuum nihil inde sperantes:* Ergo sunt contrarii.

Tentavit Deus veteris testamenti Abraham, Deus novi testamenti neminem tentat; Jac. primo:*Ipse intentator malorum est:* Ergo sunt contrarii.

Item ad idem, Deus veteris testamenti dicit*: Veniam ad te in caligine nubis;* Deus autem novi testamenti *habitat lucem inaccessibilem* ut legitur Hebræor. primo; Ergo sunt contrarii.

Item ad idem, Matthæi quinto: *Dictum est antiquis: non perjurabis, reddes autem Deo juramenta tua; ego autem dico vobis non jurare omnino;* quod ille concedit iste prohibet; Ergo etc.

Item, Exodi vicesimo primo: *Maledictus omnis qui pendet in ligno;* Sed Paulus dicit Galat. quarto: *Christus nos redemit de maledictione legis, factus pro nobis maledictum;* Ergo Deus veteris testamenti, quem dicis patrem Christi, maledixit Christum, sed constat quod pater non maledicit filium, ergo ille non est pater ejus, imo est malus et contrarius cui maledicit.

Item ad idem, Deus veteris testamenti promittit terrain ut ibi; *Dabo vobis terram fluentem lac et mel.* Ecce deliciæ terrenæ. Deus autem novi testamenti promittit regnum cœlorum, requiem æternam, delicias cœlestes ut ibi: *Invenietis requiem animabus vestris.* Ergo ipsi sunt diversi et contrarii.

Item ad idem, Deus novi testamenti dicit Matthæi sexto: *Jugum meum suave est et onus meum leve.* Deus autem veteris testamenti imponit jugum importabile, Deuteronomii vicesimo octavo, ubi maledixit illos qui non servaverunt illa quæ præceperat, de quo jugo dicit Petrus: *cur vos imponere tentatis nobis jugum quod nec vos nec patres vestri portare potuistis?* Ergo sunt contrarii; ille enim malus et iste bonus.

Item ad idem, Exodi quarto: *si dixerint mei, quod est nomen ejus qui misit me* etc. *respondit Dominus: sic dices ad eos: qui est misit me ad vos.* Ecce Deus veteris testamenti translator est, qui non vult nomen ejus manifestare; sed dicit *qui est* etc. Ita enim asinus et bos est qui est. Deus autem novi testamenti nomen suum manifestat per angelum suum, Lucæ secundo, *et vocabis nomen ejus Jesum.*

Deus veteris testamenti dicit Geneseos sexto: *Pænitet me fecisse hominem.* Ecce qualis Deus quem pœnitet de opere suo; ergo mutatur. Præterea pœnitentia est de peccato, ergo si pœnitet peccavit; Ergo malus fuit.

Item ad idem, Exodi tricesimo secundo: Postquam filii Israel adoraverunt{566} vitulum, dicit Deus ille Moysi: *Dimitte me, ut irascatur furor meus contra eos,* et infra: *Placatusque est Deus ne faceret malum quod locutus fuerat adversus populum suum.* Ecce quod mutatus est Deus veteris testamenti; Deus autem novi testamenti (non) immutatur, juxta illud Jacobi primo: *Omne datum est* etc.; et infra; *Apud quem non est immutatio* etc.

Item ad idem, Exodi vicesimo, Deus veteris testamenti dicit: Non *mœchaberis,* et idem Deus dicit Numerorum duodecimo: *Ecce ego suscitabo super te malum de domo tuo, et tollam uxorem tuam et dabo proximo tuo, id est, filio tuo.* Ecce non solum mœchationis quam ibi prohibuit, sed etiam incestus est procurator; ille Deus ergo malus et mutabilis.

Item ad idem, Exodi vicesimo primo: *non facies tibi sculptile nec aliquam similitudinem,* et infra, vicesimo quinto: *Facies duo cherubim aurea.* Ecce quanta mutabilitas, *facies* et *non facies.*

185

Qualis est Deus ille qui tot millia hominum submersit in diluvio etc.; habetur Geneseos sexto; et in mare rubro, Exodi decimo quinto; et in deserto, et in multis aliis locis. Si dicis quod non est crudelitas punire malos etc. quæro, si erat omnipotens et omnisciens, sciebat omnes peccaturos et futuros malos, et propter hoc damnandos, quare ergo fecierat eos? Nonne crudelis est qui homines ad hoc facit ut perdat?

Item ad idem, Exodi tricesimo secundo: *Hoc dicit Dominus*; et infra: *Ponat vir gladium super femur suum*; et infra: *Et occiderunt in illa die viginti tria millia*. Ecce qualis Deus quos habet clericos et ministros siquidem totius crudelitatis. Deus autem novi testamenti ministros pietatis; unde Joannes in canonica: *Qui diligit Deum diligit et fratrem suum*. Iste præcipit fratrem diligi, ille occidi.

Item ad idem, Numeror tricesimo quarto; Deus veteris testamenti dixit filiis Israel de gentibus illis qui erant in terra Cham: *Si nolueritis occidere eos, erunt clavi in oculis nostris et lanceæ in lateribus*. Ecce crudelis Deus qui non vult injurias dimitti. Deus autem novi testamenti dicit Matthæi sexto. *Si non dimiseritis hominibus, nec pater vester cælestis dimittet vobis peccata vestra*.

Item ad idem, Geneseos decimo nono, ubi Deus veteris testamenti justum simul et impium occidit, sicut patet in submersione Sodomæ et Gomorrhæ, ubi parvulos et adultos simul extinxit.

Item ad idem, Judicum vicesimo legitur quod cum filii Israel vellent pugnare contra filios Benjamin proper scelus quod commiserant in uxorem cujusdam fratris sui, consuluerunt Dominum si pugnandum esset contra eos, et quis esset dux belli, et expressit illis Judas, et quod pugnandum esset; unde sub hac fiducia inierunt bellum et occiderunt ex eis in primo conflictu viginti duo millia, in secundo octodecim millia, in tertio pauciores. Ecce quam crudelis et deceptor Deus, qui sic eos decepit ut perirent.

Item, Exodi quinto dicit Deus veteris testamenti: *Indurabo cor Pharaonis et non dimittet populum*; ecce crudelis Deus qui indurat ut occidat. Item, mendax Deus qui dicit *non dimittet*, et postea dimisit.

Item ad idem, Numerorum decimo quinto: Deus ille lapidare præcepit quemdam colligendum ligna in Sabbato, consultus super hoc a Moysi et Aaron. Deus{567} autem novi testamenti excusat discipulos fricantes spicas Sabbato; Ecce quam contrarii iste et ille!

In Genesi promisit Deus ille se daturum terram Chanaan Abrahæ, nec tamen dedit, ergo fuit mendax.... Quod autem objiciunt de illis qui egressi sunt de Ægypto, quibus et promisit per Moysen terram illam, et tamen omnes prostrati sunt in deserto.

Ad idem, Exodi tricesimo secundo: *Domine ostende mihi faciem tuam* et Dominus respondit:*Ego ostendam tibi omne bonum*, et postea ostendit ei omnia posteriora, id est, turpitudinem. Ecce qualis Deus!

Ad idem, Geneseos undecimo de Gigantibus qui ædificabant turrim, dixit ille Deus: *non desistent a cogitationibus suis donec eas opere compleverint*; et tamen sequitur ibidem: *Et cessaverunt ædificare*. Ecce quam mendax Deus!

Ad idem, Geneseos XXXII. dicit angelus Dei ad Jacob: *Nequaquam vocaberis ultra Jacob, sed Israel erit nomen tuum*. Et postea dicit in Exodo: *Ego sum Deus Abraham, Isaac, et Jacob*; et ita sibi contradicit; mendax igitur est ille Deus.

Dicit ille Deus: *Quis decipiet nolis Achab?... Ego ero spiritus mendax in ore omnium prophetarum ... Egredere et fac, decipies enim et prævalebis ... Dedit Deus spiritum mendacii in ore omnium prophetarum*. Ecce qualis Deus: si esset Deus veritatis constat quod non diceret: *quis decipiet* etc.

II.
BULL OF GREGORY IX. ORDERING AN EPISCOPAL INQUISITION.
(Archives de l'Inquisition de Carcassonne.—Doat, XXXII, fol. 103.)

Gregorius episcopus servus servorum Dei venerabilibus fratribus suffraganeis ecclesiæ Bisuntinensis salutem et apostolicam benedictionem. Ad capiendas vulpes parvulas, hæreticos videlicet qui moliuntur in partibus Burgundiæ tortuosis anfractibus vineam Domini demoliri, et penitus eliminandas ab ipsa suscepti cura regiminis nos hortatur. Ad nostram siquidem audientiam noveritis pervenisse quod quidam hæretici in vestris diocesibus constituti, qui metu mortis falso ad ecclesiam catholicam revertentes necnon et plures alii de hæretica pravitate convicti, ad errorem pravitatis ejusdem, quam a se abdicasse penitus videbantur, ut gravius scindere valeant catholicam unitatem sæpius revertuntur. Ne igitur per tales sub falsa conversionis specie catholicæ fidei professores corrumpere contingat, universitati vestræ per apostolica scripta præcipiendo mandamus, quatinus hujusmodi pestilentes, postquam fuerint de jam dicta pravitate convicti, si aliter puniti non fuerint, ita quod quilibet vestrum in suo diocesi ut ipsi det vexatio intellectum, in perpetuo carcere recludatis, de bonis ipsorum, si qua fortassis habent sibi vitæ necessaria prout consuevit talibus ministrantes; alioquin noventis nos venerabili fratri nostro Archiepiscopo Bisuntino nostris dedisse litteris in mandatis ut vos ad id auctoritate nostra, sublato cujuslibet appellationis impedimento, compellat. Datum Laterani, sexto Kalendas Junii, pontificatus nostri anno septimo (27 Mai. 1234).{568}

III.
BULL RELIEVING INQUISITORS FROM OBEDIENCE TO THEIR SUPERIORS.
(Archives de l'Inquisition de Carcassonne.—Doat, XXXII. fol. 15.)

Clemens episcopus servus servorum Dei dilectis filiis fratribus ordinum prædicatorum et minorum inquisitoribus hæreticæ pravitatis per diversas Burgundiæ et Lotharingiæ partes auctoritate apostolica deputatis et in posterum deputandis, salutem et apostolicam benedictionem. Catholicæ fidei negotium quod plurimum insidet cordi nostro in vestris prosperari manibus et de bono in melius procedere cupientes, ac volentes omne ab eo impedimentum et omne obstaculum removeri, præsentium vobis auctoritate mandamus quatinus in eodem negotio de divino et apostolico favore et omni humano timore postposito constanter ac intrepide procedentes circa extirpandam hæreticam pravitatem, tam de Burgondia quam de Lotharingia cum omni vigilantia omnique studio laboretis, et si forsitan magister et minister generalis, aliique priores et ministri provinciales, ac custodes seu guardiani aliquorum locorum vestrorum ordinum prætextu quorumcumque privilegiorum seu indulgentiarum ejusdem sedis dictis ordinibus concessorum ac concedendorum in posterum, vobis vel vestrum alicui seu aliquibus injunxerint seu quoquo modo præceperint ut quoad tempus et quoad certos articulos certasve personas negotio supersedeatis eidem, nos vobis universis et singulis auctoritate apostolica districtius inhibemus ne ipsis obedire in hac parte vel intendere quomodolibet præsumatis. Nos etiam privilegia seu indulgentias hujusmodi ad hunc articulum tenore præsentium revocantes, omnes excommunicationis, interdicti et suspensionis sententias, si quas in vos vel vestrum aliquos hac occasione ferri contingerit, irritas prorsus decernimus et inanes.... Non enim aliqua eis super hujuscemodi inquisitionis negotio vobis immediate a prædicta sede commisso et committendo facultas vel jurisdictio attribuitur seu potestas. Datum Viterbii, Idus Julii, pontificatus nostri anno tertio (15 Jul. 1267).

IV.
EUGENIUS IV. TO THE ARCHBISHOP OF NARBONNE.
(Archives de l'Inquisition de Carcassonne.—Doat, XXXV. fol. 184.)

Eugenius episcopus, servus servorum Dei, venerabilibus fratribus Archiepiscopo Narbonensi et ejus suffraganeis Carcassonæ, Sancti Pontii Thomeriarum, Agathensi et Aletensi episcopis, salutem et apostolicam benedictionem. Scripsit nobis vestra fraternitas dilectum filium fratrem Petrum de Turelule, inquisitorem hæreticæ pravitatis in provincia Narbonensi, intendere a nobis aliqua suum officium Inquisitionis et jurisdictionem vestram tangentia petere et impetrare, supplicastisque ut eum in brevi de eo et exorbitantiis suis a jure intenderetis sedem apostolicam informare, nollemus interea quicquam prædicto in vestrum et prælatorum provinciæ præjudicium facere aut concedere; ad quæ respondentes fatemur prædictum Inquisitorem aliquando significasse justam sibi fore quærimoniam{569} adversus nonnullos vestrum se in suo Inquisitionis officio injuste perturbantes, atque etiam pro viribus impedientes, petens sibi per nos viam et modum ostendi quibus taliter in posterum exercere possit officium, ut cum honore Dei et sui officii integritati valeret lites, jurgia, et contentiones ordinariorum effugere et declinare. Cum itaque sit nostræ intentionis prout ex officio pastoralis curæ nobis incumbere non ignoratis, et vos et ipsum Inquisitorem in vestris et suis juribus confovere, et lites ac controversias quæ fortassis inter vos vigerent cum justitia tollere ac terminare, hortamur in Domino vestram fraternitatem ut attente considerantes quod hujusmodi Inquisitores ab ecclesia fuerint instituti ad relevandum ordinarios parte sollicitudinis incumbente illis in favorem et augmentum fidei catholicæ, enervationemque et extirpationem hæreticæ pravitatis, contenti esse velitis in hac materia dispositionibus et institutis sacrorum canonum, et ad negotium hoc hæresum quo nullum in ecclesia habetur majus, prædictis Inquisitoribus assistere favoribus opportunis. Nam sic gratum erit nobis et summe acceptum quicquid favoris, commodi et adjumenti prædictis a fraternitatibus vestris juxta spem nostram præstabitur, ita molestias et illata eorum laudabili exercitio disturbia cum displicentia audiremus; pro bono autem concordiæ volumus ut gravaminibus propter quæ ab ipso Inquisitore per vos extitit appellatum ab eodem revocatis, lites quæ hodie inter vos pendent indecisæ sopiantur penitus et extinguantur, prout nos illas auctoritate apostolica in eventum revocationis antedictæ ad nos advocantes, tenore præsentium extinguimus, cassamus, et pro extinctis et cassatis haberi volumus et mandamus. Datum Florentiæ anno Incarnationis Dominicæ MCCCC quadragesimo primo Kalendas Julii pontificatus nostri anno undecimo.

V.
DISABILITIES OF DESCENDANTS OF HERETICS.
(Registrum curiæ Franciæ Carcassonæ.—Doat, XXXII. fol. 241.)

Noverint universi presentes litteras inspecturi quod nos frater Guillelmus de Sancto Sequano ordinis fratrum prædicatorum, inquisitor hæreticæ pravitatis in regno Franciæ authoritate apostolica deputatus attendentes quod secundum merita personarum debent distribui officia dignitatum, et quia expedit crimina nocentium esse nota, præsertim ilia per quæ extenditur ultio non solum in autores scelerum sed in progeniem dampnatorum, ideo nos ad instantiam procuratoris domini regis in seneschallia Carcassonæ de infrascriptis sibi copiam fieri postulantis, ad honorem Dei et fidei munimentum per nos ipsos exquisivimus et per discretum virum dominum Raimundum rectorem ecclesiæ de Mouteclaro publicum notarium Inquisitionis nostræ perquiri et inspici fecimus diligenter in libris et actis publicis Inquisitionis prædictæ, et invenimus quod anno Domini MCC quinquagesimo sexto Guiraldus de Altarippa quondam de Graoleto qui dicitur fuisse pater Guiraldi de Altarippa servientis armorum domini regis, confessus fuit in judicio coram Domino Bernardo de Monte-Atono tunc inquisitore hæreticæ pravitatis, quod viderat hæreticos et verba eorum audiverat. Item invenimus{570} quod Lombarda uxor dicti Guiraldi, quæ dicitur fuisse mater præfati Guiraldi de Altarippa servientis armorum domini regis, coram eodem inquisitore et eodem tempore confessa fuerit quod multotiens in diversis locis vidit hæreticos ct eos pluries adoravit misitque eis panem et poma et credidit eos esse bonos homines et quod posset salvari in fide eorum. Item invenimus in eisdem libris quod Raimundus Carbonelli de Graoleto, qui dicitur fuisse avunculus dicti Guiraldi servientis domini regis fuit hæreticus perfectus et per fratrem Stephanum Gastinensem et Hugonem de Boniolis tunc inquisitores hæreticæ pravitatis, et tanquam hæreticus

187

curiæ sæculari relictus et per ministros curiæ domini regis Carcassone publice, ut hæreticus et relapsus, combustus anno Domini MCC septuagesimo sexto. De quibus omnibus de nostris libris et actis publicis extractis fideliter dicto procuratori domini regis copiam fecimus, et omnibus quorum interest per ipsum fieri volumus, non ad suggilationem vel injuriam alicujus sed propter bona quæ agit vel excipit, vel propter posteros in quos parentum præfati criminis sceleratorum proserpit infamia, ne contra constitutiones domini regis vel sanctiones canonicas ad honores vel officia publica ullatenus admittantur. In cujus rei testimonium sigillum nostrum præsentibus duximus apponendum. Datum Carcassonæ decimo septimo Kalendas Julii, anno Domini MCC nonagesimo secundo.

VI.
MINUTES OF AN ASSEMBLY OF EXPERTS.
(Doat, XXVII. fol. 118.)

Anno Domini MCCC vicesimo octavo, indictione undecima, die Veneris in festo Stæ. Leocadiæ virginis, intitulata quinto Idus Decembris pontificatus SSmi. domini nostri Domini Joannis divina providentia papæ XXII. anno decimo tertio, venerabiles religiosi et discreti viri frater Henricus de Chamayo ordinis prædicatorum in regno Franciæ auctoritate regia et Germanus de Alanhano archipresbyter Narbonesii, rector ecclesiæ Capitistagni in civitate et diocesi Narbonensi auctoritate ordinaria, inquisitores pravitatis hæreticæ deputati, volentes in negotio fidei de consilio discretorum et peritorum procedere, convocarunt in aula seu palatio majori archiepiscopali Narbonæ dominos canonicos, jurisconsultos, peritos sæculares et religiosos infrascriptos (sequuntur nomina 42) qui omnes superius nominati juraverunt ad sancta Dei evangelia dare bonum et sanum consilium in agendis, unusquisque secundum Deum et conscientiam suam, prout ipsis a Domino fuerit ministratum et tenere omnia sub secreto donec fuerint publicata, et ibidem præstito juramento, lectis et recitatis culpis personarum infrascriptarum, petierunt præfati domini inquisitores consilium ab eisdem consiliariis quid agendum de personis prædictis, et divisim et singulariter de qualibet, ut sequitur:

Super culpa fratris P. de Arris ordinis Cartusiensis monasterii de Lupateria diocesis Carcassonensis omnes et singuli consiliarii supradicti, tam sæculares quam religiosi consilium dando concorditer dixerunt, contemplatione ordinis {571} sui, quod assignetur sibi pro carcere perpetuo claustrum et ecclesia monasterii supradicti, et etiam camera una, necnon et injungantur sibi certæ pœnitentiæ, sicut orationes et jejunia et alia quæ non repugnant observantiæ sui ordinis et regulæ supradictæ, et quod non puniatur in sermone publico sed in secreto, præsentibus paucis personis.

Item de personis infra proximo nominatis, auditis corum culpis dixerunt eas judicandas fore ut sequitur:
Richardum de Narbona, nulla pœna puniendum.
Guillelmum Mariæ de Honosio arbitrarie puniendum, cruces simplices, peregrinationes minores.
Favressam matrem prædicti Guillelmi arbitrarie puniendam, sine crucibus, pœnitentias minores.
Guillelmum Cathalani seniorem, Guillelmum ejus filium, Raymundum Veysiani, Bernardum Baronis, P. Lunatii, tanquam impeditores officii, cruces et pœnitentias minores.
Guillelmum Espulgue de Capitestagno immurandum.
Perretam de Flassacho valdensem impœnitentem fore exhumandum.
P. Guillelmi Canorgue de Capitestagno immurandum.
Vincentium Rayses de Caberia mortuum, si viveret, immurandum.
Gregorium Bellonis apostatam monachum, mortuum impœnitentem, exhumandum.
Guillelmum Bocardi Bourserium de Agenno habitatorem Narbonæ, mortuum, si viveret, immurandum.
Arnaudam uxorem Pontii de Biterris de Capitestagno immurandam.
Amicam uxorem P. Gaycons, ad murum.

Habitum fuit hoc consilium anno, indictione, die, loco, et pontificatu prædictis, præsentibus Arnaldo Assaliti procuratore incursuum hæresis domini regis, testibus et notariis qui hoc prædictum consilium scripserunt, etc.

VII.
INNOCENT IV. ORDERS INQUISITORS TO DIMINISH THEIR RETINUE AND AVOID EXACTIONS.
(Archives de l'Inquisition de Carcassonne.—Doat, XXXI. fol. 116.)

Innocentius episcopus servus servorum Dei dilectis filiis inquisitoribus hæreticæ pravitatis in terris nobilis viri domini Comitis Tholosani et Albiensis constitutis salutem et apostolicam benedictionem. Cum a quibusdam intellexerimus fidedignis quod vos occasione inquisitionis vobis commissæ contra hæreticam pravitatem superfluos scriptores aliosque familiares habetis pro vestræ libito voluntatis et graves exactiones fiunt a conversis ab eadem ad fidem et converti volentibus pravitate ad infamiam apostolicæ sedis et scandalum plurimorum, præsentium vobis auctoritate præcipiendo mandamus quatinus scriptorum et aliorum familiarium multitudinem onerosam ad necessarium numerum protinus {572} reducentes, a gravibus exactionibus per quas infamia potest et scandalum generari, vos et familiam vestram taliter compescatis quod honestatis vestræ titulus conservetur illæsus, et nos discretionis vestræ prudentiam merito commendare possumus.—Datum Lugduni secundo Idus Maii, pontificatus nostri anno sexto (14 Maii, 1249).

VIII.
ABUSE OF THE NUMBER OF ARMED FAMILIARS IN FLORENCE.
(Arch. di Firenze, Riformagioni, Arch. Diplom. XXVII.)

Bertrandus miseratione divina archiepiscopus Ebredunensis apostolicæ sedis nuncius circumspectis et religiosis viris inquisitoribus hæreticæ pravitatis qui in civitate et dioc. florentin. sunt et fuerint in futurum salutem in salutis autore. Quia quidam potestate sibi tradita abutentes et concessis a jure forma et modis debitis non utentes interdum favore seu alias concedunt aliqua ex quibus dampna proveniunt et scandala generantur, oportet talium abusus debito juris limitibus coartari. Cum igitur fidedigna relatione ad nostram audientiam sit deductum et nos fide probavimus oculata quod quidam inquisitores qui in civitate et dioc. florentin. prædictis vos in inquisitionis officio precesserint immoderatum et excessivum numerum consiliariorum notariorum et aliorum officialium ac familiarium licet non indigerunt eisdem sibi assumere curaverunt passim eisdem et aliis sub familiaritatis vel officii titulo diversis quæsitis coloribus portandi arma offensibilia et defensibilia licentiam concedendo ex quibus multa provenerunt scandala et multis data fuit occasio aliis qui arma portare non poterant offendendi. Nos juxta cominissam nobis circa reformationem officii inquisitionis sollicitudinem hujusmodi scandalis et quibusvis fraudibus occurrere cupieutes et volentes præfatum inquisitionis officium sic laudabiliter et feliciter servatis eidem suis privilegiis gubernari quod propterea non offendatur justitia nec ex abusu privilegiorum aliis præjudicium generetur, autoritate apostolica qua in hac parte fungimur decernimus et statuendo tenore præsentium ordinamus quod inquisitor florentinus qui est vel pro tempore fuerit possit duntaxat quatuor consiliarios seu assessores, duos notarios, et duos custodes carcerum et duodecim alios inter officiales et familiares sibi eligere et assumere et non ultra quibus possit dare licentiam arma prout consuetum est deferendi, hoc salvo quod si urgens necessitas pro inquisitionis officio immineret, possit in hujusmodi necessitatis articulo arma portandi licentiam impertiri. Illud autem præsenti ordinationi ex superhabundanti duximus inserendum quod ne ex limitatione prædicta inquisitionis detrahatur officio et in executione ipsius dispendium patiatur potestas ac priores artium florentini teneantur prout etiam sunt de jure stricti inquisitori qui est vel erit pro tempore fideles et diligentes existere et familiarios et etiam alios cum armis omni difficultate sublata tradere quoties pro capiendis malefactoribus et suspectis et aliis officium inquisitionis tangentibus exequendis per inquisitorem hujusmodi fuerint requisiti. In quorum testimonium præsentes literas fieri fecimus et nostri sigilli appensione muniri. Dat. in Castro Scarparic florentin. {573} dioc. die secunda Maii sub anno Domini MCCCXXXVII. Indict. V. Pontificatus III. Domini nostri summi pontificis.

IX.
REGULATIONS OF ARMED FAMILIARS BY THE COUNCIL OF VENICE.
(Archivio di Venezia, Misti Consiglio X. Vol. XIII. p. 192; Vol. XIV. p. 29.) 1450, 19 Augusti.

Cum facta sit conscientia quod inquisitor hæreticorum qui stat Venetiis dat licentiam XII. personis portandi arma et illam vendit per pecuniam, quod non est bene factum quod XII persone pro inquisitore portent arma per civitatem quum ad capiendos hereticos datur super talibus inquisitoribus auxilium brachii secularis, videlicet per dominos de nocte et per capita, Et propterea vadit pars quod inquisitores de cetero non possint dare licentiam nisi quatuor personis tantum sicut per consuetudinem antiquam solebant, quos quatuor quilibet inquisitor faciat presentari capitibus hujus concilii ut cognita condictione personarum possint provvidere sicut fuerit opus.

De parte—14. De non—2. Non sinceri—0.

1450 (1451), 17 Februarii.

Quod ad complacentiam Generalis minorum qui supplicavit ne inquisitori heretice pravitatis in civitate Venetiarum in suo tempore fiat novitas super custodibus et officialibus suis quos antiquitus inquisitores habuerunt. Vadit pars quod concedatur eidem quod non obstante parte capta in isto concilio die 9 Augusti 1450 mandetur officialibus de nocte quod pro honore officii observet inquisitori consuetudinem antiquam cum hoc conditione videlicet. Quod ipsi officiales associent inquisitorem ad officium faciendum et aliter sicut fuerit opus et sicut antiquitus faciebant; et propterea dentur in nota officio de nocte et capitibus sexteriorum ut videatur si actualiter faciant officium vel non, ita tamen quod non excedant numerum XII.

De parte—10. De non—5. Non sinceri—1.

X.
TRANSFER OF PRISONERS FROM ITALY TO FRANCE.
(Archives de l'Inquisition de Carcassonne.—Doat, XXXII. fol. 155.)

Nicholaus episcopus servus servorum Dei dilecto filio fratri Philippo ordinis fratrum prædicatorum inquisitori hæreticæ pravitatis in Marchia Trevisina auctoritate sedis apostolicæ deputato salutem et apostolicam benedictionem. Significarunt nobis dilecti filii Hugo de Boniolis et Petrus Arsini ordinis fratrum {574} prædicatorum, inquisitores hæreticæ pravitatis in regno Franciæ auctoritate sedis apostolicæ deputati, quod dudum in diocesi Veronensi quamplures hæretici de mandato tuo capti fuerunt et adhuc eos facis detineri captivos, quorum aliqui fore dicuntur de regno Franciæ oriundi, et unus eo in dicto regno pro episcopo hæreticorum ipsorum, secundum eorumdem hæreticorum usum habetur. Cum autem, sicut habeat eorumdem inquisitorum assertio, firma spes habeatur quod eorumdem hæreticorum dicti regni præsentia in illis partibus erit plurimum orthodoxæ fidei fructuosa, pro eo quod si contingat eorum aliquos divina gratia operante redire ad ipsius fidei unitatem, per ipsos multorum qui sunt in eodem regno prædictæ pravitatis fermento aspersi, occultata nequitia detegi poterit, et haberi plena notitia eorumdem. Nos qui tenemur exaltationem ipsius fidei totis viribus procurare, discretioni tuæ per apostolica scripta mandamus, quatinus tam illum qui, ut prædictum est, episcopus reputatur, quam alios hæreticos supradictos ejusdem regni præfatis inquisitoribus per eorum

189

certum nuncium ad te propter hoc specialiter destinandum, qui sumptibus ministrandis ab inquisitoribus supradictis sub fida custodia hæreticos ducat eosdem, deinceps sub ipsorum inquisitorum cura et jurisdictione mansuros, prius tamen diligentius inquisitis ab eisdem hæreticis ad præfatos fratres inquisitores ut præmittitur destinandis, quæ ad utilitatem ejusdem fidei et utiliorem executionem commissi tibi officii videris inquirenda transmittas. Nos enim prædictis inquisitoribus nostris damus litteris in mandatis, ut eosdem hæreticos ad ipsos per te taliter destinandos diligenter et fideliter faciant custodiri, facturi nihilominus circa illos libere in eos commissum sibi contra hæreticos officium exequendo, prout secundum Dei honori et commodo ejusdem orthodoxæ fidei viderint expedire. Datum Romæ apud Sanctum Petrum quarto Idus Februarii, pontificatus nostri anno primo (10 Feb. 1289).

XI.

ORDER OF INQUISITOR-GENERAL TO MAKE TRANSCRIPT OF RECORDS.
(Archives de l'Inquisition de Carcassonne.—Doat, XXXII. fol. 101.)

Joannes miseratione divina Sancti Nicolai in carcere Tulliano diaconus cardinalis, religiosis viris in Christo sibi dilectis fratribus ordinis prædicatorum et minorum inquisitoribus pravitatis hæreticæ in Citramontanis partibus auctoritate sedis apostolicæ deputatis, salutem in Domino nostro. Nil majus accedit affectui quam quod fidei catholicæ puritas ubique terrarum ad Dei gloriam valeat ampliari, et macula pravitatis hæreticæ de locis illis quæ infecisse dinoscitur virtutis divine cooperante subsidio per nostræ ac vestræ sollicitudinis ministerium penitus deleatur. Cum igitur hujusmodi cura negoti sit nobis ab apostolicæ sede commissa nos dilectorum nobis in Domino inquisitorum pravitatis ejusdem in regno Franciæ condignis desideriis annuentes, universitati vestræ auctoritate qua in hac parte fungimur, in virtute obedientiæ districte præcipiendo mandamus quatenus depositiones testium super pravitate ipsa jam receptorum a vobis vel recipiendorum in posterum, quia negotium Inquisitionis{575} in prædicto regno Franciæ inquisitoribus commissum eosdem contingere dinoscitur, in eo scilicet quod depositiones hujusmodi faciunt ad instructionem sibi commissi negotii ut per eas de statu personarum præfati regni habere possunt notitiam pleniorem, eisdem vel ipsorum certo et fido nuntio ad transcribendum sine difficultatis obstaculo assignetis, ut iidem inquisitores depositionibus ipsis pro loco et tempore uti possint contra personas prædicti regni, quæ per depositiones ipsas apparebunt de heresi culpabiles vel suspectæ. Datum apud Urbem veterem, decimo quarto Kalendas Junii, anno Domini MCC septuagesima tertio, pontificatus Domini Gregorii papæ decimi anno secundo.

XII.

BULL OF ALEXANDER IV. AUTHORIZING INQUISITORS TO ABSOLVE EACH OTHER.[530]
(Archives de l'Inquisition de Carcassonne,—Doat, XXXI. fol. 196.)

Alexander episcopus, servus servorum Dei dilectis filiis fratribus ordinis prædicatorum, inquisitoribus hæreticæ pravitatis in Tholosa et aliis terris nobilis viri A. comitis Pictavensis, salutem et apostolicam benedictionem. Ut negotium fidei valeatis liberius promovere, vobis auctoritate præsentium indulgemus ut si vos excommunicationis sententiam et irregularitatem incurrere aliquibus casibus ex humana fragilitate contingat vel recolatis etiam incurrisse, quia propter vobis injunctum officium ad priores vestros super hoc recurrere non potestis, mutuo vobis super hiis absolvere juxta formam ecclesiæ, ac vobiscum auctoritate vestra dispensare possitis, prout in hoc parte prioribus ab apostolica sede concessum est. Nulli ergo omnino hominum liceat etc.... Datum Anagniæ Nonis Julii pontificatus nostri anno secundo (7 Jul. 1256).

XIII.

CASE OF FALSE WITNESS.
(Doat, XXVII. fol. 204.)

Bernardus Pastoris de Marcelhano mercator, habitator Pedenacii diocesis Agathensis, sicut per ipsius confessionem, sub anno Domini MCCCXXIX., mense Maii XIX die factam et processum inde habitum apparet, veniens spontanea voluntate, non vocatus nec citatus per episcopum nec inquisitorem, sed per aliquos complices suos inductus, in domo episcopali Biterris, ubi tunc nos, frater Henricus de Chamayo, ordinis predicatorum, inquisitor Carcassonne, eramus, quamdam papiri cedulam scriptam nobis presentari et tradi per aliquos de familiaribus dicti Domini Episcopi procuravit et fecit, cujus tenor sequitur in{576} hec verba: Significatur religiose majestati domini inquisitoris heretice pravitatis in seueschallia Carcassonne, seu ejus locumtenentis, quod cum eo anno Begguini heretici et de heresi dampnati fuissent combusti juxta castrum de Pedenaco, mandate domini nostri regis et domini Inquisitoris, mandato summi Pontificis et domini Episcopi Agathensis; hinc est quod quidam perverso spiritu imbutus, adherens heretice pravitati, perversum animum suum ad fidem heresis perversis operibus ac hereticis et dampnosis suasionibus immittens, eorum perversa opera sequendo, quadam die post combustionem hereticorum et specialiter post combustionem cujusdam vocati Formayro et ejus sociorum, Raimundus Barseti, notarius, catholice fidei spernens doctrinam, et mandata Apostolica et domini nostri regis, et dicti domini Agathensis Episcopi, si potuisset, impugnando, et, quod deterius est, si adherentes habuisset, contra fidem Catholicam infringendo, accessit ad locum ubi dictus Formayro et alii superius nominati sunt combusti, et flexis genibus tanquam adoraret eorum nequitiam, accepit de ossibus dictorum combustorum hereticorum et de heresi dampnatorum et pro heresi, justo mandato domini nostri summi pontificis ac domini nostri regis legitime combustorum, et ipsa ossa in pallio sive sindone involvens cum multa reverentia ac si essent reliquie sanctorum, accepit ac secum asportavit, et cum per quosdam supervenientes peteretur quid faciebat ibi ipse Raimundus respondit: "Ego colligo de ossibus istorum combustorum, vere martirum, quia pro certo ipsi

190

erant sanioris fidei quam illi qui eos fecerant comburi, et de hoc habeo fidem meam, et ipsi erant optimi Christiani, et cum magno prejudicio et contra jus sunt combusti, et credo eos martires et eorum fidem laudo et credo quod sunt in Paradiso." Sic tunc testes infrascripti ejus vesaniam et incredulitatem ac etiam hereticam pravitatem increpantes, dixerunt dicto Raimundo: "Ut quid talia facitis et talia dicitis ac asseritis rebellionem Catholice fidei, quia certe nos credimus quod quidquid per sanctam Ecclesiam fit, digne et juste fiat, quia si non essent reperti heretici et pro heresi dampnati, jam non devinissent ad taliam sententiam." Ad quod respondens dictus Raimundus Barseti dixit hec verba vel similia: "Deberent teneri pro bonos christianos et veros martires, et hic non possem non credere quod non sint boni christiani," et nihil aliud posset sibi dari intellegi contra suam opinionem predictam. Quare supplicatur vestre Magnifice Dignitati ut ex vestro officio super premissis per vos adhibeatur remedium opportunum, et ad informandum vos nominantur testes, Imbertus de Ruppefixa, domicellus, Joannes Maurendi. Qua quidem cedula ut premittitur presentata et per nos recepta, dictum Bernardum ad nostram presentiam fecimus evocari, qui in judicio constitutus, juratus de veritate dicenda postmodum recognovit se fecisse fieri et dictari eamdem per magistrum Guillelmum Lombardi clericum et procuratorem Pedenacii habitatorem et scribi per Petrum clericum magistri Arnaudi Vasconis notarii dicti loci ad instantiam et instructionem Guillelmi Masconis de Pedenacio apotecarii, qui ipsam cedulam seu substantiam facti super quo formata fuit, conscientibus aliquibus aliis complicibus inferius nominandis primitus scripsit manu propria in vulgari, et postmodum eam sic in vulgari scriptam fecerunt formari et transcribi in forma predicta. Vocatis autem Joanne Maurendi, Guillelmo Masconis, Imberto de Ruppefixa, Durando de Podio, Guillelmo{577} de Casulis, a quibus idem Bernardus primo asserebat se audivisse narrari factum predictum, in dicta cedula expressum, et quod a principio, ut dixit, credebat esse verum, et coram nobis, Inquisitore predicto, uno post alium singulariter in judicio constitutis ac medio juramento interrogatis, si sciebant factum, prout in ipsa cedula continebatur fuisse verum, et primo respondentibus se nihil scire de ipso facto, nisi per auditum dici alienum, excepto dicto Joanne Maurendi, qui asseruit ipsum factum fore verum et deposuit de scientia et de visu, tandem prefatis Joanne Maurendi et Imberto de Ruppefixa in dicti Bernardi presentia affrontatis, et in judicio constitutis, et de veritate dicenda juratis, negaverunt unus post alium se dixisse predicto Bernardo factum predictum, et aliquid scire de ipso facto, excepto dicto Imberto qui, cum dicto Joanne Maurendi, finaliter asseruit se scire et vidisse, prout in culpa sua inferius postea recitanda plenius est expressum. Quibus omnibus premissis sic actis, habita suspicione per nos, Inquisitorem predictum, ex verisimilibus conjecturis et circumstantiis in eisdem tunc notatis, de consilio discretorum ibi presentium, eosdem Bernardum, Joannem, Guillelmum et Imbertum in carcere fecimus detineri; qui omnes sic detenti et in carcere reclusi, per paucos dies, apud Biterrim fuerunt auditi, interrogati et super premissa cedula plenius examinati, tandemque post multas exhortaciones, interrogationes et requisitiones eis factas, falsitatem et machinationem per eos factam inimicabiliter et dolose contra dictum Raimundum aperuerunt, unus post alium, non tamen ex toto nec clare donec fuerunt in dicto carcere per dies multos detenti et apud Carcassonam adducti. Dictus tamen Imbertus fuit primus qui predictam falsitatem et machinationem apperuit et detexit, non tamen ex integro donec omnes predicti quatuor, scilicet Bernardus Pastoris, Joannes Maurendi, Imbertus et Guillelmus fuerunt apud Carcassonam adducti et in ipso muro detenti. Demum vero dictus Bernardus post multas exhortaciones, inductiones et deductiones, effusis lacrymis, modum et seriem totius tractatus et machinationis predicte, falsitatis et cedule fabricationis et consentie in eis, corde gemebundo, detexit ac confessus fuit, quod, licet a principio dixisset se credere contenta in ipsa cedula fore vera, quod ab ipsis Joanne Maurendi, Guillelmo Masconis, et Imberto predictis se audivisse asseruerat, finaliter tamen bene perpendit ex dictis predictorum et ex circumstanciis in dicto tractatu habitis, et firmiter credidit quod predicta omnia in ipsa cedula contenta prout contra dictum Raimundum Berseti proposita erant non essent vera sed falsa et eidem Raimundo imposita falso et mendaciter, per malevolentiam et inimicitiam quam ipse et alii predicti et quidam alii de Pedenacio quos nominat, querebant vel habebant contra vel apud istum Raimundum Berseti ex causas quas in sua confessione expressit, et hoc etiam credebat et perpendebat antequam redderet cedulam predictam, sicut dixit, quodque in itinere dum ipse qui loquitur et dictus Joannes Maurendi ibant apud Biterrim ad redendam cedulam predictam dixit ipse loquens dicto Joanni: "Pectus multum me sollicitat non reddere istam cedulam," et dictus Joannes Maurendi respondit quod bene redderet eam nisi esset ibi pro teste scriptus; et hoc audito ipse Bernardus respondit: "Melius est quod estis testes et ego ipsam presentabo, quia quando sunt plures testes melius probabitur factum predictum." Item, quando fuerunt Biterrim,{578} ipse Bernardus Pastoris fecit dictum Joannem Maurendi recedere et reverti postmodum, ne, si videretur per dominum inquisitorem esset suspectus quod se ingereret in testem, non vocatus nec citatus, et postea fecit eum cum aliis citari, et eisdem citatis, ministravit expensas in cena, non tamen de pecunia sua aliorum consentientium in predictis. Item, quamdam informationem seu inquestam que fiebat in curia regia seu vicarii regii Bitterris contra dictum Raimundum Berseti super quibusdam casibus officium Inquisitionis minime tangentibus, tam ad expensas proprias quam aliorum, prosequebatur pro viribus et ducebat in odium et malum dicti Raimundi Berseti, non obstanti quod crederet contenta in ipsa cedula non esse vera, et quod etiam dixisset Joanni Maurendi et Guillelmo Mascon predictis se non credere ea fore vera nec adhibere fidem dictis eorumdem, et quod etiam sibi respondissent: "Vos, si est verum aut non, solus debetis ferre testimonium." Interrogatus quare ergo reddebat dictam cedulam ex quo sciebat eam contiuere falsitatem, respondit quod propter suum malum et suam ruinam et quod volebat quod propter illa ipse Raimundus Berseti haberet inde malum et dampnum. Interrogatus quare credebat inde malum eventurum dicto Raimundo Berseti, si ipsa cedula vel contenta in ea probarentur, respondit se nescire modum curie domini Inquisitoris, tamen sciebat, ut dixit, eadem contenta in ipsa cedula esse hereticalia, et quod dictus Raimundus propter hoc caperetur et in carcere poneretur et detineretur et postmodum remitteretur domino Episcopo Biterrensi et quod ipse episcopus posset de ipso Raimundo facere inquestam, sciens tum, ut dixit, quod dictus dominus Episcopus portabat tunc eidem Raimundo Berseti malam voluntatem, et quod non fecisset illi nisi malum et dampnum, credens tunc, ut dixit et desiderans quod ipse Raimundus condempnaretur ad perdendum officium suum, scilicet notariatus, et quod perderet magnam vel majorem partem bonorum suorum, et quod hoc sibi dixerant aliqui de complicibus predictis et aliis, quod talia erant in dicta cedula que, si probarentur, et causa bene duceretur, dictus Raimundus perderet magnam partem bonorum suorum committens predicta. Dixit se penitere de predictis.

XIV.

HOPELESSNESS OF DEFENCE.

(MSS. Bibl. Nat., fonds latin, nouvelles acquisitions, 139, fol. 33.)

Anno quo supra XIIII Kal. Februarii (19 Jan. 1252) P. Morret comparuit coram magistris inquisitoribus apud Carcassonam et requisitus si volebat se deffendere de hiis que in instructione inventa sunt contra eum et si volebat ea recipere dixit quod non. Item requisitus dixit quod habebat inimicos, videlicet B. de Beo et sorores ejus pro eo quod habuit causam cum eis, tamen postmodum pacificatum fuit inter eos. Item B. Seguini est inimicus suus. Item Savrina est inimica sua quia ipsa dicebat quod rem habuerat cum filia sua. Et requisitus si aliud volebat dicere vel proponere ad deffensionem suam dixit se nichil aliud scire, et fuerunt sibi publicata dicta testium in inquisitione contra ipsum inita in{579} presentia domini episcopi et dictorum inquisitorum. Et facta publicatione iterum fuit requisitus semel, secundo et tertio si volebat aliquid aliud dicere ad deffensionem suam vel aliquas legitimas exceptiones proponere, dixit quod non, nisi sicut dixerat; et fuit sibi assignata dies super hiis que inventa sunt contra eum in inquisitione et sibi publicatis in presentia prædictorum ... ad audiendam deffinitionem suam in octava Sti Vincentii (29 Jan.) in burgo. (Registre de l'Inquisition de Carcassonne.)

XV.

BULL OF GREGORY XI. RELEASING A "PEXARIACH."

(Doat, XXXV. fol. 134.)

Gregorius episcopus servus servorum Dei dilecto filio inquisitori heretice pravitatis in partibus Carcassonensibus, auctoritate apostolica deputato, salutem et apostolicam benedictionem. Humilibus supplicum votis libenter annuimus eaque favore prosequimur opportuno; sane petitio pro parte Bidonis de Podio Guillermi, laici, Burdegalensis diocesis, nobis nuper exhibita, continebat quod ipse qui dudum cum nonnullis dampnatis societatibus per regnum Francie discurrentibus, qui de Pexariacho nuncupabantur, et de heresi fuerunt vehementer suspecte, per heresim hujusmodi quam secundum quod testes contra cum super hoc producti deposuerunt, confessus, exititerat ad perpetuum carcerem condempnatus et in eo ex tunc continue stetit, suam penitentiam humiliter faciendo, et vere penitens et a predicta heresi discedens ad gremium et unitatem sancte matris ecclesie redire desiderat quamplurimum et affectat; quodque illi qui eum propter hujusmodi heresim auctoritate apostolica condemnarunt, liberandi eum ab hujusmodi carceribus, quamvis sit contritus et redire velit, ut perfertur, nullam habent potestatem, quare pro parte dicti Bidonis nobis fuit humiliter supplicatum ut providere ei in premissis de benignitate apostolica dignaremur; nos, hujusmodi supplicationibus inclinati, discretioni tue prefatum Bidonem si in judicio conscientie tue tibi videatur, quod ad hoc ipsius Bidonis merita suffragantur, liberandi a predicto carcere et sibi alias penitentias salutares auctoritate apostolica imponendi, hujusmodi heresi per eum primitus abjurata, tibi tenore presentium concedimus facultatem. Datum apud Pontem-sorgie, Avenionensis diocesis, secundo Idus Maii, Pontificatus nostri anno primo (14 Maii, 1371).

XVI.

MONITION OF THE ARCHBISHOP OF NARBONNE IN 1329 TO PROTECT PENITENTS WEARING CROSSES.

(Doat, XXVII. fol. 107.)

Quoniam illis qui pœnitentiam sibi impositam proper crimen hæresis agunt improperia obloquentium vel detrahentium quandoque dant materiam retrahendi{580} a via veritatis et pœnitentias facere omittendi, potissime quando de crucibus vel de pœnitentiis aliis sibi impositis irrisiones et detractiones eis inferuntur, idcirco nos Archiepiscopus, Episcopi, Inquisitores et Commissarii antedicti volentes talium obloquentium detrahentium et deridentium verbositatibus et malitiis obviare, et eos pœnitentiatos in suo bono proposito confovere, monemus canonice semel secundo et tertio ac peremptorie omnes et singulos utriusque sexus cujuscumque conditionis aut status existant et nihilominus in virtute sanctæ obedientiæ eisdem auctoritate apostolica inhibemus ne quis cujuscumque conditionis aut status existat audeat vel præsumat dictis personis pœnitentiatis vel crucesignatis occasione prædicti criminis improperium dicere vel dictum crimen retrahere vel quomodolibet imputare, intimantes omnibus tenore præsentis edicti quod eisdem detractoribus improperatoribus irrisoribus et oblocutoribus, si qui fuerint et de transgressione hujus edicti nostri legitime constiterit, cruces similes imponemus et alias procedemus contra eos secundum quod de jure et provincialibus conciliis prælatorum extiterit procedendum. Monemus insuper dictos crucesignatos et pœnitentiatos ut dictas cruces eis impositas humiliter continuo infra domum et extra portent, et sine ipsis crucibus infra domum vel extra ullatenus incedant, intimantes eisdem quod si eorum aliqui sine dictis crucibus prominentibus et apparentibus infra domum vel extra incedere præsumpserint ipsos tanquam hæreticos et impœnitentes reputabimus et eos puniemus animadversione debita prout in Valentino et Biterrensibus conciliis est ordinatum.

192

XVII.
Oath Administered to Jailor of Inquisition.
(Archives de l'Inquisition de Carcassonne.—Doat, XXXII. fol. 125.)

Anno Domini MCC octuagesimo secundo, sexta feria (vel) Sabbato infra octavas Apostolorum Petri et Pauli (3 Julii, 1282), fuit injunctum et districte mandatum et per juramentum Radulpho custodi immuratorum et Bernardæ uxori suæ per fratrem Joannem Galandi inquisitorem, in præsentia fratris P. regis prioris, fratris Joannis de Falgosio et fratris Archembaudi quod de cætero non teneat scriptorem aliquem in muro nec equos, nec ab aliquo immuratorum mutuum recipiant nec donum aliquod. Item nec pecuniam illorum qui in muro decedunt, retineant, nec aliquid aliud, sed statim inquisitoribus denuncient et reportent. Item quod nullum incarceratum et inclusum extrahat de carcere. Item quod immuratos pro aliqua causa extra primam portam muri nullo modo extrahat, nec domos intrent nec cum eo comedant. Item nec servitores qui deputati sunt ad serviendum aliis occupent in operibus suis, nec eos nec alios mittant ad aliquem locum sine speciali licentia inquisitorum. Item quod dictus Radulphus non ludat cum eis ad aliquem ludum, nec sustineat quod ipsi inter se ludant, et si in aliquo de prædictis inveniantur culpabiles ipso facto incontinenter de custodia muri perpetuo sint expulsi. Actum coram prædicto inquisitore in testimonio prædictorum et mei Pontii præpositi notarii, qui hæc scripsi. {581}

XVIII.
Royal Letters Concerning the Confiscations at Albi.
(Doat, XXXIV. fol. 131.)

Universis presentes litteras inspecturis, Petrus Textor, notarius Domini Regis, tenens locum nobilis viri domini Raynaldi de Nusiacho, domini nostri regis militis, ejusque vicarii Albie et Albigesii, salutem et presentibus dare fidem. Noveritis nos vidisse, tenuisse et diligenter inspexisse quosdam patentes litteras excellentissimi principis et domini clare memorie Sancti Ludovici Dei gratia Francorum regis, ejus sigillo cereo viridi et filis sericis viridibus et rubeis in pendenti sigillatas, inter cetera continentes quoddam capitulum cujus de verbo ad verbum tenor sequitur: "In hunc modum est sciendum quod immobilia que nobis et successoribus nostris advenient de heresibus et faidamentis hereticorum debemus nos et successores nostri et tenemur vendere vel alienare infra annum, talibus personis que facient episcopo et ecclesie Albiensi et successoribus suis servicium et alia que tenebantur facere eis veteres possessores pro rebus iisdem; si vero nos vel successores nostri non vendiderimus vel alienaverimus infra annum immobilia hujusmodi, episcopus Albiensis vel successores sui in secundo anno et in tertio accipiet auctoritate propria illa immobilia et possidebit et faciet fructus suos, et si nos vel successores nostri infra tertium annum non vendiderimus vel alienaverimus predicta ut dictum est, episcopus Albiensis et successores sui ex tunc habeant et retineant auctoritate propria possessionem et proprietatem omnium predictorum pleno jure." In cujus visionis et inspectionis testimonium, nos dictus locumtenens dicti domini vicarii sigillum autenticum curie Albie domini nostri regis huic presenti vidimus in pendenti duximus apponendum. Datum Albie, die Veneris post festum beati Vincentii Martyris, anno Domini MCCCIII. (23 Januarii, 1304).

Philippus Dei gratia Francorum rex seneschallo Tholosano vel ejus locumtenenti salutem. Ex parte dilecti et fidelis noster episcopi Albiensis nobis fuit expositum quod super incursibus et faidimentis condemnatorum de heresi, inter Sanctum Ludovicum avum nostrum et dictum episcopum quedam ordinatio facta fuit, quod nos medietatem bonorum immobilium ipsorum condemnatorum ad manum nostram devenientium tenemur extra manum nostram ponere infra annum, et si infra primum et secundum annum dicta bona non fuerint vendita, idem episcopus in tertio anno dictorum bonorum fructus facit suos, et si bona hujusmodi condemnatorum in tertio anno vendita non fuerint, in quarto anno tam in possessione quam in proprietate dictus episcopus bonorum ipsorum efficitur dominus in solidum, et habet idem episcopus electionem dicta bona retinendi pro pretio pro quo alii venderentur, prout in litteris inde confectis et sigillo regio in cera viridi sigillatis dicitur plenius contineri, et quod gentes et nonnulli officiarii vestri seneschallie vestre et quidam alii dictam ordinationem que retroactis temporibus servata fuit, infringunt et infringere ac contra eam venire nituntur indebite et de novo; quare mandamus vobis quatinus si, vocatis procuratore nostro et aliis evocandis, vobis constiterit ita esse, dictam ordinationem {582} juxta dictarum litterarum continentiam faciatis ratione previa firmiter observari, ea que contra ipsius ordinationis tenorem in dicti episcopi prejudicium indebite et de novo facta fuisse inveneritis ad statum debitam taliter reducentes quod super hoc ad nos non reperitur querela. Actum apud Novum Mercatum, die decima septima Augusti, anno Domini MCCCVI.

(Doat, XXXV. fol. 94.)

Philippus Dei gratia Francorum rex, Tholose et Carcassone Seneschallis aut eorum locumtenentibus salutem. Exposuerunt nobis nostri super incursibus heresis senescalli Carcassone et episcopi Albiensis procuratores quod, cum incursus heresis civitatis Albie et districtus ejusdem ad nos et ad dictum episcopum equis partibus pertineant, nonnullique dicte civitatis pro heresis crimine fuerint condempnati, et per hujusmodi condempnationem bona ipsorum nobis et dicto episcopo confiscata; nihilominus tamen nostri et episcopi procuratores predicti debita que per nonnullas personas diversorum locorum dictis condempnatis debebantur, quorum obligationes in dicta civitate celebrate fuerunt et ibidem exsolvi promisse, voluerunt exigere et nostris et episcopi, ut decet, rationibus applicare, quidam barones, nobiles et prelati quibus dicti debitores sunt subditi, nitentes dicta debita per dictos suos subditos contracta, sibi applicare, dicentes quod ad eos pertinet confiscatio

193

ipsorum debitorum, dictos procuratores in exactione debitorum hujusmodi impedire nituntur indebite, cum in dicta civitate contracta et solvi promissa, ut predicitur, fuerint, sicut dicunt: quare mandamus vobis et vestrum cuilibet, ut pertinebit ad eum, quatinus, si vocatis evocandis, summarie et de plano constiterit de premissis, dictos barones nobiles et prelatos ab impedimento predicto opportunis remediis desistere compellentes, predicta talia debita per dictos procuratores pro nobis et dicto episcopo levari et exigi, et debitores ad ea solvendum compelli permittatis et faciatis, ac ipsa exacta nobis et dicti episcopi rationibus applicari; et cum vos propter debatum hujusmodi de predictis debitis plura per manum nostram ut superiorem, levari et exigi fecisse dicamini, de quibus ipse episcopus partem ipsum contingentem non habuit, ut dicit; si premissa vera sint, de hac parte episcopum ipsum contingente, eidem expeditionem fieri faciatis. Datum Parisius, decima sexta die Martii, anno Domini MCCCXXIX.

XIX.

GIFT TO INQUISITOR FROM THE CONFISCATIONS.
(Doat, XXXI. fol. 171.)

Alfonsus filius regis Franciæ, Pictavensis et Tholosanus comes, universis presentes litteras inspecturis salutem in Domino. Notum facimus quod nos libere et pie concedimus et donamus Egidio clerico, inquisitori de heresi in partibus Tholose de cujus servitio nos laudamus, intuitu pietatis, centum solidos Tholosanos[585] annui redditus, in terra Raimundi de Vaure, militis, diocesis tholosane, sita in territorio Sancti Felicis et in feodo, que terra devenit ad nos incursa pro crimine heretice pravitatis, tenenda ab eodem et etiam possidenda quamdiu vixerit pacifice et quiete ita tamen quod post ejus decessum ad nos seu successores nostros libere revertatur, et si inveniretur quod plus valeret tempore date presentium litterarum, illud non intelligimus concessisse nec donasse, ita tamen quod illam terram vel redditum alienare non possit sine nostra licentia speciali. In cujus rei testimonium presentibus litteris sigillum nostrum duximus apponendum, salvo jure quolibet alieno. Actum apud hospitale juxta Corbolium, anno Domini MCCLI., mense Julii.

XX.

CHARLES OF ANJOU'S INSISTENCE AS TO CONFISCATED PROPERTY.
(Archivio di Napoli, Anno 1272, Reg. 15, Lettera C, fol. 77.)

Scriptum est seneschallo Provincie etc. Olim vicario et subvicario quandam Massilie dedisse dicimur in mandatis ut cum maria Roberta de Massilia mulier accusata de crimine heresis antequam ad carcerem occasione predicte criminis finaliter condempnaretur quamdam domum suam predicti criminis occasione ad nostram curiam legitime devolvendam vendiderit fraudulenter, ipsi vel eorum alter inquirerent de premissis diligentius veritatem, et si rem invenirent ita esse dictam domum ad opus nostre curie revocantes facerent ipsam publice subastari, rescripturi nobis quantum de ea poterat inveniri: ipsi vero mandatum nostrum in hac parte ducentes penitus in contemptum id facere non curarunt. Unde nos presenti vicario et subvicario Massilie sub obtentu gratie nostre districte precipimus ut ipsi vel alter eorum super premissis inquisita diligenter veritate si eamdem domum invenerint ad nostram curiam occasione hujusmodi pertinere ipsam ad opus ipsius curie nostre revocantes ipsam subastari faciant rescripturi nobis quantum de ea poterit inveniri. Quia tamen ipsum negotium plurimum nobis cordi existit, volumus et fidelitati tue precipiendo mandamus quatenus in premissis committi non patiatis negligentiam vel defectum, et si forsan procurator curie nostre in provincia occupatus aliis hiis interesse nequiverit alium qui degat Massilie statuas ut executioni predictorum omnium intersit prout de jure fuerit et utilitati nostre curie videatur expedire. Datum Capue XIIII. Januarii prime indictionis.

(On the next following folio is a similar letter addressed to the viguier and sous-viguier.)

END OF VOL. I.

FOOTNOTES:

[1] Johann. Saresberiens. Polycrat. lib. IV. cap. iii.—Honor. Augustod. Summ. Glor. de Apost. cap. v., viii.—Innocent PP. III. Regest. de Negot. Rom. Imp. xviii.; Ejusd. Serm. de Sanctis vii.; Serm. de Diversis iii.—Eymerici Direct. Inquisit. Ed. Venet. 1607, p. 353.

[2] Gratiani P. I. Dist. LXII.—Concil Lateran. IV. c. xxiii.-xxv.—Isambert, Anciennes Loix Françaises, I. 145.—P. Damiani Lib. I. Epist. ii.

[3] Innocent. PP. III. Regest. I. 261.—P. Cantor. Verb. abbrev. cap. cv.—Alex. PP. III. Epist. 395.—Cæsar. Heisterb. Dial. Mirac. Dist. VI. c. 5.—Concil. Rotomag. ann. 1050 c. 2.—Rodolphi Glabri Hist. Lib. v. c. 5.—Guibert. Noviogent. de Vita sua Lib. III. c. 2.—Joann. Saresberiens. Polycrat. Lib. VII. c. 19.—Hist. Monast. Andaginens. c. 81.—Ruperti Tuitens. Chron. S. Laurent. c. 28, 45.—Hist. Monast. S. Laurent. Leodiens. Lib. v. c. 62, 121-3.—Chron. Cornel. Zantfliet ann. 1305.
A story very similar to that of Philip Augustus is told of the Chancellor of Roger of Sicily and three competitors for the see of Avellana—Joann. Saresberiens. ubi sup.

[4] P. Cantor. Verb. abbrev. cap. xxxvi.—Chron. Turon. ann. 1097.—Ivon. Carnotens. Lib. I. Epp. lxvi., lxvii.

[5] Chron. Senonens. Lib. v. cap. xiii.-xv.—Chron. S. Trudon. Lib. v.—Fulbert. Carnotens. Epist. 112.—Metzleri de Viris Illust. S. Gallens. Lib. ii. cap. 28, 30, 36, 38, 39, 40, 41, 43, 45, 49, 53, 54, 56, 57, 60.—Martene Collect. Ampliss. I. 1188-9.—Vaissette, Hist. Gén. de Languedoc. T. IV. p. 7 (Ed. 1742).—Gerhohi Reichersperg. Exposit. in Psalm lxiv. cap. 34.—Ejusd. Lib. de Ædificio Dei cap. 5.—Cæsar. Heisterbac. Dial.

Mirac. Dist. II. cap. 9.—Matt. Paris. Hist. Angl. ann. 1196.—Rog. Hovedens. ann. 1197.—Benedicti Gesta Henrici II. ann 1188.—Baggiolini, Dolcino e i Patarini, p. 53 (Novara, 1838).—Martene Thesaur. II. 90-93, 99, 100, 150, 151, 192.

A clerical rhymer of the thirteenth century describes the prelates of the day—

"Episcopi cornuti
conticuere muti;
ad prædam sunt parati
et indecenter coronati,
pro virga ferunt lanceam
pro infula galeam.

"sicut fortes
incedunt
et a Deo discedunt.
ut leones feroces
et ut aquilæ veloces,
ut apri frendentes
exacuere dentes."

Carmina Burana, p. 15 (Breslau. 1883).

[6] P. Cantor. Verb. abbrev. cap. liv.—Pet. Blesens. Epist. ccxl.—Cæsar. Heisterb. Dial. Mirac. Dist. II. c. 27, 28; Dist. VI. c. 20.—Varior. ad Alex. PP. III. Epist. xxi. (Migne, Patrolog. CC. 1379).—Pet. Blesens. Tract. quales sunt P. II. IV.

[7] Innocent. PP. III. Regest. I. 277; XIV. 125; XVI. 63, 158.—II. 34; VII. 84.—III. 24; VII. 75, 76; VIII. 106; IX. 66; X. 68; XIII. 88; XV. 93. See also II. 236; VI. 216; X. 182, 194; XI. 142;XII. 24, 25; XV. 186, 235; XVI. 12.—Gollut, République Séquanoise (Ed. Duvernoy, Arbois, 1846, pp. 80, 1724).—La Porte du Theil (Académie des Inscriptions, Notices des MSS. III. 617 sqq.).—Opusc. Tripartiti P. III. cap. iv. (Fasciculi Rer. Expetendarum et Fugiendarum, II. 225, Ed. 1690).

In May, 1212, Legate Arnauld is addressed as Archbishop-elect of Narbonne (Innocent. PP. III. Regest. XV. 93, 101), but in the necrology of the Abbey of Saint-Just of Narbonne, Berenger, at his death, Aug. 11, 1213, is qualified as archbishop (Chron. de S. Just, Vaissette, Ed. Privat, VIII. 218).

[8] P. Cantor. Verb. abbrev. cap. 71.—S. Bernardi Tract. de Mor. et Offic. Episc. c. vii. No. 25.—Gesta Treviror. Archiep. cap. 92.—Prutz, Malteser Urkunden und Registen, München, 1883, p. 38.—Guillel. Nangiac. Contin. ann. 1305.—Hist. Prior. Grandimont. (Martene Ampliss. Coll. VI. 122, 135-137).—Matt. Paris Hist. Angl. ann. 1245, 1248, 1250, 1252, 1255, 1256.—Hincmari Epist. xxxii. 20.—Hildeberti Cenoman. Epist. Lib. ii. No. 41, 47.—S. Bernard. de Consideratione Lib. i. cap. 4.—Innocent. PP. III. Gesta xli.—Ejusd. Regest. I. 330; II. 265; v. 33, 34; X. 188.—Gregor. PP. IX. Bull. *Desiderantes plurimum*(Potthast Regesta, I. 673).—Chron. Augustan, ann. 1260.—Stephani Tornacens. Epist. 43.—Gualt. Mapes de Nugis Curialium Dist. II. cap. VII.

[9] Can. 43, Extra Lib. I. tit. iii.—Petri Exoniens. Summula Exigendi Confessionis (Harduin. VII. 1126).—Concil. Herbipolens. ann. 1187 c. 37.—Concil. apud Campinacum ann. 1238 c. 1, 2, 7.—Concil. apud Castrum Gonterii ann. 1253 can. unic.—C. Nugariolens. ann. 1290 c. 3.—C. Avenionens. ann. 1326 c. 49; ann. 1337 c. 59.—C. Bituricens. ann. 1336 c. 5.—C. Vaurens. ann. 1368 c. 10, 11.—Lucii. PP. III. Epist. 252.—Innocent. PP. III. Regest. Lib. I. Epist. 235, 349, 405, 456, 536, 540; II. 29; III. 37; VI. 120, 233, 234; VII. 26; X. 15, 79, 93; XI. 144, 161, 275; XV. 218, 223; Supplem. 234.—Berger, Registre d'Innocent. IV. pp. lxxvi-lxxvii., No. 2591, 3214, 3812, 4086.—Theiner Vet. Monument. Hibern. et Scotor. No. 196, p. 75.—De Reiffenberg, Chron. de Ph. Mouskes, I. ccxxv.

When the comprehensive annual curse, known as the Bull in Cæna Domini, came in fashion, falsifiers of papal letters were included in its anathemas, until the abrogation of the custom in 1773.

[10] Fascic. Rerum Expetendarum et Fugiendarum II. 7, 254-255 (Ed. 1690).

[11] P. Cantor. Verb. abbrev. cap. 24.—Cf. Petri. Blesensis Epist. 23; Johann. Saresberiens. Polycrat. Lib. VII. cap. 21, Lib. VIII. cap. 17.

[12] Concil. Juliobonens. ann. 1080 c. 3, 5.—Concil. Bremens. ann. 1266.—Eadmer. Hist. Novor. Lib. IV.—Concil. Melfitan. ann. 1284 c. 5.—P. Cantor. Verb. abbrev. cap. 24, 79.—Innocent. PP. III. Regest. X. 85; XII. 37.—Pet. Blesensis Epist. 209.

[13] Concil. Rotomag. ann. 1231 c. 48.—P. Cantor. Verb. abbrev. cap. 23.—Innocent. PP. III. Regest. I. 376.—Chron. Andres. Monast.—Narrat. Restaur. Abbat. S. Mart. Tornacens. cap. 113, 114.—Joann. Saresberiens. Polycrat. Lib. v. cap. 15. Cf. Lib. VI. cap. 24.

[14] P. Cantor. Verb. abbrev. cap. 86.

[15] Concil. Lemovicens. ann. 1031.—Concil. Avenionens. ann. 1209 c. 1.—Concil. Lateranens. ann. 1215 c. 10.—Millot, Hist. Litt. des Troubadours, II. 61.

[16] S. Bernard. Epistt. 271, 274, 276.—Can. 2, 3, Extra Lib. i. Tit. xiii.—Thomassin, Discip. de l'Église. P. IV. Lib. ii. cap. 38.—Gaufridi Vosiensis Chron. ann. 1181.—Concil. Turon. ann. 1231. c. 16.—Concil. Lugdun. ann. 1274 c. 12.—P. Cantor. Verb. abbrev. cap. 55, 60, 61.—Innocent. PP. III. Regest. XI. 142.—Even a pontiff such us Innocent III. was not above intruding his dependants upon the churches everywhere. His registers are full of such missives.

[17] Concil. Lateran. III. ann. 1179 c. 13, 14; IV. ann. 1215 c. 29.—Innocent. PP. III. Regest. I. 82, 191, 471.—P. Cantor. Verb. abbrev. cap. 31, 32, 34. 80.—Honor. PP. III. Epist. ad Archiep. Bituricens. ann. 1219.—Urbani. PP. V. Constit. 1367 (Harduin. Concil. VII. 1767).—Isambert. Anc. Loix Franç. I. 252.—Matt. Paris. Hist. Angl. ann. 1246 (Ed. 1644 p. 483)—Wadding. Annal. Minor, ann. 1238, No. 8.—D'Argentré, Collect. Judicior. de Nov. Error. I. I. 143.

The correspondence of the papal chancery under Innocent IV., as preserved in the official register, for the first three months of 1245, embraces three hundred and thirty-two letters, and of these about one fifth are dispensations to sixty-five persons to hold pluralities (Berger, Registres d'Innoc. IV. t. I.). A considerable proportion of the remainder are licenses for violations of canon law, showing how exhaustless were the vices of the clergy as a source of profit to the curia. For the rapacity with which the benefices of the dying were sought and disputed, see ibid. No. 1611.

[18] Clement. PP. IV. Epist. 456. (Martene Thesaur. II. 461).—Alcuini Epist. i. ad Arnon. Salisburg. (Pez Thesaur. II. i. 4).—Decreti P. II. Caus. XIII. Gratiani Comment, in Q.I. cap. i; Caus. XVI. Q. i. cap. 42, 43, 45-47, 56, 57; Caus. XVI. Q. vii. cap. 1-8.—Extra Lib.III. tit. xxx.—Concil. Rotomag. ann. 1189 c. 23.—Concil. Wigorn. ann. 1240 c. 44, 45.—Concil Mertonens. ann. 1300.—Concil. apud Pennam Fidelem ann. 1302 c. 7.—Concil. Maghfeldens. ann. 1332.—Concil. Londin. ann. 1342 c. 4, 5.—Concil. Nimociens. ann. 1298 c. 16.—Concil. Nicosiens. ann. 1340 c. 1.—Concil. Marciac. ann. 1326 c. 30.—Concil. Vaurens. ann. 1368 c. 68-70.—Gerhohi Reichersperg. Lib. de Ædificio Dei c. 46.

[19] Cæsar. Heisterbac. Dial. Mirac. Dist. iii. cap. 40, 41.—Hist. Monast. S. Laurent. Leodiens. Lib. v. cap. 39.—Innocent. PP. III. Regest. I. 220; II. 104.—Pet. Cantor. Verb. abbrev. cap. 27-29, 38-40.—Grandjean, Registre de Benoit XI. No. 975.—Concil. Lateran. IV. ann. 1215, c. 63-66.—Concil. Rotomag. ann. 1231, c. 14.—Teulet, Layettes II. 306, No. 2428.—Const. Provin. S. Edmund. Cantuar. ann. 1236, c. 8.—Synod. Wigorn. ann. 1240, c. 16, 26, 29.—Concil. Turon. ann. 1239, c. 4, 17.

[20] Synod. Andegav. ann. 1294, c. 3.—Capit. Car. Mag. II. ann. 811, cap. 5.—Concil. Cabillon. II. ann. 813, c. 6.—Concil. Turonens. III. ann. 813, c. 51.—Concil. Remens. ann. 813.—Concil. Mogunt. ann. 813, c. 6.—Can. 10, Extra Lib. III. tit. xxvi.—Concil. Narbonn. ann. 1227, c. 5.—Concil. Tolosan. ann. 1228, c. 5; ann. 1229, c. 16.—Concil. Rotomag. ann. 1231. c. 23.—Concil. Arelatens. ann. 1234, c. 21; ann. 1275, c. 8.—Constit. Provin. S. Edmund. Cantuar. ann. 1236, c. 33.—Concil. Albiens. ann. 1254, c. 11.—Concil. Andegav. ann. 1206; 1300.—Respons. Episc. Carcassonn. ann. 1275 (Martene Thesaur. I. 1151).—Concil. Nemausiens. ann. 1284, c. 8.—Concil. Reatinens. ann. 1303, c. 8.—Concil. Cameracens. ann. 1317.

[21] Decreti. II. Caus. xiii. Q. 2.—Can. 1-10, Sexto Lib. III. Tit. xxviii.—Anon Zwetlens. Hist. Rom. Pontif. No. 155 (Pez Thesaur. I. iii. 383).—Narrat. Restaur. Abbat. S. Martini Tornacens. cap. 86-89.—Synod. Wigorn. ann. 1240, c. 50.—Ripoll Bullar. Ord. Prædic. VII. 5.—Grandjean, Registre de Benoit XI. No. 974.—Innocent. PP. III. Regest. VII. 165.—G.B. de Lagrèze, La Navarre, t. II. p. 165.—Concil. Avenion. ann. 1326, c. 27; ann. 1237, c. 32.—Teulet, Layettes II. 306, No. 2428.—Concil. Nimociens. ann. 1296, c. 17.—Constit. Joann. Arch. Nicosiens. ann. 1321, c. 10.—Concil. Vaurens. ann. 1368, c. 63, 64.

[22] Cæsar. Heisterbac. Dial. Mirac. Dist. III. cap. 27.—P. Cantor. Verb. abbrev. cap. 138.—Löwenfeld Epistt. Pont. Rom. ined. No. 92, 114 (Lipsiæ, 1885).—See the Author's "Historical Sketch of Sacerdotal Celibacy," 2d edition, 1884.

[23] Stephani Tornacens. Epist. XII.—Innocent. PP. III. Regest. VI. 183; VIII. 192-193; X.209-210, 215; XV. 202. For the subsequent career of Waldemar of Sleswick, see Regest. XI.10, 173; XII. 63; XIII. 158; XV. 3; Supplement. 187, 224, 228, 243. Cf. Arnold. Lubecens. VI.18; VII. 12, 13; and Vaissette, Hist. Gén. de Languedoc, IV. 80 (ed. 1742). For details of clerical immunity, see the author's "Studies in Church History," 2d edition, 1883.

[24] Concil. ap. Campinacum ann. 1238, c. 1, 6.

[25] Varior. ad Alex. PP. III. Epist. XCV. (Migne, Patrolog. CC. 1457). Cf. Pet. Blesens. Epist. XC.—Innocent. PP. III. Regest. I. 386, 476, 483, 499; V. 159; VIII. 12; IX. 209; XIII. 132;XV. 105.—Pet. Cantor. Verb. abbrev. cap. 44.—Gerhohi Lib. de Ædificio Dei cap. 33; Ejusd. Exposit. in Psalm. lxiv. cap. 35.—Chron. S. Trudon. Libb. III., IV., V.—Hist. Vezeliacens. Libb. II.-IV.—Chron. Senoniens. Libb. IV., V.—Cæsar. Heisterbac. Dial. Mirac. Dist. IV. cap. 65-67. For ample details as to the immorality of the monasteries, see the author's "History of Celibacy."

[26] Cæsar. Heisterbac. Dial. Mirac. Dist. I. cap. 3, 24, 31.—Hist Monast. Andaginens. cap. 34.

[27] Gregor. PP. I. Dialog. IV. 55.—D'Achery Spicileg. III. 382.—Chron. S. Trudon. Lib.VI.

[28] Augustin. de Op. Monachor. ii. 3.—Cassiani. de Cœnob. Instit. ii. 3.—Hieron. Epistt. XXXIX.; CXXV. 16.—Regul. S. Benedicti. cap. 1.—S. Isidor. Hispal. de Eccles. Offic. II. xvi. 3, 7.—Ludov. Pii de Reform. Eccles. cap. 100.—Smaragd. Comment. in Regul. Benedict. c. 1.—Ripoll Bull. Ord. FF. Prædic. I. 38.—Cæsar. Heisterbac. Dial. Mirac. Dist.VI. cap. 20.—Catalog. Varior. Hæreticor. (Bib. Max. Patrum. Ed. 1618, t. XIII. p. 309).

[29] Brevis Hist. Prior. Grandimont.—Stephani Tornacens. Epistt. 115, 152, 153, 156, 162.

Prior Peter's fear that the convent would be converted into a market-place and a fair is illustrated by the complaint of the Council of Béziers in 1233, that many religious houses were in the habit of retailing their wine within the sacred enclosure, and attracting consumers by having jugglers, actors, gamblers, and strumpets there.—Concil. Biterrens. ann. 1233, c. 23.

[30] Giberti Gemblac. Epistt. v. vi.

[31] Petri Exoniens. Summ. Exigendi Confess. ann. 1287 (Harduin. VII. 1128).—Cæsar. Heisterbac. Dial. Mirac. Dist. III. cap. 45.—Martene Ampliss. Coll. I. 357.

196

[32] P. Damiani Opusc. V.—Concil. Trident. Sess. vi. Decret. de Justific. c. 16, 30.—Migne, Encyclopédic Theologique. t. XXVII. pp. 59-63, 118.—Abælardi Ethica, cap. 25.—Cap. 14 Extra Lib. v. tit. iii.—Concil. Lateran. IV. c. 72.—Alani de Insulis contra Hæret. Lib. II. cap. xi.—Gregor. PP. IX. Bull. 29 Apr. 1228; 18 Jul. 1237 (Potthast Regesta, I. 705, 884).—Addis and Arnold's Catholic Dict. s. v. *Portiuncula.*—Lib. Conformitatum S. Fran. Lib. II. tract. ii. (fol. 135-138. Ed. 1513).—Bonifacii PP. VIII. Bull. *Antiquorum habet.*—Concil. Claromont. ann. 1195, c. 2.—Urbani PP. II. Synodalis Concio.—Concil. Lateran. IV. can. ult.—Le Grand d'Aussy, Fabliaux, I. 379, 392.—Prediche del B. Frà Giordano da Rivalto (Firenze, 1831, I. 253).—Nicolai PP. IV. Bull. *Illuminit,* ann. 1291.—Gregor. PP. XI. Bull. *Dudum,* 23 Apr. 1372.

The mediæval doctrine of indulgence is truly expressed by Alonso, Bishop of Avila, in 1443, when disculpating himself to Eugenius IV. from an accusation of doubting the papal power: "Papa etiam potest absolvere ab omnibus peccatis et potest dare plenariam indulgentiam, liberando homine a tota pœna Purgatorii, scilicet faciendo quod non veniet in illum etiamsi multa pœna (peccata) commiserit" (D'Argentré, Collect. Judic. de novis Error. I. ii. 241). Yet when an enthusiastic Franciscan taught at Tournay, in 1482, that the pope at will could empty purgatory, the University of Paris qualified the proposition as doubtful and scandalous (Ibid. I. ii. 305). The same year the University again interfered, when the church of Saintes, having procured a bull of indulgence from Sixtus IV., announced publicly that, no matter how long a period of punishment had been assigned by divine justice to a soul, it would fly from purgatory to heaven as soon as three sols were paid in its behalf to be expended in repairing the church (Ibid. 307). In 1518 the university was obliged to repeat its condemnation of the same promises made to those who would contribute a *teston* for the crusade which was always under way and never attempted (Ib. 355). Yet the doctrine thus condemned by the university was pronounced to be unquestionable Catholic truth by the Dominican Silvestro Mozzolino, in his refutation of Luther's Theses, dedicated to Leo X. (F. Silvest. Prieriatis Dialogus, No. 27). As Silvestro was made general of his order and master of the sacred palace, it is evident that no exceptions to his teaching were taken at Rome. Those who doubt that the abuses of the system were the proximate cause of the Reformation can consult Van Espen, Jur. Eccles. Universi P. II. tit. vii. cap. 3 No. 9-12. Cf. Ibid. P. II. tit. xxxvii. cap. 6 No. 43-46, for their continuance into the eighteenth century.

The modern commercial spirit has not failed to take advantage of the indulgence. The Libreria Religiosa of Barcelona is enabled to advertise that various Spanish prelates have granted an indulgence of 2320 days (fifty-eight quarantaines) to every one who will read or hear read a chapter or even a single page of any of its publications.

[33] Concil. Turon. ann. 1236, c. 1.—Établissements de S. Louis, Liv. i. cap. 84.—Berger, Les Registres d'Innocent IV. No. 2230.

[34] Matt. Paris. Hist. Angl. ann. 1251 (p. 553, Ed. 1644).—Chron. Turon. ann. 1226.—Joannis PP. XXII. Regest. IV. 73, 74, 76, 77, 95, 97, 99.—Baluz. et Mansi Miscell. III. 242.—Concil. Ravennat. ann. 1314, c. 20.

[35] Concil. Avenion. ann. 1326, c. 3.—Concil. Marciacens. ann. 1326, c. 45.—Concil. Vaurens. ann. 1368, c. 127.—Concil. Narbonn. ann. 1374, c. 27.

The magic character attributed to these formulas of devotion is well illustrated by the story of Thierry d'Avesnes, who, during a raid into the territories of Baldwin of Mons, burned the convents of St. Waltruda of Mons, and St. Aldegonda of Maubeuge. Thereupon a holy hermit had a vision in which he saw the two angry saints demanding from the Virgin satisfaction for their injuries. This the Virgin refused, because Ada, the wife of Thierry, rendered to her the most grateful service by repeating the Ave Maria sixty times a day—twenty standing, twenty on her knees, and twenty prostrate. The saints still insisted on their wrongs, and the Virgin at length promised them revenge, when it could be inflicted without injury to Ada. Some years afterwards Thierry incautiously procured a divorce from her on the plea of consanguinity, because she remained barren after twenty years of marriage, and in a short time, while hunting, he was ambushed and slain by an enemy. His nephew and successor, Joscelin, took warning by this, and was very particular in constantly repeating the Ave Maria, and forcing his troopers to do likewise, so that, although he wrought much evil, yet he made a good ending.—Narrat. Restaur. S. Martini Tornacens. cap. 57.

Somewhat similar is the story of the knight, who, though cruel and revengeful, had such veneration for the cross that he never passed one without descending from his horse and adoring it. Once, when riding alone through a dense forest, he was assailed by the kinsmen of a noble whom he had slain, and was forced to seek safety in flight. Coming to a cross-road, where stood a cross, he dismounted and knelt before it, when his enemies, coming up, were struck with sudden blindness, and groped vainly around, while he rode quietly away.—Lucæ Tudensis de Altera Vita Lib. III. cap. 6.

[36] Concil. Lateran. IV. c. 62.—P. de Pilichdorf contr. Waldenses cap. xxx.—Concil. Biterrens. ann. 1246, c. 5.—Concil. Cenomanens. ann. 1248.—Concil. Burdegalens. ann. 1255, c. 2.—Concil. Vienn. ann. 1311 (Clementin. Lib. v. tit. ix. c. 2).—Concil. Remens. ann. 1303.—Concil. Carnotens. ann. 1325, c. 18.—Martene Thesaur. IV. 858.—Martene Ampliss. Collect. VII. 197, etc.—Concil. Moguntin. ann. 1261, c. 48.—La Secchia Rapita, xii. 1. For the repression of these abuses after the Reformation see cap. 1, 2 in Septimo iii. 15.

[37] Gesta. Consulum. Andegavens. iii. 23.—Roger. Hoveden. ann. 1177.—Innocent. PP. III. Regest. IX. 243.—Cæsar. Heisterbac. Dial. Mirac. Dist. VIII. cap. 53.—Muratori. Antiq. Med. Ævi Dissert. lviii.—Anon. Passaviens. adv. Waldens. cap. 5 (Mag. Bib. Pat. XIII. 301).

197

[38] Hartzheim. Concil. German. III. 543.—Campana, Storia di San Piero Martire Lib. II. cap. 3.—Cæsar. Heisterbac. Dial. Mirac. Dist. IX. cap. 6, 8, 24, 25.

[39] Cæsar. Heisterbac. Dial. Mirac. Dist. X. cap. 56.—Wibaldi Abbat. Corbeiens. Epist. 157.—P. Cantor. Verb. abbrev. cap. 29.

[40] Cæsar. Heisterbac. Dial. Mirac. Dist. III. cap. 2, 3, 6; Dist. v. cap. 3.

[41] S. Bernardi Serm. de Conversione cap. 19, 20.—Ejusd. Serm. 77 in Cantica cap. 1.—Cf. Ejusd. Serm. 33 in Cantica cap. 16; Tract. de Moribus et Offic. Episc. cap. vii. No. 25, 27, 28.—De Consideratione Lib. III. cap. 4, 5.—Pothon. Prumiens. de Statu Domus Dei Lib.I.

[42] Cod. Diplom. Viennens. No. 163.—P. Cantor. Verb. abbrev. cap. 57, 59—Guiberti Abbat. Gemblacens. Epist. 1.—S. Hildegardæ Revelat. Vis. X. cap. 16.

[43] Honor. PP. III. Epist. ad Archiep. Bituricens. (Martene Collect. Amplis. I. 1149-1151; Thesaur. Anecdot. I. 875-877).—Fascic. Rer. Expetendarum et Fugiendarum, II. 251 (Ed. 1690).—W. Preger, Beiträge zur Geschichte der Waldesier, München, 1875, pp. 64-67.

[44] Guill. Pod. Laurent. Chron. Prœm.—Narrat. Restaur. Abbat S. Martini Tornacens. cap. 38.— Panniers Walthers von der Vogelweide sämmtliche Gedichte, No. 110, p. 118. Cf. No. 85, 111-113.

[45] From "La Gesta de Fra Peyre Cardinal," Raynouard, Lexique Roman, I. 464. See also pp. 446, 451. Cardinal was of noble birth and high consideration at the courts of Aragon and Toulouse; he was born in 1206, and is said to have lived until 1306. He was no heretic, although "los fals clerques reprendia molt."—(Miquel de la Tor, Vie de Peire Cardinal, ap. Meyer, Anciens Textes p. 100.)—See also his Sirvente, "Un sirventes vuelh for dels autz glotos" (Raynouard, Lexique Roman, I. 447).

[46] Pelayo, Heterodoxos Españoles I. 405 (Madrid, 1880).—Petri Venerab. Opp. pp. 650 sqq. (Ed. Migne).—F. Francisci Pipini Chron. cap. 16.—Rigord. de Gest. Phil. Aug. ann. 1210.—Concil. Paris. ann. 1210.—Gregor. PP. IX. Bull. *Cum salutem*, 29 Apr. 1231.—S. Bernardi de Consideratione Lib. i. cap. 4.

For the adoration paid to Aristotle by the schoolmen of the twelfth century see John of Salisbury's Metalogicus Lib. ii. c. 16.

[47] Reinerii contra Waldenses cap. 3.—Tractatus de Modo procedendi contra Hæreticos (MSS. Bib. Nat. Coll. Doat XXX. 185 sqq.).—Lucæ Tudensis de Altera Vita Lib. III. cap. 7-10.—P. de Pilichdorf contra Waldenses cap. 16.—Passaviens. Anon. (Preger, Beiträge, pp. 64-67).—Raynouard, Lexique Roman, V. 471.

[48] Concil. Roman. ann. 1059, can. 3.—Lambert. Hersfeld. ann. 1074.—Gregor. PP. VII. Epist. Extrav. 4; Regist. Lib. IV. Ep. 20.—Concil. Remens. ann. 1131, c. 5.—Concil. Lateran. II. ann. 1139, c. 7.—c. 5, 6, Decret. I. xxxii.; c. 15; I. lxxxi.—Gerhohi Dial. de Different. Cleri. Cf. Ejusd. Lib. contr. duas Hæreses c. 3, 6; Dialogus de Clericis Sæcul. et Regular.—Anon. Libell. adv. Errores Alberonis (Martene Ampliss. Collect. IX. 1251-1270).—Can. 10 Extra Lib. III. tit. ii.—D'Argentré, Collect. Judic. de novis Erroribus, I. ii. 154.— Fortalicium Fidei, fol. 62 *b* (Ed. 1494). The importance of the question in the twelfth century is shown by the number of canons devoted to it by Gratian.

[49] Hartzheim Concil. German. III. 763-766.—Meyeri Annal. Flandriæ Lib. IV. ann. 1113-1115.— Sigeberti Gemblacens. Contin. Valcellens. ann. 1115.—P. Abælardi Introd. ad Theolog. Lib. II. cap. 4.— Trithem. Chron. Hirsaug. ann. 1127.—Vit. S. Norbert. Archiep. Magdeburg, cap. iii. No. 79, 80.

[50] Sigebert. Gemblac. Continuat. Gemblac. ann. 1146.—Ejusd. Continuat. Præmonstrat. ann. 1148.— Roberti de Monte Chron. ann. 1148.—Guillel. de Newburg. Lib. I. cap. 19.—Otton. Frising. de Gest. Frid. I. Lib. I. cap. 54, 55.—Hugon. Rothomag. contr. Hæret. Lib. III. cap. 6.—Schmidt, Histoire des Cathares, I. 49.

[51] Saige, Les Juifs du Languedoc. P. I. ch. ii.; P. II. ch. ii. (Paris, 1881). The same causes were at work in Spain, where the faithful complained that they were not allowed to persecute the Jew (Lucæ Tudens. de altera Vita Lib. III. cap. 3), and missionary work among the slaves of Jews was rendered costly by forcing the bishop of the diocese to pay to the master an extortionate price for every slave converted to Christianity and thus set free, for Jews could not hold Christian slaves. They were also relieved from the oppressive tax of the tithe (Innocent. III. Regest. VIII. 50; IX. 150). Even until late in the thirteenth century we find Jews freely holding real estate in Languedoc. See MSS. Bib. Nat. Coll. Doat. T. XXXVII. fol. 20, 146, 148, 149, 151, 152.

For the independence of the communes, see Fauriel's edition of William of Tudela, Introd. pp. lv. sq., and Mazure et Hatoulet, Fors de Béarn, p. xliii.

[52] Jonæ. Aureliens. de Cultu Imaginum.—Petri Venerab. Tract. contra Petrobrusianos.—P. Abælardi Introd. ad Theolog. Lib. II. cap. 4.—Alphonsi a Castro adv. Hæreses Lib. III. p. 163 (Ed. 1571).—Fisquet, La France Pontificale, Embrun, p. 848.

[53] S. Bernardi Epistt. 241, 242.—Gesta Pontif. Cenomanens. (D. Bouquet T. XII. pp. 547-551, 554).— Hildebert. Cenoman. Epistt. 23, 24.—S. Bernardi Vit. Prim. Lib. III. cap. 6; Lib. VII. p. iii. ad calcem; Lib. VII. cap. 17.—Guill. de Podio-Laurent. cap. 1.—Alberic. Trium Font. Chron. ann. 1148.

[54] Matt. Paris. Hist. Angl. ann. 1151.—S. Bernardi Epist. 472.—Hereberti Monachi Epist. (D. Bouquet. XII. 550-551).

[55] S. Bernardi Epistt. 189, 195, 196, 243, 244.—Gualt. Mapes de Nugis Curialium Dist. I. cap. xxiv.— Otton. Frisingens. de Gestis Frid. I. Lib. I. cap. 27; Lib. II. cap. 20.—Harduin. Concil. VI. ii. 1224.—Martene Ampliss. Collect. II. 554-558.—Guntheri Ligurin. Lib. III. 262-348.—Gerhohi Reichersperg. de Investigat. Antichristi I.—Baronii Annal. ann. 1148, No. 38.—Jaffé Regesta, No. 6445.—Vit. Adriani PP. III. (Muratori III.

441, 442).—Sächsische Weltchronik, No. 301.—Cantù, Eretici d'Italia, I. 61-63.—Tocco, L'Eresia nel Medio Evo, pp. 242, 243.—Comba, La Riforma in Italia, I. 193, 194.—Bonghi, Arnaldo da Brescia, Città di Castello, 1885.

[56] Lucii PP. III. Epist. 171.—Bonacursi Vit. Hæreticor. (D'Achery T.I. 214, 215).—Constit. General. Frid. II. ann. 1220 § 5.—Ejusd. Constit. Ravennat. ann. 1232.—Conrad. Urspergens. ann. 1210.—Pauli Æmilii de Rebus. Gest. Fran. Lib. VI. p. 316 (Ed. 1569).—Nicolai PP. III. Bull. *Noverit Universitas*, 5 Mart. 1280.—Julii PP. II. Bull *Consueverunt*, 1 Mart. 1511.—Innocent. PP. III. Regest. II. 228.—Joann. Andreæ Gloss. super cap. Excommunicamus (Eymerici Direct. Inquisit. p. 182). The name of the Poor Men of Lyons was likewise forgotten, for Andreas's only remark with respect to them is that poverty is not a crime in itself.

The differences between the Italian and French Waldenses are set forth in a very interesting letter from the former to the German brethren, subsequently to a conference held at Bergamo in 1218. This was discovered about twelve years ago by Wilhelm Preger in a MS. of the Royal Library of Munich, and is printed in his Beiträge zur Geschichte der Waldesier im Mittelalter, 1875.

[57] Chron. Canon. Laudunens. ann. 1173 (Bouquet XIII. 680).—Steph. de Borbone s. Bellavilla Lib. de Sept. Donis Spiritus, P. IV. Tit. vii. cap. 3 (D'Argentré Coll. Judicior. de Nov. Error. I. i. 85 sqq.)—Richard. Cluniacens. Vit. Alex. PP. III. (Muratori III. 447).—David Augustens. Tract. de Paup. de Lugd. (Martene Thesaur. V. 1778).—Monetæ adv. Cath. et Waldens. Lib. v. cap. 1 § 4.—Pet. Sarnens. cap. 2.—Passaviens. Anon. ap. Gretser (Mag. Bib. Pat. Ed. 1618, T. XIII. p. 300).—Petri de Pilichdorf contr. Hæres. Waldens. cap. 1.—Pegnæ Comment. 39 in Eymerici Direct. Inquis. p. 280.

The pretension of the Waldenses to descend from the primitive Church through the Leonistæ and Claudius of Turin is, I believe, now generally abandoned. See Edouard Montet, Histoire Litt. des Vaudois, Paris, 1885, pp. 32, 33; Prof. Emilio Comba, in the Rivista Christiana, Giugno, 1882, pp. 200-206, and his Riforma in Italia, I. 233 sqq.—Bernard Gui, in his Practica, P. v. (MSS. Bib. Nat. Coll. Doat. T. XXX. fol. 185 sqq.), following Richard of Cluny and Stephen of Bourbon, places the rise of Peter Waldo about 1170, and the Canon of Laon gives the date of 1173.

The time and place of Peter Waldo's death are unknown. His French disciples affectionately revered his memory and that of his assistant Vivet, to the extent of asserting, as a point of belief, that they were in Paradise with God; the Lombard branch, however, would only prudently admit that they might be saved if they had satisfied God before death; both sides were obstinate, and at the Conference of Bergamo, in 1218, this promised to make a schism (Rescript. Paup. Lombard. 15.—W. Preger, Beiträge zur Geschichte der Waldesier, pp. 58, 59).

Waldensian literature long retained the impress given to it by Waldo of stringing together extracts from the Fathers of the Church. The slavishness with which these were followed is curiously exemplified in an exposition of Canticles analyzed by M. Montet (op. cit. p. 66). The verse "Take us the little foxes, the little foxes that spoil the vines" (Cant. ii. 15) in mediæval exegesis was traditionally explained by the ravages of heretics in the Church. In the papal bulls urging the Inquisition to redoubled activity the heretics are habitually alluded to as the foxes which ravage the vineyard of the Lord. If any originality could be looked for in Waldensian exposition, we might expect it in this passage, and yet Angelomus, Bruno, and Bernard are duly quoted by the Waldensian teacher to show that the foxes are heretics and the vines are the Church.

[58] Chron. Canon. Laudunens. ann. 1177, 1178 (Bouquet XIII. 682).—Stephani de Borbone 1. c.—Richard. Cluniac. 1. c.—David Augustens. 1. c.—Monetæ 1. c.—Gault. Mapes de Nugis Curialium Dist. 1. cap. xxxi.—Lucii PP. III. Epist. 171.—Conrad. Ursperg. ann. 1210—Bernardi Fontis Calidi adv. Waldenses Liber.

[59] Alani de Insulis contra Hæreticos Lib. II.—Disputat. inter Cathol. et Paterin. (Martene Thesaur. V. 1754).—Rescript. Pauperum Lombard. 21, 22 (W. Preger, Beiträge, pp. 60, 61).—Eymerici Direct. Inquis. p. ii. q. 14. (pp. 278, 279).—Petri Sarnaii Hist. Albigens. cap. 2.—In 1321, a man and wife brought before the Inquisition of Toulouse both refused to swear, and they alleged as a reason, in addition to the sinful nature of the oath, the man that it would subject him to falling sickness, the woman that she would have an abortion (Lib. Sententt. Inq. Tolosan. Ed. Limborch, p. 289).

In the persecution of the Waldenses of Piedmont towards the close of the fourteenth century, one of the crucial questions of the inquisitors was as to belief in the validity of the sacraments of sinful priests.—Processus contra Valdenses (Archivio Storico Italiano, 1865, No. 39, p. 48).

[60] Rivista Cristiana, Marzo, 1887, p. 92.—Pegnæ Comment. 39 in Eymerici Director. p. 281.—Steph. de Borbone 1. c.—Concil. Gerundens. ann. 1197 (Aguirre, V. 102, 103).—Marca Hispanica, p. 1384.

[61] See the Sentences of Pierre Cella in Doat, XXII—Montet, Hist. Litt. des Vaudois, pp. 116 sq.

[62] Tract. de Paup. de Lugd. (Martene Thesaur. V. 1792).—Wadding. Annal. Minor. Ann. 1332, No. 6.—Bern. Guidon. Practica P. v. (Doat, XXX.).—Montet Hist. Litt. pp. 38, 44, 45, 89, 142.—Haupt, Zeitschrift für Kirchengeschichte, 1885 p. 551.—Pet. Cœlest. (Preger, Beiträge, pp. 68, 69).—Kaltner, Konrad von Marburg, pp. 69-71.—Rescript. Paup. Lombard. §§ 4, 5, 17, 19, 22, 23.—Nobla Leyczon, 409-413; cf. Montet. pp. 49, 50, 103, 104, 143.—Passaviens. Anon. cap. 5 (Mag. Bib. Pat. XIII. 300).—Disput. inter Cath. et Paterin. (Martene Thesaur. V. 1754).—David Augustens. (ibid. p. 1778).—Lucæ Tudens. de altera Vita Lib. I. cap. 4-7.—Tract. de modo procedendi contra Hæret. (Doat XXX.).—Index Error. Waldens. (Mag. Bib. Pat. XIII. 340).—P. de Pilichdorf contra Waldens. cap. 34.—Lib. Sententt. Inq. Tolosan. pp. 200, 201.—Nobla Leyczon, 17-24, 387-405, 416-423.

Yet it was impossible to resist the contagion of superstition. The Pomeranian Waldenses, in 1394, are described as believing that if a man died within a year after confession and absolution, he went directly to heaven. Even speaking with a minister preserved one from damnation for a year. There is even a case of a legacy of eight marks for prayers for the soul of the deceased.—Wattenbach, Sitzungsberichte der Preuss. Akad. 1886, pp. 51, 52.

[63] Passaviens. Anon. cap. 5.—Bernard. Guidon. Practica P. v.—David Augustens. (Martene Thesaur. V. 1786).—Steph. de Borbone, l. c.—Wattenbach, ubi sup.—Lib. Sententt. Inq. Tolosan. p. 352.

[64] Wattenbach, Sitzungsberichte der Preuss. Akad. 1886, p. 51.—Lib. Sentt. Inq. Tolosan. p. 367.— Anon. Passaviens. cap. 7, 8.—Refutat. Error. Waldens. (Mag. Bib. Pat. XIII. 336).—David Augustens. (Martene Thesaur. V. 1771-1772).—Archivio Storico Italiano, 1865, No. 38, pp. 39, 40.—Rorengo, Memorie Istoriche, Torino 1649, p. 12.—Even as late as the end of the fourteenth century, in the extensive inquisitions of the Celestinian Peter, from Styria to Pomerania, there is no allusion to immoral practices. (Preger, Beiträge, pp. 68-72; Wattenbach, ubi sup.).

For the ascetic tendency of the Waldenses, recognizing vows of chastity, and the seduction of nuns as incest, see Montet, pp. 97, 98, 108-110. For the merit of fasting, see p. 99.

[65] Lib. Sententt. Inquis. Tolosan. p. 367.—Anon. Passaviens. cap. 1, 3, 7, 8.—Refutat. Error. Waldens. (Mag. Bib. Pat. XIII. 336).—David Augustens. (Martene Thesaur. V. 1771, 1772, 1782, 1794).—P. de Pilichdorf contra Error. Waldens. cap. 1.—Innocent PP. III. Regest. II. 141.—La Nobla Leyczon, 368-373.—Frat. Jordani Chron. (Analecta Franciscana, T. I. p. 4. Quaracchi, 1885).

[66] MSS. Bib. Nat. Coll. Moreau, 1274, fol. 72.

[67] Bonacursi Vit. Hæreticorum (D'Achery I. 211, 212).—Lucii PP. III. Epist. 171.—Muratori Antiquitat. Dissert. IX.—Constit. General. Frid. II. ann. 1220, § 5.—Lucæ Tudens. de altera Vita Lib. III. cap. 3.—Anon. Passaviens. contra Waldens. cap. 6.—P. de Pilichdorf contra Waldens. cap. 12.—Hoffman, Geschichte der Inquisition, II. 371.—Schmidt, Hist. des Cathares, II. 284.

[68] Mosaic. et Roman. Legg. Collat. tit. XV. § 3 (Hugo, 1465).—Const. 11, 12, Cod. I. v.—P. Siculi Hist. de Manichæis.—Zonara Annal. tom. III. pp. 126, 241, 242 (Ed. 1557).—Findlay's Hist. of Greece, 2d Ed. III. 65.

The Bogomili (Friends of God), another Manichæan sect, whose name betrays their Slav or Bulgarian origin, have been cited as a link connecting the Paulicians and the Cathari, but incorrectly, although they may have had some influence in producing the moderated Dualism of a portion of the latter. Their leader, Demetrius, was burned alive by Alexis Comnenus in 1118 after a series of investigations more creditable to the zeal of the emperor than to his good faith. They continued to enjoy a limited toleration until the thirteenth century, when they disappeared.—See Annæ Comnenæ Alexiados Lib. XV.—Georgii Cedreni Hist. Comp. sub ann. 20 Constant.—Zonaræ Annal. t. III. p. 238.—Balsamon. Schol. in Nomocanon tit. X. cap. 8.—Schmidt, Hist. des Cathares, I. 13-15; II. 265.

About the middle of the eleventh century Psellus describes another Manichæan sect named Euchitæ, who believed in a father ruling the supramundane regions and committing to the younger of his two sons the heavens and to the elder the earth. The latter was worshipped under the name of Satanaki—(Pselli de Operat. Dæmon. Dial.).

[69] P. Siculi op. cit.—Bleek's Avesta, III. 4.—Haug's Essays, 2d ed. pp. 244, 249, 286, 367.— Yajnavalkya, I. 37.

For the corresponding tenets of the Cathari, see Radulf. Ardent. T. I. p. II. Hom. xix.—Ermengaudi contra Hæret. Opusc.—Epist. Leodiens. ad Lucium PP. III. (Martene. Ampl. Collect. I. 776-778).—Ecberti Schonaug. Serm. contra Catharos, Serm. I. viii. xi.—Gregor. Episc. Fanens. Disput. Catholici contra Hæret.— Monetæ adv. Catharos Lib. I. cap. 1.—Arch. de l'Inq. de Carcassonne (Coll. Doat, XXXII. f. 93).—Rainerii Saccon. Summa.—Cæsar. Heisterbac. Dial. Mirac. Dist. v. cap. 21.—Lib. Sentt. Inquis. Tolosan. pp. 92, 93, 249 (Limborch).—Lib. Confess. Inq. Albiens. (MSS. Bib. Nat. fonds latin 11847).—Trithem. Chron. Hirsaug. ann. 1163.

In a MS. controversial tract against the Cathari, dating from the end of the thirteenth century, the writer, following Moneta, states that their objections to the Old Testament sprang from four roots: first, the contradiction which seemed to exist between the Old and New Testaments; second, the changefulness of God himself, manifest in Scripture; third, the cruel attributes of God in Scripture; fourth, the falsehood ascribed to God. A single example will suffice of the arguments which the heretics advanced in support of their position. "They quote Genesis iii. 'Behold, Adam has become as one of us.' Now God says this of Adam after he had sinned, and he must have spoken truth or falsehood. If truth, then Adam had become like him who spoke and those to whom he spoke; but Adam after the fall had become a sinner, and therefore evil. If falsehood, then he is a liar; he sinned in so saying and thus was evil." To this logic the orthodox polemic contents himself with the answer that God spoke ironically. Throughout the tract the reasoning ascribed to the Cathari shows them to possess a thorough acquaintance with Scripture, and the use which they made of it explains the prohibition of the Bible to the laity by the Church.— Archives de l'Inq. de Carcassonne, Coll. Doat, XXXVI. 91. (See Appendix.)

Yet the Catharan ritual published by Cunitz quotes Isaiah and Solomon. (Beiträge zu den theolog. Wissenschaften, B. IV. 1852, pp. 16, 26.)

[70] Tract. de Modo Procedendi contra Hæreticos (MSS. Bib. Nat. Coll. Doat, XXX. fol. 185 sqq.).—Rainerii Saccon. Summa.—E. Cunitz in Beiträge zu den theol. Wissenschaften, 1852, B. IV. pp. 30, 36, 85.

[71] Rainerii Saccon. Summa.—Lib. Confess. Inquis. Albiens. (MSS. Bib. Nat. fonds latin, 11847).—Coll. Doat, XXII. 208, 209; XXIV. 174; XXVI. 197, 259, 272.—Lib. Sentt. Inquis. Tolosan. pp. 10, 33, 37, 70, 71, 76, 84, 94, 125, 126, 137-139, 143, 160, 173, 179, 199.—Bern. Guidon. Practica P. IV. V. (MSS. Bib. Nat. Collect. Doat. T. XXX.).—Landulf. Senior Hist. Mediolan. ii. 27.—Anon. Passaviens. contra Waldens. cap. 7.—Processus contra Valdenses (Archivio Storico Italiano, 1865, No. 39, p. 57). The description in the text of the form of heretication, by Rainerio Saccone, is confirmed in its details by the depositions of witnesses before the Inquisition of Toulouse, showing that the form was essentially the same throughout the churches.—Doat, XXII. 224, 237 sqq.; XXIII. 272, 344; XXIV. 71. See also Vaissette III. Preuves, 386, and Cunitz, Beiträge zu den theolog. Wissenschaften, 1852, B. IV. pp. 12-14, 21-28, 33, 60.

The practice of the Endura among the Cathari of Languedoc has been investigated with his customary thoroughness by M. Charles Molinier (Annales de la Faculté des Lettres de Bordeaux, 1881, No. 3). It was not always limited to three days, and its rigor may be guessed by a single example. Blanche, the mother of Vital Gilbert, caused her infant grandchild to be "consoled" while sick, and then prevented the mother, Guillelma, from giving it milk till it died (Lib. Sententt. Inq. Tolos. p. 104). Molinier's theory that the custom was of comparatively late introduction is confirmed by the absence of any allusion to it in the ritual published by Cunitz (loc. cit.), but that it was not confined to Languedoc is shown by the Anon. Passaviens. and the evidence in the Piedmontese trials of 1388 (Arch. Storico, ubi sup.).

A case in which the Consolamentum was administered to an insensible patient who subsequently recovered is recorded in the sentences of Pierre Cella (Doat, XXI. 295), and also several instances in which young girls were "perfected" at a very early age, and wore the vestments for limited periods of two or three years (ibid. 241. 244).

[72] S. Bernardi Serm. lxvi. in Cantica, cap. 3-7.—Ecberti Schonaug. Serm. i. v. vi. contra Catharos.—Bonacursi Vit. Hæreticor.—Gregor. Fanens. Disput. Cathol. contra Hæreticos cap. 1, 2, 11, 14.—Monetæ adv. Catharos Lib. I. cap. 1.—Cunitz (Beiträge zu den theol. Wissenschaften, 1852, p. 14).—Radulf. Coggeshall. Chron. Anglic. (D. Bouquet, XVIII. 92, 93).—Evervini Steinfeldens. Epist. ad S. Bernard, cap. 3.—Concil. Lombariens. ann. 1165.—Radulf. Ardent. T. I. p. II. Hom. xix.—Ermengaudi contra Hæret. Opusc.—Bonacursus contra Catharos (Baluz. et Mansi, II. 581-586).—Alani de Insulis contra Hæret. Lib. I.—Monet adv. Catharos. Lib. IV. cap. vii. § 3.—Rainerii Saccon. Summa.—Lib. Sententt. Inq. Tolosan. pp. 111, 115.—Coll. Doat, T. XXX. fol. 185 sqq.; XXXII. fol. 93 sqq.—Stephan. de Borbone (D'Argentré, Coll. Judic. de novis Error. I. i. 91).—Archiv. Fiorent. Prov. S. Maria Novella, Giugno 26, 1229.

In the early days of the Inquisition a certain Jean Teisseire, summoned before the tribunal of Toulouse, defended himself by exclaiming, "I am not a heretic, for I have a wife and I lie with her, and have children, and I eat flesh, and lie, and swear, and am a faithful Christian."—(Guillel. Pelisso Chron. Ed. Molinier, Anicii 1880, p. 17). See also the Sentences of Pierre Cella, Coll. Doat, XXI. 223.

[73] Rainerii Saccon. Summa.—Tocco, L'Eresia nel Medio Evo, p. 75.—Gregor. Fanens. Disput. cap. iv.—Monetæ adv. Catharos Lib. I. cap. 1, 2, 4, 6.—Alani de Insulis contra Hæret. Lib. I.—Ecberti Schonaug. Serm. i., xiii. contra Catharos.—Ermengaudi contra Hæret. Opusc. cap. 14.—Millot, Hist. Litt. des Troubadours, II. 64.—Lib. Sententt. Inq. Tolosan. p. 84.—Gest. Episcop. Leodiens. Lib. II. cap. 60, 61.—Stephan, de Borbone (D'Argentré, Collect. Judic. de nov. Error. I. i. 90).—Muratori Antiq. Ital. Diss. lx.

Among the early Christians there was a strong tendency to adopt the theory of transmigration as an explanation of the apparent injustice of the judgments of God. See Hieron. Epist CXXX. ad Demetriadem, 16.

[74] Lucæ Tudens. de altera Vita Lib. III. cap. ii.

Before ridiculing the Catharan theory of Dualism, we must bear in mind how strong is the tendency in this direction of sensitive and ardent souls, who keenly feel the imperfections of man's nature and its contrast with the possibilities of an ideal. Thus Flacius Illyricus, the fervid reformer, about 1560, came perilously near to the Catharan myths, and gave rise to a warm controversy by maintaining that original sin was not an accident, but the substance in man; that the original image of God was, through the Fall, not replaced, but metamorphosed into an image of Satan, a transformation of absolute good into absolute evil; a theory which, as he was warned by his friends Musæus and Judex, must necessarily lead to Manichæism.—See Herzog, Abriss der gesammten Kirchengeschichte, III. 313.

Orthodox asceticism also trenches closely on Manichæism in its denunciation of the flesh, which it treats as the antagonist and enemy of the soul. Thus, St. Francis of Assisi says, "Many, when they sin or are injured, blame their enemy or neighbor. This should not be so, for every one has his enemy in his power, namely, the body through which he sins. Thus blessed is that servant who always holds captive and guards himself against that enemy delivered to him, for when he does thus no other visible enemy can hurt him" (S. Francisci Admonit. ad Fratres No. 9). And in another passage (Apoph. xxvii.) he describes his body as the most cruel enemy and worst adversary, whom he would willingly abandon to the demon.

According to the Dominican Tauler, the leader of the German mystics in the fourteenth century, man in himself is but a mass of impurity, a being sprung from evil and corrupt matter, only fit to inspire horror; and this opinion was fully shared by his followers even though they were overflowing with love and charity (Jundt, les Amis de Dieu, Paris, 1879, pp. 77, 229).

Jean-Jacques Olier, the founder of the great theological seminary of St. Sulpice, in his "Catechisme Chrétien pour la vie interieure," which I believe is still in use there as a text-book, goes as far as Manes or Buddha in his detestation of the flesh as the cause of man's sinful nature—"Je ne m'étonne plus si vous dites qu'il faut haïr sa chair, que l'on doit avoir horreur de soi même, et que l'homme, dans son état actuel, doit étre maudit ... En verité, il n'y a aucune sorte de maux et de malheurs qui ne doivent tomber sur lui à cause de sa chair."—See Renan, Souvenirs de l'enfance et de jeunesse, p. 206.

With such views it is simply a question of words whether the creator of such an abomination as the crowning work of the terrestrial universe is to be called God or Satan; he certainly cannot be the Good Principle.

[75] Processus contra Valdenses (Archivio Storico Italiano, 1865, Nos. 38, 39).—S. Bernardi Serm. in Cantica lxv. cap. 5; lxvi. cap. 1.—Gregor. Fanens Disputat. cap. 17.—Anon. Passaviens. contra Waldens. cap. 7.—Radulf. Coggeshall. Chron. Anglic. (D. Bouquet, XVIII. 93).—Concil. Remens. ann. 1157, c. 1.—Ecberti Schonaug. contra Catharos Serm. i. cap. 1.—Cunitz, Beiträge zu den theol. Wissenschaften, 1852, B. IV. pp. 4, 12-14.—Lucæ Tudens. de altera Vita Lib. II. cap. 9; Lib. III. cap. 5.—Lami, Antichità Toscane, p. 550.

The Cathari probably had Romance versions of the New Testament as early as 1178, when we find the cardinal legate disputing at Toulouse with two Catharan bishops whose ignorance of Latin was a subject of ridicule, while they seem to have been ready enough with Scripture.—Roger. Hoveden. Annal. ann. 1178. See also Molinier, Annales de la Faculté des lettres de Bordeaux, 1883, No. 3.

Abbot Joachim bears testimony to the external virtues of the Cathari of Calabria, and the advantage which they derived from the vices of the clergy.—Tocco, L'Eresia nel Medio Evo, p. 403.

The story of the sacrament made from the bodies of children born of promiscuous intercourse was widely circulated and variously applied. It was related in the eleventh century of the Euchitæ by Psellus (De Operat. Dæmon.) and continued to be told of successive heretics—even of the Templars.

[76] Ecberti Schonaug. contra Catharos Serm. I. cap. 2.—Cæsar. Heisterbac. Dial. Mirac. Dist. v. cap. 18.—Lucæ Tudensis de altera Vita Lib. II. cap. 9; Lib. III. cap. 9, 18.

[77] Anon. Passaviens. c. 6.—Processus contra Valdenses (Arch. Storico Ital. 1865, No. 39, p. 57).

[78] Radulpli Glabri Lib. III. c. 8.—Landulf. Senior. Mediolan. Hist. II. 27.—Cæsar. Heisterbac. Dial. Mirac. Dist. V. c. 19.—Trithem. Chron. Hirsaug. ann. 1163.—Guill. de Newburg. Hist. Anglic. Lib. II. c. 13.—Guillel. Nangiac. ann. 1210.—Chron. Turon. ann. 1210.—Radulf. Coggeshall Chron. Anglic. (D. Bouquet. XVIII. 93).—Bernard. Guidon. Practica P. IV. (Doat, XXX.).—S. Bernardi Serm. in Cantic. LXV. c. 13.—Lucæ Tudens. de altera Vita Lib. III. c. 21.—Constitt. Sicular. Lib. I. tit. i.

The story of the young girl of Cologne assumes a somewhat mythical air when we find it repeated by Moneta as occurring in Lombardy (Cantù, Eretici d'Italia, I. 88); but this only enforces the universal tribute to the marvellous constancy of the heretics.

[79] Radulf. Coggeshall l.c.—Pauli Carnotens. Vet. Aganon. Lib. VI. c. iii.—Campana, Storia di San Piero Martire, Lib. II. c. 2, p. 57.—Fragment, adv. Hæret. (Mag. Bib. Pat. XIII. 341).—Cf. Trithem. Chron. Hirsaug. ann. 1315.

[80] Schmidt, Hist. des Cathares, I. 15-21.—Muratori Anecdota Ambrosiana, II. 112.—Guillel. Tyrii Lib. II. c. 13.—Innocent. PP. III. Regest. II. 176; III. 3; v. 103, 110; VI. 140, 141, 212.—See also the curious letter of a Patarin in Matt. Paris, Hist. Angl. ann. 1243 (Ed. 1644 p. 413).

[81] Gerberti Epist. 187.—Radulphi Glabri Lib. ii. c. 11, 12.—Epist. Leodiens. ad Lucium PP. II. (Martene Ampliss. Collect. I. 776-8).

[82] Ademari S. Cibardi Hist. Lib. III. c. 49, 59.—Pauli Carnot. Vet. Aganon. Lib. VI. c. 3.—Frag. Hist. Aquitan. et Frag. Hist. Franc. (Pithœi Hist. Franc. Scriptt. xi. pp. 82, 84).—Radulf. Glabri Hist. III. 8, IV. 2.—Gesta Synod. Aurel. circa 1017 (D'Achery I. 604-6).—Chron. S. Petri Vivi.—Synod. Atrebat. ann. 1025 (Labbe et Coleti XI. 1177, 1178; Hartzheim. Concil. German. III. 68).—Landulf. Sen. Mediol. Hist. II. 27.—Gesta Episcop. Leodiens. cap. 60, 61.—Hermann. Contract. ann. 1052.—Lambert. Hersfeldens. Annal. ann. 1053.—Schmidt, Hist. des Cathares, I. 37.—Radulf. Ardent. T.I.P. ii. Hom. 19.

Bishop Wazo's complaint that pallor was considered a positive proof of heresy was by no means a new one. In the fourth century it was regarded as sufficient to betray the Gnostic and Manichæan asceticism of the Priscillianists (Sulpic. Severi Dial. III. cap. xi.), and Jerome tells us that the orthodox who were pale with fasting and maceration were stigmatized as Manichæans (Hieron. Epist. ad Eustoch. c. 5). To the end of the twelfth century pallor continued to be regarded as a diagnostic symptom of Catharism (P. Cantor. Verb. abbrev. c. 78).

[83] Guibert. Noviogent. de Vita sua Lib. III. c. 17.—Schmidt, op. cit. I. 47.—Martene Thesaur. I. 336.

[84] Epist. Leodiens. ad Lucium PP. II. (Martene Ampl. Coll. I. 776-778).—Alex. PP. III. Epist. 2 (ibid. II. 628).—Concil. Remens. ann. 1157.—Hist. Monast. Vezeliacens. Lib. IV. ann. 1167.—Cæsar. Heisterbac. Dial. Mirac. Dist. v. c. 18.—Radulf. Coggeshall ubi sup.—Innocent. PP. III. Regest. IX. 208.

[85] Alex. PP. III. Epist. 118, 122.—Varior. ad Alex. PP. III. Epist. No. 16.—Annal. Aquiciuctens. Monast. ann. 1182, 1183.—Guillel. Nangiac. ann. 1183.

[86] Histor. Trevirens. (D'Achery II. 221, 222).—Alberic. Trium Font. Chron. ann. 1200.—Evervini Steinfeld. Epist. (S. Bernardi Epist. 472).—Trithem. Chron. Hirsaug. ann. 1163.—Ecberti Schonaug. contra Catharos Serm. VIII.—Schmidt, I. 94-96.

[87] Guillel. de Newburg Hist. Anglic. Lib. II. c. 13.—Matt. Paris. Hist. Anglic. ann. 1166 (p. 74).—Radulf. de Diceto ann. 1166.—Radulf. Coggeshall (D. Bouquet, XVIII. 92).—Assize of Clarendon, Art. 21.—Petri Blesens. Epist. 113.—Schmidt, I. 99.

[88] The nomenclature of the heresy is quite extensive. The sectaries called themselves Cathari, or the pure. The origin of the term Patarin has been the subject of considerable dispute, but there would seem to be no doubt that it arose in Milan about the middle of the eleventh century, during the civil wars resulting from the papal efforts to enforce celibacy on the Milanese married clergy. In the Romance dialects *pates* signifies old linen; rag-pickers in Lombardy were called Patari, and the quarter inhabited by them in Milan was known, even up to the last century, as Pattaria, or Contrada de' Pattari. Even to-day there are in Italian cities quarters or streets of that name (Schmidt, II. 279). In the eleventh-century quarrels the papalists held secret meetings in the Pattaria, and were contemptuously designated by their antagonists as Patarins—a name which was finally recognized and accepted by them (Arnulf. Mediolanens. Lib. III. cap. 11; Lib. IV. c. 6, 11.—Landulf. Jun. c. 1.—Willelmi Clusiens. vita Benedicti Abbat. Clusiens. c. 33.—Benzon. Comm. de Reb. Henrici IV. Lib. VII. c. 2). As the papal condemnation of clerical marriage was stigmatized as Manichæan, and as the papalists were supported by the secret heretics, followers of Gherardo di Monforte, the name was not unnaturally transferred to the Cathari in Lombardy, when they became publicly known, and it spread from there throughout Europe. In Italy the word Cathari, vulgarized into Gazzari, was also commonly used, and came gradually to designate all heretics; the officials of the Inquisition were nicknamed Cazzagazzari (Cathari hunters), and even accepted the designation (Muratori Antiq. Diss, LX. Tom. XII. pp. 510, 516), and the word is still seen in the German Ketzer. The Cathari, from their Bulgarian origin, were also known as Bulgari, Bugari, Bulgri, Bugres (Matt. Paris, ann. 1238)—a word which has been retained with an infamous signification in the English, French, and Italian vernaculars. We have seen above that from the number of weavers among them they were also known in France as Texerant, or Textores (cf. Doat, XXIII. 209-10). The term Speronistæ was derived from Robert de Sperone, bishop of the French Cathari in Italy (Schmidt, II. 282). The Crusaders who met the Paulicians (Παυλικιανοι) in the East brought home the word and called them Publicani, or Popelicans. More local designations were Piphili or Pifres (Ecbert. Schonaug. Serm. I. c. 1), Telonarii or Deonarii (D'Achery, II. 560), and Boni Homines, or Bonshommes. The term Albigenses, from the district of Albi, where they were numerous, was first employed by Geoffroy of Vigeois, in 1181 (Gaufridi Vosens. Chron. ann. 1181), and became generally used during the crusades against Raymond of Toulouse.

The various sects into which the Cathari were divided were further known by special names, as Albanenses, Concorrezenses, Bajolenses, etc. (Rainerii Saccon. Summa. Cf. Muratori Dissert. LX.).

In the official language of the Inquisition of the thirteenth century, "heretic" always means Catharan, while the Vaudois are specifically designated as such. The accused was interrogated "Super facto hæresis vel Valdesiæ."

[89] Schmidt, I. 63-5.—Muratori Antiq. Dissert. LX. (p. 462-3).—Raynald. Annal. ann. 1199 No. 23-5; ann. 1205 No. 67; 1207 No. 3.—Lami, Antichità Toscane, p. 491.—Innocent. PP. III. Regest. I. 298; II. 1, 50; v. 33; VII. 37; VIII. 85, 105; IX. 7, 8, 18, 19, 166-9, 204, 213, 258; X. 54, 105, 130; XV. 189; Gesta cxxiii.

[90] Schmidt I. 38.—Chron. Histor. Episc. Albigens. (D'Achery III. 572).—Udalr. Babenb. Cod. II. 303.—Concil. Tolosan. ann. 1119 c. 3.—Concil. Lateran. II. ann. 1139 c. 23.—Concil. Remens. ann. 1148 c. 18.

[91] Concil. Turon. ann. 1163 c. 4.—Concil. Lombariense ann. 1165 (Harduin. VI. II. 1643-52).—Roger de Hoveden. ann. 1176.—D. Vaissette, Hist. Gén. de Languedoc, III. 4—Löwenfeld, Epistt. Pont. Roman. inedd. No. 247 (Lipsiæ, 1885).

[92] D. Bouquet, XIV. 448-50.—D. Vaissette, III. 4. 537.

[93] Roger. Hoveden. Annal. ann. 1178.—D. Vaissette, III. 46-7.

[94] Benedict. Petroburg. Vit. Henrici. II. ann. 1178.—Alexander. PP. III. Epist. 395 (D. Bouquet, XV. 950-960).

[95] Roger. Hovedens. Annal. ann. 1178.—Schmidt, I. 78.—Martene Thesaur. I. 992.—Rob. de Monte Chron. ann. 1178.—Benedict. Petroburg. Vit. Henrici II. ann. 1178.

Roger Trencavel of Béziers was no heretic (see Vaissette, III. 49) and his treatment of the Bishop of Albi and disregard of the missionary bishops shows the complete contempt into which the Church had fallen, even among the faithful.

[96] Concil. Lateran. III. ann. 1179 c. 27.

[97] Gaufridi Vosens. Chron. ann. 1181.—Roberti Autissiodor. Chron. ann. 1181.—Alberic. Trium Font. Chron. ann. 1181.—Guillel. Nangiac. ann. 1181.—Chron. Turonens. ann. 1181.—D. Vaissette, III. 57.—Guillel. de Pod.-Laurent. c. 2.

[98] Stephani Tornacens. Epist. 92.—Gaufridi Vosens. Chron. ann. 1183.—Gualt. Mapes de Nugis Curialium Dist. I. c. xxix.—Guillel. Nangiac. ann. 1183.—Rigord. de Gest. Phil. Aug. ann. 1183.—Guillel. Brito

de Gest. Phil. Aug. ann. 1183.—Ejusd. Philippidos Lib. I. 726-45.—Grandes Chroniques, ann. 1183.—Du Cange s. vv. *Cotarellus, Palearii*.

[99] Lucii PP. III. Epist. 171.—Concil. Monspeliens. ann. 1195.

[100] Innocent. PP. III. Serm. de Tempore XII.—Guillem. de Tudela, c. ii.—Gualt. Mapes de Nugis Curialium Dist. I. c. xxx.—Guillel. de Pod.-Laurent. Proœm.; cf. cap. 3, 4.—Cæsar. Heisterbac. Dist. v. c. 21.—Stephani Tornacens. Epist. 92.—Anon. Passaviens. (Bib. Mag. Pat. XIII. 299).—Schmidt, I. 200.

[101] Innocent. PP. III. Serm. de Diversis III.

[102] Innocent. PP. III. Serm. de Diversis VI.; Regest. VII. 165, X. 54.—Honor. PP. III. Epist. ad Archiep. Bituricens. (Martene Ampl. Collect. I. 1149-51).

In 1250 Robert Grosseteste, Bishop of Lincoln, told Innocent IV. at Lyons that the corruption of the priesthood was the cause of the heresies which afflicted the Church (Fascic. Rer. Expetend. et Fugiend. II. 251. Ed. 1690).

[103] Roberti Autissiodor. Chron. ann. 1198-1201.—Hist. Episcopp. Autissiodor. (D. Bouquet, XVIII. 725-6, 729).—Petri Sarnens. Hist. Albigens. c. 3.—Innoc. PP. III. Regest. II. 63, 99; v. 36; VI. 63, 239; IX. 110; X. 206.—Potthast, No. 9152.—Alberic. Trium Font. Chron. ann. 1200.—Chron. Canon. Laudunens. ann. 1204 (D. Bouquet, XVIII. 713).

[104] Regest. II. 141, 142, 235.—Gesta Treviror. c. 104.

[105] Villani Cronica, Lib. v. c. 90.—Diez, Leben und Werke der Troubadours, 424.—Guill. Pod. Laur. cap. 47.—Vaissette, Éd. Privat, VIII. 558.—Petri Sarnensis Hist. Albigens. c. 1.—Vaissette, Éd. 1730, III. 101.

[106] Guillel. Nangiac. ann. 1207.—Vaissette, III. 128, 132.—Guillel. Pod. Laurent. c. 6, 7.—Regest. VIII. 115-6.—For the condition of other sees—Carcassonne, Vence, Agde, Ausch, Narbonne, Bordeaux—see Regest. I. 194; III. 24; VI. 216; VII. 84; VIII. 76; XVI. 5.

For the biography of Foulques, or Folquet, of Marseilles, who, after being favored by Raymond V., became the most bitter enemy of Raymond VI., see Paul Meyer ap. Vaissette, Éd. Privat, VII. 444. Dante places him in the heaven of Venus, together with Cunizza, the lascivious sister of Ezzelin da Romano (Paradiso, IX.). It is related of him that once when preaching against the heretics he compared them to wolves and the faithful to sheep. A heretic whose eyes had been torn out and his nose and lips cut off by Simon de Montfort, arose and said, "Did you ever see sheep bite a wolf thus?" to which Foulques rejoined that de Montfort was a good dog who had thus bitten the wolf. A more pleasing trait is seen in the story that he gave alms to a poor heretic beggar-woman, saying that he gave it to poverty and not to heresy.—Chabaneau (Vaissette, Éd. Privat, X. 292).

[107] Regest. I. 92, 93, 94, 165, 395; II. 122, 123, 298; III. 24; v. 96; VII. 17, 75; VIII. 75, 106; IX. 66; X. 68; XIII. 88; XIV. 32; XVI. 5.—Vaissette, III. 117.

[108] Petri Sarnens. c. 1, 17.—Vaissette, III. 129, 134-5; Preuves, 197.—Regest. VI. 242-3.

[109] Pet. Sarnens. c. 3.—Vaissette, III. 133, 135—Guillem de Tudela iv. My references to the poem which passes under the name of Guillem de Tudela are to Fauriel's edition (1837). A metrical version by Mary-Lafon appeared in 1868, since when M. Paul Meyer has issued a critical edition with abundant apparatus.

[110] Regest. VII. 76, 77, 79, 165.

[111] Regest. VII. 210, 212; VIII. 94, 97; IX. 103.—Havet, L'Hérésie et le bras seculier (Bibliothèque de l'École des Chartes, 1880, 582).

[112] Guillel. de Pod. Laurent, c. 8.—Pet. Sarnens. c. 1.

[113] Pet. Sarnens. c. 3.

[114] Pet. Sarnens. c. 3, 5.—Rob. Autissiodor. ann. 1207.—Guillel. Nangiac. ann. 1207.—Guillel. de Pod. Laurent, c. 8.—Concil. Narbonn. ann. 1208.—Regest. IX. 185.

[115] Pet. Sarnens. c. 3, 4.

[116] Regest. X. 69.

[117] Pet. Sarnens. c. 3, 6, 7.—Regest. X. 149, 176; XI. 11.

[118] Vaissette, Éd. Privat, VIII. 557.—Hist. du Comte de Toulouse (Vaissette, III. Pr. 3, 4).—Guill. de Pod. Laurent. c. 9.—Pet. Sarnens. c. 9.—Rob. Autissiodor. ann. 1209.—Guill. Nangiac. ann. 1208.—Regest. XI. 26; XII. 106.—Guillem de Tudela, v.

[119] Regest. XI. 26, 29, 30, 31, 32, 33.—Archives Nationales de France J, 430, No. 2.—Hist. du C. de Toul. (Vaissette, III. Pr. 4).

[120] Alberti Stadens. Chron. ann. 1212.—Chronik des Jacob v. Königshofen (Chron. der deutschen Städte IX. 649).—Regest. XI. 234; XV. 199.

[121] Guillel. Briton. Philippidos VIII. 490-529.—Regest. XI. 156, 157, 158, 159, 180, 181, 182, 231, 234.—Vaissette, III. Pr. 4, 96.—Vaissette, Éd. Privat, VIII. 559, 563.—Pet. Sarnens. c. 10, 14.—Guill. de Tudela viii., lvi., cliv.—Alberti Stadens. Chron. ann. 1210.—Cæsar. Heisterb. Dial. Mirac. Dist. v. c. 21.—Reineri Monach. Leodiens. Chron. ann. 1210, 1213.—Chron. Engelhusii (Leibnitz Script. Rer. Brunsv. II. 1113).

[122] Guill. de Pod. Laurent. c. 13.—Vaissette, III. Pr. 4, 5.—Regest. XI. 232.

[123] Pet. Sarnens. c. 11, 12.—Regest. XII. post Epistt. 85, 107.

[124] Regest. ubi sup; XII. 89, 90, 106, 107.

[125] Regest. XI. 230; XII. 97, 98, 99.—Guillem de Tudela, xiii.—Vaissette, III. Pr. 10.

[126] Pet. Sarnens. c. 15.—Guillem de Tudela, xi., xiv.—Vaissette, III. Pr. 7.

[127] Regest. XII. 108.—Pet. Sarnens. c. 16.—Vaissette, III. 168; Pr. 10, 11.—Guill. de Pod. Laurent, c. 13.—Guillem de Tudela xvi.-xxiii., xxv.—Roberti Autissiodor. Chron. ann. 1209.—Cæsar. Heisterb. Dial. Mirac. v. 21.

[128] Guillem de Tudela, xiii., xiv.—Vaissette, III. 169, 170; Pr. 9, 10.

[129] Regest. XII. 108; XV. 212.—Pet. Sarnens. c. 17.—Vaissette, III. Pr. 11-18.—Guillem de Tudela, xxiv.-xxxiii., xl.—Guillel. Nangiac. ann. 1209.—Guill. de Pod. Laurent, c. 14.—A. Molinier, ap. Vaissette, Éd. Privat, VI. 296.

Dom Vaissette (III. 172) cites Cæsarius of Heisterbach as authority for the statement that four hundred and fifty of the inhabitants of Carcassonne refused to abjure heresy, of whom four hundred were burned and the rest hanged. The silence of better-informed contemporaries may well render this doubtful, especially as Cæsarius assigns the incident to a city which he terms Pulchravallis (Dial. Mirac. Dist. v. c. 21).

[130] Regest. VII. 229; XV. 212; XVI. 87.—Fran. Tarafæ de Reg. Hisp.—Löwenfeld, Epistt. Pontif. ined. p. 63.—Lafuente, Hist. de Esp. V. 492-5.—Mariana, Hist. de Esp. XII. 2.—L. Marinæi Siculi de Reb. Hisp. Lib. X.—Diez, Leben und Werke der Troubadours, 424.—Vaissette, III. 124.—Gest. Com. Barcenon. c. 24.

[131] Pet. Sarnens. c. 16-18.—Joann. Iperii. Chron. ann. 1201.—Geoff. de Villehardouin, c. 55.—Alberic. Trium Font. ann. 1202.—Guillem de Tudela, xxxv.

[132] Pet. Sarnens. c. 17bis.—Vaissette, III. Pr. 19.—Regest, XII. 108.—Pierre de Vaux-Cernay asserts that de Montfort was able to retain but thirty knights, but this is manifestly an exaggeration.

[133] Concil. Avenion. ann. 1209.—D'Achery Spicileg I. 706.—Pet. Sarnens. c. 20-26, 34.—Vaissette, III. Pr. 20.—Guillem de Tudela, xxxvi.—Regest. XII. 108, 109, 122, 123, 124, 125, 126, 129, 132, 136, 137; XIII. 86.—Teulet, Layettes, I. 340, No. 899.

By a very curious exegetical effort, the Dominicans succeed in convincing themselves that Innocent's letter confirming Albi to de Montfort (XIII. 86) is an approbation of the Dominican Order and a proof that de Montfort was a member of it (Ripoll Bullar. Ord. FF. Prædicat. T. VII. p. 1).

[134] Guill. de Pod. Laurent, c. 17, 18.—Guillel. Nangiac. ann. 1210.—Rob. Autissiodor. Chron. ann. 1211.—Vaissette, III. Pr. 29, 35.—Guillem de Tudela, xlix., lxviii.—lxxi., lxxxiv.—Regest. XVI. 41.—Chron. Turon. ann. 1210.—Pet. Sarnens. c. 37, 52, 53.—Teulet, Layettes, I. 371, No. 968.

[135] Vaissette, III. Pr. 20, 23, 232-3.—Pet. Sarnens. c. 33, 34.—Guillem de Tudela, xl., xlii., xliii.—Regest. XII. 152, 153, 154, 155, 156, 168, 169, 170, 171, 173, 174, 175, 176.—Teulet, Layettes, I. 368, No. 968.

[136] Vaissette, III. Pr. 24-5, 234.—Guillem de Tudela, xliv.—Teulet, loc. cit.

[137] Pet. Sarnens. c. 39.—Regest. XIII. 188, 189; XVI. 39.—Guillem de Tudela, lviii.—Teulet, Layettes, I. 360, No. 948.

[138] The sole authority for this extraordinary document is Guillem de Tudela (lix., lx., lxi.), followed by the Historien du Comte de Toulouse (Vaissette, III. Pr. 30. Cf. Text p. 204 and notes p. 561, also Hardouin VI. II. 1998). Though generally accepted by historians, I cannot regard it as genuine, and its only explanation seems to me that it was manufactured by Raymond to arouse the indignation of his people.

[139] Guill. de Pod. Laurent, c. 16, 17.—Pet. Sarnens. c. 43, 47, 49, 53, 54, 55.—Vaissette, III. Pr. 234.

[140] Vaissette, III. Pr. 38-40, 234-5.—Guill. de Pod. Laurent, c. 18.—Guillem de Tudela, lxxx.-lxxxiii.—Teulet, Layettes, I. 370, No. 968; 372, No. 975.

[141] Pet. Sarnens. c. 75.—Guill. de Pod. Laurent, c. 23.

[142] Pet. Sarnens. c. 60.—Vaissette, III. 271-2.—Rod. Tolet. de Reb. Hispan. VIII. 2, 6, 11—Rod. Santii Hist. Hispan. III. 35.

[143] Pet. Sarnens. c. 59-64.—Regest. XV. 102, 103, 167-76.

[144] Pet. Sarnens. c. 66.—Regest. XVI. 39.

[145] Pet. Sarnens. c. 65.—Regest. XV. 212.—A. Molinier (Vaissette, Éd Privat, VI. 407).

[146] Regest. XV. 212; XVI. 42, 47.

[147] Regest. XVI. 39, 42, 43.—Pet. Sarnens. c. 66.

[148] Regest. XVI. 40, 41, 43, 44, 45, 46, 47.

[149] Pet. Sarnens. c. 66, 70.—Regest. XVI. 48.

[150] Pet. Sarnens. c. 66-8.—Regest. XVI. 87.—Raynouard, Lexique Roman, I. 512-3.

[151] Pet. Sarnens. c. 69, 70.—Vaissette, III. Note XVII.—A. Molinier (Vaissette, Éd. Privat, VII. 256).

[152] Pet. Sarnens. c. 70-3.—Guillel. de Pod. Laurent. c. 21-22.—Guillel. Nangiac. ann. 1213.—Vaissette, III. Pr. 52-4.—Guillem de Tudela, CXXV.-CXL.—Zurita, Añales de Aragon, Lib. II. c. 63.—De Gestis Com. Barcenon. ann. 1213.—Bernard d'Esclot, Cronica del Rey en Pere, c. 6.—Campana, Storia di San Piero Martire p. 44.—Tamburini, Ist. dell' Inquisizione, I. 351-2.—Comentarios del Rey en Jacme c. 8 (Mariana, IV. 267-8).

Don Jayme himself, then a child in his sixth year, was still in the hands of de Montfort as a hostage, and if the Catalan chroniclers speak truth, it was with difficulty that the young king was recovered, even after Innocent III. had ordered his release.—L. Marinæi Siculi de Reb. Hispan. Lib. X.—Regest. XVI. 171.

[153] Pet. Sarnens. c. 74-8.—Regest. XVI. 167, 170, 171, 172.—Guill. de Pod. Laurent. c. 24, 25.—Vaissette, III. 260-2; Pr. 239-42.—Teulet, Layettes, I. 399-402, No. 1068-9, 1073.

[154] Pet. Sarnens. c. 80, 81, 82.—Harduin. Concil. VII. II. 2052.—Innocent. PP. III. Rubricella.—Teulet, Layettes, I. 410-16, Nos. 1099, 1113-16.—Guill. de Pod Laurent, c. 24, 25.

[155] Pet. Sarnens. c. 82.—Vaissette, III. 269; Pr. 56.

[156] Radulph. Coggeshall ann. 1213.

[157] Chron. Fossæ Novæ: ann. 1215.

[158] Guillem de Tudela, cxlii.-clii.—Vaissette, III. 280-1; Pr. 57-63.—Teulet, Layettes, I. 420, No. 1132.—Pet Sarnens. c. 83.—D'Achery I. 707.—Molinier, L'Ensevelissement du Comte de Toulouse, Angers, 1885, p. 6.

[159] Pet. Sarnens. c. 83.

[160] Guillem de Tudela, cliii.-viii.—Guill. de Pod. Laurent. c. 27-8.—Vaissette, III. Pr. 64-66.—Pet. Sarnens. c. 83.

[161] Pet. Sarnens. c. 83-6.—Guill. de Pod. Laurent, c. 28-30.—Vaissette, III. 271-2; Pr. 66-93.—Guillem de Tudela, clviii.-ccv.—Raynald. Annal. ann. 1217 No. 52, 55-62; ann. 1218 No. 55.—Martene Ampliss. Collect. I. 1129.—Annal. Waverliens. ann. 1218.—Bernardi Iterii Chron. ann. 1218.—Chron. Lemovicens. ann. 1218.—Guillel. Nangiac. ann. 1218.—Chron. Turonens. ann. 1218.—Roberti Autissiodor. Chron. ann. 1218.—Chron. S. Taurin. Ebroicens. ann. 1218.—Chron. Joan Iperii ann. 1218.—Chron. Laudunens. ann. 1218.—Chron. S. Petri Vivi Senonens. Append. ann. 1218.—Alberici Trium Font. Chron. ann. 1218.

[162] Teulet, Layettes, I. 454, No. 1271; pp. 461-2, No. 1279-80; p. 466, No. 1301; p. 475, No. 1331; p. 511, No. 1435; p. 518, No. 1656.—Vaissette, III. 307, 316-17, 568; Pr. 98-102.—Raynald. Annal. ann. 1218, No. 54-57; ann. 1221, No. 44, 45.—Archives Nationals de France J. 430, No. 15, 16.—Guillel. de Pod. Laurent, c. 31-33.—Guillel. Nangiac. ann. 1219-1220.—Bernardi Iterii Chron. ann. 1219.—Robert. Autissiodor. Chron. ann. 1219.—Chron. Laudunens. ann. 1219.—Chron. Andrens. ann. 1219.—Alberici Trium Font. Chron. ann. 1219.—Martene Thesaur. I 884.—Rymer, Fœdera, I. 229.

[163] Vaissette, III. 319; Pr. 275, 276.—Raynald. Annal. ann. 1222, No. 44-47.—Guill. de Pod. Laurent, c. 47.—Teulet, Layettes, I. 546, No. 1537.

[164] Guill. de Pod. Laurent. c. 34.—Vaissette, III. 306, 321-4.—Molinier, L'Ensevelissement de Raimond VI.

[165] Vaissette, III. Pr. 276, 282.—Teulet, Layettes, I. 561, No. 1577.—Raynald. Annal. ann. 1222, No. 48.—Matt. Paris ann. 1223, p. 219.

[166] Alberici Trium Font. Chron. arm. 1223.—Guill. de Pod. Laurent, c. 34.—Vaissette, III. Pr. 290.—Raynald. Annal. ann. 1223, No. 41-45.—Teulet, Layettes, II. 24, No. 1631.

[167] Vaissette, III. Pr. 285, 291-3.—Gesta Ludovici VIII. ann. 1224.

[168] Rymer, Fœdera I. 271.—Vaissette, III. 339-40: Pr. 283.—Raynald. Annal. ann. 1224, No. 40.—Gesta Ludovici VIII. ann. 1224.—Chron. Turonens. ann. 1224.—Guillel. Nangiac. ann. 1224.—Epistolæ Seculi XIII. Tom. I. No. 240 (Monument. Hist. German.).

[169] Vaissette, III. Pr. 284, 296.—Vaissette, Éd. Privat, VIII. 804.—Baluz. Concil. Narbonn. pp. 60-64.—Gesta Ludovici VIII. ann. 1224.—Concil. Montispessulan. ann. 1224 (Harduin. VII. 131-33).—Grandes Chroniques, ann. 1224.—Guillel. Nangiac. ann. 1224.

[170] Vaissette, III. Pr. 284-5.—Schmidt I. 291.—Coll. Doat, XXIII. 269-70.—Rymer, Fœd. I. 273, 274, 281.—Raynald. Annal. ann. 1225, No. 28-34.—Teulet, Layettes, II. 47, No. 1694.

[171] Chron. Turonens. ann. 1225.—Matt. Paris ann. 1225, pp. 227-9. A poetaster of the period, in describing the council, depicts Raymond's discomfiture with emphasis:
"Et s'i vint li quens de St. Gille,
Ki n'i fist vallant une tille
De sa besougne, quant vint là,
Qu' escuméniies s'en r'ala,
Ausi com il i fu venus,
Voire plus, s'il pot estre plus."
—Chronique de Philippe Mousket, 25385-90.

[172] Chron. Turonens. ann. 1225.—Matt. Paris ann. 1225, pp. 227-8.—Possibly the chroniclers may be guilty of exaggeration, for the letters of Honorius only ask for a single prebend in each cathedral and collegiate church (Martene Thesaur. I. 929). In either case the encroachments of Rome were only postponed, for in 1385 Charles le Sage complained that nearly all the benefices of France were practically held by the cardinals, who carried the revenue to Italy, so that the churches were falling to ruin, the abbeys deserted, the orphanages and hospitals diverted from their purpose, divine service had ceased in many places, and the lands of the Church were uncultivated. To remedy this, he seized all such revenues and ordered them to be expended on the objects for which they had been given to the Church (Ibid. I. 1612).

[173] Matt. Paris ann. 1226, p. 229.—Vaissette, III. 349.—Rymer, Fœd. I. 281.—Martene Collect. Nova, p. 104; Thesaur. I. 931.

[174] Waddingi Annal. Minorum ann. 1225, No. 14.—Vaissette, III. Pr. 305, 318.—Teulet, Layettes, II. 75, No. 1758; p. 79, No. 1768; p. 90, No. 1794.

[175] Vaissette, III. Pr. 300, 308-14.—Teulet, Layettes, II. 68-9, No. 1742-3.—Matt. Paris ann. 1226, p. 229.—Chron. Turonens. ann. 1225, 1226.

[176] Chron. Turonens. ann. 1226.—Teulet, Layettes, II. 72, No. 1751.

[177] Matt. Paris ann. 1226.—Teulet, Layettes, II. 71, 78, 81, 84, 85, 87, 89, 90, 91, 648-9.—Guillel. de Pod. Laurent. c. 35.—Vaissette, III. 354, 364.—Chron. Turonens. ann. 1226.—Guillel. Nangiac. ann. 1226.— Gesta Ludovici VIII. ann. 1226.

The city of Agen seems to have remained faithful to Raymond (Teulet, II. 82).

[178] Gesta Ludovici VIII. ann. 1226.—Matt. Paris ann. 1226.—Chron. Turonens. ann. 1226.—Guillel. de Pod. Laurent. c. 36, 38.—Alberti Stadens. Chron. ann. 1226.—Vaissette, III. 363.

[179] Chron. Turonens. ann. 1226, 1227.—Martene Ampliss. Collect. I. 1210-13.—Potthast Regesta, 7897, 7920.—Vaissette, III. Pr. 323-5.—Guillel. Nangiac. ann. 1227.—Guillel. de Pod. Laurent. c. 38.—Matt. Paris ann. 1228.—Martene Thesaur. I. 940.—Concil. Narbonnens. ann. 1227 can. 13-17.—Vaissette, Éd. Privat, VIII. 265.

Letters of the Archbishop of Sens and Bishop of Chartres, in 1227, promising to pay to the king a subsidy for the crusade against the Albigenses are preserved in the Archives Nationales de France, J. 428, No. 8.

[180] Bernard. Guidon. Vit. Gregor. PP. IX. (Muratori, S.R.I. III. 570-1).—Guillel. de Pod. Laurent, c. 38, 39.—Teulet, Layettes, II. 144, No. 1980.—Potthast Regesta, 8150, 8216, 8267.—Raynald. Annal. ann. 1228, No. 20-4.—Martene Thesaur. I. 943.—Vaissette, III. 377-8; Pr. 326-9, 335.

[181] Harduin. Concil. VII. 165-72.—Vaissette, III. 375; Pr. 329-35, 340-3.—Teulet, Layettes, II. 147-52, No. 1991-4; pp. 154-57, No. 1998-99, 2003-4.—Guill. de Pod. Laurent. c. 47.

[182] Martene Ampliss. Collect. I. 1225.—Vaissette, III. 375, 412.—Teulet, Layettes, II. 155, No. 2000.— Raynald. ann. 1237, No. 31.—Rob. de Monte Chron. ann. 1238.—Potthast Regest. 10469, 10516-17, 10563, 10579, 10666, 10670, 10996.—Cf. Berger, Les Registres d'Innoc. IV. No. 2763-69.

For the sums raised in England in 1234 by selling releases of Crusaders' vows see Matt. Paris ann. 1234, p. 276.

[183] Bern. Guidon. Vit. Gregor. PP. IX. (Muratori S.R.I. III. 572).

[184] Tertull. de Baptism, c. 15.—Concil. Chalced. Act. I.

[185] Augustin. Epist. 185 ad Bonifac. c. iii. § 12.—Cf. Cypriani de Unit. Eccles.—C. 3 Extra, v. 7.

[186] Tertull. Apologet. c. xxiv.; Lib. ad Scapulam ii.; adv. Gnosticos Scorpiaces ii, iii.—Cypriani Epist. 54 ad Maximum; de Unitate Ecclesia; Epist. 4 ad Pomponium c. 4, 5.—Firm. Lactant. Div. Instit. v. 20.

[187] Lib. XVI. Cod. Theod. Tit. v. II. 1, 2.—Sozomen H.E. I. 21; II. 20, 22, 30; III. 5.—Socrat. II. E. I. 9; IV. 16.—Ammian. Marcell. XXII. 5.

[188] Sulp. Sever. Hist. Sacræ II. 47-51; Ejusd. Dial. III. 11-13.—Prosp. Aquitan. Chron. ann. 385-6.—St. Martin could hardly have anticipated that a time would come when a pope would cite the murder of Priscillian as an example to be followed in the case of Luther; and, in spite of Maximus's excommunication by St. Ambrose, characterize him as one of the "veteres ac pii imperatores." (Epist. Adriani PP. VI. Nov. 15, 1522 ap. Lutheri Opp. T. II. fol. 538 a.)

[189] Chrysostomi in Matthæum Homil. XLVI. c. 2. Cf. Homil. de Anathemate c. 4.—Augustini Epist. 100 ad Donatum c. 2; Epist. 139 ad Marcellinum; Epist. 105 c. 13; Enchirid. c. 72; Contra Litt. Petiliani Lib. II. c. 83.

[190] Hieron. Epist. 109 ad Ripar.; Comment. in Naum I. 9.—Leonis PP. I. Epist. 15 ad Turribium.— Lib. XVI. Cod. Theodos. Tit. v. ll. 9, 15, 34, 36, 51, 56, 64.—Constt. 11, 12 Cod. Lib. I. Tit. v.—Novell. Theod. II. Tit. vi.—Pauli Diac. Histor. Lib. XVI.—Basilicon Lib. I. Tit. 1-33.

[191] Cod. Eccles. African. c. 67, 93.—Augustin. Epist. 185 ad Bonifac. c. 7.—Ejusd. contra Cresconium Lib. III. c. 47.—Possidii Vit. Augustini c. 12.—Leonis PP. I. Epist. 60.—Pelagii PP. I. Epistt. 1, 2.—Isidori Hispalens. Sententt. Lib. III. c. li. 3-6.—Balsamon. in Photii Nomocanon Tit. ix. c. 25.—Victor. Vitens. de Persecutione Vandalica Lib. LII.—Victor. Tunenens. Chron. ann. 479.—Sidon. Apollin. Epistt. VII. 6.—Isidor. Hist. de Regg. Gothor. c. 50.—Pelayo, Heterodoxos Españoles, I. 195 sqq.—Legg. Wisigoth. Lib. XII. Tit. ii. l. 2; Tit. iii. ll. 1, 2 (cf. Fuero Juzgo cod. loc.).

[192] Mag. Biblioth. Pat. IX. II. 875.—Chron. Turonens. ann. 878.—Concil. Ratispon. ann. 792.—C. Francfortiens. ann. 794.—C. Romanum ann. 799.—C. Aquisgran. ann. 799.—Alcuini Epistt. 108, 117.— Agobardi Lib. adv. Felicem c. 5. 6.—Nic. Anton. Bib. Vet. Hispan. Lib. VI. c. ii. No. 42-3 (cf. Pelayo, Heterod. Españ. I. 297, 673 sqq.).—Hincmari Remens. de Prædestinat. II. c. 2.—Annal. Bertin. ann. 849.—Concil. Carisiacens. ann. 849 (cf. C. Agathens. ann. 506 c. 38).—Cap. Car. Mag. ann. 789 c. 44.—Capitul. Add. III. c. 90.

For the slenderness of the disabilities inflicted on Jews under the Carlovingians see Reginald Lane Poole's "Illustrations of the History of Medieval Thought," London, 1884, p. 47.

[193] Burchardi Decret. Lib. XIX. c. 133-4.—Gesta Episcopp. Leodiens. Lib. II. c. 60, 61.—Hist. Andaginens. Monast. c. 18.—Martene Ampliss. Collect. I. 776-8.

[194] Dom Bouquet, XI. 497-8.—Bernardi Serm. in Cantica LXIV. c. 8; LXVI. c. 12.—Alex. PP. III. Epistt. 118, 122.—Pet. Cantor. Verb. abbrev. c. 78, 80.

[195] Concil. Turonens. ann. 1163 c. 4.—Trithem. Chron. Hirsaug. ann. 1163.—Concil. Remens. ann. 1157 c. 1.—Guillel. de Newburg Hist. Angl. ii. 15.—Innoc. III. Regest. I. 94, 165.—Contre le Franc-Alleu sans Tiltre, Paris, 1629, pp. 215 sqq.—H. Mutii Chron. Lib. XIX. ann. 1212.—Böhmer, Regesta Imperii V. 110.— Muratori Antiq. Ital. Diss. LX. (T. XII. p. 447).—Hist. Diplom. Frid. II. T. II. pp. 6-8, 422-3; IV. 301; V. 201.— Constitt. Sicular. Lib. I. Tit. 1.—Treuga Henrici (Böhlau, Nove Constit. Dom. Alberti, Weimar, 1858, p. 78, cf. Böhmer Regest. V. 700).—Sachsenspiegel, II. xiii.—Schwabenspiegel, cap. 116 No. 29; cap. 351 No. 3 (Ed.

Senckenb.).—Archivio di Venezia, Codice ex Brera No. 277.—El Fuero real de España, Lib. IV. Tit. I. ley 1.—Isambert, Anc. Loix Françaises I. 230-33, 257.—Harduin. Concil. VII. 203-8.—Établissements, Lib. I. ch. 85.—Livres de Jostice et de Plet, Liv. I. Tit. iii. § 7.—Beaumanoir, Cout. du Beauvoisis, XI. 2, XXX. 11.—2 Henry IV. c. 15 (cf. Pike, History of Crime in England I. 343-4, 489).

It is true that both Bracton (De Legibus Angliæ Lib. III. Tract ii. cap. 9 § 2) and Horne (Myrror of Justice, cap. I. § 4, cap. II. § 22, cap. IV. § 14) describe the punishment of burning for apostasy, heresy, and sorcery, and the former alludes to a case in which a clerk who embraced Judaism was burned by a council of Oxford, but the penalty substantially had no place in the common law, save under the systematizing efforts of legal writers, enamoured of the Roman jurisprudence, and seeking to complete their work by the comparison of treason against God with that against the king. The silence of Britton (chap. VIII.) and of the Fleta (Lib. I. cap. 21) shows that the question had no practical importance.

[196] Cæsar. Heisterbac. Dial. Miracular. Dist. v. c. 33.—Mosaic. et Roman. Legg. Collat. Tit.XV. § 3 (Hugo, 1465).—Const. 3 Cod. IX. 18.—Cassiodor. Variar. IV., XXII., XXIII.—Gregor. PP. I. Dial. I. 4.—Gloss. Hostiensis in Cap. *ad abolendam*, No. 11, 13 (Eymerici Direct. Inquisit. pp. 149-150); cf. Gloss. Joan. Andreæ (Ibid. p. 170-1).—Repertorium Inquisitorum s. v. *Comburi*(Ed. Valent. 1494; Ed. Venet. 1588, pp. 127-8).

[197] Concil. Autissiodor. ann. 578 c. 33.—C. Matiscon. II. ann. 585 c. 19.—C. 30 Decreti P. II. Caus. xxiii. Quæst. 8.—C. Lateran. IV. ann. 1215 c. 18.—C. Burdegalens. ann. 1255 c. 10.—C. Budens. ann. 1268 c. 11.—C. Nugaroliens. ann. 1303 c. 13.—C. Baiocens. ann. 1300 c. 34.—Lib. Sentt. Inq. Tolosan. p. 208.—Bernard. Guidonis Practica (MSS. Bib. Nat., Coll. Doat, T. XXX. fol. 1. sqq.).

[198] Honor. Augustod. Summ. Glor. de Apost. c. 5.—Ivon. Decret. IX. 70-79.—Gratiani Decret. P. II. Caus. xxiii. q. 5.—Radevic. de Gest. Frid. I. Lib. II. c. 56.—Concil. Lateran. II. ann. 1139 c. 23.—Concil. Lateran. III. ann. 1179 c. 27 (cf. C. Tolosan. ann. 1119 c. 3; C. Remens. ann. 1148 c. 18; C. Turonens. ann. 1163 c. 4).—Lucii. PP. III. Epist. 171.

[199] Böhmer, Regest. Imp. V. 86.—Innocent. PP. III. Regest. de Negot. Rom. Imp. 189.—Muratori Antiq. Ital. Dissert. III.—Hartzheim Concil. German. III. 540.—Cod. Epist. Rodolphi I. Auct. II. pp. 375-7 (Lipsiæ 1806).—Theod. Vrie, Hist. Concil. Constant. Lib. III. Dist. 8; Lib. VII. Dist. 7.—Thom. Aquin. de Principum Regimine Lib. I. c. xiv.; Lib. III. c. x., xiii.-xviii.—Lib. v. Extra. Tit. vii. c 13 § 3.—Concil. Tolosan. ann. 1229 c. 5.—Concil. Narbonn. ann. 1244 c. 15, 16.—Zanchini de Hæret. c. v.—Beaumanoir, Coutumes du Beauvoisis, XI. 27.—See also the sermon of the Bishop of Lodi at the condemnation of Huss, Von der Hardt, III. 5.

The treatise "De principum regimine," though not wholly by St. Thomas Aquinas, was the authoritative exponent of the ecclesiastical theory as to the structure and duties of government. See Poole's "Illustrations of the History of Medieval Thought," p. 240.

[200] Post. Const. 4, Cod. Lib. I. Tit. v.—Post. Libb. Feudorum.—Lib. Juris Civilis Veronæ c. 156.—Schwabenspiegel, Ed. Senckenb. cap. 351; Ed. Schilteri c. 308.—Potthast Regesta No. 6593.—Innoc. PP. IV. Bull. *Cum adversus*, 5 Jun. 1252; Bull. *Ad aures*, 2 Apr. 1253; 31 Oct. 1243; 7 Julii 1254.—Bull. *Cum fratres*, Maii 9 1252.—Urbani. IV. Bull. *Licet ex omnibus*, 1262 § 12.—Wadding Annal. Minor ann. 1258, No. 7; ann. 1260, No. 1; ann. 1261, No. 3.—c. 6 Sexto v. 2 c. 1, 2 in Septimo v. 3.—Von der Hardt, T. IV. p. 1519.—Campana, Vita di San Piero Martire, p. 124.—De Maistre, Lettres à un Gentilhomme Russe sur l'Inquisition Espagnole, Ed. 1864, *pp.* 17-18, 28, 34.

A thirteenth-century writer argued the matter more directly than De Maistre—"Papa noster non occidit, nec præcipit aliquem occidi, sed lex occidit quos papa permittit occidi, et ipsi se occidunt qui ea faciunt unde debeant occidi."—Gregor. Fanens. Disput. Cathol. et Patar. (Martene Thesaur. V. 1741).

More historically true is the assertion of an enthusiastic Dominican in 1782, who, after quoting Deut. XIII. 6-10, declares that its command to slay without mercy all who entice the faithful from the true religion is almost literally the law of the holy Inquisition; and who proceeds to prove from Scripture that fire is the peculiar delight of God, and the proper means of purifying the wheat from the tares.—Lob u. Ehrenrede auf die heilige Inquisition, Wien, 1782, pp. 19-21.

The hypocritical plea for mercy was commenced in good faith by Innocent III. in the case of clerks guilty of forgery who were degraded and delivered to the secular courts.—c. 27 Extra v. 40.

[201] Urbani PP. II. Epist. 256.—Zanchini de Hæret. c. xviii.—Innoc. PP. III. Regest. XI. 26.—Lucæ Tudens. de altera Vita II 9.

[202] S. Raymundi Summæ Lib. I. Tit. v. §§ 2, 4, 8; Tit. VI. § 1.—This continued to be the doctrine of the Church. Zanghino Ugolini includes in his enumeration of heresies neglect to observe the papal decretals, being an apparent contempt for the power of the keys (Tract. de Hæret. c. ii.). This authoritative work was printed in Rome, 1568, at the expense of Pius V., with a commentary by Cardinal Campeggi, and was reprinted with additions by Simancas in 1579. My references are made to a transcript from a fifteenth-century MS. of the original in the Bibliothèque Nationale, fonds latin, 12532.

[203] S. Thom. Aquinat. Summæ Sec. Sec. Q. XI. art. 3, 4.

[204] Cypriani Epist. I.—Chrysost. Hom. de Anathemate.—Leon PP. I. Epist. 108 c. 2.—Gelasii PP. I. Epistt. 4, 11.—Concil. Roman. II. ann. 494.—Evagrii H.E. Lib. IV. c. 38.—Vigilii Constit. de Tribus

Capitulis.—Facundi Epist. in Defens. Trium Capitt.—Concil. Constantinop. II. ann. 553 Collat. VII.—Concil. Hispalens. II. ann. 618 c. 5.—Concil. Constantinop. III. ann. 680 Tom. XII.-Jaffé Regesta, 303.—Synod. Roman. ann. 898 c. 1.—Chron. Turonens. (Martene Ampliss. Collect. V. 978-80).—Ivon. Carnotens. Epist. 96; Ejusd. Panorm. Lib. v. c. 115-123.—Lucii PP. III. Epist. 171.—Lib. v. Extra Tit. vii. c. 13.—Gratian. Decret. II. Caus. XI. Q. iii. c. 36, 37, 38.—F. Pegnæ Comment. in Eymerici Direct. Inquis. p. 95.—Innocent. PP. III. Regest. IX. 213.—Lib. III. Extra Tit. xxviii. c. 12.—Lib. v. in Sexto Tit. i. c. 2.—Eymeric. Direct. Inquis. p. 104.

[205] Hist. Diplom. Frid. II. Introd. pp. cdlxxxviii., cdxcvi.; II. 6-8, 422-3; IV. 409-11, 435-6; V. 459-60.— Fazelli de Reb. Siculis Decad. II. Lib. viii.—Alberic. T. Font. Chron. ann. 1228.—Raynald. Annal. ann. 1220, No. 23.—Richard de S. Germano Chron. ann. 1233.

[206] Mr. John Fiske has developed the contrast between the military and industrial spirit and the theory of corporate responsibility with his accustomed admirable clearness in his "Excursions of an Evolutionist," Essays VIII. and IX.

The theory of solidarity is clearly expressed in Zanghino's remark "Quia in omnes fert injuriam quod in divinam religionem committatur" (Tract. de Hæres. c. xi.).

[207] Ademari S. Cibardi Hist. Lib. III. c. 36.—Dooms of Æthelstan, III. vi. (Thorpe, I. 219).—Bracton. Lib. III. Tract, i. c. 6.—Legg. Villæ de Arkes § 26. (D'Achery III. 608).—Hist. Diplom. Frid. II. Introd. p. cxcvi.; IV. 444.—Godefrid. S. Pantal. Annal. ann. 1233.—Fazelli de Reb. Siculis Decad. II. Lib. viii. p. 442.—Isambert. Anc. Loix Franç. I. 295.—Legg. Opstalbom. §§ 3, 4.—Treuga Henrici c. 1224 (Böhlau, Nove Constitut. Dom. Alberti, Weimar, 1858, pp. 76-77).—Registre Criminel du Châtelet de Paris, *passim* (Paris, 1861).—Beaumanoir, Coutumes du Beauvoisis, c. 30, No. 12.—Antiqua Ducum Mediolan. Decreta, pp. 187-88 (Mediolani, 1654).— Legg. Capital. Caroli V. c. 103-197 (Goldast. Constitt. Imp. III. 537-55).—London Athenæum, Mar. 15, 1873, p. 338.—R. Christian. V. Jur. Danic. art. 7.—Willenburgii de Except. et Pœnis Cleric, p. 41 (Jenæ, 1740).—5 Henry IV. c. 5.—Description of Britaine, Bk. III. c. 6 (Holinshed's Chronicles Ed. 1577 I. 106).—London Athenæum, 1885 No. 3024, p. 466.

It has seemed to me, however, that a sensible increase in the severity of punishment is traceable after the thirteenth century, and I am inclined to attribute this to the influence exercised by the Inquisition over the criminal jurisprudence of Europe.

[208] Lucæ Tudens. de altera Vita Lib. III. c. 15.—T. Aquinat Summ. Sec. Sec. Q. X. Artt. 3, 6.—Von der Hardt, T.I.P. XVI. p. 829.—Nic. Eymerici Direct. Inquis. Præfat.

[209] Galton, Inquiries into Human Faculty, pp. 66-68.—Cæsar. Heisterbac. Dial. Mirac. Dist.IV.

As early as the fourth century the tendency of exaggerated asceticism to affect the mind was noted, and St. Jerome had the common-sense to point out that such cases required a physician rather than a priest (Hieron. Epist. CXXV. c. 16).

[210] Martene Thesaur. V. 1817, 1820.—Urbani PP. IV. Bull. *Licet ex omnibus*, 20 Mart. 1262, § 13.— Clem. PP. IV. Bull. *Præ cunctis mentis*, 23 Feb. 1266 (Arch. de l'Inq. de Carc., Doat, XXXII. 32).

[211] Tamburini, Storia Generale dell' Inquisizione, I. 362-5, 561.—Chron. Veronens. ann. 1233 (Muratori S.R.I. VIII. 626, 627).

[212] Gregor. PP. I. Homil. in Evangel. XL. 8.—Pet. Lomb. Sententt. Lib. IV. Dist. 50 §§ 6, 7. Peter Lombard even presses into service a passage from St. Jerome which had no such significance (Hieron. Comment. in Isaiam Lib. XVIII. c. LXVI. vers. 24).—St. Bonaventuræ Pharetræ IV. 50.—S. Thomæ Aquinat. contra Impugn. Relig. cap. XVI. §§ 2, 3.

[213] S. Thomæ Aquinat. Summ. Sec. Sec. Q. X. art. 8, 12.—Zanchini de Hære. c. ii.

[214] Chron. Laudunens. ann. 1198.—Ottonis de S. Blasio Chron. (Urstisius I. 223 sq.).—Joann. de Flissicuria (D. Bouquet, XVIII. 800).—Rob. Autissiodor. Chron. ann. 1198, 1202.—Rog. Hoveden. Annal. ann. 1198, 1202.—Rigord. de Gest. Phil. Aug. ann. 1195, 1198.—Guillel. Brit. de Gest. Phil. Aug. ann. 1195.— Grandes Chroniques, ann. 1195, 1198.—Jacob. Vitriens. Hist. Occident. c. 8.—Radulph. de Coggeshall ann. 1198, 1201.—Chron. Cluniacens. ann. 1198.—Chron. Leodiens. ann. 1198, 1199.—Alberic. T. Font. Chron. ann. 1198.—Geoff. de Villehardouin c. 1.—Annal. Aquicinctin. Monast. ann. 1198.—Joann. Iperii Chron. ann. 1201-2.

[215] Pet. Sarnens. c. 6.—Guillel. Pod. Laur. c. 8.—Innoc. PP. III Regest. XI. 196, 197; XII. 17.

[216] Innocent. PP. III. Regest. XI. 98; XII. 67, 69; XIII. 63, 78, 94; XV. 90, 91, 92, 93, 96, 137, 146.— Ripoll. Bull. Ord. FF. Prædic. I. 96.—Berger, Registres d'Innoc. IV. No. 2752.

[217] Bremond de Guzmana Stirpe S. Dominici, Romæ, 1740, pp. 11, 12, 127, 133, 288.

[218] Bern. Guidon. Tract. Magist. Ord. Prædicat. ann. 1203-6.—Nic. de Trivetti Chron. ann. 1203-9.

[219] Pet. Sarnens. c. 7.—Innoc. PP. III. Regest. IX. 185.—Paramo de Orig. Offic. S. Inquis. Lib. II. Tit. 1, c. 2, §§ 6, 7.—Nic. de Trivetti Chron. ann. 1205.—Chron. Magist. Ord. Prædic. c. 1.—Bern. Guidon. Hist. Fundat. Convent. (Martene Ampl. Collect. VI. 439).

[220] Lacordaire, Vie de S. Dominique. p. 124.—Nic. de Trivetti Chron. ann. 1203.—Jac. de Voragine Legenda Aurea, Ed. 1480, fol. 88*b*, 90*a*.

As St. Francis had the distinguishing peculiarity of the Stigmata, so the Dominicans boasted that their founder had the special characteristic that when his tomb was opened the odor of sanctity exhaled from it was a delicious scent from paradise hitherto unknown, so penetrating in quality that it pervaded the whole land, and so persistent that those who touched the holy relics had their hands perfumed for years.—Prediche del Beato Frà Giordano da Rivalto, Firenze, 1831, I. 47.

[221] Nic. de Trivetti Chron. ann. 1215.—Bernardi Guidonis Tract, de Magist. Ord. Prædic. (Martene Ampl. Coll. VI. 400).—Hist. Ordin. Prædic. c. 1 (Ib. 332).

[222] Nic. de Trivetti loc. cit.—Chron. Magist. Ord. Prædic. c. 1.—Bernard. Guidonis loc. cit.—Concil. Lateran. IV. c. xiii.—Harduin. Concil. VII. 83.

[223] Hist. Ordin. Prædicat. c. 1, 2, 3.—Chron. Magist. Ordin. Prædicat. c. 1.—Bernard. Guidonis Tract. de Magist. Ord. Prædic. (Martene Ampliss. Coll. VI. 332-4, 400).

[224] Bernard. Guidon. Tract de Ordin. Prædic. (Martene Ampl. Collect. VI. 400, 402-3).—Ejusd. Hist. Fund. Convent. Prædic. (Ib. 446-7).—Hist. Ordin. Prædic. c. 9.—Nic. de Trivetti Chron. ann. 1220, 1228.—Chron. Magist. Ordin. Prædic. c. 3.—Constit. Frat. Prædic. ann. 1228, Dist. I. c. 22; II. 26, 34 (Archiv für Literatur-und Kirchengeschichte, 1886, pp. 209, 222, 225).

[225] Nic. de Trivetti Chron. ann. 1215, 1217, 1218.—Chron. Magist. Ord. Prædic. c. 2.—Hist. Ordin. Prædic. c. 1, 5.—Bern. Guidon. Tract. de Magist. Ord. Prædic. (Martene Ampl. Coll. VI. 401).—Hist. Convent. Parisiens. Frat. Prædic. (Ib. 549-50).

[226] Bern. Guidon. Tract. de Magist. (Martene VI. 403-4).—Ejusd. Hist. Convent. Prædic. (Ib. 459).—Nic. de Trivetti Chron. ann. 1221, 1243, 1276.—Hist. Ordin. Prædic. c. 7.—Mag. Bull. Roman. I., 73, 74, 77, 94.

An enumeration of the Dominican Order made in 1337, at the request of Benedict XII., showed about twelve thousand members. Preger, Vorarbeiten zu einer Geschichte der deutschen Mystik (Zeitschrift für die hist. Theol. 1869, p. 12).

[227] Bonaventuræ Vit. S. Fran. c. I., c. II. No. 1-4.

[228] S. Bonavent. c. II., III.

This account is doubtless colored by the result and adapted unconsciously to the successive stages of a formal religious organization. At first, however, the brethren were not expected to abandon their ordinary pursuits. They were required to follow their regular handicraft, earning their livelihood, and not living on alms except in case of necessity. See the First Rule, as reconstructed by Prof. Karl Müller, Die Anfänge des Minoritenordens, Freiburg, i. B., 1885, p. 186.

[229] Bonavent. Vit. Franc. c. IV. No. 10.—Frat. Jordani Chron. (Analecta Franciscana I. 6. Quaracchi, 1885).—Waddingi Annal. Minorum ann. 1260, No. 14.—Th. de Eccleston de Adventu Minorum Collat. 2.

[230] Frat. Jordani Chron. (Analecta Franciscana I. 3).—S. Francisci Colloq. IX.—Liber Conformitatum, Lib. I. Fruct. 9 (Ed. 1513, fol. 77a).—Potthast Regesta No. 7108.

The dates and details of the successive Rules drawn up by Francis are involved in considerable obscurity. The subject has been discussed with much acuteness by Karl Müller, op. cit.

[231] B. Francisci Regul. II.

[232] Lib. Conformitatum Lib. II. Fruct. 5, fol. 155b.

[233] Bonavent. Vit. Francis, c. 8.—Lib. Conformitatum Lib. I. Fruct. 1, fol. 13a; Lib. III. Fruct. 3, fol. 210a.—Thomæ de Eccleston de Adventu Minorum Collat. XII.—Alex. PP. IV. Bull.*Quia longum* ann. 1259—Wadding, ann. 1256, No. 19.—Mag. Bull. Roman. I. 79, 108.—Potthast Regesta No. 10308.—See also Mr. J.S. Brewer's eloquent tribute to the Franciscans in his preface to the Monumenta Franciscana (M.R. Series).

In 1496 the University of Paris condemned as scandalous and savoring of heresy the attempts of the Franciscans to assimilate their patron to Christ.—(D'Argentré, Coll. Judic. de nov. Error. I. ii. 318.)

When the Dominicans claimed for St. Catharine of Siena the honor of the Stigmata, Sixtus IV., in 1475, issued a bull prohibiting her being represented with them, as they were reserved for St. Francis (Martene Ampliss. Collect. VI. 1386). They had not as yet been vulgarized by La Cadière and Louise Lateau.

[234] S. Francis. de Perfecta Lætitia; Ejusd. Epistt. xi., xv.—Waddingi Annal. ann. 1298, No. 24-40.—Cantù, Eretici d'Italia, I. 128.

[235] Lib. Conform. Lib. I. Fruct. 8, fol. 47.—Thom. de Eccleston Collat. I.—Frat. Jordani Chron. c. 27 (Analecta Franciscana I. 10).—S. Francis. Collat. Monasticæ, Collat. 20.

[236] Waddingi Annal. ann. 1262, No. 3, 4, 8; ann. 1273, No. 12.

[237] S. Francis. Collat. Monast. Collat. 5.—Ejusd. pro Paupertate obtinenda Oratio.—Lib. Conform. Lib. III. Fruct. 4, fol. 215a.

[238] S. Francis. Colloq. 27.—Th. de Eccleston de Adventu Minorum Collat. 1, 2.

[239] Philip. Bergomat. Supplem. Chronic. Lib. XIII. ann. 1215.—Bonavent. Vit. S. Fran. c. IV. No. 5; c. XI—Regula Fratrum Sororumque de Pœnitentia.—Potthast Regest. No. 6736, 7503, 13073.—Chron. Magist. Ordin. Prædicat. c. 2, 9.—Raynald. Annal. ann. 1233, No. 40.—Nicolai PP. IV. Bull. *Supra montem*, ann. 1289.

[240] Chron. Augustens. ann. 1250.—Matt. Paris. ann. 1252.

[241] Pierre de Fontaines, Conseil, ch. xxi. art. 8.—Le Grand d'Aussy, Fabliaux, II. 112-3.—The existence of the "droit de marquette" has been questioned, but without reasonable ground. The authorities may be found in the author's "Sacerdotal Celibacy," 2d Ed. p. 354.

[242] Matt. Paris ann. 1251 (pp. 550-2).—Guillel. Nangiac. ann. 1251.—Amalrici Augerii Vit. Pontif. ann. 1251.—Bern. Guidon. Flor. Chronic. (Bouquet, XXI. 697). A similar extraordinary movement took place in

1309 (Chron. Corn. Zanflict ann. 1309), and another, on a larger scale, in 1320 (Guill. Nangiac. Contin. ann. 1320.—Grandes Chroniques V. 245-6.—Amal. Auger. Vit. Pontif. ann. 1320).

[243] Monach. Paduan. Lib. III. ann. 1260.—Chron. F. Francisci Pipini ann. 1260.—Gesta Treviror. Archiep. c. 268.—Closener's Chronik (Chron. der deutschen Städte, VIII. 73, 104).—Lami, Antichità Toscane, p. 617.—Verri, Storia di Milano, I. 264.

[244] Potthast Regest. No. 8324, 8326, 9775, 10905, 11169, 11296, 11319, 11399, 11415.—Ripoll. I. 99.—Matt. Paris ann. 1234 (pp. 274-6).—Wadding. Annal. ann. 1295, No. 18.—Mag. Bull. Roman. I. 174.—Ripoll II. 40.

The exemption of the Mendicants from all local jurisdiction save that of their own Orders was a source of almost inconceivable trouble in every portion of Christendom. When, for instance, in 1435, the legates of the Council of Basle were on their way to Brünn to settle the terms of pacification with the Hussites, they were called upon in Vienna to silence a Franciscan whose abusive sermons created disorder, and it was with much trouble that they forced him to admit that, as representing a general council, they had authority to discipline him. On their arrival at Brünn they found the public agitated over a dreadful scandal, the Dominican provincial having seduced a nun of his own order. The woman had borne a child to him, and no steps had been taken against him. The ordinary judicial machinery of the Church was utterly powerless to deal with him, and the precautions which the legates deemed it prudent to take before they ventured to commence proceedings show how arduous and dangerous they felt the task to be, though when they got to work they sentenced him to deposition and imprisonment on bread and water.—Ægidii Carlerii Liber de Legationibus (Monument. Concil. General. Sæc. XV. T. I. pp. 544-8, 553, 555, 557, 563-6, 572, 577, 587, 590, 595). This, however, seems to have been a mere *brutum fulmen*, as there is no allusion to any attempt to execute the sentence.

[245] Potthast No. 11040, 11041:—The usefulness of the Mendicants in aiding the papacy to unlimited domination is seen in the condemnation, by the University of Paris, in 1429, of the Franciscan Jean Sarrasin for publicly teaching that the whole jurisdiction of the Church is derived from the pope. He was forced to admit that it was bestowed by God on the several classes of the hierarchy, and that the authority of councils rested, not on the pope, but on the Holy Ghost and the Church (D'Argentré, Coll. Judic. de nov. Error. I. ii. 227).

[246] Richard, de S. Germano Chron. ann. 1229, 1239.—Potthast Regesta No. 10725, 13360.—Ripoll I. 158, 172.—Hist. Diplom. Frid. II. T. VI. pp. 405, 699-701, 710-11. Waddingi Annal. ann. 1246, No. 4; ann. 1253, No. 35-6.—Martene Ampliss. Coll. II. 1192.—Barbarano de' Mironi, Hist. Eccles. di Vicenza, II. 73.

[247] Potthast Regesta No. 7380, 8027, 8028, 10343, 10363, 10364, 10365, 10804, 10807, 10906, 10956, 10964, 11008, 11159.—Martene Thesaur. V. 1812.—Hist. Diplom. Frid. II. T. III. p. 416.—Gest. Archiep. Trevirens. c. 190-271.

[248] Martene Ampliss. Collect. I. 1146-9.—Innoc. PP. III. Regest. XV. 240.—Berger, Registres d'Innocent IV. No. 2712.

[249] Constit. Frat. Prædic. ann. 1228, Dist. II. cap. 32, 33 (Archiv. für Litt. und Kirchengeschichte, 1886, p. 224).—Innoc. PP. III. Regest. IX. 185.—S. Francis. Orac. XXII.—Ejusd. Regul. Sec. c. 9.—Stephan. de Borbone (D'Argentré, Collect. Judic. de nov. Error. I. I. 90-1).—Bern. Guidon. (Martene Ampl. Collect. VI. 530).—Potthast Regest. No. 6508, 6542, 6654, 6660, 7325, 7467, 7468, 7480, 7890, 10316, 10332, 10386, 10629, 10630, 10657, 10990, 10999, 11006, 11299, 15355, 16926, 16933.—Martene Thesaur. I. 954.—Concil. Narbonn. ann. 1227 c. 19.—Baluz. Concil. Gall. Narbon. App. pp. 156-9.

There were not many prelates like Robert Grosseteste of Lincoln, who wrote to both Jordan and Elias, the generals of the two Orders, to let him have friars, as his diocese was large and he required help in the duties of preaching and hearing confessions.—Fascic. Rer. Expetend. et Fugiend. II. 334-5. (Ed. 1690).

[250] Brev. Hist. Ord. Prædic. (Martene Ampl. Coll. VI. 357).—Extrav. Commun. Lib. III. Tit. vi. c. 8.—Concil. Nimociens. ann. 1298, c. 17.—Constit. Joann. Archiep. Nicos. ann. 1321, c. 10.—C. Avenionens. ann. 1326, c. 27; ann. 1337, c. 82.—C. Vaurens. ann. 1368, c. 63, 64.—Epistt. Sæculi XIII. T.I. No. 437 (Monument. Germ. Hist.).—Berger, Les Registres d'Innoc. IV. No. 1875-8, 3252-5, 3413.—Ripoll I. 25, 132-33, 153-4; II. 61, 173; VII. 18.—Matt. Paris ann. 1234, p. 276; ann. 1235, pp. 286-7; ann. 1255, p. 616.—Potthast Regesta No. 8786a, 8787-9, 10052.—Trithem. Annal. Hirsaug. ann. 1268.—Conc. Biterrens. ann. 1233, c. 9.—C. Arelatens. ann. 1234, c. 2.—C. Albiens. ann. 1254, c. 17, 18.—S. Bonaventuræ Libell. Apologet. Quæst. 1.—Abbat. Joachimi Concordiæ v. 49.

The details of the disgusting quarrels over the dying and dead are impressively set forth in a composition attempted by Boniface VIII., in 1303, between the clergy of Rome and the Mendicants (Ripoll II. 70). The constant litigation on the subject was one of the chief grievances of the spiritual section of the Franciscans (Hist. Tribulationum, *ap.* Archiv für Litteratur-u. Kirchengeschichte, 1886, p. 297).

[251] Alex. PP. Bull. *Quasi lignum vitæ.*—Waddingi Annal. ann. 1255, No. 2.—Dupin, Bib. des Auteurs Éccles. T. X. ch. vii.

For the exemption of students from secular jurisdiction see Berger, Registres d'Innocent IV. No. 1515.—Molinier (Guillem Bernard de Gaillac, Paris, 1884, pp. 26 sqq.) gives a good account of the educational organization of the Dominicans at this period.

[252] Waddingi Annal. ann. 1234, No. 4, 5; ann. 1255, No. 3.—Brev. Hist. Ord. Præd. (Martene Ampl. Coll. VI. 356-7).—Potthast Regesta No. 15562.—Matt. Paris, ann. 1253, p. 590.

William of St. Amour was a pluralist. Not satisfied with a canonry of Beauvais and a church with a cure of souls, we find him, in 1247, obtaining of Innocent IV. a dispensation to hold another cure.—Berger, Les Registres d'Innoc. IV. No. 3188.

[253] Waddingi Annal. ann. 1254, No. 3; ann. 1255, No. 5.—Brevis Historia (Martene VI. 357).—Martene Thesaur. I. 1059.

[254] Waddingi Annal. ann. 1254, No. 20; ann. 1255, No. 1.—Ripoll I. 266-7.

[255] Ripoll I. 289, 291, 296, 298, 301, 306, 308, 311, 312, 320, 322, 324, 333, 334, 336, 342, 345, 350.—Matt. Paris ann. 1255, pp. 611, 616.—Wadding. Annal. ann. 1255, No. 4; ann. 1256, No. 20-37.—Fasciculus Rer. Expetend. II. 18 sqq. Ed. 1690.—Mag. Bull. Roman. I. 112.—D'Argentré Collect. Judicior. de nov. Error. I. I. 170 sqq.—Guill. Nangiac. Gesta S. Ludov. ann. 1255.—Grandes Chroniques, IV. 373-4.—Bern. Guidon. Flor. Chron. (Bouquet, XXI. 698).

[256] Ripoll I. 346, 348, 349, 352-3, 372, 375-9.—Waddingi Annal. ann. 1256, No. 38; ann. 1257, No. 1-4, 6; ann. 1259, No. 3-6; ann. 1260, No. 10.—Clement. PP. IV. Bull. *Virtute conspicuos*, ann. 1265.—Dupin, Bib. des Auteurs Éccles. T.X. ch. vii.

When, in 1632, an edition of St. Amour's works was published in Constance (Paris) the Dominicans had sufficient influence with Louis XIII. to obtain its suppression in a savage edict. All the copies were seized: to retain one was punishable with a fine of three thousand livres, and it was declared a capital offence for a bookseller to have a single copy for sale (Mosheim de Beghardis, p. 27). The "Pericula Novissimorum Temporum" had, however, been printed, with two of St. Amour's sermons, by Wolfgang of Weissenburg in his "Antilogia Papæ," Basle, 1555, and this was reprinted in London in 1688, and embodied by Brown in his edition of the "Fasciculus Rerum Expetendarum et Fugiendarum" in 1690.

[257] Bonavent. Apol. Pauperum. Resp. I. c. 1.—Waddingi Annal. ann. 1269, No. 6-8.

[258] Ripoll I. 338.

[259] Clement PP. IV. Bull. *Providentia*, ann. 1268.—Ripoll I. 341, 344.—Ptol. Lucens. Hist. Eccles. Lib. XXIII. c. 21, 24-5.—Henr. Steronis Annal. ann. 1287, 1299.—Annal. Dominican. Colmariens. ann. 1277.—Waddingi Annal. ann. 1291, No. 97; ann. 1303, No. 32.—Concil. Valentin. ann. 1255.—Concil. Ravennat. ann. 1259.—Martene Ampliss. Collect. II. 1291.—Concil. Remens. ann. 1287.—Salimbene Chronica, pp. 371, 378-9.—Guillel. Nangiac. ann. 1298; Ejusd. Continuat. ann. 1351.—Revelat. S. Brigittæ Lib. VI. c. 63; cf. Lib. I. c. 41.—c. 2 Extravagant. Commun. III. vi.—c. 1. Ejusd. v. 7.—Ripoll II. 92-3.—P. de Herenthals Vit. Joann. XXII. ann. 1233.—Martene Thesaur. I. 1368.—c. 2 Extravagant. Commun. v. iii.—Alph. de Spina Fortalicium Fidei, fol. 61a (Ed. 1494).—Hecker, Epidemics of the Middle Ages, p. 30 (Babington's Transl.).—Fascic. Rer. Expetend. et Fugiend. II. 466 (Ed. 1690).—Theiner Monument. Hibern. et Scotor. No. 634, p. 313.—Cosentino, Archivio Storico Siciliano, 1886, p. 336.—Concil. Salisburgens. ann. 1386, c. 8.—Gudeni Cod. Diplom. III. 603.—D'Argentré, Collect. Judic. de Novis Error, I. II. 178.

During the Black Death, of one hundred and forty Dominicans at Montpellier, but seven survived; in Marseilles, of a hundred and sixty, not one. The mortality in the Franciscan Order was reckoned at one hundred and twenty-four thousand four hundred and thirty-four members, which is a manifest exaggeration.—Hoffman, Geschichte der Inquisition, II. 374-5.

[260] D'Argentré, Collect. Judic. de nov. Error. I. II. 180-4, 242, 251, 340, 347, 352, 354, 356.—Religieux de S. Denis, Hist. de Charles VI., Liv. XXIX. ch. 10.—Gersoni Sermo contra Bullam Mendicantium.—Alph. de Spina Fortalicium Fidei. fol. 61 (Ed. 1494).—C. 2 Extravagant. I. 9.—Ripoll III. 206, 256, 268.—Wadding. ann. 1457, No. 61.—H. Cornel. Agrippæ Epistt. II. 49.—Raynald. Annal. ann. 1515, No. 1.—Concil. Lateran. Sess. XI. (Harduin. IX. 1832).—Erasmi Epist. 10 Lib. XII. (Ed. 1642, pp. 585-6).

[261] Potthast Regest. No. 8326, 9172, 11299.—Martene Thesaur. V. 1816, 1820.

[262] S. Francis. Collat. Monast. Collat. XXI., XXV.—Ejusd. Prophet. XIV., XV.—Ejusd. Epist. 6, 7.—Pet. Rodulphii Hist. Seraph. Relig. Lib. I. fol. 177-8.—Th. de Eccleston de Adv. Minorum Collat. XII.—Waddingi Annal. ann. 1253, No. 30.—S. Bonavent. Opp. Ed. 1584, T.I. pp. 485-6.—Matt. Paris. ann. 1243 (p. 414).—S. Brigittæ Revelat. Lib. IV. c. 33.

[263] Bonavent. Vit. S. Francis, c. 9.—Lacordaire, Vie de S. Dominique, pp. 182-3.—Potthast Regest. No. 7429, 7490, 7537, 7550, 9130, 9139, 9141, 10350, 10383, 10421, 11297.—Raynald. ann. 1233, No. 22, 23; ann. 1237, No. 88.—Hist. Ordin. Prædicat. c. 8 (Martene Ampliss. Coll. VI. 338).—Chron. Magist. Ordin. Prædicat. c. 3 (Ibid. 350-1).—Waddingi Annal. ann. 1258, No. 1; ann. 1278, No. 10, 11, 12; ann. 1284, No. 2; ann. 1288, No. 3, 36; ann. 1289, No. 1; ann. 1294, No. 10-12; ann. 1492, No. 2; ann. 1493, No. 2-8.—Rodulphii Hist. Seraph. Relig. Lib. I. fol. 120.—Paramo de Orig. Offic. S. Inquisit. p. 238.

In 1246 Innocent IV. received a very civil letter from Melik el-Mansur Nassir, the ruler of Edessa, expressing his regret that mutual ignorance of each others' language prevented his engaging in theological disputation with the Dominicans sent for his conversion.—Berger, Registres d'Innoc. IV. No. 3031.

[264] Campana, Vita di San Piero Martire, p. 257.—Juan de Mata, Santoral de San Domingo y San Francisco, fol. 13.—Zurita, Añales de Aragon, Lib. II. c. 63.—Ricchinii Proœm. ad. Monetam, Dissert. I. p. xxxi.—Paramo de Orig. Off. S. Inquis. Lib. II. Tit. ii. c. 1.—Pegnæ Comment. in Eymeric. p. 461.—Chron. Magist. Ord. Prædic. c. 2 (Martene Ampl. Coll. VI. 348).—Monteiro, Historia da Santo Inquisição P. I. Liv. I. c. xxv., xlviii.

It is an interesting illustration of the softened temper of the nineteenth century to see, in 1842, the learned and zealous Dominican, Lacordaire, writing his "Vie de S. Dominique" to prove the impossibility of Dominic's participation in the cruelty of the Inquisition exactly one hundred years after an equally learned and zealous Dominican, Ricchini, had claimed the Inquisition as the glorious work of the saint. Yet since the time of Lacordaire there has been a reaction, and M. l'Abbé Douais does not hesitate to state, on the authority of Sixtus V., that "Saint Dominique aurait ainsi reçu une délégation pontificale pour l'Inquisition après l'année 1209" (Sources de l'Histoire de l'Inquisition, Revue des Questions Historiques, 1 Oct. 1881, p. 400).

[265] Gregor. PP. IX. Bull. *Ille humani generis*. Ap. 22, 1233.—Potthast Regesta, No. 9143, 9152, 9153, 9155, 9386, 9388, 9995, 10362.—Innoc. PP. IV. Bull. *Inter alia*, 20 Oct. 1248 (Baluze et Mansi I. 208).—Archives de l'Inq. de Carcassonne (Coll. Doat, XXXI. fol. 21).—Archives de l'Évêché d'Albi (Ib. XXXI. 255).

[266] Concil. Narbonn. ann. 1235.—Concil. Biterrens, ann. 1233; ann. 1246.—Concil. Albiens. ann. 1254 c. 17, 18.—Martene Thesaur. V. 1806, 1808-10, 1817, 1819-20.—Ripoll I. 38.—Aguirre Concil. Hispan. VI. 155-6.—Raynald. Annal. ann. 1233, No. 40, 59 sqq.—Waddingi Annal. ann. 1246, No. 2; ann. 1254, No. 7, 8; ann. 1257, No. 17; ann. 1259, No. 3; ann. 1277, No. 10; ann. 1286, No. 4; ann. 1288, No. 14-16.—Rodulphii Hist. Seraph. Relig. Lib. I. fol. 126*b*.—Potthast Regesta, No. 9386, 9388, 9762, 9766, 9993, 10052, 11245, 15304, 15330, 15069.

[267] MSS. Bib. Nat. Coll. Doat, XXI. 143; XXXII. 15.—Matt. Paris Hist. Angl. ann. 1243 (p. 414).—Guill. Pod. Laur. c. 43.—Raynald. ann. 1238, No. 51.—Harduin. Concil. VII. 1319.—Paramo de Orig. Inq. p. 244.—Wadding Annal. ann. 1238, No. 6, 7; ann. 1266, No. 8; ann. 1277, No. 10; ann. 1291, No. 14.—Potthast No. 16132.—Sixti PP. IV. Bull. *Sacri Prædicatorum*, 26 Jul. 1479.—Martene Thesaur. II. 346, 353, 359, 451.—Ripoll II. 82, 164, 617, 695.

The disturbances at Marseilles show the favoritism always manifested towards the Mendicants. Two clerks, whom the Dominicans had procured to depose falsely against the inquisitor, were punished with perpetual prison, degradation, and inability to hold benefices; the bishop who had listened to them was suspended from his office and jurisdiction, while the friars who had suborned the perjury and caused the whole trouble were let off with rendering humiliating apologies and transferred to another province. (Martene ubi sup.) There has been some dispute as to whether Frà Filippo Bonaccorso was a Franciscan or a Dominican. Wadding (l. c.) prints a bull of 1277 in which he is addressed as a Franciscan, but one in the Coll. Doat, T. XXXII. fol. 155, characterizes him as a Dominican.

[268] Anon. Cartus. de Relig. Orig. c. 309 (Martene Ampl. Coll. VI. 68).—Lib. Conformitatum, Lib. I. Fruct. ii. fol. 16*b*.—MSS. Bib. Bodleian., Arch. S. 130.

[269] S. Bernard. Serm. LXVI. in Cantic. c. 12.—Hist. Vizeliacens. Lib. IV.—Concil. Remens. ann. 1137 c. 1.—Cæsar. Heisterb. Dial. Mirac. III. 16, 17; v. 18.—Guibert. Noviogent. de Vita sua Lib. III. c. 18.—Pet. Cantor. Verb. abbrev. c. 78.—Innoc. PP. III. Regest. XIV. 138.—Alex. PP. III. Epist. 74.—C. 8 Extra V. XXXIV.—C. Lateran. IV. c. 18.

[270] Chron. Laudunens. Canon, ann. 1204 (D. Bouquet, XVIII. 713).—Chronolog. Roberti Autissiodor. ann. 1201.—Innocent PP. III. Regest. XIV. 15; XVI. 17.

[271] Martene Ampl. Collect. I. 776-8.—Alex. PP. III. Epist. 118, 122; Varior. ad Alex. III. Epist. 16.—Hist. Vizeliacens. Lib. IV.—Guibert. Noviogent. l. c.

[272] Hartzheim Concil. German. I. 76, 85-6.—Capit. Car. Mag. ann. 769, c. 6; Capit. II. ann. 813, c. 1.—Gratiani Decret. P. I. Dist. X. I have elsewhere considered in some detail the growth of the spiritual jurisdiction of the Church, through the False Decretals, in the anarchy accompanying the fall of the Carlovingian empire. See "Studies in Church History," 2d Ed. pp. 81-7, 326-39.

[273] S. Bernardi de Consideratione Lib. I. c. 4.—Rogeri Bacon Op. Tert. c. xxiv.—Pet. Blesens. Epist. 202.—Concil. Rotomag. ann. 1231 c. 48. For the rapidity with which the Church assimilated the Roman law see the collection of decretals by Alexander III. *post Concil. Lateran.*

[274] Fournier, Les Officialités du moyen âge, Paris, 1880, pp. 256 sqq., 273-4.—Cap. 19, 21, §§ 1, 2, Extra v. 1.

[275] Fr. 13, Dig. I. (Ulpian.).—Allard, Histoire des Persecutions, Paris, 1885, p. iii.—Capit. Car. Mag. I. ann. 802; III.. ann. 810; III. ann. 812.—Capit. Ludov. Pii V., VI. ann. 819; ann. 823, c. 28; Capit. Wormatiens. ann. 829.—Caroli Calvi Capit. apud Carisiacum ann. 857; Edict. Pistens. ann. 864.—Carolomanni Capit. ann. 884.—Guillel. Nangiac. Gest. S. Ludov. ann. 1255 (D. Bouquet, XX. 394, 400).—Ducange, s. v. *Inquisitores*.—Les Olim, T. III. pp. 169, 181, 211, 231, 358, 471, 501, 522, 529, 616.—Assisæ de Clarendon § 1 (Stubbs's Select Charters, p. 137, cf. p. 25).—Stubbs's Constitutional History, I. 99-100, 313, 530, 695-6.—Lib. Juris Civilis Veronæ c. 171 (Ed. 1728, p. 130).—Carta de Logu cap. xvi.(Ed. 1805, pp. 30-2).

[276] Reginon. de Eccles. Discip. Lib. II. c. 1-3.—Burchardi Decret. Lib. I. c. 91-4.—Gratiani Decret. P. II. c. XXXV. Q. vi. c. 7.—C. 7 Extra II. xxi.—Matt. Paris ann. 1246 (Ed. 1644, p. 480).

[277] Lucii PP. III. Epist. 171.

[278] Concil. Avenionens. ann. 1209 c. 2.—Concil. Monspessulan. ann. 1215 c. 46.—Douais, Les sources de l'histoire de l'Inquisition (Revue des Questions Historiques, 1 Oct. 1881, p. 401).—C. Lateran. IV. c. 2.

[279] Concil. Narbonn. ann. 1227 c. 14.—Lucæ Tudens. de altera Vita c. 19.—Concil. Biterrens. ann. 1234 c. 5.

[280] Potthast No. 7260.—Concil. Tolosan. ann. 1229 c. 1, 2.—Guill. de Pod. Laur. c. 40.—Guill. Pelisso Chron. Ed. Molinier, p. 18.

[281] Concil. Arelatens. ann. 1234 c. 5.—Concil. Turonens. ann. 1239 c. 1.—Concil. Biterrens. ann. 1246 c. 1.—Concil. Albiens. ann. 1254 c. 1.—Archives de l'Inq. de Carcassonne (Coll. Doat, XXX. 250).—Vaissette, III. Pr. pp. 385-6.—Raynald Annal. ann. 1237, No. 32.—Archives de France, J. 430, No. 19-20.—Archivio di Firenze, Riformagioni, Classe v. fol. 80.—Archives de l'Inq. de Carcassonne (Doat, XXXI. 230).

[282] Lami, Antichità Toscane, pp. 484, 504, 524.—Muratori Antiq. Ital. Diss. LX. (T. XII. p. 447).—D'Achery Spicileg. III. 588, 598.—Charvaz, Origine dei Valdesi, Torino, 1838, App. No. xxii.—Isambert, Anc. Loix Fran. I. 228.—Corio, Hist. Milanese, ann. 1228-9.—Hist. Diplom. Frid. II. T. III. p. 466.

[283] De Lagrèze, La Navarre Française, I. xxi; II. 6.—Concil. Lateran. IV. c. 3 (C. 13 Extra v. vii.).

[284] Hist. Diplom. Frid. II. T. II. pp. 4-6, 422; T. IV. pp. 6-8, 299-302; T. V. pp. 201, 279-80. The coronation-edict, which formed the basis of all subsequent legislation against heresy, was drawn up by the papal curia, and sent, a fortnight before the ceremony, to the Legate Bishop of Tusculum, with orders to procure the imperial signature and return it, so that it could be published under the emperor's name in the church of St. Peter (Raynald. ann. 1220, No. 19.—Hist. Dipl. I. II. 880). Nothing could seem a plainer duty to an ecclesiastic of the time than that the Church should stimulate the temporal ruler to the sharpest persecution of heresy.

It was doubtless the outlawry of heretics pronounced by the edicts of Frederic which enabled the Inquisition to establish the settled principle that the heretic could be captured and despoiled at any time and by any person, and that the spoiler could retain his goods—provided always that he was not an official of the Holy Office (Tract. de Inquisitione, Doat, XXXVI.).

[285] Hist. Diplom. Frid. II. T. II. p. 7.—Post Libb. Feudorum.—Post constt. iv. xix. Cod. I. v.—Innoc. PP. IV. Bull. *Cum adversus*, 1243, 1252, 1254; Bull. *Orthodoxæ*, 27 Apr., 14 Maii, 1252.—Alex. PP. IV. Bull. *Cum adversus*, 1258.—Ejusd. Bull. *Cupientes*, 1260.—Clement. PP. IV. Bull. *Cum adversus*, 1265.—Wadding. Annal. Minor. ann. 1261, No. 3; ann. 1289, No. 20.—Urbani PP. IV. Bull. *Licet ex omnibus*, 1262, § 12.—Epistt. Sæculi XIII. No. 191 (Monument. Hist. German.).—Eymerici Direct. Inquis. Ed. Pegnæ, 1607, p. 392.—Innoc. PP. IV. Bull. *Ad aures*, 2 Apr. 1253.—Sclopis, Antica Legislazione del Piemonte, p. 440.—Bernardi Comens. Lucerna Inquisit. s.v. *Executio*, No. 3.—Archivio di Firenze, Riformagioni, Classe II. Distinz. 1, No. 14.—Potthast No. 7672.—C. 2 in Septimo, v. 3.

[286] Isambert, Anc. Loix Fran. I. 230-33; III. 126.—Harduin. Concil. VII. 203-8.—Guill. de. Pod. Laur. c. 42.—Établissements, Liv. I. ch. 85, 123.—Livres de Jostice et de Plet, Liv. I. Tit. iii. § 7.

[287] Archives Nat. de France, J. 426, No. 4.—Martene Ampliss. Collect. VII. 123-4.—Bernard. Guidon. Practica P. IV. (Coll. Doat, XXX.).—Clem. PP. IV. Bull. *Præ cunctis*, 23 Feb. 1266.

In 1229 the Council of Toulouse had already prohibited all laymen from possessing any of the Scriptures, even in Latin (Concil. Tolosan. ann. 1229, c. 14).

[288] Raynald. Annal. ann. 1231, No. 13, 18.—Ripoll I. 38.—Ricobaldi Ferrar. Hist. Impp. ann. 1234.—Paramo de Orig. Offic. S. Inq. p. 177.—Richardi di S. Germano Chron. ann. 1231.—C. 15 Extra v. vii. (In this canon "noluerint" is evidently an error for "voluerint").—Hartzheim Concil. German. III. 540.

[289] Constit. Sicular. Lib. I. Tit. 1.—Hist. Diplom. Frid. II. T. IV. pp. 435, 444.—Rich. de S. Germano Chron. ann. 1233.—Giannone, Istoria Civile di Napoli, Lib. XVII. c. 6; XIX. 5.

[290] Lami, Antichità Toscane, pp. 493-4, 509-10, 546.

[291] Lami op. cit. 511, 519-22, 528, 531, 543-4, 546-7, 554, 557, 559.—Archiv. di Firenze. Prov. S. Maria Novella 1227, Giugn. 20; 1229, Giugn. 24; 1235, Agost. 23.—Ughelli, Italia Sacra, III. 146-7.—Ripoll I. 69, 71.

[292] Ripoll I. 45, 47.—C. 8 § 8, Sexto v. 2.—Gregor. PP. XI. Bull. *Ille humani generis; Licet ad capiendos*.—Potthast No. 9143, 9152, 9235.—Arch. de l'Inq. de Carcassonne (Doat, XXXI. 21, 25).

[293] Potthast No. 9263; cf. No. 9386, 9388.—Guill. de Pod. Laur. c. 43.—Coll. Doat, XXI. 143, 153.—Ripoll I. 66.

Guillem Arnaud generally qualifies himself as acting under commission from the legate, but sometimes as appointed by the Dominican provincial. In several sentences on the Seigneurs de Niort, in February and March, 1236, he acts with the Archdeacon of Carcassonne, both under legatine authority. As yet there was evidently no settled organization (Coll. Doat, XXI. 160, 163, 165, 166).

[294] Vaissette, III. Pr. 364, 370-1.—Concil. Tolosan. ann. 1229.—Concil. Biterrens. ann. 1234.—Concil. Arelatens. ann. 1234.—Concil. Narbonn. ann. 1244.—Coll. Doat, XXI. 143, 155, 158.

[295] Vaissette, III. 452.—Concil. Biterrens. ann. 1246.—Berger, Les Registres d'Innocent IV. No. 2043, 3867, 3868.—Arch. de l'Inq. de Carcass. (Doat, XXXI. 68, 74, 75, 77, 80, 152, 182).—Potthast No. 12744, 15805.—MSS. Bib. Nat., fonds latin, No. 9992.—Concil. Valentin. ann. 1248 c. 10.—Baluz. Conc. Narbonn. App. p. 100.

The system devised by the councils of Languedoc became generally current. In 1248 Innocent IV. ordered the Archbishop and Inquisitor of Narbonne to send a copy of their rules of procedure to the Provincial of Spain and Raymond of Pennaforte, to be followed in the Peninsula (Baluz. et Mansi I. 208); and their canons are frequently cited in the manuals of the mediæval Inquisition.

[296] Concil. Biterrens. ann. 1246.—Arch. de l'Inq. de Carcass. (Doat. XXVII. 7, 156; XXX. 107-9; XXXI. 149, 180, 216).—Vaissette, III. Pr. 479, 496-7.—Martene Thesaur. I. 1045.—Ripoll I. 194.—Innoc. PP.

IV. Bull. *Licet ex omnibus*, 30 Mai, 1254.—Concil. Albiens. ann. 1254 c. 24.—Alex. PP. IV. Bull. *Licet ex omnibus*, 20 Jan. 1257; Ejusd. Bull. *Ad capiendum*, ann. 1257.—Clement. PP. IV. Bull. *Licet ex omnibus*, 17 Sept. 1265.— Gregor. PP. X. Bull. *Præ cunctis mentis*, 20 Apr. 1273.—Lib. Sententt. Inq. Tolosan. *passim.*—C. 17 Sexto v. 2.— Eymeric. Direct. Inq. p. 580.—Albert. Repert. Inq. s. v. *Episcopus.*—Zanchini Tract. de Hæret.XV.—Isambert, II. 747.—Pegnæ Comment, in Eymeric. p. 578.

[297] Wadding. Annal. Minorum ann. 1288, No. 17.—C. 1 Extrav. Commun. v. iii.

[298] Innoc. PP. IV. Bull. *Ad extirpanda*, ann. 1252 (Mag. Bull. Roman. I. 91).—Ejusd. Bull.*Orthodoxæ*, 1252 (Ripoll I. 208, cf. VII. 28).—Ejusd. Bull. *Ut commissum*, 1254 (Ibid. I. 250).—Ejusd. Bull. *Volentes*, 1254 (Ib. I. 251).—Ejusd. Bull. *Cum venerabilis*, 1253 (Mag. Bull. Roman. I. 93-4).—Ejusd. Bull. *Cum in constitutionibus*, 1254 (Pegnæ App. p. 19).—Alex. PP. IV. Bull.*Cum secundum*, 1255 (M. B. R. I. 106).—Ejusd. Bull. *Exortis in agro*, 1256 (Pegnæ App. p. 20).—Ejusd. Bull. *Exortis in agris*, 1256 (Ripoll I. 297).—Ejusd. Bull. *Delecti filii*, 1256 (Ripoll I. 312).—Ejusd. Bull. *Cum vos*, 1256 (Ripoll I. 314).—Ejusd. Bull. *Fœlicis recordationis*, 1257 (M. B. R. I. 106).— Ejusd. Bull.*Implacida*, 1257 (M. B. R. I. 113).—Ejusd. Bull. *Implacida*, 1258 (Potthast No. 17302).—Ejusd. Bull. *Ad extirpanda*, 1259 (Pegnæ App. p. 30).—Clement. PP. IV. Bull. *Ad extirpanda*, 1265 (M. B. R. I. 148-51).— Ejusd. Bull. *Ad extirpanda*, 1266 (Pegnæ App. p. 43).—Archivio di Firenze, Riformagioni, Classe II. Distinzione, 1, No. 14.

About 1330 Bernard Gui (Practica P. IV.—Coll. Doat, XXX.) quotes the provisions of the bull as still among the privileges of the Italian inquisitors.

[299] Bernard. Guidon. Gravamina (Coll. Doat, XXX. 90 sqq.).—Concil. Narbonn. ann. 1229 c. 1, 2.— Concil. Albiens. ann. 1254 c. 3, 5, 8.—Archives de l'Inq. de Carcass. (Doat, XXX. 110-11, 127; XXXI. 250).— Vaissette, III. Pr. 528-9, 536.—Archivio di Napoli, Registro 6, Lett. D. fol. 180.—Eymerici Direct. Inquis. pp. 390-1, 560-1.—Bernardi Guidon. Practica P. IV. (Doat, XXX.).

It was sometimes a work of some labor and time for the inquisitor to obtain his royal letters-patent. When, in 1269, the Franciscans Bertrand de Roche and Ponce des Rives were appointed inquisitors of Forcalquier, they were obliged to travel to Palermo, where Charles of Anjou happened to be residing, and whence he gave them letters, August 4, 1269, to his seneschal and other officials.—Archivio di Napoli, Registro 6, Lett. D, fol. 180.—Cf. Regist. 20, Lett. B, fol. 91.

[300] Mag. Bull. Roman. I. 118.—C. 9 Sexto v. 1.—Zanchini Tract, de Hæret. c. xxxi.—Cf. Eymerici Direct. Inq. p. 561.—Bernardi Comens. Lucerna Inquisit. s. v. *Statutum.*

[301] Bernard. Guidon. Gravam. (Doat, XXX. 107-9).—Alex. PP. IV. Bull. *Cupientes*, 15 Apr. 1255; Ejusd. Bull. *Exortis in agro*, 15 Mar. 1256.

[302] Pegnæ Append. ad Eymeric. pp. 37-8.—Zanchini Tract, de Hæret. c. xxxvii.

[303] Arch. Nat. de France, J. 431, No. 23.—Innoc. PP. IV. Bull. *Devotionis*, 2 Mai. 1245 (Coll. Doat, XXXI. 70).—Berger, Registres d'Innoc. IV. No. 1963.—Ripoll I. 132; II. 594, 610, 644.—Alex. PP. IV. Bull. *Ut negotium*, 5 Mart. 1261.—Urbani PP. IV. Bull. *Ut negotium*, 4 Aug. 1262.—Mag. Bull. Roman. I. 116, 120, 126, 139, 267, 420.—C. 10 Sexto v. 2.—Potthast No. 13057, 18389, 18419, 19559.—Bern. Guidon. Practica P. IV. (Doat, XXX.).—Eymeric. Direct. Inquis. pp. 136, 137.

It is curious that the question whether the commission of an inquisitor did not expire with the death of the appointing pope was still considered in doubt as late as 1290, when it was settled in favor of permanence by Nicholas IV. in the bull *Ne aliqui* (Potthast No. 23302). In the earlier period Alexander IV. shortly after his accession, in 1255, considered it necessary to renew the commission of even so distinguished an inquisitor as Rainerio Saccone (Ripoll I. 275).

[304] Coll. Doat, XXXI. 73; XXXII. 15, 105.—Alex. PP. IV. Bull. *Odore suavi*, 13 Mai. 1256; Ejusd. Bull. *Catholicæ fidei*, 15 Jul. 1257; Ejusd. Bull. *Quod super nonnullis*, 9 Dec. 1257; Ejusd. Bull. *Meminimus*, 13 Apr. 1258.—Clem. PP. IV. Bull. *Licet ex omnibus*, 30 Sept. 1265.—C. 1, 2, Clementin. v. 2.—Bern. Guidon. Gravam. (Doat, XXX. 114).

[305] Wadding, ann. 1323, No. 17; ann. 1327, No. 5; ann. 1339, No. 1; ann. 1347, No. 10, 11; ann. 1375, No. 30; ann. 1432, No. 10, 11; ann. 1474, No. 17-19.—Archivio di Firenze, Prov. del Convento di S. Croce 26 Ott. 1439.—Ripoll II. 324, 421, 570-1.—Sixti PP. IV. Bull. *Sacri*, 16 Jul. 1479, § 11.

[306] Eymeric. pp. 540-9, 553.—Archivio di Firenze, Prov. del. Conv. di. S. Croce, 16 Apr. 1418.

[307] Eymerici Direct. Inquis. p. 559.—Greg. PP. X. Bull. 20 Apr. 1273 (Martene Thes. V. 1821).— Zanchini de Hæret. c. viii.—Johann. PP. XXII, Bull. *Ex parte vestra*, 3 Jul. 1322 (Wadding. III. 291).—C. 16 Sexto V. 2.—C. 3 Extrav. Commun. V. 3.—Arch. de l'Inq. de Carcassonne (Doat, XXVII. 204).

[308] Pegnæ App. ad Eymeric. pp. 66-7.—Arch. de l'Inq. de Carcass. (Doat, XXXII. 143, 147).— Eymeric. Direct. Inq. pp. 537-8.—Albert. Repert. Inq. Ed. 1494, s.v. *Delegatus.*—Franz Ehrle, Archiv für Litteratur-u. Kirchengeschichte, 1886, p. 158.—Lami, Antichità Toscane, p. 583.—Archivio di Firenze, Riformagioni, Classe V. No. 129, fol. 46, 62-70.—Martene Ampl. Collect. VI. 344.

[309] MSS. Bib. Nat., fonds latin, No. 4270, fol. 146. In the trial of Friar Bernard Délicieux, in 1319, it was held that he was guilty of "impeding" the Inquisition because, among other acts, he had been concerned in enlarging somewhat the powers of the agents appointed by the city of Albi to prosecute their appeal to Pope Clement V. against their bishop and inquisitor (Ib. fol. 165).

215

[310] Concil. Turonens. ann. 1239 c. 1.—C. Biterrens. ann. 1246 c. 1.—C. Albiens. ann. 1254 c. 1, 21.—C. Insulan. ann. 1251 c. 2.—Tract. de Paup. de Lugduno (Martene Thesaur. V. 1793).

[311] Arch. de l'Inq. de Carcass. (Doat, XXXV. 85, 184).—Ripoll II. 299, 311; III. 135.

[312] D'Argentré, Collect. Judic. I. I. 185, 234.—Harduin. Concil. VII. 1065-8, 1864.—Capgrave's Chronicle, ann. 1286.—Nic. Trivetti Chron. ann. 1222 (D'Achery III. 188).—Bracton. Lib. III. Tit. ii. cap. 9, § 2.—Myrror of Justice, cap. I. § 4, cap. II. § 22; cap. IV. § 14.—5 Rich. II. c. 5.—Rymer's Fœdera, VII. 363, 447, 458.—2 Henr. IV. c. 15.—Concil. Oxoniens. ann. 1408 c. 13.—2 Henr. V. c. 7.—25 Henr. VIII. c. 14.—1 Edw. VI. c. 12, § 3.—1 Eliz. c. 1, § 15.—29 Car. II. c. 9.—London Athenæum, May 31, 1873; Nov. 29, 1884.

[313] Wright, Proceedings against Dame Alice Kyteler, Camden Soc. 1843.—Wadding. Annal. ann. 1317, No. 56; ann. 1335, No. 5, 6.—Theiner Monument. Hibern. et Scotor. No. 531-2, p. 269; No. 570-1, p. 286; No. 599, p. 299.

[314] Wadding. Annal. ann. 1421, No. 1.

[315] Paramo, pp. 252-3.—Monteiro, Historia da Santo Inquisição, P. I. Lib. I. c. 59.—Ripoll II. 299, 310; III. 9, 110.

[316] Wadding, ann. 1290, No. 2; ann. 1375, No. 27, 28.

It is worthy of note that in the Latin kingdom of Jerusalem heresy seems to have been justiciable by the lay court, and the heretic knight was entitled to be judged by his peers.—Assises de Jerusalem, Haute Court, c. 318 (Ed. Kausler, Stuttgart, 1838, p. 367-8).

[317] Trésor des Chartes du Roi en Carcassonne (Doat, XXI. 34-49).—Lib. Confess. Inquis. Albiæ (MSS. Bib. Nat., fonds latin, 11847).—Archives Nat. de France, J. 431, No. 22-29.—Vaissette, III. 446.—Coll. Doat, XXVII. 161.—Molinier, L'Inquisition dans le midi de la France, Paris, 1880, pp. 275-6.

[318] Mag. Bull. Roman. I. 122.—Wadding. Annal. ann. 1265, No. 3.—Arch. de l'Inq. de Carcassonne (Coll. Doat, XXXII. 32).—Martene Thesaur. V. 1818—C. 17 Sexto v. 2.—C. 1 Extrav. Comm. v. 3.—Eymeric. Direct. Inquis. pp. 539, 580-1.—C. 1, § 1, Clement, v. 3.

Urban's bull of 1262 is virtually the same as his "*Præ cunctis*" of 1264, printed by Boutaric, Saint-Louis et Alph. de Toulouse, pp. 443 sqq.

[319] Vaissette, III. 515.—Archidiac. Gloss. sup. c. 17, 20 Sexto v. 2.—Harduin. VII. 1017-19.—C. 17, 19 Sexto v. 2.—C. 1, Clement, v. 3.—Concil. Melodun. ann. 1300, No. 4.—Bernard. Guidon. Hist. Conv. Albiens. (Bouquet, XXI. 767).—Albert. Repert. Inquis. s.v. *Episcopus*.—Guid. Fulcod. Quæst. I.—Ripoll I. 512; VII. 53.—Joann. Andreæ Gloss, sup. c. 13 § 8 Extra, v. vii.—Eymeric. Direct. Inquis. pp. 626, 637, 650.—C. 1 Extrav. commun. v. 3.—Bernard. Guidon. Practica P. IV. (Doat, XXX.).—Bernardi Comens. Lucerna Inquis. s.v. *Bona hæreticorum*.

As early as 1257 we find that the Inquisition had already extended its jurisdiction over usury as heresy (Alex. PP. IV. Bull. *Quod super nonnullis* [Arch. de l'Inq. de Carcass. Doat, XXXI. 244]—a bull which was repeatedly reissued. See Raynald. Annal. ann. 1258, No. 23; Potthast Regesta 17745, 18396; Eymeric. Direct. Inquis. Ed. Pegnæ, p. 133. Cf. c. 8 § 5 Sexto v. 2). The Council of Lyons, in 1274 (can. 26, 27), in treating of usury, alludes only to its punishment by the Ordinaries. The Council of Vienne, in 1311, directed inquisitors to prosecute those who maintained that usury is not sinful (c. 1 § 2 Clementin. v. 5); but Eymerich (Direct. Inquis. p. 106) deprecates attention to such matters as an interference with the real business of the Inquisition. Zanghino lays down the rule that a man may be a public usurer, or blasphemer, or fornicator without being a heretic, but if he, in addition, manifests contempt for religion by not frequenting divine service, receiving the sacrament, observing the fasts and other ordinances of the Church, he becomes suspect of heresy, and can be prosecuted by the inquisitors (Zanchini Tract. de Hæres. c. XXXV.).

We shall see that usury became a very profitable subject of exploitation by the Inquisition when the diminution of heresy deprived it of its legitimate field of action. As the offence was one cognizant by the secular courts (see Vaissette, IV. 164), there was really no excuse for the exercise of spiritual jurisdiction over it.

[320] Coll. Doat, XXVII. 7; XXXIV. 87.—Concil. Bergamens. ann. 1311, Rubr. 1.—MSS. Bib. Nat. Coll. Moreau. 1274, fol. 72.—Lib. Sententt. Inq. Tolosan, pp. 268, 282, 351-2.

[321] W. Preger, Meister Eckart und die Inquisition, München, 1869.—Denifle, Archiv für Litteratur-und Kirchengeschichte, 1886, pp. 616, 640.—Raynald. ann. 1329, No. 70-2.—Gustav Schmidt, Päbstliche Urkunden und Regesten, Halle, 1886, p. 223.—Cf. Eymeric. Direct. Inquis. pp. 453 sqq.

The power of the Inquisition over the specially exempted orders of the Mendicants varied at times. Jurisdiction was conferred by Innocent IV., in 1254, by the bull *Ne comissum vobis* (Ripoll I. 252). About two hundred years later, Pius II. placed the Franciscans under the jurisdiction of their own minister-general. In 1479 Sixtus IV., by the golden bull *Sacri prædicatorum*, § 12, forbade all inquisitors from prosecuting members of the other Order (Mag. Bull. Roman. I. 420). Soon afterwards Innocent VIII. prohibited all inquisitors from trying Franciscan friars; but, with the rise of Lutheranism, this became inexpedient, and in 1530 Clement VII., in the bull *Cum sicut*, § 2, removed all exemptions, and again made all justiciable by the Inquisition (Mag. Bull. Rom. I. 681), which was repeated by Pius IV. in the bull *Pastoris æterni*, in 1562 (Eymeric. Direct. Inq. Append. p. 127; Pegnæ Comment. p. 557).

Whether a bishop could proceed against an inquisitor for heresy was a debatable question, and one probably never practically tested. Eymerich holds that he could not, but must refer the matter to the pope; but Pegna, in his commentaries, quotes good authorities to the contrary (Eymeric. op. cit. pp. 558-9).

[322] Concil. Parisiens, ann. 1350 c. 3, 4.—Arch, de l'Inq. de Carcassonne (Doat, XXXV. 132).—Archives de l'Évêché d'Albi (Doat, XXXV. 187).—Eymerici Direct. Inquis. p. 529.—Sprengeri Mall. Maleficar. P. III. Q. 1.—Ripoll II. 311, 324, 351.—Cornel. Agrippæ de Vanitate Scientiarum, cap. XCVI. Yet a bull of Nicholas V. to the inquisitor of France in 1451 seems to render him independent of episcopal co-operation (Ripoll III. 301).

[323] C. 17 Sexto v. 2.—See the "Modus examinandi hæreticos" printed by Gretser (Mag. Bib. Patrum XIII. 341) prepared for a German episcopal Inquisition.

[324] Coll. Doat, XXXVII. 7; XXIX. 5.

[325] Coll. Doat, XXX. 132; XXXII. 155.

[326] Coll. Doat, XXXV. 18.

[327] Bern. Guidon. Practica P. IV. ad finem (Doat, XXX.). This sketch of the model inquisitor seems to have been a favorite. I find it in another MS. Tractatus de Inquisitione (Doat, XXXVI.).

[328] Gregor. PP. IX. Bull. Ille humani generis, 20 Mai. 1236 (Eymeric. App. p. 3).—Vaissette, III. 410-11.—Guill. Pod. Laur. c. 43.—Concil. Biterrens. ann. 1246, Append, c. 1.—Arch. de l'Inq. de Carcassonne (Doat, XXXI. 5).—Raynald. ann. 1243, No. 31.—Innoc. PP. IV. Bull. Quia sicut, 19 Nov. 1247 (Potthast 12766.—Doat, XXXI. 5).—Ejusd. Bull. Ad extirpanda § 31.—Anon. Passaviens. (Mag. Bib. Pat. XIII. 308).—Doctrina de modo procedendi (Martene Thesaur. V. 1809-11).—Alex. PP. IV. Bull. Cupientes, 4 Mart. 1260 (Mag. Bull. Rom. I. 119).—Ripoll I. 128.—Guill. Pelisso Chron. Ed. Molinier, p. 27.—Bernardi Guidon. Practica P. IV. (Doat, XXX.).—Eymeric. Direct. Inquis. pp. 407-9.—MSS. Bib. Nat., fonds latin, No. 14930, fol. 220.

[329] Guill. Pod. Laur. c. 43.—Vaissette, III. 402, 403, 404; Pr. 386.—Raynald. ann. 1243, No. 31.—Concil. Narbonn. ann. 1244 c. 1.—Concil, Biterrens. ann. 1246, Append. c. 2, 5.—Arch. de l'Inq. de Carc. circa 1245 (Doat, XXXI. 5).—Guid. Fulcod. Quæst. IT.—Bern. Guidon. Practica P. IV. (Doat, XXX.).—Eymerici Direct. Inquis. pp. 407-9.—Practica super Inquisit. (MSS. Bib. Nat., fonds latin, No. 14930, fol. 227-8).—Archivio Storico Italiano, 1865, No. 38, pp. 16-17.

[330] B. Guidon, loc. cit—Ripoll I. 46.

[331] C. 2 Clement, v. iii.—Bern. Guidon Gravam. (Doat, XXX. 117, 128).—Ripoll II. 610.—In 1431 Eugenius IV. dispensed with the rule in the case of an inquisitor appointed in his thirty-sixth year (Ripoll III. 9).

[332] Concil. Biterrens. ann. 1246 c. 4.—Molinier, pp. 129, 131, 281-2.—Hauréau, Bernard Délicieux, p. 20.—Wadding. Annal. ann. 1261, No. 2.—Urbani PP. IV. Bull. Ne catholicæ fidei, 26 Oct. 1262.—Bernardi Guidonis Practica, P. IV. (Doat, XXX.).—Eymerici Direct. Inq. p. 557, 577.—Archivio di Napoli, MSS. Chioccarello T. VIII.; Ibid. Registro 6, Lett. D. f. 35.

[333] C. 11, 19, 20 Extra I. 29.—Concil. Biterrens. ann. 1246 c. 3.—Coll. Doat, XXV. 230.—Urbani PP. IV. Bull. Licet ex omnibus, 20 Mart. 1262.—Guid. Fulcod. Quæst. IV.—C. 11 Sexto v. 2.—C. 2 Clement. v. 3.—Bernardi Guidon. Practica P. IV. (Doat, XXX.).—Eymerici Direct, pp. 403-6.—Zanchini Tract. de Hæret. c. xxx.

It is not easy to understand why, in 1276, the Lombard Inquisitors Frà Niccolò da Cremona and Frà Daniele Giussano assembled experts in Piacenza to determine whether they had power to appoint delegates, when the question was decided in the negative (Campi, Dell' Historia Ecclesiastica di Piacenza, P. II. p. 308-9).

[334] Archives de l'Évêché d'Albi (Doat, XXXV. 136, 187).—Zanchini Tract. de Hæret. c.XV.—Eymerici Direct. p. 407.

[335] Coll. Doat, XXII. 237 sqq.—Innoc. PP. IV. Bull. Licet ex omnibus, 30 Mai. 1254.—Bernardi Guidon. Practica P. IV. (Doat, XXX.).—Clement PP. IV. Bull. Præ cunctis, 23 Feb. 1266.—C. 11, § 1 Sexto v. 2.—Concil. Biterrens. ann. 1246 c. 4.—Alex. PP. IV. Bull. Præ cunctis, 9 Nov. 1256.—Archives de l'Inq. de Carcassonne (Doat, XXXIV. 11).—Molinier, L'Inquis. dans le midi de la France, pp. 219, 287.—Eymeric. Direct. Inq. p. 426.

[336] Bern. Guidon. Practica P. IV. (Doat, XXX.).—Urbani PP. IV. Bull. Licet ex omnibus, ann. 1263, §§ 6, 7, 8 (Mag. Bull. Roman. I. 122).—C. 1 § 3 Clement v. 3.—Coll. Doat, XXX. 109-10.—Eymeric. Direct. Inq. p. 550.

The peculiar importance attached to the notariate and the limitations imposed on its membership are seen in the papal privileges issued for the appointment of notaries. Thus there is one of November 27, 1295, by Boniface VIII. to the Archbishop of Lyons authorizing him to create five; one of January 28, 1296, to the Bishop of Arras to create three, and one of January 22, 1296, to the Bishop of Amiens to create two. (Thomas, Registres de Boniface VIII., I. No. 640 bis, 660, 678 bis.)

In 1286 the Provincial of France complained to Honorius IV. of the scarcity of notaries in that kingdom, and was authorized to create two (Ripoll II. 16).

[337] Guill. Pelisso Chron. Ed. Molinier p. 28.—Concil. Narbonn. ann. 1244 c. 6.—Concil. Biterrens. ann. 1246 c. 31, 37.—Concil. Albiens. ann. 1254 c. 21.—Alex. PP. IV. Bull. Licet vobis, 7 Dec. 1255; Ejusd. Bull. Præ cunctis, 9 Nov. 1255, 13 Dec. 1255.—Lib. Sentt. Inq. Tolosan. pp. 198-9.—Coll. Doat, XXXIV. 104.

[338] Arch. de l'Inq. de Carcass. (Doat, XXXIV. 123).—Ripoll I. 356, 396.—Vaissette, III. 406; Pr. 467.—Coll. Doat, XXXI. 105, 149.—Molinier, p. 35.—Bern. Guidon. Hist. Conv. Carcass, (D. Bouquet, XXI. 743).—Lib. Sentent. Inquis. Tolos. p. 232.

[339] Paramo de Orig. Offic. S. Inquis. p. 102.—Pegnæ Comment, in Eymeric. p. 584.—Arch. de l'Inq. de Carcassonne (Doat, XXXI. 70; XXXII. 143).

[340] Statuta Pistoriensia, c. 109 (Zachariæ Anect. Med. Ævi, p. 23).—Lib. Juris civilis Veronæ, ann. 1228, c. 104, 183 (Veronæ, 1728).—Statut. criminal. Communis Bononiæ, Ed. 1525, fol. 36 (cf. Barbarano de' Mironi, Hist. Eccles. di Vicenza, II. 69).—Antiqua Ducum Mediolan. Decreta (Ed. 1654, p. 95).—Statuta Criminalia Mediolani, Bergomi, 1594, cap. 127.—Actes du Parl. de Paris, I. 257.—Vaissette, Éd. Privat, X. Pr. 610.

[341] Arch. de l'Inq. de Carcass. (Doat, XXXI. 81).—Archivio di Napoli, MSS. Chioccarello T. VIII.; Registro 3, Lett. A, fol. 64; Registro 6, Lett. D, fol. 35.—Coll. Doat, XXX. 119-20.—C. 2 Clement, v. 3.—Johann. PP. XXII. Bull. *Exegit ordinis*, 2 Mai. 1321.—Archivio di Firenze, Riformagioni, Archiv. Diplom. XXVII., LXXVIII.-IX.; Riform. Classe. II. Distinz. 1, No. 14.—Villani, Cronica, Lib. XII. c. 58.—Archivio di Venezia, Misti, Cons. X. Vol. XIII. p. 192; Vol. XIV. p. 29.—Eymeric. Direct. Inq. pp. 374-5.—Bernard. Guidonis Practica P. IV. (Doat, XXX.).—Zanchini Tract. de Hæret. c. xxxi.—Urbani PP. IV. Bull. *Licet ex omnibus*, 1262 (Mag. Bull. Rom. I. 123).—Bernardi Comens. Lucerna Inquisit. s.v. *Inquisitores*, No. 14.

For further authorities on the subject, see Farinacii de Hæresi Quæst. 182, No. 89-94.

[342] Concil. Albiens. ann. 1254 c. 7.—Eymeric. Direct. Inquis. 392-402.—Gloss. Hostiens. super. Cap *Excommunicamus*, § *Moneamus*.—Gloss. Joan. Andreæ sup. eod. loc.—Lib. Sentent. Inq. Tolosan. pp. 1, 7, 36, 39, 292.—Archives de l'Inq. de Carcassonne (Doat, XXVII. 118).—Isambert, Anc. Loix Françaises, IV. 364-5.—Ogniben Andrea, I Guglielmiti del Secolo XIII., Perugia, 1867, p. 111.—Alex. PP. IV. Bull. *Quæsivistis*, 28 Mai. 1254.

As in France the office of bailli was a purchasable one, while the incumbent was forbidden to sell it, it is evident that he would be loath to endanger its tenure by risking disobedience to inquisitorial demands.—Statuta Ludov. IX. ann. 1254, c. xxv.-vii. (Vaissette, Éd. Privat, VIII. 1349).

[343] Zanchini Tract. de Hæret. c. 5.—Coll. Doat, XXI. 226, 308.—Bern. Guidon. Practica P.IV. (Doat, XXX.).—Concil. Narbonn. ann. 1244 c. 8.—Concil. Biterrens. ann. 1246 c. 34.—Practica super Inquisit. (MSS. Bib. Nat., fonds latin, No. 14930, fol. 223-4).

[344] C. 1, § 1, Clement v. 3.—Eymeric. Direct. Inq. p. 580.—Coll. Doat, XXXI. 57.—Bernardi Guidon. Practica P. IV. (Doat, XXX.).—Coll. Doat, XXX. 104.—Lib. Sentent. Inq. Tolosan. passim, especially pp. 208-10.—Ibid. p. 300.—Archivio Storico Italiano, No. 38, p. 26 sqq.—Curiosità di Storia Subalpina, 1874, p. 215.

[345] Alex. PP. IV. Bull. *Cupientes*, 15 Apr. 1255.—Ejusd. Bull. *Præ cunctis*, 9 Nov. 1256.—Urbani PP. IV. Bull. *Licet ex omnibus*, § 10, 1262 (Mag. Bull. Rom. I. 122).—Bern. Guidon. Practica P. IV. (Doat, XXX.).—Zanchini de Hæret. c. XV.—Bernardi Comens. Lucerna Inquisitor, s. v. *Advocatus.*—Coll. Doat, XXI. 143; XXVII. 156-62, 232; XXXI. 139.—Doctrina de modo procedendi (Martene Thesaur. V. 1795).—Tractatus de Inquis. (Doat, XXXVI.).—MSS. Bib. Nat., fonds latin, No. 14930, fol. 205.

[346] Coll. Doat, XXVII. 118, 140, 156, 162.

[347] Coll. Doat, XXVII. 118, 131, 133.—Eymerici Direct. Inq. p. 630.—Bernard. Comens. Lucerna Inquisitor. s. v. *Advocatus.*

[348] Lami, Antichità Toscane, pp. 557-9.—Coll. Doat, XXXI. 139.—MSS. Bib. Nat., fonds latin, No. 9992.—Alex. PP. IV. Bull. *Præ cunctis*, § 15, 9 Nov. 1256.

[349] Eymeric. Direct. Inquis. pp. 503-12.—Doctrina de modo Procedendi (Martene Thesaur. V. 1795-6).—Tract. de Paup. de Lugduno (Ib. 1792).—Lib. Sentent. Inquis. Tolosan. pp. 1, 6, 39, 98.

[350] Lib. Sentent. Inquis. Tolosan. pp. 37, 39-93, 99-175, 178-9.

[351] Lib. Sentent. Inq. Tolosan. pp. 252-4.—MSS. Bib. Nat., fonds latin, 11847 *ad finem.*—Arch. de l'Inquis. de Carcassonne (Doat, XXXI. 83, 94-5).—Guid. Fulcod. Quæst. v.—Alex. PP. IV. Bull. *Cupientes*, 4 Mart. 1260.—Urbani PP. IV. Bull. *Licet ex omnibus*, § 11, 1262.—Ejusd. Bull. *Præ cunctis*, 2 Aug. 1264.—C. 2 Sexto v. 2.—Bern. Guidon Practica P. IV. (Doat, XXX.).—Zanchini Tract. de Hæret. c. viii.—Concil. Narbonn. ann. 1244 c. 20.—Eymeric. Direct. Inquis. pp. 461-5.

[352] Archivio di Napoli, Registro 3, Lett. A, fol. 64.—Wadding. ann. 1359, No. 1-3.

[353] Lib. Sentent. Inq. Tolosan. pp. 350-1.

[354] Ripoll I. 285.

[355] Ripoll I. 434.—Pegnæ Comment. in Eymeric. pp. 406-7.—Wadding. Annal. Regest. Nich. PP. III. No. 10.—Arch. de l'Inq. de Carcassonne (Doat, XXXII. 101).—Raynald. ann. 1278, No. 78.—MSS. Bib. Nat., fonds latin, No. 14930, fol. 218.

[356] Paramo de Orig. Offic. S. Inquis. pp. 124-5.—Wadding. Annal. ann. 1294, No. 1.—Milman, Latin Christianity, IV. 487.

[357] Arch. de l'Inquis. de Carcassonne (Doat, XXXI. 5, 103).—Zanchini Tract. de Hæret. c. ix.

In the Cismontane Inquisition the preliminary oath seems only to pledge the accused to tell the truth as to himself and others (Eymeric. p. 421). In Italy, however, it was the more elaborate affair described in the text. In the trials of the Guglielmites at Milan, in 1300, the accused were, in addition, made to impose on themselves, in case of violating its pledges, a forfeit varying from ten to fifty imperial lire, to secure which they pledged to the inquisitor all their property, real and personal, and renounced all legal defence. Moreover, this pecuniary penalty was not to relieve them from the canonical punishment attendant upon the non-fulfilment of the obligations assumed. This, I presume, was the official formula customary in the Lombard Inquisition.—Ogniben Andrea, I Guglielmiti del Secolo XIII., Perugia, 1867, pp. 5-6, 13, 27, 35, 37, etc.

In some witch trials of 1474 in Piedmont the oath to tell the truth was enforced with excommunication and *"tratti di corde,"* or infliction of the torture known as the strappado, varying from ten to twenty-five times— and also with pecuniary forfeits.—P. Vayra (Curiosità di Storia Subalpina, 1875, pp. 682, 693).

[358] Zanchini Tract. de Hæret. c. ii.

[359] Eymeric. Direct. Inquis. pp. 413-17.—Archivio di Napoli, Reg. 138, Lett. F, fol. 105.

To appreciate the contrast between the processes of the Inquisition and of the secular courts, it will suffice to allude to the practice of the latter in Milan in the first half of the fourteenth century. An accuser bringing a criminal action was obliged to inscribe himself and to furnish ample security that in case of failure he would undergo the fitting penalty and indemnify the accused for all expenses; in default of security he was to remain in jail until the end of the trial. The judge was, moreover, bound to render his decision within three months.

If the judge proceeded by inquisition he was obliged to give the accused notice in advance. The latter was entitled to counsel and to have the names and testimony of the witnesses communicated to him, and the judge was required, under a penalty of fifty lire, to complete the matter within thirty days.—Statuta Criminalia Mediolani, e tenebris in lucem edita, Bergami, 1594, c. 1-3, 153.

It is true that, under the influence of the Inquisition, the lay courts outgrew these wholesome provisions against injustice, but meanwhile it is important to bear them in mind when considering the secrecy, the delays, and the practical denial of justice in every way which characterized the proceedings against heretics. The gradual demoralization of the secular courts under these influences was a subject of complaint. In 1329 the consuls of Béziers represented to Philippe de Valois that his judges were neglecting to take from accusers proper security to indemnify the accused in case of the failure of the prosecution, and the king promptly ordered the abuse to be corrected.—Vaissette, Éd. Privat, X. Pr. 687.

[360] Doctrina de modo procedendi (Martene Thesaur. V. 1805).—Molinier, L'Inquisition dans le midi de la France, pp. 186-7.

[361] Concil. Tolosan. ann. 1229 c. 10.—Concil. Biterrens. ann. 1244 c. 31.—Concil. Albiens. ann. 1254 c. 5.—Modus examinandi hæreticos (Mag. Bib. Patrum XIII. 341).—Joan. Andreæ Gloss. sup. c. 13 Sexto v. 2.—Pegnæ Comment. in Eymeric. p. 490.—Bernardi Comens. Lucerna Inquis. s. vv. *Minor, Torturæ* No. 33.

[362] C. 8 Extra II. 14.—Concil. Narbonn. ann. 1244 c. 19.—Concil. Biterrens. ann. 1246 c. 8; Append. c. 14.—Guid. Fulcod. Quæst. VI.—Coll. Doat, XXI. 143.—Eymeric. Direct. Inq. pp. 382, 495, 528-31.—Lib. Sententt. Inq. Tolosan. pp. 175, 367-74.—Zanchini Tract. de Hæret. c. ii., viii., ix.—MSS. Bib. Nat., fonds latin, No. 14930, fol. 221.—Bernardi Comens. Lucerna Inquisit. s. vv. *Contumax, Convincitur.*—Concil. Lateran. IV. ann. 1215 c. 28.—Hist. Diplom. Frid. II. T. II. p. 4.—Concil. Albiens. ann. 1254 c. 28.—Alex. PP. IV. Bull. *Consultationi vestræ,* 28 Mai. 1260.—C. 13 Extra. v. 38 (cf. Concil. Trident. Sess. 25 de Reform. c. 3).—Arch. de l'Inq. de Carcass. (Doat, XXXI. 83).—Bernardi Comens. Lucerna Inquisit. s. v. *Procedere,* No. 10.

[363] Muratori, Antiquitat. Ital. Dissert. 60.—Zanchini Tract. de Hæret. c. xxiv., xl.—Lami, Antichità Toscane, p. 497.

[364] Alex. PP. IV. Bull. *Præ cunctis,* § 11, 9 Nov. 1256.—Ejusd. Bull. *Cupientes,* 10 Dec. 1257; 4 Mart. 1264.—Urbani PP. IV. Bull. *Licet ex omnibus,* 1262 (Mag. Bull. Rom. I. 122).—Ejusd. Bull. *Præ cunctis,* 2 Aug. 1264.—Clement. PP. IV. Bull. *Præ cunctis,* 23 Feb. 1266.—C. 20 Sexto v. 2.—Joan. Andreæ Gloss. sup. cod.—C. 2 Clement. v. 11.—Bernardi Guidonis Practica P. IV. (Doat, XXX.).—Eymeric. Direct. Inq. p. 583.

[365] Doctrina de modo procedendi (Martene Thesaur. V. 1811-12).—Concil. Biterrens. ann. 1246, Append. c. 16.—Arch. de l'Inq. de Carcassonne (Doat, XXVII. 156, 162, 178).—Bern. Guidon. Gravamina (Doat, XXX. 102).—Ejusd. Practica (Doat, XXIX. 94).—Eymeric. Direct. Inquis. pp. 631-33.—Jacob. Laudens. Orat. ad Concil. Constant. (Von der Hardt. III. 60).—Paramo de Orig. Offic. S. Inquis. pp. 32-33.—Zanchini Tract. de Hæret. c. ix.

[366] Eymeric. Direct. Inq. pp. 413, 418, 423-4, 461-5, 521-4.—Zanchini Tract. de Hæret. c. ix.— Bernardi Comens. Lucerna Inquisit. s. v. *Impœnitens.*—Albertin. Repert. Inquis. s. v.*Cautio.*

The contrast between this and the secular jurisprudence of the thirteenth century is illustrated in the charter granted by Alphonse of Poitiers to the town of Auzon (Auvergne), about 1260. Any one accused of crime by common report could clear himself by his own oath and that of a single legal conjurator, unless there was a legitimate plaintiff or accuser; and no one could be tried by the inquisitorial process without his own consent.—Chassaing, Spicilegium Brivateuse, Paris, 1886, p. 92.

[367] Bernard. Guidon. Practica P. IV., v. (Doat, XXX.).—Concil. Biterrens. ann. 1246, Append, c. 16.— Tractat. de Paup. de Lugdun. (Martene Thesaur. V. 1791-4).—Anon. Passaviens. (Mag. Bib. Pat. XIII. 308).— Const, xvi. Cod. I., v.—Molinier, L'Inquisition dans le midi de la France, p. 240.—Lib. Sententt. Inq. Tolosan. p. 147,—Epist. Petri Card. Alban. (Doat, XXXI. 5).—Bernard. Guidon. Gravamina (Doat, XXX. 114).

[368] Bernard. Guidon. Practica P. v.(Doat, XXX.).—Modus examinandi Hæreticos (Mag. Bib. Pat. XIII. 342).—Tractat. de Paup. de Lugd. (Martene Thesaur. V. 1793-4).—MS. Vatican, No. 8668(Ricchini, Prolog.ad

219

Monetam, p. xxiii.).—Anon. Passav.(Mag. Bib. Pat. XIII. 301).—Molinier, L'Inq. dans le midi de la France, p. 234.—Alex. PP. IV. Bull. *Quod super nonnullis*, § 10, 15 Dec. 1258.

[369] Tract, de Paup. de Lugduno (Martene Thes. V. 1792).—Cf. Bernard. Guidon. Practica P. v. (Doat, XXX.).

[370] Practica super Inquisitione (MSS. Bib. Nat., fonds latin, No. 14930, fol. 221).

[371] Tract. de Paup. de Lugduno (Martene Thesaur. V. 1793).—Eymeric. Direct. Inq. pp. 433-4.— Modus examinandi Hæreticos (Mag. Bib. Pat. XIII. 341).

[372] Tract, de Paup. de Lugduno (Martene Thesaur. V. 1787-88).—Eymeric. p, 434.—Archives de l'Inq. de Carcass. (Doat, XXVII. 150).

[373] Wadding. Annal. ann. 1228, No. 45.—Nideri Formicar. Lib. III. c. 10.

[374] Eymeric. Direct. Inquis. 514, 521.—Concil. Biterrens. ann. 1246, Append. c. 17.—Innoc. PP. IV. Bull. *Illius vicis*, 12 Nov. 1247.—Lib. Confess. Inq. Albiens. (MSS. Bib. Nat., fonds latin, 11847).—Bernard. Guidon. Practica P. v. (Doat, XXX.).—Doctrina de modo procedendi (Martene Thesaur. V. 1795).—Molinier, l'Inq. dans le midi de la France, p. 330.—Archives de l'Inq. de Carcass. (Doat, XXVII. 7 sqq.).—Lib. Sententt. Inq. Tolosan. pp. 22, 76, 102, 118-50, 158-62, 184, 216-18, 220-1, 228, 244-8, 266-7, 282-5.—Archives de l'Inq. de Carcassonne (Doat, XXXIV. 89).—Archives de l'hôtel-de-ville d'Albi (Doat, XXXIV. 45).—Coll. Doat, XXXIV. 189.

[375] Archives de l'Inq. de Carcassonne (Doat, XXXI. 57).—Vaissette, III. Pr. 551-3.—Tract, de Paup. de Lugd. (Martene Thesaur. V. 1787).—Joann. Andreæ Gloss, sup. c. 1, Clement, v. 3.—Bernard. Guidon. Practica P. v. (Doat, XXX.).—Arch. de l'Inq. de Carcassonne (Doat, XXXIV. 45).

[376] Superstition and Force, 3d Ed. 1878, pp. 419-20.—Lib. Jur. Civ. Veronæ, ann. 1228, c. 75.— Constit. Sicular. Lib. I. Tit. 27.—Frid. II. Edict. 1220. § 5.—Innoc. PP. IV. Bull. *Ad extirpanda*, § 26.—Concil. Autissiodor. ann. 578 c. 33.—Concil. Matiscon. II. ann. 585 c. 19.—Alex. PP. IV. Bull. *Ut negotium*, 7 Julii, 1256 (Doat, XXXI. 196); Ejusd. Bull. *Ne inquisitionis*, 19 Apr. 1259.—Urban. PP. IV. Bull. *Ut negotium*, 1260, 1262 (Ripoll, I. 430; Mag. Bull. Rom. I. 132).—Clement. PP. IV. Bull. *Ne inquisitionis*, 13 Jan. 1266.—Bern. Guidon. Pract. P. IV. (Doat. XXX.).—Pegnæ Comment. in Eymeric. p. 593.—Archivio di Napoli, MSS. Chioccarello, T. VIII.—Historia Tribulationum (Archiv für Litt. u. Kirchengeschichte, 1886, p. 324).

The earliest allusion to the use of torture in Languedoc is in 1254, when St. Louis forbade its use on the testimony of a single witness, even in the case of poor persons.—Vaissette, Éd. Privat, VIII. 1348.

[377] Chassaing, Spicilegium Brivatense, p. 92.—Vaissette, IV. Pr. 97-8.—Archives de l'hôtel-de-ville d'Albi (Doat, XXXIV. 45 sqq.).—Lib. Confess. Inq. Albiens. (MSS. Bib. Nat., fonds latin, 11847).—Lib. Sententt. Inq. Tolosan. pp. 46-78, 132, 169-74, 180-2, 266-7.—Bern. Guidon. Practica P. IV. v. (Doat, XXX.).

[378] C. 1, § 1, Clement, v. 3.—Bern. Guidon. Gravamina (Doat, XXX. 100, 120).—Eymeric. Direct. Inq. p. 422.—Zanchini Tract. de Hæret. c. xv.

[379] Eymeric. Direct. Inq. pp. 453-5.—Bern. Guidon. Practica P. v. (Doat, XXX.).—Zanchini Tract. de Hæret. c. ix., xiv.—Processus contra Waldenses (Archivio Storico Italiano, No. 38, pp. 20, 22, 24, etc.).—Pauli de Leazariis Gloss. sup. c. 1, Clem. v. 3.—Silvest. Prieriat. de Strigimagar. Mirand. Lib. III. c. 1.—Bernard. Comens. Lucerna Inquisit. s. vv. *Jejunia, Torturæ*.

That the Clementines had practically fallen into desuetude is shown by Carlo III. of Savoy, in 1506, procuring from Julius II. as a special privilege that in his territories the inquisitors should not send to prison or pronounce sentence without the concurrence of the episcopal ordinaries, and this was enlarged in 1515 by Leo X. by requiring their assent for all arrests.—Sclopis, Antica Legislazione del Piemont. p. 484.

[380] Eymeric. Direct. Inq. pp. 480, 592, 614.—Zanchini Tract. de Hæret. c. ix.—Bernardi Comens. Lucerna Inquis. s. vv. *Indicium, Torturæ* No. 19, 25.

[381] Eymeric. Direct. Inq. pp. 480-2.—MSS. Bib. Nat., funds latin, No. 4270, fol. 101, 146.—Responsa prudentum (Doat, XXXVII. 83 sqq.).—Bernardi Comens. Lucerna Inquis. s. vv.*Confessio, Torturæ*.

The care with which the inquisitors concealed the means by which confessions were procured is illustrated in the ratification obtained from Guillem Salavert in 1303, of his confession made three years before. He is made to declare it "esse veram, non factam vi tormentorum, amore, gratia, odio, timore, vel favore alicujus, non subornatus nec inductus minis vel blanditiis, seu seductus per aliquem, non amens nec stultus sed bona mente," etc. (MSS. Bib. Nat., fonds latin, No. 11847). Yet Salavert belonged to a group of victims on whom, as we shall see hereafter, torture was unsparingly used.

[382] Eymeric. Direct. Inquis. p. 481.—Bernardi Comens. Lucerna Inquis. s. vv. *Confessio. Impœnitens, Torturæ* No. 48.—Responsa prudentum (Doat, XXXVII. 83 sqq.)—Arch. de l'Inq. de Carcass. (Doat, XXVII. 126; XXXII. 251).—Lib. Sententt. Inq. Tolosan. pp. 266-7.—Zanchini Tract. de Hæret. c. xxiii.

[383] Fortescue de Laudibus Legum Angliæ, c. xxvii.

[384] Bernardi Comens. Lucerna Inquisit. s. vv. *Infamia, Inquisitores* No. 7.

[385] Fournier, Les officialités an moyen âge, pp. 177-8.—C. 14 Extra II. 23.—Bern. Guidon. Practica P. IV. (Doat, XXX.).

[386] Concil. Narbonn. ann. 1244 c. 29.—Trésor des chartes du roi en Carcassonne (Doat, XXI. 34).— Molinier, L'Inquisition dans le midi de la France, p. 342.—Livres de Jostice et de Plet, Liv. I. Tit. iii. § 7.

[387] Concil. Albiens. ann. 1254 c. 27.—Guid. Fulcod. Quæst. IX.—Bern. Guidon. Practica P.IV. (Doat, XXX.).—Lib. Confess. Inq. Albiens. (MSS. Bib. Nat., fonds latin, 11847).—Ripoll, I. 72.

[388] Eymeric. Direct. Inq. pp. 376-81.—Zanchini Tract. de Hæret. c. iii.

[389] Archidiaconi Gloss. super c. xi. § 1 Sexto v. 2.—Joann. Andreæ Gloss. sup. c. xiii. § 7 Extra v. 7.— Eymeric. Direct. Inquis. pp. 445, 615-16.—Guid. Fulcodii Quæst. XIV.—Zanchini Tract. de Hæret. c. xiii., xiv.—Bern. Guidon. Practica P. IV. (Doat, XXX.).

In the lay courts, if a witness swore to the innocence of the accused and subsequently changed his testimony, the first statement was held good and the second was rejected, but in cases of heresy the incriminating evidence was always received.—Ponzinibii de Lamiis c. 84.

[390] C. 17 Cod. IX. ii. (Honor. 423).—Pseudo-Julii Epist. II. c. 18 (Gratiani Decret.) P. II. caus. v. Q. 3, c. 5.—Pseudo-Eutychiani Epist. ad Episcopp. Siciliæ.—Gratiani Comment. in Decret. P. II. caus. II. Q. 7, c. 22; caus. VI. Q. 1, c. 19.—Hist. Diplom. Frid. II. T. IV. pp. 299-300.—Guill. Pod. Laur. c. 40.—Alex. PP. IV. Bull. *Consuluit*, 6 Mai. 1260 (Doat, XXXI. 205); Ejusd. Bull. *Quod super non nullis*, 9 Dec. 1257; 15 Dec. 1258.—C. 5 Sexto v. 2.—C. 8 § 3 Sexto v. 2.—Concil. Biterrens. ann. 1246 c. 12.—Jacob. Laudun. Orat. in Conc. Constant. (Von der Hardt III. 60).—MSS. Bib. Nat., fonds latin, No. 14930, fol. 221.—Zanchini Tract. de Hæret. c. xi., xiii.—Eymeric. Direct. Inq. pp. 602-6.

Under the contemporary English law, criminals and accomplices were rejected as accusers, even in high-treason (Bracton, Lib. III. Tract. ii. cap. 3, No. 1).

[391] Bernardi Comens. Lucerna Inquisit. s. v. *Testis*, No. 14.—Concil Albiens. ann. 1254 c. 18.—Coll. Doat, XXII. 237 sqq.

In the German feudal law of the period no witness was admitted below the age of eighteen.—Sächsisches Lehenrechtbuch, c. 49 (Daniels, Berlin, 1863, p. 113).

[392] Eymeric. Direct. Inq. pp. 611-13.—Concil. Narbonn. ann. 1244 c. 25.—Concil. Biterrens. ann. 1246 c. 14.—Arch. de l'Inq. de Carcass, (Doat, XXXI. 149).

[393] Guid. Fulcod. Quæst. VIII.—Pegnæ Comment. in Eymeric. p. 601.—Zanchini Tract. de Hæret. c. xiii.—Doctrina de modo procedendi (Martene Thesaur. V. 1802).

Heresy, of course, was a "reserved" case for which the ordinary confessor could not give absolution. Thus a man of Realmont in Albigeois who repented of having been present at a Catharan conventicle went to a Franciscan and confessed, accepting the penance imposed of the minor pilgrimages and some other penitential acts. On his return from their performance, however, he was seized by the Inquisition, tried and imprisoned.—Vaissette, IV. 41.

[394] Bernardi Comens. Lucerna Inquisit. s.v. *Probatio*, No. 3.—Archidiac. Gloss. sup. c. xi. § 1 Sexto v. 2.—Guill. Pod. Laur. c. 40.—Bern. Guidon. Gravamina (Doat, XXX. 102).—Concil. Narbonn. ann. 1244 c. 22.—Concil. Biterrens. ann. 1246 c. 4, 10.—Arch. de l'Inq. de Carc. (Doat, XXXI. 5).—Innoc. PP. IV. Bull. *Cum negotium*, 9 Mart. 1254; Ejusd. Bull. *Ut commissum*, 21 Jun. 1254.—Alex. PP. IV. Bull. *Licet vobis*, 7 Dec. 1255; Ejusd. Bull. *Præ cunctis*, § 6, 9 Nov. 1256; Ejusd. Bull. *Super extirpatione*, § 9, 1258.—Clem. PP. IV. Bull. *Licet ex omnibus*, 17 Sep. 1265.—Ejusd. Bull. *Præ, cunctis*, 23 Feb. 1266.—Guid. Fulcod. Quæst. xv.—MSS. Bib. Nat., fonds latin, No. 14930, fol. 221.—C. 20 Sexto v. 2.—Bern. Guidon. Practica P. iv. (Doat, XXX.).—Responsa Prudentum (Doat, XXXVII.).—Eymeric. Direct. Inq. pp. 450, 610, 614, 626, 627. Cf. Pegnæ Comment, pp. 627-8.—MSS. Bib. Nat., fonds latin, No. 4270.—Bernardi Comens, Lucerna Inquisit. s.v. *Nomina*.—Mladenovic Relatio (Palacky Documenta Joannis Hus, pp. 252-3).

[395] Responsa Prudentum (Doat, XXXVII.).—Bernardi Comens. Lucerna Inquis. s. v.*Tradere*.—Zanchini Tract. de Hæret. c. ix.

[396] Lib. Confess. Inq. Albiens. (MSS. Bib. Nat., fonds latin, 11847).—Lib. Sententt. Inq. Tolosan. pp. 96-7, 180, 393.—Arch. de l'Inq. de Carcass. (Doat, XXVII. 118, 133, 140, 149, 178, 204-16).—Eymeric. Direct. Inq. p. 521.—Zanchini Tract. de Hæret. c. xiv.

[397] Lib. Sententt. Inq. Tolosan. pp. 297, 393.—Arch. de l'Inq. de Carcassonne (Doat, XXVII. 119, 133, 140, 241).—Pegnæ Comment. in Eymeric. p. 625.—Zanchini Tract. de Hæret c. xiv.

[398] Concil. Lateran IV. ann. 1215 c. 8.

So, in 1254, St. Louis orders that in all criminal cases where the inquisitorial process is used, the whole proceedings shall be submitted to the accused.—Vaissette, Éd. Privat, VIII. 1348.

[399] Concil. Biterrens. ann. 1246, Append, c. 8.—Concil. Campinacens. ann. 1238 c. 14.—Contre le Franc-Alleu sans Tiltre, Paris, 1629, p. 216.—Fournier, Les Officialités, etc. p. 289.—C. 11, Extra v. 7.—Concil. Valentin, ann. 1248 c. 11.—Concil. Albiens. ann. 1254 c. 23.—Bernard. Guidon. Practica. P. IV. (Doat, XXX.).—Eymeric. Direct. Inquis. pp. 446, 452, 565, 568.—MSS. Bib. Nat., fonds latin, No. 14930, fol. 220.— Bernardi Comens. Lucerna Inquisitor, s. vv.*Advocatus, Defensor*.—C. 13, § 7, Extra v. 7.—Alex. PP. IV. Bull. *Cupientes*, 4 Mart. 1260.—Arch. de l'Inq. de Carcassonne (Doat, XXXIV. 123).—Vaissette, IV. 72.

[400] Guid. Fulcod. Quæst. xv.—Eymeric. Direct. Inq. pp. 446, 450, 607, 610, 614.—Zanchini Tract. de Hæret. c. ix., xli.—Litt. Petri Albanens. (Doat, XXXI. 5).

In the register of the Inquisition of Carcassonne from 1249 to 1258 M. Molinier has found two cases in which the accused was allowed to introduce evidence in his favor. In one of these G. Vilanière called two witnesses to prove an alibi; in the other Guilleim Nègre brought forward a letter of reconciliation and penitence. In neither case was the defendant successful (L'Inq. dans le midi de la France, p. 346).

[401] Coll. Doat, XXXI. 149.—Bernardi Comens. Lucerna Inquisit. s.v. *Taciturnitas.*

[402] Registre de l'Inq. de Carcassonne (MSS. Bib. Nat., fonds latin, Nouv. Acquis. 139, f. 33, 44, 62).— Practica super Inquisitione (MSS. Bib. Nat., fonds latin, No. 14930, fol. 212).

[403] Concil. Biterrens. ann. 1246, Append. c. 18.—Doctrina de modo procedendi (Martene Thesaur. V. 1813).—Coll. Doat, XXVII. 97-8; XXIX. 27; XXXIV. 123; XXXV. 61; XXXVIII. 166.—Lib. Sententt. Inquis. Tolosan. pp. 33-4.—Molinier, L'Inquis. dans le midi de la France, p. 287.—Alex. PP. IV. Bull. *Olim ex parte,* 24 Sept.; 13 Oct. 1258; Urbani PP. IV. Bull. *Idem,* 21 Aug. 1262 (Mag. Bull. Rom. I. 117).

[404] Bernardi Comens. Lucerna Inquisit. s.v. *Recusatio.*—Bern. Guidon. Practica P. IV. (Doat, XXX.).— Zanchini Tract. de Hæret. c. ii., vii.—Concil. Narbonn. ann. 1244 c. 26.—Concil. Biterrens. ann. 1246 c. 9.— Eymeric. Direct. Inq. p. 572.

[405] MSS. Bib. Nat., fonds latin, No. 4270, fol. 139.

[406] Pegnæ Comment. in Eymeric. p. 675.—Zanchini Tract. de Hæret. c. xxix.—Eymeric. Direct. Inq. pp. 453-55.—Grandes Chroniques. ann. 1323.—Guill. Nangiac. Contin. ann. 1323.—Chron. de Jean de S. Victor. Contin. ann. 1323.—Bernardi Comens. Lucerna Inquisitor, s. vv.*Appellatio, Exceptio* No. 2.

[407] Vaissette, III. 462; Pr. 447.—Coll. Doat, XXXI. 152, 169, 283; XXXII. 69; XXXV. 134.—Potthast No. 10292, 10311, 10317, 18723, 18895.—Ripoll, I. 287.—Coll. Doat, XXXV. 134.

[408] Molinier, L'Inquisition dans le midi de la France, pp. 332-33.—Responsa Prudentum (Doat, XXXVII.).—Bern. Guidon. Practica P. v. (Doat, XXX.).—Eymeric. Direct. Inquis. p. 474.—Zanchini Tract. de Hæret. c. xli.

[409] C. 1 Clement, v. 3.—Bern. Guidon. Gravamina (Doat, XXX. 112).

[410] Hist. Diplom. Frid. II. T. II. p. 4.—Concil. Tolosan. ann. 1229 c. 18.—Concil. Albiens. ann. 1254 c. 16.—Concil. Tarraconens. ann. 1242.—Eymeric. Direct. Inquis. pp. 376-8, 380-4, 494-5, 500.—Concil. Biterrens. ann. 1246, Append. c. 31, 36.—Zanchini Tract. de Hæret. v., vii., xx.—Doctrina de modo procedendi (Martene Thesaur. V. 1802).—Gersonis de Protestatione consid. xii.—Bernardi Comens. Lucerna Inquisit. s. v. *Præsumptio,* No. 5.—Isambert, Anc. Loix Françaises, IV. 364.

It is somewhat remarkable that Cornelius Agrippa maintains that the law expressly forbade the Inquisition from meddling with cases involving mere suspicion, or the defending, reception, and favoring of heretics (De Vanitate Scientiarum, cap. XCVI.).—His contemporary, the learned jurist Ponzinibio, calls special attention to the fact that mere suspicion, even when not accompanied by evil report, is sufficient to justify proceedings in case of heresy, though not in other crimes.—(Ponzinibii de Lamiis c. 88).

[411] Concil. Tarraconens. ann. 1242.—Eymeric. Direct. Inq. pp. 376-8, 475-6.—Bernardi Comens. Lucerna Inquis. s. vv. *Practica, Purgatio.*—Albertini Repertor. Inquisit. s. v. *Deficiens.*—Gregor. PP. XI. Bull. *Excommunicamus,* 20 Aug. 1229.—Zanchini Tract. de Hæret. c. vii., xvii.—Martini App. ad Mosheim de Beghardis, p. 537.

[412] Concil. Narbonn. ann. 1244 c. 6, 12.—Muratori Antiq. Ital. Dissert. LX.—Doctrina de modo procedendi (Martene Thesaur. V. 1800-1).—Eymeric. Direct. Inq. pp. 376, 486-7, 492-8.—Lib. Sententt. Inq. Tolos. pp. 67, 215.

[413] Guid. Fulcod. Quæstt. XIII., XV.—Ripoll, I. 254.—Archives de l'Inq. de Carcassonne (Doat, XXXI. 139).—Archives de l'Évêché d'Albi (Doat, XXXV. 69).—Lib. Sententt. Inq. Tolosan. p. 32.—Eymeric. Direct. Inquis. pp. 465, 643.—Zanchini Tract. de Hæret. c. XX.

In the sentences of Bernard de Caux, 1246-8, though imprisonment is treated as a penance, the expression is more mandatory than in later proceedings (MSS. Bib. Nat., fonds latin, 9992).

[414] Arch. de l'Évêché d'Albi (Doat, XXXV. 69).—Arch. de l'Inq. de Carcassonne (Doat, XXVII. 232).—Concil. Narbonn. ann. 1234 c. 5.—Concil. Biterrens. ann. 1246, Append. c. 29.—Eymeric. Direct. Inq. pp. 506-7.—Zanchini Tract. de Hæret. c. xvi.—Guid. Fulcod. Quæst. XV.

[415] Tamburini, Istoria dell' Inquisizione, I. 492-502.—Bern. Corio, Hist. di Milano, ann. 1252.—Arch. de l'Inq. de Carcassonne (Doat, XXXI. 201).—Ripoll, I. 244, 280, 389.

[416] Concil. Tarraconens. ann. 1242.—Innoc. PP. IV. Bull. *Noverit universitas,* 1254 (Mag. Bull. Rom. I. 103).—Bern. Guidon. Practica P. IV. (Doat, XXX.)—Eymeric. Direct. Inquis. pp. 368-72, 376-8.—Zanchini Tract. de Hæret. c. xxxiii.

[417] Concil. Narbonn. ann. 1244 c. 3.—Concil. Biterrens. ann. 1246, Append. c. 28.—Coll, Doat, XXI. 200.—MSS. Bib. Nat., fonds latin, No. 9992.

[418] Paramo de Orig. Offic. S. Inquis. Lib. II. Tit. i. c. 2, § 6.—Martene Thesaur. I. 802.—Coll. Doat, XXXI. 1.

[419] Archives de l'Inq. de Carcassonne (Doat, XXXI. 255).—Coll. Doat, XXVII. 136.

[420] Concil. Tarraconens. ann. 1242.—Concil. Narbonens. ann. 1244 c. 1.—Concil. Biterrens. ann. 1246, Append. c. 6.—Bern. Guidon. Practica (Doat, XXIX. 54).—MSS. Bib. Nat., fonds latin, No. 14930, fol. 214.

[421] Coll. Doat, XXI. 222.—Wadding. Annal. ann. 1300, No. 1.—Cf. Molinier, L'Inq. dans le midi de la France, pp. 400-1.

[422] Arch. de l'Inq. de Carcassonne (Doat, XXXVII. 11).—Lib. Sententt. Inq. Tolosan. pp. 1, 340-1.

[423] Wadding. Annal. ann. 1238, No. 7.—Concil. Narbonn. ann. 1244 c. 2.—Concil. Biterrens. ann. 1246, Append, c. 26, 29.—Berger, Les Registres d'Innocent IV. No. 3508, 3677, 3866.—Coll. Doat, XXXI. 17.—Vaissette. III. Pr. 468.—MSS. Bib. Nat., fonds latin, nouv. acq. 139, fol. 8.—Molinier, L'Inq. dans le midi de la France, pp. 408-9.—Lib. Sententt. Inq. Tolos. pp. 284-5.—Coll. Doat, XXI. 185, 186, 217.

[424] C. Biterrens. ann. 1246, Append. c. 26.—Lib. Sententt. Inq. Tolosan. pp. 8, 13, 130, 228.

In Italy the crosses appear to be of red cloth (Archiv. di Firenze, Prov. S. Maria Novella, 31 Ott. 1327).

At an early period there is a single allusion to another "*pœna confusibilis*" in the shape of a wooden collar or yoke worn by the penitent. This occurs at La Charité, in 1233, and I have not met with it elsewhere (Ripoll, I. 46).

[425] Concil. Narbonn. ann. 1229 c. 10.—Statut. Raymondi ann. 1234 (Harduin. VII. 205).—Concil. Biterrens. ann. 1234 c. 4.—Concil. Tarraconens. ann. 1242.—Concil. Narbonn. ann. 1244 c. 1.—Concil. Valentin. ann. 1248 c. 13.—Concil. Albiens. ann. 1254 c. 4.—MSS. Bib. Nat., fonds latin, nouv. acq. 139, fol. 2.

[426] Coll. Doat, XXI. 185 sqq.—Concil. Biterrens. ann. 1246 c. 6.—Molinier, l'Inquis. dans le midi de la France, p. 412.—Lib. Sententt. Inq. Tolosan. p. 350.

[427] Molinier, op. cit. p. 404, 414-15.—Bernard. Guidon. Gravamina (Doat, XXX. 115).—Ejusd. Practica P. II. (Doat, XXIX. 75).—Arch. de l'Inq. de Carc. (Doat, XXXVII. 107, 135, 149).—Eymeric. Direct. Inq. pp. 496-99.

[428] Vaissette, III. Pr. 386.—Lami, Antichità Toscane, p. 560.—Concil. Narbonn. ann. 1244 c. 17.—Innoc. PP. IV. Bull. *Quia te*, 19 Jan. 1245 (Doat, XXXI. 71).—Molinier, op. cit. pp. 23, 390.—Concil. Biterrens. ann. 1246, Append, c. 27.—Practica super Inquisit. (MSS. Bib. Nat., fonds latin, No. 14930, fol. 222).—Innoc. PP. IV. Bull. *Cum a quibusdam*, 14 Mai. 1249 (Doat, XXXI. 81, 116).—Coll. Doat, XXXIII. 198.—Ripoll, I. 194.—Eymeric. Direct. Inq. pp. 648-9, 653.—Zanchini Tract. de Hæret. c. xix., xx., xli.—Archivio Storico Italiano, No. 38, pp. 27, 42.—Campi, Dell' Hist. Eccles. di Piacenza, P. II. p. 309.—Coll. Doat, XXI. 185 sqq.

[429] Bernardi Comens. Lucerna Inquisit. s.v. *Pœnam*.

[430] Arch. de l'Inq. de Carcassonne (Doat, XXXI. 152).—Archives Nationales de France, J. 430, No. 1.—Berger, Les Registres d'Innoc. IV. No. 4093.—Vaissette. IV. 460, 462.—Molinier, op. cit. pp. 173, 283-4, 391, 396, 397.—Lib. Sententt. Inq. Tolos. p. 40.—Bern. Guidon. Practica (Doat, XXIX. 83).—Coll. Doat, XXXI. 292.—Arch. de l'Inq. de Carcassonne (Doat, XXXV. 192).—Zanchini Tract, de Hæret. c. xix.

[431] Arch. de l'Inq. de Carcassonne (Doat, XXVII. 236).—Concil. Narbonn. ann. 1244 c. 19.—Concil. Albiens. ann. 1254 c. 25.—Guid. Fulcod. Quæst. VII.—Practica super Inquisit. (MSS. Bib. Nat., fonds latin, No. 14930 fol. 221-2).—Molinier, op. cit. pp. 365, 392.—Bernardi Comens. Lucerna Inquisit. s. v. *Inquisitores*, No. 18.

[432] Concil. Narbonn. ann. 1244 c. 17.—C. Biterrens. ann. 1246, Append. c. 15.—Innoc. PP. IV. Bull. *Cum venerabilis*, 29 Jan. 1253; Bull. *Cum per nostras*, 30 Jan. 1253; Bull. *Super extirpatione*, 30 Mai. 1254.—Alex. PP. IV. Bull. *Super extirpatione*, 13 Nov. 1258, 20 Sept. 1259; Bull. *Ad audientiam*, 23 Jan. 1260.—Berger, Les Registres d'Innoc. IV. No. 3904.—Ripoll, I. 69, 71, 223-4, 247.—Lami, Antichità Toscane, p. 576.—MS. Bib. Nat., fonds latin, nouv. acquis. 139 fol. 43.—Eymeric. Direct. Inquis. p. 638.—Zanchini Tract. de Hæret. c. xix.—Bern. Guidon. Practica P. v. (Doat, XXX.).—Albert. Repert. Inq. s. v. *Cautio*.

The right to offer bail, except in capital offences, was one thoroughly recognized by the secular law. See, for instance, Isambert, Anc. Loix Franç. III. 57.

[433] Molinier, op. cit. pp. 299-302.—Arch. de l'Inq. de Carcassonne (Doat, XXXIV. 5. It is perhaps worthy of note that Ripoll, in printing this bull of Boniface VIII., T. II. p. 61, discreetly suppresses the details of inquisitorial wrong-doing).—Grandjean, Registres de Benoît XI. No. 169, 509.—Chron. Girardi de Fracheto Contin. ann. 1303 (D. Bouquet, XXI. 22-3).—Articuli Transgressionum (Archiv. für Litt. u. Kirchengeschichte, 1887, p. 104).—C. 1, § 4, c. 2 Clement, v. 3.—Bernard. Guidon. Gravamina (Doat, XXX. 118-19).—Coll. Doat, XXXV. 113.—Ripoll, VII. 61.—Archivio di Firenze, Riformagioni, Classe XI. Distinz. I. No. 39.—Villani, Cronica, XII. 58.—Alvar. Pelag. de Planct. Eccles. Lib. II. art. vii.—Eymeric. Direct. Inq. p. 332.—Decamerone, Giorn. I. Nov. 6.—Archives administratives de Reims, III. 641.

The strictness with which the canons against usury were construed is illustrated in a case decided by the University of Paris in 1490. The Faculty of Theology was consulted as to the righteousness of a contract under which a certain church had bought for three hundred livres an annual rent of twenty livres arising from certain lands, with the right of recalling the purchase-money after two months' notice; while by a separate agreement the land-owner had the right of redemption for nine years. This is doubtless a specimen of the means adopted of evading the prohibition of interest payment, which must have grown frequent with the development of commerce and industry. The contract ran for twenty-six years before it was questioned and referred to the University. A commission of twelve doctors of theology was appointed, who discussed the subject thoroughly, and reported, eleven to one, that the contract was usurious, and that the annual payments must be computed as partial payments on account of the purchase-money (D'Argentré, Collect. Judic. de nov. Error. I. II. 323).

[434] Cornel. Agrippa de Vanitate Scientiar. cap. XCVI.

[435] Molinier, op. cit. p. 307.—Eymeric. Direct. Inq. p. 650, 685.

[436] Constt. v., VIII. § 3, Cod. I. v.—Assis. Clarendon. Art. 21.—Lami, Antichità Toscane, p. 124.—Hist. Diplom. Frid. II. T. IV. pp. 299-300.—Lib. Juris Civilis Veronæ c. 156 (Ed. 1728, p. 117).—Alex. PP. IV.

Bull. *Ad extirpanda*, § 21.—Concil. Tolosan. ann. 1229 c. 6.—Statut. Raymondi ann. 1234 (Harduin. VII. 203).—Vaissette, III. Pr. 370-1.—Concil. Biterrens. ann. 1246, Append. c. 35.—Concil. Albiens. ann. 1254 c. 6.—Établissements, Liv. I. c. 36.—Siete Partidas, P. VII. Tit. xxvi. l. 5.—Bern. Guidon. Practica (Doat, XXIX. 89).—Lib. Sententt. Inq. Tolosan. pp. 4, 80-1, 168.

[437] Isambert, Anc. Loix Françaises, IV. 364; V. 491.—Ripoll, I. 252.—Arch. de l'Inq. de Carcassonne (Doat, XXVII. 248).—Sachsenspiegel, Buch III. Art. I.—Zanchini Tract. de Hæret. c. xxxix., xl.

[438] Lib. Sententt. Inq. Tolosan. 280.—Arch. de l'Inq. de Carc. (Doat, XXXV. 122).

[439] Zanchini Tract. de Hæret. c. X.

[440] Gregor. PP. IX. Bull. *Excommunicamus*, 20 Aug. 1229.—Concil. Narbonn. ann. 1229 c. 9.—Hist. Diplom. Frid. II. T. IV. p. 300.—Concil. Arelatens. ann. 1234 c. 6.—Vaissette, III. Pr. 314.

Gregory's bull, as inserted in the canon law, provides perpetual imprisonment for those who "*redire noluerint*" (C. 15, § 1, Extra v. vii.), which is self-evidently an error for "*voluerint*," as the previous section directs that persistent heretics are to be handed over to the secular arm. Besides, Frederic's Ravenna decree, issued soon after, in prescribing lifelong imprisonment for converts, speaks of this being in accordance with the canons.

[441] Concil. Tarraconens. ann. 1242.—Concil. Narbonn. ann. 1244 c. 9, 19.—Concil. Biterrens. ann. 1246, Append, c. 20.—Coll. Doat, XXI. 152.—MSS. Bib. Nat., fonds latin, No. 9992.—Bern. Guidon. Practica P. IV. (Doat, XXX.).

[442] Lib. Sententt. Inq. Tolos. *passim*, pp. 347-9.—Eymeric. Direct. Inq. p. 507.—MSS. Bib. Nat., fonds latin, No. 9992.—Practica super Inquisit. (MSS. Bib. Nat., fonds latin, No. 14930, fol. 222).

[443] Arch. de l'Inq. de Carcassonne (Doat, XXXIII. 143).—Concil. Biterrens. ann. 1246 c. 23, 25.—Eymeric. Direct. Inq. p. 507.

[444] Arch. de l'hôtel-de-ville d'Albi (Doat, XXXIV. 45).—Bern. Guidon. Gravam. (Doat, XXX. 100).—Lib. Sententt. Inq. Tolos. pp. 32, 200, 287.—Arch. de l'Inq. de Carcassonne (Doat, XXVII. 136, 156).—MSS. Bib. Nat., fonds latin, No. 9992.

The cruelty of the monastic system of imprisonment known as *in pace*, or *vade in pacem*, was such that those subjected to it speedily died in all the agonies of despair. In 1350 the Archbishop of Toulouse appealed to King John to interfere for its mitigation, and he issued an *Ordonnance* that the superior of the convent should twice a month visit and console the prisoner, who, moreover, should have the right twice a month to ask for the company of one of the monks. Even this slender innovation provoked the bitterest resistance of the Dominicans and Franciscans, who appealed to Pope Clement VI., but in vain.—Chron. Bardin. ann. 1350 (Vaissette, IV. Pr. 29).

The hideous abuse of keeping a prisoner in chains was forbidden by the contemporary English law (Bracton, Lib. III. Tract, i. cap. 6).

[445] Lib. Sententt. Inq. Tolos. pp. 102, 153, 231, 252-4, 301.—Muratori Antiq. Dissert. LX. (T. XII. p. 519).—Bern. Guidon. Practica P. v. (Doat, XXX.).—Arch. de l'Inq. de Carcassonne (Doat, XXVII. 7).

[446] Beaumanoir, Coutumes du Beauvoisis, cap. 51, No. 7.—G.B. de Lagrèze, La Navarre Française, II. 339. In the accounts of the Sénéchausseé of Toulouse for 1337 there is an item of twenty sols expended in Nov., 1333, for straw for the prisoners to lie on, lest they should perish with cold during the winter. Other items, amounting to eighty-three sols eleven deniers, for the repairs of the fetters and shackles which they wore shows the rigor of their confinement.—Vaissette, Éd. Privat, X. Pr. 798-99.

[447] Concil. Tolosan. ann. 1229 c. 11.—Concil. Valentin. ann. 1234 c. 5.—Concil. Narbonn. ann. 1244 c. 4.—Coll. Doat, XXXI. 157.—Concil. Biterrens. ann. 1246, Append. c. 23, 27.—Innoc. PP. IV. Bull. *Cum sicut*, 1 Mart. 1249 (Doat, XXXI. 114).—Concil. Albiens. ann. 1254 c. 24.—Guid. Fulcod. Quæst. X.

[448] Molinier, op. cit. p. 435.—Vaissette, III. Pr. 536.—Vaissette. Éd. Privat, VIII. 1206.—Arch. de l'hôtel-de-ville d'Albi (Doat, XXXIV. 45).—Bern. Guidon. Gravam. (Doat, XXX. 109).—Isambert. Anc. Loix Françaises, IV. 364.—Vaissette, Éd. Privat, X. Pr. 693-4, 813-14.—Les Olim, III. 148.—Hauréau, Bernard Délicieux, p. 19.—Archivio di Napoli, Reg. 113, Lett. A, fol. 385; Reg. 154, Lett. C, fol. 81; MSS. Chioccorello, T. VIII.

[449] Arch. de l'Inq. de Carcassonne (Doat, XXVII. 14, 16).—Muratori Antiq. Dissert. LX. (T. XII. pp. 500, 507, 529, 535).—Lib. Sententt. Inq. Tolos. pp. 252-4, 307.—Tract., de Hæres. Paup. de Lugd. (Martene Thesaur. V. 1786).

[450] Practica super Inquisit. (MSS. Bib. Nat., fonds latin, No. 14930, fol. 222).—Molinier, op. cit. p. 449.—Arch. de l'Inq. de Carcassonne (Doat, XXXII. 125; XXXVII. 83).

[451] Les Olim, III. 148.—Archives de l'hôtel-de-ville d'Albi (Doat, XXXIV. 45).—Bern. Guidon. Gravam. (Doat, XXX. 105-8).—Ejusd. Practica P. IV. c. 1.—Eymeric. Direct. Inq. p. 587.—Bernardi Comens. Lucerna Inquisit. s. v. *Carcer*.

The passage in the *Practica* alluded to occurs in MSS. Bib. Nat., fonds latin, No. 14579, fol. 258. The allusion to the Clementines is not in the MS. printed by Douais, Paris, 1885, p. 179.

In 1325 Bishop Richard Ledred of Ossory availed himself of the Clementine canon to claim supervision over the imprisonment of William Outlaw, whom he threw into the Castle of Kilkenny on a charge of fautorship of sorcerers—there being, apparently, no episcopal jail.—Wright's Proceedings against Dame Alice Kyteler, Camden Soc. 1843, p. 31.

[452] Lib. Sententt. Inq. Tolos. pp. 8, 13, 14, 19, 25, 26, 29, 158-62, 246-8, 255-61.—Arch. de l'Inq. de Carcassonne (Doat, XXVII. 7, 131; XXVIII. 164).

[453] Concil. Narbonn. ann. 1244 c. 7.—Innoc. PP. IV. Bull. *Ut commissum*, 20 Jan. 1245 (Doat, XXXI. 68).—Vaissette, III. Pr. 468.—Concil. Biterrens. ann. 1246, Append. c. 20.—Zanchini, Tract, de Hæret. c. xxi., xxxviii.

[454] Arch. de l'Inq. de Carcassonne (Doat, XXVII. 2, 192).

[455] Lib. Sententt. Inq. Tolosan. pp. 40, 118, 122, 137, 139, 146, 147.—Bern. Guidon. Practica (Doat, XXIX. 85).—Ejusd. P. v. (Doat, XXX.).—Concil. Biterrens. ann. 1246, Append. c. 21, 22.—Vaissette, III. Pr. 467.—Practica super Inquisit. (MSS. Bib. Nat., fonds latin, No. 14930, fol. 222, 224).—Pegnæ Comment. in Eymeric. p. 509.—Zanchini Tract. de Hæret. c. xx.

[456] Concil. Arelatens. ann. 1234 c. 11.—Concil. Albiens. ann. 1254 c. 26.—Lib. Sententt. Inq. Tolosan. pp. 162-7, 203, 246-7, 251-2.—Zanchini Tract. de Hæret. c. xxvii.

[457] Const. 5 Cod. IX. viii.—Concil. Tolosan. ann. 1229 c. 10.—Hist. Diplom. Frid. II. T. IV. pp. 8, 302.—Innoc. PP. IV. Bull. *Ut commissum*, 21 Jun. 1254.—Alex. PP. IV. Bull. *Quod super nonnullis*, 9. Dec. 1257 (Doat, XXXI. 244).—Raynald. ann. 1258, No. 23.—Potthast No. 17745, 18396.—Eymeric. Direct. Inq. p. 123.—C. 15, Sexto v. ii.

[458] Eymeric. Direct. Inquis. p. 571.—Arch. de l'Inq. de Carcassonne (Doat, XXXII. 156).—Regist. Curiæ Franciæ de Carcassonne (Doat, XXXII. 241).—Bernardi Comens, Lucerna Inquisit. s. v. *Inquisitores*, No. 19.—Lib. Sententt. Inq. Tolosan. Index.—Wadding. Regest. Nich. PP. III. No. 10.

[459] Ripoll, I. 208, 394.—Tractatus de Inquisitione (Doat, XXXVI.).—Bern. Guidon. Practica P. IV, (Doat, XXX.).—Eymeric. Direct. Inquis. 360-1.

[460] Constt. 13, 15, 17 Cod. I. v.; 2, 3, 4, 7, 8, 9 Cod. IX. xlix.; 5, 6 Cod. IX. viii.

[461] Constt. Sicular. Lib. I. Tit. 3.—Concil. Turon. ann. 1163 c. 4.—Lucii PP. III. Epist. 171.—Innoc. PP. III. Regest. II. 1.—Cap. 10 Extra v. 7.

It was probably in obedience to the canon of Tours that, in 1178, the property of Pierre Mauran of Toulouse was declared forfeited to the count, and he was allowed to redeem it with a fine of five hundred pounds of silver (Roger. Hoveden. Annal. ann. 1178).

The decree of Alonso II. of Aragon against the Waldenses, in 1194, referred to above (p. 81) (Pegnæ Comment. 39 in Eymeric. p. 281), inflicts confiscation on all who favor the heretics, but there are no traces of its enforcement, or of the subsequent canons of the Council of Girona in 1197 (Aguirre V. 102-3). The same may be said of the edicts of Henry VI., in 1194, repeated by Otho IV. in 1310 (Lami, Antichità Toscane, p. 484).

[462] Innoc. PP. III. Regest. XII. 154 (Cap. 20 Extra v. xl.).—Isambert, Anc. Loix Françaises I. 228, 232.—Harduin. VII. 203-8.—Vaissette, III. Pr. 385.—Concil. Albiens. ann. 1254 c. 26.—Innoc. PP. IV. Bull. *Cum fratres*, ann. 1252 (Mag. Bull. Roman. I. 90).

Confiscation was an ordinary resource of mediæval law. In England, from the time of Alfred, property, as well as life, was forfeited for treason (Alfred's Dooms 4—Thorpe I. 63), a penalty which, remained until 1870 (Low and Pulling's Dictionary of English History, p. 469). In France murder, false-witness, treachery, homicide, and rape were all punished with death and confiscation (Beaumanoir, Coutumes du Beauvoisis XXX. 2-5). By the German feudal law the fief might be forfeited for a vast number of offences, but the distinction was drawn that, if the offence was against the lord, the fief reverted to him; if simply a crime, it descended to the heirs (Feudor. Lib. I. Tit. xxiii.-iv.). In Navarre, confiscation formed part of the penalties of suicide, murder, treason, and even of blows or wounds inflicted where the queen or royal children were dwelling. There is a case in which confiscation was enforced on a man because he struck another at Olite, which was within a league of Tafalla, where the queen chanced to be staying at the time (G.B. de Lagrèze, La Navarre Française II. 335).

[463] Guid. Fulcod. Quæst. XV.—Coll. Doat, XXI. 154; XXXIII. 207; XXXIV. 189; XXXV. 68.—MSS. Bib. Nat., fonds latin, No. 9992.—Coll. Doat, XXVIII. 131, 164.—Responsa Prudentum (Doat, XXXVII. 83).—Grandes Chroniques, ann. 1323.—Les Olim, T. I. p. 556.—Guill. Pelisso Chron. Ed. Molinier, p. 27.— Practica super Inquisit. (MSS. Bib. Nat., fonds latin, No. 14930, fol. 224).—Coll. Doat, XXVII. fol. 118.

In 1460, when the nearly extinct French Inquisition was resuscitated to punish the sorcerers of Arras, confiscation formed part of the sentence.—Mémoires de Jacques du Clercq, Liv. IV. ch. 4.

[464] Coll. Doat, XXXI. 175.—Zanchini Tract. de Hæret. c. xviii., xxv., xxvi., xli.—Archivio Storico Italiano, No. 38, p. 29.

[465] Lami, Antichità Toscane, 560, 588-9.—Zanchini Tract. de Hæret. c. xxvi.—Archiv. di Firenze, Prov. S. Maria Novella, Nov. 18, 1327.—Archivio di Napoli, Regist. 253, Lett. A, fol. 63.

[466] Hist. Diplom. Frid. II. T. III. p. 466.—Kaltner, Konrad v. Marburg u. die Inquisition, Prag, 1882, p. 147.—Mosheim de Beghardis, p. 347.

[467] Harduin. VII. 203.—Concil. Biterrens. ann. 1233 c. 4; ann. 1246, Append. c. 35.—Concil. Albiens. ann. 1254 c. 26.—Coll. Doat, XXI. 151.—Guid. Fulcod. Quæst. xv.—Isambert Anc. Loix Françaises, I. 257.— Arch. de l'Inq. de Carcassonne (Doat, XXXI. 263).—Bernardi Comens. Lucerna Inquisit. s. v. *Filii*.

[468] Archives de l'Inq. de Carcassonne (Doat, XXXI. 152).—Berger, Registres d'Innoc. IV. No. 1844.— MSS. Bib. Nat., fonds latin, No. 9992.—Lib. Sententt. Inq. Tolosan. pp. 158-62.—Arch. de l'Inq. de

Carcassonne (Doat, XXVII. 98).—Eymeric. Direct. Inquis. pp. 663-5.—Zanchini Tract. de Hæret. c. xviii., xix., xxv.

[469] Archives de l'Évêché de Béziers (Doat, XXXI. 35).—Potthast No. 12743.—Isambert, I. 257.—C. 14 Sexto v. 2.—Zanchini Tract. de Hæret. c. xxv.—Livres de Jostice et de Piet, Liv. I. Tit. iii. § 7.

[470] Hoffmann, Geschichte der Inquisition, II. 370.—Lucii PP. III. Epist. 171.—Innoc. PP. IV. Bull. *Ad extirpanda*, § 34.—Ejusd. Bull. *Super extirpatione*, 30 Mai. 1254 (Ripoll, I. 247).—Alex. PP. IV. Bull. *Discretioni* (Mag. Bull. Rom. I. 120).—Potthast No. 18200.

[471] Nich. PP. IV. Bull. *Habet vestræ*, 3 Oct. 1290.—Raynald. ann. 1438, No. 24.—Lami, Antichità Toscane, pp. 588-9.—Alv. Pelag. de Planctu Eccles. Lib. II. art. 67.—Archivio di Firenze, Riformagioni, Classe v. No. 110; Classe XI. Distinz. I, No. 39.

[472] Archivio di Napoli, Registro 9, Lett. C, fol. 90; Regist. 51, Lett. A, fol. 9; Reg. 98, Lett. B, fol. 13; Reg. 113, Lett. A, fol. 194; MSS. Chioccorelli, T. VIII.

[473] Albizio, Risposto al P. Paolo Sarpi, p. 25.—Sclopis, Antica Legislazione del Piemont, p. 485.

[474] Zanchini Tract. de Hæret. c. xix., xxvi., xli. Cf. Pegnæ Comment. in Eymeric. p. 659.—Grandjean, Registre de Benoît XI. No. 299.—Raynald. ann. 1438, No. 24.—Bernardi Comens. Lucerna Inquis. s. v. *Bona hæreticorum*, No. 6, 8. As early as 1387, in the sentences of Antonio Secco on the Waldenses of the Alpine valleys, the confiscations are declared to be solely for the benefit of the Inquisition (Archivio Storico Italiano, No. 38, pp. 29, 36, 50).

It must be placed to the credit of Benedict XI, that, in 1304, he authorized Frà Simone, Inquisitor of Rome, to restore confiscations unjustly made by his predecessors and to moderate punishments inflicted by them if he considered them too severe (Grandjean, No. 474).

[475] Alonsi de Spina Fortalicii Fidei, Lib. II. Consid. xi. (fol. 74 Ed. 1594).

[476] MSS. Bib. Nat., fonds latin, No. 14930, fol. 224.—Livres de Jostice et de Plet, Liv. I. Tit. iii. § 7.—Vaissette, III. 391.—Les Olim, I. 317.—MSS. Bib. Nat., fonds latin, No. 11847.—Concil. Insulan. ann. 1251 c. 3.—Teulet, Layettes, II. 165.—Concil. Biterrens. ann. 1246 c. 4.—Vaissette, Éd. Privat, VIII. 975.—Baluz. Concil. Narbonn. Append. pp. 96-99.—Coll. Doat, XXXV. 48. Cf. Berger, Registres d'Innoc. IV. No. 1543-4, 1547-8.—Vaissette, IV. 170.—Baudouin, Lettres inédites de Philippe le Bel, Paris, 1886, p. xl.

In spite of the general sense of equity manifested by St. Louis, he was by no means indifferent to acquisitions justified by the spirit of the age. In 1246 there seems to have been a raid made upon the Jews of Carcassonne, who were thrown into prison. In July St. Louis writes to his seneschal that he wants to get from them all that he can; they are, therefore, to be held in strict duress, while the amount which they can be made to pay is to be reported to him. In August he writes that the sum proposed is not satisfactory, and the seneschal is instructed to extort all that he can.—Vaissette, Éd. Privat, VIII. 1191-2.

[477] A. Molinier (Vaissette, Éd. Privat, VII. 284-94; VIII. 919).—Coll. Doat, XXXIV. 131, 135, 189; XXXV. 93.—Urbani PP. IV. Epist. 62 (Martene Thesaur. II. 94).—Bern. Guidon. Hist. Conv. Albiens.—Vaissette, III. Pr. 467, 500.—Arch. de l'Inq. de Carcass. (Doat, XXXI. 143, 146).

[478] C. Molinier, L'Inquisition dans le midi de la France, p. 101.—Les Olim, III. 1126-9, 1440-2. See also I. 920.

[479] Archives de l'Évêché d'Albi (Doat, XXXV. 83).—Les Olim, I. 556.—Archivio di Napoli, Regist. 4, Lett. B, fol. 47.—Archives de l'Évêché de Béziers (Doat, XXXI. 35).—Concil. Biterrens. ann. 1246 c. 3.—Isambert, Anc. Loix Françaises, I. 257.—C. 19 Sexto v. 2.—MSS. Bib. Nat., fonds latin No. 11847.—Collect. Doat, XXXV. 68.—Molinier, L'Inq. dans de midi de la France, p. 102.—Vaissette, Éd. Privat, X. Pr. 370 sqq.

[480] Boutaric, Saint Louis et Alphonse de Poitiers, Paris, 1870, pp. 455-6.—Douais, Les sources de l'histoire de Inquisition (Revue des Questions Historiques, Oct. 1881, p. 436).—Coll. Doat, XXXII. 51, 64.

[481] Archives de l'Évêché d'Albi (Doat, XXXIII. 207-72).—Coll. Doat, XXXV. 93.—Les Olim, II. 111.

[482] Bernardi Comens. Lucerna Inquis. s. v. *Bona hæreticor.*—Archidiac. Gloss. sup. c. 19 Sexto v. 2.—Archivio di Napoli, Regist. 15, Lett. C, fol. 77, 78.

The English law of felony was also retroactive, and all alienations subsequent to the commission of the crime were void (Bracton, Lib. III. Tract. ii. cap. 13, No. 8).

[483] Coll. Doat, XXXII. 309, 316.

[484] Les Olim, II. 147.—Doat, XXVI. 253.

[485] Archives Générales de Belgique, Papiers d'État, v. 405.—Mémoires de Jacques du Clercq, Liv. IV. ch. 4, 14.

In Arras a charter of 1335, confirmed by Charles V. in 1369, protected the burghers from confiscation when condemned for crime by any competent tribunal.—Duverger, La Vauderie dans les États de Philippe le Bon, Arras, 1885, p. 60.

[486] C. 6, 8, 9, 14, Sexto XII. 26.—Bernardi Comensis Lucerna Inquis. s. v. *Bona hæreticorum.*—Eymeric. Direct. Inquis. pp. 570-2.—Zanchini Tract. de Hæret. c. xxiv.—J.F. Ponzinib. de Lamiis c. 76.

Severe as was the contemporary English law against felony, it had at least this concession to justice, that a felon had to be convicted in his lifetime; his death before conviction thus prevented confiscation (Bracton, Lib. III. Tract. ii. cap. 13, No. 17).

[487] Lami, Antichità Toscane, pp. 497, 536-7.—It is true that when, in 1335, Henri de Chamay, Inquisitor of Carcassonne, sent to the papal court the depositions against the memory of eighteen persons accused of heretical acts committed between 1284 and 1290, and asked for instructions, the decision was that no reliance was to be placed on the testimony of witnesses who mostly contradicted themselves, and who only swore to what they had heard long before. Three previous investigations against the same persons had been held without reaching a conclusion, and the papal advisers assumed that there had been good reasons for dropping the matter.—Vaissette, Éd. Privat, IX. 401.

How the system worked is seen in the complaint made in 1247 to St. Louis, by Guillem Pierre de Vintrou, that the royal seneschal of Carcassonne had seized his property derived through his mother, because his grandfather, seventeen years after death, had been accused of heresy. St. Louis thereupon ordered an examination and report.—Vaissette, Éd. Privat, VIII. 1196.

[488] Vaissette, Éd. Privat, VIII. 1641.

[489] Zanchini Tract. de Hæret. c. xxvii.—Isambert, Anc. Loix Françaises, I. 257.

Yet there is a case in 1269 in which a creditor of two condemned heretics applies to Alphonse of Poitiers to be paid out of the confiscations, and Alphonse orders an inquiry into the circumstances.—Vaissette, Éd. Privat, VIII. 1682.

[490] Lami, Antichità Toscane, p. 593.—Archivio di Firenze, Riformagioni, Classe v. No. 110.

[491] MSS. Bib. Nat., fonds latin, No. 14930, fol. 228.—Guid. Fulcod. Quæst. III.—Archivio di Napoli, Regist. 6, Lett. B, fol. 35; Reg. 10, Lett. B, fol. 6, 7, 96; Reg. 11, Lett. C, fol. 40; Reg. 13, Lett. A, fol. 212; Reg. 51, Lett. A, fol. 9; Reg. 71, Lett. M, fol. 382, 385, 440; Reg. 98, Lett. B, fol. 13; Reg. 113, Lett. A, fol. 194; Reg. 253, Lett. A, fol. 63; MSS. Chioccorello, T. VIII.

[492] Concil. Tolosan. ann. 1229 c. 9.—Concil. Albiens. ann. 1254 c. 24.—Harduin. VII. 415.—Archives de L'Évêché de Béziers (Doat, XXXI. 35).—Concil. Biterrens. ann. 1246 c. 22.—D. Bouquet, T. XXI. pp. 262, 264, 266, 278, etc.—Vaissette, Éd. Privat, VIII. 1206, 1573.—Archives de l'Inq. de Carcassonne (Doat, XXXI. 250).—Archivio di Napoli, Regist. 20, Lett. B, fol. 91.

The care with which Alphonse looked after the proceeds of the confiscations is seen in his demand for an account from his seneschal, Jacques du Bois, March 25, 1268 (Vaissette, Éd. Privat, VIII. 1274).

[493] Molinier, L'Inquisition dans le midi de la France, p. 308.—Bern. Guidon. Fundat. Convent. Prædicat. (Martene Thesaur. VI. 481).—Boutaric, Saint Louis et Alphonse de Poitiers, pp. 456-7.

[494] Coll. Doat, XXXIV. 189.—In 1317 the result had been much less. We have the receipt of the royal treasurer of Carcassonne, Lothaire Blanc, to Arnaud Assalit, dated Sept. 24, 1317, for collections during the year ending the previous St. John's day, amounting to four hundred and ninety-five livres six sols eleven deniers, being the balance after deducting wages and expenses (Doat, XXXIV. 141).

[495] Doat, XXXV. 79, 100.—Vaissette, Éd. Privat, X. Pr. 705, 777, 783.

[496] Potthast No. 13000, 15995.—Monteiro, Historia da Santo Inquisição, P.I. Lib. II. c. 34, 35.

[497] Mosheim de Beghardis pp. 356-63.

[498] Eymeric. Direct. Inquis. pp. 652-3.

[499] Vaissette, Éd. Privat, X. Pr. 791-2, 802.—Raynald. ann. 1375, No. 26.—Wadding, ann. 1375, No. 21, 22; 1409, No. 13.—Isambert, Anc. Loix Françaises, V. 491.—Martene Ampl. Collect. VIII. 161-3.

[500] Bernard. Guidon. Practica P. IV. (Doat, XXX.).

[501] Coll. Doat, XXI. 143.—MSS. Bib. Nat., fonds latin, No. 9992.—Doctrina de modo procedendi (Martene Thesaur. V. 1807).—Lami, Antichità Toscane, pp. 557, 559.—Lib, Sententt. Inq. Tolosan. pp. 2, 4, 36, 208, 254, 265, 289, 380.—Eymeric. Direct. Inquis. pp. 510-12.

[502] Pegnæ Comment, xx. in Eymeric. p. 124.—Tract. de Paup. de Lugd. (Martene Thesaur. V. 1792).—S. Thom. Aquinat. Summ. Sec. Sec. Q. XI. Art. 3.—Eymeric. Direct. Inquis. pp. 510-12.—Tract. de Inquisit. (Doat, XXX.).—Bern. Guidon. Practica P. IV. (Doat, XXX.).—A. de Spina Fortalic. Fidei Ed. 1494 fol. 76a.—MSS. Bib. Nat., fonds Moreau, No. 444, fol. 10. Cf. Archiv. di Napoli, Reg. 6, Lett. D, fol. 39; Reg. 13, Lett. A, fol. 139.—Coll. Doat, XXXIV. 189.—Malleus Maleficarum P. II. Q. i. c. 2.—Albizio, Risposto al P. Paolo Sarpi, p. 30.

Gregory IX. had no scruple in asserting the duty of the Church to shed the blood of heretics. In a brief of 1234 to the Archbishop of Sens he says, *"nec enim decuit Apostolicam Sedem in oculis suis, cum Madianita coeunte Judeo, manum suam a sanguine prohibere, ne si secus ageret non custodire populum Israel.... videretur."*—Ripoll I. 66.

Friar Heinrich Kaleyser was a celebrated doctor of theology, and was subsequently Inquisitor of Cologne (Nider. Formicar. v. viii.).

[503] C. 18 Sexto v. 2.—Concil. Albiens. ann. 1254 c. 22.—Eymeric. Direct. Inq. pp. 372, 562.—Pegnæ Comment. in Eymeric. p. 564.—Guid. Fulcod. Quæst. x.—Alex. PP. IV. Bull. *Ad audientiam*, 1260 (Eymeric. Append. p. 34).—Bern. Guidon. Practica P. IV. (Doat, XXX.).—Alex. PP. IV. Bull. *Quæsivisti*, 1260 (Ripoll I. 393).—Wadding. Annal. ann. 1288, No. 20.—Zanchini Tract. de Hæret. c. xviii.—Fortalicii Fidei fol. 74b.—Bernardi Comens. Lucerna Inquisit. s. v. *Executio*, No. 1, 8.

[504] Guill. Pod. Laur. cap. 48.—Les Olim, I. 317.—Vaissette, Éd. Privat, VIII. 1674. X. Pr. 484, 659.—Baluz. et Mansi, II. 257.

[505] Vaissette, III. 410.—Wadding. Annal. ann. 1288, No. xix.—Hoffmann, Geschichte der Inquisition, II. 391.—Bernardi Comens. Lucerna Inquisit. s. v. *Executio*, No. 6.—Innoc. PP. VIII. Bull. *Dilectus filius*, 1486 (Pegnæ App. ad Eymeric. p. 84).—Leo. PP. X. Bull. *Honestis*, 1521 (Mag. Bull. Rom. I. 617).—Albizio, Risposto al P. Paolo Sarpi. pp. 64-70.

[506] Rodrigo, Historia Verdadera de la Inquisition, Madrid, 1876, I. 176-77.—Von der Hardt, IV. 317-18.

[507] Von der Hardt, III, 50-1.

[508] Concil. Arelatens. ann. 1234 c. 6.—Concil. Tarraconens. ann. 1242.—Concil. Biterrens. ann. 1246, Append. c. 17.—Bern. Guidon. Practica P. IV. (Doat, XXX.).—Eymeric. Direct. Inquis. pp. 514-16.—Anon. Passaviens. c. ix. (Mag. Bib. Pat. XIII. 308).—Zanchini Tract. de Hæret. c. xviii.—Lib. Sententt. Inq. Tolosan. p. 6.

[509] Concil. Narbonn. ann. 1244 c. 26.—Concil. Biterrens. ann. 1246, App. c. 9.—Eymeric. Direct. Inquis. pp. 376-77, 521-4.—MSS. Bib. Nat., fonds latin, No. 9992.—Lib. Sententt. Inq. Tolos. pp. 379-80.—Zanchini Tract, de Hæret. c. xxiii.

[510] Lucii PP. III. Epist. 171.—Hist. Diplom. Frid. II. T. IV. p. 300.—Concil. Narbonn. ann. 1244 c. 11.—Gregor. PP. IX. Bull. *Ad capiendas* (Vaissette, III. Pr. 364).—Epistt. Sæcul. XIII. No. 514 (Mon. Germ. Hist.).—Ripoll I. 55.—Concil. Tarraconens. ann. 1242.—Doctrina de modo procedendi (Martene Thesaur. V. 1800).—Concil. Biterrens. ann. 1246, App. c. 20.—Coll. Doat, XXI. 148, 292,—Lami, Antichità Toscane, p. 560.

[511] Arch, de l'Inq. de Carcassonne (Doat, XXXI. 5, 139, 149).—MSS. Bib. Nat., fonds latin, No. 9992.—Martene Thesaur. I, 1045.—Vaissette, III. Pr. 479.—Molinier, L'Inq. dans le midi de la France, pp. 387-8, 418.—Anon. Passaviens. (Mag. Bib. Pat. XIII. 308).—Tract. de Paup. de Lugd. (Martene Thesaur. V. 1791).—Doctrina de modo procedendi (Ibid. 1807).—Practica super Inquisit. (MSS. Bib. Nat., fonds latin, No. 14930, fol. 206, 212, 213, 222, 223).—Concil. Biterrens. ann. 1246, App. c. 33.

[512] Boutaric, Saint Louis et Alphonse de Poitiers, pp. 453-4.

[513] Ripoll I. 254.—C. 4 Sexto v. 2.—Potthast No. 17845.—S. Thom. Aquin. Sec. Sec. Q. xi. Art. 4.—Eymeric. Direct. Inq. p. 331, 512.—Lib. Sententt. Inq. Tolos. p. 36.—Zanchini Tract. de Hæret. c. xvi.

[514] Lib. Sententt. Inq. Tolosan. pp. 2-4, 22, 48, 63, 76, 81-90, 122, 142, 149, 150, 198-99, 230, 232, 287-88.

[515] Alex. PP. IV. Bull. *Quod super nonnullis*, 9 Dec. 1257, 15 Dec. 1258, 10 Jan. 1260.—Urban. PP. IV. Bull. *Quod super nonnullis*, 21 Aug. 1262.—Can. 8 Sexto v. 2.—Bern. Guidon. Practica P. IV. (Doat, XXX.).—Eymeric. Direct. Inq. p. 331.—Bernardi Comens. Lucerna Inquis. s. v. *Relapsus*.—Zanchini Tract. de Hæret. c. xvi.

[516] Concil. Narbonn. ann. 1244 c. 13.—Doctrina de modo procedendi (Martene Thesaur. V. 1802, 1808).—Bern. Guidon. Practica P. IV. (Doat, XXX.).—Eymeric. Direct. Inq. p. 386.

[517] Concil. Narbonn. ann. 1244 c. 13.—Concil. Biterrens. ann. 1246, Append, c. 33.—Concil. Valentin. ann. 1248 c. 13.—Archives de l'Évêché d'Albi (Doat, XXXV. 69).—Alex. PP. IV. Bull. *Ad audientiam*, 1260 (Mag. Bull. Rom. I. 118).—Guidon. Fulcod. Quæst. XIII.—Bern. Guidon. Practica P. IV. (Doat, XXX.).—Lib. Sententt. Inq. Tolosan. pp. 177, 199, 350, 393.—MSS. Bib. Nat., fonds latin, nouv. nequis. No. 139, fol. 2.—Eymeric. Direct. Inquis. p. 643.—Zanchini Tract, de Hæret. c. x.—Bern. Comens. Lucerna Inquisit. s. v. *Fuga*, No. 5.—Albertini Repertor. Inquisit. s. vv. *Deficiens, Impœnitens.*

[518] Bern. Guidon. Fund. Conv. Prædicat. (Martene Thesaur. VI. 481-3).—Coll. Doat, XXI. 143, 146.—MSS. Bib. Nat., funds latin, No. 9992.—Molinier, L'Inq. dans le midi de la France, pp. 73-4.

[519] Eymeric. Direct. Inquis. p. 513.—Tract. de Paup. de Lugd. (Martene Thesaur. V. 1792).

[520] Mladenowie Narrat. (Palacky Monument. J. Huss II. pp. 321-4).—Landucci, Diar. Fiorent. p. 178.

[521] Coll. Doat, XXXIV. 189.

[522] Guillel. Pelisso Chron. Ed. Molinier p. 45.—Coll. Doat, XXXIV 189.

[523] Sozomen. H. E. II. 20.—Constt. vi.; xvi. § I, Cod. I. 5.—Auth. Novell. CXLVI. c. 1.—Rigord. de Gest. Phil. Aug. ann. 1210.—Petri Venerab. Tract. contra Judæos c. iv.—D'Argentré, Collect. Judicior. de nov. Erroribus I. I. 132, 146-56, 349.—Potthast. No. 10759, 10767, 11376.—Ripoll, I. 487-88.—Pelayo, Heterodoxos Españoles, I. 509.—Coll. Doat, XXXVII. 125, 246.—Harduin. Concil. VII. 485.—S. Martial. Chron. ann. 1309 (Bouquet, XXI. 813).—Lib. Sententt. Inq. Tolos. pp. 273-4.—Bern. Guidon. Practica (Doat, XXIX. 246).—Raynald. ann. 1320, No. 23.—Wadding. ann. 1409, No. 12.—C. 1 in Septimo v. 4.

In the Paris condemnation of 1248 the Talmud only is specified, though in the examination mention is made of the Gloss of Solomon of Troyes, and of a work which from its description would seem to be the Toldos Jeschu, or history of Jesus, which so excited the ire of the Carthusian, Ramon Marti, in his *Pugio Fidei*, and of all subsequent Christians (cf. Wagenseilii Tela Ignea Satanæ, Altdorfi, 1681). No one can read its curious account of the career of Christ from a Jewish standpoint without wondering that a single copy of it was allowed to reach modern times.

[524] Bern. Guidon. Gravam. (Doat, XXX. 101).

[525] Extrav. Commun. Lib. v. Tit. viii. c. 1.—Amalrici Augerii Vit. Pontif. ann. 1316-17.—Bern. Guidon. Vit. Joann. XXII.

[526] Theod. a Niem de Schismate Lib. I. c. 42, 45, 48, 50, 51, 52, 56, 57, 60.—Gobelin. Personæ Cosmodrom. Aet. VI. c. 78.—Chronik des J. v. Königshofen (Chron. der Deutschen Städte, IX. 598).—Raynald. ann. 1362, No. 13; 1372, No. 10.—Poggii Hist. Florentin. Lib. II. ann. 1376.

[527] I have treated this subject at some length in an essay on torture (Superstition and Force, 3d Edition, 1878), and need not here dwell further on its details. The student who desires to see the shape which the inquisitorial process assumed in later times can consult Brunnemann (Tractatus Juridicus de Inquisitionis Processu, Ed. octava, Francof. 1704), who attributes its origin to the Mosaic law (Deut. XIII. 12; XVII. 4), and vastly prefers it to the proceeding *per accusationem*. Indeed, a case in which *accusatio* failed or threatened to fail could be resumed or continued by *inquisitio* (op. cit. Cap. I. No. 2, 15-18). It supplied all deficiencies and gave the judge almost unlimited power to convict.

The manner in which the civil power was led to adopt the abuses of the Inquisition is well illustrated in a Milanese edict of 1393, where the magistrates, in proceedings against malefactors, are ordered to employ the inquisitorial process "*summarie et de plano sine strepitu et figura juditii*" and to supply all defects of fact "*ex certa scientia*" (Antiq. Ducum Mediolan. Decreta. Mediolani, 1654, p. 188). A comparison of this with the Milanese jurisprudence of sixty years earlier, quoted above (p. 401), will show how rapidly in the interval force had usurped the place of justice.

[528] Fortescue de Laudibus Legum Angliæ cap. xxii.—As late as 1823 there is a case in which a court in Martinique condemned a man to the galleys for life for "vehement suspicion" of being a sorcerer (Isambert. Anc. Loix Françaises, XI. 253).

[529] There is evidently something lacking here. It can doubtless be supplied from Moneta, p. 151. "Et e contrario Deuteronomii, 15, v. 9, dicit legislator: *Dominaberis nationibus plurimis et nemo tibi dominabitur.*"

[530] It was this bull which enabled inquisitors to administer torture. A date several years later has usually been assigned to it.

s

Made in the USA
Middletown, DE
22 December 2015